THE 100
GREATEST AMERICANS
OF THE 20TH CENTURY

ALSO BY PETER DREIER

Jewish Radicalism: A Selected Anthology
(New York: Grove Press, 1973), coeditor with Jack Nusan Porter

The Next Los Angeles:
The Struggle for a Livable City, 2nd ed.
(Berkeley: University of California Press, 2006),
coauthor with Regina Freer, Bob Gottlieb, and Mark Vallianatos

Place Matters: Metropolitics for the 21st Century,
2nd ed. (Lawrence: University Press of Kansas, 2004),
coauthor with John Mollenkopf and Todd Swanstrom

Regions That Work:
How Cities and Suburbs Can Grow Together
(Minneapolis: University of Minnesota Press, 2000),
coauthor with Manuel Pastor, Eugene Grigsby, and Marta Lopez-Garza

Up Against the Sprawl:
Public Policy and the Making of Southern California
(Minneapolis: University of Minnesota Press, 2004),
coeditor with Jennifer Wolch and Manuel Pastor

The 100 GREATEST AMERICANS of the 20TH CENTURY

A SOCIAL JUSTICE HALL of FAME

PETER DREIER

NATION
BOOKS
New York

Published by Nation Books, A Member of the Perseus Books Group
116 East 16th Street, 8th Floor
New York, NY 10003

Nation Books is a copublishing venture of the
Nation Institute and the Perseus Books Group.

Books published by Nation Books are available at special discounts for bulk purchases in the
United States by corporations, institutions, and other organizations. For more information,
please contact the Special Markets Department at the Perseus Books Group, 2300 Chestnut
Street, Suite 200, Philadelphia, PA 19103, or call (800) 810-4145, extension 5000, or e-mail
special.markets@perseusbooks.com.

Designed by Trish Wilkinson
Set in 10.5 point Adobe Garamond Pro

Library of Congress Cataloging-in-Publication Data

Dreier, Peter, 1948–
    The 100 greatest Americans of the 20th century : a social justice hall of fame / Peter
Dreier.
        p. cm.
    Includes bibliographical reference.
    ISBN 978-1-56858-681-6 (pbk. : alk. paper) — ISBN 978-1-56858-694-6 (e-book)
1. Social reformers—United States—Biography. 2. Political activists—United States—
Biography. 3. Social change—United States—History—20th century. 4. Social
justice—United States—History—20th century. 5. United States—Social conditions—
20th century. 6. United States—History—20th century—Biography. I. Title. II. Title:
One hundred greatest Americans of the twentieth century.
E747.D74 2012
920.073—dc23
[B]   2012004704

10 9 8 7 6 5 4 3 2

To my daughters, Amelia and Sarah

Contents

Acknowledgments

THIS BOOK celebrates the achievements of the movements that have made America a more humane country by profiling their key leaders—the 100 greatest Americans of the 20th century.

Over many years, I have been privileged to know scholars, organizers, activists, journalists, and social critics who have helped me understand the role of progressive ideas and movements in shaping our nation's history and culture. None was more important than Michael Harrington, who inspired and mentored me. I have also learned a great deal from my friends Dick Flacks, David Moberg, John Atlas, Jan Breidenbach, Harold Meyerson, Frances Fox Piven, Nelson Lichtenstein, and Maurice Isserman.

Researching and writing this book was a great deal of fun, in large part because I was constantly in contact with interesting people who helped me at every stage. The idea for the book was hatched after *The Nation* magazine published my article "The Fifty Most Influential Progressives of the Twentieth Century," as its October 4, 2010, cover story. The article triggered an avalanche of letters and e-mails, praising it, attacking it for leaving out certain people, or criticizing it for including others. The article did what I had hoped it would do: generate interest in and debate about the people I listed and the movements they represented. Thanks to Katrina Vanden Heuvel, Richard Kim, and Peter Rothberg at *The Nation* for publishing and giving shape to the original article, and to Katrina for encouraging me to expand it into a book.

At Nation Books, Carl Bromley and Marissa Colón-Margolies demonstrated consistent support and enthusiasm for this project. Their editorial skills guided me at every stage of the research and writing. *The Nation*'s Frank Reynolds tracked down all the photographs used in the book.

I reached out to many historians, biographers, journalists, sociologists, political scientists, and others for help in selecting, researching, and writing about the 100 people included in the book. Lucy Knight, Dick Flacks, Ron Cohen, Donald Cohen, John Atlas, Harold Meyerson, Steve Greenhouse, and Nelson Lichtenstein made suggestions about whom to include or leave out. They also made valuable comments on multiple chapters of the book.

Jamie Angell, Chris Myers Asch, Steve Bingham, Jeff Blum, Eileen Boris, Clayborne Carson, Ellen Cassedy, Sue Chinn, Charles Cobb, Norm Cohen, Julie York Coppens, Ken Dingledine, Denis Dison, Kathleen Dolan, Bill Domhoff, Rebecca Edwards, Steve Fraser, Josh Freeman, Herb Gans, Bob Gottlieb, Raymond Gregory, Thomas Hauser, Michael Honey, Maurice Isserman, Madeline Janis, Chana Kai Lee, Mark Levinson, Deborah Martinson, Joe McCartin, John McDonough, S. M. Miller, JoAnn Mort, Philip Nell, Jim Newton, Beverly Palmer, Richard Parker, Miriam Pawel, Nolan Porterfield, Bruce Raynor, JoAnn Robinson, Mark Rogovin, Frank Roosevelt, Richard Rothstein, Jodi Rudoren, Michael Sell, Helen Selsdon, Kathryn Sklar, Daniel Soyer, Rick Valelly, Abbie Van Nostrand, Paul von Blum, Jim Vrabel, Robin Walker, Susan Ware, Howard Winant, and Goetz Wolff supplied important information or reviewed specific chapters that helped me improve the book. Beth Baker, Doug Hess, and Guido Girgenti provided indispensible research assistance.

My students and colleagues at Occidental College have provided a wonderful environment for teaching, writing, and political engagement. In particular, I would like to thank Sylvia Chico, Bob Gottlieb, and Martha Matsuoka.

My wife, Terry Meng, and our daughters, Amelia and Sarah, understood how passionate I was about this project and cut me a lot of slack during the year and a half I spent researching and writing the book. I appreciate their love, support, and curiosity.

Introduction

THROUGHOUT THE 20th century, American pioneers fought to make the United States a more humane and inclusive country. They called for women's suffrage, laws protecting the environment and consumers, an end to lynching, the right of workers to form unions, a progressive income tax, a federal minimum wage, old-age insurance, the eight-hour workday, and government-subsidized health care and housing. When these ideas were first advanced, their pioneering advocates were considered impractical idealists, utopian dreamers, or dangerous socialists. Now we take these ideas for granted. The radical ideas of one generation have become the common sense of the next.

These accomplishments did not occur because progress is inevitable or because a set of benevolent "haves" took pity on the "have-nots" of society. "If there is no struggle there is no progress," said Frederick Douglass, the African American abolitionist, adding, "Power concedes nothing without a demand." The credit for these achievements goes to the activists who fought to take their ideas from the margins to the mainstream. We all stand on the shoulders of earlier generations of reformers, radicals, and idealists who challenged the status quo of the day.

The 20th century is a remarkable story of progressive accomplishments against overwhelming odds. But it is not a tale of steady progress. At best, it is a chronicle of taking two steps forward, then one step backward, then two more steps forward. The successful battles and social improvements came about in fits and starts. We tend to view history as a pendulum that swings between periods of reform (such as the Progressive Era, the Depression, and the 1960s) and periods of reaction. But activists pushed for and won reforms in every decade—indeed, every year—of the century. When pathbreaking laws are passed—such as the Nineteenth Amendment (which granted women suffrage in 1920), the Fair Labor Standards Act of 1938 (which created the minimum wage), the Civil Rights Act of 1964 (which outlawed many forms of racial discrimination), and the Clean Air Act of 1970—we often forget that those milestones took decades of work by thinkers, activists, and politicians.

Frances Fitzgerald's 1979 book, *America Revised: History Schoolbooks in the Twentieth Century,* reveals the ways generations of Americans were deprived of an accurate sense of their own history. Throughout the 20th century, most Americans were taught history that downplayed conflict and dissent and celebrated instead America's march toward progress as led by heroic political, business, and military leaders. This sanitized and inaccurate view still pervades much of what young Americans learn about our history.

As a result, most Americans know little about the fascinating activists, thinkers, and politicians and the exciting movements and struggles that are responsible for most of the best aspects of contemporary American society. That history is not taught in most high schools. It cannot be found on the major television networks or on the History Channel. Indeed, our history is under siege.

In recent years, the most flagrant misinterpreter of America's progressive past has been Glenn Beck, the right-wing television and radio pundit who has offered his audience a wildly inaccurate history of civil rights, unions, and other progressive movements. For example, on his Fox News show on July 18, 2010, Beck claimed that the civil rights movement "has been perverted and distorted" by people claiming that Martin Luther King Jr. supported "redistribution of wealth." In fact, King voiced such ideas during the last few years of his life. For example, during a trip to Mississippi in 1968 he called for a "radical redistribution of economic power."

King is widely considered one of the greatest Americans of the 20th century and, indeed, since the nation's founding. Today we view him as something of a saint. His birthday is now a national holiday. His name adorns schools and street signs. But in his day, in his own country, many people in positions of power, and not just southern racists, considered King a dangerous troublemaker. He was harassed by the FBI and vilified in the media. Despite this, he helped change America's conscience, not only with regard to civil rights but also about economic opportunity, poverty, and peace. He pushed the country to fulfill its great promise, making it more democratic, more fair, and more humane.

Who Are the Greatest?

What makes someone eligible to be considered one of the "greatest Americans of the 20th century"? Some of the people profiled in this book are as well-known as King. Others are far more obscure. What they share with King is a commitment to social justice and a record of accomplishment, of using their talents to help achieve important progressive change.

The great Americans expressed this commitment in three ways. Some were organizers and activists who mobilized or led grassroots movements for democracy and equality. Others were writers, musicians, artists, editors, scientists, lawyers, athletes, and intellectuals who challenged prevailing ideas and inspired Americans to believe that a better society was possible. Finally, many were politicians—presidents, members of Congress, mayors and city council members, and some who ran for office and lost. They gave voice to social justice movements in the corridors of power and translated their concerns into new laws that changed society. Quite a few of the 100 greatest Americans played more than one of these roles.

Over the years, several magazines, including *Time*, *Life*, and the *Atlantic*, have compiled lists of the "greatest," "most important," or "most influential" Americans. Not surprisingly, there is some overlap among the people included on those lists and the individuals included in this book's Social Justice Hall of Fame. King, Eleanor Roosevelt, Albert Einstein, Jackie Robinson, Rachel Carson, and Margaret Sanger make everyone's lists.

But the other lists also include 20th-century Americans who may have been great in their specific fields of endeavor but who did not contribute to making America a more just, equal, or democratic society. These include business leaders John Rockefeller (Standard Oil), Henry Ford (Ford Motors), Walt Disney (Walt Disney Company), Thomas Watson (IBM), Sam Walton (Walmart), Ray Kroc (McDonalds), and Bill Gates (Microsoft); inventors Thomas Edison (the light bulb), Wilbur and Orville Wright (the airplane), and Willis Carrier (the air conditioner); writers Ernest Hemingway and T. S. Eliot; banker A. P. Giannini; developer William Leavitt; evangelist Billy Graham; baseball player Babe Ruth; singer Elvis Presley; Hollywood mogul Louis B. Mayer; composer Richard Rodgers; scientist James Watson; aviator Charles Lindbergh; and politician Ronald Reagan. Some of them actively opposed movements for social justice.

The reformers and radicals profiled in this book—from Eugene Debs, Jane Addams, and W. E. B. Du Bois in the early years of the century to John Lewis, Gloria Steinem, and Michael Moore at its end—exercised influence not only because of the huge number of people they mobilized but also because of the moral force of their ideas. They influenced Americans' attitudes about right and wrong, the treatment of different groups, and the role of government in society.

All activists, across the political spectrum, believe that what they are doing expresses their loyalty to the nation's core values. Some just call this "fairness." Others call it "patriotism." Indeed, the ways we Americans express our patriotism are as diverse and contentious as our nation. To some people, patriotism means "my country—right or wrong." To others, it means loyalty to a set of political and philosophical principles and thus requires dissent and criticism when those in power violate those standards. As King said in a speech during the bus boycott in Montgomery, Alabama, in 1955, "The great glory of American democracy is the right to protest for right."

The 100 greatest Americans of the 20th century—listed chronologically by birth—were therefore all patriots as well as dissenters. To them, America stood for basic democratic values—economic and social equality, mass participation in politics, free speech and civil liberties, first-class citizenship for women and racial minorities, and a welcome mat for the world's oppressed people. They did not agree on everything. But those included in the Social Justice Hall of Fame often joined forces when it came to battles over specific issues, such as granting women the vote, ending lynching, giving workers the right to unionize, enacting Social Security and a minimum wage, expanding health care, adopting progressive taxes, and pushing business to act more responsibly.

But the 20th century was more than a series of battles over specific issues. It was also an ongoing struggle over values and ideas. Throughout the century, Americans debated big, visionary questions. What kind of society do we want? How much inequality and poverty is justifiable in a wealthy nation? What is the proper balance between individual liberty and social justice? What is the appropriate role of government in protecting workers, consumers, and the environment, particularly from abuse by corporations? How do we address the demands for equality and fair treatment of workers, women, African Americans, immigrants, homosexuals, and others?

A Mosaic of Movements

Each of these 100 profiles can be read separately, but it will be quickly apparent that every individual was part of a mosaic of movements for social justice. These Americans linked their careers, talents, and achievements to collective efforts to make America a more democratic and equitable society. They spent most of their lives as activists for change. So it should not be surprising that many of these 100 individuals knew each other, were members of many of the same organizations, and participated in many of the same events.

These 100 people helped move America forward by organizing movements, pushing for radical reforms, popularizing progressive ideas, and spurring others to action. Some of them are identified with a particular issue—for example, women's rights or the environment—but most of them were involved in broad crusades for economic and social justice, revealing the many connections between different movements across generations.

Anthropologist Margaret Mead once said, "Never underestimate the power of a small group of people to change the world. In fact, it is the only way it ever has." Mead was both right and wrong. A small group of people can get things started. But significant progressive change—the battle for more democracy—only happens when large numbers of people get involved from the bottom up. Some limit their involvement to voting for candidates who voice their hopes and commit to fighting for laws that embody new rights. Others attend meetings, write letters to newspapers, sign petitions, donate money, and lobby their elected officials. Others join rallies and demonstrations, boycott, go on strike, and participate in sit-ins and other forms of civil disobedience. Movements succeed because thousands, and sometimes millions, of people bring their diverse talents and commitments to bear on what may seem like intractable moral problems.

Consider Rosa Parks. She is often portrayed as an exhausted middle-aged seamstress from Montgomery who, wanting to rest her tired feet after a hard day at work, simply violated the city's segregation law by refusing to move to the back of the bus. She is therefore revered as a selfless individual who, with one spontaneous act of courage, triggered the Montgomery bus boycott and became, as she is often called, the "mother of the civil rights movement." Often overlooked in this story is a much larger history: before Parks's stand, several other women had refused to give up their seats on buses, but those incidents triggered no larger protest. Because of her reputation as a veteran activist and her web of friendships, word of Parks's arrest spread quickly. E. D. Nixon, a leader of the National Association for the Advancement of Colored People (NAACP) and a union organizer, posted Parks's bond and asked for permission to use her case to challenge the city's bus segregation laws in court and in the streets. Jo Ann Robinson, an African American professor at the all-black Alabama State College and a leader of Montgomery's Women's Political Council (WPC), mimeographed thousands of leaflets urging Montgomery's blacks to stay off the city buses on Monday, when Parks would appear in court. Nixon, Robinson, and others circulated the leaflets among the city's segregated school system, churches, civic groups, and workplaces. Black teachers, for example, encouraged students in the city's segregated schools to take the leaflets home to parents. Robinson and Nixon asked black ministers to use their Sunday sermons to spread the word. The one-day boycott proved enormously effective. As King would later recall, "A miracle had taken place. The once dormant and quiescent Negro community was now fully awake." Within a few days, the boycott leaders had formed a new group, the Montgomery Improvement Association, and elected a reluctant Rev. Martin Luther King Jr. as president.

On December 5, 1955, the first day of the boycott, thousands of Montgomery's black citizens crowded into Holt Street Baptist Church for the Montgomery Improvement Association's first mass meeting. Inspired by King's words—"There comes a time when people get tired of being trampled over by the iron feet of oppression"—they voted unanimously to continue the boycott. The boycott lasted for 381 days. Although many African Americans walked to and from work during the boycott, the Montgomery Improvement Association also organized an elaborate private taxi plan with more than 200 cars as a parallel transportation system, an enormous undertaking. Drivers (including a handful of sympathetic whites) picked up and dropped off blacks who needed rides at designated points. Black community activists organized fund-raisers to raise money for gas and car repairs to keep the carpool system going. About 17,000 African Americans—almost all of the city's black bus riders—participated in the boycott, despite threats from employers and others that doing so could cost them their jobs. Throughout the year, boycott leaders successfully used church meetings, sermons, rallies, and songs to help maintain not just the black community's spirits but also its commitment to nonviolent tactics and its resolve against the opposition of the city's white business and political leaders. The boycott worked. The desegregation of Montgomery's buses inspired others across the South, catalyzing a new wave of civil rights activism.

As this example suggests, all movements need leaders as well as rank-and-file activists. There are many types of leaders in social movements—some leaders organize, others inspire by speaking, writing, singing, or producing art, others explain and educate, others raise money and keep the movement's organizations running.

One of the remarkable aspects of the lives of these 100 greatest Americans was their success in building organizations. No struggles for justice succeed without organization. We generally associate grassroots movements with relatively well-known mass-membership groups—like the National Woman Suffrage Association, the NAACP, the United Auto Workers (UAW), the Student Nonviolent Coordinating Committee (SNCC), the American Civil Liberties Union (ACLU), the Service Employees International Union, Planned Parenthood, and the Sierra Club—that can mobilize large numbers of people.

Another feature of the progressive movement is the small political parties—such as the Socialist Party, the Communist Party, the Women's Party, the American Labor Party, and the Green Party—that compete for votes in elections. The leaders and candidates of these parties rarely expect to win public office. They use political campaigns to raise issues, attract new followers, and push the mainstream parties to adopt some part of their platforms (which mainstream parties may do, but typically without acknowledging that they borrowed the ideas).

Often overlooked in the examination of progressive movements are the relatively small institutions that play a big role as catalysts. As you read the profiles, you will learn about Hull House, the National Consumers League, the Women's Trade Union League, the Highlander Folk School, Brookwood Labor College, the American Friends Service Committee, the Fellowship of Reconciliation, the War Resisters League, the Industrial Areas Foundation, the Catholic Worker, the Southern Conference for Human Welfare, the Midwest Academy—organizations that recruited, trained, and educated thousands of the key activists of the 20th century. And you will encounter publications like the *Appeal to Reason,* the *Call, The Nation,* and the *Progressive,* among others, which incubated and disseminated ideas. These small groups and publications kept the flame of social justice alive through difficult times, when conditions were bleak. They brought new activists into the progressive movement and fostered a sense of hope and possibility.

Outsiders and Insiders

The leaders, organizations, and movements that made America a more just society all had to learn how to balance the tension between outsiders and insiders.

Progressive insiders—typically elected officials, their advisers, and lobbyists—see their job as pushing through legislation that can alter living conditions, incomes, and access to opportunity. Lawmaking involves the art of compromise, which requires individuals adept at brokering deals, negotiating, and forging consensus.

Progressive outsiders—activists, protesters, reformers, and radicals—need different skills. They often view compromise as "selling out" by politicians tied to corporate and elite interests. Activists often believe that the influence of campaign contributions and the trade-offs required by legislative give-and-take make most elected officials undependable allies.

American history reveals that progressive change comes about when both insider and outsider strategies are at work. To gain any significant reforms, insiders and outsiders need each other. Boycotts, strikes, civil disobedience, and mass marches—outsider strategies—help put new issues on the agenda, dramatize long-ignored grievances, and generate media attention. This type of agitation gets people thinking about things they had not considered before and can change public opinion. Savvy liberal and progressive elected officials understand that they need "radical" protestors to change the political climate and make reform possible. When "disruption" is taking place in the streets, policymakers can appear statesmanlike and moderate in forging compromises to win legislative victories. For example, Abraham Lincoln was initially reluctant to divide the nation over the issue of slavery, but he eventually gave voice to the rising tide of abolitionism, a movement that had started decades earlier and was gaining momentum but could not succeed without an ally in the White House.

Heroes but Not Saints

None of the people in the Social Justice Hall of Fame was (or is) a saint. They all had vision, courage, persistence, and talent, but they also made mistakes. Some had troubled personal lives. Some expressed views that many progressives considered objectionable.

Margaret Sanger endorsed eugenics. Theodore Roosevelt's "big stick" imperialism outraged many progressives, as did Earl Warren's support for rounding up Japanese Americans and putting them in internment camps during World War II. Theodor Geisel's racist depictions of Japanese Americans in his editorial cartoons (under his pen name Dr. Seuss) for the radical newspaper *PM* contradicted his lifelong support for tolerance. Jackie Robinson's attack on Paul Robeson reflected Cold War tensions; Robinson later said he regretted his remarks. Many progressives admire Lyndon Johnson's commitment to civil rights and to fighting poverty but cannot forgive his expansion of the war in Vietnam. Senator Paul Wellstone voted in favor of the 1996 Defense of Marriage Act, which outlawed federal recognition of same-sex marriage, although he later said he regretted his stance on the issue.

Some of these views may be understandable in their historical context. It is important to recognize that although these 100 individuals were pioneers in most aspects of their thinking, they could not entirely transcend the political realities and social prejudices of their times.

Who Was Left Out?

The list does not include people who lived into the twentieth century but whose major achievements occurred in the previous century. This group includes labor organizer Mary Harris "Mother" Jones (1837–1930), environmentalist John Muir (1838–1914), journalist Jacob Riis (1849–1914), Knights of Labor leader Terence Powderly (1849–1924), agrarian Populist leader Mary Lease (1850–1933), economist and sociologist Thorstein Veblen (1857–1929), and African American journalist, feminist, and antilynching crusader Ida B. Wells (1862–1931).

The 20th century was filled with many courageous, heroic, and visionary thinkers and doers who breathed life into key movements for progressive change. No single list of 100 people can come close to capturing all the figures who deserve a place in the century's Social Justice Hall of Fame. Because they were part of collective crusades, they shared responsibilities—and achievements—with other leaders who played important roles in these movements. Readers who want to learn more about these efforts might want to explore the lives of one or more of the following fifty people (listed by date of birth) who deserve to be included on an expanded Social Justice Hall of Fame roster.

1. Julia Lathrop, social worker and social reformer (1858–1932)
2. Mary White Ovington, journalist and NAACP founder (1865–1951)
3. Lillian Wald, social worker and social reformer (1867–1940)
4. Stephen S. Wise, rabbi and social reformer (1874–1949)
5. Charles Beard, historian (1874–1948)
6. Mary McLeod Bethune, educator (1875–1955)
7. William English Walling, civil rights activist and NAACP founder (1877–1936)
8. Elizabeth Gurley Flynn, labor activist (1890–1964)
9. David Dubinsky, labor leader and president of the International Ladies' Garment Workers Union (1892–1982)
10. Paul Douglas, economist and U.S. senator (1892–1976)
11. Lewis Mumford, social critic (1895–1990)
12. Aaron Copland, composer (1900–1990)
13. Linus Pauling, scientist and peace activist (1901–1994)
14. Margaret Mead, anthropologist (1901–1978)
15. John Steinbeck, novelist (1902–1968)
16. Benjamin Spock, pediatrician and antiwar activist (1903–1998)
17. H. L. Mitchell, Southern Tenant Farmers Union organizer (1906–1989)
18. Edward R. Murrow, journalist (1908–1965)
19. Fred Ross Sr., community organizer (1910–1992)
20. Joseph Rauh, labor lawyer (1911–1992)
21. Paul Goodman, social critic (1911–1972)

22. Jonas Salk, scientist (1914–1995)
23. Daniel Berrigan, Catholic priest and antiwar activist (1921–)
24. William Appleman Williams, historian (1921–1990)
25. Harold Washington, congressman and mayor of Chicago (1922–1987)
26. Grace Paley, writer (1922–2007)
27. Anne Braden, civil rights activist (1924–2006)
28. James Baldwin, writer (1924–1987)
29. Robert Kennedy, U.S. senator and presidential candidate (1925–1968)
30. Phillip Burton, U.S. congressman (1926–1983)
31. Allen Ginsberg, poet (1926–1997)
32. Tony Mazzocchi, labor activist (1926–2002)
33. Harry Belafonte, performer (1927–)
34. Adrienne Rich, writer (1929–2012)
35. Dolores Huerta, United Farm Workers organizer (1930–)
36. Frances Fox Piven, political science and sociology professor (1932–)
37. Jonathan Kozol, social critic and education reformer (1936–)
38. Julian Bond, civil rights activist (1940–)
39. Phil Ochs, folksinger (1940–1976)
40. Bernice Johnson Reagon, singer and musicologist (1942–)
41. Ernesto Cortés, community organizer (1943–)
42. Randall Forsberg, antiwar activist (1943–2007)
43. Arthur Ashe, athlete (1943–1993)
44. Wade Rathke, community organizer (1948–)
45. Holly Near, singer and feminist (1949–)
46. John Sayles, filmmaker (1950–)
47. Andy Stern, union organizer and president of Service Employees International Union (1950–)
48. Miguel Contreras, union organizer and leader of Los Angeles County Federation of Labor (1952–2005)
49. Cornel West, philosopher and activist (1953–)
50. Barbara Kingsolver, writer (1955–)

Each generation of Americans faces a different set of economic, political, and social conditions. There are no easy formulas for challenging injustice and promoting democracy. Many historians—most prominently Howard Zinn in *A People's History of the United States* and Eric Foner in *The Story of American Freedom*—have chronicled the story of America's utopians, radicals, and reformers, reminding us of their successes and failures. Every generation needs to retell this story, reinterpret it, and use it to help shape the present and future. Unless we know this history, we will have little understanding of how far we have come, how we got here, and how progress was made by the moral convictions and courage of the greatest Americans.

20th-Century Timeline

1900 ▸ International Ladies' Garment Workers Union founded.

1901 ▸ New York State passes a landmark Tenement House Act.

▸ Socialist Party founded.

1903 ▸ W. E. B. Du Bois's *The Souls of Black Folk* published.

▸ National Women's Trade Union League founded.

1905 ▸ Industrial Workers of the World (IWW, or Wobblies) founded.

1906 ▸ Upton Sinclair's *The Jungle* published.

▸ Meat Inspection Act and Pure Food and Drug Act passed.

1909 ▸ *La Follette's Magazine* founded (later renamed *The Progressive*).

▸ NAACP founded.

▸ "Uprising of the 20,000": female shirtwaist makers in New York strike against sweatshop conditions.

1910 ▸ Milwaukee voters elect Socialist Emil Seidel as mayor, elect a Socialist Party majority to the city council, and elect Socialist Victor Berger to Congress.

1911 ▸ Triangle Shirtwaist Factory fire.

▸ Feminist writer Charlotte Perkins Gilman publishes *The Man-Made World,* one of several of her books that advocate for women's economic and social freedom and redefine gender roles.

1912 ▸ Woodrow Wilson (Democrat) beats William Howard Taft (Republican), Theodore Roosevelt (Progressive) and Eugene Debs (Socialist) for president.

▸ Socialist Party has about 120,000 members, and 1,039 Socialist Party members hold public office, mostly in local cities and towns.

▸ Bread and Roses textile strike in Lawrence, Massachusetts.

1913 ▸ Alice Paul and Lucy Burns organize the Congressional Union, later known as the National Woman's Party, to organize for women's suffrage and women's rights.

1914 ▸ Congress passes Clayton Antitrust Act to break up corporate monopolies.

▸ Ludlow Massacre: John D. Rockefeller's private army kills thirteen women and children and seven men in a Colorado coal miners strike.

1916 ▸ Fellowship of Reconciliation founded.

▸ Jeannette Rankin of Montana becomes the first woman elected to the US House of Representatives.

1917 ▸ United States enters World War I.

1919 ▸ Palmer Raids begin: FBI arrests and deports radicals; seizes and shuts down radical publications.

▸ Four million American workers (one of every five) walk out in a great strike wave, including national clothing, coal, and steel strikes, a general strike in Seattle, Washington, and a police strike in Boston, Massachusetts.

1920 ▸ Eugene Debs wins almost 1 million votes (3.5 percent) for president while in jail for opposing World War I.

▸ American Civil Liberties Union founded.

▸ Nineteenth Amendment passed, legalizing women's suffrage.

1921 ▸ Margaret Sanger founds American Birth Control League (later called Planned Parenthood).

1924 ▸ The Immigration Act of 1924 limits the annual number of immigrants who can be admitted from any country to 2 percent of the number of people from that country already living in the United States in 1890, down from the 3 percent cap set by the Immigration Restriction Act of 1921.

1925 ▸ Brotherhood of Sleeping Car Porters, the first African American labor union, founded.

1929 ▸ The Great Depression begins.

1932 ▸ Norris-La Guardia Act passed, prohibiting federal injunctions in most labor disputes.

▸ Franklin D. Roosevelt elected president.

▸ Myles Horton cofounds the Highlander Folk School in Tennessee.

1933 ▸ Dorothy Day founds Catholic Worker.

1934 ▸ San Francisco general strike.

1935 ▸ Congress passes the National Labor Relations (Wagner) Act.

▸ Congress passes the Social Security Act.

▸ Mary McLeod Bethune organizes the National Council of Negro Women.

> ▸ Progressive unionists form the Committee for Industrial Organization (CIO) within the American Federation of Labor (AFL).

1936 ▸ Southern Conference for Human Welfare founded.

1937 ▸ Auto workers win a sit-down strike against General Motors in Flint, Michigan.

▸ Brotherhood of Sleeping Car Porters wins contract with the Pullman Company.

1938 ▸ Congress passes Fair Labor Standards Act, which establishes the first minimum wage and forty-hour week.

▸ Congress of Industrial Organizations (CIO) forms as an independent federation.

1939 ▸ Saul Alinsky founds Back of the Yards Neighborhood Council in Chicago.

1940 ▸ Congress passes the Alien Registration Act (Smith Act).

▸ Woody Guthrie writes "This Land Is Your Land."

1941 ▸ A. Philip Randolph threatens a march on Washington, D.C., to protest racial discrimination in defense jobs.

▸ President Roosevelt signs Executive Order 8802 prohibiting racial discrimination in defense industries and creating the Fair Employment Practices Committee. Randolph calls off the march.

▸ US troops enter combat in World War II.

1942 ▸ Congress of Racial Equality (CORE) founded.

1946 ▸ Winston Churchill's iron curtain speech in Missouri marks the beginning of the Cold War.

▸ Largest strike wave in US history.

1947 ▸ Congress passes Taft-Hartley Act, which restricts union members' activities.

▸ Jackie Robinson integrates major league baseball.

▸ CORE begins Journey of Reconciliation (first Freedom Rides) to challenge segregation.

1948 ▸ President Harry S. Truman desegregates the armed services with Executive Order 9981.

▸ Former vice president Henry Wallace campaigns for president on the Progressive Party ticket.

1950 ▸ Harry Hay cofounds Mattachine Society, first homosexual rights group.

1953 ▸ I. F. Stone founds *I. F. Stone's Weekly.*

▸ Arthur Miller's play *The Crucible* premieres.

1954 ▶ US Supreme Court rules in *Brown v. Board of Education* that school segregation is unconstitutional.

1955 ▶ Montgomery activists organize bus boycott.

▶ AFL merges with CIO to form AFL-CIO.

▶ Daughters of Bilitis, the first lesbian organization in the United States, founded.

1956 ▶ C. Wright Mills's *The Power Elite* published.

▶ Sierra Club gains national recognition for successfully protesting the construction of the Echo Park Dam in Dinosaur National Monument in Utah.

1957 ▶ Committee for a SANE Nuclear Policy founded.

1958 ▶ John Kenneth Galbraith publishes *The Affluent Society*.

▶ Albert Bigelow—a former lieutenant commander in the US Navy who commanded three combat vessels in World War II—sets out from San Pedro, California, with four crewmen aboard the *Golden Rule*, a small sailboat, to protest nuclear testing in waters off the Marshall Islands, located in the western Pacific between Guam and Hawaii.

1960 ▶ College students in Greensboro, North Carolina, organize the first sit-in at Woolworth's lunch counter.

▶ Student Nonviolent Coordinating Committee (SNCC) founded.

▶ CBS broadcasts Edward R. Murrow's *Harvest of Shame* documentary about miserable conditions for migrant farm workers.

1961 ▶ Freedom Rides begin.

▶ Bay of Pigs invasion.

1962 ▶ US Supreme Court decides the *Baker v. Carr* case about political reapportionment, which led to what was then called the "one man, one vote" standard.

▶ Michael Harrington publishes *The Other America* about widespread poverty.

▶ Rachel Carson publishes *Silent Spring* about dangers of pesticides.

▶ Students for a Democratic Society (SDS) publishes its Port Huron Statement manifesto.

▶ Bob Dylan writes "Blowin' in the Wind."

1963 ▶ Betty Friedan's *The Feminine Mystique* published.

▶ March on Washington for jobs and freedom.

▶ John F. Kennedy assassinated.

1964 ▶ Congress passes Lyndon Johnson's major antipoverty legislation, the Economic Opportunity Act.

- ▸ Civil rights activists organize Mississippi Freedom Summer voter registration project.
- ▸ Congress passes the Civil Rights Act.
- ▸ Congress passes the Wilderness Act.
- ▸ Congress passes the Gulf of Tonkin Resolution authorizing US combat troops in Vietnam.

1965 ▸ US Supreme Court decides *Griswold v. Connecticut*, striking down prohibition of use of contraceptives by married couples.

- ▸ Watts riots in Los Angeles.
- ▸ Congress passes the Voting Rights Act.
- ▸ Malcolm X assassinated.
- ▸ United States sends troops to Vietnam.
- ▸ First "teach-in" on the Vietnam War held at the University of Michigan.
- ▸ The Motor Vehicle Air Pollution Control Act sets the first federal automobile emission standards.

1966 ▸ Betty Friedan cofounds National Organization for Women.

- ▸ United Farm Workers union signs a contract with DiGiorgio Fruit Corporation after a strike and consumer boycott.

1967 ▸ President Johnson appoints Thurgood Marshall as the first African American to sit on the Supreme Court.

- ▸ Riots in Detroit, Michigan, Newark, New Jersey, and other cities.
- ▸ In *Loving v. Virginia*, US Supreme Court finds the state antimiscegenation laws are unconstitutional, ending all race-based legal restrictions on marriage.

1968 ▸ Tet offensive in Vietnam.

- ▸ Martin Luther King Jr. assassinated in Memphis during garbage workers strike.
- ▸ Robert Kennedy assassinated in Los Angeles during presidential campaign.
- ▸ Congress passes Fair Housing Act.

1969 ▸ The Santa Barbara oil well blowout spills over 200,000 gallons of oil into the ocean over eleven days.

- ▸ Stonewall riot in Greenwich Village catalyzes the gay liberation movement.

1970 ▸ First national Earth Day.

- ▸ National Guard shoots antiwar protesters at Kent State and Jackson State.

▸ Arkansas Community Organization for Reform Now (ACORN) founded.

▸ Congress passes the Clean Air Act.

▸ Congress passes the Occupational Safety and Health Act.

▸ Congress passes the National Environmental Policy Act (NEPA), requiring every federal agency to prepare an environmental impact statement (EIS) for any legislation.

▸ President Richard Nixon works with Congress to establish the Environmental Protection Agency (EPA).

▸ Dennis Hayes organizes a movement to unseat "The Dirty Dozen," twelve members of Congress with poor records on environmental policy.

1971 ▸ Greenpeace activists sail from Vancouver, British Columbia, to Amchitka, Alaska, intent on stopping a scheduled US nuclear test.

1972 ▸ Congress passes the Consumer Product Safety Act.

▸ *Ms.* magazine founded.

▸ Congress passes Title IX of Education Amendments to the Civil Rights Act of 1964.

▸ DDT banned in the United States.

1973 ▸ US Supreme Court's *Roe v. Wade* ruling legalizes abortion.

▸ American Psychiatric Association removes homosexuality from its official list of mental disorders.

▸ Congress passes the Endangered Species Act.

1974 ▸ Coalition of Labor Union Women founded.

1976 ▸ Toxic Substances Control Act mandates the EPA to control all new and existing chemical substances being used in the United States.

1977 ▸ Gay rights activist Harvey Milk elected to the San Francisco Board of Supervisors.

▸ Congress passes the Community Reinvestment Act outlawing racial discrimination in lending (redlining).

1978 ▸ Protests by residents of Love Canal, a neighborhood in Niagara Falls, New York, lead to revelations that up to 21,000 tons of toxic waste had been dumped in the canal by the Hooker Chemical Company from 1942 to 1952, causing significant numbers of birth defects, abnormalities in children, and miscarriages.

1979 ▸ Nuclear accident at Three Mile Island in Pennsylvania.

1980 ▸ Congress passes Superfund legislation, which mandates cleanup of abandoned hazardous waste sites by the parties responsible.

▸ Ronald Reagan elected president.

1981 ▸ President Reagan breaks air traffic controllers strike.

     ▸ AFL-CIO rallies 400,000 in Washington, D.C., on Solidarity Day.

1982 ▸ Nuclear freeze rally in New York City draws 1 million people in association with the special session on disarmament at the United Nations.

     ▸ Wisconsin becomes the first state to outlaw discrimination on the basis of sexual orientation.

1984 ▸ EMILY's List founded to expand campaign contributions to women and feminist candidates.

1986 ▸ In *Meritor Savings Bank v. Vinson*, the US Supreme Court finds that sexual harassment is a form of illegal job discrimination.

1990 ▸ Congress passes the Americans with Disabilities Act.

1992 ▸ Service Employees International Union's Justice for Janitors campaign organizes thousands of low-paid, immigrant service workers in Los Angeles and other cities.

     ▸ Riots occur in Los Angeles after a jury acquits four white Los Angeles Police Department officers accused of beating Rodney King.

     ▸ Bill Clinton elected president.

1993 ▸ Congress passes the Family and Medical Leave Act.

1994 ▸ The Violence Against Women Act tightens federal penalties for sex offenders, funds services for victims of rape and domestic violence, and provides for special training of police officers.

1997 ▸ Students Against Sweatshops persuades Duke University to require manufacturers of items with the Duke label to sign a pledge that they will not use sweatshop labor—the first victory of the campus antisweatshop movement.

1999 ▸ More than 75,000 human-service workers are unionized in Los Angeles County.

     ▸ Union and environmental activists join forces for the "Battle in Seattle" protests at World Trade Organization meeting to challenge free trade.

2000 ▸ Vice President Al Gore wins the popular vote over George W. Bush in the presidential race. The US Supreme Court overturns popular and Electoral College vote and gives Bush the presidency.

THE 100
GREATEST AMERICANS
OF THE 20TH CENTURY

Tom Johnson
(1854–1911)

IN THE late 1800s and early 1900s, American cities were a tangle of corruption. Big business was growing in size and political influence, exploiting immigrants from abroad and migrants from rural areas in the burgeoning factory system. Bribery of local officials was widespread, giving businesses private monopolies over key public services, which were typically run inefficiently. Cities were starved for cash, but businesses paid little taxes.

With help from crusading journalists, middle-class reformers, and trade unions, a wave of progressive local officials sought to improve working and living conditions for the urban working class. Reform mayors in Cleveland, Toledo, and Cincinnati, Ohio; Detroit, Michigan; Jersey City, New Jersey; Philadelphia, Pennsylvania; Los Angeles, California; Bridgeport, Connecticut; and many other cities fought to tax wealthy property owners, create municipal electricity and water utilities, and hold down transit fares. They enacted and strengthened laws to establish building codes, moves guaranteed to make them unpopular with slum landlords. They worked alongside unions and reformers to enact laws to make factories safer. During strikes, they would not allow local police to protect strikebreaking "scabs." They expanded the number of municipal parks and recreation programs and improved local schools, especially for immigrants and their children. They hired competent administrators to run municipal agencies to clean up the corruption and inefficiency.

Tom Johnson, the mayor of Cleveland between 1901 and 1909, was the most effective of the progressive reform mayors. He was a wealthy businessman—one of a significant number of rich reformers who became "traitors" to their class, although in Johnson's case it was a class he had climbed into through hard work and influence peddling, not one he was born into.

Johnson was a municipal entrepreneur who expanded the powers of local government to challenge business influence in Cleveland. As mayor, he lowered streetcar fares, created municipally owned public baths, adopted government inspection standards for milk and meat, and expanded the city's park system. Johnson appointed Rev. Harris Cooley as his director of charities and correction.

Cooley created a 2,000-acre farm colony outside the city; it included the Cleveland Workhouse—designed to rehabilitate, not just punish, criminals—as well as the tuberculosis sanatorium and a progressive reform school for boys.

Journalist **Lincoln Steffens** called Johnson "the best Mayor of the best-governed city in the United States."

Johnson's father had fought for the Confederacy during the Civil War, and his family had owned slaves. While living in Louisville, Kentucky, Johnson quit school, took an office job with a street railway company, and worked his way up to superintendent. He invented a pay-box for trolleys and became wealthy from licensing the patent. In 1876, he purchased his own railway line in Indianapolis and then invested in other firms, including steel mills and railway companies across the Midwest. He would purchase broken-down streetcars and make minimal repairs, then use his political clout and bribes to get local officials to extend the railway system, selling them the reconditioned streetcars for huge profits. He acknowledged, "I am bound to do the best I can for myself. And so I rush in and grab all the monopolies I can get my hands on." One of Johnson's fiercest enemies was Hazen Pingree, the reform mayor of Detroit (1890–1897), who battled Johnson over rising streetcar fares.

Johnson hated being ridiculed by Mayor Pingree and other Detroit civic leaders for his influence peddling, and he had a crisis of conscience. He began to deplore the corrupt business and political practices that had brought him wealth. He entered politics. But after serving several uneventful terms in Congress, he returned to Cleveland to run for mayor, inspired by Pingree and by the radical ideas of Henry George (author of an influential 1879 book, *Progress and Poverty*).

Johnson was elected Cleveland's mayor in 1901 on a platform of "home rule, 3-cent fare, and just taxation." Before he became mayor, he observed, "The public utility corporations are a bunch of thieves. I ought to know. I was one of them." Johnson believed that public utilities—including electric plants, railroads, and trash-removal services—should be regulated, taxed, and even owned by local governments. "If you do not own them they in turn will own you," he said. "They will rule your politics, corrupt your institutions and finally destroy your liberties."

Under Johnson's administration, the city took over garbage collection and disposal and street cleaning, eliminating the bribery and corruption associated with those activities when they had been controlled by private firms. He cleaned up Cleveland's Water Department, lowered rates, and, as a result, improved public health. State law thwarted Johnson's plan to establish a municipal streetcar system, but he outmaneuvered his opponents by pressuring the city's private streetcar company to lease its properties to a municipal traction company, controlled by a five-person board appointed by the mayor.

Johnson's greatest legacy was his successful battle to create a municipally-owned electrical utility, the Municipal Light Company, known as Muny Light. He thought a public utility would provide an alternative to—and a check on—

Cleveland Electrical Illuminating Company (CEI), the powerful private company that had a monopoly at the time. Johnson's efforts triggered the opposition of the private utilities' owners and other business leaders, including the Chamber of Commerce. They warned it would lead to socialism. Despite occasional phases of poor management, Muny Light has provided Cleveland's residents with relatively cheap electricity. (In 1983 its name was changed to Cleveland Public Power.) Several times since the early 1900s, Cleveland's business leaders tried to persuade city officials to sell Muny Light. (In the 1970s, after Mayor Dennis Kucinich refused to do so, the business establishment worked successfully to defeat him for reelection.)

A Democrat, Johnson was extremely popular among Cleveland's working-class voters and gained a national reputation as an incorruptible reformer. After only one term as mayor, Johnson became the Democrats' candidate for Ohio governor in 1903. He campaigned for state taxation of railroad companies and other public utilities. He lost the election but continued to serve as mayor, winning three more terms.

Johnson was Cleveland's mayor at the same time that **Robert M. La Follette** became governor of Wisconsin. Both paved the way for other progressive big-city mayors and governors who viewed their role as allies of labor unions, housing advocates, and other reform movements. These include Emil Seidel and Daniel Webster Hoan (Milwaukee's Socialist Party mayors from 1910 to 1912 and from 1916 to 1940, respectively), **Hiram Johnson** (California's governor from 1911 to 1917), Al Smith (New York's governor from 1918 to 1920 and 1922 to 1928), **Floyd Olson** (Minnesota's governor from 1931 to 1936), Frank Murphy (Detroit's mayor from 1930 to 1933 and later Michigan's governor from 1937 to 1939), and **Fiorello La Guardia** (New York City's mayor from 1934 to 1945). They demonstrated the positive role that progressive and efficient government could play in improving people's daily lives. Johnson's Cleveland was a laboratory of Progressive Era reform that inspired activists elsewhere and laid the foundation for **Franklin D. Roosevelt**'s New Deal.

Robert M. La Follette Sr. (1855–1925)

CREDIT: Library of Congress, Prints and Photos Division. National Photo Company Collection

IN 1921, Senator Robert M. La Follette of Wisconsin had to decide whether to seek reelection. He was scheduled to give a major speech before the Wisconsin legislature, and his aides urged him to tone down the fiery antiwar rhetoric.

La Follette had opposed US involvement in World War I. In 1917, two days after President Woodrow Wilson's call for the United States to enter the war, La Follette attacked Wilson's decision: "The poor who are always the ones called upon to rot in the trenches have no organized power," La Follette said. "But oh, Mr. President, at some time they will be heard. . . . There will come an awakening. They will have their day, and they will be heard."

After the war, La Follette continued to voice these views. He called for investigations of corporate "war profiteers" and defended socialist **Eugene Debs** and others who had been jailed for their opposition to the war. Some Wisconsinites, as well as many Washington, DC, insiders and newspapers, condemned him as a traitor. La Follette realized his speech before the state legislature would be an important turning point in his political career. He pounded the lectern and clenched his fist into the air. "I am going to be a candidate for reelection to the United States Senate," he boomed. "I do not want the vote of a single citizen under any misapprehension of where I stand: I would not change my record on the war for that of any man, living or dead."

After a moment of stunned silence, the crowd erupted into thunderous applause. Even one staunch critic, standing at the back of the chamber with tears running down his cheeks, told a reporter: "I hate the son of a bitch. But, my God, what guts he's got."

Perhaps La Follette simply had a better understanding of Wisconsin voters. They reelected him that year with 80 percent of their votes.

"Fighting Bob" La Follette spent his entire political career—as a US congressman (1885–1890), governor of Wisconsin (1901–1906), US senator (1907–1925), and candidate for president (1924)—challenging militarism and corporate power. During his life and after his death, La Follette inspired generations of reformers and radicals.

Born in Dane County's Primrose township, La Follette worked as a farm laborer before enrolling at the University of Wisconsin in 1875, graduating four years later. The following year he ran successfully for district attorney. In 1884 he was elected to Congress on the Republican ticket, but he was defeated by a Democrat in 1890.

After returning home, the state's Republican leader, Senator Philetus Sawyer, offered La Follette a bribe to fix a court case against several former state officials. Not only did La Follette refuse the bribe, but he also publicly denounced the way money was used to corrupt democracy. For the next ten years, as a leader of the progressive wing of the Republican Party, La Follette spoke out against the political influence of the railroad and lumber barons who dominated his own lo-cal party. In 1900 he ran for governor pledging to clean up the corruption. He gave an average of ten to fifteen speeches a day. He won handily.

While he was governor, the state became a laboratory for progressive reform that influenced progressive movements and farmer-labor alliances in other states and the New Deal three decades later. La Follette weakened the power of big business and party machines by enacting campaign spending limits and direct primary elections, which gave voters the right to choose their own candidates for office. He supported measures that doubled the taxes on the railroads, broke up monopolies, preserved the state's forests, protected workers' rights, defended small farmers, and regulated lobbying to end patronage politics.

Elected to the US Senate in 1906, La Follette became a leader of the Senate's progressives. In 1909, as the progressive movement grew across America, La Fol-lette launched a publication that became a major voice for radical ideas. It was originally called *La Follette's Magazine*. Its goal, La Follette wrote, was "winning back for the people the complete power over government—national, state, and municipal—which has been lost to them." The magazine championed women's suffrage, led the fight to stay out of World War I, criticized the post-war Palmer Raids as a violation of civil liberties, and supported workers' rights and control of corporate power. Although never a commercial success, the magazine was popular among progressive farmers and working people and helped raise La Follette's na-tional profile even more. In 1928 it was renamed *The Progressive*. Since his death, the publication has remained a major voice of dissent and is still published in Madison, Wisconsin.

Breaking again from his party, La Follette supported Democrat Woodrow Wilson in the 1912 presidential election over former president **Theodore Roo-sevelt** (a fellow Republican running on the Bull Moose Party ticket), William Howard Taft (the Republican candidate), and Eugene Debs (the Socialist candi-date). But after the election, La Follette became Wilson's biggest Senate foe over the issue of US involvement in the European war. He was one of only six sena-tors to vote against Wilson's declaration of war. As Wilson rounded up antiwar radicals, including Debs, La Follette became the dissenters' biggest defender. "Never in all my many years' experience in the House and in the Senate," he told his Senate colleagues, "have I heard so much democracy preached and so little practiced as during the last few months."

After the war, La Follette advocated measures to protect workers and consumers against big business, for women's suffrage, for a progressive income tax, and for farm loan programs. He also continued to attack "war profiteers" who had backed US involvement in World War I and even profited from it. Many La Follette–watchers viewed his momentous 1922 reelection victory as a vindication of his anticorporate and antiwar stances.

A coalition of unions, socialists, and farmers convinced La Follette to run for president in 1924 as an independent progressive. During the campaign, La Follette called for government takeover of the railroads, elimination of private utilities, workers' right to organize unions, easier credit for farmers, outlawing of child labor, stronger protection for civil liberties, an end to US imperialism in Latin America, and a requirement for a plebiscite before any president could declare war. He promised to "break the combined power of the private monopoly system over the political and economic life of the American people" and decried "any discrimination between races, classes, and creeds"—far ahead of most political figures.

La Follette won almost 5 million votes (about one-sixth of the popular vote). He came in first in Wisconsin and second in eleven Western states and won working-class districts of major cities. Since then, no radical candidate for president has ever won that many votes. Less than a year later, in June 1925, the seventy-year-old La Follette died of a heart attack.

Not only did La Follette forge a popular labor-farmer alliance, but his legacy also included the many activists who worked in his campaigns and whose work and ideas shaped American politics for many decades. Harold Ickes Sr., an influential adviser to La Follette's 1924 campaign, became part of **Franklin D. Roosevelt**'s inner circle and a major architect of the New Deal. In 1964, only two US senators—Democrat Ernest Gruening of Alaska and Republican Wayne Morse of Oregon—courageously voted against the Gulf of Tonkin Resolution, which **Lyndon B. Johnson** used to get the authority to take military action in Vietnam without a declaration of war. Gruening, a one-time editor of *The Nation*, had served as spokesman for La Follette's 1924 campaign. Morse was a Wisconsin native, born in 1900, who told *Time* magazine in 1956 that his fondest memory as a young man was lapping up liberal philosophy "at the feet of the great Robert La Follette Sr."

In 2011, Wisconsinites organized a mass movement to protest Republican governor Scott Walker's steep budget cuts and attacks on workers' collective bargaining rights. At rallies and in the media, many protesters invoked the memory of a previous Republican governor who made Wisconsin a laboratory for progressive reform and whose bust stands in front of the state capitol building. Under La Follette, columnist Bill Wineke wrote in 2011, Wisconsin had "championed the rights of working people and upheld the dignity of the unfortunate."

CREDIT: Associated Press

Eugene Debs
(1855–1926)

IN 1920, Eugene Victor Debs ran for president from a cell in the federal prison in Atlanta, Georgia, convicted for opposing World War I. Heading the Socialist Party ticket, Debs won nearly a million votes—3.5 percent of the popular vote—in a four-way race that also included the Democrats, Republicans, and Progressives. The vote was a tribute to Debs, a beloved figure in many parts of America, but it was also a reminder of the young country's propensity for official repression when confronted with dissent and protest.

Debs was both a fierce patriot and a fiery radical. He came to his socialist politics gradually, even reluctantly. Perhaps because of this he could persuade and agitate audiences with his radical message, for he embodied the best of America's ideals of justice, compassion, and fairness.

Debs looked like a bald Sunday School teacher, all six and a half feet of him, with a kind face and an aura of optimism and hope. His political and social views emerged from his Christian upbringing in the heartland of Indiana. He absorbed the small-town values of skilled workers striving to join the middle class and the virtues of hard work, frugality, and benevolence.

The son of Alsatian immigrant retail grocers, Debs was born and raised in Terre Haute, Indiana. As a youth, he loved reading the fiery speeches of dissidents like Patrick Henry and John Brown and soon began attending lectures by such well-known orators as James Whitcomb Riley, abolitionist Wendell Phillips, and suffragist Susan B. Anthony. He left school at fourteen to work as a paint scraper in the Terre Haute railroad yards. He quickly rose to a job as a locomotive fireman. He was laid off during the depression of 1873, found another job as a billing clerk for a grocery company, and never worked for a railroad company again. But he remained close to his railroad friends, who admired his leadership skills. When the Brotherhood of Locomotive Firemen (BLF) organized a chapter in Terre Haute in 1875, Debs signed up as a charter member and was elected recording secretary.

Debs originally viewed the BLF as a kind of charitable and fraternal organization, helping injured workers and, if necessary, their widows and children. He opposed strikes and the violence that often accompanied them, even though the police and company thugs often caused the violence. After the railroad strike of 1877—the first truly national strike in US history, which ended in defeat for the unions after heavy government repression—Debs gave a speech defending the union from charges, widespread in the press, that it had encouraged violence. Debs got a rousing reception and was soon named grand secretary of the national union and editor of its magazine. Under Debs's editorship, the magazine became a leading labor voice, its readership expanding far beyond BLF members.

In addition to this union job, Debs embarked on a political career. He served two terms as city clerk of Terre Haute and was elected to the Indiana State Assembly in 1884, but after one term he decided that the labor movement was a better way to achieve his reformist goals. He still believed in the possibility of industrial cooperation and discouraged workers from participating in confrontations with employers or the government.

In the mid-1880s, the railroad companies—which had once provided well-paying jobs to their skilled workers—began reclassifying occupations and cutting wages. This led to a series of major strikes, each of which was crushed by the railroad companies. The companies hired private thugs to use violence against strikers and pitted the different railroad brotherhoods against each other, hiring scab employees from different trades to replace the strikers.

These events shook Debs's thinking. As late as 1886, Debs, along with other railroad brotherhood officials, refused to support the Knights of Labor strike against Jay Gould's railroad company. When the fledgling American Federation of Labor that year led a national general strike for the eight-hour workday, Debs was silent. But with this new strike wave, Debs began to question whether big corporations could ever be trusted to work cooperatively with workers or to support political democracy.

In 1891, realizing that railroad workers were easily divided and could not prevail against the growing economic and political power of the corporations, Debs left the BLF. He saw the need for an industry-wide union organization that would unite all railroad workers. His guiding principle became the Knights of Labor slogan: "An injury to one is the concern of all." In 1893, Debs brought together union leaders from the different crafts at a meeting in Chicago and founded the American Railway Union (ARU).

The ARU's membership grew quickly. It was the first large national industrial union, a forerunner of the great industrial unions that emerged in the 1930s, and it won its first major test. In response to a strike, the Great Northern Railroad in 1893 capitulated to almost all the union's demands.

The next year, the Pullman Company laid off workers and cut wages but did not lower rent in the company-owned houses or prices for groceries at the company store where workers were required to shop. Workers from Pullman asked the ARU for support. Some Chicago civic leaders, including **Jane Addams,** tried to arrange behind-the-scenes diplomacy to settle the strike, but Pullman refused to negotiate. So Debs and the ARU called for a national boycott (or a "sympathy strike") of Pullman cars. The ARU's 150,000 members in over twenty states refused to work on trains pulling the cars. They went on strike, not to win any demands of their own but to help several thousand Pullman workers win their strike. But the railroads found a sympathetic judge who ruled that the boycott was interfering with the US mail and issued an injunction to end the boycott. The ARU refused to desist, so President Grover Cleveland—a Democrat and a foe of the labor movement—sent in federal troops. ARU leaders, including Debs, were arrested on conspiracy charges. Debs and his union compatriots were sentenced to six-month jail terms for disregarding the injunction.

Debs used his six months in prison to think about what had gone wrong with his union organizing. He decided that the collusion between the ever-larger corporations and the federal government, including the courts and the National Guard, could not be undone by union activism alone. Redeeming American democracy from its corporate stranglehold required political action. Because both Republican and Democratic presidents called in troops to stop working-class victories, Debs was convinced that America needed a new political party, one whose base would be made up of workers and their unions.

Milwaukee's Socialist leader **Victor Berger** visited Debs in jail, bringing a copy of Karl Marx's *Das Kapital*. Debs read it carefully and began to consider the potential of socialism as an alternative to capitalism. After his release, he traveled to Chicago by train, and was astonished to see a crowd of over 100,000 people gathered in the pouring rain to greet him.

Debs helped organize the Social Democratic Party, a new party modeled on similar growing mass organizations in Europe. He ran for president on the party's ticket in 1900 and received 88,000 votes. The next year, the Social Democrats merged with some members of the Socialist Labor Party to form the Socialist Party of America. Debs ran again for president in 1904, this time attracting 400,000 votes. In 1905, he joined with other union activists and radicals to start the Industrial Workers of the World (IWW), the "Wobblies," as they were known. But although he and the Wobblies shared a belief in organizing all workers into "one big union," Debs did not share their opposition to political action, to running candidates for office. The IWW favored what they called "direct action" instead, including seizing direct control of industry through mass strikes.

Debs resigned from the IWW in 1908 and ran for president a third time, doing no better than in 1904. But by 1910, America's mood was changing. Dozens of Socialists won victories in local and state races for office, advancing a specific agenda of radical reforms, including women's right to vote, child labor laws, and workers' rights to join unions and when necessary to strike, as well as workplace safety laws for workers in railroads, mines, and factories. Two years later, they expanded their victories, and Debs polled nearly 1 million votes for president. He would have garnered more votes, but two other candidates—Democrat Woodrow Wilson and Progressive Party candidate (and former president) **Theodore Roosevelt**—stole some of the Socialists' thunder, diverting the votes of workers, women, and consumers with promises of such "progressive" reforms as women's suffrage, child labor laws, and workers' right to organize unions. One cartoonist drew a picture of Debs skinny-dipping while Teddy Roosevelt made off with his clothes.

Debs was a tireless campaigner but could not expect sympathetic coverage in the mainstream press. The socialist newspapers—the *Appeal to Reason* in the Midwest and the *Jewish Daily Forward* in New York, in particular—covered his campaign and had large readerships. Still, Debs had to travel to get the word out, taking trains from city to city, speaking wherever a crowd could be assembled. Without microphones, Debs had to speak loudly and dramatically; his words rippled through the crowd as people relayed the speech to one another.

Despite Debs's defeat in 1912, he won over 10 percent of the vote in Arizona, California, Idaho, Montana, Nevada, Oklahoma, Oregon, and Washington State. His campaign helped fellow Socialists win elections throughout the country. That year, about 1,200 Socialist Party members held public office in 340 cities, including seventy-nine mayors in cities including Milwaukee, Buffalo, Minneapolis, Reading, and Schenectady.

In 1917, President Wilson asked Congress to declare war on Germany and its allies. That move catalyzed widespread opposition from within the Senate (led by **Robert M. La Follette**) and by civil libertarians, religious pacifists, and Socialists, led by Debs. Congress passed the Espionage Act, which made it illegal to incite active opposition to US involvement in the war. Federal agents arrested scores of Socialists, Wobblies, and other dissidents. Though ill, Debs delivered a series of antiwar speeches; he was arrested, charged with impeding the war effort, convicted, and sentenced to ten years in federal prison.

On September 18, Debs delivered his most famous speech in a Cleveland federal courtroom upon being sentenced to prison. His opening remarks remain some of the most moving words in American history:

> Your Honor, years ago I recognized my kinship with all living beings, and I made up my mind that I was not one bit better than the meanest on earth. I said then, and I say now, that while there is a lower class, I am in it, and while there is a criminal element I am of it, and while there is a soul in prison, I am not free.
>
> I listened to all that was said in this court in support and justification of this prosecution, but my mind remains unchanged. I look upon the Espionage Law as a despotic enactment in flagrant conflict with democratic principles and with the spirit of free institutions.
>
> Your Honor, I have stated in this court that I am opposed to the social system in which we live; that I believe in a fundamental change—but if possible by peaceable and orderly means.

Two years later Debs ran for president on the Socialist ticket for the fifth and final time. The slogan on a campaign poster in 1920 read, "From Atlanta Prison to the White House, 1920." A popular campaign button showed Debs in prison garb, standing outside the prison gates, with the caption: "For President, Convict No. 9653." Debs received nearly a million votes.

On Christmas Day 1921, President Warren G. Harding, a Republican, freed Debs and twenty-three other prisoners of conscience. By the time they were released, the socialist movement that Debs had helped build was dead, a victim of government repression and internal factional fighting between opponents and supporters of the new Bolshevik regime in Russia. But many of the ideas that Debs and the Socialist Party championed—including women's suffrage, child labor laws, unemployment relief, public works jobs, and others—took hold after his death.

Louis Brandeis
(1856–1941)

LOUIS BRANDEIS was a crusading progressive lawyer and US Supreme Court justice. Appointed to the Supreme Court by Woodrow Wilson in 1916, he served until 1939. As a "people's lawyer" in Boston, he fought railroad monopolies, defended workplace and labor laws, and helped create policies to limit corporate abuses of consumers and workers—an approach that is now called "public interest" law. He believed that fighting injustice involved more than courtroom combat. He wrote books and articles in order to influence public opinion, advised many politicians and reform groups who shared his commitment to taming corporate power, and arguably had as much, perhaps even more, influence on American ideas and policy *before* joining the Supreme Court as he did during the twenty-three years he served on the highest court.

Born in Louisville, Kentucky, and raised in a secular Jewish family, Brandeis entered Harvard Law School at age nineteen and graduated in 1877 with the highest grades in the school's history. With his classmate and law practice partner Samuel Warren, he wrote one of the most famous law articles in history, "The Right to Privacy," published in the December 1890 *Harvard Law Review*. In it, they argued that people have "the right to be let alone."

By the early 1890s, Brandeis's law practice was a financial success, which gave him the freedom to pick and choose clients, including many public causes, without asking for money. This made Brandeis one of the first pro bono lawyers. Although he was a skilled and successful litigator, he preferred the roles of broker, mediator, and adviser.

In 1894, prodded by his friend Alice Lincoln, a Boston philanthropist and crusader for the poor, Brandeis spent nine months and held fifty-seven public hearings investigating the awful conditions in Boston's public poorhouses, where the temporarily jobless were crowded together with the mentally ill and hardened criminals. At one hearing he said, "Men are not bad and men are not degraded largely by circumstances because they desire to be so. . . . It is the duty of every man . . . to help them up and let them feel that there is some hope for them in life." The publicity from the hearings pressured Boston's officials to reform the city's poor laws to provide better food and housing. Brandeis also waged a successful fight to stop financier J. P. Morgan's efforts to merge his giant New Haven Railroad with its chief competitor, the Boston and Maine Railroad, which would have given Morgan a virtual monopoly on rail transportation in New England.

Fearing the influence of big business over everyday life, he also led a campaign to prevent a private transit corporation from controlling Boston's municipal subway system, and he persuaded the state legislature to adopt a savings-bank life insurance system.

Brandeis's most influential legal case was the 1908 US Supreme Court ruling in *Muller v. Oregon*. In 1907, Brandeis's sister-in-law Josephine Goldmark, along with **Florence Kelley,** head of the National Consumers League, persuaded Brandeis to defend Oregon's maximum-hour law for women. At issue was whether a state could limit the hours that women could work. Employers argued that Oregon's law was an infringement on the "freedom of contract" between employers and their employees. Brandeis presented his case by documenting the "clear connection between the health and morals of female workers" and the hours that they were required to work. His legal argument was relatively short, but he included more than 100 pages of documentation—pulled together by Kelley and Goldmark—including reports from social workers, doctors, factory inspectors, and other experts.

The Supreme Court upheld Oregon's law. Brandeis's groundbreaking approach to legal briefs soon came to be known as the "Brandeis Brief," one based on data as well as legal theory, and it became widespread over the next century.

Brandeis viewed the power of big business as a serious threat to a good society. The greatest problem the American people faced, he wrote in *The Curse of Bigness*, "is the problem of reconciling our industrial system with the political democracy in which we live." The antidote to the excess of corporate power was what he called "industrial democracy," which meant, in part, giving workers a voice through their labor unions. In 1907, Brandeis had served as the lawyer for Boston's cloak manufacturers during an acrimonious labor dispute, getting a court injunction against picketing, which crushed the strike. Three years later, however, Brandeis plunged into a crusade to bring industrial democracy to New York's clothing industry. That year, over 60,000 cloak makers, mostly men, went on strike in what was called the "Great Uprising."

Operating as a neutral mediator, Brandeis sought to bring the manufacturers (represented by their Cloak, Suit, and Skirt Protective Association) and the workers (represented by the International Ladies' Garment Workers Union) together to hammer out an industry-wide agreement. With Brandeis's nudging, the two sides signed the Protocol of Peace, an agreement that set minimum industry standards on wages, hours, piece rates, and sanitation (workplace safety and health). In addition, Brandeis hoped that the protocol would make strikes less likely.

Many observers, including Brandeis, viewed the protocol as a major milestone, recognizing that both owners and workers had a shared stake in efficiency and prosperity. Soon the agreement covered the entire industry and laid the foundation for future workplace reforms during the New Deal. But the protocol's weakness was that it was a voluntary agreement, not a government regulation, and not all manufacturers signed on. One such holdout was the Triangle Shirtwaist Company, where, on March 25, 1911, 146 immigrant workers, mostly young girls, perished in a tragic fire in a factory where conditions violated many of the protocol standards (see the profile of **Frances Perkins**).

Brandeis's writings and activism changed not just the law but also American attitudes about the need to restrain corporate power. His 1914 book *Other People's Money—And How the Bankers Use It* carefully showed how the interlocking network of directors of banks (whom he called "the dominant element in our financial oligarchy") and of railroads, insurance companies, and other corporations gave J. P. Morgan and a handful of other corporate titans undue influence over the economy and the political system. They were not even putting their own money at risk, Brandeis explained, which allowed them to make more reckless decisions than they otherwise would have. These oligarchs, Brandeis wrote, thus achieved "the supposedly impossible feat of having their cake and eating it too."

Brandeis shared some of the progressives' preference for regulation, but unlike most progressives, he was generally skeptical of "the curse of bigness" in both business *and* government. He thought the most proconsumer approach to restraining corporate power was to break huge corporations and overlapping trusts into smaller firms, which he believed would catalyze more competition and weaken their grip on political power.

Using his expertise on corporate practices, he served as one of President Wilson's key economic advisers, persuading the president to create the Federal Reserve System and the Federal Trade Commission and to push for the Clayton Antitrust Act and the Sixteenth Amendment, ratified in 1913, which allowed Congress to levy an income tax. Brandeis believed that public disclosure of big corporations' huge fees, commissions, salaries, and profits would mobilize voter anger. "Publicity is justly commended as a remedy for social and industrial diseases," Brandeis wrote. "Sunlight is said to be the best of disinfectants."

After winning the White House in 1912, Wilson hoped to appoint Brandeis as his secretary of commerce, but when the news leaked to the press and sparked intense opposition, he picked someone else. Four years later, Wilson's nomination of Brandeis to the Supreme Court was, at the time, the most hotly debated in American history. Former president William Howard Taft, along with six former presidents of the American Bar Association, signed a letter urging the Senate to reject Brandeis as unfit. Abbott Lawrence Lowell, the president of Harvard University (Brandeis's alma mater), along with other upper-class Bostonians, signed a letter opposed to Brandeis, the first Jew to be nominated to the Supreme Court. "In all the anti-corporate agitation of the past," wrote the *Wall Street Journal* about Brandeis, "one name stands out. . . . Where others were radical, he was rabid." A combination of anti-Semitism, opposition to Brandeis's views on big business, and partisan politics influenced the controversy. Finally, on June 1, the Senate confirmed Brandeis by a vote of 47–22; he was supported by all Democrats but one and by three progressive Republicans (including **Robert M. La Follette**).

On the Supreme Court, Brandeis was a key architect of rulings to protect free speech and to strengthen the right to privacy. During several decades of dramatic changes in public policy, Brandeis was typically on the side of progressive reform, but with his own twist. Brandeis viewed states as "laboratories" for innovative public policies. Not surprisingly, at a time when states were enacting a variety of progressive laws protecting workers and consumers, Brandeis advocated judicial constraint, encouraging his Court colleagues to give state legislators the benefit of the doubt. "The most important thing we do is not doing," he said about the Court.

Despite his personal skepticism about bigger government, he voted to uphold President **Franklin D. Roosevelt**'s New Deal programs, which often faced challenges in the courts on the grounds that they exceeded government's right to regulate business.

On some matters, however, Brandeis opposed FDR, including his effort to increase the number of seats on the Supreme Court as a means of reducing challenges to his legislation. In 1935, Brandeis voted with the Court majority in *Schecter Brothers v. the United States* to nullify the 1933 National Industrial Recovery Act, which allowed the federal government to establish codes of fair practice to limit cutthroat competition within each industry.

Brandeis's other major crusade was American Zionism. He was a secular Jew who celebrated Christmas. But he supported the idea of Jews' having a homeland, based on social justice and Jewish prophetic principles. At the time, many German Jews—who were more affluent, more assimilated, and more eager to be viewed as patriotic Americans than Eastern European immigrants—were unsympathetic to European Zionism. In 1914 Brandeis was elected chair of the Provisional Committee for General Zionist Affairs and spent much of his time and energy rallying fellow Jews as well as non-Jews in support of a Jewish state. Brandeis died in 1941, seven years before Israel's birth.

Clarence Darrow
(1857–1938)

CREDIT: Associated Press

CLARENCE DARROW was the most famous lawyer of the first half of the 20th century, celebrated by many and hated by others for defending radicals, reformers, underdogs, and dissidents.

Darrow's parents—his mother was a suffragist; his father was a fervent abolitionist—raised Clarence to love reading, to be skeptical of religion, and to admire dissenters, many of whom were guests in the Darrow home. Darrow started practicing law in Ohio in 1878 and was a typical small-town lawyer, but he aspired to play on a larger stage. After moving to Chicago in 1887, Darrow became a Democratic Party activist and a close friend of Judge John Peter Altgeld. He was greatly influenced by Altgeld's 1884 book *Our Penal Machinery and Its Victims*, which criticized the criminal justice system for favoring the rich over the poor.

Chicago at the time was a hotbed of union and radical activism. One of the most contentious issues of the day concerned the Haymarket Square bombing, which had occurred the year before Darrow moved to Chicago. During a rally to support workers striking for an eight-hour workday, police moved in to clear the crowd. Someone threw a bomb at the police, killing at least one officer. Another seven policemen were killed during the ensuing riot, and police gunfire killed or injured some of the protestors in the crowd. After a controversial investigation, seven anarchists were sentenced to death for murder; others were sentenced to fifteen years in prison. The anarchists won global notoriety, being seen as martyrs by many radicals and reformers, who viewed the trial and executions as politically motivated.

The more Darrow learned about the case, the more he regretted not being able to help defend the Haymarket dissidents. So when his friend Altgeld was elected Illinois governor, Darrow persuaded him to pardon the anarchists who had been imprisoned for the Haymarket Square bombing. The pardon triggered a firestorm of public protest and destroyed Altgeld's political career; he lost his reelection bid in 1896.

In 1890 Darrow became an attorney for the Chicago and Northwestern Railway. But when the workers for the Pullman Palace Car Company went on strike in 1894, Darrow resigned from his financially rewarding corporate job to defend them against the railroad (see the **Eugene Debs** profile). The strike by the American Railway Union, the first industry-wide union, triggered a national crisis. When Eugene Debs, the union president, was charged with conspiracy to obstruct the US mail and with contempt of court for disobeying a court injunction, Darrow became Debs's attorney. Debs and other union leaders were eventually convicted, but Darrow had established himself as the nation's leading labor lawyer.

Over the next fifteen years, Darrow defended workers and their unions against criminal prosecutions in communities where business groups dominated local politics and courts. The war between capital and labor often involved violence, espionage, and propaganda, with business commanding a huge advantage. The courtroom was hardly neutral territory, but Darrow managed to succeed against these odds, often persuading juries with his eloquent oratory. His legal accomplishments made headlines, but he also pursued a busy schedule of giving talks, participating in debates, and writing articles, as well as supporting candidates for public office.

In 1905, he joined with **Upton Sinclair**, Jack London, William English Walling, and other radicals to form the Intercollegiate Socialist Society. In 1921 the society changed its name to the League for Industrial Democracy, and the league had a significant influence on generations of American activists. Darrow gave lectures at Hull House, the settlement house founded by **Jane Addams**. He spoke out against anti-Semitism in the wake of brutal pogroms against Jews in Russia. He was one of the first members of the National Association for the Advancement of Colored People (NAACP) (founded in 1909) and even advocated interracial marriage.

In 1907, Darrow's national profile expanded with his successful defense of **William "Big Bill" Haywood**, the leader of the Western Federation of Miners (WFM) and a newly formed radical union, the Industrial Workers of the World. Haywood and two other WFM leaders were charged with plotting to murder Frank Steunenberg, the former governor of Idaho, who was an ardent foe of organized labor. Darrow's closing statement to the jury included these words:

> Gentlemen, it is not for him alone that I speak. I speak for the poor, for the weak, for the weary, for that long line of men who in darkness and despair have borne the labors of the human race. The eyes of the world are upon you, upon you twelve men of Idaho tonight. If you should decree Bill Haywood's death, in the great railroad offices of our great cities men will applaud your names. If you decree his death, amongst the spiders of Wall Street will go up paeans of praise for those twelve good men and true who killed Bill Haywood. In every bank in the world, where men hate Haywood because he fights for the poor and against the accursed system upon which the favored live and grow rich and fat—from all those you will receive blessings and unstinted praise.

The jury found Haywood not guilty, and Darrow's reputation grew.

A few years later however, Darrow's career imploded. In 1911 he defended the brothers James and John McNamara, active members of the iron workers' union, against a charge of killing twenty-one people by blowing up the headquarters of the *Los Angeles Times*, a powerful and vehemently antiunion newspaper. Radicals and union activists who had rallied to the McNamaras' cause were stunned when, on the first day of the trial, the brothers changed their previous plea of innocent to guilty. Word also leaked that Darrow had attempted to bribe two of the jurors. Darrow was charged with misconduct. In one bribery trial, the jury found him not guilty; the other trial resulted in a hung jury. His reputation sullied, the event ended his career as a labor lawyer. Jeb Harriman was a member of Darrow's defense team and during the trial was also running for mayor of Los Angeles on the Socialist Party ticket. Harriman was on the verge of possible victory, but the Mc-Namaras' confession derailed his campaign and ended his political career. The trial also set back California's union movement, which took decades to recover.

With the decline of his labor law practice, Darrow began a new career as a criminal lawyer. His sympathy for the underdog meshed with his growing belief that social conditions shaped human behavior. In his 1922 book *Crime: Its Cause and Treatment,* Darrow argued that criminals were often victims of forces over which they had no control. He thus opposed capital punishment and was a founding member of the American League to Abolish Capital Punishment.

His most famous and controversial criminal case was his 1924 defense of two wealthy Chicago college students who had kidnapped and murdered a fourteen-year-old boy just to see if they could get away with it. The defendants—Nathan Leopold and Richard Loeb—were hardly underdogs or sympathetic figures. Darrow took the high-profile case in order to save them from the death penalty. He introduced testimony from psychiatrists, hoping to persuade the judge that Leopold and Loeb were not responsible for their actions and should be sentenced to life in prison instead of death. Remarkably, he succeeded, adding to his reputation as a brilliant defense attorney.

Darrow repeated this success in another case the following year. The NAACP retained Darrow to represent Ossian Sweet, an African American medical doctor, and his family. When Sweet and his family moved into a bungalow house in an all-white neighborhood on the east side of Detroit, they were confronted by a hostile crowd of hundreds of people who assaulted them, threw rocks through a window, and shouted racial slurs. To protect themselves, occupants of the house fired shots into the crowd, killing one person and seriously wounding another. The police arrested Sweet, his wife, and nine others. Judge Frank Murphy, who later became a reformist mayor of Detroit and governor of Michigan, permitted Darrow to introduce evidence of past discrimination and violence against blacks to show that the shooting was an act of self-defense based on fear. "I know just as well as I know that you twelve men are here at this minute," Darrow said in his closing statement, "that if this had been a white crowd defending their homes, who killed a member of a colored mob, no one would have been arrested, no one would have been on trial. My clients are here charged with murder, but they are really here because they are black." After an all-white jury deadlocked, Murphy declared a mistrial. Murphy presided over a second trial the following year, and this time, following what many consider Darrow's most eloquent closing argument, the jury found Sweet and the other defendants not guilty.

Darrow gained the most international visibility when he helped defend John Scopes, charged with violating a Tennessee statute prohibiting teaching the theory of evolution in public schools. The 1925 trial is famous primarily for Darrow's sharp questioning of William Jennings Bryan—a former Nebraska congressman and US secretary of state—who took the stand as an expert on the Bible. In 1896 Darrow had supported Bryan's Democratic campaign for president, but twenty-nine years later, Darrow skillfully cross-examined the great orator about his strict interpretation of the Bible, making him look foolish and disoriented. He made Bryan reluctantly concede that the words of the Bible could not always be taken literally.

Darrow's defense of Scopes failed, however. His client was convicted and fined $100. Although he lost the case, Darrow's defense of science—what some have called a national biology lesson—won him accolades and cemented his reputation as a brilliant defender of unpopular and progressive causes. In 1927 Darrow and the American Civil Liberties Union appealed the case before the Tennessee Supreme Court. Scopes's conviction was overturned on a technicality, but the antievolution law remained on the books for many more years.

Theodore Roosevelt
(1858–1919)

THEODORE ROOSEVELT always seemed ready to go to war—against other countries, against business titans, and against his fellow Republicans. As president (1901–1909) and as the Progressive Party's candidate for president (in 1912), he believed that a strong chief executive should use the power of the federal government to lift up the downtrodden and bring the country and the world into the new industrial

CREDIT: Associated Press

age. In doing so, he significantly expanded the influence of the presidency. In foreign policy, Roosevelt was an imperialist, a militarist, and a jingoist who sometimes justified his views with racist stereotypes. In the domestic arena, he was a reformer who usually sided with workers and consumers against big business. The force of his colorful personality often stirred controversy even among his allies. Because of this, he often missed opportunities to accomplish his goals. But in several key arenas—particularly taming the power of corporate America—he achieved important progressive triumphs that moved the country toward greater democracy and social justice.

Born to a wealthy family, Roosevelt was frail and sickly as a child and was often bullied. In response, he began a strict regimen of exercise and weight lifting and developed a rugged physique as a teenager. For the rest of his life, he advocated the "strenuous life," including exercise, mountain climbing, hunting, and frequent treks in the wilderness. He graduated from Harvard in 1880, briefly studied law at Columbia University, but dropped out to pursue politics. In 1881, at age twenty-three, he won a seat in the New York Assembly as a Republican.

He lost a campaign for mayor but leveraged his connections into an appointment to the US Civil Service Commission and then, in 1895, into an appointment to the presidency of the New York City Police Board. When Republican William McKinley was elected president in 1896, he reluctantly appointed Roosevelt assistant secretary of the navy to pay off a political favor. Roosevelt used the position to prepare the navy to invade Cuba and the Philippines in retaliation for the explosion of the US battleship *Maine* in Havana harbor, which Roosevelt and the US press blamed on Spain. Once the Spanish-American War began in 1898, Roosevelt resigned his post to command a volunteer cavalry division, known as the Rough Riders, in Cuba. He led a daring charge up San Juan Hill and returned a war hero. A prodigious self-promoter, he used his new celebrity to win the governorship of New York that year.

To make sure that Roosevelt did not run again for governor, New York's Republican powerbrokers persuaded McKinley to make Roosevelt his vice presidential running mate in 1900. The vice presidency was viewed as a do-nothing position, but Roosevelt campaigned feverishly and helped McKinley defeat populist Democrat William Jennings Bryan by a huge margin. But in September 1901, only nine months after taking office, McKinley was assassinated, making Roosevelt, at age forty-two, the youngest president in the nation's history.

In foreign affairs, Roosevelt's goal was to expand America's fledgling empire, export its values, and increase its global influence, using diplomacy when possible but using force when necessary. Viewing the United States as the global police force, his motto was to "speak softly and carry a big stick." Under Roosevelt, the United States intervened in the Philippines, Panama, Santo Domingo (now the Dominican Republic), and elsewhere, but he also used diplomacy to settle the Russo-Japanese war and a colonial dispute among Germany, England, and France that led to France's undisputed control over Morocco and, eventually, British control over Egypt.

Roosevelt's claim to a place in the progressive pantheon rests with his efforts to curb the growing power of America's big corporations and to preserve America's natural resources.

In his first message to Congress in December 1901, only two months after assuming the presidency, Roosevelt warned, "There is a widespread conviction in the minds of the American people that the great corporations known as the trusts are in certain of their features and tendencies hurtful to the general welfare." He called for tougher business regulation and for the business world to be rid of its "crimes of cunning." These words understandably shook up the nation's business leaders as well as most of Roosevelt's fellow Republicans. The first sign that he was not bluffing came quickly. Without even telling his cabinet, he asked Attorney General Philander Knox to prepare a suit against the Northern Securities Company, a huge railroad trust run by J. P. Morgan, for violating the Sherman Antitrust Act. Morgan, the nation's most powerful capitalist, had contributed $10,000 to Roosevelt's gubernatorial campaign in 1898 and had lots of friends in Congress. He quickly arranged to meet with Roosevelt, and he brought with him two of the most influential Senate Republicans, Marcus Hanna of Ohio and Chauncey Depew of New York, both with close ties to business. Roosevelt was willing to go toe to toe with Morgan to make a point: the president, representing the American people, was more powerful than corporations.

Fortunately for Roosevelt, the US Supreme Court backed him up and ordered the company dismantled. He soon became known as a trustbuster, the champion of the average American against big business. That reputation helped him win reelection but alienated many other Republicans. The reality, though, was that the Northern Securities case was the high point of Roosevelt's trust-busting. In his seven years as president, his administration filed forty-three other antitrust suits but won a major victory in only one, against the beef trust. The courts did not share his enthusiasm for breaking up big corporations.

Roosevelt scored much bigger victories trying to regulate corporations instead of breaking them up. Indeed, the public was probably more interested in gaining protection from corporate abuses against workers and consumers than in turning megatrusts into smaller corporations. Roosevelt was particularly impressed, and repulsed, after reading **Upton Sinclair**'s 1906 book *The Jungle,* which exposed the filthy and unsafe conditions in the meatpacking industry, conditions that endangered workers and consumers alike. Progressive reformers had tried for years to pass federal legislation to clean up these workplaces, but industry had too much clout. Once Roosevelt embraced the issue, he used all the powers of persuasion and publicity at his command. He pushed Congress to pass two landmark laws: the Meat Inspection Act and the Pure Food and Drug Act. For the first time, the federal government took responsibility for the health and safety of America's food and drugs. These laws, and the precedents they set, have had a much more lasting impact on American society than any of the antitrust laws.

Roosevelt also put his power and personality behind the Hepburn Act to increase the powers of the Interstate Commerce Commission to regulate railroad companies' shipping rates. When it appeared that the bill was dying in Congress because of pressure from the railroads, Roosevelt went on a speaking tour to whip up public support, knowing that the press would follow him and report his speeches and the audiences' approval. The publicity worked, and Congress passed the legislation. Roosevelt was using the "bully pulpit," a term he coined to describe how he used his position and personality to put issues on the agenda and mobilize public opinion.

Roosevelt's experiences hiking and mountain climbing gave him an appreciation for wilderness that was rare at a time when most Americans thought their destiny was to exploit nature and expand the frontier. "We do not intend that our natural resources shall be exploited by the few against the interests of the many," he wrote. He was the first president to make conservation a national priority. He fought for and signed the 1902 Newlands Reclamation Act, which used funds from the sales of federal lands to build reservoirs and irrigation works to support agriculture in the West. He issued executive orders to create 150 new national forests, which expanded the size of protected land from 42 million to 172 million acres. He also created five national parks, eighteen national monuments, and fifty-one wildlife refuges.

In 1902, when 140,000 Pennsylvania coal miners went on strike, Roosevelt used his bully pulpit to negotiate a settlement. He feared a major coal shortage in the middle of winter and escalating heating costs. He had no official authority to intervene, but that did not stop him, for he sensed that the public wanted a strong president who would get his hands dirty solving problems. The mine owners had a long tradition of using private thugs and violence to destroy labor unions. George F. Baer, the president of one of the largest Pennsylvania coal companies, once told a clergyman that "the rights and interests of the laboring man" would best be protected "not by labor agitators, but by the Christian men to whom God in his infinite wisdom had given control of the property interests of the country." Not surprisingly, he refused to negotiate. Roosevelt had not been particularly sympathetic to labor unions, but in the face of the potential national crisis, he lost patience with the mine owners. The mine owners refused his invitation to meet union leaders at the White House. They wanted him to send federal troops to break the strike and force the miners back to work. Instead, he threatened to use troops to seize the mines and operate them under government auspices. By late October, with both the midterm elections and cold weather fast approaching, Roosevelt got the two sides to settle their differences, with the miners winning a substantial pay increase. Roosevelt called the agreement a "square deal" for both sides, and the term soon became the watchword for his domestic agenda.

True to his word, Roosevelt did not run for reelection in 1908. But four years later, when he was still only fifty-four years old, the itch had not subsided, and he decided to challenge President William Howard Taft, an ally of big business, for the Republican nomination. When he lost, he and supporters bolted from the Republican Party and formed the Progressive Party, often known as the Bull Moose Party. With California governor **Hiram Johnson** as his running mate, Roosevelt campaigned on a "new nationalism" platform of economic and social reform, including women's suffrage, a minimum wage for women, an eight-hour workday, a system of old-age insurance, a national health service, a federal securities commission, and the direct election of US senators. The 1912 election pitted Roosevelt against Taft, New Jersey governor Woodrow Wilson (the Democratic candidate), and Socialist **Eugene Debs**. Wilson won 41.9 percent of the vote to Roosevelt's 27.4 percent, Taft's 23.1 percent, and Debs's 6 percent. By splitting the Republican vote with Taft, Roosevelt essentially handed the presidency to Wilson.

It was not until another Roosevelt, **Franklin D. Roosevelt,** entered the White House that America would see a president with the personality and political skills to build on Roosevelt's progressive foundation.

Florence Kelley (1859–1932)

Florence Kelley (third from left) with fellow factory inspectors in New Orleans, Louisiana, 1914.
CREDIT: Photographer: Lewis Wickes Hine, Library of Congress Prints and Photographs Division, Washington, D.C./National Child Labor Committee Collection

IN 1871, William Kelley took his twelve-year-old daughter Florence on a tour of a western Pennsylvania steel mill and glass factory so she would appreciate the wonders of America's new industrial age. The father was mesmerized by the mill's new Bessemer converter (a huge fiery cauldron that turns molten pig iron into steel) and the factory's assembly-line operation for making bottles.

But Florence was shocked more than impressed. Touring the steel mill at two in the morning, she witnessed the "terrifying sight" of "boys smaller than myself—and I was barely twelve years old" carrying heavy pails of drinking water for the men. These little boys, Kelley thought, "were not more important than so many grains of sand in the molds." Visiting the glass factory at night a few weeks later, she observed that a glassblower stood in front of each furnace. Near each blower were the "dogs," as the boys were called, whose job it was to clean and scrape bottle molds, a tedious and dangerous task in the dark and hot factory. Kelley never forgot these images, or her impression "of the utter unimportance of children compared with products, in the minds of the people whom I am among."

Kelley did more than any other 20th-century American to rectify the awful conditions of child labor. She was a leading organizer to stop sweatshops and a major advocate for working women. She helped lead the battle for groundbreaking local, state, and federal labor laws, including laws mandating a minimum wage and an eight-hour workday. To this end, she became a pioneer in conducting social and statistical research into workplace abuses and in developing strategies—such as factory inspections and consumer organizing—to put pressure on state legislatures and Congress to improve working conditions. She believed that women with her class privileges had a moral duty to push government and society to protect vulnerable people. "We that are strong," she wrote as a young woman, "let us bear the infirmities of the weak."

Kelley was raised in an activist family. Her father, William, was a Jacksonian Democrat whose strong opposition to slavery led him to help found the Republican Party in 1854. He served fifteen terms as a congressman from Philadelphia; while in Congress, he championed high wages for working men. Early in her life, Florence was impressed by her great-aunt Sarah Pugh, a Quaker and an active abolitionist who refused to use cotton or sugar because they were made with slave labor.

At a time when few women attended college, Kelley's father—an early advocate of women's suffrage—encouraged her to further her education. She graduated from Cornell University in 1882 as a member of the Phi Beta Kappa Society. She applied to the graduate school of the University of Pennsylvania but was turned down because of her sex. Revealing her early commitment to working women, she founded the New Century Guild for Working Women in Philadelphia and taught evening classes there. She then decided to attend the University of Zurich, the first European university to grant degrees to women. There she joined the growing circle of students excited by socialism. Her mind, she recalled, "was tinder awaiting a match." The socialist critique of capitalism helped Kelley understand the exploitation of women and children that she had observed in American and British factories and the racism that her family had fought against. While living in Germany, she translated Friedrich Engels's book *The Condition of the Working Class in England in 1844*—the first English version, still in print today—and began a correspondence with Engels, Karl Marx's coauthor and benefactor.

In Zurich she met Lazare Wischnewetsky, a Russian medical student and fellow socialist, whom she married in 1884. The couple had three children. In 1891, to escape Wischnewetsky's physical abuse, Kelley and her children moved to Chicago. There she resumed using her maiden name, although she insisted on being called "Mrs. Kelley" so her children would not be considered illegitimate.

In Chicago, Kelley lived at Hull House, the pioneering settlement house founded by **Jane Addams** to serve the working-class immigrants in the surrounding neighborhood (see the profiles of Addams and **Alice Hamilton** for more information about Hull House).

Since 1879, the labor movement had been agitating for laws to end the exploitation of child workers. In 1892, Kelley convinced the Illinois Bureau of Labor

Statistics to hire her to investigate working conditions in Chicago's garment industry. That year, the US commissioner of labor, Carroll D. Wright, asked Kelley to
conduct a survey of Chicago's slums. Kelley uncovered children as young as three
working in sweatshops. She found women forced to work past exhaustion, workers
who risked pneumonia, and children with burns and other injuries due to dangerous conditions. Many were illiterate and had never attended school because they
had to work instead. Her troubling findings—some of them collected in *Hull
House Maps and Papers,* published in 1894—contributed to public outrage over
the living and working conditions of Chicago's poor. With her intimate knowledge
of these terrible conditions, Kelley took state legislators, including those from rural
areas, on tours of tenement sweatshops, hoping that they would be as outraged as
she was.

As a result of Kelley's research and organizing work, in 1893 the Illinois legislature passed the first factory law limiting work for women to eight hours a day
and prohibiting the employment of children under the age of fourteen. An employer who wanted to hire a child between the ages of fourteen and sixteen had
to obtain an affidavit from a parent or guardian certifying the child's age as well
as a doctor's proof of physical fitness.

To ensure that factories across the state complied with the new laws, the progressive governor of Illinois, John Peter Altgeld, in 1893 appointed Kelley to be
the chief factory inspector. She issued skillfully written reports that stirred controversy and brought public attention to ongoing abuses. At one factory, someone
fired a warning shot at her. She also discovered that many government officials, including lawyers in the Cook County district attorney's office, were not eager to
prosecute employers who violated the state's factory laws. Kelley would bring to
light clear cases of abuse—such as that of an employer who forced an eleven-year-
old boy to work with a "poisonous fluid" that paralyzed his right arm—but public
officials would refuse to prosecute. She was so angry at the legal system that she
took evening classes at Northwestern University School of Law and earned her law
degree in 1894. Kelley persisted with her day job until 1897, when Governor John
Tanner—Altgeld's successor, who had close ties to business interests—fired her.

Frustrated by these legal and political setbacks, Kelley helped forge a new
strategy to improve working conditions. With Ellen Henrotin (the wife of an influential Chicago banker and the president of the General Federation of Women's
Clubs), Kelley created the Illinois Consumers' League to mobilize women to use
their purchasing power to improve the conditions of factory workers. In 1899,
Kelley was recruited to direct the newly formed National Consumers League
(NCL). She moved to New York and took up residence at the Henry Street Settlement, founded by Lillian Wald.

For the rest of her life, Kelley worked at the NCL, turning it into a powerful
group that changed public awareness of oppressive working and living conditions
and influenced many of the most important pieces of social and workers' rights

legislation in the first third of the century. Kelley organized middle-class, elite, and trade-union women who were becoming conscious of their power as consumers. In 1902, for example, a group of Jewish housewives in New York's Lower East Side neighborhood organized a successful boycott of butchers who raised the prices of kosher meat. Kelley recognized that middle-class consumers, mostly women, could be mobilized to protest the practices of businesses that abused their workers and took advantage of consumers. One of Kelley's most successful strategies was educating consumers about the conditions facing the workers who produced their clothing. Kelley pioneered a consumers' "white label" on clothing to certify that garments had been produced without child labor and under working conditions that obeyed state laws—an idea that environmental and consumer organizations later adopted. The NCL urged consumers to shop in responsible stores on its "white list."

Kelley traveled constantly, helping build sixty NCL chapters in twenty states. She spoke to unions, women's clubs, settlement houses, college students, legislative committees, and other groups to build support for NCL and its reform causes. "She had the voice and the presence of a great actress," observed **Frances Perkins,** one of Kelley's protégés who became **Franklin D. Roosevelt**'s secretary of labor and continued crusading for the same causes as her mentor.

During Kelley's lifetime, judges generally ruled in favor of business. But Kelley played a key role in one of the most important proworker court decisions in American history, *Muller v. Oregon.* Kelley, along with her NCL colleague Josephine Goldmark, persuaded **Louis Brandeis** in 1907 to defend Oregon's ten-hour law for women and compiled the sociological and medical data that Brandeis used to document the harmful effects of long working days on women's health. After this ruling, the NCL and other groups were able to push more state legislatures to adopt a variety of protective labor laws. By 1913 nine states had adopted minimum-wage laws for women. These laws became the basis for the portion of the Fair Labor Standards Act of 1938 that extended minimum-wage laws to men.

In 1902, she and Lillian Wald organized the New York Child Labor Committee, and two years later they created the National Child Labor Committee to push for state laws to protect children. Finally, in 1912, the national group's organizing efforts persuaded Congress to create the federal Children's Bureau, and President William Howard Taft appointed Julia Lathrop, a Hull House resident, as its first director. Using the bureau's research findings, Kelley helped lobby Congress to pass the Keating-Owen Child Labor Act of 1916 and the Sheppard-Towner Act, a 1921 law that gave the Children's Bureau the authority to conduct research and pay for services to combat maternal and infant mortality.

In 1909, she helped organize the National Association for the Advancement of Colored People. A strong pacifist and Quaker, she opposed America's imperialist adventures in the early 1900s, and in 1919 she became a founding member of the Women's International League for Peace and Freedom. She served as president of the Intercollegiate Socialist Society (1918–1920), frequently speaking on campuses to recruit students to the cause of radical reform. Kelley was an active member, and for several years the vice president, of the National Woman Suffrage Association. After the adoption in 1920 of the Nineteenth Amendment, which gave women the right to vote, she led the movement to continue the social justice agenda of the suffrage movement through the founding of the League of Women Voters and the Women's Joint Congressional Committee.

Principled, brilliant, impatient, and self-confident, Kelley never backed away from a fight. "Explosive, hot-tempered, determined, she was no gentle saint," said Frances Perkins. At Kelley's funeral, her friend Newton Baker observed, "Everyone was brave from the moment she came into the room."

John Dewey
(1859–1952)

John Dewey with his family, New York, 1950
CREDIT: AP Photo/John Rooney

JOHN DEWEY died in 1952, but conservatives still blame him for destroying the nation's public education system. In mid-2011, conservative blogger Frank Miele described Dewey as "the socialist educator and philosopher who wrought a revolution by insisting that we teach children what they want to learn instead of what they should learn." Conservatives view Dewey as the father of "progressive education," which they define as schools without a standard curriculum or rules for student behavior, thus inviting chaos, lack of respect for teachers, and a "do your own thing" morality.

Dewey was the most influential philosopher of the first half of the 20th century. In 1950, historian Henry Steele Commager wrote, "It is scarcely an exaggeration to say that for a generation no major issue was clarified until Dewey had spoken."

Dewey's ideas about learning and schools have little in common with what conservatives think of today as "progressive" education. He did not believe that schools should primarily be "child-centered," permitting students to study whatever interested them. He believed that all students should learn history, science, math, and other traditional subjects, but that they should be taught in ways that piqued their curiosity and that taught them to enjoy learning as a way to solve problems.

Unfortunately, most public schools at the time resembled the ones Dewey had attended (and did not like). They emphasized rote learning, memorization, and recitation. Teachers were primarily disciplinarians who motivated students by fear and humiliation. They taught by drilling knowledge into students, who were expected to be, in Dewey's words, "ductile and docile." There were no clear standards to determine who was and was not qualified to teach.

In contrast, Dewey believed that education should help students develop their full potential as human beings. He argued that schools and the curriculum should evolve along with new scientific discoveries and new ideas. In *The School and Society* (1899), Dewey wrote that students learn best in an environment of "embryonic community life, active with types of occupations which reflect the life of the larger society, and permeated throughout with the spirit of art, history, and science."

Teachers, Dewey believed, should constantly innovate. Not only did they have to master their subject areas, but they also had to be familiar with the emerging field of child psychology and practiced in creative classroom techniques. Most important, according to Dewey, schools should promote democracy by teaching students how to analyze and solve problems, to engage in class discussions, and to learn by experience—not just memorize. Schools should be vibrant laboratories where students learn *how* to learn, not just *what* to learn.

Over a long career, in forty books and hundreds of articles, Dewey wrote about aesthetics, logic, and epistemology, but his major influence was on ideas about education and democracy. A psychologist as well as a philosopher, he was a leader of a new American-based school of philosophy called pragmatism, which challenged the then-mainstream Platonist view that civilization's core ideas were fixed. Dewey believed that philosophy should address real-world problems.

Dewey grew up in Burlington, Vermont, the son of a shopkeeper who recited Shakespeare and Milton around the house. After graduating from the University of Vermont in 1879, he taught school in Vermont and Pennsylvania and then went to graduate school in philosophy at Johns Hopkins University. His mentors at Johns Hopkins emphasized new German scientific research methods as the best way to arrive at the truth. They also embraced new techniques in psychology, pioneered in Europe, that involved observing human behavior.

After getting his Ph.D. in 1884, Dewey briefly taught at the University of Michigan, where he met his wife, Alice Chipman, who had also been a school-teacher. She got Dewey interested in the practical problems of public education. Dewey was a founding member of the Michigan Schoolmasters Club, a joint project of college and high school teachers. As he traveled around the state monitoring the quality of college preparation courses, he developed his ideas about ways to improve teaching and learning.

Dewey was recruited to teach at the newly founded University of Chicago. While there he created a "laboratory school" where he could test his ideas about education. It opened its doors in 1896 with 16 elementary students and two teachers in three rooms. By 1903 it had 140 students, twenty-three teachers, and ten graduate assistants.

The school was based on Dewey's view that students learn best while engaged in activities that require them to solve problems on their own and with other students. In this way, each student is a member of the "community," with roles, tasks, and responsibilities. At Dewey's school, students learned about reading and math by engaging in projects such as cooking and crafting. The children planted a garden, which provided a practical way to learn about soil chemistry, botany, the role of farming in human history, and the physics of light and water.

As the students got older, the curriculum became more complex and abstract, but the underlying philosophy remained the same. Dewey's educational theories mirrored his political and social views. Dewey did not want to educate children to become passive cogs in the existing industrial and political order. For

Dewey, a vibrant democracy required active citizens who did more than vote periodically, who could solve problems in their communities and workplaces. Thus, progressive education was integral to progressive politics.

Throughout his career, Dewey led by example, writing essays for the *New Republic* and *The Nation* and lending his voice and influence to building a progressive movement. He became a trustee of Hull House soon after it opened. He enjoyed exchanging ideas with **Jane Addams, Alice Hamilton,** and other Hull House leaders, whose ideas about "learning by doing" and engaging citizens in changing society mirrored his.

When Dewey moved to teach at Columbia University, he continued to speak out frequently for workers' rights, women's rights, and civil rights. His wife was an active feminist and influenced Dewey's thinking. One day he joined a women's suffrage parade. Someone handed him a picket sign and he began marching down Fifth Avenue. He was puzzled by the laughter of people as he walked past them until he looked at the placard. It read, "Men Can Vote. Why Can't I?"

Soon after Dewey and others founded the National Association for the Advancement of Colored People (NAACP) in 1909, Alice invited a group of African American women to their apartment to support them and to enlist them in the women's suffrage crusade. Hearing about the meeting, the building owner sent Dewey a letter forbidding any more integrated gatherings in the apartment. The NAACP promptly organized a meeting at the Ethical Culture building to protest the landlord's bigotry. Dewey's involvement in the American Association of University Professors (he was its first president in 1915), the New York City Teachers Union (1916), and the American Civil Liberties Union (in 1920) was motivated by his concern over the arbitrary and unjust firing of professors and teachers for expressing their views on social and political issues. In 1900, for example, economist Edward Ross lost his job at Stanford University because Jane Lathrop Stanford, the widow of the university's founder Leland Stanford, did not like his views on immigrant labor and railroad monopolies. In 1917, during World War I, Columbia University's board passed a resolution that imposed an oath of loyalty to the US government on the faculty and student body. Although Dewey ultimately supported Woodrow Wilson's war policy, he worried that the war was leading to dangerous restrictions on free speech and academic freedom. When the war ended, the United States fell into the hysterical Red Scare, including the infamous Palmer Raids, which jailed and deported leading socialists and other radicals, including **Eugene Debs.** Frustrated by the failure of the League of Nations, Dewey later joined the movement to outlaw war and establish a world court to settle international disputes.

As early as 1933 Dewey warned about the rise of Nazism. In 1936 he was one of eighteen philosophers who boycotted a meeting of the German Philosophical Association in Berlin. Although Dewey harshly criticized capitalism for "stunting" workers by denying them a share in controlling their work, he condemned Marxism, Stalinism, and communism for violating individual freedom.

In the 1940s a backlash began against Dewey's "learning by doing" ideas, which had influenced public education and teacher training. Columbia University president Nicholas Butler and University of Chicago president Robert Hutchins, among others, sought to redesign their curricula to emphasize traditional learning and focus on "great books." Dewey countered, "President Hutchins calls for liberal education of a small, elite group and vocational education for the masses. I cannot think of any idea more completely reactionary and more fatal to the whole democratic outlook."

After Dewey died, at the age of ninety-two, conservatives during the Red Scare and the McCarthy era began to link his progressive education ideas with communism. In 2005, the right-wing magazine *Human Events* ranked Dewey's *Democracy and Education* number five on its list of the "Ten Most Harmful Books of the 19th and 20th Centuries," sandwiched between *The Kinsey Report* and *Das Kapital*.

More fitting was the long obituary in the *New York Times* of June 2, 1952. It said, "His convictions were those of an essentially honest man, and although he might well have sat back to criticize the general order of things, he took an active part in the attempt to create a third political party, to lend his voice and influence to help the down-trodden, to do away with oppression in this country and elsewhere, and to strive for a finer universal education."

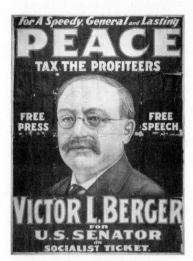

For A Speedy, General and Lasting **PEACE** TAX THE PROFITEERS FREE PRESS FREE SPEECH **VICTOR L. BERGER** FOR **U.S. SENATOR** ON **SOCIALIST TICKET.**

CREDIT: Wisconsin Historical Society/
WHI-1901

Victor Berger
(1860–1929)

DURING THE first quarter of the 20th century, two political forces—**Robert M. La Follette**'s progressivism and Victor Berger's socialism—made Wisconsin a showcase for radical change. As the first Socialist elected to Congress, Berger organized the Socialist Party into an effective political organization, building on a base of Milwaukee's large German immigrant population and its strong labor movement. Milwaukee in those days was, according to historian David Shannon, a "city of beer, German Brass bands, and bourgeois civic efficiency, . . . the strongest center of Socialist strength in the country." Victor Berger was the center of Milwaukee socialism.

Berger was born in 1860 in Austria-Hungary to well-to-do parents and attended universities in Budapest and Vienna. He came to the United States in 1878, settled in Milwaukee, and soon became a German-language teacher in its public schools.

Berger was president of his local of the Typographical Union and a frequent delegate to the American Federation of Labor conventions. For years, he published newspapers in both German and English, distributing free editions to all Milwaukee homes on the eve of elections. In 1892 he bought the *Wisconsin Vorwaerts* (Forward), a daily German-language newspaper affiliated with the Socialist Labor Party (SLP).

In 1900 he joined with **Eugene Debs** to form the Social Democratic Party, which merged the following year with the SLP to form the Socialist Party of America. Berger closed the *Vorwaerts* and began a new paper, the *Social Democratic Herald,* which carried on its masthead the description "Official Paper of the Federated Trades Council of Milwaukee and the Wisconsin State Federation of Labor." He was later editor of the *Milwaukee Herald,* an English-language labor paper owned primarily by the Brewery Workers union.

It was Berger who introduced Debs to socialism. In 1894 Debs was sentenced to six months in prison in Woodstock, Illinois, for violating a federal antistrike injunction during the Pullman strike. In jail, Debs read voraciously and began questioning many core beliefs, including his longtime membership in the Democratic Party. According to Debs: "Victor L. Berger—and I have loved him ever since—came to Woodstock, as if a providential instrument, and delivered the first impassioned message of socialism I had ever heard—the very first to set 'the wires humming in my system.'"

Berger turned Milwaukee's Socialist Party into a powerful political machine, using the newspaper, the backing of the unions, and the electoral strength of the German immigrant population. In 1910 Milwaukee voters elected Emil Seidel, the first Socialist mayor of a major city; the Socialists also won a majority of seats on the city council and the county board. At the same time, they made Berger the first Socialist elected to the US Congress. Both Seidel and Berger lost in 1912, but in 1916 Milwaukee voters elected another Socialist, Daniel Hoan, as their mayor and reelected him through 1940. Berger was reelected to Congress in 1918.

When they gained power in Milwaukee, the Socialists built new sanitation systems, municipally owned water and power systems, and community parks. They championed public education for the city's working-class children. Proud of their efficient public services, they constantly boasted about Milwaukee's excellent public sewer system under the Socialist municipal government. As both praise and irony, they were often known as "sewer socialists."

In Congress, Berger sponsored bills providing for old-age pensions, government ownership of the radio industry, abolition of child labor, self-government for the District of Columbia, and a system of public works for relief of the unemployed, and he put forward resolutions for the withdrawal of federal troops from the Mexican border, for the abolition of the Senate (which was then not yet elected directly by the voters and was called the "millionaires' club"), for women's suffrage, and for federal ownership of the railroads.

But Berger was criticized by the Socialist Party's left wing because, they argued, these measures, even if passed, would not add up to socialism. They criticized Berger's "step at a time" brand of socialism. In fact, one of Berger's favorite mottoes was, "Socialism is coming all the time. It may be another century or two before it is fully established."

These differences came to a head at the Socialist Party's 1912 convention, just as the party was gaining some success at electing members to local offices and launching Debs's campaign for president. The left wing of the party was identified with the Industrial Workers of the World (IWW), the "Wobblies," who believed in direct action rather than elections. At the meeting, Berger spoke bluntly about the split within the party's ranks: "Anarchism is eating away at the vitals of our party. If there is to be a parting of the ways, if there is to be a split— and it seems that you will have it, and must have it—then, I am ready to split right here. I am ready to go back to Milwaukee and appeal to the Socialists all over the country to cut this cancer out of our organization." Berger's wing of the party prevailed. They kicked IWW leader **William "Big Bill" Haywood** off the Socialist Party's national executive committee, prompting some of the left-wing faction to leave the party.

Like Debs, Berger was a leader in opposing the US entry into World War I. In an editorial on the mayoral election in the *Milwaukee Leader*, Berger wrote that the Socialist Party gave each voter a chance "to register his vote in favor of an immediate, general and democratic peace or for a bloody, long, drawn-out plutocratic war."

After declaring war, Congress passed the Espionage Act to restrict opposition to the war effort. Americans could be imprisoned for "making false statements with intent to interfere with the operation or success of the military or naval forces." The law allowed the US Postal Service to block any mail "advocating or urging treason, insurrection, or forcible resistance to any law of the United States."

In 1918 Berger ran for the US Senate from Wisconsin. In his campaign he demanded the return of American troops from Europe and a system of taxation on war industries that would "take every penny of profits derived from the sale of war supplies." He put up fifty billboards in Milwaukee that said, "WAR IS HELL CAUSED BY CAPITALISM. SOCIALISTS DEMAND PEACE. READ THE PEOPLE'S SIDE. *MILWAUKEE LEADER*. VICTOR L. BERGER, EDITOR."

During the campaign, Socialist meetings were harassed by organized mobs and local chambers of commerce. Berger had difficulty hiring halls in which to speak outside Milwaukee. Socialist Party members distributing campaign literature were arrested without cause. Berger's paper, the *Milwaukee Leader* (which he started in 1911 and which had a statewide circulation) was banned from the mails, so it could only be circulated in and near Milwaukee. In February 1918, in the middle of the campaign, Berger and four other Socialists were indicted under the Espionage Act. Despite this harassment, Berger won 26 percent of the vote statewide in the April Senate election. Berger was more successful the following November, when Milwaukee voters returned Berger to the congressional seat he had held from 1911 to 1913.

On February 20, 1919, Berger was convicted and sentenced by Judge Kenesaw Landis to twenty years in federal prison for his opposition to World War I. In April 1919 his colleagues in Congress expelled him by a 309–1 vote. Wisconsin's governor, Emanuel Philipp, called a special election to fill Berger's seat in December of that year, and again Berger won, only to be refused his seat still another time by a 328–6 margin.

Berger appealed Landis's decision, and the US Supreme Court overturned it on January 31, 1921, ruling that Landis had improperly presided over the case after the filing of an affidavit of prejudice. Berger had been defeated for reelection in 1920, but he was reelected in 1922 and seated; he remained in Congress until 1927. Defeated again in 1928, Berger returned to Milwaukee and resumed his newspaper career until his untimely death in a streetcar accident the next year.

CREDIT: Frances Benjamin Johnston/
Frances Benjamin Johnston Collection
(Library of Congress)

Charlotte Perkins Gilman
(1860–1935)

CHARLOTTE PERKINS GILMAN was a pathbreaking feminist, humanist, and socialist
whose lectures, novels, short stories, magazine articles, and nonfiction books challenged
the dominant ideas about women's role in society and helped shape the movement for
women's suffrage and women's rights. By the
late 1800s, Gilman was the most important
feminist thinker in the United States. She
combined economic and sociological writings
with fiction and utopian thinking, giving her
a wide appeal.

Gilman came from a remarkable lineage.
Her great-uncles and great-aunts included
the well-known minister Henry Ward Beecher, the noted theologian Edward
Beecher, the abolitionist minister and author Charles Beecher, the educator
Catharine Beecher, the suffragist Isabella Beecher Hooker, and Harriet Beecher
Stowe, the abolitionist and novelist (most famous for *Uncle Tom's Cabin*). Despite
this impressive bloodline, Gilman grew up in a poor family in Providence, Rhode
Island. Her father abandoned his wife, who had to depend on family charity and
was forced to move frequently. As a girl, Gilman wrote stories in her diary that typically involved a young woman who—often through some magical device—
overcomes the limits of her life. With an older woman as her guide, she achieves
personal salvation and overcomes evil in society. These themes—of independent
women surmounting social boundaries, not simply as individuals but as part of a
broader social reconstruction—appear in Gilman's influential writings throughout
her life.

Gilman briefly attended college, married a local artist in 1884, and gave birth
to her only child the following year. She soon fell into a severe depression, suffering what today we would call a nervous breakdown. In 1888, she moved to
California with her daughter and got a divorce. To earn money and pay back her
debts, she began writing stories and poems, publishing them in various journals
and magazines; she worked for a time as an editor and writer for the Pacific Coast
Woman's Press Association. Her autobiographical short story "The Yellow Wallpaper," published in 1892, described a woman who suffers a mental breakdown
after three months of being trapped at home staring at the yellow wallpaper. The

story was a powerful statement about the restrictions domestic life placed on women and had a significant influence in women's circles. Gilman was one of many people inspired by Edward Bellamy and his utopian novels *Looking Backward: 2000–1887,* published in 1888 and set in a socialist America in the year 2000, and its sequel, *Equality,* published in 1897. She soon became a popular lecturer, traveling around the country talking to women's clubs, social groups, and workingmen's associations, where she not only discussed Bellamy's radical ideas but also talked about women's issues. Gilman could not take her daughter with her on the road, so she put the girl in the care of her ex-husband—a decision that was reported in the newspapers and was considered scandalous.

Gilman was probably the most effective debater among suffragettes at the time. At Susan B. Anthony's invitation, she addressed the 1896 conference of the National American Woman Suffrage Association in Washington, DC, and testified before Congress in favor of women's suffrage.

As a writer and lecturer, she popularized new ideas about women's equality. Her book *Women and Economics: The Economic Factor Between Men and Women as a Factor in Social Evolution* (1898) garnered international attention. She followed this controversial book with *The Home* (1903), *Human Work* (1904), *The Man-Made World* (1911), a collection of poems, *Suffrage Songs and Verses* (1911), that included the poem "The Socialist and the Suffragist," and many other books.

In the debate over gender equality, Gilman's views were somewhat ambivalent. At times she contended that women and men shared a common "humanity," but at other times she argued that women's essential nature was superior to that of men—more nurturing and cooperative.

Gilman argued that maternal skills were not natural and that women needed training to be good mothers. "The ideal woman," Gilman wrote, "was not only assigned a social role that locked her into her home, but she was also expected to like it, to be cheerful and gay, smiling and good-humored." She skewered what she considered a male-centered culture for oppressing women in many ways—including in its limited views about women's "beauty" and clothing (such as corsets and high-heel shoes).

Gilman believed that women would be equal to men only when they were economically independent. The unpaid labor that women perform in the home—child rearing, cooking, cleaning, and other activities—was, she believed, a form of oppression. Society had to accept the idea of women, even married women, having careers. She encouraged women to work outside the home and maintained that men and women should share housework. But she went further, arguing that marriage itself had to be modernized to meet new realities. As much as possible, she believed, housekeeping, cooking, and childcare should be done by professionals, not by biological parents. To Gilman, the very idea of "motherhood" was outdated in a modern society. Children, she believed, should be raised in communal nurseries and fed in communal kitchens rather than in individual homes.

Girls and boys, she thought, should be raised with the same clothes, toys, and expectations.

Some of Gilman's fellow feminists tried to put her ideas into action. For example, in 1915, after a lobbying campaign by the Feminist Alliance, New York City's school system changed its policies and permitted women to continue teaching after they married and even after they had children.

Between 1909 and 1916 Gilman wrote and published *The Forerunner,* a socialist magazine devoted to women's emancipation and radical social change. There she published many of her own essays, articles, and stories and serialized seven of her novels. In her utopian novel *Herland* (1915), the author visits an island community of women organized around the principle of New Motherhood, where cooperation in all spheres of life has replaced male domination, competition, and war. In 1915 she was among the prominent women (led by **Jane Addams**) who founded the Woman's Peace Party to protest against World War I.

Gilman played an important role in shaping public opinion, disseminating radical ideas, and encouraging women (and men) to change their thinking about gender roles. She left it to other feminists, such as **Alice Stokes Paul,** to lead organizations like National Woman Suffrage Association and the National Woman's Party and to organize the demonstrations, hunger strikes, and other tactics that resulted in passage of the Nineteenth Amendment in 1920, giving women the right to vote.

Jane Addams (1860–1935)

Jane Addams with
Hull House children,
1933.
CREDIT: Associated Press

JANE ADDAMS was a key Progressive Era reformer, the founder of the settlement house movement, the "mother" of American social work, a champion of women's suffrage, an antiwar crusader, and the 1931 winner of the Nobel Peace Prize. She carved out a new way for women to become influential in public affairs when many doors were closed to them.

Addams's mother died when she was two. Jane and her four surviving siblings were raised by her father, John Addams, a businessman, banker, and landowner who served as an Illinois state senator from 1854 to 1870. Her evangelical Christian upbringing and her father's abolitionist views influenced her commitment to social reform. One of the first generation of women to earn a college degree, she graduated from Rockford Female Seminary in 1881. She passed the first-year exams at the Women's Medical College in Philadelphia, but back problems put her in the hospital immediately afterward and led to surgery nine months later. Never very good at science, she abandoned the idea of a career in medicine and began to search for some other career.

Even as a college graduate, Addams's options were limited. Affluent women were expected to be happy as wives, mothers, and charity volunteers. A turning point came when she read about a new idea, the settlement movement, and about a settlement house that had been established in London. During a tour of Europe soon after, she visited that house, Toynbee Hall, which was a social and cultural center in Whitechapel, one of east London's grittier working-class neighborhoods. It was founded to introduce male students at Oxford University, influenced by the ideas of Fabian socialism and social Christianity, to the realities of urban poverty. Even before her visit to London, Addams had proposed to her college friend Ellen Gates Starr that they start a settlement house in Chicago. Starr agreed, and Addams had found her career.

In 1889 Addams used the money she inherited after her father's death to cofound with Starr the nation's first settlement house in an industrial, mostly immigrant neighborhood of Chicago. They rented a run-down mansion named after its one-time owner, Charles Hull. Hull House was a place where prosperous young women and men could learn about the lives of working people and put into action their idealistic ideas of closing the divide between the social classes. The immigrants, many of whom did not speak English, lived in crowded, neglected tenements and worked in nearby factories.

Hull House offered clubs and classes and worked to be a good neighbor. Its residents opened a kindergarten, organized book-discussion groups and activities for children, nursed the sick, and started a lecture series on labor reform issues. Gradually, new facilities were added: an art gallery, a public kitchen, a gym, a coffee house, a cooperative boarding club for girls, a book bindery, an art studio, a music school, a drama group, a circulating library, and an employment bureau. By its fourth year, Hull House was host to 1,000 people every week.

Addams lived among workers who were organizing into unions and made friends with club women who had been politically active long before she arrived. After labor activist **Florence Kelley** joined the Hull House group in 1892, Hull House became a hub of social activism on labor issues and Addams became more deeply involved in the growing progressive movement.

Addams believed that well-educated upper-middle-class people should be the political allies of working people. Over the years, Addams and other Hull House residents, working alongside labor activists, pushed to end child labor and advocated for widows' pensions (the precursor to Social Security), unemployment insurance, the minimum wage, labor-organizing rights, safe workplaces, affordable housing, special courts for juveniles, and freedom of speech. Addams first supported labor legislation in 1893, when she lobbied to reform sweatshops that employed small children. A representative of a manufacturers' association offered to donate $50,000 to Hull House if Addams would "drop this nonsense about a sweat shop bill." Addams said she would rather see Hull House close than accept a bribe.

Addams often used her connections among Chicago's business and civic powerbrokers to raise money for Hull House, lobby for reforms, and intervene in political conflicts. During the 1894 Pullman strike, she was the most active member of the Citizens' Arbitration Committee, created to try to mediate the conflict between the company and the union. Addams knew George Pullman, who had built his railroad car company on Chicago's southern outskirts, and she fiercely hoped that Pullman would agree to meet with the Pullman chapter of the American Railway Union (led by **Eugene Debs**). Her efforts were unsuccessful, but her refusal to side with Pullman against the workers alienated some of Hull House's wealthy benefactors, who stopped their donations.

Addams often served as a mediator in management-labor disputes, but she always affirmed workers' right to organize, a position that put her at odds with many powerful friends and acquaintances. In an 1895 essay, "The Settlement as a Factor in the Labor Movement," Addams wrote that "the organization of working people was a necessity" in order to "translate democracy into social affairs." Those who did not recognize that "an injury to one" must be "the concern of all," she observed, had fallen "below the standard ethics of (the) day."

Hull House was the first settlement house in a white neighborhood to have an African American resident. Addams spoke out against lynching at the invitation of fellow Chicagoan Ida Wells-Barnett, invited **W. E. B. Du Bois** to speak at Hull House, and was a cofounder of the National Association for the Advancement of Colored People (NAACP). As African Americans moved in greater numbers to Chicago and the Hull House neighborhood, they were welcomed at the settlement house.

Addams worked through local, state, and national groups to achieve the social reforms she fought for. She was a member of the National Child Labor Committee, a cofounder and board member of the Women's Trade Union League, a member of the Chicago Board of Education, a vice president of the Illinois Equal Suffrage Association, a vice president of the National American Woman Suffrage Association, a founding board member of the NAACP and the American Civil Liberties Union, and a member of the Progressive Party's National Committee. The high point of her involvement in organized politics was in 1912, when she seconded the nomination of **Theodore Roosevelt** for president at the Progressive Party convention and campaigned for him in the midwestern states. Roosevelt said afterward that if he had been elected, he would have named Addams to his cabinet.

Addams and Hull House inspired many others to start settlement houses in other cities, the majority of them headed by women. By 1913 there were over 400 settlements in thirty-two states. Settlement houses laid the groundwork for the new profession of social work and for the emerging field of community organizing, but their other great influence was as places that educated generations of activists in a wide range of social and economic reform movements. Many of the most influential reformers and radicals in the 20th century were connected with the settlement house movement, including Lillian Wald, Mary Simkhovitch, Mary McDowell, **Alice Hamilton, Florence Kelley, Frances Perkins, John Dewey, Roger Baldwin, Norman Thomas,** and **Eleanor Roosevelt**.

Addams's activism did not stop with domestic issues. In 1893 she joined the small and struggling Chicago Peace Society. She was attracted to the peace movement because of her belief in nonviolence, inspired by the writings of Leo

Tolstoy. She gave her first speech about war and peace at an anti-imperialism rally in 1899, after the United States, having purchased the Philippines, began its war against those fighting for their independence.

When she opposed World War I, she argued that pacifists were patriots too and that killing was no way to settle international disputes. During the war, she cofounded the Woman's Peace Party, whose agenda was peace and women's rights, and cofounded what would eventually be called the Women's International League for Peace and Freedom. She served as the league's president until a few years before her death.

Lincoln Steffens
(1866–1936)

CREDIT: Associated Press

LINCOLN STEFFENS was the undisputed king of muckrakers. His exposés of corruption shocked the nation, changed public opinion, and provided ammunition for reformers. A man of warmth, humor, and compassion, Steffens was a social chameleon, mixing with all sorts of people, including Wall Street bankers, social reformers, union activists, and Tammany Hall bosses, who over the years educated him on the insidious ways of municipal corruption. His goal was not simply to uncover graft but to eliminate what he called "the affliction of privilege in American society."

Raised in a wealthy family in Sacramento, California, Steffens was an indifferent student if the subject bored him but a serious scholar when his interest was piqued. He did poorly at the University of California, but he convinced his father to pay for him to study art and philosophy in Germany and France for three years. He returned to the United States in 1892, landing his first job in New York as a reporter for the *Evening Post*.

In 1902, while working for *McClure's Magazine,* Steffens traveled to St. Louis, Missouri, and met Joseph W. Folk, a crusading prosecutor, who gave the journalist a guided tour of business and political corruption. That October, *McClure's* published what many consider the first muckraking article, "Tweed Days in St. Louis," which earned Steffens a national reputation. Steffens wrote, "Go to St. Louis and you will find the habit of civic pride in them. The visitor is told of the wealth of the residents, of the financial strength of the banks, and of the growing importance of the industries; yet he sees poorly paved, refuse-burdened streets, and dusty or mud-covered alleys; he passes a ramshackle firetrap crowded with the sick and learns that it is the City Hospital."

In St. Louis every transaction, including getting legislation passed or defeated, involved a bribe. The exposé had such an impact that the magazine sent Steffens around the country to uncover other scandals, which resulted in a series of articles. In 1904 they were published as a book, *The Shame of the Cities,* making Steffens one of the most famous journalists in the nation.

He next set his sights on state governments. As he recalled in his 1931 *Autobiography*, states had the same unhappy pattern as city administrations: "the same methods, the same motives, purposes, and men, all to the same end: to make the State officials, the Legislature, the courts, parts of a system representing the special interests of bribers, corruptionists, and criminals." His 1906 book, *The Struggle for Self-Government*, inspired reformers, as did his stories of valiant fighters trying to right political wrongs, collected in his 1909 book, *Upbuilders.*

In 1906 Steffens and his colleagues Ida Tarbell and Ray Stannard Baker launched their own publication, *American Magazine,* to expand their investigative efforts. But Steffens wanted to go beyond exposing wrongdoing. He wanted the magazine to propose solutions, an idea his colleagues rejected. Unsatisfied, Steffens soon left the magazine to work as a freelancer. In 1908 he interviewed and wrote an admiring profile of Socialist **Eugene Debs,** who was running for president, in *Everybody's* magazine.

The following year, Steffens thought he had found his opportunity to remedy municipal corruption when Edward Filene, a wealthy department store magnate and progressive philanthropist, invited him to Boston. Filene wanted to turn Boston into a model of social reform. Filene was as well connected as anyone in Boston, and for almost a decade he and a handful of other progressives (mostly business and professional men, including **Louis Brandeis**), tried to challenge the corruption of the city's political machine. They hoped to advance public health and education reforms and to win popular control over street railway, gas, and subway franchises, but they had little success. Filene secured $10,000 from the Good Government Association (GGA) and asked Steffens to spend a year in the city investigating Boston's political corruption and then to draft a plan for change. Steffens interviewed business leaders, social workers, reporters, Harvard professors, and others. He visited neighborhoods, collected statistics, gave speeches, and was toasted at receptions in his honor as Boston's municipal savior. One of his talks at Harvard mesmerized two students—Walter Lippmann and John Reed—who would become his protégés and then famous progressive writers themselves.

But by the time Steffens was ready to write his report, Filene's business colleagues in the GGA had gotten cold feet. Much to Steffens's and Filene's chagrin, they balked at even modest reforms, such as an increase in taxes, much less municipal ownership of key utilities. Discouraged, Steffens never finished the book he had planned to write.

After Steffens's wife died in 1911, he took solace in his Christian faith. He was particularly inspired by Sam "Golden Rule" Jones, a wealthy businessman and reform mayor of Toledo, who in both his business and his political practices lived by Christian principles of charity and compassion. Steffens wrote a series of articles about applying these principles in the real world.

In 1911, to test his ideas, Steffens traveled to Los Angeles, where the controversial trial of the two McNamara brothers was taking place. The brothers, union activists involved in a bitter citywide labor dispute, were accused of dynamiting the *Los Angeles Times* building, killing twenty-one employees in the process. Steffens met with Harrison Gray Otis (who owned the *Times*), leaders of the business community, and **Clarence Darrow** (who represented the brothers) and other members of the defense team. Steffens then hatched a plan to apply the Christian principle of "do unto others." In his plan, the brothers would plead guilty (which many believed they were), but the judge would show them leniency. In exchange, the city's labor leaders would call off an ongoing strike and begin negotiations.

But the deal fell apart when church ministers the Sunday before the verdict preached vengeance and denounced Steffens's proposal. "It is no cynical joke, it is literally true, that the Christian churches would not recognize Christianity if they saw it," Steffens wrote. "They came like the cries of a lynching mob and frightened all the timid men who had worked with us—and the judge."

After his experiences in Boston and Los Angeles, Steffens gave up hope that exposing corruption or proposing practical solutions would, on their own, lead to reform. Entrenched business interests, he concluded, would always outwit and outlast the reformers. Steffens became an unabashed revolutionary and looked for examples elsewhere that American radicals might follow. In December 1914 he boarded a ship from New York to Veracruz to see for himself what the Mexican Revolution was all about. He was trying to determine which of two competing leaders of the revolution—Francisco "Pancho" Villa or Venustiano Carranza—was the one to support. "I thought of a trick I used to practice in making a quick decision in politics at home," he wrote in his autobiography. "I'd ask Wall Street, which is so steadily wrong on all social questions. If I could find out which side Wall Street was on, I could go to the other with the certainty of being right." So he sat down with the "big business men with Mexican interests," who were happy to tell him why Villa was the better man. He then set sail to meet Carranza.

Steffens did not speak Spanish, but Carranza later said the American journalist "speaks our language"—that of revolution. Carranza asked Steffens to advise the revolutionaries on developing a constitution, but Steffens was there to learn, not to teach. In 1916, upon his return, he wrote an article in *Everybody's* magazine arguing that the greatest danger to the revolution was potential American military intervention at the behest of US and Mexican business interests. Senator **Robert M. La Follette** and the Woman's Peace Party, echoing Steffens's view, sought to mobilize opposition to sending US troops. Steffens met with President Woodrow Wilson and urged him to hold off on a planned counterrevolutionary invasion of Mexico. Wilson had already ruled out an invasion but flattered Steffens by telling him that his firsthand account of Mexican politics had been persuasive.

Next, Steffens traveled to Russia to witness that country's unfolding revolution. After seeing the emerging socialist state, he famously said, "I have seen the future and it works." But Steffens's enthusiasm for the Soviet Union did not last.

By the time he wrote his autobiography in 1931, he had become disillusioned with communism. Frustrated by reform and disenchanted by revolution, Steffens could not see the important role he had played in shaping American public opinion and in making it easier for Progressive Era activists to build a movement to strengthen democracy.

Hiram Johnson
(1866–1945)

CREDIT: Harris & Ewing/Library of Congress Prints and Photographs Division/Harris & Ewing Collection

IN THE late 1800s and early 1900s, the Southern Pacific Railroad was one of the most powerful corporations in the country, and certainly the most politically influential in California. The company consolidated its power by purchasing other railroads, then charging monopoly rates to carry freight, which angered farmers and other shippers. It used devious methods to purchase land to expand its lines, and it evicted farmers, homeowners, and businesses against their will. It became the largest landowner and largest employer in California. When people resisted its power, it used its political influence to get its way. The Southern Pacific owned—or at least rented—many members of city councils, the state legislature, and California's congressional delegation.

One of Southern Pacific's staunchest allies was Grove Johnson, a company attorney who served in the California legislature (1878–1882) and the US Congress (1895–1897). Although he favored some liberal ideas, such as women's suffrage and compulsory public education, he also exemplified the close links between business and politics during the Gilded Age.

Grove Johnson's son, Hiram, however, as the governor of California from 1911 to 1917, spearheaded a movement to curb the influence and abuses of big business. First as a reform Republican, then as a Progressive Party candidate, Johnson focused on the Southern Pacific, reining in the company with laws to regulate corporations. Johnson's pledge to "kick the Southern Pacific out of politics in California" was politically popular. Once elected, he ended the company's tight grip on state government and, by doing so, became California's first politician with a national reputation.

Johnson was born in Sacramento, the state capital, where his father practiced law and politics. He studied law at the University of California, Berkeley, was admitted to the bar in 1888, and joined his father's law practice. Their personal and political disagreements led Hiram to move to San Francisco in 1902. There he opened a law practice and quickly became a prominent attorney whose dramatic oratory persuaded juries and provided good quotations for the local newspapers.

In 1906 the city's district attorney made Johnson an assistant prosecutor for a series of corruption trials that included the trials of San Francisco's mayor, the city's political boss, and some of the city's most prominent businessmen, all of them implicated in a corruption scandal involving bribes from major utility companies. Eventually Johnson took over the prosecution team and won convictions, bolstering his reputation as a courageous lawyer and reformer.

He was increasingly drawn into the widening circle of reformers and radicals across California, who had three overlapping goals. First, they wanted to challenge corporate influence in government and the corruption of municipal and state politics, epitomized by the sway of the Southern Pacific Railroad, but also practiced by other sectors of big business. Second, they wanted to give ordinary voters a stronger voice in government by enacting "direct democracy" laws allowing citizens to recall corrupt politicians and enact legislation through initiatives (to propose new laws) and the referendum (to block existing laws), thus circumventing the influence of business groups over elected officials. They also supported giving women the right to vote. Finally, they sought to create a social safety net to cushion the hardships of poverty, unemployment, old age, and harsh working conditions.

In 1910 the Lincoln-Roosevelt League, the reform wing of California's Republican Party, convinced Johnson to run for governor. He won the party's nomination and beat his Democratic opponent. Soon after his victory, Johnson visited the east to confer with former president **Theodore Roosevelt,** Senator **Robert M. La Follette,** and other progressive Republicans. When he returned to California, Johnson initiated a whirlwind of activity, leading the most successful progressive legislative session in US history. He persuaded the state legislature to support measures calling for the initiative, referendum, and recall and to pass a law allowing voters to elect US senators (who until then had been chosen by the state legislature), giving California voters more direct power than voters in any other state. Despite Johnson's own ambivalence on women's suffrage, California gave women the right to vote in 1911, nine years before passage of the Twentieth Amendment to the US Constitution. He also persuaded the legislature to provide free textbooks to children in public schools.

To rein in big business, Johnson convinced the legislature to give the state Railroad Commission additional powers to set the rates that railroads could charge (a major victory over Southern Pacific) and to regulate privately owned utilities that provided water, gas, streetcar service, and electricity. Despite opposition from some upper-class progressives who disliked unions, Johnson pushed through laws to help workers, including workmen's compensation laws (requiring employers to compensate workers for workplace injuries), restrictions on child labor, and the nation's first eight-hour workday law that applied to female employees.

This remarkable wave of reform made Johnson a national figure. In the 1912 presidential election, when Theodore Roosevelt challenged his fellow Republican, President William Howard Taft, he asked Johnson to run as his vice presidential partner. After Taft won the GOP nomination at the party's convention, Roosevelt and Johnson led a revolt among Republican reformers. They created the Progressive Party, whose platform reflected a national version of the ideas they had enacted in California and other states. With Johnson's help, Roosevelt won the popular vote in California, but he came in second nationwide.

After his defeat, Johnson, still governor of California, expanded the state's progressive legislative agenda. The state created an Industrial Welfare Commission, which had the authority to establish a state minimum wage, a quarter century before Congress passed a federal wage law. The legislature also created an Industrial Accident Commission (to implement the workmen's compensation law) and the Commission on Immigration and Housing (to address the plight of migrant farmworkers), and it appointed union members, feminists, and other progressive activists to serve on these commissions.

Johnson's reform agenda was so popular that when he sought reelection in 1914—on the Progressive Party ticket rather than as a Republican—he got more votes than the Republican and Democratic candidates combined. Having achieved almost everything he had set out to do as governor, Johnson ran for the US Senate in 1916 and was elected on the Republican ticket. In 1920, he sought the Republican nomination for president but lost to the probusiness conservative Warren G. Harding.

California voters reelected Johnson four more times to the Senate, where he remained until his death in 1945. As a progressive Republican, he was a strong supporter of **Franklin D. Roosevelt**'s economic and social programs. Indeed, the sweeping overhaul of California politics that Johnson engineered—along with such counterparts as La Follette in Wisconsin—helped lay the foundation for the New Deal. Despite his party affiliation, he was one of the Senate's strongest union allies. For example, he led the investigation into the labor conditions in the West Virginia coal mines.

In the Senate, Johnson reluctantly supported America's involvement in World War I but soon became a leading isolationist, opposing US participation in the League of Nations (and later in the United Nations) and resisting US preparations for World War II. He died on the day the United States dropped the atomic bomb on Hiroshima.

Although he served in the Senate for twenty-eight years, he spoke his most memorable words soon after taking office. Referring to the debate over the US entry into World War I, he said, paraphrasing Aeschylus, "The first casualty when war comes, is truth."

W. E. B. Du Bois
(1868–1963)

ON AUGUST 28, 1963, more than 250,000 Americans assembled at the Lincoln Memorial to participate in the March on Washington for Jobs and Freedom. It was the largest rally in American history up to that time, and it has since become famous as the occasion for Rev. **Martin Luther King Jr.**'s "I Have a Dream" oration. Before King spoke, however, Roy Wilkins, the longtime head of the National Association for the Advancement of Colored People (NAACP), addressed the crowd. Toward the end of his remarks, Wilkins announced that W. E. B. Du Bois, who had helped found the NAACP in 1909, had died the day before in Ghana at age ninety-five. Wilkins explained, "Now, regardless of the fact that in his later years Dr. Du Bois chose another path, it is incontrovertible that at the dawn of the twentieth century his was the voice that was calling to you to gather here today in this cause. If you want to read something that applies to 1963 go back and get a volume of *The Souls of Black Folk* by Du Bois published in 1903."

Few at the March on Washington had heard of Du Bois, whose writings were mostly forgotten. He had not been actively involved in the civil rights movement of the 1950s and 1960s. The "another path" that Du Bois had chosen late in his life was black nationalism and communism, which most civil rights leaders, including King and Wilkins, rejected in favor of racial integration and social democracy.

Today, however, Du Bois is recognized as one of the monumental intellectual and political figures of the 20th century and certainly the most influential African American intellectual of the era. In the almost half century since the March on Washington, his reputation as a brilliant sociologist, historian, polemicist, novelist, and editor has been restored, his writings reprinted, and his life reported in several prize-winning biographies. Author of eighteen books, Du Bois's writings challenged America's ideas about race and helped lead the early crusade for civil rights.

William Edward Burghardt Du Bois was born in 1868, five years after the Emancipation Proclamation, in Great Barrington, Massachusetts, a town with about 50 African Americans out of 5,000 inhabitants. The valedictorian of his high school class, Du Bois attended Fisk University, a black liberal arts college in Nashville, Tennessee, and spent the summer teaching in a rural school. These were his first encounters with southern segregation, about which he would later write prolifically. After two years at Fisk, he transferred to Harvard and graduated cum laude in 1890. Five years later he earned his doctorate in history, the first African American to receive a Ph.D. from Harvard. His dissertation was published in 1896 as *The Suppression of the African Slave Trade to the United States of America, 1638–1870,* in the Harvard Historical Series.

While working as an instructor in sociology at the University of Pennsylvania, Du Bois wrote *The Philadelphia Negro: A Social Study* (1899), the first case study of an American black community, as well as reports on black farmers and businessmen and on black life in southern communities. These works established Du Bois as the first great scholar of black life in America at a time when lynching and other forms of violence against blacks were intensifying and southern states were enacting Jim Crow laws to strengthen white supremacy. In an 1897 essay in the *Atlantic Monthly,* "Strivings of the Negro People," Du Bois first outlined his concept of blacks' "double consciousness"—the tricky balancing act of reconciling pursuit of assimilation into the American mainstream with maintenance of pride in one's black identity. That essay became the basis for his most enduring book, *The Souls of Black Folk* (1903), a collection of penetrating essays on African American culture, religion, history, and politics. It was there that Du Bois wrote the statement for which he is probably most famous: "The problem of the twentieth century is the problem of the color line—the relation of the darker to the lighter races of men in Asia and Africa, in America and the islands of the sea." (Most Americans only know the first half of the statement.)

Du Bois hoped his research would bring about change by exposing whites to the brutal realities of segregation. But he soon realized that political agitation was also needed to change attitudes and to dismantle America's racial system. He hoped that well-educated African Americans—a group he called the "talented tenth"—would develop the leadership capacity to carry out that political effort.

To further that goal, Du Bois and other scholars and professionals met secretly in Buffalo, New York, in 1905 and founded the Niagara Movement to demand full equality for African Americans. "We want full manhood suffrage and we want it now," its manifesto said. "We are men! We want to be treated as men. And we shall win." The Niagara Movement challenged the views of the nation's most prominent African American educator, Booker T. Washington. In his famed "Atlanta Compromise" speech ten years earlier Washington had argued that black advancement would come primarily through accommodation and vocational education.

From 1897 to 1910, Du Bois was professor of economics and history at Atlanta University. He founded and edited the journals *Moon* (1906) and *The Horizon* (1907–1910) as outlets for the Niagara Movement. The movement attracted some black socialists, and Du Bois—influenced by the writings of Henry George, Jack London, and others—described socialism as "the one great hope of the Negro in America" in a 1907 article in *The Horizon*. He joined the Socialist Party in 1911 but left the next year to support Democrat Woodrow Wilson's campaign for president. He continued to consider himself a Socialist but was rarely in sync with the party's activities or satisfied with its commitment to racial equality. In turn, some black Socialists, such as **A. Philip Randolph,** criticized Du Bois for concentrating on the elite, with his focus on the "talented tenth," rather than building a mass movement that included black workers and farmers.

Although Du Bois never completely abandoned his "talented tenth" views, he devoted many of his most productive years to building the NAACP, which eventually became the largest grassroots organization among African Americans. Echoing the focus of the Niagara Movement, the NAACP's goal was to secure the rights guaranteed in the US Constitution's Thirteenth, Fourteenth, and Fifteenth Amendments, which promised an end to slavery, the equal protection of the law, and universal adult male suffrage, respectively.

From 1910 to 1934 Du Bois abandoned academia and served as the NAACP's director of publicity and research and as a member of its board of directors. He also served as editor of the *Crisis,* a magazine that became a highly visible and often controversial forum for criticism of white racism, lynching, and segregation and that gave exposure to young African American writers, poets, academics, and agitators. He devoted an entire issue of the magazine to the issue of women's suffrage. In 1934 Du Bois resigned from the NAACP board and from the *Crisis* because of his support for African American–controlled institutions, schools, and economic cooperatives, which challenged the NAACP's commitment to integration.

From 1934 to 1944 Du Bois was chairman of the Department of Sociology at Atlanta University, where he continued writing about the history and condition of black Americans, producing, among other works, *Black Reconstruction* (1935). In 1940 he founded *Phylon,* a social science quarterly. He returned to the NAACP as director of special research from 1944 to 1948.

Du Bois was long an advocate of international human rights and of Pan-Africanism, which addressed the condition of people of African descent around the world. He attended the first Pan-African Congress in England in 1900, and in 1919, 1921, 1923, and 1927 he organized a series of Pan-African congresses condemning colonialism, with delegations made up of intellectuals from Africa, the West Indies, and the United States.

In 1945 Du Bois served as a consultant to the newly formed United Nations. As the Cold War escalated, the US government increasingly harassed Du Bois for his left-wing activism and his attacks on US imperialism and European colonialism. In 1948 the NAACP, fearful of being identified with radicals, fired Du Bois. That year, he supported **Henry Wallace**'s Progressive Party campaign for president. From 1949 to 1955 he headed the Council on African Affairs, an anticolonialist group. In 1949 he was chairman of the Peace Information Center in New York, which promoted the Stockholm Peace Petition to ban nuclear weapons, a movement that the US government characterized as communist-inspired. Du Bois and other officers of the center were indicted by a federal grand jury on a charge of failing to register as foreign agents. They were acquitted after a trial in which the chief defense counsel was Congressman **Vito Marcantonio** of Manhattan. In 1950 Du Bois ran unsuccessfully for the US Senate on the left-wing American Labor Party ticket. In 1953 the US State Department revoked Du Bois's passport.

Increasingly disillusioned with the United States, Du Bois officially joined the Communist Party in 1961 and moved to Ghana at the invitation of its president, Kwame Nkrumah. Nkrumah asked Du Bois to serve as director of the *Encyclopedia Africana*, a project that Du Bois had been working on for many years. Du Bois soon renounced his US citizenship and became a citizen of Ghana. As a result, he was not active in the civil rights movement, although his writings eventually had enormous influence on civil rights activists, on the emerging field of black studies, and on the growing understanding of the anticolonial views within the world's poor nations.

William "Big Bill" Haywood (1869–1928)

ONE OF the most famous radical labor leaders of the early 20th century, William Haywood's imposing physical size and loud oratory earned him the nickname "Big Bill." However, because of his advocacy of militant direct action in labor and Socialist Party organizing, he was also called "the most dangerous man in America."

Haywood's stepfather was a miner, and the family often lived in mining camps around Salt Lake City, Utah, when not living in the city itself. Haywood entered the mines at the age of fifteen. Although Haywood tried other occupations in the ensuing years, he returned to mining, eventually settling for several years in Silver City, Idaho. There Haywood joined the labor movement. In 1886 he was a charter member of the Western Federation of Miners (WFM) local in Silver City. By 1900 he was president of the local and joined the national executive board. Shortly afterward, Haywood moved to Denver, Colorado, and began working for the WFM full-time, editing its journal, *Miners' Magazine*, and serving as secretary-treasurer.

The WFM was one of the more militant unions in the nation, operating in mining towns that occasionally experienced dramatic uprisings by miners and violent reprisals from mine owners (who sometimes relied on government troops to impose order). The Rockefeller and Guggenheim financial empires—owners of some of the largest mining companies at the time—rightly saw the WFM as a threat to their economic interests. After moving to Colorado, Haywood helped orchestrate a statewide struggle by miners, lasting approximately three years, which brought him into conflict with the courts and the governor.

In 1905 Haywood formed the Industrial Workers of the World (IWW) with **Eugene Debs** and Daniel De Leon, among others. The IWW's philosophy was to organize those who had been left out of the craft labor organizing movement. They advocated the creation of "one big union" for all workers, regardless of skill, race, or industry. Haywood's leadership role at the IWW brought him to national attention and infamy, but it was his connection to the WFM that nearly sent him to the gallows.

In 1906, not wishing to engage in time-consuming legal procedures to extradite radicals, private police (headed by James McParland, a Pinkerton agent) and law enforcement officials forcibly moved Haywood and two other labor leaders from Colorado to Idaho. There the three were charged with organizing a bombing that had killed Idaho's former governor Frank Steunenberg. (The bombing was allegedly in retaliation for Steunenberg's use of federal troops to indiscriminately round up hundreds of men and hold them in crowded makeshift jails, sometimes for months on end, during the violent labor conflicts in Coeur d'Alene in the late 1890s.)

The trial was a national sensation. President **Theodore Roosevelt** called the defendants "undesirable citizens," but supporters were able to raise $250,000 for their defense. Haywood was defended by **Clarence Darrow,** who both criticized the prosecution's reliance on a Canadian drifter and criminal as their main witness and portrayed the trial as nothing more than an attack on labor. Haywood was acquitted in 1907. (Another defendant, labor activist George Pettibone, was acquitted in a separate trial, and the charges against the third defendant, WFM president Charles Moyer, were eventually dropped.)

Haywood's vocal support for sabotage and other militant tactics resulted in tension between him and Socialist Party leaders, and he was removed from the party's national executive committee. He continued to support the IWW's organizing of migrant farmworkers, loggers, copper miners, and textile workers and led several major strikes.

In 1912, in Lawrence, Massachusetts, 25,000 workers, mostly immigrant women, went on strike after the mill owners cut their already meager pay. The strikers demanded a 15 percent pay increase and a fifty-four-hour workweek. Haywood, Elizabeth Gurley Flynn, Joseph Ettor, and other experienced IWW organizers went to Lawrence to help organize the workers. The strikers were met with brutal violence from local police and militia, who turned fire hoses on workers and sent strikers to jail. This generated public sympathy for the plight of the workers and outrage at the police brutality. The IWW and Socialists organized strike relief, including medical care, food, and funds for the families. They also arranged for the children of strikers to be sent to New York, where supporters, mostly wealthy women, found temporary homes for them. Nurses, including **Margaret Sanger,** accompanied the children on the trains.

The national reaction pressured the mill owners to give in to the strikers' demands. The walkout became known as the "Bread and Roses" strike because one of the women reportedly carried a picket sign that read, "We Want Bread, but Roses Too!" This became a rallying cry among the Lawrence strikers and then an anthem for workers elsewhere, a demand not only for economic justice but also for human rights and dignity.

These successes demonstrated the Wobblies' ability to do two things. First, the IWW could organize elaborate strikes involving workers who were recent immigrants from several nations and spoke many different languages. Second, the IWW appealed to workers in a wide range of industries. News coverage of these events made Haywood a popular speaker in intellectual circles.

World War I brought labor shortages, which gave the IWW a stronger hand in negotiations over working conditions. However, the IWW's opposition to US entry into World War I and its strikes during the war brought them into conflict with the federal government. Once again, Haywood became the target of investigations. In September 1917 the Department of Justice arrested more than 100 IWW officers, including Haywood, on charges including espionage and sedition. Almost a year later, a federal trial in Chicago ended (in August 1918) with convictions and lengthy sentences for Haywood and dozens of codefendants.

Haywood was freed on bail while appealing his conviction. He returned to public speaking, focusing on various political prisoners in the United States. His final appeal failed in April 1921, and Haywood left the country, reappearing in the Soviet Union later that year. In the last seven years of his life, Haywood was given some organizing assignments by the Soviets, but he soon retired to the Lux Hotel in Moscow and married a Russian woman. Haywood frequently entertained visitors from America, but health problems (including diabetes and alcoholism) led to his early death at age fifty-nine. Some of his ashes were interred in the Kremlin Wall, and the rest were interred at Forest Home Cemetery (formerly Waldheim Cemetery) in Forest Park, Illinois, next to the graves of the victims of the 1886 Haymarket Massacre.

Alice Hamilton
(1869–1970)

ALICE HAMILTON was a physician whose patient was America's working class. She was a brilliant scientist and an untiring reformer who founded the field of occupational medicine, which has helped save tens of millions of workers from unnecessary workplace injuries, diseases, and deaths. She is a giant in the annals of public health not only because of her important research but also because she helped educate and mobilize the public and promoted legislation to protect workers and their communities. The first woman professor at Harvard Medical School and the first to receive the prestigious Lasker Award in public health, Hamilton faced and overcame enormous obstacles due to gender discrimination. It is an ironic symbol of her pioneering accomplishments that one of her distinctions is having been listed in a book of eminent scientists called *Men of Science,* published in 1944.

CREDIT: Library of Congress Prints and Photographs Division/George Grantham Bain Collection

Born to an affluent family, Hamilton was raised in the growing industrial city of Fort Wayne, Indiana, and educated at home and at Miss Porter's School, a finishing school in Connecticut. She received her medical degree from the University of Michigan in 1893. (In 1900 only 5 percent of American physicians were women. By 1960 that number was still only 6 percent. Today it is about half). After internships in Minneapolis and Boston, she spent a year studying at universities in Munich and Leipzig in Germany. Neither university had permitted women students before, but they allowed Hamilton to attend lectures in bacteriology and pathology if she promised to remain inconspicuous to male students and professors.

In 1897 she accepted a teaching position at the Women's Medical School of Northwestern University in Chicago and moved into Hull House, where she could bring together her scientific training and her zeal for social reform. She had heard **Jane Addams** speak at her Methodist church in Fort Wayne years earlier and was drawn to the culture and commitment of the settlement house.

Hamilton opened a well-baby clinic for poor families in the Hull House neighborhood. She learned about the daily lives of these families. She observed the strange deaths that blighted them, the prevalence of lead palsy and wrist drop (both the result of lead poisoning), and the significant number of widowed women. Hamilton quickly realized that these problems were not simply medical issues but the result of social and economic conditions.

The rise of big industrial cities and overcrowded working-class neighborhoods had led to new dangers in workplaces and communities. Journalists, union activists, and others had written and organized against dangerous workplaces. But scientists in Europe—such as Sir Thomas Oliver, whose 1902 book *Dangerous Trades* influenced Hamilton—had devoted much more attention to these problems than their American counterparts. Hamilton decided to change this.

In 1902 Chicago was struck with a typhoid epidemic. Hamilton recognized that flies were transmitting the disease because of the haphazard way that sewage was disposed of. She brought this to the attention of the Chicago Health Department, which was reorganized to address the issue. She also observed that the health problems suffered by many poor immigrants were connected to unsafe conditions and noxious chemicals, especially lead dust, that they were exposed to at work. In 1908 Hamilton published one of the first scientific articles on occupational disease in the United States, and she was soon a recognized expert on the topic.

Hamilton combined the new laboratory science of toxicology with "shoe leather epidemiology"—firsthand visits to workplaces to examine conditions and track down examples of workers poisoned by exposure to lead and other toxins. Workers were often too intimidated by their bosses to talk to Hamilton at work, so she visited them at home, where they could speak more openly. With the help of the American Association for Labor Legislation and the American Public Health Association—along with the public outrage triggered by her friend **Upton Sinclair**'s 1906 novel *The Jungle*, which exposed the awful conditions in Chicago's slaughterhouses—Hamilton's research reached a wide audience. Her work was so persuasive that it led to sweeping state and federal reforms to improve workers' health and safety.

In 1910 Illinois governor Charles Deneen created the Occupational Disease Commission, the first such agency in the world, and appointed Hamilton director. Speaking to a group of executives in the lead industry, she described the consequences to workers' health of inhaling and ingesting lead in their factories. "All the factories in Illinois and St. Louis are so dangerous to their women that they would be closed by law in any European country," Hamilton told them. Recalling those experiences in her 1943 autobiography, Hamilton wrote, "There is something strange in speaking of 'accident and sickness compensation.' What could 'compensate' anyone for an amputated leg or a paralyzed arm, or even an attack of lead colic, to say nothing of the loss of a husband or son?"

Hamilton was a prime mover in campaigns to pass several workers' compensation laws in Illinois over the opposition of business groups. These laws reflected a radical new idea: that workers were entitled to compensation for the injuries and health problems they sustained on the job. After Hamilton issued her report on workers' compensation, Charles Neill, the U.S. commissioner of labor, asked her to replicate her research on a national level. She examined hazards posed by exposure to lead, arsenic, mercury, organic solvents, and radium (used in the manufacture of watch dials). One of her studies examined the poisonous effects of manufacturing explosives, a study undertaken during World War I at the request of the National Research Council. She stayed in this unsalaried position from 1911 to 1921, when her program was canceled after probusiness Republicans regained control of the White House.

In 1919, Hamilton was offered a position in the new Department of Industrial Medicine. This made her the first woman appointed to the Harvard Medical School faculty, but the school imposed three conditions on her employment: she would not be allowed to use the Faculty Club, she would have no access to football tickets, and she would not be allowed to march in commencement processions. At Harvard all her students were male, because the school did not admit women students until World War II. Hamilton, however, insisted on some conditions of her own: she would only be required to teach one semester a year so she could continue her investigations and return to Hull House for part of each year.

Hamilton served on the League of Nations Health Committee between 1924 and 1930, which led her to explore industrial health conditions in other countries. Her books, including *Industrial Poisons in the United States* (1925) and *Industrial Toxicology* (1934), were pioneering works and widely cited.

Despite these remarkable accomplishments, when Hamilton retired from Harvard in 1935, at age sixty-six, she was still ranked as an assistant professor, which means that she never received a promotion.

Although best known for her scientific work, Hamilton was deeply involved in many reformist and radical causes throughout her career—not surprising for someone who spent many years in Hull House's stimulating environment. Along with Jane Addams and Emily Balch, she was part of the delegation that traveled to Europe to encourage the end of World War I. The group later became the Women's International League for Peace and Freedom.

From 1944 to 1949 she served as president of the National Consumers League, the activist group that had played a key role in many of the important workers' rights, child labor, and women's workplace reforms of the 20th century. While in her eighties and nineties, Hamilton took an active role in campaigning against the hysteria of McCarthyism and the Cold War. In 1963, at ninety-four, she signed an open letter to President John F. Kennedy asking for an early withdrawal of US troops from Vietnam.

Hamilton died on September 22, 1970, at the age of 101. Three months later, Congress passed the landmark Occupational Safety and Health Act, a major legacy of Hamilton's scientific and political work.

CREDIT: Associated Press

Emma Goldman
(1869–1940)

EMMA GOLDMAN did *not* say the famous line that is often attributed to her: "If I can't dance, I don't want to be in your revolution." But those words do express her sentiments. She was a serious radical, an anarchist, and she believed that she was fighting for people's right to enjoy themselves, free of unjust and inhumane restrictions.

"I want freedom, the right to self-expression, everybody's right to beautiful, radiant things," Goldman said. "Anarchism meant that to me, and I would live it in spite of the whole world—prisons, persecution, everything. Yes, even in spite of the condemnation of my own closest comrades I would live my beautiful ideal."

How did Goldman expect her ideal society to come about? Another quotation accurately summarizes her view: "If voting changed anything, they'd make it illegal." Goldman liked to party, but she did not believe in political parties or in achieving change through the slow, incremental process of elections, reforms, and policy debates. She did not have a blueprint or a roadmap to change the world, but she nevertheless encouraged Americans to join the revolutionary movement, not only to dance but to challenge arbitrary authority, even through violence if necessary.

Goldman was an eloquent and dazzling speaker and writer who advocated anarchism, free speech, women's suffrage, birth control, workers' rights, the eight-hour workday, and free universal education without regard to race, gender, or class. She preached a brand of uncompromising revolutionism and absolute personal freedom that won many converts but alienated many more radicals and reformers—and provoked the opposition of the political establishment, who frequently sought to silence, jail, or deport her.

Born in Lithuania to a family of Russian-Jewish shopkeepers, Goldman moved with her family in 1881 to St. Petersburg. There, she embraced Russia's revolutionary movement but lived in an atmosphere of fear, as the czar's secret police crushed any dissent. Her father put her to work in a corset factory and began pressuring her into an arranged marriage. She resisted, and in 1885 the sixteen-year-old Goldman set sail for America in the company of her older half sister, Helena. As they sailed into New York Harbor, Goldman rejoiced at "the free country, the asylum for the oppressed of all lands." "We, too," she thought, "would find a place in the generous heart of America."

Goldman ended up in Rochester, New York, where she worked in a clothing factory and had a brief, unhappy marriage to another worker. Conditions in America were better than they had been in Russia, but the pace of work was faster, the discipline was harsher, and the pay ($2.50 for a ten-and-a-half-hour day) made it nearly impossible to make ends meet.

Already a radical, Goldman was inspired by the events surrounding the Haymarket bombing in 1886. During a rally in Chicago's Haymarket Square protesting police brutality against workers striking for the eight-hour workday, someone threw a bomb and killed a police officer. Eight anarchists were tried and convicted of murder, triggering an international protest movement. Outraged by what she viewed as a travesty of justice, Goldman began to read everything she could about anarchism and soon embraced the cause.

She moved to New York City in 1889 and quickly became part of that city's bohemian and anarchist worlds. There she met her lifetime partner, Alexander Berkman, a fellow anarchist. In 1892 she was an accessory to Berkman's failed attempt to assassinate steel tycoon Henry Clay Frick in revenge for Frick's brutal treatment of workers during the Homestead Steel strike. Berkman spent fourteen years in prison for this crime, but Goldman escaped indictment because of insufficient evidence. She became a prominent public figure, promoting revolutionary anarchism in speeches, pamphlets, and books.

In 1893 she was arrested and tried again for urging a crowd of hungry unemployed workers in New York's Union Square to rely on street protest rather than voting to obtain relief. In court, Goldman based her defense on the right of free speech. She lost and spent ten months in jail on Blackwell's Island, where she apprenticed as a nurse to the inmates.

When President William McKinley was shot in 1901 by Leon Czolgosz, the police quickly sought to implicate Goldman, because Czolgosz had recently attended one of her lectures in Cleveland, Ohio. Goldman and other anarchists were arrested, but she was released, again for lack of evidence.

In 1903 Goldman helped found the Free Speech League in New York City in response to a new federal law that barred anarchists from entering the country. The group was one of several that laid the groundwork for what eventually, more than a decade later, became the American Civil Liberties Union.

Goldman claimed that she opposed violence in theory, but she often defended it in practice by blaming government and business leaders for instigating violence against dissidents. "As an anarchist, I am opposed to violence," Goldman said. "But if the people want to do away with assassins, they must do away with the conditions which produce murderers."

While working as a nurse and midwife among poor immigrant workers on the Lower East Side in the 1890s, Goldman became convinced that birth control was essential to women's sexual and economic freedom. She influenced the young **Margaret Sanger,** encouraging her campaign against the Comstock Law, which prohibited the distribution of birth control literature. Goldman was arrested at least twice for violating the anti–birth control law—and saw her arrests as yet more evidence that freedom of speech was linked to other causes.

Indeed, Goldman was frequently arrested and jailed while lecturing on such topics as birth control and opposition to the draft, and sometimes her talks were banned outright. Goldman edited an anarchist literary and political magazine, *Mother Earth*, from 1906 to 1917. Starting in 1917, Goldman spent two years in prison in Missouri for her opposition to the draft during World War I. She was often called "Red Emma."

In December 1919 the US government stripped Goldman of her citizenship and deported her, Berkman, and other radicals to Russia. Goldman and Berkman grew quickly disillusioned with the Russian Revolution, which they viewed as corrupt and authoritarian. After two years, they left Russia, moved to Europe, and determined to expose the persecution, terrorism, and harsh economic conditions they had witnessed. Goldman wrote a series of articles for the *New York World* that became part of her 1923 book *My Disillusionment in Russia*.

She and Berkman eventually settled in France, where she wrote her autobiography, *Living My Life* (1931). Except for a brief visit in 1934, she was denied entry into the United States for the rest of her life, but upon her death in May 1940 she was allowed burial in Chicago's Waldheim Cemetery, near the graves of the Haymarket martyrs.

Lewis Hine
(1874–1940)

CREDIT: Lewis W. Hine/Courtesy of
George Eastman House, International
Museum of Photography and Film

THE SKY had not yet begun to brighten on a chilly February morning in 1911 when the first workers arrived at the seafood cannery in Biloxi, Mississippi. Slipping in after them was a slender man carrying cumbersome camera equipment. Photographer Lewis Hine was not allowed in the cannery. But he had no qualms about sneaking in at five in the morning, as he knew the managers would not arrive until hours later. He would return again at noon in a rowboat, tying up to the cannery dock, to get within striking distance of his subjects.

One was Manuel, who, at just five years old, was already a veteran shrimp picker. In the photograph taken by Hine, Manuel is round-cheeked and round-tummied, with a serious expression. Barefoot, he stands facing the camera, dressed in a checkered shirt, short pants, and a soiled apron, wearing a fisherman's cap on his head. In each hand he holds a strainer pot. Behind him is an immense mound of oyster shells.

Hine had traveled to Biloxi on behalf of the National Child Labor Committee, a group formed in 1904. One of the great documentary photographers, he journeyed to factories, mills, fields, and mines to document how America's children toiled. His images played a major role in the enactment of child labor laws in the United States.

Hine was born in Oshkosh, Wisconsin, above a popular Main Street restaurant that his parents owned. His father died when Lewis was seventeen years old. He worked as a hauler at a furniture factory, toiling thirteen hours a day, six days a week, to help support his mother and sister. But in 1893, during an economic downturn, the factory closed. He picked up odd jobs, splitting firewood and making deliveries. (Delivery boys were later a favorite subject in his work.) When he was hired as a bank janitor, he studied stenography at night and was promoted to secretary.

Hine's life began to change when he met Frank Manny, who became his mentor, introducing him to the ideas of **John Dewey** and, later, Felix Adler, the founder of the Ethical Culture movement. Hine enrolled at the teachers' college in Oshkosh, where Manny taught, and then spent a year at the University of Chicago. When Manny became superintendent of the Ethical Culture School in

New York City, he offered Hine a job teaching geography and natural history. While teaching, Hine completed his degree in education at New York University.

The Ethical Culture School, founded by Adler, was progressive and experimental. It based its curriculum on humanist values that helped lay the groundwork for Hine's future work. Although Hine had never picked up a camera before, Manny suggested he become the school photographer. He took pictures of school activities, set up a darkroom, and started a camera club.

Manny used Hine's emerging photography skills to teach students about social conditions, in particular the conditions facing the waves of immigrants coming through Ellis Island. Manny urged Hine to portray the dignity and worth of the newcomers, in part to help counter a growing anti-immigrant sentiment. Hine, with Manny as his assistant, lugged his rudimentary photography equipment to Ellis Island. He never photographed people without their permission, and in the cacophony of languages, he had to pantomime his requests to take a picture. Using an old box camera, glass-plate negatives, and magnesium flash powder that he had to ignite manually, he managed to capture beautiful images of people just arriving from Europe. He returned to Ellis Island many times over the coming years, taking 200 photographs in all.

After graduating from New York University, Hine began graduate studies in sociology at Columbia University. This prepared him for an assignment with Arthur and Paul Kellogg, who ran the reform-oriented magazine *Charities and The Commons* (later renamed *Survey*). They asked Hine to take pictures for the *Pittsburgh Survey*, a pioneering six-volume sociological study of conditions in that urban industrial city funded by the Russell Sage Foundation.

Hine followed in the footsteps of documentary photographer Jacob Riis, who captured the squalid conditions of New York's tenements in his 1890 masterpiece *How the Other Half Lives*. But whereas Riis photographed his subjects as helpless victims, beaten down by an oppressive system, Hine sought to present his subjects as people with pride and dignity, often tough and defiant, who held out hope for a better world. Hine was known for inviting his subjects to reveal what they wished of themselves rather than trying to catch them or coax them into wearing expressions of anguish or emptiness. Historian Robert Westbrook credits Hine with engaging his subjects with "decorum and tact," rarely taking candid shots but instead encouraging eye contact with the camera lens.

Hine worked with advocacy organizations that were trying to ban child labor. One of his pictures is of a mother and her four children sitting around the kitchen table, in a New York tenement lit by an oil lamp, all making paper flowers. "Angelica is three years old," he noted. "She pulls apart the petals, inserts the center, and glues it to the stem, making 540 flowers a day for five cents."

In 1908 the National Child Labor Committee (NCLC) offered Hine full-time work as an investigative photographer. He traveled around the country, photographing doffer boys in cotton mills, cigar makers, coal breakers, cannery workers, berry and tobacco pickers, laundry workers, even glassworkers—all under the age of sixteen. To gain access to factories and mills, he would pose as a fire inspector, a Bible salesman, or an industrial photographer. When that failed, he would linger at plant gates, asking children if he could take their picture. His years of teaching, combined with a gentle demeanor, allowed him to connect well with youngsters.

In a speech to the National Conference of Charities and Correction in 1909 entitled "Social Photography: How the Camera May Help in the Social Uplift," Hine argued that "the great social peril is darkness and ignorance." Social reformers, he said, need to expose the terrible living and working conditions that are invisible to many Americans. "The average person believes implicitly that the photograph cannot falsify. Of course, you and I know that this unbounded faith in the integrity of the photograph is often rudely shaken, for, while photographs may not lie, liars may photograph."

Hine was a stickler for individual details, recording whenever possible children's names, ages, working hours, and wages. He was particularly moved by the young boys laboring in coal mines. Of their work, he wrote, "It's like sitting in a coal bin all day long, except that the coal is always moving and clattering and cuts their fingers. Sometimes the boys wear lamps in their caps to help them see through the thick dust. They bend over the chutes until their backs ache, and they get tired and sick because they have to breathe coal dust instead of good, pure air." While he was at a Pennsylvania mine, two boys fell in the chute and were smothered to death.

Hine's photographs made visible the long-ignored plight of working children. They were used in brochures and booklets, news and magazine articles, exhibits and public lectures. His work played an important role in the movement to enact federal and state child labor laws (which were often paired with compulsory education laws to keep children in school), culminating in 1938 with the Fair Labor Standards Act, which included strong protections for children.

Hine continued to document child labor for a decade. In 1918 he left the NCLC and went to work for the American Red Cross, traveling to Europe to document the lives of refugees who were uprooted during World War I.

During the 1920s, wanting to focus on more-uplifting subjects, he began a series of portraits honoring American workers. His final major project was to document the construction of the Empire State Building. Although by then in his mid-fifties, he scrambled to dizzying heights to photograph work that he felt captured the uplifting nature of the human spirit. These photos were published in his 1932 book, *Men at Work*.

In 1936 Hine was appointed head photographer for the National Research Project of the New Deal's Works Progress Administration. But the next year, when the Farm Security Administration hired photographers to document the working and living conditions of poor and working-class Americans, Hine was not among those hired. The project director, Roy Stryker, said that Hine was difficult to work with. In addition, Hine's approach of allowing his subjects to pose for the camera may not have been in sync with the other photographers' notions of documentary social realism.

Hine's life ended in misfortune. Viewed as outmoded in a time when candid shots were in vogue, he could not find work. He lost his home and ended up on welfare, dying in poverty within a year of his wife's death. Only after his death was his work once again appreciated. Along with Riis, he is recognized as the father of documentary social photography, an inspiration to many younger photographers—including Paul Strand and others who joined the radical Photo League, as well as Dorothea Lange, Walker Evans, Margaret Bourke-White, Gordon Parks, and Milton Rogovin, who all used the camera as a weapon in the struggle for social reform. Today thousands of Hine's images have been preserved at major institutions, including the Library of Congress.

CREDIT: Associated Press/JC

Robert F. Wagner Sr.
(1877–1953)

IF **FRANKLIN D. ROOSEVELT** was the New Deal's pilot, Robert F. Wagner Sr. was its copilot. As a US senator from New York, he pushed through bills to create Social Security, provide workers with unemployment insurance and compensation for workplace injuries, construct government-subsidized housing for working-class families, and give workers the right to form unions and bargain collectively. These and other progressive laws faced enormous opposition from business groups, most newspapers, and many of his Senate colleagues, but Wagner—who saw himself as the labor movement's strongest ally in Congress—used his remarkable political skills to outmaneuver his opponents.

Wagner did not begin his political career as a progressive crusader. When he was elected to the New York State Assembly in 1904 and the state Senate four years later, he was part of the Democratic Party's Tammany Hall political machine, known for its graft and corruption and for trading votes for jobs and other favors. But a tragedy—the Triangle Shirtwaist factory fire in 1911 that killed 146 garment workers—transformed Wagner.

Born in Germany, Wagner came to America with his parents at eight years old in 1885. His father, unable to find work in his own craft, became a janitor, in part because the tenement building's landlord gave him a free basement apartment as a part of his income. Young Robert sold newspapers and delivered groceries before and after school to help the family. The valedictorian of his high school class, Wagner attended City College, where he was quarterback of the football team and graduated in 1898. Two years later he completed New York Law School and began practicing law.

Like many young lawyers at the time, Wagner's ambition and interest in public service led directly to Tammany Hall. He used his talents as a public speaker to help energize crowds on behalf of Tammany's candidates. By age twenty-six, he was a candidate himself and was elected to the state legislature. Charles Murphy, the Tammany boss, admired Wagner's skills, and in 1910 he passed over more experienced politicians to install the thirty-three-year-old as the youngest Senate leader in New York history.

The state's Democratic power brokers depended on immigrants' votes and could not ignore their growing protests over miserable working, housing, and public health conditions in New York City's factories and tenements. In November 1909 over 20,000 shirtwaist makers, led by the International Ladies' Garment Workers Union, walked off their jobs. In July of the following year, another group of garment workers—over 60,000 cloak makers, mostly men this time—went on strike. The strikers demanded better pay, shorter hours, and safer workplaces.

On March 25, 1911, on a Saturday at 4:45 p.m., close to quitting time, a fire broke out on the eighth and ninth floors of the Triangle Company building. Factory foremen had locked the exit doors to keep out union organizers and to keep workers from taking breaks and stealing scraps of fabric. Other doors only opened inward and were blocked by the stampede of workers struggling to escape. The ladders of the city's fire engines could not reach high enough to save the employees. As a result, workers burned or jumped to their deaths. Experts later concluded that the fire had probably been caused by a cigarette dropped on a pile of "cut aways," or scraps of cloth, that had been accumulating for almost three months.

News of the fire spread quickly, catalyzing public opinion and energizing a broad coalition of unlikely allies, including immigrants, muckraking journalists, clergy, unionists, socialists, and the wives and daughters of some of the city's wealthiest businessmen. On April 6, 30,000 New Yorkers marched—and hundreds of thousands more lined the march's route—behind empty hearses to memorialize the fire's victims. Numerous rallies, broadsides, and editorials called for legislative action ranging from fire safety codes to restrictions on child labor.

In response, New York governor, John Alden Dix, created the Factory Investigating Commission, a pioneering body with broad subpoena powers and teams of investigators. He put Wagner and his State Assembly counterpart, Al Smith, in charge of the investigation.

Some reformers figured that the commission was a political ploy to avoid doing anything by studying the problem until the public forgot about the tragedy. But Wagner and Smith accepted their responsibility with incredible zeal, hiring leading reformers to staff the blue-ribbon group. They took the commission members up and down the state holding hearings, visiting over 3,000 factories, and interviewing almost 500 witnesses. They found buildings without fire escapes and bakeries in poorly ventilated cellars with rat droppings. Only 21 percent of the bakeries even had bathrooms, and most of them were unsanitary. Children—some as young as five years old—were toiling in dangerous canning factories. Women and girls were working eighteen-hour days.

There was fierce opposition from the business community, but Wagner and Smith, fortified by a vibrant progressive movement, ignored it. In the first year, the commission proposed and the legislature quickly passed a package of laws requiring mandatory fire drills, automatic sprinklers, and outward-swinging doors that were to remain unlocked during work hours. They also created rules on the storage and disposal of flammable waste, and they banned smoking from the shop floor. In the second year, the legislature passed additional reforms. They set the maximum numbers of workers per floor; they established codes requiring new buildings to include fireproof stairways and fire escapes. They required employers to provide clean drinking water, washrooms, and toilets for their employees, and they gave labor commission inspectors the power to shut down unsanitary tenement sweatshops. Finally they ruled that women could work no more than fifty-four hours a week and that children under eighteen could not work in dangerous situations.

The duo's impressive leadership in shepherding these landmark reforms through the legislature catapulted Smith to the governor's office in 1918 and Wagner (after a seven-year stint as a New York State Supreme Court justice) to the US Senate in 1926.

In Washington, Wagner displayed the same talent for reform. His two greatest achievements occurred in 1935 when Congress passed the National Labor Relations Act (often called the Wagner Act), guaranteeing labor's right to organize into unions, and the Social Security Act, which provided old-age pensions. Wagner played a key role in almost every major New Deal program. He helped draft and sponsor the National Industrial Recovery Act of 1933, which established the National Recovery Administration to administer codes of fair practice within each industry, including the first federal minimum wage.

Wagner also led the successful fight to pass the 1937 US Housing Act, which provided the first significant government subsidies for low-cost housing. Wagner hoped the bill would stimulate construction jobs to build public housing. But some of the more radical components of Wagner's proposal were clipped after aggressive lobbying by the real estate industry, the banks, the lumber industry (which feared that public housing would be built with concrete and steel, not wood), and the US Chamber of Commerce. The provision that spurred new housing sponsored by unions, cooperatives, and nonprofit housing groups was killed. Wagner had intended public housing to be for middle-class families as well as the poor. But after World War II, the real estate industry recognized the pent-up demand for housing and, fearing competition from public housing (which it claimed was an opening wedge for socialism), sabotaged the program by pressuring Congress (in the 1949 Housing Act) to limit it to the very poor.

Short and stocky, with a heavy New York accent (for example, saying "woik" for "work"), Wagner mastered the details of the legislative process and found ways to persuade more-conservative colleagues to support liberal laws. But Wagner was not simply FDR's point man in Congress. He was more progressive and bolder than the president and frequently had to persuade FDR to support his proposals, often with the help of labor unions and other groups. But in two significant arenas—lynching and national health care—Wagner's efforts failed.

In 1932 African Americans—who had typically supported the Republican Party out of loyalty to Abraham Lincoln and the abolitionists—switched to the Democrats and helped elect FDR. The National Association for the Advancement of Colored People hoped that once in office, FDR would support federal legislation to end lynching, especially because his wife, **Eleanor Roosevelt,** had been a longtime opponent of lynching. In 1935 Wagner, along with Senator Edward Costigan of Colorado, agreed to draft a bill punishing sheriffs who failed to protect their prisoners from lynch mobs. But FDR refused to support the bill, worried that southern white voters—almost all of them loyal Democrats—would abandon the party. The legislation helped stir a national debate over the issue, and the bill received support from many members of Congress, but the opposition of southern Democrats defeated it.

In 1943 Wagner cosponsored the first meaningful national health insurance bill introduced in Congress. The American Medical Association, which feared government intrusion into medical practice, immediately labeled the bill "socialized medicine" and launched a campaign to kill it. With his attention diverted by World War II, FDR did not embrace Wagner's proposal. The bill never reached the floor of either house of Congress.

Despite these setbacks, Wagner's accomplishments improved the lives of hundreds of millions of Americans over many generations. According to *Time* magazine, which put Wagner's photo on its March 19, 1934, cover, Wagner "never forgot what a working man's life was like." Pick any law designed to help common people, the *New York Times* noted in its May 5, 1953, obituary, "and the chances are that either Bob Wagner's name is attached to it as a sponsor, or else he was one of its more active legislative protagonists."

Upton Sinclair
(1878–1968)

CREDIT: Associated Press

"I AIMED at the public's heart," said Upton Sinclair, "and by accident hit its stomach." Sinclair was referring to the response to his best-selling 1906 novel *The Jungle*, about conditions in Chicago's meatpacking industry. The book focused on the horrible conditions under which immigrants and their families worked and lived in the "Packinghouse" area of Chicago. Sinclair portrayed the grueling life of Lithuanian immigrant Jurgis Rudkus, whose backbreaking job in the slaughterhouse and miserable slum housing nearby almost destroys his soul as well as his body. But readers focused instead on Sinclair's graphic descriptions of the unsanitary process by which animals became meat products. The public outrage triggered by the book—based on Sinclair's two-month visit to Chicago during a bitter stockyard strike in 1904—led Congress to pass the Pure Food and Drug Act and the Meat Inspection Act in 1906, the first federal laws regulating corporate responsibility for consumer products.

A Pulitzer Prize–winning author, Sinclair wrote ninety books, mostly factual studies of powerful institutions or novels that exposed social injustice. In 1934, in the depths of the Depression, he ran for and was almost elected governor of California on the End Poverty in California (EPIC) platform.

Born into a comfortable Baltimore, Maryland, family, he entered City College of New York at age fifteen. He began writing sketches—mostly adventure stories—for magazines to pay his expenses. After graduation, he became a full-time writer. His first novel, *Springtime and Harvest* (1901), was a modest success.

Around this time Sinclair began reading Karl Marx and the radical economist Thorstein Veblen and joined **Eugene Debs**'s three-year-old Socialist Party. J. A. Wayland, the editor of the *Appeal to Reason,* a socialist newspaper, challenged Sinclair to write a novel about "wage slavery." So Sinclair headed to Chicago to investigate conditions in the meatpacking industry. A handful of powerful companies controlled the industry, using their political influence to keep the government off their backs. Livestock from midwestern farms were sent to company pens in Chicago, slaughtered, and packed into consumer products. The companies recruited immigrants from Eastern and Central Europe who performed backbreaking work in filthy and dangerous conditions. Many workers stood all day on floors covered with blood, meat scraps, and foul water. They worked six days a week, ten hours a day, and earned pennies an hour.

In *The Jungle*, Sinclair turned his observations into the gruesome details of Jurgis's daily life in Chicago's slums and slaughterhouses. He described workers falling into open cooking vats, amputated fingers being ground into sausage, and diseased cattle being hit with sledgehammers and processed through the slaughterhouses. In one scene, he describes the infiltration of rats:

> There would be meat stored in great piles in rooms; and the water from leaky roofs would drip over it, and thousands of rats would race about on it. It was too dark in these storage places to see well, but a man could run his hand over these piles of meat and sweep off handfuls of the dried dung of rats. These rats were nuisances, and the packers would put poisoned bread out for them; they would die, and then rats, bread, and meat would go into the hoppers together.

Sinclair serialized his story in the *Appeal to Reason* and then published the series as a book. It sold 100,000 copies in the first year and was quickly translated into seventeen languages. It even led to a brief upsurge in vegetarianism. President **Theodore Roosevelt,** who had seen soldiers die from eating rotten meat during the Spanish-American War, invited Sinclair to the White House and pushed Congress to pass the first consumer safety laws.

The Jungle turned Sinclair into a national celebrity. He used the money from the book to start what he hoped would be a socialist experiment in communal living. He purchased a former boys' school in Englewood, New Jersey, and renamed it Helicon Hall. Although many famous people—William James, **Emma Goldman, Lincoln Steffens,** and **John Dewey** among them—visited Helicon Hall, newspapers wrote scandalous stories about it, gossiping about "free love" experiments that were probably fiction. In March 1907 the building mysteriously burned down.

Sinclair lost his money, but he kept writing at a hectic pace. In *The Metropolis* (1908), he described the morally bankrupt social world of New York's fashionable rich. In *The Moneychangers,* published the same year, he used fiction to attack financier J. P. Morgan. In *King Coal* (1917), he wrote about the Ludlow Massacre, in which John D. Rockefeller's coal empire called out the state militia and private thugs to put down a coal miners strike by killing twenty people, both workers and members of their families. *The Profits of Religion* (1917) is an incendiary attack on organized religion. *The Brass Check* (1920) indicted the American newspaper business and its business-friendly journalism. *Goose Step* (1923) dealt with the corruption of higher education as a tool of big business. *Oil!* (1927) exposed the corruption of California's oil industry. In *Boston* (1928), Sinclair wrote a two-volume fictionalized account of the Sacco-Vanzetti case, in which two Italian immigrants, Nicola Sacco and Bartolomeo Vanzetti, both anarchists, were unfairly convicted and executed for murder.

In 1916 Sinclair and his second wife moved to California, settling in Pasadena and then Monrovia, both suburbs of Los Angeles. There he got involved in radical politics. Sinclair ran on the Socialist ticket for the US House of Representatives (1920), for the US Senate (1922), and for governor (1926 and 1930), winning few votes but using the campaigns to promote his left-wing views.

After **Franklin D. Roosevelt** was elected president in 1932, Sinclair figured he might have more influence running for office as a Democrat. Like most Socialists, he supported the New Deal but thought it did not go far enough, allowing business to undermine its more ambitious goals. Sinclair joined the Democratic Party, wrote a sixty-four-page pamphlet outlining his economic plan—*I, Governor of California and How I Ended Poverty,* which he published himself—and declared his intention of running in the Democratic primary for California governor in 1934.

Sinclair's plan focused on the idea of "production for use." The thousands of factories that were either idle or working at half capacity would be offered the opportunity to rent their plants to the state of California, hire back their workers, and run their machinery "under the supervision of the state." The workers would turn out goods and would own what they produced. Similarly, farmers, who were producing huge quantities of unsold foodstuffs, would be invited by the state to bring their produce "to [state] warehouses," where they would "receive in return receipts which will be good for . . . taxes." The farmers' food would be "shipped to the cities and made available to the factory workers in exchange for the products of *their* labor."

Much to Sinclair's surprise, his pamphlet became a best seller across California. And his campaign turned into a grassroots movement. Thousands of people volunteered for his campaign, organizing EPIC clubs across the state. The campaign's weekly newspaper, the *EPIC News,* reached a circulation of nearly 1 million by primary day in August 1934.

The campaign allowed Sinclair to present his Socialist ideas as commonsense solutions to California's harsh economic conditions. Sinclair shocked California's political establishment (and himself) by winning the Democratic primary. Dozens of other progressive candidates, running on the EPIC platform, also won Democratic primary races for the legislature. Many experts predicted that Sinclair had a good chance to beat the sitting Republican governor Frank Merriam, a colorless politician trying to defend the GOP's probusiness views at a time of massive unemployment and misery.

A few days after the primary, Sinclair took a train to meet FDR in Hyde Park, New York, hoping to persuade the popular president to endorse him. FDR's progressive advisers, including his wife **Eleanor Roosevelt** and Harry Hopkins, thought he should support Sinclair, but his more conservative aides, including his political director, Jim Farley, feared that Sinclair was too radical and would hurt the Democrats' chances of winning a big victory in the congressional midterm elections that year. The president made no endorsement that day, nor would he do so later on.

Despite FDR's stance, Sinclair's campaign took off. Fearing a Sinclair victory, California's powerful business groups mobilized an expensive and effective dirty-tricks countercampaign. Almost every day, the right-wing *Los Angeles Times* mocked Sinclair by publishing quotations from his books taken out of context. The papers only covered Merriam's campaign, ignoring Sinclair's daily speeches and events. One Hollywood studio produced a phony newsreel, with actors playing jobless hoboes riding trains to California to take advantage of Sinclair's promised welfare handouts. The newsreel was shown in movie theaters across the state as if it were a documentary.

Then FDR's aide Farley sent an emissary to California to cut a deal with Merriam. If the Republican governor would support the New Deal, FDR would not endorse Sinclair. FDR's silence hurt Sinclair. On election day, Merriam got 48 percent of the vote, and Sinclair got 37 percent of the vote—twice the total for any Democrat in the state's history. A third candidate (promoted by conservative Democrats to take votes away from Sinclair) got 13 percent.

Sinclair's campaign had such reach that his ideas pushed the New Deal to the left. After the Democrats won a landslide midterm election in Congress that year, FDR launched the so-called Second New Deal, including Social Security, major public works programs, and the National Labor Relations Act.

In California, Sinclair's campaign had a lasting impact. A state long dominated by the Republicans became a two-party state. Two dozen EPIC candidates won election to the state legislature, including future members of Congress Augustus Hawkins (California's first black member of Congress) and Jerry Voorhis. The following year, several labor, progressive, and radical organizations in Los Angeles formed the United Organization for Progressive Political Action, and three of its candidates won election to the city council. Another EPIC supporter, Culbert Olson, was elected governor in 1938. The EPIC clubs continued and became the foundation of the state's burgeoning liberal Democratic movement, the California Democratic Clubs, which helped elect liberal Edmund "Pat" Brown as governor in 1958. Sinclair's EPIC campaign inspired many younger progressives to challenge business-oriented candidates in Democratic primaries, including **Tom Hayden** in his insurgent 1976 primary campaign against incumbent US senator John Tunney.

After the election, Sinclair returned to writing novels. *The Flivver King: A Story of Ford-America* (1937) is a fictionalized indictment of Henry Ford and his use of "scientific management" to replace skilled workers and impose rigid and dehumanizing conditions in his factories. The United Auto Workers published the book to educate and agitate its members, only months before the landmark sit-down strike in Flint, Michigan. Between 1940 and 1953 he wrote eleven novels based on the character Lanny Budd, who always finds himself in the middle of decisive moments in history. One of them, *Dragon's Teeth* (1942), about the rise of Nazism in Germany, won the Pulitzer Prize for fiction.

CREDIT: Associated Press

Albert Einstein
(1879–1955)

WHEN *TIME* selected Albert Einstein as its "Person of the Century" in its December 31, 1999, issue, it was the fourth time (including 1929, 1946, and 1979) that the scientist had appeared on the magazine's cover. Einstein was the world's first celebrity scientist. During a visit to California in 1931, Einstein, then living in Europe, asked to meet actor Charlie Chaplin, also an international celebrity and political radical. Chaplin invited him to the premier of the film *City Lights.* As they posed for photographers, Chaplin commented, "They cheer for me because they all understand me and they cheer for you because nobody understands you."

People who know almost nothing about Einstein's scientific accomplishments (except perhaps that he created something called the "theory of relativity" or that he is connected with the formula $E = mc^2$) associate his name and image (including the unruly hair and the baggy sweater) with "genius." *Time* picked the physicist as its Person of the Century because he "changed forever the way the rest of us saw the heavens and ourselves." But Einstein also represented science's potential to change the world itself—to enlist rational thinking and technology to improve the conditions in which we live. Conversely, he also represented science's potential, as in the case of advanced weapons of war, to destroy the world.

Einstein understood this moral and practical dilemma. He did not believe that scientific knowledge, on its own, would save the world. It could be used for good or evil, depending on who had the power to harness science and technology. He thus spent much of his life, in Europe and (after 1933) in the United States, working for peace and social justice. Einstein was a pacifist, a humanist, a socialist, and a Zionist. As a scientist, Einstein was a reluctant celebrity, but he recognized that he could use his fame and reputation to promote causes to make the world more humane and democratic. He did so willingly, joining forces with other scientists and activists to challenge the political establishment.

At different times in his life he was harassed by both the German and the US governments for his political views. During the Cold War, the FBI's file on Einstein grew to over 1,800 pages, listing dozens of allegedly "subversive" organizations that he supported. As biographer Jim Green noted, "his mail was monitored, his phone tapped, his home and office searched and his trash examined." Senator Joseph McCarthy called Einstein an "enemy of America."

Einstein's passions for science and justice were forged early in his life in Germany. His parents were secular, middle-class Jews. At age five, he was fascinated to learn that invisible forces could move the needle on a compass, sparking a lifelong interest in invisible forces. Seven years later, he read what he called his "sacred little geometry book," which triggered another lifelong passion. At one of his schools, the Prussian-style educational system stifled his original mind and shaped his skepticism toward arbitrary authority. One teacher even told him that he would never amount to anything. Until Einstein was in his midtwenties, it looked as if his teacher might have been correct.

After attending school in Germany and Switzerland, Einstein entered Zurich's Swiss Federal Polytechnic School in 1896 to become a teacher of physics and mathematics. He earned his diploma in 1901, became a Swiss citizen, but was unable to find a teaching job. He eventually got a job as a technical assistant in the Swiss Patent Office. On the job and in his spare time, Einstein devoted himself to physics.

Einstein earned his doctorate in 1905. That year he published several physics papers that solidified his reputation as a pioneering scientist and, we now know, altered the entire field of modern physics. His biggest scientific breakthrough came in 1919. Two expeditions—one to the Príncipe Island off the west coast of Africa, the other to Sobral in northern Brazil—were sent to test Einstein's prediction that starlight would be deflected near the sun. A solar eclipse provided evidence supporting his general theory of relativity, which predicted that light would be bent by the sun's gravitational field. In November 1919 the results were announced in London at a joint meeting of the Royal Society and the Royal Astronomical Society. This catapulted Einstein to international fame. The *Times of London*'s headline read, "Revolution in Science—New Theory of the Universe—Newton's Ideas Overthrown—Momentous Pronouncement—Space 'Warped.'" Einstein was invited to lecture around the world, including in the United States in 1921, his first US visit. Wherever he went, huge crowds followed him—and not just scientists.

In 1922 he was awarded the Nobel Prize in physics "for his services to Theoretical Physics, and especially for his discovery of the law of the photoelectric effect."

Einstein's first serious political activities occurred during World War I, when he got involved with a number of organizations that opposed German militarism and the war. He was one of a handful of intellectuals who signed a manifesto opposing Germany's entry into war. He called nationalism "the measles of mankind."

Einstein found hope in the Gandhian movement in India and its emphasis on civil disobedience. In a speech in New York in September 1930, he challenged fellow pacifists to replace words with deeds. If only 2 percent of those called up for military service refused to fight, he said, governments would be powerless, because they could not send so many people to prison.

As a Jew, a radical, and a well-known figure, Einstein was an obvious target for Nazi hatred. The Nazis branded Einstein's science "Jewish physics," organized conferences and book burnings to denounce Einstein and his theories, and disrupted his lectures. Understandably, Einstein feared for his life. He and his wife Elsa were visiting the United States in 1933 after Hitler became German chancellor. Rather than return to Berlin, Einstein took a position at the Institute for Advanced Study in Princeton, New Jersey. He renounced his German citizenship and seven years later became a US citizen. In 1934 he identified the arms industry as "the hidden evil power behind the nationalism which is rampant everywhere." But that year, seeing the Nazi threat, he also called on the United States and the European nations to prepare for a war against Germany, and he reversed his earlier views about refusing military service. He criticized the US government's neutrality in the Spanish Civil War, which he, like many others, viewed as a battle between fascists and antifascists.

In 1939, more than two years before the United States entered World War II, Einstein wrote to President **Franklin D. Roosevelt** warning about the possibility that Germany might be able to build an atomic bomb. He urged the president to mobilize America's scientific community to conduct the research needed to develop atomic weapons. Roosevelt responded quickly, telling Einstein that he had organized a committee to study the issue. Ironically, when America's best scientists moved to Los Alamos, New Mexico, in 1941 for the Manhattan Project to develop the first atomic bomb, Einstein—whose findings had laid the groundwork for the project—was not invited. Years later, the release of FBI files revealed that Einstein had been blacklisted from the project because of his long involvement with peace and socialist organizations. In 1953 he publicly urged Americans to refuse to testify before the House Un-American Activities Committee, the key organ of the Cold War witch hunts.

Einstein would later regret writing his letter to Roosevelt. He was horrified by the human carnage that accompanied the US bombing of Japan in 1945, and he worried about the escalation of the arms race and nuclear weapons during the Cold War. In 1954 he told his friend Linus Pauling, "I made one great mistake in my life—when I signed the letter to President Roosevelt recommending that atom bombs be made; but there was some justification—the danger that the Germans would make them."

Although he retired from the Institute for Advanced Study in 1945, he continued to speak out on public issues for the rest of his life. In 1946 he became chair of the new Emergency Committee of Atomic Scientists, formed to stop the spread of nuclear weapons, including the hydrogen bomb. Interviewed on **Eleanor Roosevelt**'s television program in 1950, Einstein said, "The idea of achieving security through national armament is, at the present state of military technique, a disastrous illusion." In 1955, shortly before his death, Einstein and philosopher Bertrand Russell persuaded nine other prominent scientists to sign the Russell-Einstein Manifesto calling for the abolition of atomic weapons and of war itself. In 1948 Einstein supported **Henry Wallace**'s Progressive Party campaign for president; he was part of a coalition of radicals and progressives who admired Wallace's opposition to the Cold War, his pro-union views, and his support for civil rights.

A victim of anti-Semitism as a young scientist in Germany, Einstein became a vocal advocate for a Jewish state that he hoped would liberate Jews from persecution and encourage the flowering of Jewish culture. He hoped that Jews and Arabs would be able to share power and coexist in one county and was disappointed when that did not happen. Once Israel was created in 1948, he became a strong supporter of the nation, which was founded on socialist principles. In 1952 Israel's prime minister, David Ben-Gurion, offered Einstein the presidency of Israel, a ceremonial position. Einstein was flattered but declined. However, he continued to raise funds and promote the Hebrew University of Jerusalem, which he had helped establish and which became a world-renowned institution.

Einstein coupled his radical views on international relations with equally radical analysis of politics and economics. In a 1931 article, "The World as I See It," he wrote, "I regard class distinctions as unjustified, and, in the last resort, based on force." In a famous 1949 essay, "Why Socialism?" published in the first issue of the journal *Monthly Review,* he wrote that "the crippling of individuals" is "the worst evil of capitalism." He criticized capitalism's "economic anarchy" and the "oligarchy of private capital, the enormous power of which cannot be effectively checked even by democratically organized political society." He believed that a socialist economy had to be linked to a political democracy; otherwise, the rights of individuals would be threatened by an "all-powerful and overweening bureaucracy." It was this radical humanism that led him to oppose the communism of the Soviet Union.

Einstein often spoke out for the civil rights of African Americans. He joined a committee to defend the Scottsboro Boys, nine Alabama youths who in 1931 were falsely accused of rape and whose trial became a cause of protest by leftists around the world. He lent his support to the National Association for the Advancement of Colored People, and he corresponded with **W. E. B. Du Bois.** In 1946 he accepted an invitation from the singer and activist **Paul Robeson** to cochair the American Crusade to End Lynching, which the FBI considered a subversive organization because its members included radicals trying to pressure President Harry S. Truman to support a federal law against lynching. That year, almost a decade before the Montgomery bus boycott sparked the modern civil rights movement, Einstein penned an essay, "The Negro Question," in which he called American racism the nation's "worst disease." While effusively praising America's democratic and egalitarian spirit, Einstein noted that Americans'

"sense of equality and human dignity is mainly limited to men of white skins."
Having lived in the United States for little more than a decade, Einstein wrote,
"The more I feel an American, the more this situation pains me."

From early adulthood until he died, the rational scientist was also a passionate citizen of the world. A year before his death, Einstein explained that he wrote
and spoke out on public issues "whenever they appeared to me so bad and unfortunate that silence would have made me feel guilty of complicity."

CREDIT: Associated Press

Margaret Sanger
(1879–1966)

WHEN FEDERAL agents arrived at Margaret Sanger's home with a warrant for her arrest in 1914, she calmly ushered the men into her cluttered living room and quietly spent the next three hours explaining why she had mounted a campaign to promote birth control, especially to women of little means. She had been indicted by a grand jury on nine counts of breaking federal laws against distribution of birth control information with her newsletter the *Woman Rebel.* The potential prison sentence was forty-five years. By the time Sanger completed her persuasive argument, the agents agreed with her. Nevertheless, they said she had broken the law, and they had no power to rescind the warrant.

Throughout her life, Margaret Sanger ran afoul of the law in her quest to promote women's health and birth control.

Born Margaret Higgins, she was the sixth of eleven children in a working-class family in Corning, New York. Her father, Michael Higgins, a stonemason, was a freethinking atheist who gave Margaret books about strong women and encouraged her idealism. Her mother, Ann, was a devout Catholic and the strong and loving mainstay of the family. When her mother died from tuberculosis at age fifty, Sanger had to take care of the family. She always believed her mother's many pregnancies had contributed to her early death.

Sanger longed to be a physician, but she was unable to pay for medical school. She enrolled in nursing school in White Plains, New York, and as part of her maternity training delivered many babies—unassisted—in at-home births. Some of the women had had several children and were desperate to avoid future pregnancies. Sanger had no idea what to tell them.

Soon after her 1902 marriage to architect and would-be painter William Sanger, she became pregnant, developed tuberculosis, and had a very difficult birth, followed by a lengthy illness and recovery. The young family moved from New York City to the suburbs for Margaret's health, but two babies and eight years later, Sanger insisted that they return to the city.

In the city the Sangers were part of a left-wing circle that included John Reed, **William "Big Bill" Haywood, Lincoln Steffens,** and **Emma Goldman.** Goldman had been smuggling contraceptive devices into the United States from

France since at least 1900 and greatly influenced Sanger's thinking. Sanger joined the Socialist Party and the Industrial Workers of the World, providing support for its strikes in Lawrence, Massachusetts, in 1912 and in Paterson, New Jersey, in 1913. Sanger also returned to nursing, working as a visiting nurse and midwife at Lillian Wald's Henry Street Settlement in the Lower East Side. Again, women repeatedly asked her how to prevent future pregnancies. In those days poor women tried a range of quack medicines and dangerous methods to end pregnancies, including knitting needles. A turning point for Sanger came when one of her patients died from a self-induced abortion. Sanger decided her life's mission would be fighting for the right of low-income women to control their destinies and improve their health through family planning.

The Sangers went to France, which was then, with regard to contraception, the most progressive nation. After learning as much as she could from the French, she returned to the United States and launched her newsletter the *Woman Rebel* in 1914, with considerable backing from unions and feminists. As Sanger and her friends sat around her dining room table addressing newsletters, they brainstormed what to call their emerging movement for reproductive freedom. From that conversation, the term "birth control" was born. Encouraging working-class women to "think for themselves and build up a fighting character," Sanger wrote that "women cannot be on an equal footing with men until they have full and complete control over their reproductive function."

Sanger also began writing on women's issues for the *Call,* a socialist newspaper. She developed two columns that later became popular books, *What Every Mother Should Know* (1914) and *What Every Girl Should Know* (1916). When she covered the topic of venereal disease, she went up against the US postal inspector Anthony Comstock, a one-man army against all things sexual. In 1873 Congress had passed the Comstock Law, which made illegal the delivery or transportation of "obscene, lewd, or lascivious" material and banned contraceptives and information about contraception from the mails.

Comstock censored her column, the first of many run-ins. He then seized the first few issues of the *Woman Rebel* from Sanger's local post office. She got around him by mailing future issues from different post offices. Thousands of women responded to the newsletter, anxious for information on contraception.

Sanger's next project was an educational pamphlet, *Family Limitation,* which described clearly and simply what she had learned in France about birth control methods such as the condom, suppositories, and douches. She planned to print 10,000 copies, but there was great demand from labor unions, representing members from Montana copper mines to New England cotton mills. She scraped up enough money to print 100,000. Over the years, 10 million copies would be printed, and the pamphlet was translated into thirteen languages. In the 1920s in Yucatán, Mexico, feminists distributed the pamphlet to every couple requesting a marriage license.

But before she could distribute *Family Limitation* in the United States, Sanger had to go to court for the *Woman Rebel*, whose distribution was the "crime" for which she had received the arrest warrant. With very little time to prepare her defense and faced with a judge who seemed hostile to her cause, she made the snap decision to jump bail and flee, alone, to England. While in Europe, she visited a birth control clinic in Holland run by midwives, where she learned about a more effective method of contraception, the diaphragm, or "pessary."

By the time Sanger returned to the United States, Comstock had died. Her hopes were raised that the laws might not be so vigorously enforced and that she might not have to stand trial. A well-publicized open letter to President Woodrow Wilson, signed by nine prominent British writers, including H. G. Wells, supported Sanger and her work. Newspapers wrote about Sanger's notoriety, and she gained sympathy when they reported that her five-year-old daughter, Peggy, had died suddenly of pneumonia. In the face of public pressure, the government dropped the case, but the laws remained on the books.

Sanger opened the nation's first birth control clinic in October 1916 in the Brownsville section of Brooklyn, primarily serving immigrant Jewish and Italian women. She, her sister Ethel Byrne (a registered nurse), and Fania Mindell (who helped translate for the immigrant patients) rented a small storefront space and distributed flyers written in English, Yiddish, and Italian advertising the clinic's services. Sanger smuggled in diaphragms from the Netherlands and tried to recruit a physician to properly fit them in her patients, but no doctors were willing to face possible imprisonment. Although doctors were allowed to provide men with condoms as protection against venereal disease, they were not allowed to provide women with contraception.

Instead, Sanger and Byrne provided the services. The first day the clinic opened, they saw 140 women. Women—some from Pennsylvania and Massachusetts—stood in long lines to avail themselves of the clinic's services. After nine days, the vice squad raided the clinic, and Sanger spent the night in jail. As soon as she was released, she returned to work. Again, the police came, and this time they forced her landlord, a Sanger sympathizer, to evict them.

Following the eviction, Sanger, her sister, and two others were arrested for "creating a public nuisance." Ethel was the first to be convicted, and she responded to her sentence of thirty days of hard labor by going on a hunger strike. After four days, the judge ordered her to be force-fed; it was the first time this punishment had been used in the American penal system. Headlines around the nation publicized her plight. "The whole country seemed to stand still and anxiously watch this lone woman's fight against an iniquitous law," wrote a reporter for the *Birth Control Review* in 1917. Ethel almost died before Sanger was able to secure a pardon from the governor and rescue her.

Sanger's trial began on January 29, 1917. She was also convicted, but the judge offered her a suspended sentence if she would agree not to repeat the offense. She refused. Offered a choice of a fine or a jail sentence, she chose the latter and spent thirty days in jail.

Sanger appealed her conviction, and a year later the New York Court of Appeals upheld her conviction. However, the judge ruled that physicians could legally prescribe contraception for general health reasons rather than exclusively for venereal disease.

Sanger continued to fight for the right to disseminate birth control information and to import contraceptives from abroad. She launched the monthly *Birth Control Review* in 1917 and started the American Birth Control League (the precursor to Planned Parenthood) in 1921, focusing particularly on physicians, nurses, and social workers. Two years later she opened the Birth Control Clinic Research Bureau in New York, the first legal clinic to distribute contraceptive information and fit diaphragms, directed by women doctors. But it was not until 1936 that a federal district court in New York City ruled that the US government could not interfere with the importation of diaphragms for medical use.

Feminists and progressive reformers were divided over Sanger's crusade for birth control. **Alice Hamilton,** Crystal Eastman, and Katharine Houghton Hepburn (mother of actress Katharine Hepburn) supported Sanger, but others, such as **Charlotte Perkins Gilman** and Carrie Chapman Catt, thought that birth control would increase men's power over women as sex objects.

To the detriment of her reputation and the cause of reproductive freedom, Sanger was also attracted to aspects of the eugenics movement. In the 1920s, some scientists viewed eugenics as a way to identify the hereditary bases of both physical and mental diseases. Some, however, viewed it as a means of creating a "superior" human race. Among them were leading Nazis, who opposed birth control or abortion by healthy or "fit" women in order to promote a white master race. In fact, the Nazis banned and burned Sanger's books on family planning.

Sanger's primary focus was on freeing women who lived in poverty from the burden of unwanted pregnancies, but by embracing eugenics, she appeared to be crossing the line in troubling ways. For example, in a 1921 article, "The Eugenic Value of Birth Control Propaganda," she argued that "the most urgent problem today is how to limit and discourage the over-fertility of the mentally and physically defective." Although many of the eugenics movement's leaders were racists and anti-Semites who promoted involuntary sterilization in order to help breed a "superior" race, Sanger was not among them. Her embrace of eugenics was intended to stop individuals from passing down mental and physical diseases to their descendents. She believed that reproductive choices should be made on an individual basis. She always repudiated the use of eugenics, including sterilization, for specific racial or ethnic groups. In the 1920s, when anti-immigrant sentiment reached a peak and some scientists sought to justify restricting immigration by claiming that some ethnic groups were mentally and physically inferior, Sanger spoke out against the stereotyping that led to the Immigration Act of 1924.

In 1930, with the support of **W. E. B. Du Bois,** the Urban League, and the *Amsterdam News* (New York's leading black newspaper), Sanger opened a family-planning clinic in Harlem, staffed by a black doctor and a black social worker. In 1939, encouraged by Du Bois, Reverend Adam Clayton Powell Jr. of Harlem's powerful Abyssinian Baptist Church, journalist Ida Wells, sociologist E. Franklin Frazier, educator Mary McLeod Bethune, and other black leaders, Sanger expanded her efforts to the rural South, where most African Americans lived.

Sanger remained an activist for birth control and women's rights throughout her life. She helped found the International Planned Parenthood Federation in 1952. She spent the end of her career raising money for research. Her efforts contributed to the development of the birth control pill.

In 1961, Estelle Griswold, executive director of Planned Parenthood of Connecticut, opened a birth control clinic in New Haven with Dr. C. Lee Buxton, a licensed physician and professor at Yale's medical school. They were arrested in November 1961 for violating a state law prohibiting the use of birth control. They appealed the case to the US Supreme Court, which in 1965 ruled in *Griswold v. Connecticut* that the law violated the right to marital privacy. The case established a woman's right to control over her personal life and made birth control legal for married couples. This paved the way for *Roe v. Wade*, the landmark 1973 Supreme Court ruling that recognized a woman's right to choose abortion.

John L. Lewis
(1880–1969)

CREDIT: Associated Press

ON OCTOBER 19, 1935, at the annual conference of the American Federation of Labor (AFL) in Atlantic City, New Jersey, John L. Lewis rose to ask his union colleagues to support a major organizing drive among workers in the nation's key industries, including automobiles, steel, rubber, and electronics. As president of the United Mine Workers of America (UMWA), Lewis was becoming increasingly frustrated by the AFL's unwillingness to invest resources to build an industrial labor movement. As soon as Lewis began speaking, William Hutcheson—AFL vice president and head of the United Brotherhood of Carpenters and Joiners of America, who represented the old guard leaders of craft unions—interrupted to raise a point of order, arguing that the convention had already rejected Lewis's idea. "Is the delegate impugning my motives?" Lewis thundered, according to *Time* magazine. Lewis then stomped down the aisle to Hutcheson, "tapped him menacingly on the shoulder, [and] shouted something about 'mighty small potatoes.'" Hutcheson responded with what *Time* called a "fighting phrase." Lewis punched his nemesis with his fist. Hutcheson countered with "an ineffective right," and then Lewis struck Hutcheson hard enough that he sprawled to the floor.

The battle between the two labor titans made headlines, but more importantly it cemented Lewis's reputation as a tough union leader willing to fight for his ideas and for American workers. The next morning, Lewis brought together other supporters of industrial unionism, who soon agreed to break off from the AFL and form the Committee for Industrial Organization (CIO; later called the Congress of Industrial Organizations). *Time* acknowledged the stakes: "If the A. F. of L. were to reorganize its hundreds of jealous craft unions into comprehensive associations of workers within single industries, most economists agree that Labor would be enormously benefited." With Lewis as its president, the CIO spearheaded the most successful union-organizing drive in America's key industrial sectors. In the midst of the Depression and then during and after World War II, the CIO mobilized millions of workers and eventually helped lift them into the middle class.

For much of the 1920s and through the 1940s, John L. Lewis was the labor movement's most visible public figure. With a deep, booming voice and huge bushy eyebrows that moved up and down as he spoke (often pounding on the lectern for emphasis), he was well known to most Americans, even those with no direct link to unions. He was the leader of UMWA at a time when coal was the backbone of the American economy and when a strike of coal miners could dramatically disrupt the nation's daily life.

Because he represented the power of the burgeoning labor movement, presidents sought his advice or, in some instances, tried to figure out how to outmaneuver him. Corporate leaders feared him and sought to weaken his influence. By the end of his life, Lewis had played a leading role in the development of many essential features of Americans' working life, such as health and retirement benefits, restrictions on child labor, and limits on the number of hours and days workers could be required to work.

Lewis was born in Lucas, Iowa, to Welsh immigrants, and he followed his father into the coal mines of south-central Iowa. After moving to Illinois, he began to demonstrate his skills in labor organizing. He became president of the local UMWA chapter in 1909. In 1911 he began to travel the nation as a special field representative for the AFL, advising labor-organizing efforts.

In the first two decades of the 20th century, the growing demand for coal allowed the UMWA to expand rapidly, although not without resistance from the coal industry owners, judges, and local police. Because an adequate supply of coal was critical to America's efforts during World War I, Lewis worked with federal officials to guarantee peaceful labor relations in the mine industry, in exchange for substantial wage increases for miners.

Lewis became vice president of the UMWA in 1917 and then president early in 1920, a position he held on to tightly for forty years.

When Lewis assumed leadership of the UMWA it was the largest trade union in the country, with approximately 400,000 members. But the unionized mines faced intense competition from nonunion operators (particularly in the South) as well as from fuel oil. Many miners were displaced by machines, which could cut faster and more cheaply. By 1932 the union's membership had fallen dramatically. The New Deal gave Lewis and the UMWA another chance. Lewis and the labor movement successfully fought for passage of a section in the National Industrial Recovery Act (NIRA) of 1933 that secured the right of workers to organize unions.

Lewis gambled the UMWA's dwindling treasury on an all-out organizing drive. Because miners worked in dangerous jobs and often lived in isolated mining towns, they developed strong bonds with each other and a strong sense of opposition to mine owners. (In 1931 Florence Reece, the wife of a UMWA organizer, wrote the song "Which Side Are You On?" during a bitter struggle with mine owners in Harlan County, Kentucky.) Lewis figured out how to turn that culture into an organizing asset. In coalfields across the country, Lewis and his union organizers told miners, "The President wants you to join the union!" In many places, mine operators used scabs, private militias, and the support of local law enforcement to try to undermine the UMWA.

Within months after the National Recovery Administration was established in 1933, 92 percent of the country's coal miners were organized. After this, Lewis sought support from the AFL to organize other key industries, eventually pushing the AFL to pledge to organize the labor movement on an industrial basis. But the AFL did not commit the staff or other resources necessary to launch major organizing drives. Lewis's fisticuffs with Hutcheson symbolized the breach between the AFL and the more radical union leaders committed to a bigger and more militant movement. Lewis was not a socialist or a communist, but he respected the dedication and toughness of the radicals and hired many of them to help wage organizing drives.

After unions helped pass the National Labor Relations (Wagner) Act of 1935, Lewis seized the opportunity. He committed UMWA funds to support organizing drives in the rubber, auto, glass, and steel industries, each of which succeeded. Lewis assigned his own staff to help each drive, stayed in touch with each union's leaders, and personally negotiated the agreements with General Motors and US Steel. Those successes led in 1938 to the formal launch of the CIO, which was soon bigger than the AFL.

In 1936 Lewis and **Sidney Hillman** founded Labor's Non-Partisan League, the first union political action committee (PAC). The labor PAC helped reelect President **Franklin D. Roosevelt.** But as war loomed in Europe, Lewis stood firmly against US involvement. He was also upset at FDR for staying on the sidelines during a major steel strike in 1937. Lewis refused to back FDR for a third term in 1940 and endorsed the GOP candidate Wendell Willkie instead. Not surprisingly, few workers followed Lewis's lead. Having alienated many of his labor counterparts, who were solidly behind FDR, Lewis resigned as president of the CIO soon after the election. Two years later, he broke with the industrial union movement he had helped create and took the UMWA out of the CIO.

After the United States entered the war in 1941, the UMWA agreed to a no-strike pledge to support the war effort. But under Lewis's leadership, the UMWA routinely violated the pledge, most notably in 1943 when half a million workers walked off the job. Most Americans were angry at Lewis, some calling him a traitor. FDR thought he had no choice but to threaten to seize the mines with federal troops and draft the miners into the army. FDR's tactic was only partly successful. Some steel mills closed for weeks, and power shortages crippled production. Lewis led another major coal strike in 1946, which led the media to vilify him as a power-hungry union leader.

After World War II, Lewis continued as president of the UMWA, which remained an influential force in the coalfields and in politics but which lost some of its sway as the nation became less dependent on coal. As the coal industry slipped into a long, slow decline and oil replaced coal as the nation's number-one source of energy, Lewis fought to protect the income, safety, and job security of miners. At a 1947 congressional hearing about an explosion of coal dust in a Centralia, Illinois, mine that killed 111 workers, Lewis stated, "If we must grind up human flesh and bone in the industrial machine we call modern America, then before God I assert that those who consume coal and you and I who benefit from that service because we live in comfort, we owe protection to those men first, and we owe security to their families if they die."

In 1948 the UMWA won a historic agreement establishing medical and pension benefits for miners, financed in part by a royalty on every ton of coal mined. The union also acknowledged management's right to automate and close unprofitable operations. In return, it secured high wages and expanded benefits in the remaining mines. Lewis also led the campaign for the first Federal Mine Safety Act, passed in 1952.

During the height of his influence, many Americans viewed Lewis not only as a powerful union leader but also as a voice of conscience, boldly challenging big corporations to respect workers with decent pay, health insurance and pensions, funds for widows and children, and safer workplaces. But Lewis's most important contribution was in leading the labor movement into a new era of industrial unionism and using workers' labor and voting power to make America a more humane society.

CREDIT: Associated Press

Helen Keller
(1880–1968)

IN 2009 a bronze statue of Helen Keller was unveiled at the US Capitol. The statue shows the blind Keller standing at a water pump. It depicts the moment in 1887 when her teacher Anne Sullivan spelled "W-A-T-E-R" into one of Keller's hands while water streamed into the other hand of the seven-year-old girl. This was Keller's awakening, when she made the connection between the word Sullivan spelled into her hand and the tangible substance splashing from the pump, whispering "wah-wah," her way of saying "water." This scene, made famous in the play and the film *The Miracle Worker,* has long defined Keller in the public mind as a symbol of courage in the face of overwhelming odds. "Some are still dismissed and cast aside for nothing more than being less than perfect," said Senate Minority Leader Mitch McConnell, the conservative Republican from Kentucky, at the unveiling ceremony for the statue. "The story of Helen Keller inspires us all."

What most Americans know about Keller they learned from *The Miracle Worker,* originally broadcast as a television play in 1957, adapted as a Broadway play two years later, and turned into a 1962 feature film starring Patty Duke as Keller and Anne Bancroft as Sullivan. Since then, it has remained one of the most popular plays performed in high schools, colleges, and regional theaters.

The play and the film reveal that after Keller went blind, she became an unruly, kicking, screaming child. With patience and determination, Sullivan, her tutor, taught her how to sign and read, overcome her disability, and learn to live in the world. *The Miracle Worker* ends with Keller's triumph in learning to sign. That is the image of Keller that has been frozen in time.

Less well known, although no less inspiring, is the fact that Keller was also an ardent Socialist, feminist, and antiwar activist.

Keller was born in 1880 on a plantation in Tuscumbia, Alabama, to Arthur Keller, a former Confederate officer and a conservative newspaper publisher, and Kate Keller, a descendant of John Adams. When she was just nineteen months old, she lost her sight and hearing as a result of a fever. She became uncontrollable, prone to tantrums, kicking, biting, and smashing anything within reach. In that era, many blind and deaf people were consigned to an asylum. Some family members suggested that this was where Helen belonged. Instead, her mother contacted the Perkins School for the Blind in Boston, which recommended that a former student, twenty-year-old Anne Sullivan, become Helen's private tutor. In 1887 Sullivan—the daughter of poor Irish immigrants and nearly blind herself—moved to the Kellers' home. She helped calm Helen's rages and helped channel her insatiable curiosity and exceptional intelligence. She patiently spelled out letters and words in Keller's hand. With Sullivan's support, Keller soon learned to read and write Braille, and by the age of ten she had begun to speak.

Her story became well known and she became a celebrity. Her family connections and fame also opened up many opportunities for Keller, including private schools and an elite college education. Mark Twain even helped create a fund to pay for Keller's education. She later acknowledged, "I owed my success partly to the advantages of my birth and environment. I have learned that the power to rise is not within the reach of everyone."

In 1900, at age twenty, Keller entered Radcliffe College, with Sullivan at her side. Keller graduated from Radcliffe magna cum laude in 1904. At Radcliffe Keller was first exposed to the radical ideas that helped her draw connections among different forms of injustice. She began to write about herself and her growing understanding of the world. In 1901, in an article entitled "I Must Speak" in the *Ladies Home Journal,* Keller wrote, "Once I believed that blindness, deafness, tuberculosis, and other causes of suffering were necessary, unpreventable. But gradually my reading extended, and I found that those evils are to be laid not at the door of Providence, but at the door of mankind; that they are, in large measure, due to ignorance, stupidity and sin."

In her investigation into the causes of blindness, she discovered that poor people were more likely than the rich to be blind. In Boston and elsewhere, she visited slums and learned about the struggles of workers and immigrants to improve their working and living conditions. In 1908 Sullivan's husband, John Macy, a socialist, encouraged Keller to read H. G. Wells's *New Worlds for Old,* which influenced her views about radical change. She soon began to devour Macy's extensive collection of political books, reading socialist publications (often in German Braille) and Marxist economists.

Her first autobiography, *The Story of My Life,* was published in 1902. Keller also began to give inspirational lectures, mostly about blindness, on behalf of the American Foundation for the Blind (AFB). But she also talked, wrote, and agitated about radical social and political causes, making her class analysis explicit in such books as *Social Causes of Blindness* (1911), *The Unemployed* (1911), and *The Underprivileged* (1931). In 1915, after learning about the Ludlow Massacre—in which John D. Rockefeller's private army killed coal miners and their wives and children in a labor confrontation in Colorado—Keller denounced him as a "monster of capitalism."

In 1909 Keller joined the Socialist Party, wrote articles in support of its ideas, campaigned for its candidates, and lent her name to help striking workers. Although she was universally praised for her courage in the face of her physical disabilities, she now found herself criticized for her political views. The editor of the *Brooklyn Eagle* attacked her radical ideas, attributing them to "mistakes sprung out of the manifest limitations of her development." In the essay "How I Became a Socialist," published in the *Call*, a socialist newspaper, in 1912, Keller wrote, "At that time, the compliments he paid me were so generous that I blush to remember them. But now that I have come out for socialism he reminds me and the public that I am blind and deaf and especially liable to error."

Keller was also a strong advocate for women's rights. She supported birth control and praised its leading advocate, **Margaret Sanger,** with whom she had many mutual friends. Keller argued that capitalists wanted workers to have large families to supply cheap labor to factories but forced poor children to live in miserable conditions. "Only by taking the responsibility of birth control into their own hands," Keller said, "can [women] roll back the awful tide of misery that is sweeping over them and their children." Keller was also an advocate of women's suffrage, writing in 1916: "Women have discovered that they cannot rely on men's chivalry to give them justice."

At an antiwar rally in January 1916 sponsored by the Woman's Peace Party at New York's Carnegie Hall, Keller said,

> Congress is not preparing to defend the people of the United States. It is planning to protect the capital of American speculators and investors. Incidentally this preparation will benefit the manufacturers of munitions and war machines. Strike against war, for without you no battles can be fought! Strike against manufacturing shrapnel and gas bombs and all other tools of murder! Strike against preparedness that means death and misery to millions of human beings! Be not dumb, obedient slaves in an army of destruction! Be heroes in an army of construction!

In 1917 she donated money to the National Association for the Advancement of Colored People, still a young and controversial civil rights organization, and wrote for its magazine. The following year, she was one of the founders of the American Civil Liberties Union. She criticized the US government's attempts to jail or deport radicals who opposed World War I, including Socialists and members of the Industrial Workers of the World, and to suppress their ideas.

In 1919 Keller played herself in a silent film about her life, *Deliverance*. The actors at the New York theater where the film was being shown were on strike, and Keller joined the union's picket line and spoke at their strike meetings. In an article for the *Call*, Keller wrote that she would "rather have the film fail than aid the managers in their contest with the players."

In 1919 she also wrote a letter, addressed to "Dear Comrade," to **Eugene Debs,** the Socialist labor leader and presidential candidate who was in jail for advocating draft resistance during World War I. She wrote, "I want you to know that I should be proud if the Supreme Court convicted me of abhorring war, and doing all in my power to oppose it."

In 1924 she supported the presidential campaign of **Robert M. La Follette,** a Wisconsin progressive. That year, in a letter to La Follette, she expressed her anger at the double standard many used in evaluating her activities:

> So long as I confine my activities to social service and the blind, they compliment me extravagantly, calling me "arch priestess of the sightless," "wonder woman," and a "modern miracle." But when it comes to a discussion of poverty, and I maintain that it is the result of wrong economics—that the industrial system under which we live is at the root of much of the physical deafness and blindness in the world—that is a different matter! It is laudable to give aid to the handicapped. Superficial charities make smooth the way of the prosperous; but to advocate that all human beings should have leisure and comfort, the decencies and refinements of life, is a Utopian dream, and one who seriously contemplates its realization indeed must be deaf, dumb, and blind.

After 1924 Keller devoted most of her time and energy to speaking and fund-raising for the American Foundation for the Blind. But she continued to support radical causes, and even when feminism began to ebb, she continued to agitate for women's rights. In 1932 she wrote an article for *Home* magazine, "Great American Women," praising feminists Susan B. Anthony, Lucy Stone, and Elizabeth Cady Stanton, and she penned a humorous article for the *Atlantic Monthly,* "Put Your Husband in the Kitchen." In 1948 she visited Hiroshima and Nagasaki, cities destroyed by American atomic bombs at the end of World War II, and spoke out against nuclear war. In 1955 at the height of the Cold War, she wrote a public birthday greeting and letter of support to Elizabeth Gurley Flynn, a leading communist activist, then in jail on charges of violating the Smith Act. In response, some supporters of the American Foundation for the Blind, for which Keller was the national face, threatened to withdraw their support. The AFB's executive director wrote to one of his trustees, "Helen Keller's habit of playing around with communists and near communists has long been a source of embarrassment to her conservative friends."

Indeed, the FBI kept Keller under surveillance for most of her adult life for her radical views, but she never saw a contradiction between her crusade to address the causes of blindness and her efforts to promote economic and social justice.

Toward the end of her career, as she was speaking at a midwestern college, a student asked, "Miss Keller, is there anything that could have been worse than losing your sight?" Keller replied: "Yes, I could have lost my vision."

Frances Perkins
(1880–1965)

Frances Perkins, center, during an inspection tour of the San Francisco tower of the Golden Gate Bridge, 1935. CREDIT: Associated Press

ON MARCH 25, 1911, Frances Perkins was having afternoon tea with her friend Margaret Morgan Norrie, a wealthy New Yorker descended from two signatories to the Declaration of Independence. They met at Norrie's elegant redbrick townhouse over-looking Washington Square Park in Greenwich Village. But their conversation was interrupted by the sound of fire engine bells. A big fire had erupted on the other side of the square. From the townhouse, they could see flames engulfing the top floors of a ten-story building. Holding up her long skirt, the thirty-year-old Frances ran to the fire scene and realized that the building housed the Triangle Shirtwaist Company, one of the city's largest garment factories, which employed immigrant girls in miserable overcrowded conditions.

Perkins saw workers huddled on the top floors unable to escape because the exit doors had been locked and there were no fire escapes. She saw other workers hanging from the windows by their hands, clinging desperately. She noticed that the city fire trucks' ladders could not reach the top floors, and she witnessed the awful sight of workers jumping or falling to their deaths from the eighth and ninth floors. In total, 146 workers, most of them young immigrant women, died in the Triangle fire. The experience of witnessing that tragedy, Perkins later explained, "seared on my mind as well as my heart—a never-to-be-forgotten reminder of why I had to spend my life fighting conditions that could permit such a tragedy."

The Triangle fire may have deepened her commitment, but Perkins was al-ready involved in progressive causes, including the battle to improve working conditions in New York City's sweatshops. At the time, she was an activist with the New York Consumers League. Later, as New York State's industrial commis-sioner and as **Franklin D. Roosevelt**'s secretary of labor for twelve years, Perkins played a pivotal role in most of the important social and workplace legislation, including Social Security and the federal minimum wage, enacted during the first half of the 20th century.

Perkins grew up in a comfortable middle-class Republican family in Worces-ter, Massachusetts. At Mount Holyoke College, she was deeply influenced by an economic history course that required her to visit factories in the nearby industrial city of Holyoke and interview workers about their working conditions. She was also affected by reading *How the Other Half Lives,* Jacob Riis's exposé of New York's slums. In February 1902, during her senior year, Perkins attended a campus talk by **Florence Kelley,** head of the National Consumers League. Perkins was impressed by Kelley's fiery speech, her combination of radicalism and pragmatism, and her nonconformist lifestyle as a divorced woman with three children working to save the world. Eventually, Kelley, who also came from a middle-class Republican family, became Perkins's role model and mentor.

After graduation, Perkins took a series of teaching positions in Connecticut, Massachusetts, and Chicago. In her spare time, she volunteered at settlement houses in each city, including Hull House. One of her duties was to try to collect wages for workers who had been cheated by their employers, a responsibility that took her into the homes of the city's poorest residents. In Chicago, she gained more firsthand exposure to dangerous factory conditions and slum housing.

In 1907 she took a $50-a-month job with the Philadelphia Research and Protection Association, a reform group. She exposed the exploitation of young immigrant and African American women by bogus employment agencies that promised good jobs but lured them into prostitution. She applied for jobs herself to uncover the agencies' practices. She visited fleabag lodging houses and terrible factories, supplying information to the press and city officials.

Perkins moved to New York in 1909 to study at Columbia University. The city was bursting with protest and with a growing progressive movement that included union activists, clergy, muckraking journalists, socialists, and even upper-class women (including the wives of some of New York's wealthiest men), feminists who cared about the problems of working women. After earning her master's degree in economics and sociology in 1910, Perkins spent the next two years as head of the New York Consumers League. She conducted studies of unsafe and unsanitary workplaces, such as cellar bakeries, that exploited women and children, forcing them to work in dangerous conditions. She became an expert in workplace dangers and firetraps. Collaborating closely with Kelley, she lobbied the state legislature for a bill limiting the workweek for women and children to fifty-four hours. She also became active in the women's suffrage movement, marching in suffrage parades and giving street-corner speeches.

Following the Triangle fire, and in response to the outcry, New York's governor, John Alden Dix, created the Factory Investigating Commission, a pioneering body with broad subpoena powers and teams of investigators. Its leaders, legislators **Robert F. Wagner** and Al Smith, asked Perkins to lead the investigation of mercantile shops. As Perkins recalled:

> We used to make it our business to take Al Smith, the East Side boy, to see the women, thousands of them, coming off the ten-hour night shift on the

rope walks in Auburn. We made sure that Robert Wagner personally crawled through the tiny hole in the wall that gave egress to a steep iron ladder covered with ice and ending 12 feet from the ground, which was euphemistically labeled "Fire Escape" in many factories. We saw to it that the austere legislative members of the Commission got up at dawn and drove with us for an unannounced visit to a Cattaraugus County cannery and that they saw with their own eyes the little children, not adolescents, but 5, 6, and 7-year olds, snipping beans and shelling peas. We made sure that they saw the machinery that would scalp a girl or cut off a man's arm.

Perkins recognized the importance of working-class organization, but she also understood the necessity of forging coalitions to push for progressive legislation. Many of Perkins's upper-class friends provided financial and political support for the causes she worked on. She also forged friendships with politicians, even those she disagreed with, because she knew they could someday be helpful in passing reform legislation.

One of those politicians was Smith, the state assemblyman who surprised many New Yorkers by successfully pushing for factory reforms after the Triangle fire. After he was elected governor in 1918, Smith appointed Perkins to the State Industrial Commission and named her its chair in 1926. Three years later, Franklin Roosevelt, then New York governor, named her the state's industrial commissioner. In that capacity, she expanded factory investigations, reduced the workweek for women to forty-eight hours, and championed minimum wage and unemployment insurance laws.

After FDR's victory in the 1932 presidential election, many progressives, including his wife, Eleanor, and **Jane Addams,** urged him to make Perkins secretary of labor, but many Americans doubted that a woman could handle such a demanding job. Even Al Smith, her former boss and admirer, remarked that "men will take advice from a woman, but it is hard for them to take orders from a woman." She proved them wrong.

As secretary of labor, Perkins drew on the New York State experience as the model for new federal programs. She was determined to create a safety net for a Depression-scarred society, securing a remarkable array of benefits for American workers. These included the National Labor Relations (Wagner) Act and the Fair Labor Standards Act, which established for the first time a minimum wage and a maximum workweek for men and women.

Perkins excelled at the "inside/outside" game. She was one of a handful of FDR's close inner circle advisers with regular access to the president. FDR trusted Perkins's political judgment and her lobbying skills. She was effective at outmaneuvering and out-arguing some of the president's more conservative advisers. She was also adept at working with labor and consumer groups, advising them on which congressmembers to lobby, what arguments to make, and when to resort to protest and rallies to draw attention to issues and help push legislation over the finish line.

Perkins consistently supported workers' right to organize unions and to pressure employers. For example, in May 1934 about 130,000 San Francisco workers—printers, streetcar operators, bakery-wagon drivers, and others—stayed home from work to show their solidarity with the city's longshoremen's union, led by **Harry Bridges,** who were on strike against the big shipping companies. The city's business leaders, as well as state and city officials, implored Secretary of State Cordell Hull, who was standing in for FDR while the president was out of the country, to mobilize federal troops to quell the general strike. Hull agreed with them. FDR's attorney general, Homer Cummings, told Perkins that a general strike was tantamount to an attempt to overthrow the government. The unflappable Perkins rushed to a naval communications facility to get a message to FDR before he heard from Hull or Cummings. He not only sided with Perkins—saying the strike should be settled through negotiations, not military force—but he also made it clear to the other cabinet members that she was in charge of handling the crisis. As Perkins predicted, the workers returned to work within two days, the employers and the union negotiated their differences, and the workers won better wages, working conditions, and a union-sponsored hiring hall.

As Perkins said, "I have come to the conclusion that the Department of Labor should be the Department *for* Labor, and that we should render service to working people."

In 1945 Perkins resigned from her position as labor secretary to head the U.S. delegation to the International Labor Organization conference in Paris. President Harry S. Truman subsequently appointed her to the Civil Service Commission, a job she held through 1953. In the last years of her life, she taught at Cornell University's School of Industrial and Labor Relations.

Franklin D. Roosevelt (1882–1945)

AS PRESIDENT, Franklin D. Roosevelt (FDR) guided the nation through two of its biggest crises: the Great Depression and World War II. His combination of optimism, political savvy, and willingness to experiment gave Americans confidence in themselves and reminded them that the national government could be a positive force in their daily lives.

Nothing in FDR's early life would have led one to predict his remarkable accomplishments. Born to privilege, a distant cousin of President **Theodore Roosevelt,** and a mediocre student at Harvard, he drew on his family connections to enter politics. He was elected to the New York State Senate in 1910 and was appointed assistant secretary of the navy by President Woodrow Wilson in 1913, playing an influential role in preparing the country for entry into World War I. In 1920, he was the Democratic nominee for vice president on a ticket with Ohio governor James Cox that lost to Republican Warren G. Harding.

In the summer of 1921, at age thirty-nine, he was stricken with polio. With remarkable courage he fought to regain the use of his legs, particularly through swimming, an experience that shaped his sympathies for the disadvantaged. In 1928 he was elected governor of New York, where (with the help of key adviser **Frances Perkins**) he carried out innovative relief and recovery programs (including unemployment insurance, pensions for the elderly, limits on work hours, and massive public works projects) that helped him win reelection in 1930 and led to his nomination as the Democratic candidate for president two years later. Pledging a "New Deal" for the American people, he defeated incumbent Republican Herbert Hoover by a landslide. In his inaugural address, Roosevelt lifted Americans' hopes by assuring them that they had "nothing to fear but fear itself."

Taking office in March 1933, more than three years into the Depression, FDR inherited a nation that had lost faith in itself and in the social order. More than 13 million Americans were jobless, and most banks were closed. Right-wing demagogues competed with a flourishing radical movement of angry farmers, veterans, workers, and others for the loyalty of the American people and politicians.

FDR had not run for president as a progressive, and he took office with no bold plan to lift America out of the Depression. But he was willing to try new ideas and recognized that his ability to push progressive legislation through Congress depended on the pressure generated by protesters—workers, World War I veterans, the jobless, the homeless, and farmers—even though he did not always welcome working closely with these constituencies. The well-worn story that ends with FDR telling a group of activists, "I agree with you. Now, go out and make me do it," has never been documented, but it is emblematic of the New Deal era. As protests escalated throughout the country, FDR became more vocal, using his bully pulpit to criticize big business and to promote policies to jump-start the economy, protect the needy, and expand workers' rights.

With his actions setting the tone, with allies like Senator **Robert F. Wagner** leading in Congress, and with unions and other grassroots groups mobilizing support, FDR instigated economic and social reforms that saved and humanized capitalism, despite the barbs of many critics, including most newspapers and business leaders—who accused his New Deal agenda of leading America to socialism.

In his first 100 days, FDR proposed and Congress enacted a sweeping program to restore the ravaged business and agriculture sectors, provide direct cash relief to the unemployed faced with starvation, and help families in danger of losing their farms and homes—all policies in line with the ideas of British economist John Maynard Keynes, who called for government jobs and deficit spending to catalyze economic recovery.

During his first two terms, FDR oversaw some of the most far-reaching economic and social legislation in the nation's history, including Social Security; protections of workers' rights to unionize; a federal minimum wage; heavier taxes on the wealthy; new regulations on banks, public utilities, and business stock transactions; a huge work relief program for the unemployed; unemployment insurance; and several government-sponsored enterprises that brought electricity and jobs to rural areas, including the Tennessee Valley Authority. The Civilian Conservation Corps put 300,000 young men to work in 1,200 camps planting trees, building bridges, and cleaning beaches. The Public Works Administration (PWA) and later the Works Progress Administration (WPA) provided jobs to millions of Americans to build schools, libraries, hospitals, airports, and roads. It also paid artists, writers, actors, and others to create murals, produce plays and musicals, and write travel guides and oral histories. Together the PWA and WPA transformed the nation's landscape, adding such landmarks as LaGuardia Airport and the Triborough Bridge (now RFK Bridge) in New York, the Golden Gate Bridge in San Francisco, the Orange Bowl in Miami, the Oregon Coastal Highway, and many others. In the process, they stimulated the economy by creating jobs and generating orders for materials that American industry could then produce.

Despite their widespread appeal, New Deal policies reflected both the biases of the era and the political compromises needed to get legislation enacted. Southern Democrats in Congress, for example, successfully insisted that the 1935 National Labor Relations (Wagner) Act exclude farmworkers, fearing that rural black sharecroppers would use the workers' rights law to unionize and threaten the South's racial caste system.

FDR directly confronted the business leaders who believed that the upper-class president was a "traitor to his class." Running for reelection in 1936, he said, "We had to struggle with the old enemies of peace—business and financial monopoly, speculation, reckless banking, class antagonism, sectionalism, war profiteering. Never before in all our history have these forces been so united against one candidate as they stand today. They are unanimous in their hate for me—and I welcome their hatred."

Through his "fireside chats," in which he spoke to the nation via radio, FDR reassured Americans that conditions would improve. Many citizens felt that they had a personal relationship with the president and wrote him letters, describing their own predicaments or thanking him for his efforts.

The New Deal helped lift America out of the worst economic disaster in the nation's history, but the country did not reach full employment until World War II. By the early 1940s FDR was focused on preparing the United States for a war against fascism. Although he supported neutrality legislation to keep the country out of the European war, he also worked to provide military and economic aid in order to strengthen nations threatened or attacked by the Nazis. After the Japanese bombed Pearl Harbor in December 1941, FDR led the nation to the brink of victory in the two-front war in Europe and Asia until he died in 1945.

FDR's initial election in 1932 (with 57.4 percent of the popular vote), subsequent landslide victory in 1936 (60.8 percent), and more narrow wins in 1940 (54.7 percent) and 1944 (53.4 percent) transformed the political landscape. The so-called New Deal coalition of rural farmers, urban workers, Jews, African Americans, and others persisted until the Nixon era. The New Deal policies established the precedent that the federal government was responsible for social welfare and for stimulating the economy through its spending policies. Although these ideas have been challenged by conservatives—most forcefully by President Ronald Reagan during the 1980s—they remain firmly entrenched in the minds of most Americans.

Rose Schneiderman
(1882–1972)

ON MARCH 25, 1911, the Triangle Shirtwaist factory fire killed 146 women workers (see **Robert F. Wagner** profile). One week later activists held a meeting at the Metropolitan Opera House to memorialize the victims. Anne Morgan, the progressive-minded daughter of Wall Street chieftain J. P. Morgan, rented the hall, hoping to mobilize the city's wealthy and middle-class reformers around a unified voice for action. Ironically, the hall's balcony seats were filled with immigrant workers, who were merely spectators, while the affluent women and men sat in the orchestra section below. Several speakers reminded the well-off participants of their responsibility to provide charity for the poor; others called for justice and laws to protect worker safety. Then Rose Schneiderman—a twenty-nine-year-old Jewish immigrant, sweatshop worker, union organizer, and Socialist—rose to speak. Having seen the police, the courts, and politicians side with garment manufacturers against the workers, she questioned whether better laws would make a difference if they were not enforced.

"I would be a traitor to these poor burned bodies if I came here to talk good fellowship. We have tried you good people of the public and we have found you wanting," Schneiderman told the 3,500 people in the hall.

> This is not the first time girls have been burned alive in the city. Every week I must learn of the untimely death of one of my sister workers. Every year thousands of us are maimed. There are so many of us for one job it matters little if 146 of us are burned to death. . . . I can't talk fellowship to you who are gathered here. Too much blood has been spilled. I know from my experience it is up to the working people to save themselves. The only way they can save themselves is by a strong working-class movement.

Schneiderman's speech not only fired up the garment workers in the balcony but also galvanized the wealthy women in the front rows. Her message reflected a lifelong commitment to building a powerful labor movement by unifying radicals and reformers. Only four foot nine, with flaming red hair, Schneiderman was already well-known as a fiery orator and union leader.

Born in Poland, Schneiderman came to New York City with her Orthodox Jewish family in 1890. Two years later her father died of meningitis. Her mother took in boarders, sewed for neighbors, and worked as a handywoman. But the family was still forced to rely on charity in order to pay the rent and grocery bills. For a time Schneiderman's mother was even forced to briefly place her three children in an orphanage. A brilliant student, Schneiderman dropped out of school at thirteen to support the family by working as a department store salesclerk. Three years later she left sales for a better paying (but more danger-ous) job as a cap maker in a garment factory.

About 70 percent of women's clothes and almost half of men's clothes in the country were produced by New York City's garment industry. Of the more than 350,000 women in the city's workforce, the majority worked in service occupa-tions, as maids, personal servants, waitresses, retail clerks, and laundresses. About one-third worked in manufacturing jobs, making and packing cigars, assembling paper boxes, making candles, and creating artificial flowers, but the heaviest con-centration of women workers—about 65,000 of them—toiled in the clothing in-dustry. Fewer than 10,000 of New York's women workers belonged to a union.

As a Socialist, Schneiderman believed in building a movement of men and women workers to change society. She recognized that women workers faced ex-tra exploitation from employers and also had to deal with sexism from male union leaders. So she put particular emphasis on organizing women and fighting for laws to protect them. As a feminist, Schneiderman joined the struggle for women's suffrage, a cause that many male union leaders—and even some female unionists—thought was secondary to the battle for workers' rights. As a pragma-tist, she recognized that workers, particularly women workers, needed allies among middle-class reformers and upper-class feminists, so she spent much of her time forging coalitions with people from different social backgrounds, such as **Eleanor Roosevelt** and **Frances Perkins**.

By 1903, at age twenty-one, Schneiderman had organized her first union shop, the Jewish Socialist United Cloth Hat and Cap Makers' Union, and had led a successful strike. By 1906 she was vice president of the New York chapter of the Women's Trade Union League (WTUL), an organization founded to help working women unionize. In 1908 Irene Lewisohn, a German Jewish philan-thropist, offered Schneiderman money to complete her education. Schneider-man refused the scholarship, explaining that she could not accept a privilege that was not available to most working women. She did, however, accept Lewisohn's offer to pay her a salary to become the New York WTUL's chief organizer.

Schneiderman's organizing efforts among immigrants paved the way for a strike of 20,000 garment workers in 1909 and 1910, the largest by American women workers up to that time. The strike, mostly among Jewish women, helped build the International Ladies' Garment Workers Union (ILGWU) into a formi-dable force. The union in turn catapulted a number of exceptional working-class women—including Fannie Cohn, Bessie Abramowitz, and Pauline Newman, as well as Schneiderman—into leadership roles. The WTUL's upper-class women—whom Schneiderman called the "mink brigade"—raised money for the workers' strike fund, lawyers, and bail money and even joined the union members on picket lines. Schneiderman was a key figure in mobilizing this diverse coalition on behalf of the landmark labor laws passed by the New York legislature after the Triangle fire.

The WTUL was based on the belief that a spirit of sisterhood could overcome ethnic and class differences among women. But Schneiderman and other working-class members often found it difficult to deal with what she considered the condescension, anti-Semitism, and antisocialism of some wealthy WTUL leaders. Schneiderman resigned in 1914 and took a job as an organizer with the ILGWU.

Schneiderman believed that working women needed the vote as well as unions to improve working conditions. She helped found the Wage Earner's League for Woman Suffrage in 1911. "I hold that the humanizing of industry is woman's business," she said at a suffrage rally. "She must wield the ballot for this purpose."

Reconciling her two passions, Schneiderman became a leading figure in both labor and feminist politics. In 1917 she went to work for the Industrial Wing of the New York Woman Suffrage Party, hoping to mobilize working women to fight for the right to vote. She also rejoined the WTUL, whose wealthy women were devoted suffragists. That year women won the right to vote in New York State. When the Republican-dominated state legislature tried to repeal some of the post-Triangle labor laws, Schneiderman, along with **Florence Kelley,** the WTUL, and the National Consumers League, successfully organized the newly enfranchised women to oppose the attempt and then to defeat antilabor legislators in the 1918 election.

In 1920 Schneiderman ran for the US Senate on the Labor Party ticket. Her platform called for the construction of nonprofit housing for workers, improved neighborhood schools, publicly owned power utilities and staple food markets, and state-funded health and unemployment insurance for all Americans. Her unsuccessful campaign increased her visibility and influence in both the labor and feminist movements but cost her some allies among middle-class reformers, who supported the Democratic candidate.

Schneiderman also—and somewhat unusually—tried to organize African American women, who were allowed access to only a handful of occupations, including work in laundries, and earned much lower pay than white women. In 1924, with the help of the Urban League, a civil rights group, Schneiderman quietly organized meetings with black women workers in various New York settlement houses. She hoped that the ILGWU would mount a unionization effort among black female laundry workers, but the union's male members balked at the idea, reflecting the racism and sexism of the period.

In 1926 Schneiderman was elected president of the national WTUL, a position she held until she retired in 1950. No longer working directly for a labor union, she focused her energies on lobbying for an eight-hour workday and for minimum-wage legislation. In 1927 the New York legislature passed a historic bill limiting women's workweek to forty-eight hours. But many male trade unionists and even some male Socialists believed that a law that applied only to women would divide the labor movement. Schneiderman persisted, arguing that such a law was needed because women earned less than men, even if they held the same jobs. Moreover, she believed, a minimum-wage law for women was a stepping-stone to a minimum wage for all workers, which the New York state legislature passed in 1933.

One of Schneiderman's closest allies was Eleanor Roosevelt, who joined the WTUL in 1922, coming into contact with working-class women and radical activists for the first time. She taught classes, raised money, and participated in the WTUL's policy debates and legislative actions. As first lady, Roosevelt donated the proceeds from her 1932–1933 radio broadcasts to the WTUL and promoted the WTUL in her columns and speeches. As Schneiderman recalled in her autobiography, Roosevelt overcame the trappings of privilege to become "a born trade unionist." Roosevelt regularly invited Schneiderman to Hyde Park to spend time with **Franklin D. Roosevelt.** Schneiderman's conversations with FDR sensitized the future governor and president to the problems facing workers and their families. Francis Perkins credited Schneiderman with giving the future president "a real understanding of the trade-union movement."

In 1933, after his inauguration as president, FDR appointed Schneiderman to the National Recovery Administration's Labor Advisory Board, the only woman to serve there. She wrote the National Recovery Administration codes for every industry with a predominantly female workforce and, along with Frances Perkins, played an important role in shaping the National Labor Relations (Wagner) Act, the Social Security Act, and the Fair Labor Standards Act.

As New York State's secretary of labor from 1937 to 1943, appointed by Governor Herbert Lehman, Schneiderman campaigned hard for the extension of Social Security to domestic workers, for equal pay for women workers, and for comparable worth (giving women and men equal pay for different jobs that have comparable value). She lent support to union campaigns among the state's increasing number of service workers: hotel maids, restaurant workers, and beauty parlor workers.

During the late 1930s and early 1940s, Schneiderman became deeply involved in efforts to rescue European Jews and to resettle them in the United States and Palestine.

She died in 1972, just as the second wave of feminism was emerging as a powerful political movement. It, too, had to deal with class and racial divisions among women, but its ranks soon included a vocal component of working women, reflected in groups like 9 to 5 (founded in 1973) and the Coalition of Labor Union Women (founded in 1974).

Fiorello La Guardia
(1882–1947)

FIORELLO LA GUARDIA'S father was a non-practicing Catholic from Italy, his mother a religious Jew. They raised their son as an Episcopalian. The five-foot-two La Guardia drew on his unusual background and extraordinary talents to become the greatest mayor in American history, transforming New York City into a modern metropolis.

During his three terms (1933–1945) as mayor, during the Depression and World War II, La Guardia ran an honest, efficient, and progressive administration that helped lift the spirit and improve the conditions of New York's polyglot working class. As mayor, La Guardia earned a national reputation as a nonpartisan reformer dedicated to civic improvement. He once said, "There is no Republican, no Democratic, no socialist way to clean a street or build a sewer, but merely a right way and a wrong way."

As the leader of the nation's largest city, he also became the voice for America's cities, insisting that the media, business, and the federal government pay attention to the distinct needs and dreams of workers and immigrants in American metropolises. From 1935 to 1945 he led the US Conference of Mayors, using his celebrity to change forever the relationship between the federal and municipal governments.

While La Guardia was still an infant, his father became an army bandmaster and the family moved west. After finishing high school in Arizona, he joined the US Consular Service in 1901, serving five years in consulates in Budapest, Hungary; Trieste, Italy; and Fiume (Rijeka), Croatia. La Guardia returned to the United States as a translator, from 1907–1910, for the US Immigration Service at Ellis Island, while studying at night at New York University law school. (He was fluent in Yiddish, German, French, Croatian, and Italian as well as English.) Watching how immigrants were mistreated by the authorities, employers, and landlords, La Guardia recalled, "I suffered a great deal because I could not help these people."

After earning his law degree, La Guardia established a kind of one-man legal-aid bureau, often offering advice and appearing in court without fee on behalf of those too poor to pay. He soon developed a reputation as an advocate for the disenfranchised. In 1916 he defeated the incumbent and was elected to Congress as a progressive Republican from the Lower East Side.

When World War I broke out, La Guardia was desperate to serve in combat. Rejected as too short, he got a friend to teach him to fly and used his political connections to get a commission in the Army Air Service with the rank of lieutenant. He served with distinction as a bomber pilot over Italy.

Returning to New York a war hero, he was elected president of the city's Board of Aldermen (city council) in 1920, then was elected to Congress in 1922 from East Harlem, and was reelected four more times. In Congress, he opposed Prohibition, advocated for child labor laws, fought for greater government oversight of Wall Street, and supported national employment insurance for jobless workers. His most important accomplishment was the 1932 Norris–La Guardia Act, which restricted the courts' power to ban or restrain strikes, boycotts, or picketing by union members.

Never a loyal Republican, in 1924 he was denied the party's nod for renomination, but he was selected instead as the nominee of the Socialist and Progressive Parties, while supporting Progressive **Robert M. La Follette** over Republican Calvin Coolidge for president. At the Progressive convention in Cleveland, Ohio, La Guardia said, "I rise to let you know that there are other streets and other attitudes in New York besides Wall Street. I speak for Avenue A and 116th Street, instead of Broad and Wall."

In 1933 La Guardia ran successfully for New York City mayor on a "Fusion" (a Liberal and Republican Party coalition) reform ticket dedicated to unseating the corrupt Tammany Hall Democratic machine. He inherited a corrupt city in chaos that was plagued by widespread joblessness and on the brink of fiscal collapse. He understood that New York City could not pay for the investment and subsidies needed to provide relief, jobs, services, and infrastructure. He took office just as the New Deal was taking hold and immediately went to Washington, DC, to seek federal help. He worked closely with **Franklin D. Roosevelt**'s administration to make New York City a laboratory of New Deal funding for large public works projects. FDR said of La Guardia, "Our Mayor is the most appealing man I know. He comes to Washington and tells me a sad story. The tears run down my cheeks and tear[s] run down his cheeks and the first thing I know he has wangled another $50 million."

Within weeks, New York received 20 percent of the entire federal Civil Works Administration funding, enough to add 200,000 jobs. During La Guardia's first five years in office, federal investments enabled New York to upgrade its decaying infrastructure and build parks, beaches, low-income housing, bridges, schools, sewers, tunnels, reservoirs, hospitals, and municipal swimming pools. He presided over massive bridge and tunnel construction projects. He transformed a dump site in Queens into the location of a grand World's Fair; the area, renamed "Flushing Meadows," is today the home of the New York Mets and the US Tennis Open. La Guardia unified the city's fragmented rapid transit system, a goal that had long eluded his predecessors; it remains the nation's most heavily used subway system.

He was an able administrator who demanded excellence from civil servants and rooted out corruption from municipal agencies. He established merit employment in place of patronage jobs and quickly fired employees who took bribes, fixed traffic tickets, or gave contracts to political cronies. He ended Tammany's long-standing practice of selling judgeships. He improved the operations of the police and fire departments. He was not above grandstanding to demonstrate his efforts to fight organized crime, such as in the newsreel footage of La Guardia smashing illegal gambling machines with a sledgehammer.

He expanded the city's social welfare services, especially for children, creating, for example, a network of well-baby clinics. He intervened and helped settle strikes, typically on the side of unions. He warned his police department not to use clubs or pistols in dispersing groups of unemployed or striking workers. During the 1934 strike by taxi drivers, for example, he criticized the taxi owners and refused to let the police ban picketing or demonstrations.

La Guardia, observed one historian, had the skills of both an accountant and a preacher. As a result, he restored faith in city government, as FDR did for the national government. He reached out to the city's many ethnic, racial, and religious groups to give them a voice in government and a sense of being part of a great municipal mosaic. In 1937 he created an international incident when, in a speech to the American Jewish Congress, he characterized Adolf Hitler as a fanatic and suggested that he be made a central figure in the upcoming World's Fair Chamber of Horrors. The German embassy made formal complaints to Washington, and Secretary of State Cordell Hull twice apologized. When the US State Department told La Guardia that the German government was concerned about the safety of German nationals and property, La Guardia appointed an all-Jewish police detail, under Captain Max Finkelstein, to protect the German consul.

La Guardia was also the first New York mayor to seriously address issues of racial discrimination in housing and employment. He forced the city's hospitals to employ black doctors and nurses. In 1945 he formed the Mayor's Committee on Baseball to pressure local teams—the Dodgers, Yankees, and Giants—to hire black players.

A colorful figure with a flair for the dramatic, known as the "Little Flower" (in honor of his first name), La Guardia seemed to be everywhere. He often appeared at fires and natural disasters. He sometimes dropped in on city departments unannounced. He occasionally conducted the municipal orchestra. In 1942 he began a series of Sunday "talks to the people" on WNYC, the municipal radio station, where he offered his views on politics and other topics. For example, during World War II when landlords announced a large rent increase, La Guardia cited statistics showing that there were practically no apartment vacancies, resulting in huge profits for the real estate industry. More than 2 million listeners tuned in to the mayor's talks—the highest ratings of any radio program in the city.

On June 30, 1945, New York's newspaper delivery drivers began a strike that would last seventeen days, refusing to distribute any paper in the city except for the prolabor paper *PM*. The next day, La Guardia used his Sunday radio program to urge listeners to gather their children around the radio. He then read the popular *Dick Tracy* comic strip from the *Daily News,* creating different voices for the various characters and, at the end, explaining the moral of that week's adventure to his young listeners. He also promised to read the Sunday comics on the air every Sunday as long as the strike continued and promised that someone from WNYC would read the daily comics every day. The next Sunday, camera crews were in the studio to film La Guardia's broadcast, assuring that the story would make the national news.

Deciding not to run for a fourth term as mayor, La Guardia left office at the start of 1946 and served briefly as director general of the UN Relief and Rehabilitation Administration.

New York had a long tradition of politicians getting rich off bribes and influence peddling. La Guardia was the opposite. After his death in 1947, his estate included a mortgaged home and $8,000 in war bonds. La Guardia's colorful life was the subject of the Pulitzer Prize–winning Broadway musical *Fiorello!*, which flourished on Broadway from 1959 to 1961.

Roger Baldwin (1884–1981)

CREDIT: Roger Nash Baldwin Papers. Public Policy Papers. Department of Rare Books and Special Collections. Princeton University Library.

DURING AND after World War I, when America was seized by a national hysteria against radicals, immigrants, and unions, Roger Nash Baldwin led the crusade to defend civil liberties. The Woodrow Wilson administration cracked down on any individual, group, or publication that opposed US involvement in the combat in Europe. The dramatic political changes in Russia following the 1917 revolution also provided America's business and political leaders with another excuse to suppress dissenters of all kinds. So, too, did the wave of over 3,000 strikes by more than 4 million workers and the race riots that gripped Chicago and other cities throughout 1919.

Wilson's attorney general, A. Mitchell Palmer, recruited J. Edgar Hoover to investigate the threat of domestic subversion. Hoover reported that radicals posed a real danger to the United States and urged that the government take dramatic action against a possible revolution. Palmer used the extraordinary wartime powers granted by the Espionage Act of 1917 and the Sedition Act of 1918 to identify and round up people and groups he considered terrorists. Palmer and Hoover orchestrated a series of well-publicized raids in over thirty cities, rounding up and arresting thousands of people whom they identified as socialists, anarchists, communists, pacifists, and others, without warrants and without regard to constitutional protections against unlawful search and seizure. These Palmer Raids particularly targeted leaders of the Socialist Party and the Industrial Workers of the World. Some were brutally treated and held without trial for many months. Others were deported, mostly to Russia. Politicians and newspapers often linked "foreigners" and "radicals," contributing to a fever of anti-immigrant sentiment, which eventually led to a wave of federal laws in the early 1920s that severely restricted immigration to the United States.

In 1917, with the nation in the grip of this orchestrated hysteria, a small group challenged these egregious abuses of basic rights and formed the National Civil Liberties Bureau, which three years later changed its name to the American Civil Liberties Union (ACLU). The group's sixty-four founders included a "who's who" of the nation's leading liberals, progressives, and radicals. They included **Jane Addams, Helen Keller, John Dewey, A. J. Muste, Rose Schneiderman, Norman Thomas,** theologian Harry Ward (a professor at the Union Theological Seminary), Elizabeth Gurley Flynn, Rabbi Judah Magnes, James Weldon Johnson, Felix Frankfurter, Morris Hillquit, Helen Phelps Stokes, and Oswald Garrison Villard.

Baldwin was the key organizer of this group and the leader of the ACLU for the next three decades. Under Baldwin, the ACLU became the nation's most influential and most controversial defender of civil liberties, a role that it continues to play today.

Raised in Wellesley, Massachusetts, an exclusive Boston suburb, Baldwin's ancestors included Mayflower Pilgrims and a general in George Washington's army. His wealthy parents were Unitarians with many prominent friends and connections. **W. E. B. Du Bois** was a frequent guest at the Baldwin house. Baldwin entered Harvard in 1901, at a time when students were absorbing the exciting mix of progressive, socialist, and other reform ideas and causes, hoping to find ways to right society's wrongs. He volunteered at the Cambridge Social Union, which provided adult education to workers, and he helped organize the Harvard Entertainment Troupers, which offered musical performances for the poor.

Soon after his graduation, he moved to St. Louis, Missouri, and with the help of **Louis Brandeis** (his father's friend), he secured a job running a settlement house, where he worked from 1906 until 1917. He became a national leader of the growing movement for child protection. He served as chief officer of the St. Louis Juvenile Court and as secretary of the National Probation Association. He also founded the sociology department at Washington University, where he taught from 1906 to 1910.

Baldwin's reform instincts were jolted when he heard a speech in St. Louis by anarchist **Emma Goldman**. He began to see the problems of the poor—which he confronted every day in his settlement house and juvenile court work—as part of the capitalist system. The remedy was not charity or social work, he thought, but "the end of poverty and injustice by free association of those who worked, by the abolition of privilege, and by the organized power of the exploited." For the rest of his life, Baldwin walked a tightrope between his day-to-day reform work and his radical beliefs.

In 1910, at the National Conference of Charities and Correction, held in St. Louis, he met Jane Addams, who became a close friend and mentor and who shared his pacifist convictions. As US involvement in World War I seemed likely, Baldwin joined the American Union Against Militarism (AUAM), which Addams had helped found in 1915 to protest the draft and to protect conscientious objectors and other antiwar dissidents. He joined its staff in 1917 and helped create a division within the AUAM to provide legal advice and aid to conscientious objectors, a division that became the National Civil Liberties Bureau (NCLB).

In 1917 Congress passed the Selective Service Act to conscript men for military service. Baldwin was drafted the following year, but as a conscientious objector, he refused to go. His arrest, trial, and conviction made headlines. He spent a year in prison, referring to it as "my vacation on the government." Upon his release, he returned to work at the NCLB. In January 1920 the group was renamed the American Civil Liberties Union, focusing on the protection of free speech, religious freedom, the right to a fair trial, the right to assembly, racial equality, and other First Amendment protections. Baldwin was named its director.

The ACLU swiftly became one of the century's major progressive organizations. A kind of nonprofit law firm, its only client, its leaders said, was the First Amendment.

In its first two decades, the ACLU was primarily devoted to protecting the First Amendment rights of antiwar dissidents and labor unions. Most judges sympathized with employers, who used court injunctions to restrict unions from picketing and demonstrating. In 1930 Baldwin organized the National Committee on Labor Injunctions to challenge the antiunion abuses of many judges. In 1932 the ACLU and its labor allies scored a major victory when Congress passed the Norris–La Guardia Act (cosponsored by Senator George Norris of Nebraska and Congressman **Fiorello La Guardia** of New York), which barred federal courts from issuing injunctions against nonviolent labor disputes.

The ACLU was constantly linking First Amendment rights to the fight for workers' rights, women's rights, racial justice, and other causes, such as police abuse. On May 15, 1923, for example, **Upton Sinclair** rose to speak on behalf of 3,000 striking longshoremen at Liberty Hill in the San Pedro neighborhood of Los Angeles. As Sinclair began reading the US Constitution, the chief of police told him to "cut out that Constitution stuff" and quickly arrested the famous muckraker. For four days, Sinclair and three other speakers were held incommunicado. Once released, Sinclair sent a letter to various supporters recruiting them to join the ACLU's new Southern California chapter.

In 1920 two Italian immigrants, Nicola Sacco and Bartolomeo Vanzetti, both anarchists, were arrested for committing a murder during a bank robbery in Braintree, Massachusetts. Like many other Americans, Baldwin was not sure whether they were innocent or guilty, but he was thoroughly convinced that the pair could not get a fair trial because the prosecution was using their anarchist beliefs and their immigrant status to convict them. The ACLU helped raise money for their legal defense and helped mobilize public opposition to the one-sided trial. An international movement of protests on behalf of Sacco and Vanzetti was unable to overturn their conviction, and they were executed on August 23, 1927.

In 1925 the ACLU hired **Clarence Darrow** to defend John Scopes, the Tennessee science teacher arrested for violating a state law prohibiting teaching evolution in public schools. Baldwin said that the trial pitted "God against the monkeys," and it soon became known as the "monkey trial." In another controversial case, the ACLU defended Mary Ware Dennett, an outspoken ACLU member, suffragist, and birth control advocate whose pamphlet *The Sex Side of Life: An Explanation for Young People* was banned by the US Postal Service as obscene. The jury in her trial took only forty minutes to convict her, but the ACLU appealed and overturned the ruling.

Baldwin and the ACLU were deeply involved with the National Association for the Advancement of Colored People (NAACP), working to stop lynching and other acts of violence perpetuated by the Ku Klux Klan and other racist groups. The ACLU's 1931 report *Black Justice* documented the systematic denial of civil rights. The ACLU participated in the defense of the Scottsboro Boys, nine young black men accused of raping two white women on an Alabama train. It was the first civil rights case to attract national publicity.

In 1933 the ACLU won one of the most influential cases against censorship in American history. The US Customs Department had banned James Joyce's novel *Ulysses* on grounds of obscenity. On behalf of its publisher, Random House, the ACLU persuaded the judge that the book was not obscene, which helped shift public opinion about censorship.

Baldwin was also an advocate of international human rights. In the 1920s he helped form the International Committee for Political Prisoners as well as the American League for India's Freedom, which supported India's independence from British colonialism. In 1927 he visited the Soviet Union, and the next year he published *Liberty Under the Soviets,* reflecting his sympathies for the Russian Revolution. But in 1939 Russia signed a treaty with the Nazis, stalling for time to avoid a war between the two countries, and Baldwin, like many leftists at the time, broke with the pro-Russia American Communists. In 1953, at the height of the Cold War, he wrote *A New Slavery: The Communist Betrayal of Human Rights*, which was highly critical of the Soviet Union.

Baldwin maintained his antiwar convictions. He joined the League Against War and Fascism and other groups that sided with the antifascist forces in the Spanish Civil War. During World War II, the federal government planned to force 110,000 Japanese and Japanese Americans from their homes and confine them to relocation camps out of fear that they would form a pro-Japan force within the United States. The ACLU took the courageous but unpopular stand of opposing the plan. Ironically, when the war was over, General Douglas MacArthur asked Baldwin to advise Harry S. Truman's administration on civil liberties issues as the United States sought to rebuild Japan and Germany.

Throughout the 20th century, Americans who opposed censorship or repression of free speech (including books, plays, and movies), who campaigned for civil rights, or who fought police abuse knew they could turn to their local ACLU chapter for help. Baldwin drew on his web of contacts among liberals and radicals alike to make the ACLU an effective advocate for social and economic justice. Although he retired from the directorship in 1950, he remained active in the organization and advocated for many causes, particularly human rights cases around the world.

Founded in response to the post–World War I antiradical hysteria, the ACLU faced a major crisis during the post–World War II Red Scare. As early as 1940 the ACLU, with Baldwin's support, had expelled Elizabeth Gurley Flynn, a member of the Communist Party, from its board on the grounds that Communists opposed civil liberties, even though the ACLU's mission was to defend the free speech rights even of those with unpopular views. In 1948 the ACLU began attaching a disclaimer to its court briefs denouncing communism, hoping to inoculate itself from the Cold War frenzy. By the 1950s many key members of ACLU's board did not want the organization to take up the cause of radicals who were blacklisted by schools, universities, Hollywood studios, government agencies, or other employers because of their political beliefs. As a result, the ACLU failed to take a strong stance protecting the civil liberties of suspected Communists and victims of McCarthyism.

On other matters, however, the ACLU remained at the forefront of battles for civil liberties and civil rights. In 1954 the ACLU joined forces with the NAACP to challenge racial segregation, leading to the US Supreme Court's historic ruling in *Brown v. Board of Education* that ended the "separate but equal" doctrine. The ACLU was also involved in the Supreme Court's 1973 *Roe v. Wade* decision that found that the right to privacy included a woman's right to decide to have an abortion. In 1977 Baldwin played an active role in one of the ACLU's most controversial cases: the defense of the American Nazi Party's right to stage a march in Skokie, Illinois, a Chicago suburb with a large Jewish population. Although the ACLU won the case when a federal court ruled that the city's ordinances designed to prevent the march were unconstitutional, many ACLU members resigned from the organization in protest. In 2003 the ACLU helped persuade the Supreme Court in *Lawrence v. Texas* to strike down a Texas law making sexual intimacy between same-sex couples a crime.

Eleanor Roosevelt
(1884–1962)

CREDIT: Associated Press

IN NOVEMBER 1938, 1,500 people, African American and white, packed into the city auditorium in Birmingham, Alabama, to kick off the four-day Southern Conference on Human Welfare. The gathering was organized to address the South's serious social problems, including poverty, poor education, and the infamous poll tax that prevented black citizens from voting. The next morning the auditorium was surrounded by police. Police Commissioner Bull Connor ordered the integrated crowd to separate their seating according to race or face arrest. The crowd obeyed, with black people sitting on one side, and white people on the other. Arriving late was the first lady, Eleanor Roosevelt, along with African American educator Mary McLeod Bethune and Aubrey Williams, head of the New Deal's National Youth Administration. Roosevelt sized up the situation and sat down on the side with the African Americans. One of the policemen tapped her on the shoulder and told her to move. Instead, she calmly moved her chair between the white and black sections and there she remained.

Throughout her life Roosevelt stuck with her principles and fought on behalf of America's most vulnerable citizens. Over time, she became friends with a widening circle of union activists, feminists, civil rights crusaders, and radicals whose ideas she embraced and advocated for both as **Franklin D. Roosevelt**'s wife and adviser and as a political figure in her own right.

Although she came from a long line of privilege, Roosevelt had a difficult childhood. Her father, Elliott Roosevelt, was an early influence on her social consciousness, taking her with him when he visited the Children's Aid Society or served up Thanksgiving dinner to newsboys. By the time Roosevelt was ten, both her parents had died. She was sent to live with her maternal grandmother, a formidable woman who wanted to groom her for New York's elite society. Her prominent relatives included her uncle, **Theodore Roosevelt,** who became president when Eleanor was seventeen.

Her early education consisted of a private tutor and a year in an Italian convent school. Her first and most influential mentor was Marie Souvestre, who ran Allenswood, a feminist, progressive boarding school for girls outside London that Roosevelt attended from 1898 to 1902. The school taught classical languages and

the arts, and Souvestre gave Roosevelt special instruction in history and philosophy. Souvestre was a demanding thinker who challenged her students with her liberal ideas against colonialism and anti-Semitism. She invited Roosevelt to be her
traveling companion through France and Italy during holiday breaks from school
and encouraged her to be an independent and confident woman.

In 1902 Roosevelt's grandmother insisted she return to the United States to
get down to the business of becoming a debutante. Roosevelt was nearly six feet
tall and willowy, with prominent teeth and a weak chin—not the social belle
that her mother had been and that her grandmother wished her to be.

Roosevelt quickly realized that she preferred volunteering with social reform
groups to going to fancy balls. From 1902 to 1903 she volunteered at the River-
ton Street Settlement House on the Lower East Side, teaching exercise and dance
to children. Unlike her peers, who arrived in carriages, she insisted on taking
public transportation, forcing herself to overcome her fears and walk even at
night through the Bowery, a low-rent area.

She also became immersed in the National Consumers League (NCL), led by
Florence Kelley. Through the NCL, she investigated and publicized dreadful
working conditions in garment factories. She also met many progressive activists
who shaped her political consciousness.

In 1902 she was riding a train when her distant cousin Franklin Delano Roosevelt, a Harvard student, happened to board, and they spent the next two hours
in easy conversation. That began their discreet romance, which he at first kept
hidden from his domineering mother. It was by accompanying Eleanor that
Franklin was first exposed to New York's dismal tenements. For the rest of their
lives together, Eleanor was FDR's unofficial guide and conscience regarding the
suffering of the poor, workers, African Americans, and women.

They were married in 1905 when she was twenty and he twenty-two, with
her Uncle Theodore walking her down the aisle. During the first several years of
marriage and young motherhood, she grew increasingly depressed under the
thumb of her mother-in-law, Sara Delano Roosevelt, who insisted on running
the household. Eleanor was able to escape Sara's domination when the couple
moved to Albany, New York, after FDR was elected to the state legislature in
1910. She learned that she had a gift for politics and soon became one of FDR's
most trusted advisers. She also lobbied for causes she believed in—eliminating
poverty, improving working conditions, women's rights, and education—and
was better at connecting with people than was FDR.

By 1916 the couple had had six children, including one son who died as a
baby. Franklin's appointment as assistant secretary of the navy in 1913 brought
the Roosevelts to Washington, DC, and was the beginning of national promi-
nence. It also marked a difficult turning point in their relationship, when Eleanor
discovered Franklin's long-term affair with her social secretary Lucy Mercer.
Deeply distressed, she offered him a divorce. They remained married, however, in
a loyal political partnership.

World War I offered Roosevelt an outlet for her organizing talents. She organized a Union Station canteen for soldiers on their way to training camps, led Red Cross activities, supervised the knitting rooms at the navy department, and spoke at patriotic rallies. She visited wounded soldiers in the hospital and led an effort to improve conditions at St. Elizabeths Hospital, a mental hospital in Washington.

During the postwar Red Scare, Roosevelt renewed her reform impulses. She became active in several groups that the attorney general, A. Mitchell Palmer, considered dangerously radical. She coordinated the League of Women Voters' legislative efforts, mobilizing members to lobby for bills. She raised money for the Women's Trade Union League, worked for bills regulating maximum hours and minimum wages for women workers, and forged friendships with such labor activists as **Rose Schneiderman,** with whom she walked picket lines. J. Edgar Hoover, a close aide to Palmer who later became FBI director, kept a file on Roosevelt for years.

As FDR's political fortunes rose—first to governor of New York in 1928 and then to president in 1932—Eleanor constantly had to find her footing as a public person. While governor, FDR was stricken with polio, leaving him unable to walk. Eleanor became his eyes and ears, investigating conditions at hospitals, asylums, and prisons.

Eleanor's involvement with reform movements prepared her to become the most influential and politically progressive first lady in American history. "No one who ever saw Eleanor Roosevelt sit down facing her husband and holding his eyes firmly [and saying] to him 'Franklin, I think you should' or, 'Franklin surely you will not' will ever forget the experience," wrote Rexford Tugwell, a key FDR aide.

She became a key player in the Democratic Party, not only mobilizing voters but also pushing the party to support progressive legislation and to give women a larger voice in party affairs. She effectively pushed FDR to appoint women (including Secretary of Labor **Frances Perkins**) to key positions in government. She developed a tight circle of close women friends who were her main confidants, including Associated Press political reporter Lorena Hickock, with whom she eventually had an intimate friendship.

When she became first lady, she devoted considerable time to those hardest hit by poverty, visiting an encampment of World War I veterans (called Bonus Marchers) in Washington, sharecroppers in the South, and people on breadlines in San Francisco and in the slums of Puerto Rico. Her public support for union organizing drives among coal miners, garment workers, textile workers, and tenant farmers (including the racially integrated and left-wing Southern Tenant Farmers Union) lent visibility and credibility to their efforts. She invited union organizers, women activists, and others to the White House and seated them next to FDR so he could hear their concerns.

In 1933 she began holding her own press conferences, for women reporters only, in part to preserve their jobs during the Depression. Her influence was such that the president often had her float ideas to journalists and others to see how they would fly politically.

Eleanor was much bolder than FDR in opposing racism, segregation, and lynching. She became a close friend of Walter White, head of the National Association for the Advancement of Colored People (NAACP), serving as his advocate within the White House, and she made a point of publicly joining the civil rights organization. Whereas FDR was worried about losing white southern votes, Eleanor took public and principled stands. On civil rights issues, she agitated; he waffled. But sometimes she prevailed. In 1939 she resigned in protest from the Daughters of the American Revolution after that organization refused to rent its Constitution Hall to opera singer Marian Anderson, who had previously sung at the White House. Instead, Roosevelt worked behind the scenes to arrange for Anderson to sing to 75,000 people at the Lincoln Memorial. In February 1940 she shared the stage with the NAACP's Roy Wilkins and the Socialist Party's **Norman Thomas** at a National Sharecroppers Week forum at a New York hotel. Before and during World War II, she worked with White, Aubrey Williams, **A. Philip Randolph,** and others to eliminate racial discrimination in the armed forces and in private defense employment.

She developed a strong voice as a public speaker and prolific writer of magazine articles and books. Her syndicated column My Day, about her life in the White House, appeared six times a week in some 180 papers around the country. She also lectured and spoke frequently on the radio.

The American people found her approachable and caring, even as she was ridiculed in the press as being both dowdy and a publicity hound. During her first year in the White House, more than 300,000 people wrote to her. She personally answered many of the letters and forwarded the rest to federal agencies for a response.

She was actively involved for decades in promoting peace and international understanding as well. She tried to convince FDR to support the Permanent Court of International Justice, commonly called the World Court, which had been set up after World War I to settle disputes among nations. Privately FDR agreed with the idea, but he considered it politically too risky and allowed the Senate to reject US membership in the court by a seven-vote margin.

Starting in 1939, as the Nazis were engaged in genocide against Jews, Eleanor fought for special legislation to admit Jewish refugees, especially children, to the United States, but without FDR's public support the idea went nowhere.

During World War II—in which all four of the Roosevelt sons served— Eleanor, then fifty-nine years old, visited troops in London and in the South Pacific. She won over Admiral William Halsey, who had derided her for what he considered her do-goodism and meddling, when she spent exhausting days personally comforting wounded soldiers. "She alone had accomplished more good than any other person, or any group of civilians, who had passed through my area," Halsey said.

After FDR's death in 1945, Eleanor assumed she would retire, but the new president, Harry S. Truman, sought her advice. He also appointed her to the five-person U.S. delegation at the first meeting of the UN General Assembly held in London in 1946. She played a surprising and pivotal role, addressing the full assembly, without notes, and swaying the vote against forced repatriation of refugees, allowing them to choose where they wished to settle.

For three years, Roosevelt lobbied, debated, and maneuvered to get the United Nations to adopt a statement on human rights. In 1948 she chaired the UN Human Rights Commission, and under her leadership the General Assembly, meeting in Paris, passed, at 3:00 a.m. on December 10, the Universal Declaration of Human Rights, still a landmark document. According to a December 10, 1988, column by Richard Gardner in the *New York Times*, "Then something happened that never happened in the United Nations before or since. The delegates rose to give a standing ovation to a single delegate, a shy, elderly lady with a rather formal demeanor, but a very warm smile. Her name, of course, was Eleanor Roosevelt."

Norman Thomas
(1884–1968)

Norman Thomas, center, Socialist Party candidate for president, leads parade in Milwaukee, Wisconsin, in 1932. CREDIT: Associated Press

IN OCTOBER 1967, eighty-two-year-old Norman Thomas—blind and crippled by arthritis and a recent automobile accident—took the podium to address a meeting of college students in Washington, DC. Many were angry at the United States for conducting what they considered an immoral and imperialist war in Vietnam. Over the previous few years of escalating demonstrations, protesters would occasionally burn the American flag. That symbolic act, inevitably highlighted on TV news and featured in the next day's newspapers, led many Americans to conclude that people who opposed the war also hated the United States. Thomas, a lifelong pacifist and Socialist, as stalwart a foe of the Vietnam folly as anyone, raised the moral stakes by proclaiming, "I don't like the sight of young people burning the flag of my country, the country I love. A symbol? If they want an appropriate symbol, they should be washing the flag, not burning it."

It was for actions like that that Thomas was often called "America's conscience." He was the nation's most visible Socialist from the 1930s through the 1960s, and he could easily have been marginalized by mainstream politics, especially when he ran for office, as he frequently did, against reform-oriented Democrats. Instead, Thomas was a constant and effective presence in battles for workers' rights, civil liberties, civil rights, peace, and feminism. He was influential because of his great moral authority, his spellbinding oratory, and his leadership of broad coalitions of radicals and reformers who put aside ideological differences to win progressive victories. The British journalist Alistair Cooke wrote about Thomas, "He always lost the election and always grew in influence and dignity with every defeat."

Thomas's father, grandfather, and great-grandfather were conservative Presbyterian pastors. After attending Princeton University, he followed in their footsteps, enrolling in Union Theological Seminary, and he was ordained a minister in 1911. But by then he had been inspired by the emerging Christian Social Gospel movement, which viewed religion as a vehicle for social reform. He turned down an offer to head the wealthy Brick Presbyterian Church on Fifth Avenue in New York City to serve an ethnically diverse parish in East Harlem, a poor neighborhood. Like many other middle-class reformers of the era, Thomas also headed a settlement house in the area to serve the needs of the poor.

Thomas was drawn to both pacifism and Christian socialism, and in 1917 he supported the antiwar Socialist candidate Morris Hillquit for mayor of New York. In a letter to Hillquit that Thomas released to the press, Thomas wrote, "I believe that the hope for the future lies in a new social and economic order which demands the abolition of the capitalistic system." The letter angered the well-off leaders of the Presbyterian hierarchy. Contributions to his church and to its charitable work with the poor fell sharply, and he resigned from the ministry and took a job running the Fellowship of Reconciliation (FOR), a pacifist group, and its magazine, *World Tomorrow.* Outraged by the government's persecution and jailing of antiwar activists, Thomas joined with **Roger Baldwin** to create the National Civil Liberties Bureau (NCLB), which was later renamed the American Civil Liberties Union (ACLU). In addition to his duties with FOR, Thomas took the helm of the NCLB after Baldwin went to prison for refusing to register for the draft.

Although he never held a pulpit or worked for a church group again, Thomas maintained his strong religious views. He wrote frequently for Christian publications until 1921, when he joined *The Nation* magazine as associate editor, and he served briefly as editor of the *New York Leader,* a short-lived socialist daily newspaper.

Thomas considered socialism an extension of liberal democracy and the Christian Gospels, and he viewed communism as the opposite of his basic values. He joined the Socialist Party just as it was facing brutal repression. Its political leaders were sometimes barred from taking office, even after winning an election. **Eugene Debs** was in jail for his opposition to World War I. When the party's meetings were not banned by local authorities, the gatherings were targeted and attacked by local thugs and right-wingers. Its foreign-born members were threatened with deportation. In addition, the Communist Party—which had close ties to Russia's revolutionary government—competed for members and siphoned off some of the Socialist Party's more left-wing activists. The Socialist Party's membership fell from more than 100,000 in 1917 to barely 12,000 by 1923.

Thomas refused to let the Socialist Party die. For years, he crisscrossed the country giving speeches to unions, women's groups, religious organizations, colleges, peace groups, civil rights organizations—wherever he could find an audience. To spread the Socialist Party message, he ran for office relentlessly, never expecting to win but always hoping to win new followers and to influence what other candidates were advocating.

After running unsuccessfully for four local and state offices on the Socialist ticket, Thomas ran for president first in 1928 and then five more times. Debs

had died in 1926, and neither of the Socialist Party's two top political leaders—
Victor Berger and Hillquit—were eligible to run for president due to their foreign birth. Thomas became the party's national leader.

In 1932, in the depths of the Depression, the Socialist platform called for old-
age pensions, public works projects, a more progressive income tax, unemployment insurance, relief for farmers, slum clearance and subsidized housing for the
poor, a shorter workweek, and the nationalization of banks and basic industries.
Thomas figured that in such desperate times, his message would appeal to voters.
But many voters who may have agreed with Thomas's views did not want to
"waste" their vote on a Socialist who had no chance to win and who might even
take enough votes away from the Democratic candidate, **Franklin D. Roosevelt,**
to keep Republican Herbert Hoover in office. Thomas had little regard for FDR,
whom he considered a wealthy dilettante and a lackluster governor of New York.
He believed FDR's 1932 platform offered few specifics except vague promises of a
"New Deal."

Thomas did not expect to win, but he was disappointed that whereas FDR
garnered 22.8 million votes (57 percent), he had to settle for 884,781 (2 percent).
When friends expressed delight that FDR was carrying out some of the Socialist
platform, Thomas responded that it was being carried out "on a stretcher." He
viewed the New Deal as patching, rather than fixing, a broken system. He wanted
FDR and Congress to socialize the banks and expand credit for job-creating businesses, including public and cooperative enterprises. Instead, FDR bailed out the
financial system with some modest regulations "and gave it back to the bankers to
see if they could ruin it again."

Although Americans rejected Thomas's bids for office, many still admired his
principled stands on issues. He remained a public figure, an eloquent and sometimes fiery speaker, frequently quoted in the news and a constant presence at rallies and conferences and in the pages of liberal and radical publications. He was
a nonstop crusader for workers' rights, women's rights (including birth control),
and civil rights.

In 1926 Thomas was arrested for speaking to the strikers in Passaic, New Jersey, challenging the local sheriff's imposition of martial law. His arrest gave the
ACLU an opportunity to obtain an injunction against the sheriff for his violation
of civil rights. In 1933 Thomas and others were attending a conference of radicals
and progressives in Washington, DC, staying at the Cairo Hotel. When the hotel
barred Floria Pinkney, an African American delegate, Thomas led a march on the
hotel and canceled the group's reservations. In 1934 Thomas persuaded H. L.
Mitchell, a former Tennessee sharecropper who ran a dry-cleaning shop in Arkansas and was a Socialist, to form the Southern Tenant Farmers Union, one of
the first racially integrated labor unions. Thomas often traveled to the rural South
to help organize the sharecroppers and was occasionally beaten and arrested.

In 1935 Thomas led a national campaign against the Ku Klux Klan and rogue
cops in Tampa, Florida. The Klan members and their police accomplices had ab-

ducted and beat three local radicals, one of whom—Joseph Shoemaker, a Socialist Party member—died from the wounds. The ACLU offered a $1,000 reward for information leading to the arrest and conviction of the guilty persons. The national attention prompted some Florida newspapers, civic and religious leaders, and the local sheriff to condemn the violence and bring the thugs to justice.

In the late 1930s, concerned that big business and FDR were preparing America for another major war, Thomas made alliances with anyone who shared his opposition, including anti-Semites and racists whose views he opposed. It was Thomas's most serious political mistake. Three days after the Japanese bombed Pearl Harbor, however, Thomas reluctantly announced his support for America's war effort. During the war, Thomas was one of the few public figures to oppose the internment of Japanese Americans. He also pleaded with FDR to allow Jewish refugees into the country to escape the Holocaust. He worked closely with **A. Philip Randolph,** an African American union leader, pushing FDR to integrate the nation's defense factories and abolish discrimination in the nation's armed forces.

Thomas vigorously protested President Harry S. Truman's decision to use the atomic bomb to destroy Hiroshima and Nagasaki. After the war, and despite his strong opposition to communism, he defended the civil liberties of American Communists during the McCarthy era.

In 1957 Thomas cofounded the Committee for a SANE Nuclear Policy to halt the escalating arms race between the United States and the Soviet Union. He spoke relentlessly on SANE's behalf. In 1960 he addressed a SANE rally in Madison Square Garden, along with Randolph, **Eleanor Roosevelt, Walter Reuther,** and singer Harry Belafonte; the rally attracted 20,000 people. In 1961, **Tom Hayden,** the leader of Students for a Democratic Society, wrote that his generation only trusted three people over thirty: sociologist **C. Wright Mills,** Socialist writer-activist **Michael Harrington,** and Thomas.

In December 1964, 2,000 Americans gathered at New York's Hotel Astor to celebrate Thomas's eightieth birthday. Thomas used the occasion to call for a cease-fire in Vietnam. He received hundreds of congratulatory telegrams from prime ministers, politicians, labor leaders, and social activists, including US Supreme Court Chief Justice **Earl Warren** and Vice President Hubert Humphrey. **Martin Luther King Jr.,** on his way to Oslo to accept the Nobel Peace Prize, taped a message to Thomas and later published it as an article entitled "The Bravest Man I Ever Met." In it, he said, "I can think of no man who has done more than you to inspire the vision of a society free of injustice and exploitation. While some would adjust to the status quo, you urged struggle. Your example has ennobled and dignified the fight for freedom, and all that we hear of the Great Society seems only an echo of your prophetic eloquence."

A plaque in the Princeton University library reads: "Norman M. Thomas, class of 1905. 'I am not the champion of lost causes, but the champion of causes not yet won.'"

A. J. Muste (1885–1967)

A.J. Muste's last arrest at an anti-war protest in New York in 1966.
CREDIT: Hope College Collection of the Joint Archives of Holland

ON MAY 21, 1959, A. J. Muste wrote to President Dwight D. Eisenhower asking him to allow a small group of peace activists to enter the Mead Missile Base in Nebraska in order to stop the construction of nuclear weapons. Muste informed the president that if they were not granted permission, he and others would engage in civil disobedience and peacefully enter the site, saying, "We do not believe that our nation has any right to engage in preparation for mass destruction by nuclear weapons or to hold the threat of such destruction over the people of other countries."

Muste never heard back from the president, so he proceeded with the plan. On July 1 the seventy-four-year-old Muste led the protestors in prayer, and then he and a small group scaled the four-and-a-half-foot barbed-wire fence surrounding the site, while others blocked trucks trying to deliver parts. They were immediately arrested. During the ensuing trial, the judge listened closely to, and seemed impressed by, Muste's arguments against the arms race between the United States and Soviet Union and the dangers of a nuclear war. In private, he told Muste that he sympathized with the goals of the protest but that he had to enforce the law. The judge sentenced Muste and the other protesters to eight days in jail, plus a six-month suspended jail sentence, one year of probation, and a $500 fine.

As a veteran labor and peace activist, Muste saw arrest and jail as just other ways to draw public attention to his message. He once wrote, "Those who undertake a revolution are obligated to try to see it through. Mass action is a mere gesture unless those who engage in it are prepared for mass arrests." Often called the "American Gandhi," Muste was the leading American peace activist of his generation. Deeply religious, he put his pacifism to work on behalf of workers' rights, civil rights, and peace by guiding small activist groups to perform acts of enormous courage that inspired others and ignited broader movements for change. He was never well-known to the general public, but he commanded enormous respect among progressives for his calmness, wisdom, and strategic brilliance. It was Muste's patience and leadership that transformed opposition to the Vietnam War from the protests of a tiny group to a mass movement.

Born in Holland, Abraham Johannes Muste was brought to the United States at age six. His parents settled in Grand Rapids, Michigan, where his father worked in a local furniture factory. They raised Muste in the strict Calvinist traditions of the Dutch Reformed Church. He graduated as class valedictorian from Hope College and was ordained a minister in 1909.

At the Union Theological Seminary, he was influenced by the Social Gospel and the activism of his fellow seminary students, leading him to abandon the biblical literalism of the Dutch Reformed Church. He voted for socialist **Eugene Debs** in the 1912 presidential election.

In 1915 he left his New York pulpit and became minister of a Congregational church outside Boston. The outbreak of World War I drew Muste to pacifism. On Easter Sunday, March 31, 1918, he preached about the futility of war shortly after one of the prominent sons of the church had been killed in the war. The congregation promptly fired him.

In 1919 striking textile workers in Lawrence, Massachusetts, appealed for help from the religious community. Muste—now a Quaker—was quickly thrust into the struggle for workers' rights and discovered that he had a talent for organizing and inspiring workers. He led the more than 15,000 strikers to a resounding victory, including winning a forty-four-hour workweek.

For several years he served as general secretary of the Amalgamated Textile Workers of America. Then, in 1921, he became director of the Brookwood Labor College outside New York City, where he helped train union activists, many of whom would play important roles in industrial union campaigns of the 1930s.

Brookwood, like the Highlander Folk School a decade later, became an important gathering place for activists, who would draw on the contacts they made there to build a progressive movement. Muste then became an itinerant labor organizer. In 1931 he helped lead a bitter strike in the silk mills of Paterson, New Jersey, where he was jailed for what the police called "unlawful assembly" but others simply call "picketing." He was also involved in major strikes in Toledo, Ohio, in 1934 and Akron, Ohio, in 1936.

In these strikes, watching business use its political influence and violence to prevent workers from organizing, Muste began to question the morality of capitalism and to revise his pacifist views. Capitalism, he believed, was a violent system, leading to hunger, joblessness, and human misery. Muste became the leader of the Workers' Party, a tiny ultraradical group. But he was quickly disillusioned by the infighting among different wings of the left, often over matters of arcane political doctrine, not organizing strategy. In 1936, while traveling in Europe, he entered the Church of St. Sulpice in Paris and was overwhelmed by a feeling of inner peace. As he recalled, a voice spoke to him, saying, "This is where you belong, in the church, not outside of it," and he decided then to rededicate his life to Christianity and pacifism, a promise he kept for the rest of his life.

From 1937 through 1940, Muste was the minister of the Presbyterian Labor Temple in New York. In 1940 he became executive secretary of the Fellowship of Reconciliation (FOR), an interfaith pacifist group, where he remained until his retirement in 1953.

Muste's uncompromising pacifism was controversial. "If I can't love Hitler, I can't love at all," he said at a Quaker meeting in 1940, before the United States had entered World War II. But even after the war began, Muste defended young men who refused military service and supported alternative public service jobs for conscientious objectors—a position that put him at odds with most other major churches, who supported the war against Nazism. To Muste's disappointment, his seventeen-year-old son enlisted in the navy. "His mother and I could not be a conscience for him," he wrote, "nor he for us. The man who goes into war having seriously thought his way to that decision is on a higher moral level than the smug pacifist who has no notion of the ambiguities and contradictions the decision involves."

Muste called for the United States to help rescue victims of Nazi persecution and protested the US internment of Japanese Americans.

In 1942, with Muste's support, FOR staffers James Farmer and George Houser founded the Congress of Racial Equality, which became an important force within the civil rights movement, dedicated to using nonviolent direct action against segregation. In 1948 Muste gave a speech at Crozer Theological Seminary, discussing Mohandas Gandhi's philosophy of nonviolence and his movement for Indian independence from British imperialism. One of the students in the audience that day was **Martin Luther King Jr.** King often credited Muste with inspiring his initial interest in nonviolence. Muste was also an influential mentor to Rev. **James Lawson, Bayard Rustin,** and other civil rights stalwarts.

In the aftermath of America's use of atomic bombs on Hiroshima and Nagasaki, Muste argued that the peace movement should focus on dismantling the country's nuclear arsenal. He faced jail and prosecution for refusing to pay income taxes used for war purposes. With **Dorothy Day,** he led public opposition to civil defense drills in New York City. In 1957, on the twelfth anniversary of the bombing of Hiroshima, Muste walked into a restricted nuclear testing area near Las Vegas and was arrested. A year later, he and others lay down in front of trucks carrying materials for the construction of an intercontinental ballistic missile base in Wyoming. In 1958 he organized a voyage of protest ships into nuclear test areas of the Pacific—a tactic later used by the environmental group Greenpeace. The next year, he led the Omaha Action after Eisenhower failed to answer his polite letter. In the early 1960s, to gain visibility for the peace and antinuclear movements, Muste organized teams of pacifists to walk from San Francisco to Moscow, Quebec to Guantánamo, and from New Delhi to Peking, carrying the message of unilateral disarmament.

During the Vietnam War, Muste alone was trusted by all the different wings of antiwar sentiment, so he was able to act as a bridge builder to hold together the fragile coalitions that made up the antiwar movement. In April 1966 he visited South Vietnam, as part of a delegation from Clergy and Laymen Concerned About Vietnam, to make contact with dissenters. After trying to organize a peace demonstration, they were arrested and deported. Nine months later, despite ill health and warnings from his doctor not to go, Muste and two other clergymen traveled to North Vietnam, where he met with North Vietnamese premier Ho Chi Minh. He returned home bearing an invitation from Minh to President **Lyndon B. Johnson** requesting him to visit Hanoi in order to discuss an end to the war.

For Muste, pacifism and nonviolence were not simply tactics. He often said, "There is no way to peace. Peace is the Way." One night, while Muste was taking part in a vigil against the Vietnam War, a reporter asked him if he really thought that by standing outside the White House holding a candle night after night, he would change the policies of the country. Muste replied, "Oh, you've got it all wrong. I'm not doing this to change the country. I do it so the country won't change me."

CREDIT: Associated Press

Alice Stokes Paul
(1885–1977)

ALICE PAUL dedicated her life to the cause of women's equality. She was an architect of the movement that led to passage of the Nineteenth Amendment in 1920, giving women the right to vote. Viewing that victory as only a first step, Paul drafted the Equal Rights Amendment in 1923 but had to wait almost fifty years—until 1972—before Congress passed it, only to watch it die when too few states ratified it. In the 1930s and 1940s she worked with the League of Nations and then the United Nations to get those institutions to adopt the principle of gender equality. In the 1960s she spearheaded a coalition that added a sexual discrimination clause to Title VII of the 1964 Civil Rights Act, a landmark law that helped break down many barriers to women's equality.

The Paul family lived outside Moorestown, New Jersey, on a 265-acre farm they called "Paulsdale," with a large house with indoor plumbing, electricity, and a telephone. But they were not typical farmers. Her father was the president of a bank. Alice and her three younger siblings had some chores to perform, but hired workers did the actual farming, and maids did the cooking and cleaning. But the Pauls were not a typical rich family, either. Although they had many material comforts, they lived quite simply given their wealth.

Alice was descended from Hicksite Quakers, the most liberal and egalitarian wing of Quakers. They believed in gender equality and in working for the betterment of society—ideals Alice's parents instilled in her from an early age. Paul's mother was a member of the National American Woman Suffrage Association and sometimes took Alice with her to women's suffrage meetings. Paul attended a Hicksite Quaker school, graduating first in her class in 1901. It was a foregone conclusion that she would attend Swarthmore College, a co-ed Quaker institution that her grandfather, Judge William Parry, had helped start in 1864.

Paul's Swarthmore professors included some of the nation's leading female academics. One of them, math professor Susan Cunningham, liked to say, "Use thy gumption." Much of Paul's political life could be summarized by those words.

After graduating from Swarthmore, Paul earned a master's degree in sociology at the University of Pennsylvania. In 1907 she moved to England to practice social work among the poor at a Quaker-run settlement house in Birmingham. One day she heard a speech by Christabel Pankhurst, the daughter of Emmeline Pankhurst, the leader of the radical wing of England's feminist movement. Paul was intrigued by the Pankhursts' motto, "Deeds not words," which they translated into direct action, including heckling, rock throwing, and window smashing, to draw attention to the cause of women's rights. Not surprisingly, the women often got arrested for such protests, which led to newspaper photos of activists being carried away in handcuffs by the police.

Hesitant at first to join their militant crusade, Paul eventually overcame her fears and was arrested and jailed several times. In prison, she and other suffragettes protested their confinement with hunger strikes. Their jailers force-fed them. Paul took solace in a motto that one of her fellow activists carved into the prison wall: "Resistance to tyranny is obedience to God."

When Paul returned to the United States in 1910, she was determined to inject the radical ideas she had learned in England into the women's rights movement. While earning her Ph.D. in economics at the University of Pennsylvania (her dissertation examined women's legal status), she joined the National American Woman Suffrage Association (NAWSA). At the suggestion of **Jane Addams,** she was soon appointed head of the committee responsible for working for a federal women's suffrage amendment.

In 1912 she moved to Washington, DC, and joined forces with Lucy Burns, another American, whom she had met when they were both arrested in a London suffrage protest. The duo began planning an elaborate parade on the eve of Woodrow Wilson's presidential inauguration, scheduled for March 4, 1913. About 8,000 college, professional, middle- and working-class women marched with banners and floats down Pennsylvania Avenue from the Capitol to the White House. The crowd watching the march was estimated at half a million people; many harassed the marchers while the police stood by. Troops were called to restore order and to help the suffragists get to their destination—six hours after the parade started. The melee generated headlines, making the issue of women's suffrage a topic of conversation around the country.

Although Wilson showed some interest in the women's cause, he said the time was not yet right. Paul never believed that Wilson was the least bit sympathetic to women's suffrage. He would only support them, she thought, if public opinion compelled him to.

In this and other respects, Paul disagreed with NAWSA leaders. They endorsed Wilson, despite his opposition to women's suffrage, hoping they could eventually convince him. They worried that Paul's tactics could trigger a backlash. They also disagreed with Paul's emphasis on winning a federal amendment. The NAWSA's main focus was on winning women the vote one state at a time, hoping to build momentum that could later lead to a federal constitutional change. By 1912, however, only nine states had granted women the vote.

In reality, the two strategies complemented each other: even if the amendment was passed by Congress, it would have to be ratified in the states, where NAWSA was building its base.

But the broader disagreements led to a split. Paul and her followers first formed the Congressional Union in 1914, which became the National Woman's Party (NWP), an organization that recruited women prepared to engage in direct action. The NWP published a weekly paper and staged demonstrations, parades, mass meetings, picketing, hunger strikes, and lobbying vigils. Suffragists released from prison, wearing prison uniforms, rode a "Prison Special" train, speaking throughout the country.

Paul's critics called her a fanatic. Her loyal followers considered her a self-sacrificing heroine who inspired women to take risks for the cause. She was a charismatic figure who not only had incredible leadership skills but also was a gifted administrator, a rare combination. Despite her Quakerism, however, she reflected some of the attitudes of her upper-class background, including prejudices against Jews and African Americans. The NWP was overwhelmingly white, middle class, and Protestant.

Starting in January 1917, the NWP organized "silent sentinels"—activists standing outside the White House holding banners asking, "Mr. President, what will you do for suffrage?" and "Mr. President, how long must women wait for liberty?" Over the next eighteen months, more than 1,000 women picketed, including Alice, every day except Sunday. Wilson initially patronized the protesters, tipping his hat to them when he passed by. But when the United States entered World War I, the president and others became irate over the idea of women picketing outside the White House while the nation was at war. Angry mobs attacked the protesters, and police began arresting them on the trumped-up charge of obstructing traffic.

Sent to a prison in Virginia, Paul and her colleagues adopted the tactics she had learned in England. They demanded to be treated as political prisoners and staged hunger strikes. Their jailers beat them and confined them to cold, unsanitary, rat-infested cells.

The press reported on the suffragists' terrible experiences in prison, and politicians and activist groups demanded their release. The public outcry played a role in Wilson's decision in 1917 to reverse his stance and announce his support for a suffrage amendment. He explained that it was a "war measure"—to stop the controversy over women's rights from dividing the country during wartime.

But it was not until the war was over, in 1919, that both the House and the Senate passed the Nineteenth Amendment. Because the suffrage movement had invested heavily in state-level campaigns, its leaders were confident they could garner the three-fourths of the states needed to ratify the amendment. By the summer of 1920, they needed just one more state to vote in favor; the Tennessee legislature met in August 1920 to vote on the issue. The deciding vote was cast by Harry Burn, at twenty-four the youngest member of the Tennessee assembly. He initially intended to vote "no" but changed his vote after receiving a telegram from his mother asking him to support women's suffrage. Women finally gained the right to vote seventy-two years after the women's suffrage movement began.

Unlike many suffragists, however, Paul viewed the victory as simply a stepping-stone toward fuller women's equality. In 1923 she announced a campaign for another constitutional amendment that read, simply, "Men and women shall have equal rights throughout the United States and every place subject to its jurisdiction." What became known as the Equal Rights Amendment (ERA) split the women's movement. The League of Women Voters, the National Consumers League, the Women's Trade Union League, and other women's groups opposed the ERA on the grounds that it would abolish protective labor legislation for women.

With Paul's backing, the ERA was introduced in every session of Congress after 1923. In 1944 both the Republicans and the Democrats included the ERA in their party platforms. When Congress began debating the Civil Rights Act of 1964, Paul helped lead a coalition to add the word "sex" to Title VII, which banned discrimination in employment. Few members of Congress understood the importance of adding just that single word.

In 1972, when Paul was eighty-seven, the new women's movement got Congress to adopt the ERA, but only thirty-five states—three short of the number needed—ratified the amendment. By then, Paul, who had been out of the limelight for many years, had become a heroine to the new generation of feminists.

When a *Newsweek* reporter asked Paul to explain her remarkable perseverance in the struggle for women's rights, she recalled an adage she had learned from her mother while she was growing up on the family farm: "When you put your hand to the plow, you can't put it down until you get to the end of the row."

Sidney Hillman
(1887–1946)

SIDNEY HILLMAN, a longtime leader of the Amalgamated Clothing Workers of America (ACWA), believed that the labor movement should embrace the cultural, intellectual, and family concerns of its members as well as their bread-and-butter economic needs— a vision called "social unionism." From the 1920s through the 1950s, ACWA members and their families could live in union-sponsored apartments and be treated in union-sponsored health clinics. They could get loans from the union-sponsored Amalgamated Bank (opened in 1923), and they could obtain life insurance from the union, too. Union members participated in union-sponsored sports leagues (including women's softball) and took vacations at a retreat owned and run by the union. The union sponsored choral groups, put on plays and musicals, organized concerts of both classical and popular music, and sponsored classes and workshops on economics, politics, and history for its members. Retired garment workers could relax at one of the union's senior citizen centers.

What Hillman, ACWA's president from 1914 to 1946, helped achieve for his own union's members he hoped to win for all American working people. Although he did not win everything he hoped for, Hillman, as a founder of the Committee for Industrial Organization (which later became the Congress of Industrial Organizations) and a key adviser to President **Franklin D. Roosevelt,** was one of the chief architects of America's social welfare system.

Born to religious parents, at age fourteen Hillman was sent to Kaunas (Kovno), Lithuania, to study to be a rabbi. Inspired by the revolutionary fervor against czarist Russia, he quickly left the seminary to get a job so he could study politics and economics at night and aid labor organizers and political activists during the day. Hillman organized typesetters for an illegal Jewish union and was twice jailed for his political activity. Already an avid reader of Russian translations of Western social thinking (including works of Karl Marx, Charles Darwin, John Stuart Mill, and Herbert Spencer), he continued his political education in jail under the tutelage of fellow prisoners involved in the revolutionary movement. After participating in a failed uprising against the czar in 1905 and fearing the resulting crackdown, Hillman fled for England.

In 1907 Hillman moved to Chicago and began working as an apprentice cutter for Hart Schaffner & Marx (HSM), the nation's largest manufacturer of men's clothing. Three years later, a dozen women HSM workers, including a radical named Bessie Abramowitz, walked off the job. They were working ninety hours a week but earning only eight or nine dollars. The company had announced another wage cut, which, on top of its failure to pay overtime wages, pushed the women to the breaking point. The walkout triggered a four-month citywide garment strike of 45,000 workers, more than half of them women.

Most of the male HSM workers made fun of the initial group of women strikers, but Hillman was more sympathetic. Abramowitz and other women workers invited him to join them at Hull House, where **Jane Addams** had offered to host strategy meetings and help mediate the strike. Two months into the strike, the leaders of the United Garment Workers (UGW) tried to settle with the company without gaining any improvements. At a mass meeting of strikers, Hillman—speaking in a combination of Yiddish and broken English—denounced the deal and urged his fellow workers to continue the strike. Now recognized as a key strike leader, Hillman—with the help of Addams and lawyer **Clarence Darrow**—negotiated a favorable settlement. He also negotiated a relationship with Bessie. The two married in 1916, and she became an important union leader in her own right.

In 1914 Hillman, Abramowitz, and other Chicago strike leaders met with other disgruntled UGW members from Baltimore and New York at the union's national convention. Angry at the native-born UGW leaders for selling out the immigrant workers, they formed a breakaway union, the ACWA. Hillman, twenty-seven at the time, was elected ACWA president and set up office in New York.

Hillman knew he had a lot to learn. Addams and Darrow introduced him to their network of leading middle-class progressives and socialists, including **Florence Kelley** of the National Consumers League, Walter Lippmann, and Felix Frankfurter, all of whom advocated some version of "industrial democracy." The reformers were outraged by the clothing industry's exploitation of its workers, particularly its abuse of women and children. They provided valuable support for the fledgling ACWA, pushing for laws to protect employees and to regulate the brutal business practices made possible by laissez-faire capitalism.

For the next three decades, Hillman oversaw ACWA's huge growth, particularly in factories making men's garments. During World War I Hillman built a partnership between the union and the federal government to maintain production and improve working conditions in factories making military uniforms. This convinced him of the importance of government protection of workers and regulation of the economy on their behalf. By 1918 the ACWA had 138,000 members, had union contracts with 85 percent of men's garment manufacturers, and had reduced the workweek to forty-four hours.

Hillman gained the loyalty of his members by making the union a part of their daily lives and by winning victories at the workplace. But he was still a Jewish radical who viewed the union movement as a vehicle for transforming society. "Messiah is arriving," he wrote his young daughter toward the end of World War I. "He may be with us any minute—one can hear the footsteps of the Deliverer—if only he listens intently. Labor will rule and the world will be free."

Although he occasionally led strikes to break a logjam and show the union's strength, Hillman became known for forging positive relations with employers. Garment workers were often employed at small firms in a highly competitive industry where shops operated on a shaky profit margin, and wages were the businesses' largest cost. Hillman's strategy was to organize workers at all skill levels within the entire industry to prevent any shop from undercutting the wages of other employees. Sometimes, Hillman would even get the union to provide loans to employers to help struggling firms improve their management.

Hillman recognized labor's potential to wield political influence if unions mobilized their members and families in elections. In 1924 he and other progressive unionists supported **Robert M. La Follette**'s presidential campaign. In 1932 the upsurge of urban working-class voters, especially in the North and Midwest, catapulted FDR into the White House and brought huge Democratic majorities in Congress.

Hillman believed that the ACWA's success in organizing workers on an industry-wide basis could be duplicated in other major sectors, particularly those (like autos, steel, and chemicals, and unlike clothing) where goods are manufactured in relatively few large factories. In 1935 Hillman joined **John L. Lewis** and others to leave the American Federation of Labor and form what would become the CIO. Two years later, Hillman became the CIO's first vice president and spurred the creation of several new unions among textile and department store workers.

Many ACWA members—particularly Jewish immigrants—were socialists who believed that the labor movement should have its own political party as it did in Europe. So in New York—where the ACWA's headquarters was located— Hillman formed the American Labor Party. Radicals and Socialists could vote for FDR and other prolabor progressive candidates (such as **Fiorello La Guardia** and **Vito Marcantonio**) on the American Labor Party ticket, while the same candidates also ran on the major party tickets.

In 1944, under Hillman's leadership, the CIO formed the nation's first political action committee (PAC). Its primary goal was to help FDR win a fourth term and to help keep the Democrats in power in Congress, but it also sought to push a progressive policy agenda, called the "People's Program," that was somewhat to the left of FDR—including a national planning board, civil rights, and federal aid to education.

Throughout the Roosevelt administration, Hillman was constantly maneuvering to win support for stronger government involvement in economic planning and workplace regulations. Hillman envisioned a greater role for government in order to rescue Americans from the Depression and to guarantee full employment and job security. He pushed for a short workweek, public works, and unemployment insurance. He argued for national planning and a "more equitable distribution of our national income" in order to increase workers' buying power and dig the economy out of the Depression.

He worked closely with key New Dealers, including Senator **Robert F. Wagner** and Secretary of Labor **Frances Perkins,** to draft and pass the National Labor Relations Act (giving workers the right to unionize) and the Fair Labor Standards Act (establishing the minimum wage and forty-hour workweek).

In 1944 Republicans and conservative newspapers spread rumors, probably apocryphal, that FDR would respond to suggestions for vice presidential candidates by saying, "Clear it with Sidney." FDR's opponents used that phrase repeatedly to claim that the president was too beholden to labor. Anti–New Dealer William Randolph Hearst's *New York Journal-American* held a "Sidney Limerick Contest" to mock Hillman and his relationship with Roosevelt. Labeling Hillman a Socialist (an accurate description), the Republicans erected billboards with the slogan: "It's YOUR country—why let Sidney Hillman run it?"

Despite the conservative attacks, the CIO-PAC's work under Hillman became the model for building electoral organization among union members. It proved so successful that years later other groups—particularly big business as well as issue advocacy groups such as the National Rifle Association and the Sierra Club—adopted the PAC model for wielding electoral clout. For Hillman, the key to success was mobilizing members to work as campaign volunteers and to vote on election day, not simply to donate money.

Hillman died in 1946, but his close associates assumed the union's leadership. By the mid-1950s, the ACWA had about 350,000 members (two-thirds of them women), representing the vast majority of workers in the men's clothing industry. The ACWA (along with the International Ladies' Garment Workers union) had significantly raised garment workers' standard of living. Union leaders justifiably boasted that they had virtually eliminated the sweatshop. Americans could fill their closets with union-made clothing.

That reality is long gone. In the 1970s the clothing industry began moving its production overseas, particularly to Asia and Latin America. By 2000, most of the clothing Americans purchased in retail stores was imported. The number of clothing workers in the United States plummeted. A new wave of immigration from Asia and Mexico kept a segment of the industry in the United States—primarily in New York and Los Angeles—but the sweatshop had returned with a vengeance. Most of the sewing factories in the United States today violate wage, overtime, and workplace health and safety conditions. Thus Hillman's enduring legacies cannot be found in America's sewing factories. His legacies are, instead, his vision of social unionism, his successful efforts to expand the CIO industrial union movement, particularly among immigrant workers, and his brilliance at mobilizing union members in political campaigns to give labor a stronger voice in US politics.

Henry Wallace
(1888–1965)

ONE OF the great "what if?" questions of the 20th century is whether America would have been different if Henry Wallace rather than Harry S. Truman had succeeded **Franklin D. Roosevelt** in the White House. Wallace opposed the Cold War, the arms race with the Soviet Union, and racial segregation. He was a strong advocate of labor unions, national health insurance, and public works jobs. He would have been, without question, the most radical president in American history. Instead, if he is remembered at all, it is as a fringe candidate who ran on the Progressive Party ticket against Truman in 1948 and garnered less than 3 percent of the popular vote. That is unfortunate, because Wallace was a remarkable public servant who, as FDR's agriculture secretary (1933–1940) and then vice president (1940–1944), was, according to **John Kenneth Galbraith,** "second only to Roosevelt as the most important figure of the New Deal."

CREDIT: Library of Congress Prints and Photographs Division/Harris & Ewing Collection

Wallace was born on an Iowa farm in 1888. After graduating from Iowa State College in 1910, he went to work for his family's newspaper, *Wallaces' Farmer,* which was widely read by farmers and was influential in educating farmers about new scientific techniques and political issues shaping agricultural life. In 1921 Wallace took over as editor when his father became secretary of agriculture in the administrations of Warren G. Harding and then of Calvin Coolidge.

Wallace had a great passion for "scientific agriculture" and a talent for agricultural research. In 1926 he started the Hi-Bred Corn Company—later renamed Pioneer Hi-Bred—to market a new high-yield corn seed he had developed during his years conducting scientific experiments on a part-time basis. The company was hugely successful, making Wallace rich and his heirs secure. (DuPont bought the business for $9.4 billion in 1999.) The new company revolutionized American agriculture.

Wallace recognized that farming followed an unpredictable boom-and-bust cycle due to the weather, overproduction, and consumers' ability to pay for food. In the 1920s almost half of all Americans made their living directly or indirectly from agriculture. Wallace saw that farmers had not shared in the decade's prosperity and that their plight worsened when the economy crashed in 1929. Between

1929 and 1932 farm income fell by two-thirds. Farm foreclosures were occurring at a record pace. Farming communities were emptying, as family farmers and sharecroppers abandoned the land looking for jobs elsewhere, a situation portrayed in John Steinbeck's 1939 novel *The Grapes of Wrath* and in the film based on it.

As Adam Cohen recounts in his 2009 book *Nothing to Fear,* these experiences radicalized many farmers throughout the farm belt. In May 1932, for example, 2,000 farmers attended a rally at the Iowa state fairgrounds and urged fellow farmers to declare a "holiday" from farming, under the slogan "Stay at Home—Buy Nothing Sell Nothing." In effect, they were urging farmers to go on strike—to withhold their corn, beef, pork, and milk until the government addressed their problems. They threatened to call a national farmers strike if Congress did not provide farmers with "legislative justice." In Sioux City, Iowa, farmers put wooden planks with nails on the highways to block agricultural deliveries. In Nebraska, one group of farmers showed up at a foreclosure sale and saw to it that every item that had been seized from a farmer's widow sold for five cents, leaving the bank with a total settlement of just $5.35. In Le Mars, Iowa, a group of farmers kidnapped Judge Charles Bradley off the bench while he was hearing foreclosure cases and threatened to lynch him if he did not agree to stop foreclosures.

Wallace, a scientist and economist as well as a farmer, believed that the solution to the farm crisis was a combination of better farm management and government relief. Both Wallace and his father had been loyal Republicans, but in 1928 the younger Wallace changed his allegiance, supporting Democrat Al Smith for president. Four years later, Wallace endorsed FDR in the pages of his newspaper. Iowa, a traditionally Republican state, gave FDR almost 60 percent of its votes. Soon after winning the presidency, FDR recruited Wallace to become his secretary of agriculture—at forty-four, the youngest member of the cabinet.

The farm belt protests continued after FDR took office in March 1933. Wallace used the growing farm rebellion to persuade the president to support a number of innovative and controversial programs, including crop subsidies, to keep farmers afloat. Wallace was the key advocate for the Agricultural Adjustment Administration, the Rural Electrification Administration, the Soil Conservation Service, the Farm Credit Administration, and school lunch programs. Wallace added programs for soil conservation and erosion control. The department sponsored research to combat plant and animal diseases, to locate drought-resistant crops, and to develop hybrid seeds to increase farm productivity.

As a result, the US Department of Agriculture changed from a marginal department into one of the largest agencies, in size and influence, in Washington. Wallace's agency was also widely considered the best-run department in the federal government.

Business groups and Republicans in Congress opposed Wallace's plans, as they did most of the New Deal initiatives. Radical farm groups, like the National

Farmers Union, thought the plans did not go far enough. But it is clear that the New Deal farm programs saved the farm economy and helped stabilize rural areas.

Wallace, **Frances Perkins,** Harry Hopkins, and Rex Tugwell formed the progressive wing of FDR's inner circle. Wallace had FDR's ear on a wide variety of issues, and he used that influence to push for policies to help industrial workers and the urban poor as well as farmers. Wallace became the New Deal's evangelist. In 1934 alone, he traveled more than 40,000 miles to all forty-eight states, delivered eighty-eight speeches, signed twenty articles, published two books, and met regularly with reporters to promote the president and his program.

Because the fate of American farming was closely linked to global issues— particularly the export and import of food, but also hunger and famine around the world—Wallace was well versed in foreign affairs. In the late 1930s he became alarmed by the rise of fascist dictatorships in Germany, Italy, and Japan. Many midwesterners, including progressives, were still isolationists, but Wallace had become a vigorous internationalist and a strong advocate for "collective security" among the United States and its allies.

During FDR's first two terms, Wallace developed a broad following among farmers, union activists, and progressives. FDR was impressed by Wallace's popularity, his intelligence, and his integrity and believed that they shared a common view of government's role in society. In the summer of 1940, having decided to run for an unprecedented third term, FDR picked Wallace to be his vice presidential running mate.

During World War II, FDR involved Wallace in many military and international matters. Wallace also traveled throughout the war-torn world. FDR encouraged him to speak out about the possible shape of the postwar world. "Henry Wallace," wrote columnist James Reston in the *New York Times* in October 1941, "is now the administration's head man on Capitol Hill, its defense chief, economic boss and No. 1 post war planner."

Wallace faced significant opposition from the conservative wing of the Democratic Party. He feuded openly with Jesse H. Jones, a one-time Texas banker and businessman who was FDR's secretary of commerce and head of the Reconstruction Finance Corporation (RFC), which controlled the purse strings for purchasing wartime supplies. Wallace and Jones disagreed over the importing of essential materials for the war effort, such as rubber from South America. Wallace knew that about 40,000 workers were needed to extract the 20,000 tons of rubber that the United States needed each year. But each year, one-third of the rubber workers died and another third were too sick to work, afflicted with malaria, malnutrition, venereal disease, contaminated water, and other conditions. To guarantee a steady supply of rubber, Wallace (with Perkins's support) wanted the United States to provide the workers with healthy food and to require labor clauses in contracts with South American suppliers that mandated health and safety standards. Jones was adamantly opposed to Wallace's proposal and rounded up allies within the Roosevelt administration (including the State Department) and in Congress, including Republican Senator Robert Taft of Ohio, who accused Wallace of "setting up an international W.P.A."

On May 8, 1942, Wallace delivered a talk in New York City that became famous for his phrase "the century of the common man." It was, his biographers John C. Culver and John Hyde note, "as pure an expression of progressive idealism as Wallace could muster." Wallace defined America's wartime mission as laying the groundwork for a peaceful world of global cooperation, "a fight between a slave world and a free world." Modern science has made it possible for everyone to have enough to eat, Wallace said, but it will require cooperation among the major nations to raise the standard of living for the common man in every corner of the world.

The speech was Wallace's response to a 1941 article by Henry Luce, the publisher of *Time* and *Life* magazines, that called for an "American century" after the war—meaning a century dominated by the United States, "to exert upon the world the full impact of our influence, for such purposes as we see fit and by such means as we see fit."

Wallace's rebuttal was very explicit. He envisioned an end to colonialism, a world in which "no nation will have the God-given right to exploit other nations. Older nations will have the privilege to help younger nations get started on the path to industrialization, but there must be neither military nor economic imperialism." Wallace was aiming for a kind of global New Deal.

Millions of copies of Wallace's speech were distributed around the world, in twenty languages. It drew praise in liberal and progressive circles, but it also stirred controversy. The British prime minister, Winston Churchill—who hoped that Britain would still have an empire to run after the war—was upset by Wallace's stark anticolonial sentiments. American business groups objected to Wallace's views about economic imperialism. The *New York Times* and, of course, Luce's publications thought it was too radical.

Wallace's speech framed the debate between progressives and conservatives. Opponents viewed Wallace as naive, a dreamer, and a radical. These opponents included influential Democrats who worried that FDR might anoint Wallace as his successor, or at least give Wallace a big enough stage from which to launch a presidential bid once FDR had retired.

Led by Robert Hannegan, chairman of the Democratic National Committee, local and state party bosses quietly lobbied FDR to replace Wallace with Senator Harry Truman of Missouri. At the 1944 Democratic convention in Chicago, they got their way. Too busy with overseeing the American war effort to get in the middle of an intraparty battle, FDR let it be known that either Wallace or Truman would be an acceptable vice presidential pick. The party bosses maneuvered to hand Truman the nomination.

Wallace was deeply hurt by FDR's failure to back him, but he realized that he was not very good at playing hardball politics. After the election, FDR appointed Wallace to be secretary of commerce, but he stripped Wallace of control of the RFC, which he left in Jones's conservative hands. Wallace had a prestigious title, but he was no longer an influential insider. After FDR died in April 1945, Wallace continued to speak out in public, often in terms critical of Truman. Within a year Truman had purged most of FDR's key appointees. In September 1946 he fired Wallace, too.

On the three major issues facing postwar America—the Cold War and the arms race (particularly the atomic bomb), strengthening New Deal social policies and boosting organized labor, and addressing segregation and racism—Wallace believed that Truman was too cautious and conservative. These were themes Wallace would pick up on when he campaigned for president against Truman on the Progressive Party ticket in 1948. He attacked Truman's support for loyalty oaths to root out communists and radicals from government jobs, unions, and teaching positions in schools and universities. He called for national health insurance, an expanded public works program, and reparations for Japanese Americans who had been interned during the war. He said it was time to elevate women to "first-class citizenship." And when Wallace campaigned in the South, he refused to speak to segregated audiences.

On foreign policy, Wallace opposed the so-called Truman Doctrine, which aimed to contain communism through military intervention if necessary. He refused to support the Marshall Plan to rebuild Europe, considering it an instrument of the Cold War. He preferred a multilateral aid program that would be administered through the United Nations. Some early polls showed that Wallace had the support of more than 20 percent of the voters. Democratic Party officials, as well as some left-leaning union leaders, feared that even if Wallace could not win the election, he might attract enough Democratic voters that the White House would fall into the hands of the Republicans. Although his campaign initially attracted support from a wide political spectrum, much of that support soon withered as critics claimed that Wallace's campaign was filled with communists.

There *were* communists in key positions within the Wallace campaign, particularly among the left-wing unions that supported him after most other unions had abandoned his crusade. In some ways, Wallace was naive about the Soviet Union. He visited the port city of Magadan in Siberia in 1944 and described it as "combination TVA and Hudson's Bay Company." In reality, it was a slave-labor camp filled with political prisoners. Only later did he acknowledge that he had been conned by his Soviet guides.

Wallace believed in what would decades later be called "détente"—finding ways to cooperate with the Soviet Union rather than getting trapped in a spiraling arms race. Even as Cold War tensions were growing, Wallace simply did not subscribe to the anticommunist hysteria that emerged after the war. "I say those who fear communism lack faith in democracy," he said.

Truman beat Republican Thomas Dewey in a historic upset. Wallace received only 2.38 percent of the national vote. He even trailed third-place Strom Thurmond, the Democratic governor of South Carolina, who was running on the segregationist Dixiecrat Party ticket.

After this humiliating defeat, Wallace bought a farm in New York State, where he enjoyed working with plants and keeping chickens and made only occasional forays into public life. He was soon forgotten or reviled as a misguided radical. It is easy to see, with 20-20 hindsight, that running as the Progressive Party's presidential candidate transformed Wallace into a marginal figure. But an honest examination of his 1948 platform reveals that most of the ideas for which he was condemned as a radical are now viewed as common sense.

A. Philip Randolph
(1889–1979)

ON JUNE 18, 1941, A. Philip Randolph and Walter White sat down with President **Franklin D. Roosevelt** at the White House. The nation was gearing up for World War II, and African Americans were consistently being excluded from well-paying jobs with private defense contractors. The two civil rights leaders wanted the commander in chief to open up defense employment to blacks. They came armed with a threat: a march on Washington, DC, to demand defense jobs for African Americans. Randolph looked FDR in the eye and told him, "Time is running out. We want something concrete, something tangible, positive and affirmative."

"How many people do you plan to bring?" FDR asked him. "One hundred thousand, Mr. President," Randolph responded. This figure staggered the president. He turned to White, who headed the National Association for the Advancement of Colored People (NAACP). "Walter, how many people will really march?" FDR asked. "One hundred thousand, Mr. President," White said without hesitation.

FDR relented. A week later, on June 25, FDR signed Executive Order 8802, which Randolph had helped draft. It stated, "There shall be no discrimination in the employment of workers in defense industries or government because of race, creed, color, or national origin." The order also created a Fair Employment Practices Committee (FEPC) to investigate reports of discrimination. Randolph called off the march.

Randolph may have been bluffing. Could he have pulled off the threatened march of 100,000 African Americans? If anyone in America could have, it would have been A. Philip Randolph, and that is what FDR feared. At the time, Randolph was the most effective African American organizer in the country, the head of the largest black labor union (the Brotherhood of Sleeping Car Porters). He was a powerful voice for civil rights and had important allies among liberals, progressives, and radicals. Twenty-two years later, his ties to the civil rights and labor movements helped him organize the 1963 March on Washington for Jobs and Freedom, which had over 250,000 participants. Both of these marches—one canceled, the other carried out—were major milestones in America's march toward economic and racial justice.

The son of an ordained minister and a seamstress, Randolph grew up in Jacksonville, Florida. An outstanding student, he attended the Cookman Institute, the only academic high school in Florida for African Americans, where he excelled in literature, drama, and public speaking, starred on the baseball team, sang solos with its choir, and was valedictorian of his graduating class of 1907.

In 1911 Randolph moved to Harlem, the cultural, political, and economic capital of black America. He worked menial jobs while taking night courses in English literature and sociology at City College and participating in the radical intellectual and political ferment of the times. He was drawn to socialism and to acting. Fusing these interests, he initially found a calling as a soapbox orator on the streets of Harlem. He met Chandler Owen, a law student at Columbia University, and they formed a number of short-lived political, community, and labor groups. One was the Brotherhood of Labor, an employment agency in Harlem, which they hoped would catalyze union organizing among black workers, but it went nowhere.

In 1917 Randolph and Chandler started the *Messenger,* which they called "the only magazine of scientific radicalism in the world published by Negroes." It mixed politics and culture, promoted the Harlem Renaissance, socialism, and labor unions. In a March 1919 editorial Randolph wrote, "The history of the labor movement in America proves that the employing classes recognize no race lines. They will exploit a White man as readily as a Black man. They will exploit any race or class in order to make profits. The combination of Black and White workers will be a powerful lesson to the capitalists of the solidarity of labor."

Through his magazine, speeches, and political campaigns, Randolph made a name for himself. A. Mitchell Palmer, President Woodrow Wilson's attorney general, labeled Randolph the "most dangerous Negro in America" and arrested him for treason for his antiwar views; he spent two days in jail but was not prosecuted.

At the time, Randolph had done little to earn Palmer's label, but that would change. In 1925 a group of black porters for the Pullman Company came to him for help organizing for better wages and improvements in working conditions. The company hired black men as porters (waiters and luggage handlers) on its railroad sleeping cars, a form of luxury travel. At its peak, the Pullman Company was the largest single employer of black men in the United States, employing 12,000. Pullman porter was among the best-paid jobs available to black men and it offered the opportunity to travel around the country. But working conditions were onerous. Many porters worked as many as 80 to 100 hours a week. They were not paid for overnight layovers and were excluded from the better jobs, such as conductor, which were reserved for whites. They relied on tips for most of their income, which meant they had to endure the racist insults and rudeness of white passengers, including the indignity of being called "George" (the name of the company founder George Pullman) rather than by their own names.

The company was politically well connected (as **Eugene Debs** had learned the hard way in 1894). Soon after Randolph and others announced the formation of the Brotherhood of Sleeping Car Porters (BSCP), the company fired union members, threatened workers with tougher or fewer assignments if they showed any prounion sentiments, and branded Randolph as a Bolshevik.

Randolph worked tirelessly, though, traveling across the country, meeting with porters, trying to keep the organization together with limited funds and outside support. The *Messenger* became the union's official publication, but Randolph also generated publicity for the union in black newspapers and in some radical publications. Randolph became the public face of the organization, drawing on a core of activist porters as his key organizers. The porters admired Randolph's hard work and integrity, but for almost ten years the BSCP had little to show for Randolph's efforts.

The New Deal changed the odds. The Railway Labor Act of 1934 gave railroad workers the right to unionize. The next year, Randolph persuaded a vast majority of porters to endorse the BSCP as their collective voice in negotiations with Pullman. That year, the American Federation of Labor (AFL) voted to grant an international charter to the BSCP. After two more years of difficult negotiations, the Pullman Company finally signed a contract with the BSCP on August 25, 1937, a major milestone.

Randolph's goal was not simply to build a union of porters but, rather, to promote the idea of trade unionism to skeptical black workers. He also sought to persuade the white labor leadership that black workers deserved their support and should be part of union drives in every industry in which they toiled.

Randolph's national stature as a black leader was enhanced in 1936 when he was drafted as president of a new organization, the National Negro Congress (NNC), made up of about 200 black groups. Its goal was to build a mass movement of blacks, mostly by working through labor unions but also by promoting civil rights. Several key Committee for Industrial Organization (CIO) unions backed the new organization, and the NNC provided support for several union campaigns, encouraging black workers to join the industrial union movement. But Randolph soon realized that many of NNC's key union supporters were Communists who expected the NNC to support Communist Party positions on foreign-policy matters, including support of the Soviet Union. Randolph had been outmaneuvered. In 1940 Randolph resigned from the NNC but kept his position with the BSCP.

By then Randolph was an important figure in the black community. Still a Socialist, still dedicated to the labor movement, and still a crusader for civil rights, Randolph embarked on what some friends told him was an impossible task: to get the president to end racial discrimination in the defense industry and even desegregate the US military.

The boom in defense spending in anticipation of US entry into World War II created good jobs for white workers but not for blacks. Only 240 out of 107,000 workers in the aircraft industry were black. Even where they were hired, they were consigned to the worst jobs. Similarly, there were only 4,700 blacks among the US

Army's half a million soldiers. Only one (of four) Negro units was being trained for combat. There were no blacks in the US Marines, the Tank Corps, the Signal Corps, or the Army Air Corps. Blacks were often trained in segregated camps and were almost always assigned support duties—digging ditches, building roads, cooking and serving meals. Even the Red Cross blood supply was segregated.

After hearing Randolph speak about these issues, **Eleanor Roosevelt** arranged for Randolph, Walter White, and T. Arnold Hill (from the Urban League) to meet with FDR on September 27, 1940.

FDR listened but did not make any promises. Secretary of the Navy Frank Knox argued that white sailors would never accept blacks as equals on the same ship. FDR's chief military and cabinet advisers opposed integration. Angered by FDR's indifference, Randolph formulated a plan and came up with a slogan: "We loyal Negro Americans demand the right to work and fight for our country." He set up a National March on Washington Committee. He enlisted the NAACP, the Urban League, the porters, and black newspapers to spread the word. They set a date: July 1, 1941.

FDR heard about the proposed march but refused to schedule another meeting with Randolph to discuss it. Randolph kept the heat on, writing FDR letters demanding a meeting and upping the number of marchers to 100,000 African Americans—a frightening idea to the president and to most white Americans. At that point, FDR asked Eleanor to contact her friend Randolph and ask him to cancel the march. FDR eventually agreed to another meeting. After he issued the executive order, Randolph canceled the march.

In reality, the FEPC did not live up to Randolph's expectations. Discrimination in wages and seniority persisted in the defense industry. The armed services remained segregated. As blacks migrated to northern cities to take the worst jobs in the defense plants, they encountered racism from whites at work and in the housing market. Nevertheless, weak though it was, the FEPC marked the beginning of federal efforts to end racial discrimination in employment. Future efforts would build on this foundation.

Although FDR had promised much more than he delivered, Randolph—and America—had learned valuable lessons about power and about organizing. Whether or not he was bluffing, Randolph faced down the president with the threat of a massive protest march. FDR reluctantly agreed to Randolph's demands. In 1948 Randolph not only again threatened mass protest if President Harry S. Truman failed to order an end to segregation in the military, but he also urged black men to resist the draft until the president relented. Truman was furious, but he signed an executive order commanding integration of the armed forces and of federal civil service jobs.

Throughout the 1950s and 1960s, Randolph kept pushing on both the labor and civil rights fronts. In 1955 he became a vice president of the AFL-CIO's Executive Council, and in 1959 he helped found the Negro American Labor Council.

In 1955 one of Randolph's BSCP protégés, E. D. Nixon, recruited a young, newly arrived minister named **Martin Luther King Jr.** to lead the Montgomery bus boycott. In 1963 the civil rights movement was gathering momentum, but the various civil rights organizations competed for attention and funding. Randolph brought them all together to organize the massive March on Washington for Jobs and Freedom. Three years later, as **Lyndon B. Johnson**'s Great Society programs stalled because of the rising cost of the Vietnam War, Randolph led a coalition of progressives to propose a Freedom Budget for the nation, calling for spending $185 billion over ten years to fight poverty.

Randolph never gave up his socialist belief that unions and their members—regardless of race—are key to the struggle to redistribute society's wealth, provide good jobs for all, and create a more democratic society. And he persisted in his belief that strategic mass action, by a coalition of progressive, liberal, and radical forces, are central to making America live up to its ideals.

CREDIT: Associated Press/Henry Burroughs

Earl Warren
(1891–1974)

WHEN REPUBLICAN president Dwight D. Eisenhower nominated California's Republican governor Earl Warren to the US Supreme Court, he thought he was appointing a conservative jurist. Later, Eisenhower reportedly said that it was the "biggest damn fool mistake" he had ever made. Warren, chief justice from 1953 to 1969, took the Supreme Court in an unprecedented liberal direction. The Warren Court, which also included liberal justices **William O. Douglas, William J. Brennan,** and Hugo Black, dramatically expanded civil rights and civil liberties.

As a county prosecutor, state attorney general, and governor, Warren was probusiness, tough on crime, and zealously antiradical, even anti–New Deal. But once he was appointed to the Supreme Court, his other traits—a strong sense of fair play and respect for individual liberties—prevailed.

Warren used his considerable political skills to guarantee that the 1954 ruling in *Brown v. Board of Education* was unanimous. In two other landmark decisions, *Baker v. Carr* (1962) and *Reynolds v. Sims* (1964), the Warren Court established the principle of "one man, one vote," which ended the overrepresentation of rural areas in state legislatures.

In another milestone case, *Gideon v. Wainwright* (1963), the Warren Court ruled that in criminal cases courts are required to provide attorneys for defendants who cannot afford their own lawyers. In *New York Times Co. v. Sullivan* (1964), the Court significantly expanded free speech by requiring proof of "actual malice" in libel suits against public officials and public figures. The 1965 *Griswold v. Connecticut* decision established the right to privacy and laid the groundwork for *Roe v. Wade* (1973), the post-Warren ruling that gave women the right to have an abortion.

Anyone who watches a cop show on television knows that criminal suspects have a "right to an attorney" and a "right to remain silent." It was the Warren Court, in *Miranda v. Arizona* (1966), that ruled that detained suspects, prior to police questioning, must be informed of their constitutional rights to an attorney and against self-incrimination.

Warren's father was a longtime employee of the Southern Pacific Railroad. He lost his job after participating in the failed Pullman strike of 1894, led by **Eugene Debs.** Warren grew up in Bakersfield, California, graduated from the University of California, Berkeley, in 1912, and then graduated from its law school two years later. He worked for a year as counsel to an oil company, spent several years in private practice, and joined the Alameda County (Oakland), California, district attorney's staff as a deputy district attorney.

After running for and serving for thirteen years as Alameda County district attorney, Warren was elected California's attorney general in 1938. In that position, he played a key role in detaining Japanese Americans during World War II. After the Japanese bombed Pearl Harbor in December 1941, Warren and others believed that Japanese Americans posed a security risk as potential spies and saboteurs on behalf of Japan. Thousands of Japanese Americans lost their property and businesses. Only in retirement did Warren acknowledge that the relocation was a mistake based on hysteria.

In 1942 Warren was elected governor, and he was reelected in 1946 and 1950. During his administration, he expanded the state's higher education system and raised gasoline taxes to develop California's highway system. In 1948 he was the Republican Party's vice presidential candidate on a ticket with Thomas Dewey, which lost to incumbent Harry S. Truman. It was the only election he ever lost.

It was an accident of timing that Warren's first major test as chief justice, one that ultimately defined his reputation as a liberal and activist jurist, was *Brown v. Board of Education.* The National Association for the Advancement of Colored People's legal team, led by **Thurgood Marshall,** had worked for years to bring cases to lower courts challenging laws mandating the segregation of public schools, hoping to chip away at the entrenched doctrine. Many of the plaintiffs took enormous personal risks to defy the Jim Crow status quo.

Finally, in December 1952, the Court heard the arguments in the *Brown* case. Under Chief Justice Fred Vinson, the Court was deeply divided on whether school segregation was constitutional. Vinson had written the Court's opinions ordering the admission of the black students to all-white universities in Texas and Oklahoma, but several of his Court colleagues believed that when it came to public schools, he favored maintaining the "separate but equal" precedent adopted in *Plessy v. Ferguson* (1896).

In June 1953 the Court ordered the reargument of the *Brown* case. Vinson died in September before the new hearing took place. In what may be an apocryphal story, Justice Felix Frankfurter, thinking about the upcoming reargument, stated that Vinson's death "is the only evidence I have ever had for the existence of God."

Eisenhower appointed Warren the chief justice before the Court heard the new arguments in the *Brown* case in December 1953. Knowing that the decision would be politically controversial, Warren sought a unanimous decision. He assigned the job of writing the opinion to himself, and then, like a shrewd politician, he met with each of his eight colleagues separately and listened to their views in order to construct a decision that they could all agree on. After he brought the last holdout, Justice Stanley Reed, on board, Warren drafted the ruling. "We cannot turn the clock back," Warren wrote. "We must consider public education in the light of its full development and its present place in American life throughout the Nation. Only in this way can it be determined if segregation in public schools deprives these plaintiffs of the equal protection of the laws."

Although the decision narrowly held that *Plessy*'s "separate but equal" formula did not apply to the field of public education, the decision was explosive in terms of its political impact. It helped trigger a new wave of civil rights activism and also catalyzed a countermovement of resistance to desegregation, particularly in the South. Warren suggested the Court delay for a year the order implementing its decision. In the *Brown II* decision, issued on May 31, 1955, the Court ordered that school districts be desegregated "with all deliberate speed."

Eisenhower was angry at Warren for the *Brown* ruling. According to Warren's memoirs, Eisenhower told him that southerners "are not bad people. All they are concerned about is to see that their sweet little girls are not required to sit in school alongside some big overgrown Negroes."

The *Brown* decision made Warren a controversial public figure. A grassroots movement emerged throughout the South, including the rise of groups such as the White Citizens Council and a new wave of Ku Klux Klan activism, to defy the Court's ruling. One hundred and one members of Congress, all from the South, signed the Southern Manifesto pledging to defy court-ordered desegregation. Billboards erected by the right-wing John Birch Society saying "Impeach Earl Warren" dotted the South and elsewhere.

Many of the Warren Court's later decisions also outraged conservatives, who believed that the Republican politician had become a judicial activist, making social policy and upending the Founding Fathers' ideas about the Constitution. During his 1968 campaign for president, Richard Nixon pledged to appoint a Supreme Court justice who would overturn the Warren Court's rulings.

Although critics have accused Warren of being a judicial activist, his decisions simply exposed the political nature of the Supreme Court and of the judiciary in general. The Court's rulings have always tended to reflect at least three overlapping influences: the ideological views of the presidents who appoint justices, current events and public opinion, and the legal outlooks of the justices. Twenty-first century rulings by Republican-appointed Court majorities—such as the 5–4 *Bush v. Gore* ruling that handed George W. Bush the presidency in 2000 and the 5–4 *Citizens United v. Federal Election Commission* decision in 2010 to give corporations the unlimited ability to contribute to political campaigns—are examples of how conservative justices often interpret the Constitution to justify their own political and ideological activist agendas.

As chief justice, Warren may have been ahead of public opinion on many civil liberties and civil rights issues, but he was in sync with what **Martin Luther King Jr.** called the arc of history, helping to bend it toward justice.

Floyd Olson
(1891–1936)

FLOYD OLSON was the 20th century's most successful third-party politician. Running on the Farmer-Labor Party (FLP) ticket, a progressive alliance of rural farmers and urban workers, Olson won three terms as Minnesota's governor, defeating Democratic and Republican candidates. He served as governor from 1931 until his death in 1936. "I am not a liberal," Olson said. "I am what I want to be—a radical."

Like his predecessors and fellow governors, **Robert M. La Follette Sr.** of Wisconsin and **Hiram Johnson** of California, Olson viewed state government as a laboratory for progressive ideas, many of which would later be adopted at the national level. Had he not died of stomach cancer at age forty-four in August 1936 during his third term as governor, his record, reputation, and legacy would be better known.

Olson was born in Minneapolis in 1891 to poor immigrant parents—a Swedish mother and Norwegian father, a railroad worker. After graduating from high school in 1909, he enrolled at the University of Minnesota but got in trouble constantly for refusing to participate in mandatory Reserve Officer Training Corps drills and for wearing a derby hat in violation of university rules. After a year, he dropped out. He took series of odd jobs in Canada and Alaska before moving briefly to Seattle, Washington, where he worked as a stevedore on the docks and joined the Industrial Workers of the World. These experiences, along with his appetite for reading, radicalized Olson.

Olson returned to Minnesota in 1913 and attended law school at night. He graduated at the top of his class, earned his degree in 1915, and began to practice law. In 1919, at age twenty-eight, he was appointed Hennepin County's assistant attorney and the next year became county attorney, a position he held for ten years. He was also active in the American Civil Liberties Union. Olson made a name for himself prosecuting corrupt businessmen and the Ku Klux Klan, which was making a comeback in some northern cities. With his reputation for honesty and courage, he won reelection in 1922 and 1926. Olson joined the Minnesota Farmer-Labor Party, which was founded in 1918 and quickly gained strength as part of an upsurge of radical populism, particularly in the Midwest. Some of its key leaders had been active in the Socialist Party (which had elected mayors in Minnesota, Wisconsin, and other states), the Non-Partisan League (a progressive political organization of farmers), and the Duluth Union Labor Party. The Minnesota Farmer-Labor Party's platform called for protection of farmers and labor union members, government ownership of some industries, and old-age insurance. By the 1920s and 1930s the FLP had successfully challenged the Republican Party's longtime domination of state politics. In those decades, the FLP elected three governors, four US senators, and eight US representatives.

In 1924, while serving as Hennepin County attorney, Olson ran for governor on the FLP ticket but lost to the Republican candidate. By the time he ran again in 1930, Minnesota's workers and farmers—their livelihoods and self-confidence destroyed by the Depression—were ready for his radical platform. He won election with 57 percent of the vote, garnering support from white-collar professionals and small business owners as well as from workers and farmers. The six foot two, handsome, and charismatic Olson easily won reelection twice. The FLP's 1934 platform called for a "cooperative commonwealth" that included public ownership of all industry, insurance, banking, and public utilities and tough regulation of business.

Despite Olson's popularity, the FLP never controlled the Minnesota legislature during his three terms as governor, and he was constantly at odds with the conservatives in the State House. Despite this, he often outmaneuvered the legislature by mobilizing union members, farmers, and small businesspersons to lobby for progressive bills that expanded public works, regulated securities, promoted consumer- and worker-owned cooperative enterprises, and conserved natural resources. Like **Franklin D. Roosevelt,** he used his oratorical skills through the new medium of radio to broadcast his views and rally rural and urban voters to win elections and lobby the legislature for his progressive agenda.

During his first term (1931–1933), the conservatives in the legislature thwarted most of Olson's programs except the funding of a major highway building program. By the time he began his second term in 1933, the Depression had gotten much worse. A quarter of Minnesotans were out of work. Farmers were devastated by falling prices, rising debt, and a serious drought. Farmers organized protests to stop sheriffs from carrying out foreclosures. In his second inaugural address, Olson outlined the situation in dire terms:

We are assembled during the most critical period in the history of the Nation and our state. An army of unemployed; some 200,000 homeless and wandering boys; thousands of abandoned farms; an ever-increasing number of mortgage foreclosures; and thousands of people in want and poverty are evidences not only of an economic depression but of the failure of government and our social system to function in the interests of the common happiness of the people. Just beyond the horizon of this scene is rampant lawlessness and possible revolution. Only remedial social legislation, national and state, can prevent its appearance.

Olson immediately took bold action. He ordered a halt to all foreclosure sales and declared a bank holiday to keep Minnesotans from withdrawing their savings and destroying the financial system.

With the state government, county governments, and school districts unable to pay their bills, Olson proposed—and the legislature reluctantly passed—a progressive income tax, Minnesota's first. Emboldened, Olson continued to press for and won more reforms. According to historian Russell Fridley in an article in *Minnesota Law and Politics*:

> [Olson's reforms included] a tax on chain stores, bank reorganization, municipally owned liquor stores, ratification of the federal amendment prohibiting child labor, large appropriations for relief, a two-year moratorium on farm foreclosures, an old-age pension system, incentives to form business cooperatives, a ban on injunctions in labor disputes, limiting hours worked by women in industrial jobs to 54 per week, creation of 13 state forests and the beginning of state protection over what became the Boundary Waters Canoe Area Wilderness. His losses were few: his plans for unemployment compensation and a state-owned hydroelectric plant were defeated, while the legislature voted to freeze state employee salaries (a measure he strongly opposed).

Olson used the power of his office to negotiate an end to the meatpackers strike against the Hormel Company. The settlement included revenue sharing for workers—a significant milestone in US labor history To end a bitter truck drivers strike that had led to the death of three workers, Olson declared martial law. Having the governor on their side helped the workers win union recognition from a reluctant employer.

Ordinary Minnesotans admired Olson for his working-class roots and his common touch. He used fiery rhetoric to inspire and mobilize his followers and to win support for his progressive programs. He said, "Minnesota is definitely a left-wing state," and he observed, "If the so-called depression deepens, the government ought to take and operate the key industries of the country." In a 1935 article in *Common Sense,* Olson wrote, "A third party must arise and preach the gospel of government and collective ownership of the means of production and distribution." At the same time, Olson was friendly with many wealthy Minnesotans who opposed his political views but who mingled with him socially at summer resorts and country clubs.

Many of Olson's supporters wanted him to run as a third-party candidate for president in 1936. He flirted with the idea. "Whether there will be a third party in 1936," Olson told an interviewer, "depends mainly on Mr. Roosevelt." He thought that Bob La Follette Jr. (the progressive Republican senator from Wisconsin and son of the late governor) or Burton Wheeler (the Democratic senator from Montana) might be the best third-party candidates. "I think I'm a little too radical," Olson acknowledged. "How about 1940?" the interviewer asked. "Maybe by then I won't be radical enough," Olson replied.

Despite the rhetorical teasing, Olson admired FDR and was not interested in challenging him. Instead, he decided to leave the governorship and run for the US Senate seat, hoping to serve as a progressive pro–New Deal voice in Washington. He was favored to win, but in late 1935, he was diagnosed with cancer. He died in August 1936, his political career cut short, forgoing a more visible role on the national stage that, some predicted, could have eventually led to the White House.

Olson's popularity, political skills, and policy program moved Minnesota decisively to the left. Under subsequent FLP governors and (after the FLP merged with the Democratic Party in 1944) under Democratic-Farmer-Labor Party leaders, Minnesota remained one of the nation's most progressive states. Olson expanded the state's public education system and created a social safety net and a government jobs program that, in tandem with the New Deal, cushioned the pain of the Depression for Minnesotans and left a legacy of buildings, highways, libraries, hospitals, conservation projects, and playgrounds that improved life for decades afterward. Olson also shaped Minnesota's ideological direction, cementing his enduring reputation for supporting high taxes, robust public services, and social compassion.

Dorothy Day
(1897–1980)

DOROTHY DAY founded the Catholic Worker movement, which was established on the principles of militant pacifism, radical economic redistribution, and direct service to the poor. She influenced generations of activists through her newspaper, the *Catholic Worker,* and through Catholic Worker houses located in urban slums, which provided food and shelter to the destitute. She had a major influence on generations of activists, including **Michael Harrington, Cesar Chavez,** Daniel Berrigan, and Philip Berrigan.

Day was raised in a bookish family, nominally Episcopalian but not religious. The Days moved around the country as her father, a sports reporter, pursued jobs. When she was a teenager, the family lived in Chicago. Upton Sinclair's novel *The Jungle* inspired her to take long walks in Chicago's poor neighborhoods. Her brother, Donald, who wrote for a progressive newspaper, the *Day Book,* encouraged her to learn about radical politics. She read about **Eugene Debs,** the Industrial Workers of the World (the Wobblies), and the Haymarket anarchists and was drawn to the ideas of anarchist Peter Kropotkin.

In 1916 Day dropped out of the University of Illinois after two years and moved to New York City, where she got involved in bohemian and radical circles. The chain-smoking Day looked for a job as a journalist, but none of the major newspapers would hire a woman reporter. Undeterred, she convinced the editor of the *Call,* a socialist paper, to pay her $5 a week. Day covered strikes and peace meetings and even interviewed Leon Trotsky, the Russian revolutionary. (He was so critical of American Socialists that Day's editor gutted the piece.) Day later wrote for other Socialist publications, including the *Masses* and the *Liberator.*

In November 1917 Day was one of forty women arrested and then briefly jailed during a rally in front of the White House to protest the brutal treatment of imprisoned suffragist **Alice Stokes Paul.** After they arrived in prison, Day and other women launched a hunger strike and were eventually freed by presidential order. It was the first of her many arrests.

As a young woman, Day rejected the sexual mores of her time. She became pregnant and had an abortion, a decision she deeply regretted, which she described in her semiautobiographical novel, *The Eleventh Virgin* (1924).

In 1924 she fell in love with botanist Forster Batterham, an atheist and anarchist who was opposed to marriage and to having children. They lived together for four years. When she became pregnant again, she was ecstatic, but Batterham opposed her decision to have the baby. Their daughter, Tamar, was born in 1926.

Day was a religious agnostic, but she occasionally attended services at Catholic churches, which she viewed as the churches of immigrants and the poor. Tamar's birth triggered a spiritual epiphany that led her to officially join the Catholic Church the next year. Gradually, her relationship with Batterham fell apart as Day grew increasingly religious.

Initially Day felt like an impostor, embarrassed at not knowing the proper rites. But her religion soon became her foundation, with prayer and Mass an important part of her daily life. In explaining her conversion later, she wrote, "My very experience as a radical, my whole makeup, led me to want to associate myself with others, with the masses, in loving and praising God."

Day began to write for Catholic publications such as *Commonweal* and *America*, where she fused socialist ideas with Catholic social teaching. In 1932 Day visited Washington, DC, to cover a Hunger March sponsored by the Communist-led Unemployment Councils. She felt herself drawn to the dispossessed marchers. She wondered why the Catholic Church was nowhere to be seen. "Is there no choice but that between Communism and industrial capitalism?" she wrote. "Is Christianity so old that it has become stale, and is Communism the brave new torch that is setting the world afire?"

That year Day met Peter Maurin, the man who would set her on her path. She called him "the French peasant whose spirit and ideas would dominate the rest of my life." Like Day, he was a journalist and a convert. He had heard of Day through the editor of *Commonweal* and he sought her out, offering to mentor her in Catholic social teaching. She later wrote that Maurin was "a genius, a saint, an agitator, a writer, a lecturer, a poor man, and a shabby tramp, all in one." He also was a compulsive talker who never stopped "indoctrinating" Day, as he put it, and anyone else who would listen.

Through Maurin's teaching, Day began to embrace the idea of poverty as a way of life, sharing with others, paring away material goods, and creating a community based on Christian love. Maurin envisioned an action program that included a newspaper, roundtable discussions, hospitality houses, and agrarian communes.

With virtually no seed money, Day launched the *Catholic Worker,* publishing the first issue on May 1, 1933. She assembled the tabloid at her kitchen table and had 2,500 copies published by the Paulist Press for $57. She and some friends hawked the paper to passersby in Union Square for a penny a copy.

Her timing could not have been better. It was the midst of the Depression, and a newspaper aimed at the downtrodden—radical but not doctrinaire—had plenty of appeal. Within a few months, the print run had increased to 25,000, and it rose to 110,000 within two years. In addition to addressing labor issues, the *Catholic Worker* tackled other topics that the regular Catholic press would not touch, including racism, lynching, and corporate greed.

As the newspaper attracted a following, Day and Maurin sought to put their principles into practice. In 1933 Day, Maurin, and a small group of followers launched the Worker School, followed by the first Catholic Worker house in a Harlem storefront. They soon rented an apartment with space for ten women, and then a place for men. The Catholic Workers continued to participate in direct action as well as service. They picketed the German consulate in 1935 to protest the rise of Nazism, walked picket lines with striking workers, and helped on breadlines. They also attempted to launch a garden commune on Staten Island as a sanctuary for people living in New York's tenement slums. However, the project was unsustainable, in part because many who made their way out from the city had little interest in hard manual work.

In 1936 they moved into two buildings in Chinatown and opened them to house the poor. The staff of these "hospitality houses" (who received only food, board, and occasional pocket money) did not try to convert their guests to Catholicism or radicalism. They imposed no conditions.

Although many in the church welcomed or at least tolerated the Catholic Worker, others were appalled, in part by Maurin and Day's acceptance of any poor person who needed help, no matter his or her background or circumstances. Day's strong personality was called "dynamic" by admirers and "domineering" by detractors. She believed not in majority rule but, rather, in inspiration by take-charge visionaries. Day never knew how she would pay the bills, but she had faith that donations would arrive, which they usually did.

By 1936 the Catholic Worker movement had opened thirty-three hospitality houses around the country. The houses all had "colorful and slightly mad characters who drifted in to partake, more or less permanently, of Worker hospitality," according to William D. Miller's biography of Day, *A Harsh and Dreadful Love.*

As a young radical, Day rejected war as serving only capitalist interests, pitting workers from different nations against each other. After her conversion to Catholicism, she remained a pacifist, based on her interpretation of Gospel teaching— but her stance was often contrary to the views of the Catholic Church. The outbreak of the Spanish Civil War tested her pacifist views. Most leaders of the Catholic Church supported the fascist general Francisco Franco, seeing the battle as one of Christianity versus communism. Day received a great deal of hate mail when she refused to take sides in the war because of her pacifist beliefs. But Day viewed Franco as Adolf Hitler's ally and was one of the founders of the Committee of Catholics to Fight Anti-Semitism.

Animosity toward her pacifism grew stronger as the United States prepared to enter World War II. Circulation of the *Catholic Worker* dropped dramatically— from 190,000 in 1938 to 50,500 in 1946.

Day never wavered. In the 1950s her strong antiwar stance led her to oppose civil defense drills, which she believed duped people into believing nuclear war was survivable. She and other Catholic Workers sat on park benches when ordered to take shelter, and for this she was arrested three times and once sentenced to a month in jail.

Day actively opposed the Vietnam War, and she was close to the Berrigan brothers, both Catholic priests, when they were jailed for draft resistance. In 1973, when she was seventy-six and in failing health, she traveled to the San Joaquin Valley in California to demonstrate with Cesar Chavez and the United Farm Workers union. Along with a thousand others, she was jailed—for the final time.

Today, the Catholic Worker movement has 185 communities around the world, including one in Uganda, which opened in 2011.

The hierarchy of the Catholic Church marginalized Day for her radicalism, but toward the end of her life she was honored by many organizations, including the University of Notre Dame. Although she was known to say, "Don't call me a saint. I don't want to be dismissed so easily," many Catholics have tried to get Day canonized by the Catholic Church for her lifetime of social and spiritual activism.

Paul Robeson
(1898–1976)

Paul Robeson arrives at New York's Idlewild Airport from England after a five-year absence in 1963.
CREDIT: Associated Press/Harry Harris

PERHAPS THE most all-around-talented American of the 20th century, Paul Robeson was an internationally renowned concert singer, actor, college football star and professional athlete, writer, linguist (he sang in twenty-five languages), scholar, orator, lawyer, and activist in the civil rights, union, and peace movements. Despite his fame, his name was virtually erased from memory by government persecution during the McCarthy era. He was blacklisted, his concerts were canceled, and his passport was revoked.

Robeson's mother, a teacher, died when Paul was six. His father, the Reverend William Drew Robeson, who had escaped from slavery at age fifteen in 1850, raised Paul and his four older siblings. Reverend Robeson served as pastor of a church in Princeton, New Jersey, until the church's white elders fired him for speaking out against social injustice. For a while he worked as a coachman, but he eventually managed to find other pulpits.

After excelling in academics and sports in high school, Robeson attended Rutgers, back then a private college, on a scholarship in 1915. He was the third black student at Rutgers and its first black football player. His own teammates roughed up the six-foot-three Robeson on the first day of scrimmage, and he constantly endured racial slurs and physical harassment from opposing players. His father had impressed upon him, he later recalled, that he was not there on his own but rather was "the representative of a lot of Negro boys who wanted to play football and wanted to go to college."

Robeson was elected to Phi Beta Kappa in his junior year and was the valedictorian of his 1919 graduating class. He won the Rutgers oratory award four years in a row. Although a member of the college glee club, he was not allowed to travel with the group or participate in its social events. He earned varsity letters in football, baseball, basketball, and track. He was twice named to the College Football All-America Team, but he was benched when Rutgers played southern teams, who would not take the field with a black player playing for the opposing team. A "class prophecy" in the college yearbook predicted that by

1940 he would be the governor of New Jersey as well as "the leader of the colored race in America."

After graduation, Robeson moved to Harlem and studied law at Columbia University, earning his degree in 1923. He helped pay for law school by playing professional football. However, when he took a job at a private law firm, his supervisors made it clear that he would never be considered a professional equal. The last straw was a white secretary's refusal to take dictation from him. He quit and never practiced law again.

Fortunately, while Robeson was in law school his wife had persuaded him to perform in small theater roles, and he quickly launched a new career as an actor and concert singer. In 1924, a year out of law school, he got the lead in Eugene O'Neill's *All God's Chillun Got Wings* at a Greenwich Village theater. Critics praised Robeson's performance, but he could not find a restaurant in that liberal neighborhood that would serve him. Next he played the central character in O'Neill's *The Emperor Jones,* about an ex-convict who escapes to a Caribbean island and sets himself up as emperor. The following year, Robeson launched his career as a concert singer with a recital of Negro spirituals. From that point on, his solo concerts and recordings were the core of his work as a performer, and he won increasing fame as an actor on stage and in film.

Robeson had a powerful bass-baritone voice and a commanding presence on stage. He was tall, handsome, and self-confident. He performed with dignity even the demeaning and stereotypical roles available to black actors at the time.

In 1928 Robeson was invited to sing the part of Joe in the London production of *Show Boat,* which had been a huge hit in New York. The musical chronicles the lives of people working on a Mississippi River showboat, but its black characters reflected the era's stereotypes. Robeson sang "Ol' Man River," which became one of his trademark songs throughout his career. In the London show he sang the original lyrics, which begin "Niggers all work on the Mississippi." Within a few years, he changed the first word to "darkies," performing the song in concerts, and when he made the film version in 1936, he transformed the opening line entirely to "There's an ol' man called the Mississippi; that's the ol' man I don't like to be." He also eventually changed the line "I'm tired of livin' and feared of dyin'" to the more militant and political "I must keep fightin' until I'm dying."

Although Robeson disliked most of his film roles for reinforcing negative stereotypes of Africans and African Americans, a few of them allowed him to play parts several notches above the typically demeaning parts available to black actors. In *The Proud Valley,* he played David Goliath, a black American miner who gets a job in a Welsh mine, joins a male choir made up of other coal miners, and eventually dies in a mine accident while saving his fellow workers. This independently produced movie, filmed on location in the Welsh coalfields, documents the harsh realities of coal miners' lives and showed Robeson's character in particular in a positive light, merging his artistic and political talents.

In 1930 he became the first black man in almost a century to play Othello in England. It would be another thirteen years, in 1943, before he performed the role in the United States; even then, having a black man play a romantic lead, especially with a white woman as Desdemona, was controversial. However, the production ran for 296 performances, a record for a Shakespeare play on Broadway.

Robeson and his family spent much of the 1930s living in England and traveling and performing throughout Europe. In England he faced less overt racial prejudice and greater social acceptance than in the United States. His travels awakened his political consciousness. In London he met Jomo Kenyatta and other young Africans who would soon lead independence movements, triggering Robeson's awareness of the emerging struggles by nonwhite peoples against colonialism.

In 1934 he visited Germany, where the Nazis had just taken power, and said the atmosphere felt like a "lynch mob." That same year he visited the Soviet Union and was impressed by the lack of racial bigotry of the Russian people.

As his fame grew, Robeson filled the world's largest concert halls and used his celebrity to speak out on political issues. In 1933 he donated the proceeds of *All God's Chillun* to Jewish refugees fleeing Hitler's Germany. At a 1937 rally for antifascist forces fighting in the Spanish Civil War he declared, "The artist must take sides. He must elect to fight for freedom or slavery. I have made my choice. I had no alternative." In New York in 1939 he starred in a network radio premiere of Earl Robinson's "Ballad for Americans," a patriotic cantata that celebrated America's racial and ethnic diversity and its tradition of dissent. Robeson and Bing Crosby recorded the piece, which was so popular that it was performed at both the Republican and Communist Party conventions in 1940.

During World War II, Robeson was at the height of his fame. His concerts of Negro spirituals and international songs drew huge audiences. His recordings sold well. In polls, Americans ranked Robeson as one of their favorite public figures. He entertained troops at the front and sang battle songs on the radio. He was a frequent presence at rallies and benefits for left-wing causes. In Los Angeles in September 1942, he gave a free concert for thousands of workers at an aviation plant.

In 1943 Robeson headed a delegation of blacks who met with the baseball commissioner Kenesaw Mountain Landis and major league baseball owners to demand the desegregation of baseball. (The Brooklyn Dodgers signed **Jackie Robinson** to a contract two years later.) In 1945 he headed an organization that challenged President Harry S. Truman to support an antilynching law.

When World War II ended and the Cold War began, Robeson's outspoken support for the Soviet Union became highly controversial. His biographer Martin Duberman suggests that privately Robeson had begun to have doubts about the Soviet Union, particularly its mistreatment of Jews. When he visited Russia in 1949, he insisted on seeing his friend Itzik Feffer, a Jewish writer, whom the Soviets had arrested. Feffer told him about widespread official anti-Semitism in the Soviet Union, including the arrests and show trials. At his concert in Moscow, Robeson made a point of talking about Feffer and then singing, in Yiddish, the anthem of the Warsaw Ghetto resistance, clearly a statement of solidarity with Russian Jewish dissidents. But when speaking in the United States, Robeson never uttered any criticism of the Soviet Union, leading many to suspect that he was a communist.

Once he was asked why, being so critical of the United States, he did not move to the Soviet Union. "Because my father was a slave, and my people died to build this country," Robeson said, "and I am going to stay right here and have a part of it."

In 1948 Robeson campaigned enthusiastically for **Henry Wallace**'s Progressive Party campaign for president.

The attacks on Robeson escalated dramatically after he spoke at the Congress of the World Partisans of Peace in Paris in 1949. Robeson said that American workers, white and black, would not fight against Russia or any other nation. In the United States, however, the media misreported his remarks, interpreting them to mean that black Americans would not defend the United States in a war against the Soviet Union.

After that, it was open season on Robeson. He was denounced by the media, politicians, and conservative and liberal groups alike as being disloyal to the United States and a shill for the Soviet Union. Even civil rights groups—eager to avoid the taint of communism—distanced themselves from Robeson, who had received the Spingarn Medal, the highest award given by the National Association for the Advancement of Colored People, only four years earlier.

In 1950 the US State Department revoked Robeson's passport, claiming that his travel overseas would be "contrary to the best interests of the United States." The loss of his passport prevented him from performing in Europe and Australia, where he was still enormously popular. His American concerts were canceled, too. Record companies stopped recording him. NBC barred Robeson from appearing on a television show with **Eleanor Roosevelt.** He received frequent death threats. Right-wing groups violently disrupted the few concerts he performed, sponsored by left-wing groups, such as a benefit concert for the Civil Rights Congress in Peekskill, New York, in August 1949. Unable to perform regularly, Robeson's income declined from $100,000 in 1947 to $6,000 in 1952.

Robeson could not travel abroad until a 1958 US Supreme Court ruling, written by **William O. Douglas,** overturned travel bans based solely on someone's beliefs and associations. He made triumphant concert tours in England, Australia, and Russia and performed at a sold-out recital at Carnegie Hall in New York, but the eight years of persecution and enforced idleness had taken a tremendous toll on his physical and mental health as well as his income. He suffered from debilitating depression and spent the last fifteen years of his life in relative seclusion.

Robeson was too isolated to play a role in the civil rights movement; his accomplishments and very existence were practically erased from public memory. It was not until the late 1970s that Robeson's admirers—boosted by the upsurge of black studies and black cultural projects, plus the waning of the Cold War—began to rehabilitate his reputation, with various tributes, documentary films, books, concerts, exhibits, and a one-man play that Avery Brooks performed on Broadway and around the country. In 1995, after five decades of exclusion for political reasons, his athletic achievements were finally recognized with his posthumous induction into the College Football Hall of Fame.

Even though Robeson's life and career were destroyed by the Red Scare, he has inspired many artists, particularly African Americans, to use their talents and celebrity to promote social justice. He opened the path for many others—including activist artists like Harry Belafonte, Ruby Dee, and Ossie Davis; more-recent black superstars like Sidney Poitier, Denzel Washington, Laurence Fishburne, and Spike Lee; and thousands of everyday activists in various struggles for social justice, who have carried on Robeson's legacy of commitment and conscience.

William O. Douglas
(1898–1980)

IN 1954 the *Washington Post* published an editorial supporting a government plan to pave a strip of land adjacent to the Chesapeake and Ohio Canal. The canal had been defunct as a mode of transportation since 1924, and in 1938 the government had purchased the right-of-way. Hoping to encourage more people to use the area, Congress suggested turning the land into a road for cars. US Supreme Court Justice William O. Douglas responded with a letter to the editor, publicly challenging the editor to accompany him on a trek along the full 185 miles of canal.

Not only did a number of *Post* editors take him up on the offer, so too did dozens of conservationists and scientists—fifty-eight in all. As word spread, members of the public joined in the hike, and schoolchildren cheered as the group passed through towns along the way. Faced with a driving snowstorm and other hardships, only nine men, including Douglas, successfully completed the eight-day hike. On the last day, Douglas organized a committee to shepherd the establishment of the Chesapeake and Ohio Canal National Historical Park, today one of the most heavily visited parks in the country.

Douglas was not only an outspoken environmentalist but also the strongest civil libertarian to ever sit on the Supreme Court. Appointed by **Franklin D. Roosevelt** in 1939 at age forty, he was both the youngest justice on the Court and the longest serving, with thirty-six years on the bench. In addition to his legal opinions, he also wrote more than thirty books.

Although he came from humble roots, his adoring mother, who called him "Treasure," always told him he was destined for greatness, even repeatedly rehearsing a mock presidential nominating speech for him when he was a small boy. His father, an itinerant preacher, died when Douglas was six, and his mother moved the family to Yakima, Washington.

Money was a constant struggle, and his education was nearly derailed several times because he could not pay tuition. He received a scholarship from Whitman College in Walla Walla, Washington, where he became a champion debater and graduated Phi Beta Kappa in 1920. After teaching school for two years, he was accepted into Columbia University Law School.

After brief stints at a Wall Street firm and teaching at Columbia, he was recruited to teach at Yale Law School in 1928 by its youthful dean, whom Douglas had met one evening while drinking—during Prohibition—at the Pelham Country Club.

With the election of FDR in 1932, Douglas set his sights on working for the administration. He became an authority on the Securities Act of 1933, publishing seven major articles on the new law. In 1934 he was asked to join the Securities and Exchange Commission and became its chair in 1937. He was a close adviser to FDR on the regulation of corporations, an issue that led many conservatives to attack the president as well as Douglas.

FDR appointed Douglas, then forty, to the Supreme Court in 1939 to replace **Louis Brandeis,** who had retired. The Senate Judiciary Committee's hearing on Douglas, which occurred only four days after the president's announcement, lasted five minutes.

Douglas carried his suspicion of corporate power to the bench, writing in his memoir *The Court Years: 1939–1975,* "I was always denounced as an activist; so were Black, Warren, Tom Clark, Brennan and others. And we were 'activists'—not in reading our individual notions of the public good into the Constitution and/or the laws, but in trying to construe them in the spirit as well as the letter in which they were enacted."

Despite his reputation as a civil libertarian, Douglas sided with the Court majority in the notorious 1944 *Korematsu v. United States* opinion affirming the constitutionality of the wartime internment of Japanese Americans.

Douglas was bored by his life on the Supreme Court, and he was politically ambitious. In 1944 FDR wanted Douglas as his vice presidential running mate after he had dumped **Henry Wallace,** but party bosses persuaded the president to pick the less controversial Harry S. Truman. Four years later, Truman offered Douglas the vice presidential nomination, but Douglas turned it down, telling friends that he did not want to be "second fiddle to a second fiddle."

Douglas remained on the Court and over time became its strongest First Amendment advocate, insisting that the US Constitution's wording that "no law" shall restrict freedom of speech should be interpreted literally. This was particularly courageous during the hysteria of the Red Scare. In *Terminiello v. Chicago* (1949), Douglas's opinion reversed Chicago's "breach of peace" ordinance, which banned speech that "stirs the public to anger, invites dispute, brings about a condition of unrest, or creates a disturbance." To hold otherwise, he wrote, "would lead to standardization of ideas either by legislatures, courts, or dominant political or community groups." Douglas wrote a spirited dissent in *Dennis v. United States* (1951), which upheld the convictions of American Communist Party members for conspiracy to teach and advocate overthrow of the government.

In 1953 Douglas granted a temporary stay of execution to Julius and Ethel Rosenberg, convicted of being Soviet spies who sold the Soviet Union the plans for the atomic bomb. He ruled that they had been condemned to die by Judge Irving Kaufman without the consent of the jury, a violation of the Atomic Secrets Act. At the request of the Eisenhower administration, Chief Justice Fred Vinson took the unusual step of reconvening the Court—sending jets around the country to bring the justices back to Washington—in order to set aside Douglas's stay. As a result of Douglas's action on the Rosenberg case, conservatives in Congress sought to impeach him, but the effort went nowhere.

Conservatives tried to impeach him again in 1970, at the behest of President Richard Nixon. According to Nixon aide John Ehrlichman, "From the beginning Nixon was interested in getting rid of William O. Douglas; Douglas was the liberal ideologue who personified everything that was wrong with the Warren Court."

Nixon told then-congressman Gerald Ford to instigate impeachment proceedings for Douglas on several grounds—everything from writing articles for sexually explicit magazines to publishing *Points of Rebellion* (1969), in which he urged the nation's young people to revolt against the establishment, to having connections with Albert Parvin, a Los Angeles businessman who asked Douglas to serve as president of his philanthropic foundation and who supposedly was connected to mob gambling interests in Las Vegas. The effort fizzled in part because a Democratic-led Congress refused to take it up and in part because Douglas was well prepared to defend himself.

On the bench he was a staunch advocate of women's rights. In 1942, in *Skinner v. State of Oklahoma,* Douglas argued in his majority opinion that states could not impose compulsory sterilization as a punishment for a crime. Twenty-three years later, in *Griswold v. Connecticut* (1965), Douglas wrote his most famous opinion. It overturned a Connecticut law that prohibited the use of contraceptives, arguing that it violated the "right to marital privacy." Douglas's "right to privacy" opinion laid the groundwork for *Roe v. Wade* (1973), giving women the right to an abortion.

Douglas was a lifelong outdoorsman and nature lover. In 1960, two years before **Rachel Carson**'s *Silent Spring* was published, he wrote a dissenting opinion in support of a small group of Long Islanders who were trying to block the spraying of DDT. In 1972, when the Court refused to let the Sierra Club sue over the Walt Disney Corporation's plan to build a resort next to Sequoia National Park, on the basis that the conservation group lacked legal standing, Douglas strenuously disagreed. In his dissent in *Sierra Club v. Morton,* he noted that if ships and corporations had standing, then so too should "valleys, alpine meadows, rivers, lakes, estuaries, beaches, ridges, groves of trees, swampland or even air." It would take five more years, but the Sierra Club eventually blocked the project. In 1976 the Sierra Club made Douglas an honorary vice president, calling him "the highest-placed advocate of wilderness in the United States."

Even Douglas's strongest supporters acknowledged that his opinions were often written hastily, that his personal life was a mess (he married four times), and that he never got over the disappointment of not being president, a position he thought he deserved. But Douglas's enduring legacy, as one of his biographers, L. A. Powe Jr., observed, is that "even in the worst of times judges can actually stand up and demand we adhere to our ideals."

Harry Bridges (1901–1990)

Harry Bridges addresses a mass meeting in San Francisco to support a union boycott of Alabama in protest of the state's segregation policies in 1965.
CREDIT: Associated Press

IN THE 1930s working on the docks, like mining and lumberjacking, was one of the most dangerous jobs in the country. Longshoremen needed powerful arms, a strong back, remarkable endurance, and incredible agility to avoid serious injuries when they loaded and unloaded heavy cargo. Dock work also required intricate cooperation among the workers, because a mistake by any one of them could put the others in danger. The shipowners expected longshoremen to work at a fast pace, but they made few concessions to improve safety.

In San Francisco, men would show up at seven in the morning in front of the Ferry Building, not knowing how many longshoremen were needed that day because that depended on the number of ships in port, the types of cargo, and the weather. The companies hired men for a day or a job in a dehumanizing process called the "shape-up." Each work crew of about sixteen men was run by a gang boss, some of whom solicited kickbacks in exchange for a job that day. Workers who complained about job conditions—or who expressed any union sympathies—were blacklisted. The Depression made the competition for jobs fiercer.

By May 1934 conditions had gotten so brutal that longshoremen, led by rank-and-file activist Harry Bridges, went out on strike, not only in San Francisco but along the entire West Coast, from San Diego, California, to Seattle, Washington. They demanded that the shipowners replace the shape-up with a hiring hall operated by the International Longshoremen's Association (ILA), the struggling dockworkers' union. The shippers tried to import scabs, but the Teamsters (the truckdrivers' union), in solidarity with the longshoremen, refused to haul any goods to or from the docks. A few thousand crewmen on the cargo ships refused to work, too.

Without goods moving in and out of the port, the city's economy—already imperiled by the Depression—sank into chaos. The business elite, with the support of police, tried to reopen the docks with replacements, but strikers held their ground, thwarting the police escorts, seizing the trucks, and dumping the cargo into the streets. Two strikers were killed, and dozens of longshoremen and cops were injured in the waterfront battle called "Bloody Thursday." The governor called in the National Guard, who restored order, but the calm was only temporary. The shipowners had not made any concessions, and the longshoremen were now angrier than ever.

A dramatic silent funeral procession down Market Street swung public opinion in favor of the strikers. Bridges urged the dockworkers to avoid further violence with police or soldiers. Instead, he called for a general strike, which he hoped would bring the shipowners to the negotiating table. The longshoremen shut down the docks. The Teamsters expanded their sympathy strike from the waterfront to the rest of the city. In total, about fifty other unions rallied to the dockworkers' side, and at least 125,000 San Francisco workers joined the general strike—the first general strike since the Seattle walkout in 1919.

The city came to a standstill. The papers called the strike a "civil war" and a "Communist-led insurrection." City and state officials asked the **Franklin D. Roosevelt** administration to send in federal troops to end the citywide shutdown, which the media warned could spread to other cities. U.S. Attorney General Homer Cummings and Secretary of State Cordell Hull were ready to grant the request, but Secretary of Labor **Frances Perkins** urged the president to show restraint. "I thought it unwise to begin the Roosevelt administration by shooting it out with working people who were only exercising their rights to organize and demand collective bargaining," she wrote in her memoirs. FDR listened to Perkins.

Pressured by the city's business leaders, the shipowners sat down with the ILA and negotiated a settlement. By October, the union won recognition, a five-cent-an-hour raise, and union hiring halls to replace the hated shape-up, using a rotation system that spread the work among the longshoremen.

Bridges emerged from the strike a national figure, a hero to workers and progressives and an enemy to the business community and conservatives. He quickly rose to president of the local ILA and then to president of its West Coast region. In 1937 he led the West Coast ILA out of the American Federation of Labor and into the Congress of Industrial Organizations (CIO). Bridges became president of the new organization, the International Longshoremen's and Warehousemen's Union (ILWU). On July 17, 1937, *Time* magazine put a photo of Bridges on its cover over the caption "Labor's Harry Bridges: A Trotsky to Lewis' Stalin?" referring to CIO head **John L. Lewis.** The economic importance of the ports gave the ILWU, and Bridges, significant influence. The union's members—which reached a peak at 62,100 in 1949—reelected Bridges president for forty years, until he retired in 1977.

The longshoremen went from being "wharf rats" to "lords of the docks." They gained safer conditions, paid holidays and vacations, and good health and retirement benefits, and they were among the highest-paid hourly workers in the country. Bridges developed a tactic, the "quickie strike," in which union members would stop work immediately to protest a violation of their contract. It usually got results. The ILWU's constitution gives rank-and-file members significant control over contracts and public positions.

Under Bridges's leadership, the union became an influential force within the labor movement and in the broader progressive world. The ILWU extended its jurisdiction to most waterfront workers on the Pacific coasts of the United States and Canada and had a strong presence in Hawaii. Bridges used the ILWU's base to support union drives by other CIO unions throughout the West.

Testifying before Congress in 1950, he called himself "an officer of a left-wing union." Asked what he meant, he said it was "a union that believes in a lot of rank-and-file democracy and control. . . . It's also a union that recognizes that from time to time it's got to stand up and fight for certain things that might not necessarily be only wages, hours, and conditions. Civil liberties, racial equality, and things like that."

Under Bridges's leadership, the ILWU was one of the first unions to be thoroughly racially integrated. In 1945, when the ILWU's Stockton, California, warehouse unit refused to admit a Japanese American into its ranks, Bridges and other officers suspended the unit until each member signed a nondiscrimination pledge. The ILWU has typically been among the country's most socially conscious unions, taking public stands on a wide range of issues, including nuclear disarmament, opposition to the Vietnam War, South African apartheid, and workers' rights around the world. Members often backed up their opposition to oppressive regimes abroad by refusing to handle cargo bound for or coming from those countries. The ILWU used its pension funds to finance construction of what the union calls "cooperative, affordable, integrated working-class housing" in San Francisco's St. Francis Square.

Bridges was born into a middle-class family in Kensington, Australia. As a teenager he worked for his father, a realtor, collecting rents and serving eviction notices. He saw how desperately poor some of the tenants were and hated taking their rent money. At sixteen he went to sea, traveling the world and seeing firsthand the miserable slums in India, East Asia, and London. He recalled, "The more I saw the more I knew that there was something wrong with the system." His uncle's prolabor political views, his travel experiences, and his participation in a rally in support of Australian strikers in 1917 led Bridges toward socialism. He was in the crew of a ship that arrived in New Orleans during a strike. He reported for picket duty and was put in charge of a picket squad. He was arrested and jailed overnight, which prompted him to join the Industrial Workers of the World, whose motto—"An injury to one is an injury to all"—he agreed with.

In 1920 he jumped ship in San Francisco after an argument with the captain over the treatment of seamen. He gave up seafaring and went to work along the San Francisco docks and eventually became the leader of the West Coast longshoremen's union.

After the 1934 general strike and until 1955, business leaders, right-wing groups such as the American Legion, and conservative politicians tried to get Bridges deported to Australia for his union activism and his radical views. Bridges was constantly under investigation by the FBI, local police departments, and Congress, who tried to prove that he was a Communist or that he had lied about being a Communist. In 1940 the US House of Representatives voted 330–42 to deport him as an "undesirable alien." The US Supreme Court heard two cases about Bridges—one charging he was a Communist, the other that he had lied when he said he had never been a member of the Communist Party. Both times the Court ruled in Bridges's favor, blocking his deportation. Its rulings enabled Bridges to become a US citizen in 1945.

Bridges always denied that he was a member of the Communist Party, although he acknowledged working with party members on union and other issues. Party members formed the core of Bridges's militant faction that led the 1934 strike and created the ILWU. In 1950, at the height of the Cold War, the CIO expelled the ILWU on the grounds that it was "Communist dominated."

ILWU members viewed Bridges as honest and incorruptible. He refused to take a salary any higher than that of the highest-paid member. When he traveled, he stayed in cheap hotels. He was consistently reelected president with more than 80 percent of the members' vote. Whereas the ILWU was a powerful voice for rank-and-file workers, the ILA, which represented dockworkers on the East Coast, was repeatedly charged with corruption and with taking employer payoffs. The 1954 Academy Award–winning film *On the Waterfront* depicts the mob influence of the ILA on the New Jersey docks. The movie's opening scene shows the workers still competing for jobs during a shape-up.

From within the union, the biggest controversy Bridges faced concerned automation. As shipowners mechanized the docks, Bridges saw that the number of jobs would inevitably decline. In 1961 the ILWU fought for and won the "mechanization and modernization agreement," which allowed cargo to be handled with mechanical loaders and to be shipped in prepacked containers, reducing labor costs and improving productivity and profits. In return, the union received generous wage and pension guarantees and no layoffs of existing workers. In 1960 it took about 16,000 longshoremen, clerks, watchmen, and foremen to move 74 million tons of cargo. By 1982 just 11,000 were able to handle 109 million tons. The agreement upset some union members, who saw the gradual decline of waterfront jobs as a loss of union influence. Others, however, viewed it as a way to share and redistribute shippers' profits with the workers as well as to make their jobs easier with labor-saving equipment.

In July 2001 the public square in front of San Francisco's Ferry Building— where dockworkers once assembled for the despised shape-up—was officially named Harry Bridges Plaza.

Langston Hughes
(1902–1967)

LANGSTON HUGHES, the poet, novelist, playwright, and short-story writer, penned "Dream Deferred," one of the most famous poems in American literary history.

> *What happens to a dream deferred?*
> *Does it dry up*
> *Like a raisin in the sun? . . .*
> *Or does it explode?*

The poem reflects Hughes's brilliance as a writer as well as his anger toward injustice, a theme that reappears in much of his work. He wrote the poem in 1951, several years before the modern civil rights movement emerged in Montgomery, Alabama in 1955. Hughes was already a well-published and respected writer, but the civil rights movement—and the explosion of interest in black studies and black literature—boosted his visibility as his writings became widely read in high schools and colleges.

Hughes was the first African American literary figure to gain widespread critical and popular acclaim. He viewed the struggles and hopes of African Americans as part of the broader movement for social and economic justice. Throughout his adult life, Hughes was a man of the left but also, like his contemporaries **Paul Robeson** and **A. Philip Randolph,** deeply involved in the black community and the freedom movement.

Hughes grew up in Kansas, Illinois, and Ohio and began writing poetry in high school. Upon graduating in 1920, he attended Columbia University for a year and absorbed the dynamic cultural scene of the Harlem Renaissance, the literary and intellectual flowering that fostered a new black identity (the "new Negro") in the 1920s and 1930s.

Hughes was a regular contributor to the two leading black-run magazines of the period—Charles S. Johnson's *Opportunity* and **W. E. B. Du Bois**'s the *Crisis*—through which he met the major artists, musicians, and political activists of the Harlem scene. In 1921 his poem "The Negro Speaks of Rivers" was published in the *Crisis*.

In 1924 Hughes was working as a busboy in a Washington, DC, hotel when the famous poet Vachel Lindsay entered the dining room. Hughes slipped several sheets of paper next to Lindsay's plate. Although annoyed by the intrusion, Lindsay nevertheless read Hughes's poem "The Weary Blues." He called for Hughes and asked him, "Who wrote this?" "I did," replied Hughes. The poem won first prize in *Opportunity*'s poetry contest, and Lindsay became one of Hughes's biggest boosters.

In 1926 Hughes published his first volume of poetry, also titled *The Weary Blues*. He was soon in demand and published other books, including *Shakespeare in Harlem, The Dream Keeper, Not Without Laughter, The Ways of White Folks, The Big Sea,* and *Popo and Fifina*. In these and in subsequent poems and stories, Hughes employed the rhythms of black music, especially jazz and blues—both little known outside the African American community at the time—which set Hughes's work apart from other writers.

Hughes portrayed the everyday lives of ordinary black people, including their joys, sorrows, music, humor, and routine encounters with racism. But unlike other prominent black poets of that era, such as Countee Cullen, Claude McKay, and Jean Toomer, Hughes sought to tell the stories of blacks in their own vernacular. Hughes was not ashamed of the African American masses. If anything, he was critical of the efforts of many middle-class black Americans to mimic the lifestyles and culture of their white counterparts.

His 1926 essay "The Negro Artist and the Racial Mountain," published in *The Nation* when Hughes was only twenty-four, became a manifesto for him and other writers and activists who asserted racial pride:

> The younger Negro artists who create now intend to express our individual dark-skinned selves without fear or shame. If white people are pleased we are glad. If they are not, it doesn't matter. We know we are beautiful. And ugly, too. The tom-tom cries, and the tom-tom laughs. If colored people are pleased we are glad. If they are not, their displeasure doesn't matter either. We build our temples for tomorrow, strong as we know how, and we stand on top of the mountain free within ourselves.

In 1926 Hughes enrolled at the historically black Lincoln University in Pennsylvania, supported by an elderly and wealthy white woman who admired his writing. (One of his classmates was **Thurgood Marshall,** a future lawyer for the National Association for the Advancement of Colored People and US Supreme Court justice.) Upon graduation in 1929, he returned to New York to resume his involvement with the Harlem Renaissance.

His first novel, *Not Without Laughter,* published in 1930, won the Harmon Gold Medal for literature. Its central character is an African American boy, Sandy, caught between two worlds. His mother works hard, demands respect, and appreciates the middle-class values of the white community around her. His father is footloose and fun loving. Through Sandy's eyes, Hughes reveals the conflicting values and attitudes within the black community, portraying the lives of the characters in intimate detail. Four years later Hughes published a collection of short stories, *The Ways of White Folks,* about the humorous but often tragic relationships between blacks and whites.

The Depression radicalized Hughes as he watched his family, friends, Harlem, and the country suffer from the economy's collapse. He published poetry in *New Masses,* a journal tied to the Communist Party. During the Depression, the party actively recruited African Americans and was one of the few interracial political groups to challenge segregation. For example, the party supported the Scottsboro Boys, nine black teenage boys unfairly accused of rape in Alabama in 1931, by raising money for their defense and publicizing the case. The party also nurtured young black activists, lifting them into leadership positions and encouraging their literary talents through its magazines and newspapers and through the John Reed Clubs, a network of organizations that supported and sponsored radical writers and artists.

In 1937 Hughes traveled to Spain to cover the Spanish Civil War for African American newspapers, reflecting the American left's support for the popular forces resisting a takeover by military strongman Francisco Franco, later the country's dictator. Hughes's political views are reflected in "A New Song," originally published in 1933 and revised five years later. America's blacks are "awakening to action," Hughes wrote, but he viewed their struggle not only as a battle against racism, but also as part of a crusade for economic justice and equality. "The Black and White world shall be one."

His 1935 play *Mulatto*—a protest against Jim Crow—became the longest running Broadway play written by an African American until Lorraine Hansberry's 1958 *A Raisin in the Sun.*

Hughes's 1936 poem "Let America Be America Again," published in *Esquire* magazine, reflected his radical views. It contrasts the nation's promise with its mistreatment of his fellow African Americans, the poor, Native Americans, workers, farmers, and immigrants. He hoped to see a day when America would no longer be divided by class and race divisions and "equality is in the air we breathe."

In 1942 Hughes began writing a column for the African American newspaper the *Chicago Defender,* which was the leading black paper in the country and was read nationwide. The column introduced the character of Jesse B. Semple, or Simple. Through Simple, Hughes displayed a remarkable eye and ear for the black experience, using humor and satire to raise serious issues about racial injustice. Simple's voice represented the black Everyman. Hughes featured Simple in his blues-musical play, *Simply Heavenly,* written in 1957. Simple says, "I'm broke, busted, and disgusted. And just spent mighty near my last nickel for a paper— and there ain't no news in it about colored folks. Unless we commit murder, robbery or rape, or are being chased by a mob, do we get on the front page, or hardly on the back." Hughes continued writing columns for twenty years and collected his Simple columns in several books.

In 1953, at the height of the Cold War, Hughes was called to testify before the Senate Permanent Subcommittee on Investigations, led by Senator Joseph McCarthy. He denied he had ever been a Communist Party member and distanced himself from his previous radical left views. In 1959, when he published *Selected Poems,* he left out some radical poems. Whether he sincerely rejected his radical past or simply accommodated himself to the realities of being a black writer trying to make a living in Cold War America is unknown. Although he abandoned his radical views, he continued to protest the social and racial conditions endured by African Americans.

By the 1950s Hughes was the most popular black poet and writer in the country, but he was primarily known within the African American community. That began to change when the civil rights movement emerged, as more Americans became interested in black history and black culture. He was often called the "Poet Laureate of the Negro Race."

During his lifetime, Hughes published fifteen volumes of poetry, ten novels and collections of short stories, twenty plays and operas (including *Mule Bone* with Zora Neale Hurston in 1931 and *Troubled Island* with composer William Grant Still in 1936), two autobiographies, four books about black history, hundreds of magazine articles and newspaper columns, and seven books for children, including books about Africa, the West Indies, jazz, and black history. He translated into English the works of the Spanish poet Federico Garcia Lorca and the Latin American Nobel laureate poet Gabriela Mistral.

Hughes's racial consciousness and pride, as well as his depictions of black life, influenced later generations of artists and activists in Africa and the Caribbean as well as in the United States. During the 1960s he inspired and supported many young black writers, helping shape a new wave of black literature. In his 1967 anthology *The Best Short Stories by Negro Writers,* Hughes included a short story by a then-unknown Georgia-born writer, Alice Walker, a student at Sarah Lawrence College. "His support for me meant more than I can say," recalled Walker, who has become one of her generation's acclaimed writers. The playwright Loften Mitchell, a generation younger than Hughes, said, "Langston set a tone, a standard of brotherhood and friendship and cooperation, for all of us to follow. You never got from him, 'I am *the* Negro writer,' but only 'I am *a* Negro writer.' He never stopped thinking about the rest of us."

Vito Marcantonio
(1902–1954)

VITO MARCANTONIO lived his entire life within a densely populated four-block area of New York City's East Harlem neighborhood. He represented the area in Congress, serving seven terms (1934–1950), proud to be its most radical member. Always controversial, he earned a national reputation as a powerful orator, brilliant parliamentarian, and defender of the disadvantaged. He led fights for major civil rights and prounion legislation and against the Cold War. During his last term, he cast the only votes against the Korean War and the witch-hunting of the House Un-American Activities Committee. His constituents—mostly Italian Americans and Puerto Ricans—stood by him despite an onslaught of negative press condemning his left-wing sympathies.

Marcantonio's father, who died in a streetcar accident when Marcantonio was in high school, was a skilled carpenter, a social step above most of the poor, rural Italian immigrants who were flocking to New York. Although nearly all children in his neighborhood dropped out of school by the eighth grade, Marcantonio and one other classmate walked four miles (to save the nickel trolley fare) to attend the closest high school, De Witt Clinton.

In high school, Marcantonio was influenced by his history teacher, a Socialist, but he was even more inspired by another teacher, Leonard Covello, who would be Marcantonio's lifelong friend and mentor. Covello, an immigrant who graduated Phi Beta Kappa from Columbia University, was dedicated to making sure that young Italians got a good education. In addition to teaching Italian, he established Casa del Popolo, an Italian settlement house in an abandoned church, and founded Circoli Italiani, a network of Italian student clubs. Covello encouraged his students to remain in their community and provide leadership.

After high school, Marcantonio enrolled at New York University. While studying law, he also helped prepare immigrants for citizenship at the Casa del Popolo settlement house. As a student with growing radical political awareness, he organized mass rent strikes, sponsored by the Harlem Tenants Association. Over the next decade he worked as naturalization director, education director, and head of men's activity at a settlement house.

During law school, he clerked in a prestigious progressive law firm where he met Joseph Brodsky, who had gained fame codefending the Scottsboro Boys. Harlem, especially its Jewish section, was already a bastion of Socialist Party voters, and Marcantonio absorbed the radical ideas circulating in the community.

Meanwhile, in 1922, **Fiorello La Guardia** was elected to Congress, and he asked Marcantonio to organize the Fiorello La Guardia Political Association. Under Marcantonio's leadership, it grew to a powerful and effective machine known for constituent service.

After graduating with a law degree in 1925, Marcantonio joined La Guardia's law practice as a clerk. He went on to become assistant US district attorney in 1930–1931.

When La Guardia was elected mayor of New York in 1933, Marcantonio ran for his vacant congressional seat. Like La Guardia, Marcantonio maintained a fluid relationship with political parties and was adept at working in coalition with multiple parties to win elections. Initially, he ran as a Republican in opposition to the Tammany Hall–controlled Democratic Party. During his congressional career, he was the candidate of the Republican, Democratic, City Fusion, All People's, and the American Labor Parties.

In 1935 *The Nation* magazine named Marcantonio to its Honor Roll for being a congressman "in the forefront of the struggle against social injustice." Major newspapers gave him a huge amount of coverage, generally incensed over his leftist politics.

Marcantonio took strong radical positions, calling for the nationalization of industry, commerce, transportation, banking, and utilities. He railed against "an economic system which permits want in a land of plenty" and proposed that the government seize factories boarded up during the Depression and reopen them for unemployed people to produce goods "for use instead of profit." (**Upton Sinclair** echoed this idea in his 1934 run for governor of California.)

In 1935, when Congress debated the pros and cons of public ownership of utilities, Marcantonio gave a fiery speech on the House floor:

If it be radicalism to believe that when God said, "Let there be light," that that light should be used for the benefit of all of the American people and not for the sole benefit of a few exploiters; if it be radicalism to believe that our national resources should be used for the benefit of all of the American people and not for the purpose of enriching just a few; if it be radicalism to smash, to abolish, and to surgically eradicate these companies which have been throttling the life of America and siphoning out the lifeblood of American consumers, then, ladies and gentlemen of this House, I accept the charge. I plead guilty to the charge; I am a radical, and I am willing to fight it out on this issue until hell freezes over.

He lost his bid for reelection in 1936 but came roaring back for the next six terms. According to his biographer Gerald Meyer, "He possessed a wide range of oratorical skills that could rivet the attention of street corner crowds, whip into a frenzy the faithful, impress his colleagues of the House, and even convince judges and juries to decide in favor of indicted leftists."

After his defeat as a nominal Republican in 1936, he became active in the newly formed American Labor Party (ALP), leading its left wing in New York State until 1941. The ALP had been formed as a way to woo garment workers away from the Socialist Party to vote for **Franklin D. Roosevelt.** The ALP gave Marcantonio the margin of victory in his 1938, 1940, and 1946 congressional races. He became president of the International Labor Defense (closely linked to the Communist Party) and led efforts to free labor activist Tom Mooney from prison and to defend West Coast labor leader **Harry Bridges,** a native of Australia, from deportation.

Marcantonio was a tireless and eloquent advocate for the foreign-born. In 1940, arguing against a proposal to exclude aliens from working on federally funded projects, he recalled that immigrants had been "induced to come here to be used as cheap labor—industrial cannon fodder of the labor exploiters," and he went on to say, "These people helped build America. Now we persecute them under the name of America." He served as vice chair and was an active supporter of the American Committee for the Protection of the Foreign Born.

Marcantonio retained the loyalty of his Italian constituency by delivering speeches in Italian—once referring to his Democratic opponent as a *testa di cappuccio* (cabbage head).

As the demographics of his district changed to include more Puerto Ricans, he embraced the cause of Puerto Rican independence, introducing five supportive bills in Congress. He learned to speak Spanish and constantly looked out for the interests of Puerto Rico as well as of his own Puerto Rican constituents. He consistently won 60 percent or more of the Puerto Rican vote.

A strong antiracist, he was a master of parliamentary maneuvering to get civil rights bills debated on the floor of Congress. In 1941 he fought for funding for the federal Fair Employment Practices Committee, proposed by Roosevelt to investigate discrimination. In 1942 he led the legislative battle to end the hated poll tax, which disenfranchised African Americans (and some poor whites) in the South. The bill passed the House but was defeated in the Senate. Each year he introduced antilynching legislation. During the war, he insisted on a federally supervised absentee ballot for soldiers (to ensure that black GIs would be able to vote in the 1944 presidential election). Mississippi congressman John Rankin led the opposition, observing that "the Gentleman from New York is harassing the white people of the Southern States."

In 1945 Marcantonio called for Commerce Secretary **Henry Wallace** to investigate discriminatory practices of professional baseball, and in 1947 he supported Adam Clayton Powell Jr.'s amendment to desegregate public facilities in the District of Columbia.

He petitioned to overturn the antilabor Taft Hartley Act and strongly supported collective bargaining rights for all workers.

Throughout his congressional career, Marcantonio's service to his constituents was legendary. People knew they could come to the Vito Marcantonio Political Association clubhouses to request assistance with jobs, immigration, public housing, legal aid, and medical care. He even gave his own money to those in need, who frequently contacted him when they were in dire straits.

Marcantonio was constantly accused of being a secret supporter of the Communist Party. He clearly took positions that paralleled the party's views and worked with party members in various community, labor, and political organizations. But he insisted, "I disagree with the Communists. I emphatically do not agree with them, but they have a perfect right to speak out and to advocate communism. I maintain that the moment we deprive those with whom we extremely disagree of their right to freedom of speech, the next thing that will happen is that our own right of freedom of speech will be taken away from us."

But the Red Scare finally brought an end to his political career, when the Democratic, Republican, and Liberal Parties banded together in 1950 to unseat him. The *New York Times* ran a series of editorials on three successive days urging his defeat. Although he won the majority of his longtime constituents in Italian Harlem, the Republican-led state legislature had redrawn his district to include Yorkville, a higher-income area made up predominantly of German American and Irish American voters, a move that contributed to Marcantonio's defeat.

After his electoral defeat, he threw his energy into his law practice. In 1951 he defended **W. E. B. Du Bois,** then in his eighties, who was charged with leading a pro-Soviet peace organization.

Marcantonio had planned to run again in 1954, but he died suddenly that year of a heart attack. He was fifty-one years old.

New York's conservative Cardinal Francis Spellman denied him a Catholic burial. But Italian Harlem gave Marcantonio an enormous send-off, with 20,000 people coming to view his body. Du Bois was among his pallbearers, and he was eulogized by **Dorothy Day.**

Virginia F. Durr (1903–1999)

Virginia Durr (left) and Rosa Parks in 1981 at Mount Holyoke College, where they received honorary doctorate degrees. CREDIT: Birmingham, Alabama, Public Library Archives, Portrait Collection

IN 1954, at the height of the Red Scare, Virginia F. Durr was forced to appear at a Senate hearing in New Orleans called by Senator James Eastland, a Mississippi segregationist. He wanted to expose "Communist influence" in the emerging civil rights movement, particularly in the Southern Conference for Human Welfare, an interracial group that had waged a campaign against the poll tax. Eastland believed that everyone in the civil rights movement was a Communist. The hearings came on the eve of the *Brown v. Board of Education* ruling, which outlawed segregation in public education, and Eastland was using Durr to discredit her brother-in-law, liberal US Supreme Court Justice Hugo Black, who had joined in the unanimous *Brown* decision.

Durr refused to answer Eastland's questions. At one point the fifty-one-year-old southern belle defiantly began to powder her nose. The frustrated Eastland finally ordered her off the stand. Reporters surrounded her, asking her what had impelled her to challenge the powerful senator. "Oh, I think that man is as common as pig tracks," Durr explained. "I guess I'm just an old-fashioned Southern snob." *Newsweek* and newspapers published photographs of Durr's nose-powdering rebellion. To liberals and progressives, Durr's combative stance was an act of courage and conscience. Most white southerners, however, viewed her as a traitor to her race and class.

Virginia Foster Durr could not have been a more unlikely candidate to become a staunch civil rights activist. She was born in a parsonage in Birmingham, Alabama, where her father, Sterling Foster, was the minister. One grandfather owned a plantation and slaves, and the other had been a Ku Klux Klan member.

In her autobiography *Outside the Magic Circle,* she confessed that she had once believed the Klan was "something noble and grand and patriotic that saved the white women of the South."

Although strong-willed even as a child, Virginia Foster seemed destined to be a well-brought-up southern lady. Her family were among the "genteel poor," who looked down on those whites who were "common." As for African Americans, she would later wonder how southerners could simultaneously hold two such conflicting images in their minds: one of the kindly servants who lovingly tended children, and another of the violent beast intent on raping white women.

The first time her values were directly challenged came in 1921, soon after she arrived at Wellesley College in Massachusetts. When she went to the dining room, she found she had been assigned to a table with an African American student. Horrified, she refused to sit there and returned to her room. The dorm housemother found her and calmly gave her the choice of sitting in her assigned seat or withdrawing from Wellesley. She took the seat. After two years at Wellesley, her family could no longer afford tuition ("The boll weevil ate my education," she later explained), and she returned to Alabama. There she fell in love with Birmingham lawyer Clifford Durr, whose family also had deep roots in Alabama. They were married in 1926.

In the early 1930s Virginia Durr grew aware of the economic troubles outside her door. Factories were closing, and "dairies were pouring milk into the gutters because they couldn't sell it." Through the Birmingham Junior League, she organized a project to distribute milk to low-income children. She drove Red Cross workers into the countryside so they could certify families for relief. She met coal miners whose bodies had been destroyed by black lung and tuberculosis. On weekends she took Cliff out to poor areas and showed him children suffering from hunger.

She was troubled that those thrown out of work blamed themselves for their plight. "They never said, 'We are destitute because U.S. Steel [a major Birmingham employer] doesn't treat us as well as they treat the mules,'" she wrote.

In 1933, at a meeting at his prominent law firm, Cliff suggested that the partners take a pay cut rather than fire some of their employees—including a stenographer with a young child and no husband—in the midst of hard times. Logan Martin, the senior partner, got angry at Cliff, a junior partner, for even suggesting the idea. That night, Cliff explained the situation to Virginia, who suggested he resign in protest. The next day, he did.

Fortunately, Cliff quickly found a job with the Reconstruction Finance Corporation, a New Deal agency. In 1941 **Franklin D. Roosevelt** appointed him to the Federal Communications Commission (FCC). There he challenged the growing power and concentration of broadcasters, many of whom opposed FDR's New Deal, and pushed to set aside radio frequencies for educational programs run by nonprofit organizations (an idea that some identified as leftist and led to his investigation by the House Un-American Activities Committee and the FBI).

The Durrs moved to Alexandria, Virginia, where Virginia enthusiastically joined in the social and political life of New Deal Washington. She attended parties where **Pete Seeger** sang folk songs and afternoon teas where **Eleanor Roosevelt** dropped by. **John L. Lewis** and his wife became her friends, as did a young New Deal bureaucrat from Texas named **Lyndon B. Johnson** and his wife, Lady Bird Johnson. Virginia was greatly influenced by civil rights activists Mary McLeod Bethune and Mary Church Terrell, among the first well-educated African Americans she had ever met.

In 1938 Virginia was a founding member of the Southern Conference for Human Welfare, which held its first meeting in Birmingham. Some 1,500 people came, "black and white, labor union people and New Dealers," Durr recalled. "Southern meetings always include a lot of preaching and praying and hymn singing, and this meeting was no exception. The whole meeting was full of love and hope. It was thrilling." There she met **Myles Horton** from the Highlander Folk School; Aubrey Williams, director of the New Deal's National Youth Administration; and other activists, both black and white, with whom she would wind up working for the next few decades.

Like almost all other white southerners, Durr came from a long line of loyal Democrats. So she shocked many friends and family members when she not only supported **Henry Wallace**'s 1948 Progressive Party presidential campaign but also ran for the US Senate on the party's ticket in Virginia. She and Wallace garnered few votes.

During the McCarthy era, right-wingers would use her involvement with the Progressive Party, along with her work against the poll tax—she was vice chair of the National Committee to Abolish the Poll Tax—as evidence of her communist sympathies.

In 1948, while Virginia was running for Senate, Cliff resigned from the FCC rather than have to administer the anticommunist "loyalty oaths" that President Harry S. Truman now required of government servants. The Durrs then moved to Denver, where Cliff worked as a lawyer for an insurance company. But after Virginia signed a petition against the Korean War, the *Denver Post* ran a story headlined, "Wife of General Counsel of Farmers Union Insurance Corporation Signs Red Petition," and Cliff lost his job.

In 1952 the Durrs moved back to Alabama, settling in Montgomery. Cliff set up a law practice and Virginia became his secretary. She worked for him for thirteen years, "but he protested every day. He said that I wasn't a proper secretary because I was too interested in the cases."

In Montgomery, Virginia joined the local Council on Human Relations, Montgomery's only interracial political organization, and its offshoot, United Church Women. None of this helped Cliff's law practice. The more they were identified as white supporters of black civil rights, the fewer white clients came through his door. Most of his clients were poor African Americans, many of whom could not afford to pay for his services. The Durrs just managed to eke out a living, often with financial help from northern friends.

Through her political work Durr met the leaders of Montgomery's black community, including Rosa Parks and E. D. Nixon, both longtime activists with the National Association for the Advancement of Colored People. During the summer of 1955 Myles Horton wrote Virginia, asking her to suggest a black person to attend a Highlander Folk School workshop about implementing the recent Supreme Court *Brown v. Board of Education* decision. Virginia went to Parks's house to ask if she would like to go. When Parks—who worked as a seamstress at the department store and occasionally sewed for the Durrs—explained that she did not have the money for bus fare to the Tennessee school, Virginia raised it. In December, a few months after returning from the workshop, Parks's refusal to move toward the back of a segregated bus triggered Montgomery's year-long bus boycott. After Parks was arrested, E. D. Nixon called Cliff to help bail her out of jail.

The Durrs remained involved in civil rights activism despite being shunned by most whites and facing tough financial circumstances. Virginia lent support during the 1955 Montgomery bus boycott and the 1961 Freedom Rides and became "the unofficial den mother for young movement activists," according to Dorothy Zellner, an organizer for the Student Nonviolent Coordinating Committee, who visited the Durrs many times at their home. "While the majority of Alabamans considered Virginia and Clifford Durr traitors, not heroes," explained Rosellen Brown, another young civil rights activist, "they represented to many of us the best of the white South, its native strength: they were sensible, outspoken, committed and only accidentally heroic."

Reflecting on her background as a southern belle trained to admire the Confederacy and the Klan, Durr wrote, "I've often thought how strange it was that those who actually did try to overthrow the government by force and violence became great honored figures in the South, whereas we, their grandchildren, were reviled because we were trying to get the vote. The South is a peculiar place."

Ella Baker speaks at a news conference in 1968.
CREDIT: Associated Press/Jack Harris

Ella Baker
(1903–1986)

LATE IN the afternoon of February 1, 1960, four young black men—Ezell Blair Jr., David Richmond, Franklin McCain, and Joseph McNeil, all students at North Carolina Agricultural and Technical College in Greensboro—visited the local Woolworth's store. They purchased school supplies and toothpaste, and then they sat down at the store's lunch counter and ordered coffee. "I'm sorry," said the waitress. "We don't serve Negroes here." The four students refused to give up their seats until the store closed. The local media soon arrived and reported the sit-in on television and in the newspapers. The four students returned the next day with more students, and by February 5 about 300 students had joined the protest, generating more media attention. Their action inspired students at other colleges across the South to follow their example. By the end of March sit-ins had spread to fifty-five cities in thirteen states. Many students, mostly black but also white, were arrested for trespassing, disorderly conduct, or disturbing the peace.

Over Easter weekend, April 16 to 18, many of those students came to Shaw University, a black college in Raleigh, North Carolina, to discuss how to capitalize on the growing momentum of the sit-ins. The fruit of the meeting was the Student Nonviolent Coordinating Committee (SNCC), an organization to translate these local actions into a wider movement. SNCC would expand the sit-in campaign, but it also used other tactics, such as freedom rides and voter registration drives, to tear down segregation. SNCC's work reinvigorated the civil rights movement.

Many accounts report that the Greensboro protest "sparked" or "catalyzed" the sit-in movement that led to SNCC's founding. But in the middle of all this was Ella Baker, a fifty-seven-year-old veteran organizer. She had spent decades traveling throughout the South for the National Association for the Advancement of Colored People (NAACP) and the Southern Christian Leadership Conference (SCLC). Long before there were Rolodexes, e-mail, and Facebook, she was famous for her vast social network of contacts. She gently encouraged the young activists to build a movement from these isolated local protests. It is no accident that SNCC's founding convention took place at Baker's alma mater.

Many of the young civil rights activists called her *Fundi,* a Swahili title for a master technician who oversees apprentices, to acknowledge Baker's role as their mentor. She eschewed a visible role, concentrating on patiently training the next generation of social change leaders. She spent more than fifty years as an organizer but was less well-known than many of those she trained and nurtured with the NAACP, SCLC, SNCC, and other organizations.

Baker grew up in rural North Carolina not far from where her grandparents had been slaves. Her mother, a former teacher and deeply religious, tutored Ella at home and coached her in public speaking. As a child, Ella was part of a supportive and tightly knit black community, where friends, relatives, and neighbors helped each other out. Her grandfather mortgaged the family farm to help feed families in need. For high school, Baker's parents sent her to the boarding school affiliated with Shaw University. She remained at Shaw for college, edited the student newspaper, and graduated as class valedictorian in 1927.

Then she moved to Harlem. Financial hardship forced Baker to set aside her dream of getting a graduate degree in sociology. Despite her college education, her race and gender limited her job prospects, and she wound up waiting on tables and working in a factory. She began to write articles for the *American West Indian News* and in 1932 found a job as an editorial assistant and office manager for the *Negro National News.*

The suffering brought on by the Depression troubled her deeply. Harlem was a hotbed of radical activism, and Baker soon got involved in local groups working on behalf of tenants and consumers. In 1931 she organized the Young Negroes' Cooperative League and became its national director. The group sponsored cooperative buying clubs and grocery stores both to reduce prices and to bring people together for collective action. In her next job, paid for by the New Deal's Works Progress Administration, she organized consumer cooperatives among housing project residents. She taught adult literacy and consumer education, often with a focus on young women and housewives. In 1935 she wrote an exposé of the exploitation of black domestic servants for the NAACP journal *Crisis.*

Baker started working for the NAACP in 1938 and three years later became its assistant field secretary. For five years, she traveled throughout the South, recruiting new members, working with local leaders to strengthen their chapters, and helping them organize campaigns against lynching, for equal pay for black teachers, and for job training. One of the leadership-training workshops she organized was attended by Rosa Parks, an active NAACP member in Montgomery, Alabama.

Baker understood that local activists in the South always risked facing financial and physical threats for their involvement with the civil rights organization.

Baker's speech at the NAACP's annual conference in 1942 outlined her focus on identifying concrete, winnable local issues that could build the organization: "What are the things taking place in our community which we should like to see changed? Take that one thing—getting a new school building; registering people to vote; getting bus transportation—take that one thing and work on it and get it done."

At the time, the NAACP's leadership was dominated by middle-class black businessmen, male professionals, and ministers, but most of its grassroots activists were working-class women and men. Baker's experiences convinced her that "strong people don't need strong leaders." She worked to cultivate what she called "group leadership" in contrast to leadership by charismatic figures or by people of higher economic status. She would carry these lessons with her the rest of her life.

In 1946 Baker left her NAACP job and returned to New York City to raise her niece. While working as the Harlem director of the American Cancer Society, she volunteered with the NAACP's New York City chapter, organizing protests demanding school desegregation. In 1952 she was the first woman elected chapter president. In 1951 and 1953 she ran for the New York City Council as a member of the Liberal Party, losing both times. It was the only time she allowed the spotlight to shine on her.

Soon after the 1955 Montgomery bus boycott erupted, Baker, **Bayard Rustin,** and Stanley Levinson (a close adviser to **Martin Luther King Jr.**) used their connections with northern liberals and unions to establish In Friendship, which raised funds and provided support for the boycott campaign. They talked extensively with King about establishing a new organization to build similar campaigns throughout the South. Rustin convinced Baker to run the new organization, SCLC. The initial plan was for her to spend six weeks based in Atlanta, but it turned into a two-and-a-half-year stint.

During this time she had many titles, but she was never given the title of director, which was reserved for a male minister. Baker bristled at the sexism and outsize egos of the ministers who ran SCLC, including King. Despite her long experience as a successful grassroots organizer, they treated her as if she were the hired help. Moreover, King and his fellow ministers lacked the time and experience to build a grassroots organization. SCLC drew on the reputations of its ministers to draw attention to racial injustice and to help sponsor voter registration drives, but it never became a mass-membership organization.

Baker was on the brink of resigning from SCLC when the student sit-in movement began in early 1960. Baker wrote, and she and King cosigned, the invitation letter to SNCC's founding meeting.

Baker took responsibility for organizing the event. The SCLC leaders figured that they could recruit the sit-in movement's leaders into forming a youth branch of the organization, but Baker counseled the young activists to shape their own organization. She expected 100 participants to attend, but more than 300 activists showed up. These included black students from fifty-six colleges and high schools across the South, a handful of white southern students, and students from northern and midwestern colleges (including representatives of Students for a Democratic Society) who had been organizing pickets at Woolworth's stores to show support for the sit-ins.

Baker made sure that students were well represented among the speakers. She enlisted as key speaker Rev. **James Lawson,** a theology student at Vanderbilt University who had organized workshops on nonviolence for students in Nashville, Tennessee, and had helped lead the sit-ins in that city.

In her closing speech, "More Than a Hamburger," Baker pushed the students to dream of how their lunch-counter sit-ins could develop into larger efforts to challenge racism in "every aspect of life." She emphasized the importance of growing grassroots group leadership rather than relying on the charisma of any individual, a not-too-subtle dig at King and his fellow ministers. The SCLC ministers asked Baker to convince the students to become part of their organization. Baker refused, but with her blessing, the students voted to form their own organization, SNCC.

SNCC might have quickly disintegrated had Baker not nurtured it and helped the students learn to run the organization on their own. She resigned from SCLC and worked as a volunteer for SNCC, supporting herself as a paid consultant for the Atlanta YMCA. She recruited Jane Stembridge, a white Virginian who was a student at Union Theological Seminary in New York, to run the Atlanta office. With Baker's support, **Bob Moses,** a black math teacher from New York who traveled to Atlanta to volunteer for SCLC's voter registration drive, soon defected to SNCC. The volunteer staff put out a newsletter, *Student Voice,* that helped give the new group an identity and helped spread the word. One of the first checks sent to help the new organization came from **Eleanor Roosevelt.**

As Baker guided SNCC's young activists, she reminded them of her belief in radical democracy: "People did not really need to be led; they needed to be given the skills, information, and opportunity to lead themselves." As students took on more leadership responsibility and worked on the Freedom Rides and voter registration, they put her ideas into practice and continued to ask Baker for advice. Those attending SNCC's marathon meetings recall that Baker, who by that time had thirty years of experience in movement building, would sit silently much of the time and then make a few comments. Reflecting on Baker's talent for listening to everybody and then summarizing what was most important, former SNCC chair Charles McDew explained, "Somebody may have spoken for 8 hours, and 7 hours and 53 minutes [of it] was utter bullshit, but 7 minutes was good. She taught us to glean out the 7 minutes."

Baker was not pleased with SNCC's turn toward "black power" in 1966 under the leadership of Stokely Carmichael. She gradually drifted away from

SNCC, but for the remainder of her life, she continued to work on progressive issues. She spent several years working on school desegregation efforts with the Southern Conference Educational Fund. She also expanded her work to include independence struggles in Puerto Rico and in Africa.

John Lewis, an SNCC leader and later a US representative from Atlanta, recalled that Baker "was much older in terms of age, but I think in terms of ideas and philosophy and commitment she was one of the youngest persons in the movement."

Theodor Geisel
(Dr. Seuss)
(1904–1991)

CREDIT: Associated Press/Burt Steel

WRITING UNDER the pen name "Dr. Seuss," Theodor Geisel was, and remains two decades after his death, the world's most popular writer of modern children's books. He wrote and illustrated forty-four children's books, characterized by memorable rhymes, whimsical characters, and exuberant drawings that have encouraged generations of children to love reading and expand their vocabularies. His books have been translated into more than fifteen languages and have sold over 200 million copies. They have been adapted into feature films, TV specials, and a Broadway musical. He earned two Academy Awards, two Emmy Awards, a Peabody Award, and the Pulitzer Prize.

Despite his popular image as a kindly cartoonist for kids, Geisel was also a moralist and political progressive whose views suffuse his stories. Some of his books use ridicule, satire, wordplay, nonsense words, and wild drawings to take aim at bullies, hypocrites, and demagogues. He believed that children's books should be both entertaining and educational. He thought that writers of children's books should "talk, not down to [children] as kiddies, but talk to them clearly and honestly as equals."

Geisel grew up in Springfield, Massachusetts. In 1925 he graduated from Dartmouth College, where he served as editor in chief of the campus humor magazine. He soon found some success submitting humorous articles and illustrations to different magazines, including *Judge,* the *Saturday Evening Post, Life, Vanity Fair,* and *Liberty,* writing as Dr. Seuss.

Geisel's work as a children's author began by accident. In 1931 an editor at Viking Press called Geisel—at the time a successful advertising illustrator—and offered him a contract to illustrate a book of children's sayings, *Boners.* The book sold well, and soon Geisel produced a sequel. Five years later, returning from Europe on a ship in rough waters and facing gale-force winds, Geisel began reciting words to the chugging rhythm of the ship's engines. He began saying, "And that is a story that no one can beat, and to think that I saw it on Mulberry Street," the name of a major thoroughfare in his hometown of Springfield. When he got back to New York, Geisel began writing and drawing a book that became *And to Think That I Saw It on Mulberry Street*. Twenty-nine publishers rejected the book, in part because children's books in verse were out of style. Finally, in 1937, Geisel found a publisher for the book. It earned good reviews, especially for its illustrations, but sold poorly, as did his next several children's books.

Horton Hatches the Egg (1940) was more successful, winning praise for its imaginative rhymes and drawings and its funny story about an elephant and a bird. *Horton* might have given Geisel the commercial boost he was hoping for, but he was preoccupied by the war in Europe, Hitler's persecution of the Jews, and America's need to prepare itself for war. He put his children's books on hold and became an editorial cartoonist for the left-wing New York City daily newspaper *PM* and then a wartime writer and illustrator for the US government and the military, helping make propaganda and training films to support the war effort.

Fervently pro–New Deal, *PM* included sections devoted to unions, women's issues, and civil rights. Geisel sharpened his political views as well as his artistry and his gift for humor at *PM*, where, from 1941 to 1942, he drew over 400 cartoons. The tabloid paper "was against people who pushed other people around," Geisel explained. "I liked that."

His work viciously but humorously attacked Adolf Hitler and Benito Mussolini. He bluntly criticized isolationists who opposed American entry into the war, especially the famed aviator (and Hitler booster) Charles Lindbergh and right-wing radio priest Father Charles Coughlin, both of whom were anti-Semites, and Senator Gerald Nye of North Dakota, an isolationist leader. Geisel's was one of the few editorial voices to decry the US military's racial segregation policies. He used his cartoons to challenge racism at home against Jews and blacks, union-busting, and corporate greed, which he thought divided the country and hurt the war effort. But Geisel also got swept up by the country's anti-Japanese hysteria and drew several cartoons, using racist caricatures of Japanese people, depicting Japanese Americans as traitors to the United States.

Many Dr. Seuss books are about the misuse of power—by despots, kings, or other rulers, including parents who arbitrarily wield authority. In a university lecture in 1947—a decade before the modern civil rights movement—Geisel urged would-be writers to avoid the racist stereotypes common in children's books and opined that America "preaches equality but doesn't always practice it." His children's books consistently reveal his sympathy with the weak and the powerless and his fury against bullies and tyrants. His books teach children to think about how to deal with an unfair world. Rather than telling them what to do, Geisel invites his young readers to consider what they should do when faced with injustice.

After the war, he occasionally submitted cartoons to publications. One 1947 drawing, published in the *New Republic*, depicts Uncle Sam looking in horror at

Americans accusing each other of being Communists. It was a clear statement of Geisel's anger at the nation's right-wing hysteria. But Geisel devoted most of his postwar career to writing children's books and quickly became a well-known and commercially successful author—thanks in part to the postwar baby boom. He was popular with parents, kids, and critics alike. First came *If I Ran the Zoo* (1950) and *Scrambled Eggs Super!* (1953).

Next came *Horton Hears a Who!* (1954), the first of Geisel's politically oriented children's books, written during the McCarthy era. It features Horton the Elephant, who befriends tiny creatures (the "Whos") whom he cannot see but whom he can hear thanks to his large ears. Horton rallies his neighbors to protect the endangered Who community. Horton observes in one of Geisel's most famous lines: "Even though you can't see or hear them at all, a person's a person, no matter how small." The other animals ridicule Horton for believing in something that they cannot see or hear, but he remains loyal to the Whos. Horton urges the Whos to join together to make a big enough sound so that the jungle animals can hear them. That can only happen, however, if Jo-Jo, the "smallest of all" the Whos, speaks out to save the entire community. Eventually he does so, and the Whos survive. Some Seuss analysts see the book as a parable about protecting the rights of minorities, urging "big" people to resist bigotry and indifference toward "small" people, and the importance of individuals' (particularly "small" ones) speaking out against injustice. Other observers, however, view the residents of Who-ville as representing the Japanese people. Despite Geisel's racist caricatures of the Japanese during the war, he was horrified by the consequences of the atomic bomb dropped on Hiroshima and came to sympathize with the helplessness of the Japanese when he visited the country after the war. His changing attitude is evident in *Horton Hears a Who!*, which Geisel dedicated to a Japanese friend. In the book, Horton represents the US government's effort to rebuild Japan as a democracy. ("I've got to protect them," Horton says, "I'm bigger than they.") Other jungle animals in the story oppose this effort, preferring revenge or indifference—much like many Americans at the time.

Geisel next wrote his most famous book, *The Cat in the Hat*, in response to a challenge. In May 1954 *Life* magazine published an article about widespread illiteracy among schoolchildren, claiming that they were not learning to read because their books were boring. William Spaulding, an editor at Houghton Mifflin, asked Geisel to write a book using the 225 words that he believed all first-graders should be able to recognize. Spaulding challenged Geisel to "bring back a book children can't put down." Within nine months, Geisel produced *The Cat in the Hat*. It was an immediate success. The book became the first in a series of Dr. Seuss's Beginner Books that combined a simple vocabulary, wonderful drawings, imaginative stories, and bizarre characters (many based on animals). In quick succession, he wrote *On Beyond Zebra!* (1955), *If I Ran the Circus* (1956), *How the Grinch Stole Christmas* (1957) and *Green Eggs and Ham* (1960), which used only fifty words.

In several early books—including *The 500 Hats of Bartholomew Cubbins* (1938), *The King's Stilts* (1939), and *Bartholomew and the Oobleck* (1949)—Geisel makes fun of the pretensions, foolishness, and arbitrary power of kings. His finest rendition of this theme is *Yertle the Turtle* (1958). Yertle, king of the pond, stands atop his subjects in order to reach higher than the moon, indifferent to the suffering of those beneath him. In order to be "ruler of all that I see," Yertle stacks up his subjects so he can reach higher and higher. Mack, the turtle at the very bottom of the pile, says,

> *I don't like to complain,*
> *But down here below, we are feeling great pain.*
> *I know, up on top you are seeing great sights,*
> *But down at the bottom we, too, should have rights.*

Yertle tells Mack to shut up. Frustrated and angry, Mack burps, shaking the carefully piled turtles, and Yertle falls into the mud. His rule ends and the turtles celebrate their freedom. The story is clearly about Hitler's thirst for power, a topic that inspired some of Geisel's most powerful *PM* cartoons But Geisel is also saying that ordinary people can overthrow unjust rulers if they understand how to use their own power. The story's final lines reflect Geisel's political outlook:

> *And the turtles, of course . . . all the turtles are free*
> *As turtles and, maybe, all creatures should be.*

The Sneetches (1961), inspired by the Protestant Geisel's opposition to anti-Semitism, exposes the absurdity of racial and religious bigotry. Sneetches are yellow birdlike creatures. Some Sneetches have a green star on their belly. They are the "in" crowd and they look down on Sneetches who lack a green star, who are the outcasts. Eventually, they all realize that neither the plain-belly nor star-belly Sneetch is superior. The story is an obvious allegory about racism and discrimination, clearly inspired by the yellow stars that the Nazis required Jews to wear on their clothing to identify them as Jewish.

The Lorax (1971) appeared as the environmental movement was just emerging, less than a year after the first Earth Day. Geisel called it "straight propaganda"—a polemic against pollution—but it also contains some of Geisel's most creative made-up words, like "cruffulous croak" and "smogulous smoke." A small boy listens to the Once-ler tell the story of how the area was once full of Truffula trees and Bar-ba-loots and was home to the Lorax. But the greedy Once-ler—clearly a symbol of business—cuts down all the trees to make thneeds, which "everyone, everyone, everyone needs." The lakes and the air become polluted, there is no food for the animals, and it becomes an unlivable place. The Once-ler only cares about making more things and more money, ignoring warnings about the devastation he's causing.

Business is business!
And business must grow,

he says. Eventually the Once-ler shows some remorse, telling the boy:

Unless someone like you
cares a whole awful lot
nothing is going to get better
It's not.

The book attacks corporate greed and excessive consumerism, themes that re-mind some readers of *How the Grinch Stole Christmas. The Lorax* was once banned by a California school district because of its obvious opposition to clear-cutting by the powerful logging industry.

In 1984 Geisel produced *The Butter Battle Book,* another strong statement about a pending catastrophe—the nuclear arms race between the United States and the Soviet Union, while Ronald Reagan was president. "I'm not anti-military," Geisel told a friend at the time, "I'm just anti-crazy." It is a parable about the dan-gers of the political strategy of "mutually assured destruction" brought on by the escalation of nuclear weapons. Geisel's satirical gifts are on display. The cause of the senseless war is a trivial conflict over toast. The battle is between the Yooks and the Zooks, who do not realize that they are more alike than different, because they live on opposite sides of a long wall. They compete to make bigger and better weapons until both sides invent a destructive bomb (the "Bitsy Big-Boy Boo-meroo") that, if used, will kill both sides. Like *The Lorax,* there is no happy ending or resolution. As the story ends, the generals on both sides of the wall are poised to drop their bombs. It is hard for even the youngest reader to miss Geisel's point.

Myles Horton
(1905–1990)

DURING THE summer of 1955 Rosa Parks attended a ten-day interracial workshop at the Highlander Folk School, a training center for union and civil rights activists in rural Tennessee. Founded by Myles Horton in 1932, Highlander was one of the few places where whites and blacks—rank-and-file activists and left-wing radicals—could participate as equals. At the workshop that Parks attended, civil rights activists talked about strategies for implementing integration.

"One of my greatest pleasures there was enjoying the smell of bacon frying and coffee brewing and knowing that white folks were doing the preparing instead of me," Parks recalled. "I was 42 years old, and it was one of the few times in my life up to that point when I did not feel any hostility from white people."

Parks was a veteran activist with the Montgomery, Alabama, chapter of the National Association for the Advancement of Colored People, challenging the Jim Crow laws that kept blacks from voting, and organizing black youths to protest the city's segregated public library system. Her experience at Highlander persuaded her that it was possible for blacks and whites to live in "an atmosphere of complete equality," without "any artificial barriers of racial segregation." So when she decided to resist Montgomery's segregation law by refusing to move to the back of the bus on December 1, 1955, she was not acting on the spur of the moment after a hard day's work. Her action was something she had been thinking about for a long time, but the workshop at Highlander six months earlier had strengthened her resolve.

Highlander's cultural workshops, led by Horton's wife Zilphia, brought activists and song leaders together to share songs and create new ones, often by revising popular songs and hymns. It was at Highlander that folksingers **Pete Seeger** and Guy Carawan first heard the song "We Shall Overcome," originally a Negro hymn that North Carolina tobacco workers had used to lift their spirits during a strike. Seeger and Carawan revised the words, quickened the tempo, and tweaked the tune, then taught the song to students involved in the sit-in movement and sang it at rallies and marches and in jails. The song eventually became a civil rights anthem around the world.

The issues have evolved over time, but Highlander has retained the Hortons' original philosophy. "We believe that education leads to action," Myles Horton said in 1972. "If you advocate just one action, you're an organizer. We teach leadership here. Then people go out and do what they want." But Horton was being somewhat disingenuous. He was a radical, and he started Highlander to help people challenge the South's class and racial caste system. The people he brought to Highlander shared some version of his progressive belief in greater economic and racial equality.

Horton was born in a log cabin near Savannah, Tennessee, in 1905. Both his parents had been schoolteachers before Horton's birth, but when the state increased its standards and required teachers to have one year of high school (which neither had), they lost their jobs. So his parents worked in factories, as sharecroppers, and at other odd jobs.

"From my mother and father," Horton wrote, "I learned the idea of service and the value of education." His mother organized classes for poor and illiterate neighbors. His father was a member of the Workers' Alliance, a union formed by employees of the New Deal's Works Progress Administration.

While in high school, Horton worked as a store clerk, at a sawmill, and in a factory making crates for shipping tomatoes. Upset at earning only a penny a crate, Horton persuaded the other employees to stop working and hold out for a pay increase. "The tomatoes kept stacking up," Horton recalled, and after two hours, they got their raise.

Horton entered Cumberland University in Tennessee in 1924 and quickly led a student rebellion against the hazing of freshmen by fraternities. The next summer, working in a Tennessee factory, he shocked his fellow workers by supporting John T. Scopes, who was on trial for teaching evolution.

In the 1920s the YMCA had campus chapters devoted to social action based on the Christian Social Gospel. During Horton's junior year, he attended a YMCA conference at Vanderbilt University in Nashville, where he had his first contact with African American and foreign students. He was angry that he was not permitted to take a Chinese girl to a restaurant or to enter a public library with a black acquaintance. He was further angered by a Labor Day speech given on campus by John Emmett Edgerton, a woolen manufacturer and a trustee of Cumberland University. Edgerton warned students that northern agitators were starting labor unions that would destroy industry and jobs in the South. To see for himself, Horton went to Edgerton's textile mill in Lebanon, Tennessee; he was shocked by the conditions and urged the workers to organize. University officials threatened to expel him if he visited the mill again.

During the summer of 1927 Horton took a job teaching Bible school classes to poor mountain people in Ozone, Tennessee, for the Presbyterian Church.

He invited the students' parents to discuss their problems, and they talked about the challenges of farming, how to get a job in a textile mill, how to test wells for typhoid, and other issues. During the course of the summer, more and more people came to Horton's sessions. For the twenty-two-year-old Horton, the people's response to his classes was a revelation. He realized that he could lead a discussion without knowing all the answers. And he could get people to talk about their problems so they could figure out for themselves how to solve them.

Inspired by these experiences, when he graduated from Cumberland, Horton enrolled at the Union Theological Seminary (UTS) in New York, where he took classes with Reinhold Niebuhr, a leading theologian who headed the Fellowship of Socialist Christians and who cofounded, with socialist **Norman Thomas,** the *World Tomorrow,* a journal dedicated to "a social order based on the religion of Jesus." While at UTS, he visited local settlement houses, Brookwood Labor College (headed by **A. J. Muste**), and several utopian cooperative communities (such as the Oneida Community) that had been formed by religious and radical groups in the 1800s. He also helped organize garment workers in New York City, and visited North Carolina to observe a textile strike.

In 1930 and 1931, as the Depression deepened, Horton took graduate courses at the University of Chicago with Robert Park and Lester Ward, two reform-oriented sociologists, and **John Dewey,** the philosopher and educational reformer. He also visited **Jane Addams** at Hull House.

These ideas and experiences strengthened Horton's resolve to connect education and social action, and when he toured Denmark's folk schools in 1931 and 1932, he discovered the pragmatic approach that would animate him for the rest of his life. The folk schools helped mobilize Danish citizens—first rural peasants, then urban workers—to deal with their social and economic problems. Horton admired the close informal relations among students and teachers and their use of culture—songs and stories—as tools for learning. He decided that he wanted to start a similar school in the South, helping ordinary people—black and white, rural and urban—to become effective activists.

In 1932 Horton joined forces with two other white southern progressives—Don West and Jim Dombrowski—to start the Highlander Folk School in Monteagle, Tennessee, about fifty-five miles northwest of Chattanooga.

Highlander began with eight students, who were motivated by a commitment to improve their communities. Horton and the students soon got involved helping striking coal miners in Wilder, Tennessee, 100 miles from Monteagle, by soliciting and distributing food and clothing. The violence used by the company against the strikers, the complicity of local government officials, the biased coverage by the newspapers, the murder of the local union president, and the near starvation conditions faced by the workers and their families shocked Horton and shaped Highlander's labor education program. The school offered practical courses in labor history, union strategies, economics, journalism, public speaking, parliamentary procedure, mimeographing and posters, drama, and music.

Within a few years, Highlander had become a training center for the Congress of Industrial Organizations (CIO) union organizers and leaders in the South. It helped coal miners, woodcutters, mill hands, and other workers. Horton and his colleagues defiantly insisted that the workshops be racially integrated, which was not only controversial but also a violation of Tennessee's laws.

Highlander began holding workshops on public school desegregation in 1953, nearly a year before the US Supreme Court's *Brown v. Board of Education* ruling and two years before the Montgomery bus boycott. Highlander became a magnet for people concerned about racial injustice and civil rights. It attracted people from high schools and colleges, churches, YMCAs, unions, and social clubs. It also sponsored racially integrated children's camps. In 1957 the twenty-eight-year-old **Martin Luther King Jr.** attended a Highlander workshop. Many people who became local leaders in the civil rights movement spent time at Highlander, as did other prominent leaders, including Andrew Young, **Fannie Lou Hamer,** Stokely Carmichael, James Bevel, Bernard Lafayette, Ralph Abernathy, and **John Lewis,** who would become a congressman from Atlanta. **Eleanor Roosevelt** was a longtime supporter and an occasional visitor. After attending a Highlander workshop, two black community leaders from South Carolina—Esau Jenkins and Septima Clark—organized Citizenship Schools where black adults could learn to read and write and thus qualify to vote.

Highlander inevitably stirred controversy. In 1954 Senator James Eastland of Mississippi, a segregationist, held Senate hearings to uncover "subversive" activities, including at Highlander. In 1957 Georgia's Commission on Education, created to counter school desegregation efforts, distributed 250,000 copies of a four-page report, "Highlander Folk School: Communist Training School," with photos of Highlander's interracial meetings. Southern newspapers labeled Highlander a Communist training camp promoting racial integration. The right-wing John Birch Society put up billboards across the South with a photo of Martin Luther King at Highlander and the caption "Martin Luther King at Communist Training School." Highlander's insurance company canceled its fire insurance, which Horton suspected was the work of segregationists trying to put Highlander out of business.

Between 1957 and 1971 the Internal Revenue Service revoked Highlander's tax-exempt status three times, a form of harassment meant to undermine its fund-raising efforts. The Ku Klux Klan marched in front of the school. In 1960 Tennessee courts ordered Highlander closed on the grounds that it had violated its charter by "permitting integration in its school work." Horton immediately relocated the school to Knoxville, Tennessee, and changed the name to Highlander Research and Education Center. In 1971 the school moved to a 100-acre mountainside farm in New Market, Tennessee.

Horton retired from Highlander in 1971, traveled around the world to explain the Highlander idea to educators, wrote his autobiography *The Long Haul,* and died in 1990. Highlander has continued as a center for social activism. It helped spawn a grassroots environmental justice movement across the South, opposing strip mining, advocating for worker health and safety, fighting pollution and toxic dumping, and supporting the antiglobalization movement by sponsoring workshops on economic human rights and fair trade.

Carey McWilliams
(1905–1980)

THANKS TO his book *Factories in the Field,* in which he named and shamed California's worst corporate abusers of migrant labor, and his role as head of California's Division of Immigration and Housing, Associated Farmers, the powerful growers' lobby, once called Carey McWilliams "the Agricultural Pest No. 1 in California, outranking pear blight and boll weevil." Republican **Earl Warren,** during his campaign for California governor in 1942, pledged that if elected his first official act would be to fire McWilliams from his government position.

For the next four decades, as an attorney, author, activist, editor, and government official, McWilliams was one of the country's most effective advocates for workers' rights, civil rights, immigrants' rights, and civil liberties. McWilliams wrote nine books and hundreds of articles that helped awaken public opinion and catalyzed crusades for reform. From 1951 to 1975 he edited *The Nation* magazine, transforming the magazine into a voice for muckraking investigative journalism.

McWilliams grew up in Steamboat Springs, Colorado, the son of a prosperous rancher and state legislator. After his father lost his fortune and committed suicide, the seventeen-year-old McWilliams moved to Los Angeles in 1922. He graduated from the University of Southern California with a law degree and took a job with a prestigious downtown law firm, but he was not happy practicing business law. He quickly became a man-about-town, hanging out with writers at night while tending to his dull legal career during the day. In his spare time, he wrote book reviews, profiles of literary figures, and articles about Southern California culture for local and national magazines.

McWilliams was radicalized by the Depression and left his literary and bohemian life behind to focus his talents on social justice. His exposure to the miserable conditions of migrant farm workers—and to the efforts of powerful growers, police, judges, and right-wing vigilantes to thwart their efforts to unionize—was the main impetus for his transformation from apolitical lawyer and literary critic to radical writer-activist.

In the early 1930s the radical Cannery and Agricultural Workers Industrial Union had been organizing migrant farm laborers, and it engaged in a series of strikes across California to better their conditions. The strikes involved Filipinos, Mexicans, and white Okies and Arkies (migrants from Oklahoma and Arkansas) who picked cotton, pears, oranges, and other crops. Associated Farmers was the key front group for the growers, funded by San Francisco and Los Angeles business groups. They hired vigilantes to break the heads of strikers and to throw tear gas canisters into crowds of striking workers, while local cops (and judges) looked the other way. Local police departments had "red squads" to infiltrate the unions and break up strikes. They arrested and jailed hundreds of union organizers and leaders for allegedly being members of the Communist Party.

McWilliams came face-to-face with what he called this "rural civil war" as a member of the American Civil Liberties Union, whose Southern California branch enlisted attorneys to monitor these violations of civil liberties and to defend the strikers in court. McWilliams not only volunteered his legal talents to the cause but also began writing about the growing menace of "farm fascism." In a 1934 article for H. L. Mencken's *American Mercury,* McWilliams described a lynching in San Jose—by a mob seeking vengeance on two men who had kidnapped and killed a local boy—that was supported by California governor Jim Rolph and the powerful Hearst newspapers. He feared that the growing discontent over Depression conditions could strengthen right-wing movements in the United States, as was taking place in Europe.

In May 1935 McWilliams and his journalist friend Herb Klein began a nine-day journey throughout California. They interviewed growers, contractors, workers, state employees, the head of Associated Farmers in Fresno, and several union organizers jailed in San Quentin State Prison. They dug into public records to see who owned the largest farms and to uncover the interconnections among the business groups, the growers, and politicians. The first account of their findings appeared in *The Nation* that July. "Terror has broken out into the open again in California," McWilliams and Klein warned. "The period is one of transition from sporadic vigilante activity to controlled fascism, from the clumsy violence of drunken farmers to the calculated actions of an economic militaristic machine."

They documented that the same "financial oligarchy" of business interests that had used vigilantes against workers in the San Francisco general strike the year before (see the profile of **Harry Bridges**) were doing battle with the thousands of hungry field workers trying to unionize. They exposed the Associated Farmers' connections to shippers, oil companies, manufacturers, bankers, and newspapers. They reported that the state police used the Associated Farmers' list of 1,000 labor radicals to harass and arrest union activists.

McWilliams's subsequent book *Factories in the Field* quickly became a national best seller. He combined his journalistic flair for telling vivid stories about real people with history, economics, and sociology to reveal the conditions under which farmworkers toiled providing food for America's tables. He traced how a handful of oligarchs had come to own so much of the good farmland, how they pitted a succession of different racial and ethnic groups—Filipinos, Chinese, Japanese, Mexicans, and whites—against each other to intensify competition for jobs, and how they had perfected a system of exploitation using cheap, mobile, and temporary workers. McWilliams paid particular attention to terror imposed on the workers by the growers, the police, and the right-wing vigilantes.

By the time *Factories in the Field* came out in July 1939, McWilliams had already been appointed head of the state Division of Immigration and Housing by Governor Culbert Olson, a progressive Democrat elected in 1938. Over his four-year term, McWilliams focused on improving housing and raising wages for farmworkers. He hired investigators and lawyers who were sympathetic to the workers and held public hearings throughout the state to expose the conditions and force growers to explain their abuses.

The growers and their political allies fought back. State legislators such as Sam Yorty (who was later mayor of Los Angeles) forced McWilliams to testify before their committees and grilled him, hoping to persuade the public that he was a Communist. The FBI spied on him, and its director, J. Edgar Hoover, put McWilliams on his Security Index, which meant that he could be sent to a detention camp in case of a national emergency.

The attacks on McWilliams, plus the publication of John Steinbeck's *The Grapes of Wrath* that same year, not only drew more attention to growers' abuses of farmworkers but also increased sales of *Factories in the Field.* The controversy over these two books brought the issue to the attention of Senator Robert La Follette Jr. (son of **Robert M. La Follette,** a former senator and governor from Wisconsin), who held hearings in California in December 1939 and invited McWilliams to testify.

McWilliams's campaign to improve farmworker conditions had made inroads, but by 1940 other issues, including the pending world war, were attracting more attention. For progressives, one of those issues was the growing assaults on civil liberties and on immigrants. Congress passed the Alien Registration Act (Smith Act), which made advocating "subversive" political ideas a crime, required "aliens" (noncitizens) to register with the government, and mandated the deportation of any alien considered "disloyal" to the United States, as defined by the whim of Congress or the attorney general.

In 1940 McWilliams was elected chairman of the American Committee for the Protection of the Foreign Born, which worked to mobilize public opposition to alien registration while also educating resident aliens about their rights and obligations under the law. Its members included philosopher **John Dewey** and labor organizer **A. Philip Randolph, Vito Marcantonio, Langston Hughes,** and **Paul Robeson.**

During and after the war, Los Angeles was caught in a frenzy of racist hysteria against Japanese Americans and Mexican Americans. McWilliams wrote a series of books that established him as the country's most influential analyst of racial intolerance and injustice. He also played a pivotal role in two high-profile campaigns to defend Mexican Americans and Japanese Americans against attacks on their civil rights. In February 1942, 120,000 Japanese Americans (two-thirds of them US citizens) were detained and put into internment camps. McWilliams later observed that "in Los Angeles, where fantasy is a way of life, it was a foregone conclusion that Mexicans would be substituted as the major scapegoat group once the Japanese were removed." Once out of government, he wrote *Prejudice* in 1944, undermining every argument used to justify detaining Japanese Americans. The book was cited repeatedly that year in the dissenting opinion in *Korematsu v. United States,* the US Supreme Court ruling that upheld the constitutionality of the internment.

On August 1, 1942, two groups of Mexican Americans brawled by a reservoir near Los Angeles that the media called Sleepy Lagoon. The next morning police found the body of Jose Diaz. The Los Angeles Police Department (LAPD) rounded up more than 600 youths—mostly Mexican Americans known as "zoot-suiters" for the ballooned pants and long coats they wore, a favorite style then with young Mexicans—on a variety of trumped-up charges. Twenty-two of them were indicted for Diaz's murder. The racist press coverage inflamed the city's racial climate and guaranteed that the defendants would not get a fair trial. The local papers blamed Diaz's death on a "crime wave" led by "zoot-suiters."

At the request of the district attorney, the judge did not allow the defendants to change their clothes during the trial so the jury could see them in their zoot suits. The judge also allowed a staffer for the Los Angeles sheriff's office to testify as an "expert witness" that Mexicans had a "blood thirst" and a "biological predisposition" to crime and killing, citing the human sacrifices of their Aztec ancestors. In January 1943 the all-white jury convicted seventeen of the defendants. Three were given life sentences for first-degree murder.

Soon after the convictions, Los Angeles erupted in racial violence. For almost a week in late May and early June, sailors and other servicemen assaulted Mexican Americans, turning East Los Angeles into a racial war zone. McWilliams described a mob of several thousand beating up every zoot-suiter they could find. "Streetcars were halted while Mexicans, and some Filipinos and Negroes, were jerked from their seats, pushed into the streets and beaten with a sadistic frenzy."

The LAPD was ordered not to arrest any of the servicemen, but more than 500 Mexican Americans were arrested on phony charges ranging from "rioting" to "vagrancy." Some local newspapers praised the attacks as a way of cleansing Los Angeles of a dangerous element. The city council adopted an ordinance banning zoot suits. McWilliams used his behind-the-scenes influence with the state attorney general to recommend a gubernatorial commission to calm the city. Governor Warren, no ally of McWilliams, recognized the wisdom of his idea and formed the commission, and the navy suspended shore leave to avoid further riots.

Due to the efforts of the Sleepy Lagoon Defense Committee, which McWilliams chaired, the state court of appeal reversed the convictions in October 1944. Although eight of the defendants had spent two years in San Quentin, the case represented a major organizing victory in the city's Mexican American community.

McWilliams's book *Witch Hunt,* published in 1950, was one of the first attacks on the intensifying anticommunist panic that would soon be labeled McCarthyism.

In 1951 McWilliams moved to New York to work for *The Nation,* assuming the role of editor in 1955. At the time, simply having a subscription to the magazine could be viewed, by congressional witch-hunters, as evidence of being a Communist or a Communist sympathizer and thus a potential victim of the blacklist. During this period, many donors to *The Nation* stopped contributing. It was banned from New York City schools.

McWilliams stood firm. The magazine became a source for investigative reporting and criticism of McCarthyism, the Cold War, the military industrial complex, and the arms race. Editorially, the magazine was an outspoken defender of free speech and civil liberties. McWilliams recruited some of the country's best foreign correspondents to inform readers about events around the world and opened its pages to such writers as Hunter S. Thompson, to academics **Howard Zinn, C. Wright Mills,** and William Appleman Williams, and to activists **Ralph Nader** and **Tom Hayden.**

The magazine provided excellent eyewitness reporting of the growing civil rights movement and later the United Farm Workers struggles in California. (**Cesar Chavez** said he learned most of what he knew about California agribusiness from McWilliams's writings.) McWilliams oversaw *The Nation*'s coverage of the growing antiwar movement, the consumer movement, and the early activities of the women's liberation movement.

McWilliams's November 1960 article "Are We Training Cuban Guerillas?" was the first to reveal the CIA's role in training Cuban exiles in Guatemala to overthrow Fidel Castro. "Public pressure should be brought to bear upon the administration to abandon this dangerous and hare-brained project," McWilliams wrote. The mainstream press failed to follow McWilliams's lead. In April 1961 the new president, John F. Kennedy, was embarrassed by the failed Bay of Pigs invasion.

Long after McWilliams left Hollywood, he continued to influence the film culture. Robert Towne's Oscar-winning original screenplay for the movie *Chinatown* (1974) was inspired by McWilliams's 1946 book *Southern California: An Island on the Land.* Luis Valdez's 1981 film *Zoot Suit,* based on events surrounding the Sleepy Lagoon murder trial, drew much of its story from McWilliams's writings. McWilliams recruited, trained, and influenced many writers and activists who shaped American politics and journalism into the late 20th and early 21st centuries.

CREDIT: Associated Press

William J. Brennan Jr.
(1906–1997)

THE APPOINTMENT of William J. Brennan Jr. to the US Supreme Court in 1956 came as a surprise to Court watchers. Many of his fellow Harvard Law School alumni could scarcely remember the unassuming Brennan, even though he had finished in the top 10 percent of his class. "As far as the knowledgeable world of Supreme Court insiders was concerned, Brennan was the anonymous man," wrote journalist David Halberstam. "Which meant in addition, it appeared, that he was the undeserving man as well, since if he was deserving, they all would have known him."

In fact, President Dwight D. Eisenhower chose him less for his brilliant mastery of constitutional law than for political reasons: Brennan was a Democrat and a Catholic, and the Republican president wanted to appeal to both groups in an election year. Only one senator, Joe McCarthy, voted against Brennan's confirmation.

When Brennan arrived in Washington to take his place on the high court, he felt like "the mule at the Kentucky Derby." But Brennan became perhaps the most influential justice in history. During his thirty-four years on the Court (spanning eight presidents), he wrote 1,360 opinions, 461 for the majority. His influence was also reflected in the language and logic of opinions written by his colleagues. Brennan combined a sharp intellect with a strong work ethic and with a sense of compassion, warmth, and humility that provoked a deep respect, even by those who disagreed with him. In 1984 the conservative magazine *National Review* regretfully acknowledged that "there is no individual in this country, on or off the Court, who has had a more profound and sustained impact upon public policy in the United States" than Brennan.

Brennan's tenure on the Court—and his opinions on a wide variety of subjects—reflected the high-water mark of progressive jurisprudence. He did not shy away from his view that the US Constitution should be an engine of social and political change. The law, he believed, should evolve with the times. He flatly rejected the notion that the Court should be guided primarily by the original intent of the Constitution's framers. Such thinking, Brennan wrote, was "little more than arrogance cloaked as humility."

Brennan served his first thirteen years on the Court under Chief Justice **Earl Warren.** Under subsequent chief justices Warren Burger and William Rehnquist, the Court no longer enjoyed a liberal majority. Brennan thus became the leader of the court's liberal wing, which was often outvoted. But even under Burger and Rehnquist, Brennan was occasionally able to knit together a narrow majority ruling that reflected his liberal principles. In his last majority opinion, on June 27, 1990, in *Metro Broadcasting v. Federal Communications Commission,* Brennan convinced several reluctant justices to join him to uphold two federal affirmative action programs designed to increase black ownership of radio and television stations. Five years later, an even more conservative Court overruled the decision.

Brennan grew up in a working-class Irish family in Newark, New Jersey. His father, William J. Brennan Sr., stoked the coal furnace at the Ballantine Brewery and was a leader in the International Brotherhood of Engineers and Oilers. He was also a political activist, elected four times to the Newark Board of Commissioners as the labor unions' candidate. As Public Safety Commissioner he oversaw the police and fire departments.

This work left its mark on his son, who would be known for his commitment to ending repressive police tactics. Referring to two of his most influential decisions, Brennan wrote, "It was the 'living' Constitution, infused with a vision of human dignity, that prohibited local police from ransacking a home without a warrant and forbade state prosecutors to compel an accused to convict himself with his own words." The senior Brennan's campaign slogan—"A square deal for all, special privileges to none"—was mirrored in many of his son's later legal decisions.

At his father's urging, Brennan got an undergraduate degree in business at the University of Pennsylvania Wharton School of Finance, graduating in 1928, before going to Harvard Law School. There, he studied under Felix Frankfurter, with whom he would later serve—and frequently disagree—on the bench. Frankfurter once remarked that he was pleased when his students were independent thinkers, "but Brennan's carrying it too far."

After completing his law degree in 1931, Brennan worked at a prominent Newark law firm where—surprisingly, given his family background—he represented management clients in labor disputes. After World War II, he was made a partner in the firm, where he became known for his expertise in labor law. But he felt increasingly uncomfortable representing management interests.

In 1949 Republican governor Alfred Driscoll appointed Brennan to New Jersey's Superior Court, and he rose quickly through the judicial system. Brennan advanced to the appellate division in 1950 and two years later to the state Supreme Court.

Upon his appointment to the US Supreme Court, Brennan became, according to Dahlia Lithwick's *New York Times* review of a Brennan biography, "an epic strategist and deal-maker who coordinated many of the Warren court's major decisions behind the scenes." He was adept at, in Brennan's words, "getting to five"—crafting his own opinions, or helping draft others' opinions, based on understanding enough about his colleagues' personal, political, and judicial views, to pull together a majority of votes.

Warren later said the most important case decided during his tenure on the Court was one written by Brennan, *Baker v. Carr* (1962), which affirmed the principle that the apportionment of legislature districts must be based on all citizens having the right to equal representation. Before then, districts within one state often varied wildly. Two years later the Supreme Court held that state legislative districts must be roughly equal in population, and virtually every legislature in the country had to redistrict. By establishing this basic democratic principle, the decision effectively shifted political power away from sparsely populated rural counties to denser urban areas.

Brennan's opinions strongly upheld and expanded civil rights and affirmative action. Harvard law professor Charles Ogletree Jr. described Brennan as "the consummate warrior for racial justice," who "spent his entire legal life trying to give [the Constitution] life and meaning for African-Americans."

Although he had to be prodded into hiring a female law clerk, on the bench Brennan was a defender of women's rights, striking down discriminatory workplace practices and advancing reproductive rights. His 1972 opinion in *Eisenstadt v. Baird* established the right of unmarried people to have access to information about contraception. In that ruling, he inserted right-to-privacy language: "If the right of privacy means anything, it is the right of the individual, married or single, to be free from unwarranted governmental intrusion into matters so fundamentally affecting a person as the decision whether to bear or beget a child." This rationale helped lay the groundwork for reproductive rights.

In 1970 Brennan's opinion in *Goldberg v. Kelly* found that New York had infringed on a welfare recipient's rights by cutting off her benefits without holding a hearing on the action, and thus violating the Fourteenth Amendment's guarantee of due process. In a 1987 speech to the Association of the Bar of the City of New York, Brennan said he viewed that decision as "injecting passion into a system whose abstract rationality had led it astray." Brennan's simple point—that bureaucrats should meet with their clients face to face—became a watershed in guaranteeing Americans their right to due process.

Brennan's famous opinion in the 1964 libel case *New York Times Co. v. Sullivan* struck a blow against limits on political dissent and free speech. The Court ruled that public officials (and later, public figures) could not recover damages for false statements about them unless the falsehoods were deliberate or reckless. The right to criticize government, Brennan wrote, is "the central meaning of the First Amendment." The amendment requires "breathing space" for free expression as an element of "a profound national commitment to the principle that debate on public issues should be uninhibited, robust, and wide-open, and that it may well include vehement, caustic, and sometimes unpleasantly sharp attacks on government and public officials."

Brennan believed in the strict separation of church and state. In 1963 he concurred with a decision to ban organized prayer in public schools, a decision the religious Brennan called his most difficult. His 1987 decision, *Edwards v. Aguillard,* overturned a Louisiana law requiring the teaching of "creation" science.

Brennan's biggest disappointment was his failure to persuade a majority of his colleagues to abolish the death penalty, which he believed was unconstitutional in two ways: He said that the death penalty was "barbaric and inhuman"—a violation of the Constitution's admonition against cruel and unusual punishment. He also believed that the workings of the criminal justice system—particularly the police and the courts—made it more likely that African Americans would end up on death row. Thus, Brennan thought, the death penalty was also unconstitutional because it was discriminatory based on race.

"The machinery chugs on unabated, belching out its dehumanizing product," he wrote toward the end of his life. "But I refuse to despair."

Brennan did not live to see the growing opposition to capital punishment emerge in the 21st century, particularly as a result of a significant number of cases in which DNA evidence revealed the innocence of prisoners on death row. In 2011 Illinois became the fourth state in four years to get rid of the death penalty, bringing the total number of states that no longer use the practice to sixteen, in addition to the District of Columbia.

In 1995 New York University School of Law established the Brennan Center for Justice, a public interest law firm, research center, and advocacy institute, to carry out Brennan's commitment to civil liberties, civil rights, free speech, and democracy.

CREDIT: Courtesy of the Library of the Jewish Theological Seminary

Rabbi Abraham Joshua Heschel (1907–1972)

IN JANUARY 1963, as the civil rights movement was gaining momentum, the National Conference of Christians and Jews sponsored a conference in Chicago entitled "Religion and Race." They invited Rabbi Abraham Joshua Heschel to deliver the keynote address. Heschel opened his speech by linking biblical history to contemporary struggles: "At the first conference on religion and race, the main participants were Pharaoh and Moses," Heschel said.

Moses's words were, "Thus says the Lord, the God of Israel, let My people go that they may celebrate a feast to me." While Pharaoh retorted: "Who is the Lord, that I should heed this voice and let Israel go? I do not know the Lord, and moreover I will not let Israel go." The outcome of that summit meeting has not come to an end. Pharaoh is not ready to capitulate. The exodus began, but is far from having been completed. In fact, it was easier for the children of Israel to cross the Red Sea than for a Negro to cross certain university campuses.

One of the 20th century's greatest theologians, Heschel not only profoundly shaped modern Judaism but also influenced Protestant and Catholic ideas about the biblical imperative to improve the world. An immigrant from Poland, Heschel had a thick Yiddish accent and looked like the stereotypical Old World rabbi, with his long white beard and his massive head of white hair, always wearing a yarmulke or a black beret. But in his last decade, he was also a man of action on the front lines of both the civil rights and the antiwar movements, speaking out, marching, and recruiting other clergy to these causes. For Heschel, from his earliest days as a student in Europe, the religious and secular worlds were deeply intertwined.

Heschel was born in Warsaw, Poland. His parents were Chasidim, members of a spiritually intense Orthodox Jewish sect, and descended from generations of distinguished rabbis. As a teenager, he demonstrated a precocious ability to understand lengthy treatises of Jewish law and to write his own commentaries on the Torah, the first five books of the Bible. He also had a personal charisma that others saw as confirmation of his spiritual and leadership qualities.

But Heschel resisted this destiny. On a daily basis, he continued to practice Orthodox rituals, but his intellectual curiosity would not allow him to follow the path chosen for him. He convinced his family to let him attend a secular university and a liberal nontraditional rabbinical college. He first went to a secular high school in Vilnius, Lithuania, then to the University of Berlin, where he received his Ph.D. in 1933 for a dissertation on the Hebrew prophets. The next year, he completed his studies at the rabbinical college. He emerged from this education well versed in Western philosophy, history, and art as well as Jewish subjects.

The 1935 publication of his revised dissertation made his reputation as a major scholar. The book advanced the then-radical thesis that the Hebrew prophets were serious critics of the social injustices of their eras but that their ideas remained relevant to injustices in contemporary times.

It would have been difficult for Heschel to avoid thinking about social injustice; his academic career began just as the Nazis took power in Germany. He was deported back to Poland in 1938, then fled to England. In 1940 he found haven at Hebrew Union College in Cincinnati, Ohio, the seminary that trained Reform Jewish rabbis, as part of an effort to rescue European Jewish scholars from the Nazis. While living in Cincinnati, he tried to rescue his family members, including his mother and sister, but without success: they were murdered by the Nazis. In 1945 he moved to the Jewish Theological Seminary (JTS) in New York City, the rabbinical seminary linked to Conservative Judaism, a branch more closely aligned with Heschel's religious views but less comfortable with what would become his progressive political activities. At JTS he published several important books on Jewish theology, including *Man Is Not Alone: A Philosophy of Religion* (1951), *The Sabbath: Its Meaning for Modern Man* (1951), *God in Search of Man: A Philosophy of Judaism* (1952), and *Man's Quest for God* (1954).

Heschel's knowledge of Christian theology led the Vatican to seek his advice when, in 1960, Pope John XXIII sought to repair relations between Catholics and Jews as part of the Ecumenical Council, the original name of the Second Vatican Council. Over four years, Heschel met with the pope's representatives and with the pope himself. He had a significant influence on what became the landmark 1965 statement "Nostra Aetate" (In our time), a turning point in Christian-Jewish relations. It reversed centuries of standard Christian teachings about Jews, including no longer blaming Jews collectively for the death of Jesus and refraining from calling for Jews to convert to Catholicism.

In 1963 Heschel was invited to a meeting of religious leaders with President John F. Kennedy. The day before the event, Heschel sent the president a telegram about civil rights, asking him to declare the nation's racial inequality a "state of moral emergency" and to act with "high moral grandeur and spiritual audacity."

It was at the 1963 "Religion and Race" conference that Heschel first met **Martin Luther King Jr.,** who delivered the final address at the meeting. They stayed in close touch, sharing both theological and political ideas. In March 1965, as state and local police attacked marchers outside Selma, Alabama, with billy clubs and tear gas, Heschel led a delegation of 800 people to FBI headquarters in New York City to protest the agency's failure to protect the demonstrators.

On Friday March 19 Heschel received a telegram from King inviting him to join another march from Selma to Montgomery. Heschel flew to Selma from New York on Saturday night and was welcomed as one of the leaders into the front row of marchers, with King, Ralph Bunche, and Ralph Abernathy. The photograph of Heschel walking arm in arm with King has become iconic of the coalition of Jews and blacks during the civil rights era. Heschel wrote, "For many of us the march from Selma to Montgomery was about protest and prayer. Legs are not lips and walking is not kneeling. And yet our legs uttered songs. Even without words, our march was worship. I felt my legs were praying."

Heschel was also the most visible traditional Jew in the antiwar movement. Having escaped Nazism, Heschel was acutely aware of the responsibilities of citizens in a democracy. "In regard to the cruelties committed in the name of a free society," he wrote, "some are guilty, all are responsible." In announcing his opposition to the Vietnam War, he cited Leviticus: "Thou shalt not stand idly by the blood of thy neighbor." Opposition to the war, he declared, was a religious obligation, "a supreme commandment." He worried that most Americans were indifferent to what he described as the criminal behavior of their elected government. "I have previously thought that we were waging war reluctantly, with sadness at killing so many people," he wrote about President **Lyndon B. Johnson**'s escalation of the war in Vietnam. "I realize that we are doing it now with pride in our military efficiency."

In October 1965 Heschel spoke at an antiwar rally at the UN Church Center and proposed a national religious movement to end the war. He quickly went to work putting that idea into practice. The National Emergency Committee of Clergy Concerned About Vietnam was founded in January 1966, with Heschel, Jesuit priest Daniel Berrigan, and Lutheran pastor Richard John Neuhaus as cochairs. Rev. **William Sloane Coffin,** the Yale chaplain, agreed to be acting executive secretary. Their first act was to send a telegram to LBJ, signed by twenty-one clergy, including Martin Luther King and Reinhold Niebuhr, urging the president to extend the bombing halt that had begun the previous Christmas and to pursue negotiations with the National Liberation Front and the North Vietnamese. Over the next few months, the group recruited additional clergy and organized rallies, fasts, vigils, and other forms of protest. Heschel drafted position papers, raised money, recruited Jewish clergy, gave numerous speeches, and led a two-day fast at a New York church to push for an end to US bombing of North Vietnam.

On January 31, 1967, the organization—renamed Clergy and Laymen Concerned About Vietnam (CALCAV) to be more inclusive—organized its first Washington, DC, rally. More than 2,000 people, clergy and laity, from forty-five states participated, including the leaders of the nation's major Jewish and Protestant denominations. They met with their congressional representatives and picketed in front of the White House. Heschel electrified the audience with his speech "The Moral Outrage in Vietnam," later published in *Fellowship*, the magazine of the Fellowship of Reconciliation: "Who would have believed that we life-loving Americans are capable of bringing death and destruction to so many innocent people? We are startled to discover how unmerciful, how beastly we ourselves can be. In the sight of so many thousands of civilians and soldiers slain, injured, crippled, of bodies emaciated, of forests destroyed by fire, God confronts us with this question: Where art thou?"

The next day, Heschel joined a small CALCAV delegation in a forty-minute meeting with Secretary of Defense Robert McNamara. They attempted, without success, to persuade him to suspend the bombing of North Vietnam and begin peace negotiations. By early 1967, CALCAV's leaders knew that King was preparing to make public his growing opposition to the war. Heschel, along with other major religious figures, accompanied him as he delivered his major antiwar address at New York's Riverside Church on April 4.

During the 1968 annual meeting of the Rabbinical Assembly, Heschel was honored by his fellow Conservative rabbis for his social activism and his contributions to Jewish scholarship. King was the keynote speaker, and the rabbis feted him by singing "We Shall Overcome" in Hebrew.

King, who called Heschel "my rabbi," was looking forward to attending a Passover Seder at Heschel's home that year, but he was assassinated a few weeks before the Jewish holiday. Heschel was the only Jew to deliver a eulogy at King's funeral service.

Rachel Carson
(1907–1964)

Rachel Carson testifies before the US Senate in 1963 to urge Congress to curb the sale of chemical pesticides and aerial spraying.

RACHEL CARSON was a marine biologist, an elegant writer, and a reluctant activist. She became a household name when her 1962 book *Silent Spring* alerted the public to the dangers that pesticides (such as DDT) have on the environment and on health. More broadly, her work questioned the chemical industry's political influence, government complicity with the industry, and scientists' faith in technology as an easy solution to most problems.

After World War II, American business embarked on a crusade to persuade Americans that science and technology could save humankind from the threats of disease, war, and hunger, could make society more efficient and productive, and could generally make life easy. Some major breakthroughs—such as Jonas Salk's discovery of a vaccine for polio—bolstered this belief in science as savior. New inventions—television, air conditioners, freezers and frozen food, fast cars, jet planes, and the first giant computers—persuaded many Americans to equate increasing technology with social and economic progress. The business crusade extended to other realms, such as support for nuclear power both as a source of energy and as a key element in the Cold War "atoms for peace" propaganda. DuPont, one of the nation's largest corporations, promoted its products through the popular slogan "Better living through chemistry."

Carson's most profound influence was creating popular skepticism of business claims about the safety of chemicals in our food, water, air, toys, clothes, and other aspects of the environment and daily life. Her work helped spark the modern environmental movement. In 1970, six years after she died, Congress established the Environmental Protection Agency. Two years later, the federal government banned the use of DDT.

Carson was a prolific and graceful writer who learned how to translate her understanding of scientific facts into works that raised public awareness about the natural world. Her specialized knowledge of marine biology, genetics, and other fields never diminished her sense of the majesty of the natural environment. "The pleasures, the values of contact with the natural world are not reserved for the scientist," she wrote. "They are available to anyone who will place himself under the influence of a lonely mountain top—or the sea—or the still-ness of a forest; or who will stop to think about so small a thing as the mystery of a growing seed."

Carson was born near Springdale, Pennsylvania, where her parents made a modest living on their small farm, now preserved as the Rachel Carson Home-stead. At the Pennsylvania College for Women (now Chatham University), Carson explored her two passions: literature and biology. Despite society's prejudice against women in science, Carson's biology teacher, Mary Scott Skinker, encour-aged her to pursue graduate school at Johns Hopkins University. She earned her masters degree in zoology and genetics in 1932 and taught for a few years at Johns Hopkins and at the University of Maryland, while spending her summer conduct-ing research at the Marine Biological Laboratory at Woods Hole, Massachusetts.

In the midst of the Depression, Carson lacked the funds to finish her Ph.D. She took a temporary position with the US Bureau of Fisheries (now the US Fish and Wildlife Service) as the writer for the *Romance Under the Seas* radio show. In 1936 the bureau hired her as a full-time biologist. She eventually became the chief editor of all publications for the bureau. She edited scientific articles and wrote pamphlets about natural resources and conservation, including a series about the national wildlife refuge system, which gave her valuable field experience.

Carson supplemented her government income by writing articles for the *Bal-timore Sun* on the delicate relationship between humans and the ecology of Chesapeake Bay. She expanded her 1937 article for *Atlantic Monthly*, "Undersea," into a book, *Under the Sea-Wind*, published in 1941. It earned critical acclaim but little popular attention.

Her next book, *The Sea Around Us* (1952), brought her fame and many sci-entific honors. "Great poets from Homer down to Masefield have tried to evoke the deep mystery and endless fascination of the ocean," the *New York Times* said in a review. "But the slender, gentle Miss Carson seems to have the best of it. Once or twice in a generation does the world get a physical scientist with literary genius. Miss Carson has written a classic in *The Sea Around Us*." The book was on the *New York Times* best-seller list for eighty-six weeks—thirty-nine weeks as the top seller—and won the National Book Award. Next came *The Edge of the Sea*, published in 1955. These three books about the ocean made Carson's repu-tation as a popular naturalist, science writer, and speaker and gave her the finan-cial independence to quit her government job and devote herself to writing.

Silent Spring marked a shift in her career—from writer to social critic and ac-tivist, challenging the practices of industry, government, and many fellow scientists.

During World War II, the United States used the insecticide DDT to kill lice and mosquitoes and to protect against outbreaks of malaria and typhus. After the war, chemical companies produced over 200 pesticides for use by farmers, foresters, and millions of suburbanites determined to keep insects off their lawns. Pesticide use grew from 125 million pounds in 1945 to 600 million pounds a decade later, but the public was generally unaware of the dangers. As early as 1945 Carson proposed an article on pesticides to *Readers Digest*, but the magazine was not interested. In 1957 DDT was sprayed as part of a mosquito-control campaign in Massachusetts, near the home of Carson's friend Olga Owens Huckins. Huckins sent Carson a letter she had written to the *Boston Herald* describing how the aerial spraying had destroyed her backyard bird sanctuary. "All these birds died horribly," Huckins wrote, but the mosquitoes remained. Worse, the state had not informed the residents about the use of the pesticide.

This information led Carson to worry about the use and abuse of science and technology. Human arrogance and power, she believed, could be used to "change drastically—or even destroy—the physical world." After four years of research, Carson's *Silent Spring* carefully documented the dangers of pesticides and herbicides. (The title referred to a spring when no birdsongs could be heard because the birds had been killed by pesticides.) She revealed the long-term presence of toxic chemicals in water and on land and its threat to animals, their habitat, and humans. Among other things, she documented the presence of DDT in breast milk.

The *New Yorker* serialized *Silent Spring* before its publication as a book in September 1962. Excerpts were also published in *Audubon* magazine. Carson called for a ban on the more harmful, long-lasting chemicals like DDT and for tighter government regulations on the manufacture and sale of other chemicals. She urged scientists to find other ways to fight pests to reduce the deadly poisons in the environment. Carson accused the chemical industry of intentionally spreading misinformation and government officials of uncritically accepting industry's claims. "The 'control of nature' is a phrase conceived in arrogance," Carson wrote, "born of the Neanderthal age of biology and philosophy, when it was supposed that nature exists for the convenience of man."

Anticipating attacks by industry, Carson and her publisher sent chapters to many noted scientists and others who would support the book's findings, including US Supreme Court Justice **William O. Douglas,** an ardent environmentalist. He publicly endorsed the book, saying, "We need a Bill of Rights against the 20th century poisoners of the human race."

As predicted, the chemical industry attacked *Silent Spring* as "sinister" and "hysterical." Industry spokespersons called Carson an alarmist. Robert White-Stevens, a biochemist for American Cyanamid and a key industry spokesperson, said that the book's claims were "gross distortions of the actual facts, completely unsupported by scientific, experimental evidence, and general practical experience in the field." He warned, "If man were to follow the teachings of Miss Carson, we would return to the Dark Ages, and the insects and diseases and vermin would once again inherit the earth," and he labeled Carson "a fanatic defender of the cult of the balance of nature." DuPont, Monsanto, and other corporations, including baby food companies, as well as the pesticide industry trade group, the National Agricultural Chemicals Association, spent hundreds of thousands of dollars to produce brochures and articles attacking Carson's credentials and promoting and defending pesticides.

The media was generally sympathetic to Carson. In a July 3, 1962, editorial, the *New York Times* wrote, "If her series [in the *New Yorker*] helps arouse public concern to immunize Government agencies against the blandishments of the hucksters and enforces adequate controls, the author will be as deserving of the Nobel Prize as was the inventor of DDT." On July 22, the *Times* ran an article with the headline "Silent Spring Is Now Noisy Summer: Pesticide Industry Up in Arms over a New Book." The story began, "The $300,000,000 pesticides industry has been highly irritated by a quiet woman author whose previous works on science have been praised for the beauty and precision of the writing." But the reviewer for *Time* magazine attacked Carson's "oversimplifications and downright errors. . . . Many of the scary generalizations—and there are lots of them—are patently unsound."

The chemical industry's campaign against *Silent Spring* brought more attention to the book, increasing public awareness and sales. It became a best seller. *CBS Reports* broadcast an hour-long television program about it, even after two major corporate sponsors withdrew their support. The industry attacks strengthened Carson's warnings about the misuse of science. "Such a liaison between science and industry is a growing phenomenon, seen in other areas as well," Carson said. "The American Medical Association, through its newspaper, has just referred physicians to a pesticide trade association for information to help them answer patients' questions about the effects of pesticides on man."

President John F. Kennedy discussed *Silent Spring* at a press conference and appointed a presidential science advisory committee to look into the problem of pesticides. Congress held hearings on the topic. Carson testified before both groups. In 1963 the Kennedy task force issued a report supporting Carson's scientific claims. The committee chairman, Jerome B. Wiesner, said the uncontrolled use of poisonous chemicals, including pesticides, was "potentially a much greater hazard" than radioactive fallout.

As the first grassroots environmental organizations emerged, they turned *Silent Spring* into a manifesto for change. Carson died in 1964 at fifty-six, unable to see the changes that her work had inspired. In the decades since, our understanding of the dangers of toxic chemicals—and our doubts about the claims of the chemical industry and others—have grown as other scientists and journalists, such as **Barry Commoner** and **Bill Moyers,** and hundreds of advocacy groups, such as the Sierra Club and Pesticide Watch, have followed in Carson's footsteps.

CREDIT: Associated Press/stf

Walter Reuther
(1907–1970)

"WE ARE the vanguard in America of that great crusade to build a better world," Walter Reuther told about 3,000 members of the United Auto Workers (UAW) at the union's 1947 convention. "We are the architects of the future."

The forty-year-old UAW president was preparing his members, many of them military veterans, for another kind of war, one that would pit unions and their progressive allies against the increasingly concentrated power of big business, a war whose battlefields would be the shop floor, the bargaining table, the voting booth, and the halls of Congress.

As a union activist who rose up from the factory floor, Reuther built the UAW into a major political force for a more humane society. He was UAW president from 1946 until his death in 1970. Under his leadership, the UAW grew to become the nation's largest union, with more than 1.5 million members. After World War II, he pushed for a large-scale conversion of the nation's industrial might to promote peace and full employment. Reuther played a key role in raising Americans' living standards and creating a mass middle class. An intellectual as well as an activist, he championed industrial democracy and mobilized union support for the civil rights movement in the 1960s.

Born in Wheeling, West Virginia, Reuther was one of five children of Valentine Reuther, a German immigrant, a Socialist, and an activist in the brewery workers' union. In 1919 Valentine took Walter and his brother Victor, ages eleven and six, to visit Socialist Party leader **Eugene Debs** at a prison outside Wheeling, where he was being held for his opposition to World War I. The visit made an indelible impression on both young Reuthers, who became committed Socialists.

Reuther quit high school at age sixteen and became an apprentice tool-and-die maker. He moved to Detroit in 1927, drawn by the Ford Motor Company's promise of high wages and a shorter workweek. He quickly established himself as one of the most skilled toolmakers at Ford's massive River Rouge plant. He characterized the industry at that time as a "social jungle" in which workers were "nameless, faceless clock numbers." Working nights, Reuther earned his high school diploma at twenty-two and took classes at Detroit City College, where he was joined by his younger brothers Victor and Roy.

The Depression deepened Reuther's already radical outlook. In 1932 he campaigned for Socialist Party presidential candidate **Norman Thomas** and was promptly fired by Ford, which kept a close eye on its employees' nonwork lives.

The following year, Walter and Victor embarked on a world tour, hoping to work at the Soviet Union's huge Gorki automobile factory, which Henry Ford had equipped. The brothers spent a year helping train the Gorki tool-and-die workers. Reuther was impressed by Russia's quick transformation into a modern industrial society, but he also saw the repression under Stalin's totalitarian regime, an experience that shaped Reuther's anticommunism during the Cold War.

Reuther returned to Detroit in 1935, but he never worked on the shop floor again. Instead, he channeled his talent and ambitions into building the fledgling auto workers' union. In 1936 he and Victor led a successful sit-down strike at the Kelsey-Hayes Wheel Company, a Ford supplier with 5,000 employees. The strike led to a settlement that doubled workers' wages. Reuther's reputation as a brilliant and courageous organizer was secured when he played a key role in planning the successful 1937 sit-down strike against General Motors (GM), a strike that crippled the company's production. GM recognized the UAW, and Chrysler soon followed suit. But Ford's antagonism toward unions meant that the third giant automaker would go to even greater lengths to resist the UAW.

On May 26, 1937, Reuther and other UAW organizers were passing out leaflets at a pedestrian overpass next to Ford's factory complex in Dearborn, Michigan. Ford's private police organization, euphemistically called the Service Department, attacked the union activists in what became known as the "Battle of the Overpass." Newspaper photographers captured Ford's thugs beating Reuther bloody. At a time of widespread pro-union sympathy, the incident was a public relations nightmare for Ford. Even so, it took almost four more years—until April 1941, when a huge strike shut down Ford's operations—before the company recognized the UAW and signed a union contract.

In 1939, when GM stalled negotiations for a new union contract, Reuther (at the time head of UAW's GM division) called for a strike, but only by tool-and-die workers. Faced with the threat of halting the retooling for its 1940 cars, GM agreed to a new contract.

In December 1940, with almost half of the nation's auto-manufacturing capacity idle, Reuther proposed a bold plan to convert idle factories to build 500 military aircraft a day. A brilliant student of industrial engineering and planning, Reuther's plan would put employees back to work, serve a patriotic goal, and put labor on an equal footing with business in planning the war economy. But the auto executives did not want to share decision making with government bureaucrats, much less with union leaders, and they rejected the idea out of hand.

Once the nation went to war, however, **Franklin D. Roosevelt** frequently consulted Reuther (whom he once called "my young red-headed engineer") on wartime production problems. Anticipating the war's end, Reuther proposed creating a three-part peace production board (with representative from business, labor, and government) to convert defense plants so they could produce railroad cars and workers' housing. To many Americans, this idea seemed like common sense. But business viewed it, correctly, as a radical shift of power, reducing business's influence in shaping the economy. One Detroit auto executive, George Romney (father of former Massachusetts governor Mitt Romney), understood Reuther's genius: "Walter Reuther is the most dangerous man in Detroit because no one is more skillful in bringing about the revolution without seeming to disturb the existing forms of society."

When the war ended, Reuther determined to put the labor movement on a more equal footing with corporate America. In 1946 he led a 116-day strike against GM. Autoworkers' buying power had eroded during the war, and the UAW demanded a 30 percent pay increase without an increase in the retail price of cars. When GM insisted that it could not meet the union's demand, Reuther challenged the company to "open its books." GM refused, but the UAW won an 18 percent wage increase.

But Reuther was making a larger point, one he would return to many times, particularly after he was elected UAW president in 1946. By demanding that GM freeze its prices, Reuther was appealing to consumers as well as to UAW members. He argued that the automobile industry—the largest and most profitable companies in the world—had a responsibility to society as well as to its stockholders and its workers. And it was the labor movement's responsibility not only to look out for its members but also to use its influence—at the bargaining table with business and in the political realm with government—to make America a more livable society for all. "What good is a dollar-an-hour more in wages if your neighborhood is burning down?" Reuther asked. "What good is another week's vacation if the lake you used to go to is polluted, and you can't swim in it and the kids can't play in it?"

Using the UAW's clout within the labor movement and with the Democratic Party, Reuther pushed a progressive postwar agenda that included national health care, economic redistribution, full employment, and job security for all.

Reuther's call for a progressive social contract among government, business, and labor was too radical for most Democrats, especially as the Cold War was heating up. So Reuther sought to achieve similar goals at the bargaining table, creating, in effect, a private welfare state for those Americans lucky enough to work for the nation's biggest corporations and to have a union contract. In 1948 the UAW got GM to agree to a historic contract tying wage increases to the general cost of living and to productivity increases. Over the next two decades, UAW members won unprecedented benefits, including enhanced job security, paid vacations, and health insurance. In 1955 the UAW won supplemental unemployment benefits that enabled UAW members to earn up to 95 percent of their regular paycheck even if they were laid off. Reuther hailed that provision as "the first time in the history of collective bargaining [that] great corporations agreed to begin to accept responsibility" for their workers during layoffs.

The union used strikes—or the threat of work stoppages—to gain these victories. It took a strike at Ford in 1949 to establish the union's right to have a voice in the speed of the assembly line. It took a 100-day strike at Chrysler in 1950 to win a pension plan.

As a result of these victories, UAW members were able to buy homes, move to the suburbs, send their children to college, take regular vacations, and anticipate a secure retirement. The UAW set the standard for other unions to win similar benefits from other major industries.

The UAW was on the front line of the civil rights movement. Reuther marched with **Martin Luther King Jr.** and other civil rights leaders in Mississippi and elsewhere. The UAW helped fund the 1963 March on Washington (which the AFL-CIO refused to endorse) and brought many of its members to the historic protest. Reuther was one of the few white speakers at the march. The UAW used its political clout to lobby for passage of the Civil Rights Act, the Voting Rights Act, and the Fair Housing Act. Reuther was also an early and generous supporter of **Cesar Chavez**'s efforts to organize farmworkers, marched with Chavez on numerous occasions, and supported the boycott of nonunion grapes and lettuce, long before other union leaders recognized the importance of the farmworkers' struggle.

Reuther advised Presidents John F. Kennedy and **Lyndon B. Johnson** to champion a bold federal program for full employment that would include government-funded public works and the conversion of the nation's defense industry to production for civilian needs. This, he argued, would dramatically address the nation's poor, create job opportunities for African Americans, and rebuild America's troubled cities without being as politically divisive as a federal program identified primarily as serving low-income blacks.

Both presidents rejected Reuther's advice. They were worried about alienating racist southern Democrats and sectors of business who opposed Keynesian-style economic planning. LBJ's announcement of an "unconditional war on poverty" in his 1964 State of the Union address pleased Reuther, but the details of the plan revealed its limitations. Testifying before Congress in April 1964, Reuther said, "While [the proposals] are good, [they] are not adequate, nor will they be successful in achieving their purposes, except as we begin to look at the broader problems [of the American economy]." He added, "Poverty is a reflection of our failure to achieve a more rational, more responsible, more equitable distribution of the abundance that is within our grasp." Reuther threw the UAW's considerable political weight behind LBJ's programs, but his critique proved to be correct.

In 1952 Reuther was elected president of the Congress of Industrial Organizations (CIO) and three years later brokered a merger with American Federation of Labor (AFL) president George Meany. By then about one-third of America's workers were union members. Reuther hoped that the AFL-CIO would spear-head a new wave of union organizing, but he was constantly frustrated by the in-difference of many unions to organizing the unorganized or to mobilizing their members for political action. The conservative Meany was part of the problem, but Reuther shared some of the blame as well. As part of the Red Scare, Reuther had expelled many of the most radical and experienced organizers and leaders from labor's ranks.

In 1966 Reuther said, "The AFL-CIO lacks the social vision, the dynamic thrust, the crusading spirit that should characterize the progressive modern labor movement." Two years later he withdrew the UAW from the AFL-CIO and forged a new labor group, the Alliance for Labor Action, with the Teamsters union. Reuther had big plans for the organization, but before it could launch any initiatives, Reuther, his wife, and two others were killed in a private plane crash in 1970.

CREDIT: Associated Press/William J. Smith

I. F. Stone
(1907–1989)

ISIDOR "IZZY" Feinstein's journalism career began at age fourteen, when he published his own neighborhood newspaper, *Progress*. Though a lackluster high school student in Haddonfield, New Jersey—graduating forty-ninth out of a class of fifty-two, and more interested in his budding reporting career than his class work— he was an avid reader and became radicalized as a teenager.

His father, who ran a dry-goods store, had immigrated to Philadelphia to escape anti-Semitic persecution in Russia. But the family found that racism and bigotry was deeply ingrained in the United States, too. When young Izzy witnessed a group of African Americans picketing the local movie theater at the opening of D. W. Griffith's film *The Birth of a Nation,* which glorified the Ku Klux Klan, it was a formative experience for the boy.

While studying at the University of Pennsylvania, he worked part-time at the *Philadelphia Inquirer,* earning $40 a week—a good wage in 1928. He dropped out in his junior year, began working at the paper full-time, and was a journalist for the rest of his life. With newspaper work, he said, he never "felt compelled to compromise with my conscience." In 1937 he changed his last name to Stone to keep readers who were too prejudiced to get past his Jewish-sounding byline, but among friends and colleagues, he was always called Izzy.

After several short stints at papers in New Jersey and Pennsylvania, he worked as an editorial writer from 1932 to 1939 for the *Philadelphia Record* and the *New York Post.* In 1937, he wrote a series of editorials for the *New York Post* attacking the US Supreme Court for knocking down key components of **Franklin D. Roosevelt**'s New Deal program as unconstitutional. In one he wrote, "Those safe, conservative majorities brought on the Civil War. Those safe, conservative majorities have stood in the path of almost every major piece of social legislation enacted by the elected representatives of the American people. To suit their ends, those safe, conservative justices have twisted the Constitution itself beyond recognition." Later that year he published his first book, *The Court Disposes,* in which he observed, "The Court can scent communism several centuries downwind, in a federal income tax or a minimum wage for chambermaids."

A few years later, the *Post,* concerned that Stone's left-wing editorials were costing the paper advertising dollars, forced him from the editorial department to the newsroom but gave him nothing to do. He soon resigned.

Stone and his wife, Esther, moved to Washington, DC, which became their permanent home. He covered the nation's capital initially as a freelancer for *The Nation,* then for *PM* (a leftist New York daily that lasted from 1940 to 1948 and whose staff included cartoonist **Theodor Geisel,** "Dr. Seuss"), the *New York Star,* the liberal *New York Post,* and the radical *Compass.* When the *Compass* folded in 1952, Stone was forty-five and had a family to support. But he was a pariah in the midst of the McCarthy era and could not find work.

Without a job, he began *I. F. Stone's Weekly* in 1953 and continued its publication through 1971. He never accepted advertisements for what he called his "four-page miniature journal of news and opinion."

As a publisher, Stone became "an independent capitalist, the owner of my own enterprise, subject to neither mortgager nor broker, factor nor patron." To get started, he used the mailing lists of the *Compass* and other publications, along with $3,500 he had received in severance pay and a $3,000 interest-free loan from a friend. He quickly had 5,000 subscribers, which swelled to 70,000 by the 1960s. Charter subscribers included **Albert Einstein, Eleanor Roosevelt,** and Bertrand Russell. "In the fifties, to find his *Weekly* in the mail was to feel a breath of hope for mankind," **Arthur Miller** recalled.

Stone researched, wrote, and edited the newsletter himself, helped only by his wife and an occasional student assistant. From the start, its influence was much greater than the size of its readership, because other journalists, politicians, and activists picked up on his leads.

Reporters and editors admired Stone's ability to unearth facts, connect the dots, ferret out the truth, and uncover patterns of lying, cover-ups, and hypocrisy by politicians and government officials regarding civil rights, civil liberties, nuclear weapons, the Cold War, Cuba, foreign policy, and war.

Stone got his stories not by cozying up to the powerful, parroting official press releases, or currying access to high-level policymakers, but by methodical tracking, following like a bloodhound the paper trail of hearings, transcripts, government documents, newspapers (he read ten a day), and foreign-language publications. In part, his methodology was developed out of necessity. He had very poor vision and hearing, making it difficult for him to cover press conferences and speeches.

He published original, critical articles about the Korean War, Senator Joe McCarthy, and FBI director J. Edgar Hoover, who read the *Weekly* compulsively. In 1953 Stone revealed that Pepsi-Cola had signed a $20,000 note for McCarthy when his bank account was overextended and that, at the same time, Pepsi was lobbying McCarthy's subcommittee to decontrol sugar.

He was unblushingly patriotic and believed, especially during the dark days of McCarthyism, that he was carrying out the Founders' desire for a truly free press. "I may be just a Red Jew son-of-a-bitch to them, but I'm keeping Thomas Jefferson alive," Stone said.

He wrote articles filled with his outrage over racial injustice, such as the murder trial of the killers of fourteen-year-old African American Emmett Till, who had been murdered in Mississippi in 1955 after reportedly flirting with a white woman. "Basically all of us whites, North and South, acquiesce in white supremacy, and benefit from the pool of cheap labor," he wrote.

In 1941 he resigned from the National Press Club when it refused service to him and his African American guest, William Hastie, a former federal judge. When Stone tried to join again in 1956, after the club was integrated, he was blackballed.

During the nuclear test ban debate in 1957, Stone pieced together a story that reporters for major newspapers missed. To undermine support for a test ban, the Atomic Energy Commission (AEC) argued that there was no way to detect nuclear testing from a great distance and thus that there would be no way to verify the agreement. Stone found a government seismologist who told him that an underground Nevada test had been detected from as much as 2,600 miles away. The AEC was forced to claim it had made an "inadvertent" error. "No agency in Washington has a worse record than the AEC for these little 'errors,'" Stone wrote. Stone published the story in his tiny *Weekly,* and it was picked up by other reporters and politicians.

Stone used this method to investigate many issues, from military spending to worker uprisings in Hungary, free speech infringement, and American arrogance abroad. In 1964 he was the first American journalist to challenge President **Lyndon B. Johnson**'s account of the Gulf of Tonkin incident, which LBJ used to justify going to war in Vietnam. Throughout the 1960s Stone exposed the government's lies about the Vietnam War with thorough documentation, providing ammunition for the antiwar movement.

In one stirring piece, written in 1965, he compared events in Selma, Alabama, and Saigon: "If the federal government handled Negro aspiration as it handles the revolt in South Vietnam, we would be sending 'counter-insurgency' teams from Fort Bragg into the South to kill civil rights agitators. We would be burning out with napalm the Negro neighborhoods in which we suspected that CORE or SNCC workers were hiding."

In 1967, with the war intensifying, he condemned the US military's practice of destroying whole villages to get a handful of guerrillas. "Imagine 30,000 Chinese troops uprooting Iowa villagers to save them from Republicanism and you get some idea of how likely this is to win—as our sentimental generals say—the hearts of the people."

Stone also wrote twelve books, including *Underground to Palestine* (1946), *This Is Israel* (1948), *The Hidden History of the Korean War* (1952), and *The Killings at Kent State: How Murder Went Unpunished* (1971).

In declining health, Stone began publishing the newsletter on a biweekly basis in 1967 and gave it up entirely in 1971. He then taught himself Greek and wrote a nonfiction mystery-thriller, *The Trial of Socrates,* published in 1988. The book, a *New York Times* best seller for nine weeks, explored why ancient Greece, a civilization known for its embrace of free speech, would execute Socrates for what he thought and said.

Controversy hounded Stone even after he died. In 1992 the right-wing magazine *Human Events* charged that he had been a Soviet spy, based on newly released documents. Stone's FBI file, released in 1994, contained 2,000 pages. According to his biographer D. D. Guttenplan, "The FBI didn't find a single piece of evidence to suggest that I. F. Stone was anything other than he seemed—an unrepentant radical who concentrated his fire on his own government's failings."

CREDIT: Associated Press

Thurgood Marshall
(1908–1993)

THURGOOD MARSHALL liked telling stories. One of his favorite concerned his days as the head of the legal arm of the National Association for the Advancement of Colored People (NAACP) in the 1930s and 1940s representing black clients facing prosecution in the South. He recalled arriving in town one day only to learn that his client had been lynched that afternoon. Another story concerned some white tourists who were visiting the US Supreme Court and mistakenly entered an elevator that was reserved for the justices. When they saw Marshall, they mistook him for the elevator operator. "First floor, please," one of them said. "Yowsa, yowsa," Marshall responded, accentuating his southern accent, then pushed the button. When the elevator reached the first floor, he ushered them out, never letting on that he was a member of the Supreme Court.

Throughout his life, Marshall—the chief architect of the legal strategy to dismantle segregation—was forced to endure such indignities, but he channeled his outrage by battling racism. As the head of the NAACP's legal arm, he worked under repressive conditions with limited budgets. His most important victory was the Supreme Court's *Brown v. Board of Education* ruling in 1954, which overturned the legality of the long-standing "separate but equal" system of racial segregation governing public education. Marshall's argument in the case relied on the Fourteenth Amendment, which gave freed slaves "equal protection of the laws." As one of his clients recalled, "until Marshall came, [that] law was whatever a white lawyer or white policeman or white judge said it was." He was already a famous lawyer, and certainly America's most prominent black attorney, when **Lyndon B. Johnson** appointed him to the Court in 1967.

Marshall grew up in segregated Baltimore, Maryland, where, he recalled, "there wasn't a single department store that would let a Negro in the front door." His mother was an elementary school teacher. His father, who had been a Pullman car waiter, worked as a steward at an exclusive, all-white yacht club. In his spare time, Marshall's father liked to visit Baltimore courtrooms and listen to the cases. He would come home and engage Marshall and his brother in lawyerly arguments. Marshall learned about the US Constitution as a young boy as punishment for being a hell-raiser in school. "Instead of making us copy out stuff on the blackboard after school when we misbehaved, our teacher sent us down into the basement to learn parts of the Constitution," Marshall recalled, "I made my way through every paragraph."

Marshall graduated with honors in 1930 from Lincoln University, where he was an outstanding debater. His classmates included entertainer Cab Calloway and writer **Langston Hughes.** Marshall wanted to attend the University of Maryland's law school, a few blocks from his home, but it barred blacks. Instead, he went to Howard University Law School in Washington, DC. His mother pawned her wedding and engagement rings to pay the entrance fees, and Marshall commuted each day from Baltimore so he could live at home and save money.

Charles Hamilton Houston, the vice dean, viewed the law school as training "social engineers" who could use the law to challenge segregation. A Harvard Law School graduate, Houston was the first black lawyer to win a case before the US Supreme Court.

Marshall graduated at the top of his class and opened a law office in Baltimore, mostly handling civil rights cases for poor clients. He earned a solid reputation as a skilled lawyer, particularly after winning a case (with Houston's help) before the state court of appeals—*Murray v. Maryland* in 1936—that challenged the University of Maryland law school's ban on black students. That year, Houston, by then the NAACP's lead attorney, recruited Marshall to join the staff, based in New York. Two years later, at age thirty, Marshall became chief counsel when Houston returned to Howard.

With Houston's help, Marshall recruited a team of brilliant activist lawyers for the NAACP. In contrast to cause lawyers, who defended individuals to advance a progressive cause, like **Clarence Darrow** and **Louis Brandeis,** Marshall's team (renamed the NAACP Legal Defense Fund) became the first public interest law firm devoted entirely to identifying cases that would change society, not just help a particular plaintiff. The team was a laboratory for cutting-edge litigation; its long-term goal was to tear down segregation by finding cases that could set precedents in lower courts and eventually reach the Supreme Court.

Before Marshall arrived at the NAACP, its legal strategy was to make "separate but equal" truly equal by fighting to get equal funding for segregated all-black schools. Marshall abandoned that approach in favor of challenging segregation itself. Some local black lawyers who had handled cases for the NAACP resigned in protest, but Marshall would not back down. He handled many of the cases himself, recruited new lawyers, and traveled around the country, especially the South, looking for plaintiffs for future cases.

He was known for his folksy courtroom style, a tactic to disarm his opponents, who often underestimated him.

As an emissary from the NAACP, Marshall was often at risk of physical harm while traveling in the South. While on the road, he usually stayed in private homes because no hotel, restaurant, or public restroom was open to him. He endured repeated death threats. Once, in Columbia, Mississippi, after an all-white jury acquitted his black clients—a rare occurrence—he was nearly lynched, with the help of local police.

Marshall argued thirty-two cases before the US Supreme Court and won twenty-nine of them. He won his first Supreme Court case, *Chambers v. Florida* (1940), at the age of thirty-two. Other landmark victories include *Smith v. Allwright* (1944), which overthrew the South's "whites only" primary system, which white southern politicians used to disenfranchise blacks, and *Shelley v. Kraemer* (1948), in which the Court declared that restrictive covenants barring blacks from buying or renting homes could not be enforced in state courts.

But *Brown* was Marshall's crowning achievement at the NAACP. In 1950 Marshall won two Supreme Court cases—*Sweatt v. Painter* and *McLaurin v. Oklahoma State Regents*—that challenged segregation in graduate schools. After these victories, he recruited plaintiffs to tackle segregation in public elementary and high schools. He sued school districts in South Carolina, Virginia, Delaware, the District of Columbia, and Kansas on behalf of local parents and students. The cases were consolidated under the Kansas lawsuit, *Oliver Brown et al. v. Board of Education of Topeka*. One of Marshall's innovations was to file a Brandeis Brief (see the profile of **Louis Brandeis**) that did not rely solely on legal theory, but also drew on studies by sociologists and psychologists that documented the harmful effects of segregation.

Marshall's opposing lawyer was John W. Davis, former solicitor general and the Democrats' presidential candidate in 1924. Considered the leading appellate lawyer in the country, Davis had argued some 140 cases before the Supreme Court. While in law school, Marshall would sometimes cut classes to watch Davis argue before the Court.

After Marshall and Davis made their arguments in 1952, the court was divided. It was only after a second round of arguments in 1954—after **Earl Warren** was appointed chief justice—that the court ruled unanimously to overturn segregation in public schools. The ruling marked a turning point in American history and lifted Marshall's national profile.

Some civil rights activists disparaged the NAACP's legal approach to dismantling segregation, contending that civil disobedience was a more effective tool to change public opinion and pressure politicians and businesses to change their practices. But when they needed attorneys, it was the NAACP they turned to. Marshall's clients included the activists who staged lunch counter sit-ins and integrated southern buses in Freedom Rides.

In 1961 President John F. Kennedy named Marshall to the federal appeals court. Southern senators held up the appointment for almost a year, challenging his legal credentials but obviously opposed to him because he was black and a civil rights pioneer. None of the 112 opinions he wrote on that court was overturned on appeal. Several of his dissenting opinions were eventually adopted as majority opinions by the Supreme Court.

Lyndon B. Johnson appointed Marshall to the Supreme Court in 1967. There he joined a strong liberal majority and advanced bold ideas expanding civil rights and free speech. In *Amalgamated Food Employees Union v. Logan Valley Plaza* (1968), Marshall's majority opinion ruled that a shopping center was a "public forum" and could not exclude picketers. His majority opinion in *Stanley v. Georgia* (1969) held that the possession of pornography in the privacy of one's home could not be subject to prosecution. In *Bounds v. Smith* (1977) he wrote the majority opinion ruling that state prisons must provide inmates with "adequate law libraries or adequate assistance from persons trained in the law."

As his liberal colleagues left the court, to be replaced by four conservative justices appointed by Richard Nixon, the court's center of gravity shifted, and Marshall became well-known for his articulate dissenting opinions. One of his best known was in a 1973 case, *San Antonio School District v. Rodriguez*, in which the court ruled by a 5–4 vote that Texas's system of funding public schools through property taxes—which meant that wealthy communities spent much more than poor ones—did not violate the Constitution's equal protection mandate. In his dissent, Marshall argued that the system "deprives children in their earliest years of the chance to reach their full potential as citizens" by denying them an equally funded public education.

Like his closest ally, Justice **William J. Brennan Jr.,** Marshall believed that the death penalty was unconstitutional under all circumstances. During a death penalty argument in 1981, Justice William Rehnquist said that the prisoner's repeated appeals had cost the taxpayers too much money. Marshall interrupted, saying, "It would have been cheaper to shoot him right after he was arrested, wouldn't it?"

In his final term, Marshall dissented in 25 of 112 cases. He became increasingly frustrated by the country's failure to carry out the provisions of the landmark rulings intended not only to dismantle legal segregation but also to bring about more racial and social equality. The angrier he got, the more he vented his frustrations in public, sometimes causing controversy, highly unusual for a Supreme Court Justice. "I wouldn't do the job of dogcatcher for Ronald Reagan," he said in a 1989 interview.

Marshall had hoped to wait to retire until a Democrat was elected president and could replace him. But when his health deteriorated, he retired in 1991 after twenty-four years on the Supreme Court. President George H. W. Bush appointed Clarence Thomas—Marshall's polar opposite on everything except skin color—to replace him.

In 2010 President Barack Obama appointed one of Marshall's former law clerks, Elena Kagan, to the Supreme Court. During the confirmation process, conservative Republican senators sought to discredit Kagan by disparaging her mentor, Marshall. On the first day of her confirmation hearings, Marshall's name came up thirty-five times. Senator Jeff Sessions of Alabama, the ranking Republican on the Judiciary Committee, criticized Marshall as a "liberal activist judge." Senate Minority Whip Jon Kyl of Arizona attacked Marshall for his "determination to protect the underdog." Marshall would have worn those attacks as a badge of honor.

CREDIT: Associated Press

Lyndon B. Johnson
(1908–1973)

"PART OF the way with LBJ" was how antiwar activists described their lukewarm endorsement of President Lyndon Baines Johnson when he was running against Republican Barry Goldwater in 1964. Activists gave Johnson grudging support for his growing embrace of civil rights and antipoverty efforts, but they could not disguise their disgust at his escalation of the Vietnam War. Nearly five decades later, that remains LBJ's divided image among liberals and progressives: as a savvy lawmaker who squandered his opportunity to make a serious assault on racial and economic injustice by spending the nation's taxes and his own political capital fighting an immoral war in southeast Asia.

LBJ's family had lived in Texas for generations, fought for the Confederacy during the Civil War, and made their living as farmers and ranchers. But LBJ's father, a one-time state legislator, piled up huge debts, lost the family farm, and plunged the family into financial hard times. As a schoolteacher with poor students in rural Texas, as an aide to a Texas congressman during the New Deal, as Texas state director of the National Youth Administration (a New Deal jobs program), as a congressman and senator, and as president, LBJ's own experience with economic hardship shaped his commitment to helping the poor.

In the 1930s Texas was part of the solid Democratic South, supporting the New Deal so long as it provided jobs and relief and did not require racial integration or encourage workers to join unions. LBJ was elected to Congress in 1937, at age twenty-eight. As an ally of **Franklin D. Roosevelt,** he brought electricity, housing, and other improvements to his district. He lost his first bid for the Senate in 1941 and stayed in the House but ultimately won a Senate seat in 1948. In 1955 his Democratic colleagues elected him majority leader. He used his legendary parliamentary skills and powers of persuasion to get reluctant senators to vote for liberal legislation.

In 1960 he threw his Texas hat into the presidential ring, but Senator John F. Kennedy from Massachusetts had wider appeal. JFK needed LBJ's help to win the South and to help pass legislation in Congress, so he asked him to be his running mate. Johnson knew he would have more power as Senate majority leader than as vice president, but he took the offer, thinking it would be a stepping-stone to the White House after eight years of a Kennedy administration. When Kennedy was killed in November 1963, Johnson achieved his goal in a way both unexpected and unwanted. But he mobilized America's sympathy for the slain president to achieve goals that JFK, a much-less-skilled legislator, could not have won.

Six months after taking office, in a commencement speech at the University of Michigan on May 22, 1964, LBJ called on the country to move not only toward "the rich society and the powerful society, but upward to the Great Society," which he defined as one that would "end poverty and racial injustice." The language was bold, designed to appeal to civil rights activists, unions, and liberals and to lay the groundwork for the upcoming election. In November he beat Goldwater in a historic landslide victory, which, along with large Democratic majorities in Congress, provided a mandate for LBJ's Great Society plan, which progressives hoped would be the next New Deal.

The Great Society is best known for its efforts to reduce poverty and promote civil rights, but it also included landmark environmental protection and conservation measures, liberal immigration laws, the creation of the National Endowment for the Arts and the National Endowment for the Humanities, the Highway Safety Act, the Public Broadcasting Act, and a bill to provide consumers with protection against dangerous and shoddy products.

Johnson called on the nation to wage a War on Poverty and backed his call with major legislative initiatives. In 1964 Congress passed the Economic Opportunity Act, and soon antipoverty programs were under way, including such programs as Head Start (early education for poor children), Legal Services (legal aid to poor families), and health care provision based in neighborhood clinics and hospitals. The antipoverty program encouraged residents of poor neighborhoods to create nonprofit community-based organizations to deliver services, build housing, and organize to gain a voice in local government. Johnson established the Department of Housing and Urban Development, appointed Robert Weaver, the first African American in the cabinet, to head it, and increased funding for low-income housing. He enacted pathbreaking job training programs, Medicare (for the elderly), and Medicaid (for the poor). Federal aid for elementary and secondary education, especially for poorer districts, was dramatically expanded.

In the context of a growing economy, the plan was effective. Between 1965 and 1968, antipoverty funding doubled, from $6 billion to $12 billion, and then doubled again to $24.5 billion by 1974 under President Richard Nixon. The poverty rate declined from 20 percent to 12 percent between 1964 and 1974.

Although LBJ grew up under Jim Crow segregation and was known to use racist epithets in conversation, he was a moderate on race issues. In 1948 he opposed President Harry S. Truman's civil rights program, but six years later he was one of the few southern Senators who refused to sign the Southern Manifesto, a pledge to resist implementing the US Supreme Court's desegregation order. He risked alienating white Texas voters by maneuvering successfully to pass the Civil

Rights Act of 1957, the first civil rights measure enacted in almost a century. He recognized his own racist sentiments but fought to overcome them, in part out of decency and in part out of a desire to win acceptance from northern liberals among his Senate colleagues and voters.

In his first address to Congress, on November 27, 1963, a few days after Kennedy was shot, LBJ told the legislators, "No memorial oration or eulogy could more eloquently honor President Kennedy's memory than the earliest possible passage of the civil rights bill for which he fought so long." Using his consummate arm-twisting skills and bolstered by ongoing civil rights protests in the South, LBJ got the Civil Rights Act—outlawing segregation in restaurants, buses, and other public facilities—through Congress and signed it on July 2, 1964.

Next on his agenda was the Voting Rights Act. On March 15, 1965, in a speech to Congress, LBJ said, "There is no Negro problem. There is no Southern problem. There is no Northern problem. There is only an American problem." He added, "It's not just Negroes, but really it's all of us, who must overcome the crippling legacy of bigotry and injustice." He concluded, "And we shall overcome."

Johnson's use of the words of the civil rights anthem symbolized his embrace of the movement. But it was an uneasy alliance. LBJ was angry at the civil rights activists who embarrassed him by challenging the segregated all-white delegation at the 1964 Democratic Party convention. But he also recognized that the willingness of activists to put their bodies on the line against fists and fire hoses had tilted public opinion. The movement's civil disobedience, rallies, and voter registration drives pricked Americans' consciences. LBJ understood that the nation's mood was changing.

At a meeting at the White House, LBJ asked **Martin Luther King Jr.** to put the protests on hold and give him a chance to bring reluctant members of Congress around. King responded that blacks had already waited too long. As LBJ's aide **Bill Moyers** recalled, King "talked about the murders and lynchings, the churches set on fire, children brutalized, the law defied, men and women humiliated, their lives exhausted, their hearts broken. LBJ listened, as intently as I ever saw him listen. He listened, and then he put his hand on Martin Luther King's shoulder, and said, in effect: 'OK. You go out there Dr. King and keep doing what you're doing, and make it possible for me to do the right thing.'"

LBJ used every arm-twisting trick he had to fashion a coalition of northern and border-state Democrats and moderate Republicans to enact the landmark Voting Rights Act. The act barred literacy tests and other obstacles to voting that were being imposed by southern states. Within four years, black voter turnout had tripled. Since then, the number of black elected officials at all levels of government has grown dramatically.

Johnson and the civil rights movement forged a productive if tense alliance. As the movement took to the streets, LBJ showed increasing resolve and moral courage to be the president from the South who brought America closer to racial and economic justice. But Johnson did not reap the political rewards for his efforts. Between 1964 and 1968, race riots engulfed many American cities, triggering a tremendous backlash among white middle-class and working-class voters, including many once-loyal Democrats.

LBJ also lost his credibility with many liberal Democrats for his zealous expansion of the Vietnam War. The number of American troops in Vietnam grew to 100,000 in 1965 and to 500,000 three years later. As antiwar protests grew in number and size, LBJ's ratings among Democratic voters dropped sharply. King's first major speech opposing the war, in August 1967, deepened the nation's antiwar feelings and ruptured the relationship between the preacher and the president.

By the spring of 1968 Johnson had concluded that he would face strong opposition in the Democratic primaries and could even lose the November election. On March 31, 1968, to the surprise of some of his own staff, LBJ announced that he would not seek reelection. Four days later, King was killed in Memphis, Tennessee, and riots broke out in a number of cities. LBJ recognized that King's murder could also spark a renewed push to pass a bill outlawing racial discrimination in housing that had been languishing in Congress. Despite being a lame-duck president, LBJ was still able to use his prodigious political skills. Within a week, on April 11, Congress passed and LBJ signed the Fair Housing Act.

LBJ predicted, correctly, that by identifying closely with the civil rights movement, the Democratic Party would lose its hold on many white southerners. Democrats also lost many white voters who blamed the party for the violence of the urban riots and the terrorist wing of the antiwar movement, as well as for the "sex, drugs, and rock and roll" culture of the hippie movement. In November 1968 appealing to what he called the "silent majority," Richard Nixon beat Vice President Hubert Humphrey for the White House, which many political analysts viewed as a rebuke of LBJ as well.

CREDIT: Associated Press/Ota Richter

John Kenneth Galbraith
(1908–2006)

DURING THE late 1950s and throughout
the 1960s, it was "conventional wisdom"
to view the United States as the quintessential "affluent society." Economist John
Kenneth Galbraith had coined these
phrases, and that they are now widely
used is a mark of his influence not only among economists but in the broader society. He used the first phrase to highlight our society's tendency to accept as normal things that should be matters of controversy and debate. He used the second
term somewhat ironically, noting that despite the postwar nation's great private
wealth, America was quite stingy when it came to meeting the needs of the poor
and shortsighted when it came to planning for its future.

Galbraith was the 20th century's best-known American economist, in part because he was able to write clearly and engagingly for a broad audience. His ideas
helped shape America's understanding of itself. He popularized the theories of
British economist John Maynard Keynes and his followers, which challenged the
view that an unregulated free market could bring about sustained prosperity and
a humane society. He grew increasingly critical of the power big corporations
wielded over consumers, workers, and the environment and concerned about the
failure of unions and government to serve as a counterweight. His writings
shaped public opinion, and his involvement in politics and government at the
highest levels shaped public policy.

Some economists, envious of Galbraith's popularity and influence, dismissed
his writings as unscientific. They were contemptuous of Galbraith's expressions
of moral outrage at America's misplaced priorities. But even his professional colleagues had to give this towering intellectual—literally as well as figuratively: he
was six foot eight—his due. In 1972 he was elected president of the American
Economic Association.

Galbraith was born on a 150-acre farm in Ontario, Canada. His father was a
schoolteacher and farmer, who led a farm-cooperative insurance company. Galbraith's mother died when he was fourteen.

At age eighteen he enrolled at Ontario Agricultural College—which he later
described as "not only the cheapest but probably the worst college in the English-
speaking world"—where he took practical farming courses. But the Depression
forced Galbraith to ask bigger questions—Why were so many farmers going bankrupt? How were prices and stability to be restored to the agricultural economy?—

so he finished his undergraduate education at the University of Toronto and then headed for the University of California, Berkeley, where he earned a master's degree in 1933 and a doctorate in agricultural economics the next year.

Like many young economists in those years, Galbraith was energized by the ideas of Keynes, who argued for government intervention in moments of crisis to address problems like severe unemployment. During his long teaching career, mostly at Harvard, Galbraith was active in politics. At age thirty-three, under **Franklin D. Roosevelt,** he was the administrator of wage and price controls in the controversial Office of Price Administration during World War II. He advised John F. Kennedy, his former Harvard student, on economic issues and served as his ambassador to India. In several memos to JFK, Galbraith warned about the potential quagmire of US military intervention in Vietnam, but other advisers had greater sway over the young president. Galbraith served as an adviser to **Lyndon B. Johnson,** helping him shape his antipoverty programs, and he wrote the president's speech outlining his Great Society agenda. He later broke with LBJ over the war in Vietnam.

Galbraith's greatest influence was as a public intellectual who shaped the national debate with best-selling books, a prolific stream of articles, and a constant presence on television, on the lecture circuit, and in his popular classes at Harvard. In his three most influential books—*American Capitalism* (1952), *The Affluent Society* (1958), and *The New Industrial State* (1967)—he held a mirror up to postwar America.

His *American Capitalism* exposed the growing concentration of corporate power, which he viewed as a threat to democracy as well as to a healthy economy. In the 1950s, at the height of the Cold War, big business went on a propaganda crusade, using radio, TV, and other means to extol the virtues of the "free market" and the dangers of government regulation, which, big business held, was only a short step from communism. Galbraith set out to debunk this. He believed that the solution was not to break up the big corporations but to regulate them through government policy.

America's postwar prosperity—suburbanization, home ownership, and new household goods like vacuum cleaners and freezers—was growing in the late 1950s when Galbraith came out with *The Affluent Society*. Galbraith was impressed with America's technological capacity to produce things, but he said that rising gross domestic product was not the best measure of a society's well-being. "An increased supply of educational services," he wrote, "has a standing in the total not different in kind from an increased output of television receivers." America needed to find a "social balance" between private and public goods.

In order to grow, Galbraith noted, corporations had to manipulate consumers, through advertising and market research, to feel unsatisfied with their existing standard of living and to demand things they did not have and did not need. As a result, America was overloaded with useless products.

Big business could persuade consumers that the next version of each product—cars, toasters, refrigerators, toys, clothes, televisions—was bigger, better, and absolutely necessary to keeping up with the Joneses. Companies designed major and expensive consumer goods, including cars, to last only a few years before falling apart in order to stimulate demand, a strategy called "planned obsolescence."

Companies also encouraged consumers to "buy now, pay later," leading many of them to overextend themselves—a trend that led to the explosion of credit cards and massive consumer debt.

Meanwhile, Galbraith warned, the nation was investing too little on public needs—education, roads, parks, scientific research to prevent diseases, health care, job training, the arts, and the invisible poor. Big corporations could move quickly to invent and produce new products and whet consumers' appetites, but democratic government was unable to move as rapidly to raise taxes and invest in public programs. America's priorities were out of whack, Galbraith explained. For example, if auto companies build more cars, government needs to invest more money on public roads and places to park. Americans have lots of vacuum cleaners for their homes, but governments have too few street-cleaning machines.

Galbraith identified the widening gap between the rich and the poor as both a moral challenge and a threat to economic stability. Only government had the capacity to deal with the boom-and-bust cycles of the capitalist economy and help those left behind in poverty. He thus proposed significant public investment to create jobs, avoid another depression, and increase social justice.

But although he was a great believer in government spending, Galbraith was not enthusiastic about rising military spending and the escalating arms race. Military Keynesianism might generate jobs, but it did not make the world safer or make America a more livable society. In *The Affluent Society* and other books, and in his advice to Democratic candidates and officeholders, Galbraith was always a skeptic about the Cold War and the influence of what Dwight D. Eisenhower called the "military-industrial complex."

The Affluent Society sold more than 1 million copies and stayed on the *New York Times* best-seller list for most of 1958. It helped lay the foundation for the liberal policies carried out by JFK and LBJ (such as Medicare, Medicaid, and low-income housing), although Galbraith thought that they were not bold enough.

With each book, Galbraith deepened his progressive analysis. In *The New Industrial State,* Galbraith's view of big business was even more critical. Most of society's long-term planning, he wrote, is done by the top managers of America's major corporations, and the power they wield has become even more concentrated as big conglomerates increasingly gobble up smaller companies. In *Economics and the Public Purpose,* published in 1973, he insisted that democratically elected government, not big corporations, should plan for society's basic needs.

During the 1980s and 1990s, as Reaganism and the dominance of conservative ideas seemed to overturn everything he believed in, Galbraith continued to

write and lecture, attacking the widening income gap, the deregulation of business, and US militarism. In *The Good Society* (1996), he warned that America
was becoming a "democracy of the fortunate."

Many of Galbraith's ideas are now, ironically, conventional wisdom. Few
economists today believe that stimulating economic growth, on its own, is sufficient to ensure a society's well-being. They acknowledge that government programs for education, health care, transportation, and other infrastructures are
necessary to guarantee a decent society and a sustainable economy. The annual
UN Human Development Report evaluates societies based on indicators of
health, education, poverty, gender equality, and other measures that reflect much
of Galbraith's thinking and that of one of his biggest admirers—Amartya Sen,
Harvard economist and Nobel laureate.

But even today, only a handful of well-known economists—among them
Paul Krugman, Robert Reich, Robert Kuttner, Dean Baker, Nancy Folbre, Jared
Bernstein, Juliet Schor, and Joseph Stiglitz—follow in Galbraith's giant footsteps, raising big questions about the overall direction of society, writing for a
broad audience, and challenging the ideological and political influence of corporate America and its allies in government. Galbraith's critique of his profession is
as true today as it was when he wrote it: "What is called sound economics is very
often what mirrors the needs of the respectably affluent."

CREDIT: Associated Press

Saul Alinsky
(1909–1972)

AFTER RIOTS erupted in the Rochester, New York, ghetto in the summer of 1964, an interracial group of clergy approached organizer Saul Alinsky to help them build a power base among low-income African Americans and challenge the influence of the city's dominant employer, Eastman Kodak, which employed only 750 blacks out of 40,000 employees. (Alinsky quipped that "the only thing Kodak has done on the race issue in America is to introduce color film.") After several months of meetings, local residents founded Freedom, Integration, God, Honor, Today (FIGHT), a community organizing group, to take on Kodak. But after the company refused to create a training and hiring program for black residents, FIGHT upped the ante. A number of FIGHT members and their churches purchased Kodak stock and pledged to attend the company's annual shareholder meeting. Kodak tried to keep protesters at a distance by holding the meeting in New Jersey, but FIGHT brought a thousand people to the meeting 600 miles away. Their action gained national media attention.

Following this, Alinsky threatened to bring 100 black people to a Rochester Philharmonic Orchestra concert after treating them to a banquet of nothing but huge portions of baked beans. The idea was to conduct the nation's first "fart-in" to embarrass Kodak, a major Philharmonic sponsor. Fortunately for the Philharmonic, FIGHT did not have to resort to that tactic, because Kodak agreed to implement the jobs program.

The battle in Rochester was typical of Alinsky's approach, which was to employ any tactic that would work to bring powerful politicians and corporations to the negotiating table with ordinary people. As he wrote in his 1971 book *Rules for Radicals,* "*The Prince* was written by Machiavelli for the Haves on how to hold power. *Rules for Radicals* is written for the Have-Nots on how to take it away."

Alinsky reshaped activism and politics in America by transferring some of the tactics of grassroots organizing from shop floors and factories to urban neighborhoods and congregations. Alinsky was widely known in the 1960s as an "agitator" and a "troublemaker," but his fame had faded somewhat (except among progressive activists) until 2008, when Republicans revived his reputation by linking Alinsky to both the major Democratic Party candidates for president. In the late 1960s Hillary Clinton had spent time with Alinsky and had written her senior thesis at Wellesley College about him. Conservatives mined her report to uncover flattering comments about Alinsky in order to tarnish her as a radical.

But the GOP honchos took even larger swipes at Barack Obama, who had been a community organizer for three years in Chicago and had acknowledged being influenced by Alinsky's writings and ideas. In her September 2008 speech accepting the GOP vice presidential nomination at the Republican convention in St. Paul, Alaska governor Sarah Palin said, "I guess a small-town mayor is sort of like a community organizer, except that you have actual responsibilities." A few days later, former New York mayor Rudy Giuliani sought to link Obama with what he called "a very core Saul Alinsky kind of almost socialist notion that [government] should be used for redistribution of wealth."

Giuliani was both wrong and right. Obama was not recruited by Alinsky's community organizing group (the Industrial Areas Foundation) but by another church-based group engaged in organizing in Chicago's poor neighborhoods. But he was right about Alinsky's outlook. Alinsky *did* believe in the "redistribution of wealth," although he never called himself a Socialist.

Alinsky was born to Orthodox Jewish parents in Chicago who divorced when he was thirteen. Over time Alinsky increasingly took after his firebrand mother.

At the University of Chicago, Alinsky took courses in the school's famed sociology department and then attended graduate courses in criminology and a few law school courses. Leaving graduate school without a degree, Alinsky joined Chicago's Institute for Juvenile Research (IJR), which was developing community projects based on the then-novel theory that crime was the result of poverty and social turmoil in neighborhoods. Alinsky developed a talent for building trusting relationships with community residents, criminals, and prisoners.

In 1938 IJR assigned Alinsky to study Chicago's Back of the Yards area, the immigrant neighborhood of about 90,000 residents made famous in **Upton Sinclair**'s *The Jungle*. Alinsky spent most of his time with leaders of the Packinghouse Workers union, who were trying to organize the employees of the major meatpacking firms that dominated the area. The union understood that it would be difficult to win a victory in the workplaces without community support, so they embraced Alinsky's efforts to build a neighborhood organization.

In Back of the Yards, Alinsky sought out local leaders involved in churches, sports leagues, neighborhood businesses, and other networks. One was Joseph Meegan. He and Alinsky gained the confidence of Chicago's auxiliary Catholic bishop Bernard Sheil, who helped them recruit young priests and parish leaders and overcome the tensions between Catholics from different ethnic backgrounds. They persuaded Sheil to speak at the 1939 founding meeting of the Back of the Yards Neighborhood Council (BYNC), where about seventy-five organizations were represented. The next day, Sheil shared the stage with Congress of Industrial Organizations president **John L. Lewis** at a rally of 10,000 people.

The alliance between the church and the union guaranteed that the BYNC would be taken seriously by the city's political and corporate power brokers. The BYNC put pressure on city officials to provide the neighborhood with school lunch and milk programs, fluoridated drinking water, an infant-health clinic, and a baseball field with floodlights. The BYNC got the city to spray weed killer in vacant lots, and it sold garbage cans to the community at a fraction of the market cost. It started a credit union to provide local residents and businesses with low-interest loans. It pressured the Works Progress Administration and the National Youth Administration to provide jobs for neighborhood residents. Its success marked the beginning of modern community organizing.

This success caught the attention of some important patrons. Bishop Sheil and Marshall Field III (newspaper publisher and heir to the Marshall Field family fortune) helped fund Alinsky's new organization, the Industrial Areas Foundation (IAF), designed to train community organizers and to build community organizations in other cities. In 1946 Alinsky published *Reveille for Radicals* describing the nuts and bolts of effective organizing. The book became the bible of community organizing until he wrote *Rules for Radicals* in 1971.

These books have not only provided organizers with a tool kit of principles and tactics but have also offered a vision for a renewed democracy. In Alinsky's view, an empowered citizen actively questions the decisions made by those in power. Alinsky was scornful of social workers, whom he thought viewed poor people as "clients" to be served by beneficent experts. He felt similarly about government antipoverty programs, which he called "political pornography," because he believed they distributed crumbs that kept people pacified. The organizer's job was to agitate people to recognize their own self-interest and then to help them mobilize to gain a stronger voice in challenging the bastions of power and privilege. Organizers, he thought, have to show people that many problems they view as personal troubles can only be addressed through collective action. Alinsky taught that confrontation and conflict were necessary to change power relations.

One way to achieve that, Alinsky believed, was to "personalize" an issue—to identify the person in government, a corporation, or another institution who has the power and authority to make a decision that will change its practices. Alinsky believed it was necessary to "rub raw the resentments of the people in the community." That meant getting people involved in small-scale battles (against unscrupulous merchants or realtors, for example) so they could experience winning, gain self-confidence, and then tackle larger targets and issues. Community organizing, he believed, taught people how to win concrete victories, and to do so through creative tactics that were fun and morale-building. He realized that compromise was the heart of democracy. It was about sharing power.

Alinsky viewed his success in Chicago as a first step in building a network of "people's organizations" around the country. These community groups, along with unions, would form the basis of a progressive movement for social justice. In 1947 Alinsky hired Fred Ross, an experienced organizer among California's migrant farmworkers. Ross built the Community Service Organization (CSO) in several cities, mostly among Latinos, recruiting new members and identifying potential leaders through house meetings and one-on-one conversations. In San Jose, California, one of the people Ross recruited was **Cesar Chavez,** who began as a leader but whom Ross soon hired and trained as an organizer. Chavez would later adopt these organizing ideas in starting the United Farm Workers union.

In the mid-1960s Alinsky began training organizers and overseeing campaigns in Rochester and Buffalo, New York; St. Paul, Minnesota; New York City; Kansas City, Missouri; and Chicago. Alinsky worked closely with African American groups in major cities, hoping to build stable organizations that could battle segregation and wield influence on a variety of issues. But he was not involved in the southern civil rights movement, whose leaders did not seek his advice. Alinsky was particularly scornful of the student New Left and the campus antiwar movement. He did not think they understood the importance of building organizations with leaders and relied too much on protests, demonstrations, and media celebrities. He considered their sometimes revolutionary rhetoric silly, utopian, and dogmatic.

Alinsky's ideas took hold and influenced organizers and activists around the country. His books and colorful campaigns brought him a great deal of attention (including a glowing profile in *Time* magazine in 1970), and he became an iconic figure among organizers.

Beginning in the 1970s, America experienced an upsurge of community organizing, what writer Harry Boyte called a "backyard revolution." Many community groups emerged and adopted Alinsky's ideas. They organized around slum housing and tenants' rights, public safety, and racial discrimination by banks (redlining), achieving some success. Environmental groups drew on Alinsky's ideas, especially those opposed to the construction of nuclear power plants or those fighting the toxic takeover of their neighborhoods, such as the battle in the polluted Love Canal neighborhood in Niagara Falls, New York.

Whereas Alinsky focused almost entirely on building neighborhood-based organizations, since his death in 1972, a number of national organizing networks with local affiliates have emerged, enabling groups to address problems at the local, state, and national levels, sometimes even simultaneously. These include the National Welfare Rights Organization, ACORN, National People's Action, PICO, Direct Action Research and Training (DART), and Gamaliel. In addition, veteran activists have created a number of training centers—including the Midwest Academy, Grassroots Leadership, the Center for Third World Organizing, the Green Corps, the AFL-CIO Organizing Institute, and the Organizing and Leadership Training Center—to nurture new generations of social change organizers.

Tens of thousands of organizers and activists have been directly or indirectly influenced by Alinsky's ideas about organizing. Most of them have been progressives, following Alinsky's instincts to challenge the rich and powerful. But the left has no monopoly on using Alinsky's techniques. After Obama took office in 2009, conservatives like Glenn Beck and the Tea Party both attacked Obama for being an Alinsky-ite and a "socialist," and they began recommending Alinsky's books as training tools for building a right-wing movement. One Tea Party leader explained, "Alinsky's book is important because there really is no equivalent book for conservatives. There's no 'Rules for Counter-Radicals.'" Freedom Works, a corporate-funded conservative group started by former Republican congressman Dick Armey, uses *Rules for Radicals* as a primer for its training of Tea Party activists.

CREDIT: Associated Press

Bayard Rustin
(1912–1987)

BAYARD RUSTIN was black, gay, a pacifist, and a radical, and thus had four strikes against him in terms of influencing mainstream America. But from the 1940s through the 1960s, he managed to use his immense talents—as an organizer, strategist, speaker, intellectual, and writer—to effectively challenge the economic and racial status quo. Always an outsider, he helped catalyze the civil rights movement with courageous acts of resistance. He was the lead organizer of the 1963 March on Washington, a job for which it seemed he had prepared his entire life.

The youngest of eight children, Rustin was raised by his grandparents in West Chester, Pennsylvania. His grandmother was a Quaker and an early member of the National Association for the Advancement of Colored People. Rustin was a gifted student, an outstanding football and track athlete, and an exceptional tenor. In high school he was arrested for refusing to sit in the local movie theater's balcony, which was nicknamed "Nigger Heaven." He attended two black colleges and then moved to New York City in 1937. He enrolled briefly at the City College of New York, where he got involved with the campus Young Communist League. He was attracted by their antiracist efforts—including their fight against segregation in the military—but he broke with the Communist Party after a few years.

While singing in nightclubs to earn money, Rustin looked for other ways to channel his prodigious energy, his outrage against racism, and his growing talent as an organizer. He found two mentors who shaped his thinking and employed him as an organizer, **A. Philip Randolph** and **A. J. Muste.** Randolph hired Rustin in 1941 to lead the youth wing of the March on Washington movement, designed to push **Franklin D. Roosevelt** to open up defense jobs to black workers as the United States geared up for World War II.

Then, under Muste's guidance, Rustin began a series of organizing jobs with several pacifist groups—the Fellowship of Reconciliation (FOR), the American Friends Service Committee, and the War Resisters League. These were small, mostly white organizations that provided Rustin with a home base. A brilliant, charismatic speaker, Rustin kept up a hectic travel schedule, preaching the gospel of nonviolence and civil disobedience on campuses, in churches, and at meetings of fellow pacifists.

In 1942 Rustin recruited a nucleus of militants to form the Congress of Racial Equality, committed to using Gandhian tactics to dismantle segregation. Rustin trained and led small groups engaged in nonviolent protests to integrate restaurants, movie theaters, barber shops, amusement parks, and department stores. That year, he was beaten by a policeman in Tennessee for refusing to move to the rear of a segregated bus. In this and subsequent actions, Rustin showed enormous courage, believing that a few people, acting as witnesses for justice, could trigger a broader mass movement—a prophecy he helped fulfill in the 1960s.

As a Quaker and conscientious objector, Rustin was legally entitled to do alternative service rather than military service during World War II, but on principle, objecting to war in general and the segregation of the armed forces in particular, he refused to serve even in the Civilian Public Service. In 1944 he was convicted of violating the Selective Service Act and was sentenced to three years in a federal prison in Kentucky.

Upon his release, he rejoined the Fellowship of Reconciliation and resumed his career as a peripatetic organizer. In April 1947 he led FOR's interracial Journey of Reconciliation, bold nonviolent acts of civil disobedience through four southern and border states to challenge segregation and a precursor to the Freedom Rides of the early 1960s. He and others were arrested in Chapel Hill, North Carolina, and Rustin spent twenty-two days on a prison camp chain gang.

In 1948 Rustin went back to work for Randolph to push President Harry S. Truman to enforce and expand FDR's antidiscrimination order. They organized protests in several cities and at the 1948 Democratic Party national convention. Their hard work paid off: Truman desegregated the military and outlawed racial discrimination in the federal civil service that year.

In the late 1940s and early 1950s, while still on FOR's staff, Rustin visited India, Africa, and Europe, making contact with activists in the various independence and peace movements. Increasingly, he viewed the struggle for civil rights in the United States as part of a worldwide movement against war and colonialism.

In 1953 Rustin was arrested for "public indecency"—having homosexual sex in a parked car—in Pasadena, California, where he had been invited to give a talk. Although Rustin was unusually open among his friends about his homosexuality, this was the first time that it had come to the public's attention. Homosexual behavior was a crime in every state. A. J. Muste fired him for jeopardizing FOR's already controversial reputation. But Randolph got him a similar job with the War Resisters League, where Rustin worked for the next twelve years.

During the next decade, Rustin played a critical but behind-the-scenes role as a key organizer within the civil rights movement. At Randolph's behest, he went to Montgomery, Alabama, in 1955 to help with the bus boycott. Rustin helped local leaders with advice on organizing a large-scale boycott, but his biggest influence was mentoring **Martin Luther King Jr.,** who had no practical organizing experience, on the philosophy and tactics of civil disobedience.

But much of that advice would be given from a distance, in phone calls, memos, and drafts of ghostwritten articles and book chapters for King. Rustin had to cut short his first visit to Montgomery because, as a former Communist and as a gay man, he was a political liability. So just at the moment when Rustin might have helped lead the mass movement that he had been working for his entire adult life, he had to do so quietly and in the shadows.

At the end of 1956, the Supreme Court ruled that Montgomery's segregated bus system was unlawful. The victory could have remained a local triumph rather than a national bellwether. Rustin, however, along with **Ella Baker** and Stanley Levinson (another King adviser), laid out the idea for building what Rustin called a "mass movement across the South" with "disciplined groups prepared to act as 'nonviolent shock troops.'" This was the genesis of the Southern Christian Leadership Conference, which catapulted King from local to national leadership. Baker was hired to build the organization, and Rustin became King's strategist, ghostwriter, and link to northern liberals and unions.

In 1963 Randolph pulled together the leaders of the major civil rights, labor, and liberal religious organizations and laid out his idea for a major march on Washington to push for federal legislation—particularly for the Civil Rights Act, which Kennedy had proposed but which was stalled in Congress. Kennedy tried to dissuade the leaders from sponsoring the march, contending that it would undermine support for the Civil Rights bill. But Randolph had faced down presidents before, and he did so again. Over the opposition of some civil rights leaders, Randolph insisted that Rustin serve as the day-to-day organizer of the March for Jobs and Freedom. Rustin pulled together a staff and organized all the logistics.

Three weeks before the march, Senator Strom Thurmond, a South Carolina segregationist, publicly attacked Rustin on the floor of the Senate by reading reports of his Pasadena arrest for homosexual behavior a decade earlier—documents he probably got from FBI director J. Edgar Hoover. Randolph defended Rustin's integrity and his role in the march, but, as John D'Emilio, Rustin's biographer, noted, thanks to Thurmond, "Rustin had become perhaps the most visible homosexual in America."

After the triumphant march, Rustin continued organizing within the civil rights, peace, and labor movements. In February 1964 he coordinated a one-day school boycott in New York City to protest the slow progress of school integration. On that day, 464,000 pupils stayed away from school. King continued to rely on Rustin's advice, but always from a safe distance, fearful the movement would be tarnished by the controversial Rustin.

After Congress passed the Voting Rights Act in 1965, Rustin—who had spent his entire life stirring up protests—wrote a much-read and controversial article, "From Protest to Politics," in the then-liberal magazine *Commentary,* arguing that the coalition that had come together for the March on Washington needed to place less emphasis on protest and instead focus on electing liberal Democrats who could enact a progressive policy agenda centered on full employment, housing, and civil rights. Rustin drafted a "Freedom Budget," released in 1967, that advocated "redistribution of wealth." Rustin's ideas influenced King, who increasingly began to talk about the importance of jobs and economic redistribution.

However, Rustin's ideas were controversial among the young Student Nonviolent Coordinating Committee (SNCC) radicals, who did not trust unions or the Democratic Party. SNCC had become a key advocate of "black power," an idea that Rustin opposed because it undermined his belief in coalition politics and racial integration.

But the two biggest obstacles to Rustin's program were the war in Vietnam, which drained resources and attention away from **Lyndon B. Johnson**'s Great Society and War on Poverty, and the urban riots that began in 1965 in Los Angeles and triggered a backlash against the civil rights movement. Rustin was among the first public figures to call for the withdrawal of all American forces from South Vietnam, but as LBJ escalated the war, Rustin muted his criticisms. He wanted to avoid alienating LBJ, Democratic leaders, and union leaders who supported the war and who funded the A. Philip Randolph Institute, which had been created in 1964 to provide Rustin with an organizational home. When King announced his strong opposition to the war in 1967, it caused a serious rift between the two men. As a result, Rustin—one of the nation's most important and courageous pacifists for three decades—was absent from the antiwar movement and lost credibility among many New Left student activists.

Rustin devoted much of the last two decades of his life to working on international human rights. He traveled around the globe, monitoring elections and the status of human rights in Chile, El Salvador, Grenada, Haiti, Poland, Zimbabwe, and elsewhere.

Ironically, Rustin's homosexuality—which had limited his activist career for decades—became a centerpiece of his last few years. Rustin did not initially embrace the burgeoning gay rights movement, which exploded after the Stonewall riot in New York City in 1969. He only began to speak publicly about the importance of civil rights for gays and lesbians during his last few years, when he was involved in a stable relationship. Thanks in part to a 2003 documentary about Rustin, *Brother Outsider,* he has become something of an icon among gay activists.

Harry Hay
(1912–2002)

CREDIT: Mark H. Thompson

DURING THE summer of 1948, at an all-male party in Los Angeles, Harry Hay began talking about the upcoming presidential election. Like other members of the Communist Party, Hay supported former vice president **Henry Wallace,** who was running on the Progressive Party ticket. Hay was a homosexual, and he wondered how he could help Wallace's campaign without announcing his sexual preference, which was a taboo topic at the time. Hay came up with the idea of creating "Bachelors for Wallace," a coy attempt to encourage other homosexuals to vote for the left-wing politician.

The group did not last long, and it would not have mattered anyway, because Wallace got less than 3 percent of the national vote. But the idea of starting an organization for homosexuals kept Hay awake at night. He wrote a political manifesto that included his then-radical notion that homosexuals were an "oppressed minority." It began, "We, the Androgynes of the world, have formed this responsible corporate body to demonstrate by our efforts that our physiological and psychological handicaps need be no deterrent in integrating 10 percent of the world's population towards the constructive social progress of mankind."

There were few people he could show his manifesto to. But in 1950 Hay and a few other men founded the first homosexual rights group in the country, the Mattachine Society. It was a courageous move, given Americans' attitudes toward homosexuals at the time. The next year, Hay's manifesto appeared in print with the title *The Homosexual in America,* published under a pseudonym, Donald Webster Cory. It was the first commercially published nonfiction account of homosexual life in the United States.

These efforts—the first assertion that homosexuals were an oppressed minority and the founding of an organization that allowed homosexuals to socialize and, eventually, to publicly organize for gay rights—made Hay a gay rights pioneer.

Hay was born in England, the son of a mining engineer. His family moved to Los Angeles when he was seven. He knew by age eleven that he was attracted to boys. He had his first homosexual encounter at fourteen. At the time, he later explained, the term "homosexual" was not included in most dictionaries. "We had no words to describe ourselves," he said. He referred to homosexuals as "temperamental guys."

Hay went to Stanford University in 1930 but soon dropped out and returned to Los Angeles to pursue an acting career. There he met Will Geer, an actor and political leftist, who became his lover. Geer introduced Hay to the city's Communist Party (as Greer later did with his friend **Woody Guthrie**). The two men got involved with the party's efforts to help organize the labor movement, organizing demonstrations in support of farmworkers and the unemployed. In 1934, during the San Francisco general strike, they raised money and food supplies for strikers and their families.

Hay supported himself by acting, doing odd jobs, and teaching part-time at the People's Educational Center, a Marxist-oriented school in downtown Los Angeles. He spent most of his nonworking time occupied with political activism, involved with several Communist Party–sponsored groups, including the Hollywood Anti-Nazi League, the League Against War and Fascism, Mobilization for Democracy, Workers' Alliance, and others.

For idealistic young people like Hay, the Communist Party was an outlet for their anger about the human suffering all around them during the Depression. They were not just complaining; they were organizing protests. The party was one of the few groups that seemed to care about the oppression of African Americans and the second-class status of women.

But the Communist Party was not at all tolerant of homosexuals. Like the rest of society, the party viewed homosexuals as deviant. It was tough enough being a Communist; party members did not want to be tainted by the even more stigmatized label that came with being gay. Hay knew the handful of other homosexual men within the party, and they secretly socialized, but they did not dare do so publicly.

When he was twenty-five, alone and depressed, Hay visited a psychiatrist, who urged him to have a heterosexual relationship, suggesting that it might change his sexual preference. In 1938 he married Anita Platky, another Communist Party activist. She knew about his homosexual past but thought he could change. They stayed together for thirteen years and adopted two daughters. But marriage did not change him. He wound up living a double life.

In 1950 Hay met Rudi Gernreich, a Viennese refugee and future fashion designer, at a Los Angeles dance studio. (Gernreich later became famous as the inventor of the miniskirt and the topless bathing suit for women in the mid-1960s.) Both men knew the same small network of homosexuals involved in left-wing politics. That year, the two men cofounded the Mattachine Society, its name coming from the 15th-century French Société Mattachine, male dancers who performed in public, sometimes satirizing social customs, but only while wearing masks. At first the society was primarily a discussion group with fewer than ten members. Whenever the Mattachines met, members brought a "cover" girl, a female friend or relative, because it was against the law in California for gay men to meet in groups. At the time, the American Psychiatric Association defined homosexuality as a mental illness.

Hay eventually resigned from the Communist Party, but he used the organizing lessons he had learned in left-wing circles to build the Mattachine Society, recruiting members gradually and promising them anonymity. One of the group's first members was Dale Jennings, another party member. In 1951 Jennings was arrested for soliciting a police officer to commit a homosexual act. It was a case of police entrapment, which was common at the time. Most gay men pled "no contest" to avoid a public trial, which could embarrass their families (for many were married) and get them fired from their jobs. But at Hay's insistence, Jennings agreed to go to trial. The Mattachine Society set up the Citizens Committee to Outlaw Entrapment to raise funds for the defense, hire a lawyer, and educate the public about police harassment of gays. On the stand, Jennings swore that yes, he was homosexual, but no, he had not solicited.

The jury acquitted him. The Mattachines declared it the first time an admitted homosexual had been freed after being charged with vagrancy and lewdness. It was the first victory for what was still a small and underground movement. But word about the case, and about the Mattachine Society, spread among homosexuals, and its membership grew, with new chapters forming around the country.

In 1953 Hay started *ONE*, the first magazine to address homosexual rights. The authors of its essays, stories, and other articles used pseudonyms. So did the writers of letters to the editor from around the country. The US Postal Service declared the magazine was "obscene," which meant it could not be sent through the mail. *ONE* sued and finally won in 1958 as part of the landmark First Amendment case *Roth v. United States*. (The magazine continued until 1967.)

As the Red Scare took hold, homosexuals, like Communists, became targets of right-wing witch-hunters. In 1953 President Dwight D. Eisenhower barred homosexuals from all federal employment, including the military, on the grounds that they were susceptible to blackmail by Communists. In 1955 Hay was called before the House Un-American Activities Committee, but he was not charged with any crime.

Many of the new members of the Mattachine Society did not share Hay's left-wing background. Indeed, many of them believed that Hay's history as a Communist would hurt what was then called the "homophile" movement. Just as the Communists had once pushed Hay to the margins for being gay, the Mattachines now expelled him for being a former Communist.

Even at its height, the Mattachine Society—and its lesbian counterpart, Daughters of Bilitis, formed in 1955—was never very visible to the general public. But the organization nurtured a generation of activists who laid the groundwork for the later gay rights movement and for a growing number of gays to emerge from the closet.

One such figure, Franklin Kameny—a World War II veteran, Harvard-trained astronomer, and Mattachine member—was dismissed from his position with the Army Map Service in 1957 for being gay. Dr. Kameny argued his case in front of the US Supreme Court, stating that the federal policy against homosexuality was "no less odious than discrimination based upon religious or racial grounds." This was the first time a civil rights case based on sexual orientation was presented before the Supreme Court. In fighting the federal government's discriminatory practices in employment, military service, security clearances, and other areas, Kameny challenged the view, widespread in psychiatric circles, that homosexuality was a mental illness. In 1969 a National Institutes of Mental Health task force also disputed this view. In 1973 the American Psychiatric Association finally came around to the same conclusion. Slowly, the public image, and self-image, of homosexuals began to change, illustrated by slogans like "Gay is good" and "I'm gay and proud."

The gay rights movement emerged as a public force with the 1969 Stonewall riot in New York City—a spontaneous demonstrations against a police raid on a gay bar. By then, however, Hay was on the sidelines of the homosexual rights crusade.

In 1963, at age fifty-one, he met John Burnside, the inventor of the teleidoscope (a variation on the kaleidoscope); Burnside became his life partner. They moved to New Mexico in 1970 and managed a trading post on a Pueblo Indian reservation north of Santa Fe. At the end of the decade, they returned to Los Angeles.

Hay resumed his involvement in the gay rights movement in 1979 when he cofounded a group called the Radical Faeries, which he viewed as a spiritual tribe more than a political organization. Unlike many gay rights activists, Hay opposed what he called "hetero-assimilation," assimilation into mainstream society. His own style of dress—the knit cap of a macho longshoreman, a pigtail, and a strand of pearls—symbolized his attitude. "Assimilation absolutely never worked at all," he told an interviewer for *The Progressive* magazine in 1998. "You may not think you are noticeable but you are." These views put Hay, ever the outsider, at odds with most of the gay rights movement.

Eventually, younger gays acknowledged Hay's role as a gay rights pioneer. In 1977 he was invited to speak at New Mexico's first gay pride march, in Albuquerque. In 1999 an ailing Hay accepted an invitation to be the grand marshal of the annual gay pride parade in San Francisco. He remained in that city—the epicenter of the gay rights movement—living in a Victorian house, painted pink.

Studs Terkel
(1912–2008)

CREDIT: Associated Press/Paul Meredith

IN 1951 *Studs' Place*, an unscripted radio drama about the owner of a greasy-spoon diner in Chicago, was doing well. The show, featuring ordinary people facing life's challenges, gave Studs Terkel, the show's star, an excuse to interview fascinating people, some of them famous. It had been running for two years and audiences loved it.

But suddenly NBC wanted to yank the program. Network executives had been informed that in the previous decade Terkel had signed petitions for groups such as the Joint Anti-Fascist Refugee Committee and the Committee for Civil Rights. As Terkel recalled in *Touch and Go,* a memoir he wrote when he was ninety-four, NBC sent an inquisitor who asked if he knew there were Communists behind the petitions.

"Suppose Communists come out against cancer?" Terkel replied. "Do we have to automatically come out for cancer?"

The show was canceled.

That was vintage Terkel: mixing progressive politics with a strong shot of humor.

He was born Louis Terkel in New York City, but he will always be associated with Chicago, where his family moved when he was eleven years old. A sickly and asthmatic child, he was the youngest of three boys born to Sam and Annie Terkel, who had emigrated to New York from the Russian-Polish border. In New York, Sam was a tailor and Annie a seamstress in a factory.

Once they moved to Chicago in 1922, his parents ran the fifty-room Wells-Grand Hotel, a boarding house whose guests included railroad firemen, seafarers, secretaries, Wobblies, and the occasional hooker. At the hotel, Terkel recalled, he felt "like the concierge of the Ritz of Paris." He remembered, "That hotel was far more of an education to me than the University of Chicago was."

As a teenager, Terkel was riveted to political debates on the radio. During the 1930s his political awareness was further nurtured at Bughouse Square, a free-speech area of a local park where an assortment of Socialists, Communists, vegetarians, Christian fundamentalists, and others would mount soapboxes and hold forth. After graduating from McKinley High School in 1928, he attended the

University of Chicago, where he earned a law degree in 1934. But he spent more time at the movies and listening to the blues than studying legal matters.

His first job was as a fingerprint classifier for the FBI. He was soon let go. Only years later, after requesting his FBI file, did he discover why. A University of Chicago professor had told the agency, "I remember [Terkel]. Slovenly, didn't care much, a low-class Jew. He is not one of our type of boys." J. Edgar Hoover himself sent a note to take Terkel off the payroll.

He became involved with the Chicago Repertory Theater Group, performing in union halls. There was another man named Louis in the group, so to avoid confusion, Terkel took the moniker "Studs," after Studs Lonigan, the protagonist in James T. Farrell's novels about Chicago's tough Irish neighborhoods. The name stuck.

In Chicago he led the life of, in his own words, "an eclectic disk jockey, a radio soap opera gangster, a sports and political commentator; a jazz critic; a pioneer in TV, Chicago style; an oral historian and a gadfly." He found work with the radio division of the Federal Writers Project, a New Deal program. One day he was asked to read a script, and he was soon performing in radio soap operas, other stage performances, and the news show. He described his voice as "low, husky, menacing," which made him a natural to play heavies. "I would always say the same thing and either get killed or sent to Sing Sing," he later recalled.

In his spare time, he helped raise funds for the Soviet American Friendship Committee and the Joint Anti-Fascist Refugee Committee. In 1942, before Terkel went into the air force, the Chicago Repertory group held a farewell party for him. Billie Holiday dropped by and sang "Strange Fruit," the hypnotic anti-lynching song, at his request. Her appearance at the party made it into his file, kept by US Army Intelligence.

In the air force, he hosted a popular radio show for the troops, a show that included music and antifascist news. Because of a perforated ear drum, he was not sent overseas, and within a year he was discharged.

Terkel's first big professional break came in 1944 when he was hired by the Meyeroff advertising agency to do radio commercials and then a sports show. When his account manager left for a different agency, he invited Terkel to come along, giving him the chance to create a new show, which he called the *Wax Museum*. Terkel, the disc jockey, played an eclectic assortment of his favorite old records, including folk music, opera, jazz, and blues. He introduced his audience to performers like folksinger **Woody Guthrie** and gospel singer Mahalia Jackson. He could occasionally invite performers or composers to sit down for an on-air interview.

When **Henry Wallace** ran for president in 1948 on the Progressive Party ticket, Terkel enthusiastically jumped on board. Terkel and musicologist Alan Lomax produced a program for Wallace during the last week of the campaign, to be aired on ABC. Along with Wallace, the program featured **Paul Robeson.**

Terkel advised Wallace, "Make believe you're addressing one person: that old farmer having a hard time, or that lost young family in a big city who don't know where to turn. Be very intimate."

Soon after Wallace's defeat, the Cold War and the Red Scare began to threaten radicals, progressives, and even sympathetic liberals. NBC executives in New York told Terkel that he could clear his record by saying he had been duped into signing left-wing petitions. He refused, and Terkel, the star and creator of *Studs' Place,* was blacklisted.

Fortunately, his wife, Ida, had steady work as a social worker at a racially integrated childcare center. In 1952 Terkel began what would become a forty-five-year relationship (until 1997) with WFMT radio. He and Vince Garrity—whom Terkel described in his memoir *Touch and Go* as "ex–office boy of Mayor Kelly, ex–bat boy for the Cubs, acquainted with every cop on the beat"—produced a program, *Sounds of the City,* that set Terkel on the path of interviewing ordinary folks. Terkel would roam the city at night with a microphone and tape recorder, uncovering all kinds of funny and moving stories. When that show ended, he had his own music and documentary program with Jimmy Unrath, a technical wizard who made up for Terkel's mechanical ineptitude. In 1963, at the suggestion of Terkel's wife, Terkel and Unrath produced a documentary called *This Train,* boarding a train organized by the National Association for the Advancement of Colored People filled with people headed from Chicago to the March on Washington.

On his radio program, a daily one-hour show, Terkel included music, commentary, and interviews with a diverse roster of guests. He had the knack of asking the right questions and getting his interviewees to relax. As a result, his subjects—who included many political activists and writers not often heard or seen on radio or TV—talked candidly and in rich detail about their lives, feelings, and ideas. Terkel made his listeners feel as if they were eavesdropping on an interesting conversation.

Terkel's first book, *Giants of Jazz,* was published in 1956, but he did not become a famous and best-selling author until André Schiffrin, editor at Pantheon Books, approached him in 1965 and suggested that he write a book, an oral history, that would capture the story of Chicago at that moment in time—in the midst of the civil rights movement, the rise of automation, and the nuclear arms race. The result was *Division Street: America,* published in 1967. Terkel edited the transcripts of his conversations with seventy people from a cross-section of Chicago—cops, teachers, cab drivers, nuns, CEOs, and others. They ranged in age from fifteen to ninety and spoke from a variety of political and religious perspectives. The book reflected Terkel's genius at interviewing people and at eliciting vivid and fascinating stories from everyday persons, a skill honed over the years on his radio program. Terkel said he made people comfortable by being respectful, by really listening to them, and by his own "ineptitude" and "slovenliness": "The ordinary person feels not only as good a being as I am; rather he feels somewhat superior," he wrote. *Division Street: America* was a success with both the critics and the public. It was the first of many books by Terkel with a similar format, showcasing the voices and views of ordinary Americans. Schiffrin next suggested he write about the Great Depression and then jobs, and Terkel produced *Hard Times* (1970) and *Working: People Talk About What They Do All Day and How They Feel About What They Do* (1974), among many other works. He won a Pulitzer for his book on World War II, *The Good War* (1984). Terkel was not the first oral historian, but he transformed the genre into a popular literary form.

Terkel believed that most people had something to say worth hearing. "The average American has an indigenous intelligence, a native wit," he said. "It's only a question of piquing that intelligence." In all his books, he was able to draw people out, creating a tapestry of conversation that revealed insights into the American character.

In addition to his radio show and books, Terkel was a frequent master of ceremonies and speaker at progressive political events, and late in his life, he resumed his acting career, appearing as a sportswriter in John Sayles's 1988 film *Eight Men Out* about the 1919 Chicago baseball scandal.

His final book, *P.S.: Further Thoughts from a Lifetime of Listening,* was released in November 2008, a few weeks after he died at the age of ninety-six.

"Curiosity never killed this cat," Terkel once said. "That's what I'd like as my epitaph."

David Brower
(1912–2000)

"THANK GOD for David Brower," said Russell Train, who headed the federal Environmental Protection Agency in the early 1970s. "He makes it so easy for the rest of us to be reasonable."

As the longtime (1952–1969) leader of the Sierra Club and as founder of the Friends of the Earth, the League of Conservation Voters, and the Earth Island Institute, Brower helped transform environmentalism from a polite cause dominated by don't-rock-the-boat upper-class conservationists to an activist movement that uses political action, including unconventional tactics, to protect wilderness areas from speculators, developers, state agencies, and the federal government.

"I wish we didn't have to be angry all the time," Brower said, "but someone has to get angry." He was angry not only at polluters and despoilers but also at other environmentalists who disparaged confrontation. For more than half a century, his activism earned him accolades as a founder of the modern environmental movement. He was often criticized for being unwilling to compromise. But he recognized that the stakes were high. "When *they* win, it's forever," he often said. "When *we* win, it's merely a stay of execution."

Born in Berkeley, California, Brower's interest in the wilderness stemmed from his family's frequent hikes into the nearby hills and camping trips in the Sierra Nevada. When Brower was eight years old, his mother lost her sight because of a brain tumor. He took her on frequent walks in the hills around Berkeley, which gave him a greater appreciation for the area's natural beauty.

Brower dropped out of the University of California, Berkeley, after two years because of financial hardship. In 1933 he joined the Sierra Club. Founded in 1892 by environmental pioneer John Muir, its initial mission was to expand the number of national parks in America. "In the 1930s," explained Muir's biographer, Stephen Fox, "most of the three thousand members were middle-aged Republicans," primarily hikers and wildlife enthusiasts.

In 1935, after working at a concession stand in Yosemite National Park, Brower became the park's publicity manager. He became increasingly alarmed over the destruction of wilderness areas by projects such as the Hoover Dam on the Colorado River, by devastating corporate logging of national forests, and by environmentally harmful mining permitted by the Federal Bureau of Land Management.

Brower was a world-class mountaineer. In the army during World War II he trained soldiers in climbing and skiing and saw combat in Italy. He led daring assaults involving hazardous rock climbing to overcome enemy positions. He received the Combat Infantryman's Badge and the Bronze Medal.

In 1952 the Sierra Club hired Brower as its first executive director. During his seventeen years in that position, Brower revitalized the organization with his ethos that public education and political action were vital to the preservation of the wilderness. In its obituary for Brower, the *New York Times* noted that he "sought to protect redwoods from loggers, animals from furriers, porpoises from tuna fishermen and the public from nuclear energy and any number of projects proposed by the Army Corps of Engineers and the Federal Bureau of Reclamation."

Under Brower, the Sierra Club led campaigns to establish ten new national parks and seashores, in California, Oregon, Washington, Tennessee, North Carolina, and Kentucky. In the 1950s he led a high-profile campaign that stopped the federal Bureau of Reclamation from building a hydroelectric dam on the Green River that would have flooded parts of Dinosaur National Monument in Utah. To win that battle, however, the Sierra Club agreed to a compromise, reluctantly giving the federal government its consent to build a dam and reservoir in the lesser-known Glen Canyon in Arizona. The Bechtel Corporation made a fortune constructing the dam and also oversaw the excavation of one of the world's biggest coal mines, Peabody Coal's Black Mesa mine, on the adjacent Navajo Reservation, which polluted the local water supply.

Later, Brower said he felt that the Sierra Club's compromise had been a huge mistake. "Polite conservationists leave no mark save the scars upon the Earth that could have been prevented had they stood their ground," he once said. Eventually this doggedness would cause friction at many of the organizations where he worked.

Frustrated by his failure to save Glen Canyon, Brower invested significant Sierra Club resources in campaigns to stop any more dams inside national parks or monuments. In a drive to prevent a dam in the Grand Canyon, the Sierra Club ran controversial full-page advertisements on the back page of the *New York Times.* The most famous of these asked readers, "Should We Also Flood the Sistine Chapel So Tourists Can Get Nearer the Ceiling?" and sparked a nationwide protest against the planned dam project. The Sierra Club also played a key role in passage of the Wilderness Act of 1964, which initially protected 9 million acres of public land and now protects over 100 million acres.

These victories brought the Sierra Club national attention and many new members. But they also angered some politicians. These power brokers successfully pressured the Internal Revenue Service (IRS) to revoke the Sierra Club's tax-exempt status in 1967 for being too "political." In response, Brower created a separate tax-exempt nonprofit, the Sierra Club Foundation, and the Sierra Club continued to engage in political battles. Brower eventually came to believe that the IRS's action was a blessing, liberating the Sierra Club to build political muscle and mobilize its growing membership to vote, lobby, and protest.

To raise public awareness about the wilderness, the Sierra Club developed coffee-table books that included stunning nature photographs, many by Ansel Adams, so readers could fall in love with the wilderness and feel a connection to conservationists' call for its preservation. "We're not blindly opposed to progress," Brower said, "we're opposed to blind progress."

Brower took an outspoken stance against development by Pacific Gas and Electric of a nuclear reactor at California's Diablo Canyon near San Luis Obispo. Some members of the Sierra Club board—with ties to the utility's executives—did not share that position, and as a result, in 1969 the board asked Brower to resign.

When Brower took over leadership of the Sierra Club, it had 7,000 members and a $75,000 annual budget. When he left, it had 77,000 members and assets of $3 million. (Today the Sierra Club has 1.4 million members.) Later in life, Brower rejoined the organization's board, held an honorary position as vice president, and received the club's John Muir Award in 1977.

Brower gained wider attention when John McPhee wrote a three-part profile of him in the *New Yorker* in 1971 and then expanded the article into a best-selling biography, *Encounters with the Archdruid;* the title reflects an insult one property developer used for Brower.

After leaving the Sierra Club, Brower founded two new organizations: the League of Conservation Voters (LCV) and Friends of the Earth (FOE).

The LCV has played an important role in electoral politics by endorsing candidates and educating and mobilizing voters. It generated lots of publicity in 1970, immediately after the first Earth Day, when (in partnership with the organization Environmental Action) it published the first scorecard rating politicians' voting records on environmental issues, including a "Dirty Dozen" list of members of Congress with the worst records. Every two years since then, the LCV has ranked every member of the House and Senate on his or her environmental voting record. This was a brilliant maneuver, helping educate the public about environmental issues, providing the media with an easy-to-report story, and giving ammunition to LCV's local and state chapters to support or oppose their congressmembers. In its first year, the LCV worked successfully to defeat several of the Dirty Dozen members seeking reelection. These reports and electoral campaigns are among Brower's most lasting legacies. The LCV claims that since 1996, forty-nine out of seventy-nine Dirty Dozen politicians have been defeated. In 2008 over 80 percent of the 1,500 candidates endorsed by LCV won their elections.

At FOE, Brower used confrontational tactics, including marches, boycotts, and sit-ins, to generate publicity and develop an ideology of radical defense of the environment. But Brower had a falling out with FOE leaders, who wanted the organization to focus more on policy research and legislation and less on protest. Brower left FOE in 1984.

Irrepressible, after leaving FOE, Brower founded yet another organization, the Earth Island Institute (EII), to promote conservation and environmental projects around the world. Its efforts to address toxic dumping and public health problems in poor communities helped push the larger environmental movement, including the Sierra Club, to recognize the class and race aspects of environmental problems. EII has launched dozens of campaigns and then spun them off as separate projects and organizations, including Rainforest Action Network, Urban Habitat, International Rivers, Energy Action, Ethical Traveler, Fiji Organic Project, International Marine Mammal Project, Reef Protection International, and Women's Earth Alliance.

Brower constantly warned that mainstream environmental organizations were too closely aligned with and were sometimes co-opted by corporations and corporate-funded foundations that disdained confrontation. By employing tactics used by suffragists, civil rights activists, and the antiwar movement—including civil disobedience aimed at corporations as well as government—Brower helped inspire a new wave of environmentalism by Greenpeace, Earth First, and other organizations. Over time, the Sierra Club, the Wilderness Society, and other mainstream groups, too, were influenced by the more radical wing of the environmental movement.

In the late 1990s Brower built bridges between environmentalists and labor unions, two movements that were often at odds, in hopes of igniting a progressive "blue-green" coalition. In 1999 he helped organize the Alliance for Sustainable Jobs and the Environment. Its initial target was Charles Hurwitz, CEO of the Houston-based Maxxam Corporation. Maxxam's Kaiser Aluminum subsidiary was locking out striking workers in five cities, and another subsidiary, Pacific Lumber Company, was clear-cutting ancient redwoods in northern California. Calling these two Maxxam-owned companies "icons of corporate irresponsibility," the alliance issued its "Houston Principles," which Brower helped craft, pledging greater cooperation in protecting jobs and fighting pollution.

In November 1999, the eighty-seven-year-old Brower participated in the "Battle in Seattle," the massive protest against the World Trade Organization that brought labor and environmental groups together again. A year later, Brower died in his home on Grizzly Peak, above Berkeley, California.

In his book *Let the Mountains Talk, Let the Rivers Run*, Brower reflected on what he had hoped to accomplish with his life: "We urge that all people now determine that an untrammeled wilderness shall remain here to testify that this generation had love for the next."

Woody Guthrie
(1912–1967)

CREDIT: Library of Congress/*New York World-Telegram* and the *Sun* Newspaper Photograph Collection

ALTHOUGH WOODY GUTHRIE wrote almost 3,000 songs, he is best known for "This Land Is Your Land," often considered America's alternative national anthem. Most Americans know the chorus—"This land is your land, this land is my land / From California, to the New York Island / From the redwood forest, to the gulf stream waters / This land was made for you and me"—and perhaps even some of the verses about the "ribbon of highways," "sparkling sands," "diamond deserts," and "wheat fields waving." But few people know the two radical verses of the song, which are usually omitted from songbooks and recordings:

> *As I went walking I saw a sign there*
> *And on the sign it said "No Trespassing"*
> *But on the other side it didn't say nothing*
> *That side was made for you and me.*

> *In the shadow of the steeple I saw my people*
> *By the relief office I seen my people*
> *As they stood there hungry, I stood there asking*
> *Is this land made for you and me?*

Guthrie penned the song in 1940 as an answer to Irving Berlin's popular "God Bless America," which he thought failed to recognize that it was the "people" to whom America belonged. In the song, Guthrie celebrates America's natural beauty and bounty but criticizes the country for its failure to share its riches. The lyrics reflect Guthrie's assumption that patriotism and support for the underdog were interconnected.

Guthrie was born in Okemah, Oklahoma, in 1912 to a middle-class family. His father was a cowboy, land speculator, and local politician who did well during the oil boom, went bankrupt during the economic downturn, and struggled throughout the 1920s; the family often lived in shacks. Both his father and mother (who was eventually institutionalized for mental illness, later revealed to

275

be Huntington's chorea) taught Woody Western songs, Indian songs, and Scottish folk tunes.

In 1931 Guthrie moved to Pampa, Texas, and formed the Corn Cob Trio and then the Pampa Junior Chamber of Commerce Band, both singing cowboy songs. In 1935 he left for California looking for a way to support his young family. He hitchhiked and rode freight trains, earning money painting signs, playing guitar, and singing in the streets and saloons along the way.

In Los Angeles, he landed a job on a local radio station singing cowboy songs as well as his own compositions. His audience—including many Okies (from Oklahoma) and Texans living in makeshift shelters in migrant camps—grew, and Guthrie began adding political and social commentary to his songs. He talked and sang about corrupt politicians, lawyers, and businessmen and praised the people who were fighting for the rights of migrant workers. Guthrie met Will Geer, an actor and left-wing activist, who introduced him to the local radical scene and traveled with him to support migrant workers' union-organizing drives.

Guthrie's songs of that period—including "I Ain't Got No Home," "Goin' Down the Road Feelin' Bad," "Talking Dust Bowl Blues," "Hard Travelin'," and "Tom Joad" (based on the hero of John Steinbeck's novel, *The Grapes of Wrath*, about migrant workers)—all reflect his growing anger and his mission to give a voice to the disenfranchised. In "Pretty Boy Floyd," Guthrie portrayed the outlaw as a Robin Hood character, contrasting him to the bankers and businessmen who exploit workers and foreclose on families' farms and homes: "Yes, as through this world I've wandered / I've seen lots of funny men / Some will rob you with a six-gun / And some with a fountain pen."

In 1939 Guthrie began writing a column, Woody Sez, for *People's World*, the Communist Party's West Coast paper, commenting on the news of the day. The next year, the party's New York paper, the *Daily Worker*, picked up the column.

Always restless, Guthrie moved to New York City in 1940 and was quickly embraced by radical organizations, artists, writers, musicians, and progressive intellectuals. He performed occasionally on radio and developed a loyal following. His admirers viewed him as an authentic proletarian, filled with homespun wisdom that energized his songs and columns. Much of Guthrie's image was the result of his own mythmaking and that of his promoters, particularly folklorist Alan Lomax. In reality, Guthrie came from a middle-class family and was a prodigious reader and self-taught intellectual.

Lomax recorded Guthrie in a series of conversations and songs for the Library of Congress in Washington, DC, that contributed to this "folksy" impression. Lomax's efforts were part of an upsurge of popular left-wing culture—fostered in part by New Deal programs like the federal theater and writers' projects—that promoted folk and traditional songs as "people's" music. In addition to Guthrie, Lomax also helped Huddie "Lead Belly" Ledbetter, an ex-convict from Louisiana.

Lead Belly played the twelve-string guitar and wrote and performed songs like "Midnight Special" and "Bourgeois Blues," which captivated liberal middle-class audiences in New York and other cities.

In New York, Guthrie joined a growing interracial circle of radical musicians, actors, poets, writers, composers, dancers, and political activists. **Pete Seeger,** Lee Hays, and Millard Lampell formed the Almanac Singers to perform songs about current events for unions, left-wing groups, and other causes. Guthrie sang on several Almanac singles and two albums, *Deep Sea Chanties* and *Sod Buster Ballads,* and often performed with the Almanacs, including in Detroit before 100,000 members of the United Auto Workers union. Guthrie wrote some of the Almanac Singers' most popular songs, including "Union Maid." He had a gift for writing songs that told stories about current events and real people but were also timeless in terms of exploring issues of justice and fairness. He was also a brilliant satirist, writing songs that made fun of business leaders, politicians, Adolf Hitler, and such right-wing figures as aviator Charles Lindbergh and Charles Coughlin, the "radio priest."

In early 1941 the Almanacs performed songs opposing President **Franklin D. Roosevelt**'s plans to enter World War II—a view that Communists applauded but that alienated many of their admirers, including **Eleanor Roosevelt.** After Germany broke its truce with Russia and invaded the country in June of that year, the Almanacs changed their tune, writing patriotic songs that embraced the war effort and the US alliance with Russia to defeat Hitler. They were back in Mrs. Roosevelt's good graces. When their songs were in sync with the New Deal, the Almanacs were courted by commercial promoters. They sang on national network radio, made records, and performed at night clubs, including the upscale Rainbow Room at Rockefeller Center. Guthrie had several regular radio gigs of his own. But the Almanac Singers' political views—including Guthrie's—were too controversial to sustain mainstream success. After Seeger joined the army and Guthrie signed up for the merchant marine (he was later drafted into the army, serving until 1945), the Almanacs broke up.

For a month in 1941 Guthrie was on the New Deal payroll, earning $266 to write songs for a documentary film about the Grand Coulee Dam, which brought electricity and jobs to Oregon and Washington. He moved to Portland, Oregon, and quickly wrote some of his most memorable songs, including "Roll on Columbia" (about the Columbia River), "Grand Coulee Dam," and "The Biggest Thing That Man Has Done."

While in the merchant marine and the army, Guthrie composed hundreds of anti-Hitler, prowar, and other songs to inspire the troops, including "All You Fascists Bound to Lose," "Talking Merchant Marine," and "The Sinking of the Reuben James." In 1943 he published his first novel, *Bound for Glory,* a semiautobiographical account of his Dust Bowl years that contributed to his reputation as a rambling troubadour. By 1946 the Red Scare had made it harder for Guthrie to find work. Many of the Congress of Industrial Organizations unions had purged their radicals and no longer welcomed Guthrie.

After the war, Guthrie returned to New York and settled in Coney Island, Brooklyn, with his second wife, Marjorie. Their son Arlo, born in 1947, became a popular folksinger following his debut antiwar hit album, *Alice's Restaurant,* in 1967. Their daughter Nora, born in 1950, later became the head of the Woody Guthrie Foundation and the founder of the Guthrie Archives.

While living in Coney Island, Guthrie composed and recorded several albums for children, including, *Songs to Grow on for Mother and Child* and *Work Songs to Grow On.* Several generations of parents have raised their kids with Guthrie's songs, many of which provided valuable lessons for living, including on such topics as friendship ("Don't You Push Me Down"), family ("Ship in the Sky"), neighborhoods ("Howdi Doo"), chores ("Pick It Up"), personal responsibility ("Cleano"), and family vacations ("Riding in My Car"). Guthrie was also connected with Brooklyn's Jewish community through his mother-in-law, the Yiddish poet Aliza Greenblatt, and wrote several songs with Jewish themes, including "Hanuka Dance," "The Many and The Few" and "Mermaid's Avenue."

In the late 1940s Guthrie's behavior became increasingly erratic, even violent. These were symptoms of Huntington's chorea, a rare hereditary degenerative disease that gradually robbed him of his health and ability to function physically. Doctors at first mistakenly treated him for everything from alcoholism to schizophrenia. In 1954 he was admitted into the Greystone Psychiatric Hospital in New Jersey, where he was finally properly diagnosed. For the last decade of his life, he was confined to hospitals, barely able to communicate. Many family, friends, and young fans—including **Bob Dylan**—came to visit him to pay their respects. Although Guthrie helped inspire the folk music revival of the late 1950s and 1960s, he was unable to enjoy it or benefit from it financially.

Since his death, Guthrie has become a cultural icon. Ramblin' Jack Elliott and Guthrie's friend Pete Seeger have been his most effective promoters, ensuring that younger generations know Guthrie's music. **Bruce Springsteen,** Ani DiFranco, the Klezmatics, and many others have recorded and reinterpreted Guthrie's songs for new audiences. At Nora Guthrie's initiative, British singer Billy Bragg and the American band Wilco explored the many unpublished Guthrie songs in his archives and set them to music, producing two albums. Guthrie was posthumously inducted into the National Songwriters' Hall of Fame, the Nashville Songwriters' Hall of Fame, and the Rock and Roll Hall of Fame.

Arthur Miller (1915–2005)

Arthur Miller (left, with his attorney Joseph Rauh, Jr.) arrives at Federal District Court in New York in 1957 for his trial for contempt of Congress charges after he refused to tell the House Un-American Activities Committee the names of the Communist writers with whom he attended meetings in New York.
CREDIT: Associated Press/William Smith

ARTHUR MILLER never forgot his introduction to Marxism. He was a teenager, playing handball in front of Dozick's drugstore in Brooklyn. While straddling his bike, waiting for his turn to play, an older boy approached him and began telling him that there were two classes of people, workers and employers, and "that all over the world, including Brooklyn, a revolution that would transform every country was inexorably building up steam." The idea was astonishing to Miller, raised in a family of businessmen who viewed workers, however necessary, as a "nuisance."

This chance encounter revolutionized his own conception of the world and of his family. "The true condition of man, it seemed, was the complete opposite of the competitive system I had assumed was normal, with all its mutual hatreds and conniving," he wrote in his autobiography.

Miller's affinity for the underdog echoed through much of his work as one of the preeminent playwrights of the American theater. He later rejected Marxism, but he never lost his commitment to progressive causes and democratic rights. His writing was shaped by the major events of his lifetime—the Depression, World War II, McCarthyism and the Cold War, the upheavals of the 1960s, and the global tensions of the Reagan era.

Miller was born into a prosperous Manhattan family. His immigrant father had established a successful company, Miltex Coat and Suit. The family had its own chauffeur. In the 1920s, "all was hope and security" in Miller's world.

But the 1929 stock market crash and the Great Depression wrecked the family fortune. The Millers moved to Brooklyn, and his father never again achieved success in business. He attempted to open another coat factory, where Arthur helped out and witnessed the company salesmen being ill-treated by buyers. He wrote a short story about the salesmen, *In Memoriam*, which planted the seed for his most famous play, *Death of a Salesman*.

For two years Miller took odd jobs, including working in an auto parts warehouse, to help out the family and to save money for college. In 1934 he talked his way into the University of Michigan, after being twice rejected because of his less-than-sterling high school academic record. (He flunked algebra three times.)

At Michigan, a significant number of students were more interested in the union organizing and sit-down strikes in nearby Flint and Detroit than in football games and fraternities. Miller joined the staff of the student newspaper, the *Michigan Daily*. In 1937 the paper sent him to Flint to cover a United Auto Workers strike at a General Motors factory. Miller saw the company using violent thugs and paid spies to infiltrate the union. Informing and betrayal would become central themes of Miller's dramatic works. Those years, Miller recalled, were "the testing ground for all my prejudices, my beliefs and my ignorance. It helped to lay out the boundaries of my life."

Miller never joined the Communist Party, but he was part of the left-wing movement that sided with workers' struggles and saw hope for the working class in the Soviet Union. Some of Miller's friends joined the Abraham Lincoln Brigade, fighting alongside antifascists in the Spanish Civil War.

Before college, Miller had seen few plays, but his interest was piqued at Michigan. "I chose theater," he recalled, because "it was the cockpit of literary activity, and you could talk directly to an audience and radicalize the people." Miller was not alone. During the Depression, many young playwrights, actors, and directors used theater as a vehicle to promote radical ideas and action. Their plays revealed the human suffering caused by economic hard times and celebrated the burgeoning protests by workers, farmers, and others. The Group Theater in New York City, founded in 1931, was one of the first efforts to present plays in a naturalistic style, sometimes called "social realism." Its members, like their counterparts in similar theater groups around the country, were inspired by European-born composer Kurt Weill and playwright Bertolt Brecht. The Group Theater's performances of Clifford Odets's plays *Waiting for Lefty* and *Awake and Sing* in 1935 helped create a new kind of Depression-era social drama. Some theater groups performed plays about current events that they called "living newspapers," designed to document injustice and inspire political action.

Miller was influenced by this combination of political idealism and social realism. The Depression had shattered the nation's social and psychological stability, and Miller's plays dramatized the family and community tensions brought about by economic hard times, war, and a repressive political climate. Miller focused on the moral responsibility of individuals and society.

Miller's early plays reflect the radical spirit of the Depression. In 1935, during his sophomore year, Miller wrote *No Villain,* which won the university's prestigious Hopwood Prize. A later rewrite, *They Too Arise,* earned a $1,250 prize from New York's Theater Guild. It told the story of a coat manufacturer facing a strike and bankruptcy. His two sons can help resolve the dilemma, but only if they compromise their principles. The father observes that they live in a dog-eat-dog world and that one has to choose sides. One of his sons responds that the solution is to "change the world."

Miller's second play, *Honors at Dawn,* is even closer to Odets's agitational style. The play opens in a giant automobile factory where autoworkers are calling for a sit-down strike. The managers try to recruit Max, the protagonist, to spy on the union, but he refuses and is fired. Later, the company owner offers the nearby university a generous donation, but only if the president fires a radical faculty member and helps identify engineering students who are union sympathizers or Communists. When the president capitulates, Max begins to understand the corrupt relationship between business and the university. He returns to the factory to help the workers organize. *Honors at Dawn* earned Miller his second Hopwood Prize.

After graduating, Miller returned to Brooklyn and began writing plays and fiction. For six months he earned $23 a week working for the New Deal's Federal Theater Project, which allowed writers and artists to patch together a living while producing theater during the Depression, a project Congress disbanded in 1939 because of the radical views of many participants. Miller also worked briefly for the Works Progress Administration, collecting oral histories in the South for the Library of Congress.

To earn money to support his wife and two children, Miller wrote radio plays for NBC's *Cavalcade of America* series and others, honing his skills with dialogue and storytelling. During the war he also worked the night shift at the Brooklyn Navy Yard. He was about to abandon playwriting but gave it one last shot with his 1947 play *All My Sons.* The play critiques an economic system that pits an individual's ethics against his desire to be successful in business. Based on a true event, it tells the story of a manufacturer's cover-up of defective plane parts that leads to the deaths of twenty-one army pilots. The play, directed by Elia Kazan, a veteran of the Group Theater, was Miller's first real commercial success, winning two Tony Awards and the New York Drama Critics' Circle Award.

Miller went on to win the Pulitzer Prize in 1949, among other major awards, for *Death of a Salesman,* the tragic story of Willy Loman and his hopeless struggle for respect. The modern tragedy, based on the life of Miller's Uncle Manny, stunned audiences and quickly came to be considered a masterpiece of American theater. It has been translated into twenty-nine languages and has been performed around the world.

The McCarthy era inspired Miller's most frequently produced work, *The Crucible,* which premiered in 1953. The play portrays the collective psychosis and hysteria engendered by the Salem witch trials of 1692. Miller made no secret of the parallels to McCarthy's anticommunist witch-hunt. By then, Miller had not been politically active in radical causes for years. But he was a vocal critic of McCarthyism and of the House Un-American Activities Committee (HUAC). That alone was enough to make him suspect.

When *Death of a Salesman* was made into a movie by Columbia Pictures, the American Legion threatened to picket theaters because of Miller's left-wing affiliations. Columbia pressed Miller to sign a declaration that he was not a Communist. He refused. Columbia then made a short film entitled *Life of a Salesman* to be shown with the main feature. The short consisted of business professors praising sales as a profession and denouncing the character of Willy Loman. Miller wrote, "Never in show-business history has a studio spent so much good money to prove that its feature film was pointless."

In 1954, when Miller tried to renew his passport to travel to Belgium to attend the first European performance of *The Crucible*, the State Department turned him down, telling the *New York Times* that it refused passports to people it believed supported communism. The next year, New York City officials caved to pressure from HUAC and refused Miller permission to film scenes of a movie he was making about juvenile delinquency in the city.

Miller was subpoenaed to testify before HUAC in 1956. This was during his marriage to Marilyn Monroe, for whom he had left his wife. According to Miller's autobiography, HUAC chair Representative Francis Walter contacted Miller's attorney the night before the hearing was to begin, offering to drop the whole thing if Walter could have his photo taken with Monroe.

Miller declined, and the hearing proceeded, lasting several days. The main evidence against him was a stack of petitions he had signed twenty years earlier as a college student. By that time, some former Communists and sympathizers who had also been called before Congress, including Clifford Odets and director Elia Kazan, not only recanted past beliefs but also gave investigators the names of others who had been part of the same groups or participated in the same events. Miller was not the only witness who refused to name names, but he was among the most well-known, so his principled stance generated significant media attention. He was cited for contempt of Congress, a crime punishable with imprisonment. He instead received a year's suspended sentence and a $500 fine—and legal bills of $40,000. In 1958 a US court of appeals overturned his conviction.

Miller continued to write short stories, films, and plays (including several about the Holocaust), but, except with *The Price*, he never again enjoyed the critical success he had with *All My Sons, Death of a Salesman, The Crucible,* and *View from the Bridge* (1956). Nevertheless, his midcentury plays secured his reputation as one of America's greatest playwrights. His work is regularly staged throughout the world.

Miller took seriously his responsibility to be an active citizen, expressing his views not only through his plays but also through his actions. During the Vietnam War, he returned to the University of Michigan to participate in the first antiwar teach-in. And as president of PEN International, an association representing literary figures, he helped transform the struggling organization into what he called "the conscience of the world writing community." Through the 1970s and 1980s, he campaigned for writers persecuted in Lithuania, South Africa, Czechoslovakia, Latin America, the Soviet Union, and even closer to home, by school boards in Illinois and Texas. Miller's works were banned in the Soviet Union as a result of his work to free dissident writers.

In 1965 Miller turned down an invitation to witness President **Lyndon B. Johnson** signing the Arts and Humanities Act. In a telegram to Johnson, he said, "The signing of the Arts and Humanities bill surely begins new and fruitful relationship between American artists and their government. But the occasion is so darkened by the Viet Nam tragedy that I could not join it with clear conscience. When the guns boom, the arts die."

Jane Jacobs
(1916–2006)

CREDIT: Associated Press/CP files, Adrian Wyld

ON APRIL 10, 1968, New York state officials scheduled a public hearing to discuss their plans for an expressway that would have sliced across Lower Manhattan and displaced hundreds of businesses and the homes of 2,000 families. The expressway's opponents, including Jane Jacobs, a writer who lived in Greenwich Village, considered the hearing a sham. Jacobs noticed that the microphone was set up so that speakers addressed the crowd, not the transportation officials seated on the stage. When speakers asked the officials questions about the project, they refused to answer, saying that they were just there to listen.

When it was Jacobs's turn to speak, she gave a blistering critique of the highway plan. Then she announced that she was going to walk up on the stage and march past the officials' table in silent protest, and she welcomed others to join her. About fifty people followed Jacobs to the stage. "You can't come up here," the top state official said. "Get off the stage." Jacobs refused, so the official summoned the police and shouted, "Arrest this woman."

Jacobs was taken to the police station and released, promising to appear in court. The next day, and for several days afterwards, her arrest was headline news. When she appeared in court on April 17, the city had changed the charges from disorderly conduct to second-degree riot, inciting a riot, criminal mischief, and obstructing public administration, all more serious criminal charges. She was told that she faced anywhere from fifteen days to one year in prison for each charge. Many of New York's leading liberals came to Jacobs's defense, offering to create a legal defense fund and writing letters and articles protesting her treatment. The charges were eventually dropped.

This was one battle in a much longer war that Jacobs had waged against top-down city planning, particularly as practiced by New York's planning and public works czar, Robert Moses. Moses was a master builder who for decades had re-shaped the physical landscape of New York City and its suburbs, bulldozing entire neighborhoods, constructing highways, bridges, parks, beaches, and housing projects, all oriented toward the car and away from public transit. From the 1940s through the 1960s, he was considered the most powerful individual in New York, even though he was never elected to any office.

But Moses met his match in Jacobs, whose only ammunition was her typewriter, her network of community activists, and her moral authority. The controversy surrounding Jacobs's arrest led New York Mayor John Lindsay to cancel the highway project. It was also the beginning of Moses's fall from power: Governor Nelson Rockefeller removed him from his positions as head of several powerful agencies. More importantly, Jacobs's victory over the expressway marked a triumph for a different view of city planning, one that she had been advocating for years, most prominently in her 1961 book *The Death and Life of Great American Cities.*

The book became the manifesto of a movement, much like **Rachel Carson**'s *Silent Spring* (1962), **Betty Friedan**'s *The Feminine Mystique* (1963), and **Ralph Nader**'s *Unsafe at Any Speed* (1965). Jacobs's book and her subsequent writings changed the way we think about livable cities. Her views have become part of the conventional wisdom of city planning.

Jacobs grew up in Scranton, Pennsylvania. Graduating from high school during the Depression, she decided to get a job rather than go to college. In 1934 she moved to New York, where she found work as a secretary in Greenwich Village. She sold a series of articles about different areas of the city—such as the flower market and the diamond district—to *Vogue* magazine, earning $40 for each at a time when she was making $12 a week as a secretary. In her spare time, she took courses at Columbia University's School of General Studies in geology, zoology, law, political science, and economics.

In 1952 *Architectural Forum* hired Jacobs as an editor, a position she held for ten years. It was there that her writings about city planning first got attention.

The 1950s was the heyday of urban renewal, the federal program that sought to wipe out urban blight with the bulldozer. Its advocates were typically downtown businesses, developers, banks, major daily newspapers, big-city mayors, and construction unions. Most planners and architects of the time joined the urban renewal chorus, convinced that big development projects would revitalize downtown business districts, stem the exodus of middle-class families to suburbs, and improve the quality of public spaces. On an assignment in Philadelphia, however, Jacobs noticed that the streets within an urban renewal project were deserted, whereas an older street nearby was crowded with people. She talked to the project architect, who described its wonderful aesthetics but seemed unconcerned with its impact on real people. Her impression was reinforced by a walking tour of East Harlem and other neighborhoods, where she came to see that the dominant ideas of city planning—bulldozing low-rise housing in poor neighborhoods and replacing it with tall apartment buildings surrounded by open space—were misguided. Planners preferred straight lines, big blocks, and order, but cities came alive when they brought out the human qualities of randomness, surprise, and social interaction.

In 1958 William Whyte, an editor at *Fortune* magazine, asked Jacobs to write an article on downtowns. The theme of the *Fortune* article became the manifesto of her book *Death and Life,* which she completed three years later: "Designing a dream city is easy. Rebuilding a living one takes imagination."

"This book is an attack on current city planning and rebuilding," she wrote in the book's opening paragraph. "It is also, and mostly, an attempt to introduce new principles of city planning and rebuilding, different and even opposite from those now taught in everything from schools of architecture and planning to Sunday supplements and women's magazines."

Jacobs's views about cities drew on her experiences living in Greenwich Village, which she considered the quintessential livable neighborhood. In 1947 she and her husband, an architect, bought a dilapidated three-story building and spent years fixing it up. She rode her bicycle to and from work.

Cities, Jacobs believed, should be untidy, complex, and full of surprises. Good cities encourage social interaction at the street level. They favor foot traffic, bicycles, and public transit over cars. They get people talking to each other. Residential buildings should be low-rise and should have stoops and porches. Sidewalks and parks should have benches. Streets should be short and should wind around neighborhoods. Livable neighborhoods require mixed-use buildings—especially those with first-floor retail establishments and housing above. She saw how "eyes on the street" could make neighborhoods safe as well as supportive. She favored corner stores over big chains and liked newsstands and pocket parks where people can meet casually. Cities, she believed, should foster a mosaic of architectural styles and heights. And they should allow people from different income, ethnic, and racial groups to live in close proximity.

Jacobs was self-taught, with no college degree or credential. She was unencumbered by planning orthodoxy, although she carefully read and thoroughly critiqued the major thinkers in the field—including Sir Patrick Geddes, Ebenezer Howard, Le Corbusier, and Lewis Mumford—who believed that high-rise towers surrounded by open spaces reflected the best combination of technology, efficiency, and modernism. Likewise, she condemned the execution of these ideas by Moses and other government planners who arrogantly believed that their own expertise trumped the day-to-day experiences of the people whose lives were affected by their decisions.

Jacobs had a profound influence on both community organizers and planners. Her efforts in New York were part of a broader grassroots movement around the country to stop government agencies, typically with business support, from destroying poor and working-class communities—a process that activists often called "Negro removal." From this cauldron emerged new leaders, new organizations, and new issues—issues such as bank redlining, tenants' rights and rent control, neighborhood crime, environmental racism, and underfunded schools. Some groups that were founded to protest against top-down plans began thinking about what they were for, not just what they were against. Hundreds of community development corporations (CDCs) emerged out of these efforts.

Jacobs also paved the way for what became known as "advocacy planning." Starting in the 1960s, a handful of urban planners and architects chose to side with residents of low-income urban neighborhoods against the power of city redevelopment agencies and their business allies. They provided technical skills (and sometimes political advice) for community groups engaged in trench warfare against displacement and gentrification. Jacobs's activist work and her writings showed people they could defeat the urban renewal bulldozer. Eventually mayors and planning agencies began to rethink the bulldozer approach to urban renaissance. In 1974 President Richard Nixon canceled the urban renewal program.

Although many developers and elected officials still favor the top-down approach, most planners and architects have absorbed Jacobs's lessons. Advocates of "smart growth" and "new urbanism" claim Jacobs's mantle, although she would no doubt dispute some of their ideas and, in particular, criticize the failure of these approaches to make room for poor and working-class residents.

Jacobs wrote several other books—including *The Economy of Cities* (1969), and *Cities and the Wealth of Nations* (1984)—but none of them had the influence of *Death and Life*, which eventually became required reading in planning, architecture, and urban studies programs.

Hailed for her visionary writing and activism, Jacobs refused to accept sainthood. She turned down honorary degrees from more than thirty institutions. She always gave credit to the ordinary people on the front lines of the battle over the future of their neighborhoods and cities.

C. Wright Mills (1916–1962)

CREDIT: Photo by Yaroslava Mills, courtesy of Nik Mills

IN THE 1950s, when most college faculty were cautious about their political views and lifestyles, C. Wright Mills burst onto the scene, a radical sociologist from Texas who rode a motorcycle to work, wore plaid shirts, jeans, and work boots instead of flannel suits, built his house with his own hands, and warned that America was becoming a nation of "cheerful robots" heading for World War III. In a 1961 article, "Who Are the Student Boat-Rockers?" activist **Tom Hayden** listed the three people over thirty whom young radicals most admired. They were **Norman Thomas, Michael Harrington,** and Mills.

The three books Mills published between 1948 and 1956—*The New Men of Power, White Collar,* and *The Power Elite*—challenged the widely held belief that American society, having triumphed over the fundamental problems of the 20th century (Depression and war), had become a model of economic success, political democracy, and social well-being. Mills, a Columbia University professor, warned about the dangers of the concentration of wealth and power. Mills's most influential book, *The Power Elite,* challenged the notion that farmers, workers, middle-class consumers, small businesses, and big businesses all had equal voices in American democracy. Instead, he described the overlapping circles of business, military, and political leaders who formed a power structure. Their big decisions determined the nation's destiny, including war and peace.

Today this is the prevailing view, but in the 1950s it was highly controversial. Mills's was a lonely voice among academic sociologists, but his books sold well, suggesting that at least some Americans were not happy with the postwar status quo.

The Cold War led to what was called the "permanent war economy" to sustain expensive new weapons systems and military bases around the world. At home, the fear of Communists and other radicals led to the hysteria of the McCarthy era, stewarded by business groups who were worried about stronger unions and higher taxes and by politicians who got into office by scaring voters about the Red menace threatening to take over the public schools, unions, Hollywood, and universities.

It was in this atmosphere that Mills began his academic career. Growing up in a middle-class family in Dallas, Texas, Charles Wright Mills studied philosophy at the University of Texas and then earned his Ph.D. in sociology at the University of Wisconsin, where he focused his research on social psychology and social theory. After a brief stint teaching at the University of Maryland, he arrived at Columbia in 1945 to work at the university's new survey research center and to teach sociology. He remained at Columbia until he died of a heart attack, at age forty-five, in 1962.

At Columbia, Mills mastered social research, particularly the skills of conducting interviews and doing large surveys, and used those skills to carry out several projects that his senior colleagues suggested. But Mills was restless. He wanted to use his academic perch to reach outside academia, influence public opinion, and help build a progressive movement.

In New York, he met a widening circle of radicals and rebels, such as novelist Harvey Swados, critic Dwight Macdonald, and labor activist J. B. S. Hardman, who expanded Mills's political horizons. He began writing essays for progressive and left-wing opinion magazines, including the *New Republic, New Leader, Partisan Review, Dissent,* and, especially, *Politics,* which criticized America's warfare state and sought ways to invigorate grassroots democracy. In his first few years at Columbia, Mills joined a network of academics who provided research to help union leaders understand the major social and economic changes facing their members. Mills's ties to the labor movement led to the first of his major books on what he called the "main drift" of American society—*The New Men of Power: America's Labor Leaders,* published in 1948.

Union membership had increased fivefold in the decade before Mills wrote the book, and unions represented one-third of nonfarm workers. Mills believed that unions could be a bulwark against America's drift toward "war and slump" by pushing to convert the war economy to civilian uses, improving workers' incomes and job security, and giving ordinary Americans a voice in government to challenge big-business power.

The New Men of Power was cautiously optimistic about the labor movement's potential. But in 1947, while he was writing the book, Congress passed the Taft-Hartley Act, over President Harry S. Truman's veto. The act weakened unions' ability to organize. Mills was also disappointed when, in the 1948 elections, the American Federation of Labor and Congress of Industrial Organizations unions (including the United Auto Workers) endorsed Truman over **Henry Wallace** and Norman Thomas (whom Mills voted for). In that political climate, few major union leaders were inclined to challenge the Cold War, the arms race, or the attacks on radical dissent. Indeed, most unions would soon purge themselves of their radical leaders as part of the Red Scare hysteria. Mills drifted away from working with progressive labor activists as his confidence in the labor movement gave way to skepticism.

Having examined the blue-collar working class, Mills turned to Americans in the professions and middle management. In his next book, *White Collar: The American Middle Classes,* published in 1951, he explored the social conditions and psychology of this growing stratum of Americans, living in urban neighborhoods and suburbs and exemplifying the "American way of life" that the nation's leaders contrasted with the drab and compliant life in Communist Russia.

Based on interviews and surveys as well as on analyses of popular culture, Mills concluded that many middle-class Americans were socially, intellectually, and politically stifled, trapped in offices in large business bureaucracies over which they had no control (including no union representation). Instead of finding pleasure and pride in craftsmanship at work, they pursued happiness and status by buying things they did not need and living without much purpose. He coined the phrase "cheerful robot" to decry the unthinking conformity of much of America's middle-class culture. Mills believed that such conformity was an aspect of what he called "mass society"—a condition of widespread political apathy that permitted business and political leaders to pursue the arms race and the potential for a nuclear war without much opposition.

Mills's critique was not unique. Throughout the 1950s and early 1960s, there were other indications that many Americans were starting to question the nation's moral and psychological condition. The 1955 novel *The Man in the Grey-Flannel Suit* (made into a film the next year) disparaged the lifestyle of middle-class managers. J. D. Salinger's popular 1951 novel *Catcher in the Rye;* the 1955 film starring James Dean, *Rebel Without a Cause;* and Paul Goodman's 1960 book *Growing Up Absurd* all depicted the alienation of middle-class youth, raging against "phonies." Malvina Reynolds's 1962 song "Little Boxes" poked fun at the look-alike housing developments in postwar suburbs and at the complacency of the people who lived in them. Best-selling books by sociologically oriented journalists—William H. Whyte's *The Organization Man* (1956) and Vance Packard's *The Hidden Persuaders* (1957) and *The Status Seekers* (1959)—expressed alarm, during the height of the Eisenhower administration, at the influence of corporate employers, advertisers, and suburban developers in shaping the daily lives of American families. Arthur Miller's 1949 play *Death of a Salesman* struck a similar chord. In 1952, two left-wing writers, William Gaines and Harvey Kurtzman, launched *MAD,* a comics magazine of political and social satire that became an instant sensation with the baby-boom generation. It poked fun at middle-class suburbia, the Cold War, and advertising. Its slogan, "What?

Me worry?" was intentionally ironic, because many Americans were quite worried about the escalating arms race, the proliferation of fallout shelters, and the possibility of a nuclear holocaust.

The Power Elite, published in 1956, was the most radical, controversial, and widely read of Mills's three major books. It caused a firestorm in academic and political circles. America has a ruling elite, Mills wrote, and its most active members—top corporate executives—have little sense of social responsibility. Rather, they work collaboratively with the top military leaders and their allies in Congress and the White House (former general and World War II hero Dwight Eisenhower was the Republican president at the time) to shape the nation's major priorities based primarily on greed and self-interest. The various interest groups that could contend for power—farmers' organizations, labor unions, big-city mayors, and others—fight over crumbs left over after the big spending decisions, particularly the military budget, have already been decided.

Mills pointed out that the corporate, military, and political elites were not separate spheres but, rather, overlapping groups at the "command posts" of society. Top corporate executives (such as Eisenhower's secretary of defense, former General Motors CEO Charles Wilson) were recruited to serve in the cabinet and on numerous committees providing advice to the White House and Congress. Retired generals and admirals (whom Mills called "warlords") went to work for major defense corporations, using their influence to argue for bigger military budgets, new weapons systems, and government contracts for their new employers. Corporate executives and Pentagon leaders lobbied members of Congress to increase the military budget, pointing out that jobs would be created in defense plants and military bases in their districts.

Mills was particularly concerned that few newspapers, academics, or religious leaders spoke out against this concentration of power. Instead, most went along with the power elite's ideology—a stance Mills called "crackpot realism," in which dangerous, irresponsible ideas are accepted by the public as normal. One such idea was the concept of "mutually assured destruction"—that a world war could be averted if both the United States and Soviet Union had enough weapons to destroy the other. Mills hated Soviet totalitarianism, but he thought the United States and the Soviet Union could cooperate to avoid a costly arms race and a possible nuclear holocaust.

Mills's critique of America's power structure was dramatically at odds with the prevailing view of American democracy taught in high schools and colleges at the time. But Mills found unlikely validation in President Eisenhower's farewell address on January 17, 1961, which warned about the "unwarranted influence" of the "military-industrial complex," an assemblage of influential players very similar to the power elite.

Along with Floyd Hunter's *Community Power Structure* (a study of Atlanta, Georgia, published in 1953), *The Power Elite* inspired hundreds of studies by academics and activists, exposing the overlapping networks of corporate influence on local and national politics. A half century later, most Americans now recognize that the biggest corporations and the very wealthy have disproportionate political influence.

By the time he wrote *The Power Elite,* Mills had given up hope that a resurgent labor could revitalize American democracy. He seemed oblivious to the burgeoning civil rights movement that had erupted in Montgomery, Alabama, in 1955. (In fact, his writings indicate that he was oblivious to issues of race.)

But Mills's books, particularly *The Power Elite,* resonated with the growing mood of discontent in the nation, particularly on the college campuses. Its influence can be seen in the Port Huron Statement, the founding manifesto of Students for a Democratic Society, written in 1962. During the last few years of his life, a few trends—the rise of student activism in the United States and Europe, the Cuban revolution in 1959, and the awakening of anticolonial movements in Africa, Asia, and South America—gave Mills a new sense of hope.

Energized by these movements, he wrote two short books—which he called "pamphlets"—aimed at a wide audience. *The Causes of World War Three* (1958), an impassioned plea for an end to the nuclear arms race, sold over 100,000 copies. *Listen, Yankee* (1960), a sympathetic look at the Cuban revolution from the viewpoint of a Cuban revolutionary, sold over 400,000 copies. In the fall of 1960, he published a "Letter to the New Left" in the British journal *New Left Review,* encouraging young radicals around the world.

Mills's writing combined analysis and outrage. He was a meticulous researcher, but he did not wish to be what he called a "sociological bookkeeper." He wrote about the fundamental questions facing American society and he had strong opinions. "I try to be objective," Mills wrote, "I do not claim to be detached."

Toward the end of his life, the mainstream media began asking Mills for his views on major issues of the day. In December 1960 he was invited to appear on the NBC television show *The Nation's Future* to debate A. A. Berle, a spokesperson for the newly elected John F. Kennedy administration, about US policy in Latin America. On the eve of the program, Mills suffered a heart attack and had to cancel the debate. He never fully recovered his remarkable energy. A second heart attack on March 20, 1962, was fatal. He never lived to see the emergence of the student and antiwar movements that his work helped inspire.

Barry Commoner
(1917–)

DESCRIBED IN 1970 by *Time* magazine as the "Paul Revere of ecology," Barry Commoner followed **Rachel Carson** as America's most prominent modern environmentalist. But unlike Carson, Commoner viewed the environmental crisis as a symptom of a fundamentally flawed economic and social system. A biologist and research scientist, he argued that corporate greed, misguided government priorities, and the misuse of technology accounted for the undermining of "the finely sculptured fit between life and its surroundings."

Commoner linked environmental issues to a broader vision of social and economic justice. He called attention to the parallels among the environmental, civil rights, labor, and peace movements. He connected the environmental crisis to the problems of poverty, injustice, racism, public health, national security, and war.

Commoner insisted that scientists had an obligation to make scientific information accessible to the general public, so that citizens could participate in public debates that involved scientific questions. Citizens, he said, have a right to know the health hazards of the consumer products and technologies used in everyday life. Those were radical ideas in the 1950s and 1960s, when most Americans were still mesmerized by the cult of scientific expertise and such new technologies as cars, plastics, chemical sprays, and atomic energy.

Commoner first came to public attention in the late 1950s when he warned about the hazards of fallout caused by the atmospheric testing of nuclear weapons. He later used his scientific platform to raise awareness about the dangers posed by the petrochemical industry, nuclear power, and toxic substances such as dioxins. Commoner was one of the first scientists to point out that although environmental hazards hurt everyone, they disproportionately hurt the poor and racial minorities because of the location of dangerous chemicals and because of the hazardous conditions in blue-collar workplaces. Commoner thus laid the groundwork for the environmental justice movement.

Commoner grew up in Brooklyn, New York, the child of Russian Jewish immigrants. He studied zoology at Columbia University and received a doctorate in biology from Harvard University in 1941. After serving in the navy during World War II, Commoner was an associate editor for *Science Illustrated* and then became a professor at Washington University in St. Louis, Missouri, a position he held for thirty-four years. There he founded, in 1966, the Center for the Biology of Natural Systems to promote research on ecological systems. He later moved the center to Queens College in New York.

While serving in the navy, Commoner discovered a disturbing unintended consequence of technology. He was put in charge of a project to devise an apparatus to allow bombers to spray DDT on beachheads to kill insects that caused disease among soldiers. The military wanted to remove the insects before troops landed. Commoner's crew discovered that the DDT sprayed from bombers effectively eliminated hordes of flies on the beach, but also that more flies soon came to feast on the tons of fish that the DDT had also killed. This lesson became a central theme for Commoner throughout his career: humans cannot take action on one part of the ecosystem without triggering a reaction elsewhere.

After the war, many scientists, including **Albert Einstein,** alarmed by America's use of the atomic bomb on Japan in 1945, began to rethink their role in society. They questioned whether dropping the bomb had been necessary for the United States to win the war. They were shocked by the scale of the damage in terms of both immediate deaths and long-term human suffering. And they worried about the potential for a prolonged arms race between the United States and the Soviet Union, which, they feared, could end in a nuclear war in which all humanity would be the losers.

As Commoner told *Scientific American* in a 1997 interview:

> The Atomic Energy Commission had at its command an army of highly skilled scientists. Although they knew how to design and build nuclear bombs, it somehow escaped their notice that rainfall washes suspended material out of the air, or that children drink milk and concentrate iodine in their growing thyroids. I believe that the main reason for the AEC's failure is less complex than a cover-up but equally devastating. The AEC scientists were so narrowly focused on arming the United States for nuclear war that they failed to perceive facts—even widely known ones—that were outside their limited field of vision.

Commoner and other scientists—including chemist Linus Pauling (a professor at the California Institute of Technology and a Nobel Prize winner)—believed they had a responsibility to sound the alarm about the potentially devastating effects of nuclear fallout. In 1956, when Adlai Stevenson ran for president as the Democratic Party nominee, he sought Commoner's advice and then called for the United States to take the lead in ending nuclear testing. In 1958 Commoner and other scientists and activists formed the Committee for Nuclear Information with the goal of educating the public to understand how, in Commoner's words, "splitting a few pounds of atoms could turn something as mild as milk into a devastating global poison." Their new publication, *Nuclear Information* (renamed *Scientist and Citizen*), was founded to discuss the responsibility of scientists to the larger society. They drafted a petition, signed by 11,021 scientists worldwide, urging that "an international agreement to stop the testing of nuclear bombs be made now." These activities created a groundswell of public opinion that eventually helped persuade President John F. Kennedy to propose the 1963 Nuclear Test Ban Treaty.

Commoner's early experience with DDT led him to espouse what scientists call the "precautionary principle"—that new chemicals and technologies should not be introduced into society if there is reason to believe that they pose a significant public health risk. They should be approved only after it can be demonstrated that they are safe. Commoner warned about the risks to human health posed by detergents, pesticides, herbicides, radioisotopes, and smog. He argued that polluting products (such as detergents and synthetic textiles) should be replaced with natural products (such as soap, cotton, and wool). He alerted the public to the negative effects of nuclear power plants, toxic chemicals, and pollution on the economy, birth defects, and diseases like asthma.

In the 1970s Commoner spoke out against the view that overpopulation, particularly in the Third World, was responsible for the increasing depletion of the word's natural resources and the deepening ecological problems. The thesis was popularized by Paul Ehrlich (in his book *The Population Bomb*) and other scientists, but Commoner challenged those who echoed the ideas of the 19th-century British thinker Thomas Robert Malthus.

As Commoner argued, it is rich nations that consume a disproportionate share of the world's resources. And it was their systems of colonialism and imperialism that led to the exploitation of the Third World's natural resources for consumption in the wealthy nations, making the poor even poorer. Without the financial resources to improve their living conditions, people in developing countries relied more heavily upon increased birthrates as a form of social security than did people in wealthier nations. As Commoner wrote, "The poor countries have high birthrates because they are extremely poor, and they are extremely poor because other countries are extremely rich." His solution to the population problem was to increase the standard of living of the world's poor, which would result in a voluntary reduction of fertility, as has occurred in the rich countries.

In *The Closing Circle* (1971), Commoner argued that our economy—including corporations, government, and consumers—needs to be in sync with what he called the "four laws of ecology":

- Everything is connected to everything else.
- Everything must go somewhere.
- Nature knows best.
- There is no such thing as a free lunch.

The Closing Circle helped introduce the idea of sustainability, a notion that is now widely accepted but was controversial at the time. As Commoner pointed out, there is only one ecosphere for all living things. What affects one, affects all. He also noted that in nature there is no waste. We can't throw things away. Therefore, we need to design and manufacture products that do not upset the delicate balance between humans and nature. We need to utilize alternative forms of energy, such as wind, solar, and geothermal power. And we need to change our consumption habits accordingly—to use fewer products with plastics (which are based on oil), aerosol cans (which harm the atmosphere), and industrial-grown food (which is produced with harmful chemicals).

In his best-selling book *The Poverty of Power* (1976), Commoner introduced what he called the "Three Es"—the threat to *environmental* survival, the shortage of *energy,* and the problems (such as inequality and unemployment) of the *economy*—and explained their interconnectedness: industries that use the most energy have the most negative impact on the environment. Our dependence on nonrenewable sources of energy inevitably leads to those resources becoming scarcer, raising the cost of energy and hurting the economy.

Commoner was neither a back-to-the-land utopian nor a Luddite opposed to modern industrial civilization. He did not place the burden of blame on the consumers who buy these products or the workers who produce them. He believed that big business and their political allies dominate society's decision making, often leading to misguided priorities, a theme that paralleled the ideas of economist **John Kenneth Galbraith** and, later, **Ralph Nader.** The corporate imperative for wasteful growth is the root cause of the crisis, Commoner believed, and must be corralled by responsible public policies demanded by a well-educated public. As Commoner told *Scientific American*: "The environmental crisis arises from a fundamental fault: our systems of production—in industry, agriculture, energy and transportation—essential as they are, make people sick and die."

Commoner's proposals for addressing these problems reflect his lifetime of pushing a progressive agenda. "What is needed now is a transformation of the major systems of production more profound than even the sweeping post–World War II changes in production technology," he told *Scientific American.* "Restoring environmental quality means substituting solar sources of energy for fossil and nuclear fuels; substituting electric motors for the internal-combustion engine; substituting organic farming for chemical agriculture; expanding the use of durable, renewable and recyclable materials—metals, glass, wood, paper—in place of the petrochemical products that have massively displaced them."

Commoner acknowledged some of the environmental movement's victories, including bans on DDT and on lead in gasoline. Commoner saw this as evidence that society can *prevent* environmental hazards by changing the way we produce and consume. But in a 2007 interview with the *New York Times,* he warned that these measures did not go far enough. "Environmental pollution is an incurable disease," he said. "It can only be prevented. And prevention can only take place at the point of production. If you insist on using DDT, the only thing you can do is stop. The rest has really been sort of forgotten about."

Many Americans embraced Commoner's ideas about workplace hazards, nuclear power plants, and recycling. But he grew frustrated by the influence of corporate America over both political parties and by the failure of the mainstream environmental movement to join forces with other progressive movements to heed his warnings and challenge the basic tenets of the free-market system.

In 1979 Commoner helped form the Citizens Party, hoping it would gain influence similar to that of the Green Party in Europe. The next year Commoner ran as the party's presidential candidate. He got on the ballot in twenty-nine states but received less than one-third of 1 percent of the national vote. Like most third parties in the American system, the Citizens Party wound up being a minor fringe force. Commoner did not run again for office, but he advised Jesse Jackson's Democratic Party presidential campaigns in the 1980s.

In the 2007 interview with the *New York Times,* the ninety-year-old Commoner remained the relentless radical: "I think that most of the 'greening' that we see so much of now has failed to look back on arguments such as my own—that action has to be taken on what's produced and how it's produced. That's unfortunate, but I'm an eternal optimist, and I think eventually people will come around."

Fannie Lou Hamer (1917–1977)

Fannie Lou Hamer speaks to Mississippi Freedom Democratic Party sympathizers outside the Capitol in Washington, DC, in 1965. CREDIT: Associated Press/William J. Smith

FANNIE LOU HAMER may be best remembered for the words chiseled on her gravestone: "I'm sick and tired of being sick and tired." But the resignation suggested in that famous phrase was not part of Hamer's constitution. She was an irrepressible fighter who fearlessly stood up to the worst elements of the Mississippi power structure during the 1960s civil rights movement.

Hamer was the youngest of twenty children born to Jim and Ella Townsend of Ruleville, Mississippi, an all-black town. The Townsends were impoverished, hard-working sharecroppers in the heart of cotton country. The family often went hungry. Shoes were a luxury that Hamer did not enjoy for many years— her mother would tie rags around her children's feet with string when winter came. Hamer was especially close to her mother, who, she once said, "was one woman in the state of Mississippi who didn't let no white man beat her kids."

She was expected to help out in the fields when she was just six years old— the same year she had a bout of polio that left her with a lifelong limp. In elementary school, she was a good student, but she was forced to stop her education in the sixth grade to work in the fields to help her family.

In the 1940s she met her husband, Perry "Pap" Hamer, who worked on the W. D. Marlow plantation. They worked together on the plantation for eighteen years until she was fired for trying to vote. She experienced racism in its many forms. In 1961 she went into a hospital to have a small uterine tumor removed; doctors performed a hysterectomy without her knowledge or permission.

She was first exposed to activism in the 1950s, when she attended meetings of the Regional Council of Negro Leadership, founded by Mississippi physician T. R. M. Howard to promote voter registration, equal schools, and other civil rights. The meetings featured speeches by northern black elected officials and by National Association for the Advancement of Colored People (NAACP) attorney **Thurgood Marshall.**

When organizers from the Student Nonviolent Coordinating Committee (SNCC) and the Southern Christian Leadership Conference came to Ruleville in August 1962, Hamer was ready. She attended a meeting at Williams Chapel Church, where, despite being a sharecropper who had grown up singing Gospel music in small rural churches, she heard freedom songs for the first time. Deeply moved, she was the first to raise her hand high when the organizers asked who would be willing to register to vote. She later said, "I guess if I'd had any sense I'd a-been a little scared."

Soon after, Hamer and seventeen other brave souls took the bus to the Sunflower County seat in Indianola, Mississippi, to try to register to vote. On the bus, she began singing hymns, such as "Go Tell It on the Mountain" and "This Little Light of Mine," to bolster the group's morale. Others had been turned away before them, but this time, she and one other, Ernest Davis, were allowed in. Before they could register, they had to take one of the infamous literacy tests designed to disenfranchise black people. Among other questions, they were required to write down the names of their employers, information that would promptly be used against them. They were also required to interpret a section of the state constitution to the satisfaction of local white officials. For Hamer, the clerk pointed to a section of the Mississippi Constitution dealing with de facto laws. As she later explained, "I knowed as much about a facto law as a horse knows about Christmas Day."

She failed the test. By the time she returned home, she had lost her job, but she had discovered her passion. She became a leader and public figure in the civil rights movement. The stout, five-foot-four Hamer had a commanding speaking and singing voice. When times grew difficult, she was the first to lead others in Gospel and freedom songs. Leading people in song to give them hope and courage became a key part of her effectiveness.

The following December she tried to register again. She was asked to interpret a section of the state constitution concerning the state legislature. She had studied the Mississippi Constitution with SNCC workers. "So that time I gave a reasonable enough interpretation," she recalled. She told the registrar that if he did not pass her this time, she would keep coming back until he did. A few weeks later, she learned that she had passed the test. (That made her one of only 28,000 black Mississippians who were registered—out of a total of 422,256 eligible black voters.) But when she tried to vote the next August in the primary election, she was told she could not because she had not been paying the poll tax for two years. She explained that she had not paid the tax because she had not been registered, but she was denied the right to vote anyway.

In 1963 she traveled throughout the South with SNCC, living on a stipend of $10 a week. She met with people in homes, churches, and elsewhere, encouraging them to register to vote. Most people remained fearful—worried about losing their jobs, about being physically assaulted or even killed, and about having their homes bombed or burned. Hamer and others organized citizenship classes, which included reading lessons, instruction on how to take the voter registration test and how to use a bank account, and lots of singing. Organizers gradually found people willing to come together to challenge the Jim Crow laws, which took self-confidence and courage. One participant observed that the classes were designed to help people "unbrainwash" themselves. Stories of Hamer's bravery spread across the South, inspiring others.

In June 1963 she and others in the group were traveling by bus through Mississippi, en route to Greenwood. They stopped at the small town of Winona, and several of the group went into the segregated café. Even though they had broken no law, they were arrested. Hamer spent a harrowing time in the Montgomery County jail where she and her comrades were beaten mercilessly with blackjacks by two African American male inmates, whom the jailers had intimidated.

In addition, Hamer and her husband were constantly harassed by local officials. For example, one day they received a $9,000 water bill—even though the Hamer house had no running water.

In 1964 Hamer was in the vanguard of Freedom Summer, educating and training busloads of idealistic volunteers, many of them college students, who came from the North to help register voters.

That year, Hamer helped found the Mississippi Freedom Democratic Party (MFDP), a pivotal part of the movement's strategy to shine a national spotlight on the disenfranchisement of African Americans in the South. Several MDFP activists ran for office in the Democratic primary, challenging white segregationist incumbents. Hamer ran against Representative Jamie Whitten, who had held the seat since 1941. She had no chance to win, because most blacks could not vote, but she used the campaign to give the MDFP project visibility and to show African Americans how the election process worked.

After organizing for months, MDFP sent an integrated delegation of sixty-eight members, including Hamer, to represent Mississippi at the 1964 Democratic Party convention in Atlantic City, New Jersey, in August. This was a direct challenge to the official all-white delegation, which brutally excluded blacks from voting. When they arrived in Atlantic City, the MFDP demanded that the national Democratic Party seat them rather than the segregated official delegation.

Hamer stood before the party's credentials committee and with television cameras rolling delivered an emotional speech, telling the world what it was like for African Americans trying to be "first-class citizens" in Mississippi. "If the Freedom Democratic Party is not seated now, I question America. Is this America?" Hamer asked. "The land of the free and the home of the brave, where we have to sleep with our telephones off the hooks because our lives be threatened daily because we want to live as decent human beings, in America?"

She spoke of her own beating and of the murders of NAACP leader Medgar Evers and of three other civil rights workers—James Chaney, Andrew Goodman, and Michael Schwerner—who only a few days earlier had been slain near Philadelphia, Mississippi.

President **Lyndon B. Johnson** called a last-minute press conference to divert press coverage from Hamer's testimony, but many TV networks ran her speech on their late news programs. The credentials committee received thousands of calls and letters in support of the MFDP. Johnson, who would soon be campaigning and hoped to avoid controversy in the national spotlight, persuaded the credentials committee to offer MFDP two at-large seats. Some of the civil rights movement's liberal allies, including Senator Hubert H. Humphrey of Minnesota (who was hoping to be LBJ's vice presidential running mate) and union leader **Walter Reuther,** urged the MFDP to accept the deal, which they viewed as an opening wedge in challenging the party's segregationist wing. Even **Martin Luther King Jr.** urged them to agree to the compromise.

Hamer rebuked Humphrey, who had long been a civil rights champion. "Do you mean to tell me that your position is more important than four hundred thousand black people's lives?" Hamer said.

Senator Humphrey, I know lots of people in Mississippi who have lost their jobs trying to register to vote. I had to leave the plantation where I worked in Sunflower County, Mississippi. Now if you lose this job of Vice-President because you do what is right, because you help the MFDP, everything will be all right. God will take care of you. But if you take [the nomination] this way, why, you will never be able to do any good for civil rights, for poor people, for peace, or any of those things you talk about. Senator Humphrey, I'm going to pray to Jesus for you.

The MFDP rejected the deal, arguing that it was too little. But they succeeded in keeping the pressure on. At the next Democratic Party convention, in 1968, Hamer was part of an integrated Mississippi delegation.

Hamer's passion was not limited to electoral politics. She wanted to change living conditions and organized several projects aimed at raising the dignity and living standards of her fellow Mississippians. She testified before US Senate committees on poverty and attended the 1969 White House Conference on Hunger.

In 1969, after years of dreaming and fund-raising help from longtime supporter Harry Belafonte and others, Hamer bought the first forty acres of land for

Freedom Farm, a cooperative for African American farmers. Of 31,000 black people in Sunflower County, only seventy-one owned land. Eventually, Freedom Farm grew to 640 acres. Members grew cash crops and vegetables for their families. In 1971 the first white family asked to move to Freedom Farm.

In 1974, despite Hamer's best efforts, Freedom Farm folded, the victim of bad weather and poor management. Meanwhile, Hamer's health was failing. Her husband worried that others took advantage of her generosity. He said, "I would come to this house and it would be so many people in here I could hardly get in the door. They came to get clothes, food, money—everything. They wore her down. She raised lots of money and she would come back and give it to people. And when she died, she didn't have a dime."

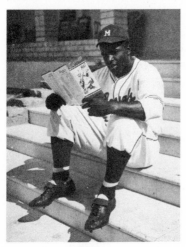

CREDIT: Associated Press

Jackie Robinson
(1919–1972)

WHEN JACKIE Robinson took the field for the Brooklyn Dodgers on April 15, 1947, he was the first black player in modern major league baseball. A half century later, America celebrated the fiftieth anniversary of his courageous triumph over baseball's apartheid system. Major League Baseball (MLB) honored Robinson by retiring his number—42—for all teams. President Bill Clinton appeared with Rachel Robinson at a Mets-Dodgers game at Shea Stadium to venerate her late husband. That year witnessed a proliferation of books, television movies, plays, symposia, museum exhibits, and academic conferences about Robinson. His hometown of Pasadena, California—which virtually ignored him during his own lifetime—finally got around to dedicating a Rose Bowl Parade in his honor.

Why so much activity to commemorate a baseball player? Because Robinson was and is more than a baseball icon. His success on the baseball diamond was a symbol of the promise of a racially integrated society. It is difficult today to summon the excitement and fervor that greeted Robinson's achievement. He did more than change the way baseball is played and who plays it. His actions on and off the diamond helped pave the way for America to confront its racial hypocrisy. The dignity with which Robinson handled his encounters with racism among fellow players and fans—and in hotels, restaurants, trains, and other public places—drew public attention to the issue, stirred the consciences of many white Americans, and gave black Americans a tremendous boost of pride and self-confidence. **Martin Luther King Jr.** once told Dodgers pitcher Don Newcombe, "You'll never know what you and Jackie and Roy [Campanella] did to make it possible to do my job."

Robinson was one of America's greatest all-around athletes. He was a four-sport star athlete at UCLA, played professional football, and then played briefly in baseball's Negro Leagues. He spent his major league career (1947 to 1956) with the Brooklyn Dodgers and was chosen Rookie of the Year in 1947 and Most Valuable Player in 1949. An outstanding base runner, with a .311 lifetime batting average, he led the Dodgers to six pennants and was elected to the Hall of Fame in 1962.

The grandson of a slave and the son of a sharecropper, Robinson was fourteen months old in 1920 when his mother moved her five children from Cairo, Georgia, to Pasadena, a wealthy, conservative Los Angeles suburb. During Robinson's youth, black residents, who represented a small proportion of the city's population, were treated like second-class citizens. Blacks were allowed to swim in the municipal pool only on Tuesdays (the day the water was changed) and could use the YMCA only one day a week.

Robinson learned at an early age that athletic success did not guarantee social or political acceptance. When his older brother Mack returned from the 1936 Olympics in Berlin with a silver medal in track, he got no hero's welcome. The only job the college-educated Mack would find was as a street sweeper and ditch digger.

Robinson's Pasadena background and personal characteristics played a role in the decision by Dodgers general manager Branch Rickey to select him out of the Negro Leagues to break the sport's color barrier. He knew that if the Robinson experiment failed, the cause of baseball integration would be set back for many years. He could have chosen other Negro League players with greater talent or more name recognition, but he wanted someone who could be, in today's terms, a role model. Robinson was articulate and well educated. Although born in the segregated Deep South, he had lived among and formed friendships with whites in his Pasadena neighborhood.

Rickey knew that Robinson had a hot temper and strong political views. As an army officer in World War II, Robinson had been court-martialed (although he was later acquitted) for resisting bus segregation at Fort Hood, Texas. But Rickey calculated that Robinson could handle the emotional pressure while helping the Dodgers on the field. Robinson promised Rickey that he would not respond to the inevitable verbal barbs and even physical abuse.

Rickey could not count on the other team owners or most major league players (many of whom came from southern or small-town backgrounds) to support his plan. But the Robinson experiment succeeded—on the field and at the box office. Within a few years, most other major league teams hired black players, although it was not until 1959 when the last holdout, the Boston Red Sox, brought an African American onto the roster.

After Robinson had established himself as a superstar, Rickey gave him the green light to unleash his temper. On the field, he fought constantly with umpires and opposing players. Off the field, he was outspoken—in speeches, interviews, and his regular newspaper column—against racial injustice. He viewed his sports celebrity as a platform from which to challenge American racism. During his playing career, he was constantly criticized for being so frank about race relations in baseball and in society. Many sportswriters and most other players—including some of his fellow black players, content simply to be playing in the majors—considered Robinson too angry and vocal.

Robinson's political views reflected the tensions of Cold War liberalism. In 1949 Rickey orchestrated Robinson's appearance before the House Un-American Activities Committee so that he could publicly criticize **Paul Robeson,** who had stirred controversy by stating in a Paris speech that American blacks would not fight in a war with Russia. As expected, Robinson challenged Robeson's patriotism. "I and other Americans of many races and faiths have too much invested in our country's welfare for any of us to throw it away for a siren song sung in bass," Robinson said.

But Robinson also seized the opportunity, a decade before the heyday of civil rights activism, to make an impassioned demand for social justice and racial integration. "I'm not fooled because I've had a chance open to very few Negro Americans," Robinson said to Congress. The press focused on Robinson's criticism of Robeson and virtually ignored his denunciation of American racism.

Shortly before his death, Robinson said he regretted his remarks about Robeson. "I have grown wiser and closer to the painful truth about America's destructiveness," he acknowledged. "And I do have an increased respect for Paul Robeson, who sacrificed himself, his career, and the wealth and comfort he once enjoyed because, I believe, he was sincerely trying to help his people."

When Robinson retired from baseball, no team offered him a position as a coach, manager, or executive. He became an executive with the Chock Full o'Nuts restaurant chain and became an advocate for integrating corporate America. He lent his name and prestige to several business ventures, including a construction company and a black-owned bank in Harlem. He got involved in these business activities primarily to help address the shortage of affordable housing and the persistent redlining (lending discrimination against racial minorities) by white-owned banks. Both the construction company and the Harlem bank later fell on hard times and perhaps dimmed Robinson's confidence in black capitalism as a strategy for racial integration.

Nevertheless, Robinson's views led him into several controversial political alliances. In 1960 he initially supported Senator Hubert H. Humphrey's campaign for president, but when John F. Kennedy won the Democratic Party nomination, Robinson shocked his black and liberal fans by endorsing and campaigning for Richard Nixon. He came to regret that support. He later worked as an aide to New York's Governor Nelson Rockefeller, the last of the major liberal Republicans who supported activist government and civil rights.

Until his death, Robinson continued speaking out. He was a constant presence on picket lines and at rallies on behalf of civil rights. He was one of the best fundraisers for the National Association for the Advancement of Colored People, but he resigned from the organization in 1967, criticizing it for its failure to involve "younger, more progressive voices." He pushed Major League Baseball to hire blacks as managers and executives and even refused an invitation to participate in an Old Timers game because he did not yet see "genuine interest in breaking the barriers that deny access to managerial and front office positions."

During 1997 much of the fiftieth anniversary celebration of Robinson's achievement—most of the news articles, movies, and museum exhibits—framed the integration of baseball as an individual's triumph over adversity, as the story of a lone trailblazer who broke baseball's color line on his athletic merits, with a helping hand from Dodger owner Branch Rickey.

But the true story of baseball's integration is not primarily the triumph of either individualism or enlightened capitalism. Rather, it is a political victory brought about by social protest, part of the larger civil rights struggle. As historian Jules Tygiel explains in *Baseball's Great Experiment*, beginning in the 1940s, the Negro press, civil rights groups, the Communist Party, progressive whites, and radical politicians waged a sustained campaign to integrate baseball. That push involved demonstrations, boycotts, political maneuvering, and other forms of pressure that would gain greater currency the following decade. Reporters for African American papers and for the Communist paper the *Daily Worker* kept the issue before the public. This protest movement set the stage for Rickey's experiment and for Robinson's entrance into the major leagues. The dismantling of baseball's color line was a triumph of both a man and movement.

By hiring Robinson, the Dodgers earned the loyalty of millions of black Americans across the country. But they also gained the allegiance of many white Americans—most fiercely, American Jews, especially those in the immigrant and second-generation neighborhoods of America's big cities—who believed that integrating the country's national pastime was a critical stepping-stone to tearing down many other obstacles to equal treatment. In fact, however, the integration of baseball proceeded very slowly after Robinson's entry into the big leagues, paralleling the slow progress of school integration in the larger society after the 1954 *Brown v. Board of Education* ruling.

Robinson recognized the paradoxes of racial progress in America. "I cannot possibly believe," he wrote in his 1972 autobiography, *I Never Had It Made*, "that I have it made while so many black brothers and sisters are hungry, inadequately housed, insufficiently clothed, denied their dignity as they live in slums or barely exist on welfare."

Robinson's crusade helped move the country closer to its ideals. His legacy is also to remind us of the unfinished agenda of the civil rights revolution.

Pete Seeger
(1919–)

ON A cold afternoon on January 18, 2009, Pete Seeger stood in front of the Lincoln Memorial and sang "This Land Is Your Land" at a preinaugural celebration, with President-elect Barack Obama and his wife, Michelle, sitting nearby on the platform, half a million people standing on the mall, and millions of people watching on television across the country and around the world. Defiantly, the eighty-nine-year-old Seeger sang two little-known stanzas of his friend **Woody Guthrie**'s patriotic anthem—one about Depression-era poverty, the other about trespassing on private property—that reflect its author's, and Seeger's, radical political views.

Performing at a presidential inaugural event was a long way from Seeger's situation during the McCarthy era of the 1950s, when he was blacklisted, barred from television and many concert halls, and forced to sing at progressive summer camps and private schools to earn a living.

Seeger is the most influential folk artist of the 20th century. No one can get a crowd singing like he can. The songs he has written, including the antiwar tunes "Where Have All the Flowers Gone?," "If I Had a Hammer," and "Turn, Turn, Turn" (whose text is drawn from Ecclesiastes), and those he has popularized, including "This Land Is Your Land," "Guantanamera," "Wimoweh," and "We Shall Overcome," have been recorded by hundreds of artists in many languages and have become global anthems for people fighting for freedom. His songs are sung by people in cities and villages around the world, promoting the basic idea that the hopes that unite us are greater than the fears that divide us.

In addition to being a much-acclaimed and innovative guitarist and banjoist, a globe-trotting minstrel and song collector, and the author of many songbooks and musical how-to manuals, Seeger has been on the front lines of every key progressive crusade during his lifetime—labor unions and migrant workers in the 1930s and 1940s, the banning of nuclear weapons and opposition to the Cold War in the 1950s, civil rights and the anti–Vietnam War movement in the 1960s, environmental responsibility and opposition to South African apartheid in the 1970s, and, always, human rights throughout the world.

During the 1920s, 1930s, and 1940s, two overlapping groups—collectors of traditional songs and American progressives—celebrated folk music and "people's music." Carl Sandburg, John Lomax, his son Alan Lomax, Lawrence Gellert, and other folklorists collected work songs, sea shanties, hillbilly songs, prison songs, African American and slave songs, and union songs. Progressives used songs not only to promote cross-cultural understanding and a sense of common humanity, but also to energize picket lines, enliven rallies, and galvanize labor unions and political campaigns. For example, the struggle by mine workers in Harlan County, Kentucky, inspired Florence Reese to write the labor classic "Which Side Are You On?"

Pete Seeger, the son of musicologists Charles and Ruth Seeger, spent two years at Harvard, where he got involved in radical politics and helped start a student newspaper, the *Harvard Progressive,* but he quit in 1938 in order to try his own hand at changing society by making music. He worked at the Library of Congress's Archive of American Folk Song (where he learned many of the songs he would sing throughout his career), traveled around with Woody Guthrie singing at migrant labor camps and union halls, and perfected his guitar- and banjo-playing skills.

In 1941, at age twenty-two, Seeger formed the Almanac Singers with Lee Hays and Millard Lampell, later joined by Guthrie, Bess Lomax (daughter of musicologist John Lomax), and several others who rotated in and out of the group. The Almanacs drew on traditional songs and wrote their own songs to advance the cause of progressive groups, the Communist Party, the Congress of Industrial Organizations unions, the New Deal, and, later, the United States and its allies (including the Soviet Union) in the fight against fascism. (For more on the Almanacs, see the profile of Woody Guthrie.) The Almanacs were part of a broader upsurge of popular progressive culture during the New Deal, fostered in part by programs like the federal theater and writers' projects. Even so, the group was hounded by the FBI, got few bookings, and was dropped by its agent, the William Morris Agency. After Seeger and Guthrie joined the military, the group disbanded in 1943.

The Almanacs cultivated an image of being unpolished amateurs. Guthrie once said that the Almanacs "rehearsed on stage." Among them, however, Seeger was the most gifted and disciplined musician, with a remarkable repertoire of traditional songs. He carefully crafted a stage persona that inspired audiences to join him, a performing style that he perfected when he began working as a soloist. Every Seeger concert involves a lot of group singing.

Immediately after World War II, American radicals and liberals sought to resume popular support for progressive unions, civil rights, and internationalism. The left's folk-music wing hoped to build on its modest successes before and during the war. In 1946 Seeger led the effort to create People's Songs (an organization of progressive songwriters and performers, dominated by but not confined to folk musicians) and People's Artists (a booking agency to help the members of People's Songs get concert gigs and recording contracts). They compiled *The People's Song Book* (which included protest songs from around the world), sponsored a number of successful concerts, and organized chapters in several cities and on college campuses.

When **Henry Wallace** ran for president on the Progressive Party ticket in 1948, his campaign relied heavily on folk music. Seeger traveled with Wallace during the campaign, distributing song sheets at every meeting or rally so that sing-alongs, led by Seeger, could alternate with Wallace's speeches.

By 1949 folk music had become increasingly popular, with performers like Burl Ives, Josh White, and others gaining a foothold in popular culture, but the folk music of this period had lost much of its political edge.

For a brief period, as a member of the Weavers folk quartet, Seeger achieved commercial success, performing several chart-topping songs that reflected his eclectic repertoire. The group was formed in 1948 by Seeger and Hays (both former Almanacs), along with Ronnie Gilbert and Fred Hellerman. They exposed audiences to their repertoire of songs from around the world as well as to American folk traditions, but without the overt advocacy of left-wing political causes. Decca Records signed the Weavers to a recording contract and added orchestral arrangements and instruments to their music, a commercial expediency that rankled Seeger but delighted Hays. The Weavers performed in the nation's most prestigious nightclubs and appeared on network television shows.

In 1950 their recording of an Israeli song, "Tzena Tzena," reached number 2 on the pop charts, and their version of Lead Belly's "Goodnight, Irene," reached number 1 and stayed on the charts for half a year. Several of their recordings—"On Top of Old Smokey," "Kisses Sweeter Than Wine," the African song "Wimoweh," and "Midnight Special"—also made the charts. Their 1951 recording of Guthrie's song "So Long It's Been Good to Know You" reached number 4.

But the Weavers' commercial success was short-lived. As soon as they began to be widely noticed in 1950, they were targeted by both private and government witch-hunters. The FBI and Congress escalated their investigations. Seeger and the Weavers were mentioned in *Red Channels* and *Counterattack,* the semi-official private guidebooks for the blacklist. A few performers, notably Josh White and Burl Ives, agreed to cooperate with the investigators and were able to resume their careers; others refused to do so, and some were blacklisted. The Weavers survived for another year with bookings and even TV shows, but finally the escalating Red Scare caught up with them. Their contract for a summer television show was canceled. They could no longer get bookings in the top nightclubs. Radio stations stopped playing their songs, and their records stopped selling. They never had another major hit record.

Seeger left the Weavers to pursue a solo career, but he was blacklisted from the early 1950s through the mid-1960s. In 1955 he was convicted of contempt of

Congress for refusing to discuss his political affiliations at a hearing called by the House Un-American Activities Committee, although he never spent time in jail. (The conviction was overturned on appeal in May 1962.) Many colleges and concert halls refused to book Seeger. He was kept off network television. In 1963 ABC refused to allow Seeger to appear on *Hootenanny,* which owed its existence to the folk music revival Seeger had helped inspire. During the blacklist years, Seeger scratched out a living by giving guitar and banjo lessons and singing at the small number of summer camps, churches, high schools and colleges, and union halls that were courageous enough to invite the controversial balladeer. In 1966, on New York City's nonprofit educational television station, he hosted a low-budget folk music program, *Rainbow Quest,* that gave exposure to many little-known country, bluegrass, and folk singers.

Eventually, however, Seeger's audience grew. In the 1960s he sang with civil rights workers at rallies and churches in the South and at the march from Selma to Montgomery, Alabama. He popularized the song "We Shall Overcome" in the United States and during his concerts around the world. In a letter to Seeger, **Martin Luther King Jr.** thanked him for his "moral support and Christian generosity." In 1967 Tom and Dick Smothers defiantly invited Seeger onto their popular CBS television variety show, the *Smothers Brothers Comedy Hour.* True to his principles, Seeger insisted on singing a controversial antiwar song, "Waist Deep in the Big Muddy." CBS censors refused to air the song, but public outrage forced the network to relent and allow him to perform the song on the show a few months later.

Seeger helped catalyze the folk music revival of the 1960s, encouraging young performers, helping start the Newport Folk Festival, and promoting the folk song magazine *Sing Out!* that he had helped launch. His book *How To Play the 5-String Banjo* taught thousands of baby boomers how to play this largely forgotten instrument. On stage, he always taught his audiences songs from around the world, often sung in their original languages, such as the South African song "Wimoweh" and "Guantanamera" from Cuba.

Many prominent musicians, including **Bob Dylan,** Bono, **Joan Baez,** the Byrds, Natalie Maines of the Dixie Chicks, Bonnie Raitt, Tom Morello, and **Bruce Springsteen** (who sang with Seeger at the Lincoln Memorial) consider Seeger a role model and trace their musical roots to his influence. Many of his eighty albums—which include children's songs, labor and protest songs, traditional American folk songs, international songs, and Christmas songs—have reached wide audiences. His travels around the world—collecting songs and performing in many languages—inspired today's world music movement. Among performers around the globe, Seeger became a symbol of a principled artist deeply engaged in the world.

In 1969 Seeger launched the group Clearwater (near his home in Beacon, New York) and an annual celebration dedicated to cleaning up the polluted Hudson River, an effort that helped inspire the environmental movement.

Through persistence and unrelenting optimism, Seeger endured and over-came the controversies triggered by his activism. In 1994, at age seventy-five, he received the National Medal of Arts (the highest award given to artists and arts patrons by the US government) as well as a Kennedy Center Honor, when President Bill Clinton called him "an inconvenient artist, who dared to sing things as he saw them." In 1996 he was inducted into the Rock and Roll Hall of Fame because of his influence on so many rock performers. In 1997 he won the Grammy Award for his eighteen-track compilation album, *Pete*.

In the 21st century, some of the nation's most prominent singers recorded albums honoring Seeger, including Springsteen's *Seeger Sessions*. PBS broadcast a ninety-three-minute documentary on Seeger's life, *The Power of Song*. In May 2009 more than 15,000 admirers filled New York City's Madison Square Garden for a concert honoring Seeger on his ninetieth birthday. The performers included Bruce Springsteen, Dave Matthews, Emmylou Harris, Joan Baez, Billy Bragg, Rufus Wainwright, Bela Fleck, Taj Mahal, Roger McGuinn, Steve Earle, Ramblin' Jack Elliott, Dar Williams, Tom Morello, Ani DiFranco, and John Mellencamp. Seeger joined in on several numbers with his banjo and also led the crowd in singing "Goodnight, Irene" and an a cappella rendition of "Amazing Grace."

Jerry Wurf
(1919–1981)

CREDIT: Walter P. Reuther Library, Wayne State University

IN APRIL 1968 Jerry Wurf, president of the American Federation of State, County, and Municipal Employees (AFSCME) flew to Memphis to support African American garbage workers who had gone on strike not only to protest unsafe conditions, abusive white supervisors, and low wages, but also to gain recognition for their union. With the help of key AFSCME staffers, and in coalition with the National Association for the Advancement of Colored People and local black ministers (led by Rev. **James Lawson**), Wurf helped draw attention to the sanitation workers' struggle.

Rev. **Martin Luther King Jr.** also flew to Memphis to support the strikers. He addressed 15,000 people—black workers, preachers, students, and a broad spectrum of the black community, joined by white unionists and liberals—at the Mason Temple. King told them, "You are reminding the nation that it is a crime for people to live in this rich nation and receive starvation wages." Wurf, a longtime civil rights activist, was one of the other speakers on the podium. In his deep, foghorn voice, he talked about the injustices shared by blacks and workers, then turned to King and said, "We know, brother, we've been the same places." When a local black minister rose to speak, he pointed to Wurf and said, "This man's skin is white. But he is a brother."

Wurf believed that garbage workers, secretaries, hospital orderlies, emergency medical technicians, childcare providers, highway laborers, office clerks, janitors, social workers, mental health workers, and food service workers deserved decent pay, health care benefits, and pensions. They should not have to give up their hopes, or their rights, just because they worked for government.

As AFSCME's president, Wurf was the labor movement's most important leader in organizing public employees. Through aggressive organizing and skillful bargaining, AFSCME grew from 220,000 members in 1964, when Wurf was elected its president, to over 1 million members at the time of his death in 1981. Other unions organized teachers, prison guards, and other public employees. Wurf's union focused on raising the standard of living for low-paid workers, who were disproportionately blacks and Latinos.

The upsurge in public-sector unionizing in the 1960s and 1970s resembled the breakthrough of industrial unionism in the 1930s. Membership in public-sector unions, led by AFSCME as well as by the American Federation of Teachers and the National Education Association, grew tenfold between 1955 and 1975, topping 4 million by the early 1970s and doubling to 8 million by 2010.

This dramatic growth occurred at a time when overall union membership was falling. The peak unionization rate was 35 percent during the mid-1950s. By 2010, it had plummeted to 12 percent. Today, government employees make up over half of the 15 million union members in the United States. As historian Joseph McCartin observed in *Dissent* magazine in spring 2011, "By default, public sector unions have become the single most effective social force capable of speaking out for a justice economy." Wurf's pathbreaking success in organizing government workers in the 1960s and 1970s is what has kept the labor movement alive today.

Wurf was born to Jewish émigrés from Austria-Hungary. His father was a tailor and textile worker. At the age of four, Wurf developed polio and spent much of his youth in a wheelchair. For the rest of his life, he walked with a limp, which did not stop him from joining picket lines or protest marches. As a Depression-era teenager in New York, he joined the Young People's Socialist League and honed his skills at soapbox oratory, passing out leaflets and debating the fine points of political theory. Wurf briefly attended New York University but dropped out to change the world. He wound up making change as a cashier at a local cafeteria, hoping to organize his fellow workers into the Hotel and Restaurant Workers Union. In the early 1940s Wurf was such a persistent and militant organizer that the Yiddish-speaking cafeteria owners he was opposing called him *Mal'ach Hamaves,* or "angel of death."

In 1947 Wurf joined the staff of District Council 37, AFSCME's New York City affiliate, and soon became its director. He inherited a corrupt, do-nothing union with fewer than 1,000 members and transformed it into a potent organizing force. By the time he left to become AFSCME's national president, District 37 had 38,000 members. Wurf's biggest breakthrough came in 1958, when he mounted a successful campaign to persuade New York mayor Robert Wagner Jr. to issue Executive Order 49, which gave unions the right to organize the city's employees. (The mayor was the son of Senator **Robert F. Wagner Sr.,** sponsor of the prolabor National Labor Relations Act, often called the Wagner Act.)

At District 37 and later as AFSCME president, Wurf committed the union not only to organizing African American employees but also to supporting the civil rights struggle. Before Wurf became AFSCME president, the union had separate white and black locals in the South, as did most unions. Wurf changed that practice. He elevated more blacks to leadership within the union and recruited more black organizers and more female organizers. In the late 1940s he was a founder of the New York chapter of the Congress of Racial Equality, a group committed to using civil disobedience to challenge segregation.

The plight of Memphis's African American sanitation workers posed a major challenge to AFSCME, which had not yet made major progress organizing public employees in the South. On January 31, 1968, twenty-two black workers were sent home when it began raining. White employees were not sent home. When the rain stopped after an hour or so, the white workers continued to work and were paid for the full day, while the black workers lost a day's pay. The next day, two sanitation workers, Echol Cole and Robert Walker, were crushed to death by a malfunctioning city garbage truck.

These two incidents epitomized the workers' long-standing grievances. The Memphis sanitation workers earned an average of about $1.70 per hour. Forty percent of them qualified for welfare to supplement their poverty-level salaries. They had almost no health care benefits, pensions, or vacations. White supervisors called black workers "boy" and would arbitrarily send them home without pay for minor infractions that would be overlooked if done by white workers. The workers asked Memphis's mayor, Henry Loeb, and the city council to improve their working conditions, but they refused to do so.

On February 12, 1,300 black sanitation workers went on strike. They demanded a pay raise, overtime pay, merit promotions without regard to race, and recognition by the city of AFSCME as their bargaining agent. For the next several months, city officials refused to negotiate with the union. In private, Mayor Loeb reportedly told associates, "I'll never be known as the mayor who signed a contract with a Negro union."

With the help of key AFSCME staffers and in coalition with black community leaders, Wurf helped organize marches and rallies to publicize the strike. In the midst of this frenzy of activity, a local judge found Wurf guilty of violating an injunction prohibiting the city garbage workers from striking. Wurf ignored the order and kept the strike going, raising money to help the strikers pay for food and rent.

Wurf was contemptuous of Mayor Loeb's racism and antiunion hostility, and he figured the movement's best strategy was to outmaneuver him by getting the city council to support the workers. On February 22, more than 700 workers packed a city council hearing to demand a settlement. The next day, Wurf helped orchestrate a mass march from city hall to Mason Temple. The Memphis police attacked the union members, ministers, and AFSCME leaders indiscriminately, using clubs and mace. Police harassed them and even arrested strike leaders for jaywalking. On March 5, 117 strikers and supporters were arrested for sitting in at city hall. Six days later, hundreds of students skipped high school to participate in a march led by black ministers. The attacks cemented the alliance between the union and the black religious and community leaders.

With tensions rising and no compromise in sight, local ministers and AFSCME invited King to Memphis to lift the strikers' flagging spirits and en-

courage them to remain nonviolent. His visit to Memphis triggered national media attention and catalyzed the rest of the labor movement to expand its support
for the strikers. On Wednesday, April 3, at the Mason Temple, King delivered
what would turn out to be his last speech, emphasizing the linked fate of the
civil rights and labor movements:

> Memphis Negroes are almost entirely a working people. Our needs are iden-
> tical with labor's needs. That is why Negroes support labor's demands and
> fight laws which curb labor. That is why the labor-hater and labor-baiter is
> virtually always a twin-headed creature spewing anti-Negro epithets from one
> mouth and anti-labor propaganda from the other mouth.

The next day, James Earl Ray assassinated King. As *Time* magazine noted at
the time, "Ironically, it was the violence of Martin Luther King's death rather
than the nonviolence of his methods that ultimately broke the city's resistance"
and led to the strike settlement. After President **Lyndon B. Johnson** ordered federal troops to Memphis and instructed Undersecretary of Labor James Reynolds
to mediate the conflict and settle the strike, Wurf led the negotiations with city
officials to reach an agreement. The city council passed a resolution recognizing
the union. The fourteen-month contract included union dues check-off, a grievance procedure, and wage increases of fifteen cents per hour.

"Let us never forget," Wurf said at the meeting where union members ratified
their new contract, "that Martin Luther King, on a mission for us, was killed in
this city. He helped bring us this victory."

In the 1960s and 1970s, Wurf's views on organizing unorganized workers
and on civil rights and his opposition to the Vietnam War put him at odds with
AFL-CIO president George Meany and the leaders of other unions. As a member of the AFL-CIO's executive council and one of its vice presidents, he was
often a dissenting voice on key issues confronting the labor movement. In 1973,
one member told *Time* magazine that the votes of the executive council "usually
range from 25 to 1 to 34 to 1, depending on how many other union chiefs are
present to vote down Jerry Wurf."

In October 14, 1973, on the opening day of the annual AFL-CIO convention,
Wurf authored a blistering column in the *Washington Post* entitled "Labor's Battle
with Itself," attacking his fellow union leaders for "fighting each other for the right
to represent workers rather than working together to organize the unorganized."
He proposed that the labor movement, which had 113 affiliated unions, reorganize itself into twenty or thirty large unions that could focus on organizing a particular industry or sector. The AFL-CIO leaders rejected Wurf's proposal without
much discussion, but the same ideas resurfaced three decades later, this time proposed by Andy Stern, the president of the Service Employees International Union.

During Wurf's last decade, hostility toward public-sector unions intensified,
especially from business groups and conservative politicians. A turning point

occurred in 1981, when President Ronald Reagan fired 11,345 unionized air traffic controllers after they launched a nationwide walkout. The attacks have escalated since then and reached a crescendo in 2011 with the attempts by Republican governors in Wisconsin, Ohio, and several other states to overturn the collective bargaining rights of public employees. Wurf would surely be frustrated by these assaults on public employees, but he would also be heartened by the progressive response, which included huge demonstrations in state capitals and public opinion polls revealing that a vast majority of Americans supported the right of government employees to unionize.

Bella Abzug (1920–1998)

Bella Abzug, left, with
Shirley Chisholm in 1971.
CREDIT: Associated Press

"THIS WOMAN'S place is in the House—the House of Representatives," declared Bella Savitsky Abzug as she launched her campaign for Congress in 1970. It was a typical Abzug quote, combining her memorable wit with an attack on an injustice: the lack of women in elected office. Working for fifty years as a lawyer, politician, and activist, Abzug championed a range of progressive causes. Best known as a pioneering feminist and antiwar crusader, she also fought for the rights of workers, minorities, gays, and lesbians and battled against McCarthyism, environmental degradation, and poverty.

Abzug's parents were Russian-Jewish immigrants who settled in New York City. Her pacifist father ran a butcher shop, which, following the onset of World War I, he renamed the Live and Let Live Meat Market. After her father died when Abzug was thirteen, her family's synagogue forbade her to recite the mourning prayer, a duty traditionally reserved for males. Bella went to the synagogue every day for a year and recited the prayer anyway. Her Jewish upbringing gave her a strong sense of outrage against anti-Semitism, discrimination against women, and other forms of injustice. As a teenager, she developed her activist skills as a member of a radical Zionist group that dreamed of creating a socialist homeland for Jews.

Abzug was born the same year that women won the right to vote. She was elected senior class president at the all-girls Walton High School. In 1941, as president of Hunter College's student government, she led demonstrations against fascism. After college, during World War II, she worked in a shipbuilding factory. She married in 1944 and three years later graduated from Columbia University Law School, where she was one of only a handful of women students but nevertheless managed to become an editor of the *Columbia Law Review*. During this time she also took courses at the Jewish Theological Seminary of America. Throughout her life Abzug maintained a deep interest in Jewish causes, including support for progressive groups in Israel.

After law school, Abzug joined a firm that represented union locals. Although she was hardly shy, she realized that some of the union leaders and even other lawyers paid less attention to her than to the male attorneys. She decided to wear wide-brimmed hats, which drew notice and soon became her trademark.

Abzug achieved early notoriety for her defense of Willie McGee, a black man who was sentenced to death in Mississippi in 1945 for allegedly raping a white woman. Abzug was hired by the left-wing Civil Rights Congress to help with McGee's appeals. The process lasted several years and became a cause célèbre among liberals and leftists both in the United States and internationally. An all-white jury had convicted McGee after just two and a half minutes of deliberation. Despite the best efforts of Abzug and other attorneys, the appeals eventually failed when the US Supreme Court refused to hear the case. McGee was executed in 1951.

During the McCarthy era, Abzug represented many clients, including actors, school teachers, and public figures, including **Pete Seeger,** who were fired for real or alleged ties to Communists or who were dragged before the House Un-American Activities Committee or the Senate Subcommittee on Internal Security.

While breaking new ground as a trial lawyer, Abzug also became involved in the peace movement. In 1961 she cofounded and served as political director of Women Strike for Peace, an organization that opposed nuclear weapons and, later, the Vietnam War. Abzug frequently led marches and rallies against nuclear proliferation.

In 1970 Abzug ran successfully for Congress, becoming only one of twelve women in the House. She was reelected two more times. Still wearing her flamboyant hats, and always candid and quotable, Abzug became a national symbol of the women's and antiwar movements in Congress and at numerous rallies and demonstrations. She ignored traditions that required new members of Congress to work below the radar screen. She quickly introduced bills to end the draft, which she compared to slavery, and to end the war in Vietnam. Her activism earned her a place on President Richard Nixon's infamous "enemies list." She voted against the 1973 War Powers Act on the grounds that it did not go far enough to limit the powers of the presidency. She wrote the Equal Credit Opportunity Act of 1974 (giving women greater access to consumer credit) and other pieces of legislation on childcare, family planning, abortion rights, Social Security for homemakers, and Title IX amendments, regulations guaranteeing women equal funding in higher education. She cosponsored the first bill in Congress on gay rights. She coauthored amendments to the Freedom of Information Act (which requires government agencies to release documents requested by the public) and authored the Water Pollution Act of 1972. She was the first member of Congress to call for Nixon's impeachment during the Watergate scandal.

During her first term in Congress, Abzug founded the National Women's Political Caucus with **Gloria Steinem** and Congresswomen Shirley Chisholm and Patsy Mink. She authored a bill that led to the federally funded National Women's Conference in 1977 that drew 2,000 delegates to Houston, Texas, to ratify a national agenda on women's rights.

"There are those who say I'm impatient, impetuous, uppity, rude, profane, brash and overbearing," Abzug said of herself. "Whether I'm any of these things, or all of them, you can decide for yourself. But whatever I am—and this ought to be made very clear at the outset—I am a very serious woman."

Abzug gave up her seat in the US House to run for the US Senate, then an all-male body, in 1976, losing in the four-candidate Democratic primary by less than 1 percent of the vote to Daniel P. Moynihan. She also lost a bid for mayor of New York City in 1977 and an attempt to regain a seat in the US House in 1978.

Abzug believed that more women should run for office, but should not just emulate the behavior of male candidates. "If a woman candidate says, 'Judge me as you would a man' it encourages voters to regard political office as the natural habitat of men, who provide the role models that a woman must emulate to succeed," Abzug explained. "This is a mistake. Women candidates have special strengths and should not try to conceal them."

Abzug remained involved in national affairs, serving on President Jimmy Carter's National Advisory Commission for Women until she was fired for criticizing the president's proposals to cut the budget for women's programs. She also founded Women USA in 1979 to register female voters. In the 1980s Abzug returned to her legal practice, and in 1984 she published *Gender Gap: Bella Abzug's Guide to Political Power for American Women.* Encouraging women to run for office, she wrote, "We can learn to become political leaders and activists, or we can sit back and let a minority of men in government, backed by powerful money and military interests, run our country and try to run the whole world. It's up to us."

Abzug made two last bids for Congress. The first was in 1986 for a seat representing suburban Westchester, outside New York City. She won the primary but lost to the incumbent Republican. In 1992 she tried to run for her old seat in Manhattan, but her campaign fizzled when party leaders failed to back her candidacy.

Despite not returning to Congress—and suffering from health problems, including a several-year battle with breast cancer—Abzug remained active through the 1990s, frequently speaking at international conferences on women's rights. She also founded the Women's Environment and Development Organization, which held an international conference on breast cancer in 1997. Geraldine Ferraro, another congresswoman from New York, summarized Abzug's legacy thus: "Now let's be honest about it. She didn't knock lightly on the door. She didn't even push it open or batter it down. She took it off the hinges forever! So that those of us who came after could walk through."

Betty Friedan
(1921–2006)

CREDIT: Associated Press

BETTY FRIEDAN'S 1963 book *The Feminine Mystique* catalyzed the modern feminist movement, helped change attitudes toward women's equality, and identified the "problem that has no name" (which feminists later labeled "sexism"). Friedan was also instrumental in organizing the National Organization for Women (NOW) and other key groups that advocated women's liberation.

Friedan was born Bettye Goldstein in Peoria, Illinois, and was raised in a prosperous family with a nursemaid, cook, and butler-chauffeur. Her Russian immigrant father ran a jewelry business, and her mother hosted bridge luncheons in their spacious home. But as Jews, the Goldsteins were never fully accepted into Peoria society. Friedan's brilliance and ambition helped her overcome anti-Semitism. In high school she wrote for the school paper, founded the literary magazine, joined the debating society, and graduated as class valedictorian.

Her academic and leadership skills blossomed when she arrived at Smith College in 1938, in the midst of the Depression's exciting political ferment. She majored in psychology, and as editor of the *Smith College Weekly,* she revitalized the paper from a bland publication filled with gossip and social news to a far more political outlet, the *Smith College Associate News (SCAN).*

At Smith, she embraced radical ideas and the labor movement as an instrument for progressive change. When maids at the college went on strike, Bettye sympathetically covered the struggle in *SCAN.* Her editorials challenged her privileged classmates to wake up to issues of social justice, workers' rights, and fascism. The summer after her junior year, she spent eight weeks at the Highlander Folk School in Tennessee, participating in a writing workshop and taking classes about unions and economics.

In 1942 she went to graduate school at University of California, Berkeley, and dropped the "e" at the end of her first name. She traveled in left-wing circles and joined a Marxist study group. But she later panicked at the implications of getting a Ph.D., imagining her future as a lonely spinster in academia. She gave up her scholarship.

Fleeing Berkeley, she moved to Greenwich Village in 1944. Her first job was as a reporter for the Federated Press, an agency that fed news stories to progressive publications and union newspapers. Her stories were popular and showed a talent for humanizing class, race, and women's issues. Her next job was with the *UE News*, the weekly paper of the United Electrical, Radio, and Machine Workers of America, a left-wing union. In 1947 she married Carl Friedan, an actor and stage producer. The first of their three children was born the following year.

There was no significant feminist movement at the time, but the Communist Party and the unions in its orbit were among the few organizations concerned about what they called the "woman question." In 1946 they started the Congress of American Women to address issues facing working-class women. As a reporter for *UE News*, Friedan often wrote about women's issues, including a popular pamphlet, *UE Fights for Women Workers*, on corporate discrimination and on the special problems faced by black women workers. In 1952, when she became pregnant with her second son, Friedan left the *UE News*.

In some respects, Friedan's experience was similar to that of millions of women who had worked during World War II and were then encouraged—by employers, the media, advertising, and government propaganda—to return to "hearth and home" as mothers and housewives after men came home. Like many women in postwar America, Friedan volunteered for a variety of community activities, though some of hers were unconventional, such as participating in rent strikes. But frustrated by the fact that she was not contributing financially to the family or using her considerable professional talents, Friedan began a freelance writing career, mostly for women's magazines like *Cosmopolitan*.

The seed of *The Feminine Mystique* was planted in 1957 when Friedan was asked to prepare an alumni questionnaire for her Smith College fifteenth reunion. She felt vaguely guilty as she worked on it, thinking of the academic star she had been and feeling she had not realized her potential.

In 1947 Ferdinand Lundberg and Marynia Farnham published *Modern Women: The Lost Sex*, which argued that American women were overeducated and that this excess of education caused discontent and prevented females from "adjusting to their role as women." The book triggered considerable controversy in the postwar era. Using the Smith questionnaire as a starting point, Friedan pitched a story to *McCall's* magazine aimed at refuting *Modern Women*'s thesis. She and two friends developed a survey, including open-ended questions "that we had not asked ourselves out loud before." They covered such topics as decision making in the family, hours of housework, feelings about being a mother, number of books read in a year, interests outside the home, and agreement, or not, with a husband's politics.

Two hundred women responded. Friedan found that those who seemed most happy and fulfilled were those who did not conform to the "role of women" and that those who were most dispirited were traditional housewives. She completed her article for *McCall's*—"Are Women Wasting Their Time in College?"—but it was rejected. When her agent sent it to *Redbook,* a male editor sent it back saying that Friedan "must be going off her rocker. Only the most neurotic housewife will identify with this." No magazine would touch it.

Frustrated but convinced she was on to something important, Friedan expanded the article into a book and worked for five years to complete *The Feminine Mystique,* which was published in February 1963.

Not aware that other women shared their troubles, many women experienced their unhappiness as a personal problem and blamed themselves for their misery. Friedan called this "the problem that has no name." Earlier books had diagnosed women's oppression and second-class status—including Elizabeth Hawes's *Why Women Cry* (1943), Simone de Beauvoir's *The Second Sex* (published in English in 1953), Mirra Komarovsky's *Women in the Modern World* (1953), and Alva Myrdal and Viola Klein's *Women's Two Roles* (1956)—but none of them tapped the vein of dissatisfaction in a way that *The Feminine Mystique* did. The book touched millions of women, aided by Friedan's accessible writing style and the luck of good timing.

The publisher initially printed only 2,000 copies, but the book's sales exploded. *The Feminine Mystique* spent six weeks on the *New York Times* best-seller list. The first paperback printing sold 1.4 million copies. *McCall's* and *Ladies' Home Journal,* magazines with a combined readership of 36 million, published excerpts.

Though the analogy was certainly overwrought, Friedan argued that women were trapped by their domestic lives, that their existence was akin to a "comfortable concentration camp." Women became helpless, almost childlike, with no privacy, cut off from the outside world, doing soul-killing work. Friedan also exposed the myriad ways that advertisers, psychiatrists, educators, and newspapers patronized, exploited, and manipulated women.

The Feminine Mystique made Friedan famous and a person to be reckoned with. She was flooded with letters from women reporting that the book had opened their eyes about their own lives and had validated their dissatisfaction with the status quo. She was asked to speak at colleges, before women's groups, and elsewhere across the nation.

Friedan's agenda for change in *The Feminine Mystique* was quite modest, especially for someone with her radical background. She wrote about the problem of workplace discrimination, but she barely mentioned the issues of childcare and maternity leave. The book had little to say about the problems confronting poor and working-class women or women of color—issues she had written about for *Federated News* and the *UE News.* She mostly encouraged women to get an education and to prepare themselves for a career beyond housework. It was not until the late 1960s and early 1970s that Friedan and others embraced a wider and more progressive agenda: the right to an abortion, protection against sexual violence and domestic abuse, the criminalization of sexual harassment and rape, the demand for childcare centers, equality with men in terms of access to financial credit and other aspects of economic life.

After the book came out, as Friedan was gaining a platform on TV and radio shows and on the lecture circuit, she described herself as an "educated house-wife." She made no reference to her experience in the left-wing movements of the late 1930s through the early 1950s. Indeed, many other women with similar backgrounds (including **Bella Abzug**)—women who played a key role in build-ing the women's liberation movement and later in creating the new academic field of women's studies—downplayed their past left-wing affiliations. Friedan believed that she and the book would have more credibility if she was seen as someone who shared the frustrations of other middle-class suburban women. Of course in 1963 the hysteria of McCarthyism and the Red Scare were still a lin-gering force in American politics and culture, and Friedan understood that her past associations with Communist and radical groups could undermine her rep-utation and destroy her growing influence.

Moreover, Friedan wanted to do more than write about women's roles. She wanted to instigate real change, and that meant renewing her activist credentials. She quickly connected with a small network of liberal, professional women who were involved with the Presidential Commission on the Status of Women, which had been created in 1961 by John F. Kennedy at the suggestion of **Eleanor Roo-sevelt.** They talked about creating a women's version of the National Association for the Advancement of Colored People, and in 1966 they formed NOW to lobby and organize for the civil rights of women. Friedan was elected president, a position she held until 1970. She became the first media celebrity of the women's liberation movement and its de facto spokesperson.

Friedan could be difficult and antagonizing, and she clashed with most radi-cal feminists on the issue of overthrowing male-dominated power structures. In-stead she believed in sharing power equally. "Some people think I'm saying, 'Women of the world unite—you have nothing to lose but your men,'" she told *Life* magazine in 1963. "It's not true. You have nothing to lose but your vacuum cleaners."

Some criticized NOW for being too focused on middle-class white women's concerns. At the same time, Friedan was also concerned that the women's move-ment would be identified as being dominated by man-hating lesbians, a stereo-type that was widespread at the time and that Friedan worried would undermine feminism's credibility.

Two years before NOW's founding, Congress passed the Civil Rights Act of 1964, which prohibits discrimination in employment on the bases of race, color, national origin, religion, and sex. Most members of Congress viewed the law pri-marily in terms of race and hardly noticed that "sex" was included. For half a century, NOW and other feminist groups have used the law—which established the Equal Employment Opportunity Commission—to fight for women's equal-ity at work.

Friedan also cofounded the National Abortion Rights Action League (origi-nally the National Association for the Repeal of Abortion Laws) in 1969. The next year—the fiftieth anniversary of the Nineteenth Amendment guaranteeing women the vote—she co-organized the Women's Strike for Equality. In 1971, a year after the defeat of the Equal Rights Amendment, Friedan joined Bella Abzug, **Gloria Steinem,** Shirley Chisholm, and others to form the National Women's Political Caucus to encourage more women to participate in politics and run for office.

Throughout her life, Friedan continued to write major books, among them *The Second Stage* (1981), *The Fountain of Age* (1993), and *Beyond Gender* (1997). In the last book, she worried that progressives had splintered into separate identity movements. She outlined an agenda for change that, ironically, was similar to the radical politics she had embraced in her younger years. In a 1995 column in *Newsweek*, she wrote,

> The problems in our fast-changing world require a new paradigm of social policy, transcending *all* "identity politics"—women, blacks, gays, the disabled. Pursuing the separate interests of women isn't adequate and is even diversionary. Instead, there has to be some new vision of community. We need to reframe the concept of success. We need to campaign—men and women, whites and blacks—for a shorter workweek, a higher minimum wage, an end to the war against social-welfare programs. "Women's issues" are symptoms of problems that affect everyone.

Howard Zinn
(1922–2010)

"If you want to read a real history book," Matt Damon's character tells his therapist, played by Robin Williams, in the film *Good Will Hunting*, "read Howard Zinn's *A People's History of the United States*. That book will knock you on your ass."

Zinn's book was already popular on college campuses, but its cameo appearance in the Academy Award–winning movie significantly boosted its sales and Zinn's name recognition. Few academics have had as wide a following as Zinn, a historian who himself became a historic figure. As a scholar, Zinn changed the way Americans view their history. He championed the notion that history should be told from the point of view of ordinary people, including society's victims and dissenters. He popularized this view with *A People's History*, first published in 1980, which has sold nearly 2 million copies and is now in its fifth edition. The book drew on and inspired the burgeoning field of social history, which focuses on the everyday lives of farmers, workers, women, African Americans, immigrants, and others—and on the movements they organized to improve living and working conditions. This perspective is now common in many American high school and college history textbooks, but it was not when Zinn first published *A People's History*.

The son of Jewish immigrants, Zinn grew up in "all the best slums in Brooklyn" before being employed as a pipe fitter at the Brooklyn Navy Yard, where he met his wife. At twenty-one he joined the military and served in the Army Air Force during World War II as a B-17 bombardier, for which he was decorated, attaining the rank of second lieutenant.

After the war Zinn lived in public housing and continued working as a manual laborer for several years, eventually taking advantage of the GI Bill to enter college as a twenty-seven-year-old freshman. Working nights in a warehouse loading trucks, Zinn studied at New York University for his undergraduate degree, then earned his master's and doctorate degrees in history from Columbia University. Zinn's master's thesis was about the 1914 coal strikes in Colorado, and his dissertation examined **Fiorello La Guardia**'s career in Congress. His 1959 book *LaGuardia in Congress* was nominated for the American Historical Association's prestigious Albert J. Beveridge Prize.

As a part of his early research, Zinn also returned to Europe to study places he had bombed during the war. Although he felt that fighting fascism had had a moral element to it, he discovered that more civilians had been killed in bombing raids over France than had been previously documented and that the US military's reasoning behind target selection was flawed.

In 1956 Zinn was hired by Spelman College, a historically black college for women in Atlanta, Georgia, to chair the history department. There he became involved in the civil rights movement, serving as an adviser to the Student Nonviolent Coordinating Committee (SNCC) and participating in protests (occasionally with his students). He wrote articles about the movement for *The Nation* and other magazines and then wrote two books—*The Southern Mystique* (1964) and *SNCC: The New Abolitionists* (1964)—drawing on his firsthand engagement and eyewitness accounts, creating history in the present tense. With historian August Meier, he lobbied to end the Southern Historical Association's practice of holding meetings at segregated hotels.

Among his students at Spelman was Alice Walker, who would become a famous novelist. She called Zinn "the best teacher I ever had." Zinn also taught Marian Wright Edelman, the civil rights activist, lawyer, and founder of the Children's Defense Fund, and Bernice Johnson Reagon, a scholar and activist who founded the musical group Sweet Honey in the Rock.

Zinn later wrote about his approach to teaching during those turbulent times: "I wanted students to leave my classes not just better informed, but more prepared to relinquish the safety of silence, more prepared to speak up, to act against injustice wherever they saw it. This, of course, was a recipe for trouble." Zinn's encouragement of civil disobedience by students and his criticism of local and national political leaders created tensions with Spelman's administrators, and Zinn was fired in 1963 despite having tenure. "I was fired for insubordination," he recalled, "which happened to be true." (In 2005 Zinn was the commencement speaker at Spelman when the school recognized his life's work with an honorary doctorate.)

In 1964 Zinn was hired by the political science department at Boston University. He was a popular teacher known for his humor and personal warmth as well as for his unwavering support for student and faculty activism. He frequently spoke at teach-ins and rallies about the war in Vietnam. In 1968, he traveled with Father Daniel Berrigan to Hanoi to receive prisoners released by the North Vietnamese. He also authored two influential books about the war—*The Logic of Withdrawal* (1967) and *Disobedience and Democracy* (1968). With **Noam Chomsky** he edited and annotated *The Pentagon Papers* (1972), classified documents exposing America's involvement in Vietnam that were leaked by defense analyst Daniel Ellsberg. Zinn also testified at Ellsberg's trial.

Zinn frequently clashed with John Silber, Boston University's autocratic president. Zinn twice led unsuccessful attempts by the faculty to remove the president, and he twice survived attempts by Silber to have him fired. Zinn was a cochair of the strike committee when Boston University professors walked out. After the strike was settled, he and four colleagues were charged with having violated their contract when they refused to cross a picket line of striking secretaries. The charges against "the BU Five" were soon dropped.

Zinn retired from the university in 1988, dismissing a lecture hall of several hundred students thirty minutes early so they could join him at a protest. Over the next twenty-two years Zinn continued publishing and public speaking, often talking to large audiences and receiving accolades for his inspiring lectures. He continued to write books about politics and history, as well as about the politics of writing history, and articles for *The Nation, Z, Boston Globe, The Progressive,* and other publications.

Zinn also wrote three plays that were produced in cities across the country— *Daughter of Venus* (about nuclear disarmament and personal commitment to social change), *Marx in Soho* (a one-man show in which Karl Marx is presented as a humane figure defending the original intent of his works), and *Emma* (a biographical play about the anarchist **Emma Goldman**).

Zinn also edited, with Anthony Arnove, *Voices of a People's History of the United States* (2004), which provides original texts by or about the heroes in *The People's History.* This collection served as the text for the made-for-television work *The People Speak,* which Matt Damon helped produce. Over the years, several collections of Zinn's works and commentary on them have been published.

Zinn's works, telling history from the view of rebels, organizers, and victims of war and colonialism, have reached millions of readers and viewers. *People's History* is used widely in high school and college courses. Some historians have criticized his most popular book as simplistic cheerleading for heroes ("the people") against villains ("the elites"). Nonetheless, as a writer, Zinn did for history what Carl Sagan did for physics and Stephen Jay Gould for evolutionary biology. He popularized and demystified topics that most academics reserve for other specialists and that many students find dull and lifeless.

Unusually for a scholar, Zinn's fame and influence justified his writing an autobiography: *You Can't Be Neutral on a Moving Train: A Personal History of Our Times* (1994), which was later made into a documentary film.

Rev. William
Sloane Coffin
(1924–2006)

IN 1961, as Rev. William Sloane Coffin disembarked from a Greyhound bus in Montgomery, Alabama, he stepped into a world he had never known. The worldly chaplain of Yale University was confronted by a crowd of angry white people hurling rocks and bricks at him and his small, racially integrated group of civil rights sympathizers. As the sweat dampened their suits, Coffin looked uncharacteristically uncomfortable.

Coffin and his comrades had not only angered southern whites. They had also gone up against John F. Kennedy's administration. Their decision to join the Freedom Rides came just as President Kennedy was preparing to go to Europe for delicate talks with the Soviet premier, Nikita Khrushchev. The last thing Kennedy wanted was a spotlight on protests back home. As historian Taylor Branch noted in *Parting the Waters*, "To Kennedy, the Coffin group represented a distressing change in the composition of the protesters. No longer confined to Quakers, kooks, students, pacifists or even Negro Gandhians, the ranks of the Freedom Riders suddenly included prominent Ivy League professors." A furious Attorney General Robert Kennedy even ordered the National Guard and federal marshals to pull back from their position of protecting the Freedom Riders. The next morning, as Coffin and the others prepared to board a bus for Jackson, Mississippi, they were arrested in the bus depot. Coffin spent his first night in jail.

The action was vintage Coffin: bold, principled, and guaranteed to put him in the headlines. The *New York Times* carried a front-page photo and *Life* magazine carried a piece, "Why Yale Chaplain Rode: Christians Can't Be Outside."

No one would have predicted that a man of Coffin's patrician background would end up being the strongest progressive voice of white Christianity during one of the nation's most turbulent times. He seemed destined instead for a life of elected office, diplomacy, or industry.

The Coffins traced their lineage to the Pilgrims. His father was a wealthy and prominent businessman and president of the Metropolitan Museum of Art's board of trustees. Bill and his brother and sister lived with their parents in a Manhattan penthouse until their world turned upside down in 1933. Their father slipped on the steps of the Met and died later that day of a heart attack.

Suddenly with greatly reduced means, Bill's mother, Catherine, moved her children to Carmel-by-the-Sea in California and later to Paris so Bill could study piano, his passion. Thanks to financial support from his uncle, Rev. Henry Coffin, he was able to continue his education at prestigious boarding schools, then at Yale, before being drafted during World War II.

During basic training, Coffin was first exposed to segregation and overt racism. But in general the Army suited him. He reveled in the chance to be physically tough, exhibit leadership, and face danger. He excelled in languages, including Russian, and in 1946 was part of an operation to forcibly repatriate prisoners of war to Joseph Stalin's Soviet Union, where they were sure to be either killed or sent to labor camps. "It was one of the worst things of my life," he told the *Boston Globe* in 2004. And it happened, he said, "because I was a good soldier." He continued, "Subsequently, it has been very easy for me to disobey a law or an order concerning life and death. You can't say 'I'm following orders.' That's a reason, but no excuse."

After the war, Coffin returned to Yale—where generations of Coffin males had gone before—and graduated with a degree in government. Then he enrolled at Union Theological Seminary (UTS), where students were urged to tackle challenging social problems and to resist serving wealthy, complacent congregations. He did an internship at a Harlem church, his first real exposure to the poor.

After working for the CIA during the Korean War, Coffin transferred from UTS to Yale Divinity School. Upon his graduation in 1956, he took a job as chaplain at Phillips Academy, then Williams College, and then, in 1958, at Yale. He spent the next eighteen years there, inspiring a generation of students with his activist vision of Christianity. As Warren Goldstein writes in *William Sloane Coffin, Jr.: A Holy Impatience*, "God, he argued, had been reduced to a quaint anachronism and an extracurricular activity. Coffin set out to change the way students thought about God and their lives."

When Coffin saw images of African Americans being beaten in Alabama, he was ready to take a stand. On the spur of the moment, he contacted his friend John Maguire from Wesleyan University, and the two managed to convince a small group to travel with them to the South.

After being jailed and making national news, Coffin returned to a storm of controversy at Yale; some alumni threatened to withhold donations unless he was fired. Much of the faculty, though, had contributed bail money to Coffin, and Yale's president Whitney Griswold strongly backed him. Coffin would be jailed two more times over the next few years, protesting segregation in Baltimore, Maryland, and in St. Augustine, Florida.

"Every minister is given two roles, the priestly and the prophetic," Coffin said, explaining his activism. "The prophetic role is the disturber of the peace, to bring the minister himself, the congregation and entire moral order some judgment."

As the Vietnam War heated up, Coffin initially hesitated to join the peace movement. His years in the army and the CIA predisposed him to support US foreign and military policy. He even preached a sermon called "Christians Could Go Either Way on the Vietnam War."

In 1965 a chance encounter with a student changed his mind. Paul Jordan confronted Coffin, bringing him a fat file of articles and speeches. Coffin stayed up through the night absorbing the material, documenting "a history of corruption, of misperceptions and missed opportunities the likes of which I had never imagined," as he later wrote. Coffin became a convert.

In August 1965 he joined his first speak-out about the war, and later that year he became involved with Clergy Concerned About Vietnam along with **Rabbi Abraham Joshua Heschel,** whose writings and activism had a significant influence on Coffin. Using his many connections, deep understanding of liberal Christian thought, and vast powers of oratory, Coffin galvanized others to action. Along with **Norman Thomas,** he became cochairman of SANE, a major peace group, and, with other clergy leaders, he met with Secretary of Defense Robert McNamara and other officials in **Lyndon B. Johnson**'s administration.

Impatient with the continued escalation of the war, Coffin turned to civil disobedience. On October 2, 1967, Coffin led a press conference at the New York Hilton releasing "A Call to Resist Illegitimate Authority," an antidraft manifesto signed by 320 prominent people, including MIT professor **Noam Chomsky,** poet Robert Lowell, and pediatrician Benjamin Spock. He also announced that Battell Chapel at Yale would be a sanctuary for students resisting the draft. Soon after, he was part of a rally of 5,000 people on Boston Common, where young men turned in their draft cards in protest. In Washington, DC, days later, Coffin and ten others tried to deliver a briefcase full of draft cards to the Justice Department, but to their frustration, Assistant Deputy Attorney General John McDonough refused to accept them.

In 1968, Coffin, Spock, and three others were indicted for conspiracy to violate the draft law. Four of the five were convicted in a well-publicized trial. The verdicts were overturned on appeal. Coffin's close connection with students and his nationwide reputation—he even inspired a *Doonesbury* cartoon character, Rev. Scot Sloan, drawn by Yale graduate Garry Trudeau—helped shield him from ongoing demands for his dismissal from Yale.

Coffin continued his peace efforts with a trip to Hanoi in 1972, where he and other clergy and peace activists accompanied three US prisoners of war on their return home.

In 1976 he stepped down from Yale, and in 1978 he became senior minister of the influential Riverside Church in New York, a bastion of liberal Christianity. At Riverside, he also oversaw a deep and divisive debate over the issue of homosexuality. Initially giving cautious lip service to tolerance, he later became strongly supportive of full equality for gay people, leading the church to vote to become "Open and Affirming"—open to gay people and affirming of them as Christians.

He left Riverside in 1987 to become the president of SANE/Freeze, the largest disarmament organization in the country. After retirement, he continued working for peace, opposing the 1991 Persian Gulf War and the 2003 invasion of Iraq. Despite his lifelong activism, Coffin did not consider himself a pacifist. During the genocide in Bosnia, he argued that there are times when international intervention with force is justified.

In the fall of 2003, invited back to preach at Riverside Church, Coffin told the congregants that there was "a huge difference between patriotism and nationalism."

"Patriotism at the expense of another nation is as wicked as racism at the expense of another race," he declared. A descendant of the Pilgrims, Coffin revealed his fervent patriotism by challenging his country to live up to its democratic values.

Malcolm X
(1925–1965)

CREDIT: Associated Press

FOR MUCH of his life, FBI agents trailed Malcolm X's every move, tapped his phone, and infiltrated meetings where he was speaking. The political and media establishment considered him a dangerous demagogue and hatemonger whose antiwhite rants could only exacerbate the nation's racial tensions. But even FBI informants could not help but be impressed with the Nation of Islam preacher. In a 1958 memo one of them described Malcolm X as "an excellent speaker, forceful and convincing. He is an expert organizer and an untiring worker" whose hatred for whites "is not likely to erupt in violence as he is much too clever and intelligent for that."

Malcolm X's influence spread much farther than his religious followers. In the early 1960s he expressed the anger of many poor urban African Americans who felt trapped in ghettos and were the victims of humiliating police brutality, underfunded schools, and job discrimination. Before Malcolm, the Nation of Islam was a relatively small religious cult. His electrifying rhetoric and charisma attracted mainstream media attention, which gave him a much larger audience. His assassination in 1965 at age thirty-nine—probably at the hands of Nation of Islam rivals who resented his celebrity—heightened his fame.

Soon after his death, Grove Press published *The Autobiography of Malcolm X.* The book, written by Alex Haley based on long interviews with Malcolm, depicts his evolution from street hustler to controversial public figure. It quickly became a best seller. Since then, it has sold millions of copies and has become one of the most powerful memoirs in history, a staple of American culture, taught in high schools and colleges. Although the book exaggerates some parts of Malcolm's story—whether because of Malcolm's telling or Haley's literary license is unclear—it is, like many autobiographies, a story of redemption. Malcolm pulled himself out of the hell of pimping, stealing, and drug dealing, finding spiritual salvation and intellectual enlightenment by virtue of an extraordinary self-discipline. He was, as his biographer Manning Marable noted, constantly evolving and reinventing himself. Toward the end of his life, Malcolm was abandoning his black separatism, embracing a more mainstream version of Islam, and revising his political views.

He was born Malcolm Little, the seventh of ten children, in Omaha, Nebraska, in 1925. As a young child, he absorbed the passion of his father. Earl Little was an itinerant Baptist preacher and an organizer for Marcus Garvey's Universal Negro Improvement Association, a black self-help organization. Malcolm's mother, Louise, was from the West Indies, the daughter of a white man she never knew.

When Malcolm was three, the family moved to Lansing, Michigan. Three years later, his father died a violent death. His battered body was found on the streetcar tracks, and many in the city's black community believed he had been murdered by white supremacists. After her husband died, Louise found it impossible to put food on the table and went on public welfare. Malcolm recalled often being "dizzy" with hunger. His mother suffered a mental breakdown and in 1939 was institutionalized for the rest of her life.

Malcolm, already a troubled youth, was uprooted, being sent first to foster care and then to a detention home. At a mostly white junior high school, he was a bright student, but he grew disillusioned when his English teacher told him it was unrealistic for him to consider being a lawyer because of his race, suggesting that he take up carpentry instead. In the summer of 1940, when he was fifteen, he moved to Boston to live with his sister Ella. There he underwent the first of many transformations. He changed himself from a small-town restless teen to a streetwise hustler who furnished marijuana and bootleg liquor to white men whose shoes he shined.

He moved to Harlem and took on the persona of Detroit Red, selling drugs and running numbers up and down the East Coast. He also became a gun-toting drug addict and robber. Arrested with stolen property, in 1946 he received a ten-year prison term—and it was in prison, he wrote, that "I found Allah and the religion of Islam, and it completely transformed my life."

He began his time in jail bitter and angry—so much so that his fellow prisoners nicknamed him "Satan." His brother Philbert wrote him in prison and introduced him to the Nation of Islam. He quenched his thirst for knowledge in the prison library, copying words from a dictionary to expand his vocabulary and reading prodigiously, tackling Plato, Aristotle, Spinoza, Kant, Nietzsche, and Schopenhauer. He joined the prison debate club and became an effective public speaker, a skill that would serve him well. At the urging of another sister, Hilda, he wrote to the Nation of Islam's leader, Elijah Muhammad. Muhammad responded, introducing Malcolm to the idea that "the white devil" was the true criminal in society.

After his release from prison in 1952, Malcolm went to Detroit to live with his brother and welcomed the chance to be part of a well-ordered, religious family that practiced Muslim traditions. His trip to Chicago to hear Elijah Muhammad speak was an electrifying experience, especially when Muhammad singled Malcolm out, asked him to stand, and told the audience about his prison conversion. After the meeting, Muhammad invited the Little family to dine in his eighteen-room home. Muhammad took a special liking to Malcolm and nurtured his leadership in the Nation of Islam.

In 1953 Malcolm Little took the name "Malcolm X" as a way of repudiating the "slave" name he had inherited as an African American. He began proselytizing door-to-door in poor Detroit neighborhoods, focusing especially on the most down-and-out. A gifted orator, he rose quickly through the ranks of the Nation of Islam, first as assistant minister of his Detroit mosque, then as a minister in Boston and Philadelphia, and finally as minister of Harlem Mosque No. 7, a congregation second in importance only to the Nation of Islam's Chicago headquarters. In those cities, and as a speaker elsewhere, he drew in new recruits with his compelling presence. He was the Nation of Islam's most gifted salesman.

During the late 1950s he was seen as the public voice of the Nation of Islam and was frequently interviewed in the media. He rejected the pacifism and integration advocated by **Martin Luther King Jr.** and the mainstream civil rights organizations. He argued instead for black nationalism, "which means that . . . the so-called Negro controls the politics and the politicians of his own community. Our people need to be re-educated into the importance of controlling the economy of the community in which we live, which means that we won't have to constantly be involved in picketing and boycotting other people in other communities in order to get jobs."

He espoused the primacy of racial dignity. In a 1964 radio interview, he encouraged "the black man to elevate his own society instead of trying to force himself into the unwanted presence of the white society."

Malcolm's indictment of white racism struck a chord with black Americans, especially those living in the urban ghettos. His fiery words—such as calling whites "blue-eyed devils"—struck fear into many white Americans, who imagined that Malcolm X was fomenting an armed rebellion by ghetto residents. He was portrayed in the media as an apostle of violence. Malcolm's words were tough talk, but as the FBI informant recognized, they were more a matter of arming blacks psychologically to overthrow the negative self-images imposed by white racism. Malcolm was preaching black pride, much as Garvey had done a generation earlier and much as the Student Nonviolent Coordinating Committee and the Black Panthers did in the mid- and late-1960s when they proclaimed, "Black is beautiful."

Although Malcolm said that the choice was between "the ballot or the bullet," he clearly preferred the ballot. In April 1964, speaking in Cleveland at an event sponsored by the pacifist Congress of Racial Equality, Malcolm X said that President **Lyndon B. Johnson** and the Democrats in Congress should pass the Civil Rights Act if they wanted to avoid a black uprising. He observed:

> All of us have suffered here, in this country, political oppression at the hands
> of the white man, economic exploitation at the hands of the white man, and
> social degradation at the hands of the white man. Now in speaking like this, it

doesn't mean that we're anti-white, but it does mean we're anti-exploitation, we're anti-degradation, we're anti-oppression. And if the white man doesn't want us to be anti-him, let him stop oppressing and exploiting and degrading us. Whether we are Christians or Muslims or nationalists or agnostics or atheists, we must first learn to forget our differences.

The Nation of Islam was an inward-looking cult. Its members were told to avoid politics and not to vote. In contrast, Malcolm recognized that the civil rights movement had energized black Americans to demand full citizenship and an end to Jim Crow in the South and discrimination in the North. Although Malcolm regularly taunted civil rights leaders as "lackeys" and "Uncle Toms," he also admired Martin Luther King Jr., **A. Philip Randolph, Bayard Rustin,** and others for their courage and movement-building skills. He even occasionally sought common ground with them. In 1962, for example, Malcolm joined with Los Angeles civil rights leaders to protest the killing of Ronald Stokes—an unarmed Muslim who had been a friend of his—in a parking lot. Elijah Muhammad objected to his consorting with the civil rights groups and his protesting against political authorities. It is no accident that Malcolm's most important protégé and convert—boxer Cassius Clay, renamed **Muhammad Ali**—spoke out against the Vietnam War, a stance not approved by Elijah Muhammad.

By 1963 Malcolm had discovered that his spiritual leader was hardly an ascetic, as he demanded of followers, but, rather, had fathered several children through extramarital affairs. He confronted Muhammad about his activities, which further alienated him from his one-time mentor. Malcolm was also beginning to doubt the "white devil" theory, in part because of his encounters with light-skinned Arab Muslims during an international tour in 1959.

After President Kennedy was assassinated in November 1963, Malcolm defied Elijah Muhammad's instructions and spoke out publicly, saying that the murder in Dallas represented "the chickens coming home to roost." Angry that Malcolm's inflammatory words might put the Nation of Islam at risk, Elijah Muhammad prohibited him from speaking for ninety days.

Politically, intellectually, and spiritually, Malcolm had outgrown the Nation of Islam. In March 1964 he broke with the group, knowing that doing so might mean he would be targeted for assassination.

Soon after founding a new group, the Muslim Mosque in New York, Malcolm went on a transformative two-month tour of Africa and the Middle East, including a *hajj* (pilgrimage) to Mecca. This journey further challenged his views, opening his mind to the potential for good in all people, regardless of race. He disavowed black separatism. He became a Sunni Muslim and changed his name again, to El-Hajj Malik El-Shabazz. His faith in black economic self-help and entrepreneurial capitalism shifted to socialism. As he wrote in a letter from Mecca to his assistants in Harlem:

You may be shocked by these words coming from me. But on this pilgrimage, what I have seen, and experienced, has forced me to *re-arrange* much of my thought-patterns previously held, and to *toss aside* some of my previous con-clusions. . . . In the words and in the actions and in the deeds of the "white" Muslims, I felt the same sincerity that I felt among the black African Mus-lims of Nigeria, Sudan, and Ghana. . . . I could see from this, that perhaps if white Americans could accept the Oneness of God, then perhaps, too, they could accept *in reality* the Oneness of Man—and cease to measure, and hin-der, and harm others in terms of their "differences" in color.

Until his death, he toured internationally, especially in Africa. He saw paral-lels between the anticolonial struggles in Africa and the struggles of African Americans. In June 1964 he formed the Organization of Afro-American Unity, and in July he attended the African Summit Conference in Cairo, appealing to the delegates of thirty-four nations to bring the cause of America's black people before the United Nations.

Malcolm X was assassinated in 1965 as he was giving a speech at the Audu-bon Ballroom in New York. Three members of the Nation of Islam were found guilty of the murder, although controversy continues over who was ultimately responsible.

Cesar Chavez
(1927–1993)

CREDIT: Associated Press/George Widman

MANY PEOPLE thought Cesar Chavez was crazy to think he could build a union among migrant farmworkers. Since the early 1900s, unions had been trying and failing to organize California's agricultural workers. Whether the workers were Anglos, Chinese, Japanese, Filipinos, or Mexican Americans, these efforts met the same fate. The organizing drives met fierce opposition and always flopped, vulnerable to growers' violent tactics and to competition from a seemingly endless supply of other migrant workers desperate for work. So when Chavez left his job as a community organizer in San Jose in 1962 and moved to rural Delano to try, once again, to bring a union to California's lettuce and grape fields, even his closest friends figured he was delusional.

Within a decade, however, the United Farm Workers (UFW) union had collective bargaining agreements with most of California's major growers. Pay, working conditions, and housing for migrant workers improved significantly. Millions of Americans boycotted lettuce and grapes to put economic pressure on the growers to sign a contract with the union. A young governor named Jerry Brown signed a bill giving California's farmworkers the right to unionize—something they lacked (and still lack) under federal labor laws.

Chavez became a national hero, a symbol of courage and fortitude, for leading a nonviolent revolution to organize farmworkers. His work fomented enormous pride and solidarity among Hispanics in California and across the nation. To those who ever doubted that Chavez could build an effective union among America's poorest and most vulnerable workers, in the face of a large, powerful, and conservative agribusiness industry, he responded, "Si se puede," "Yes, we can."

When Chavez was growing up, his family owned a small farm in Arizona, but they lost it to foreclosure when he was eleven years old. The sight of the Anglo grower, who bought the land at auction, bulldozing the family's farmhouse, trees, and crops left an indelible impression on the young Cesar. That early memory would later fuel a determination to help Mexican American farmworkers gain power and respect. "If I had stayed there," Chavez later said about his family's farm, "possibly I would have been a grower. God writes in exceedingly crooked lines."

Instead, the Chavez family joined the roughly 300,000 migrant workers who followed the crops to California every year. The family often slept by the side of the road, moving from farm to farm, from harvest to harvest, living in over-crowded migrant camps. Cesar attended thirty-eight different schools until he finally gave up after finishing the eighth grade.

Chavez experienced the daily humiliations of being a brown-skinned migrant worker: physical punishment from an Anglo teacher when he unthinkingly began speaking Spanish in class, police harassment, segregated seating at the local movie theater, denial of service at restaurants. These compounded the abuse Chavez and other migrants faced in the fields, where growers had dictatorial control and where workers toiled in the broiling sun for meager wages, living in shacks and lacking toilet facilities.

Chavez spent two years in the navy during World War II. Returning home, he married, moved to San Jose's Mexican barrio, and took whatever jobs he could find in the nearby fields or in a lumberyard.

His life changed when he met Father Donald McDonnell, a local priest who introduced him to the writings of St. Francis of Assisi and Mohandas Gandhi and discussed nonviolence as a strategy for change, and Fred Ross, a community organizer and colleague of **Saul Alinsky.** Ross recruited Chavez to the Community Service Organization (CSO), which helped Mexican Americans in urban barrios deal with immigration and tax problems, taught them how to organize against police brutality and discrimination, and ran voter registration drives. Chavez quickly became a leader, and in 1952 Ross hired the twenty-five-year-old as an organizer. Chavez was a successful organizer and eventually became the CSO's statewide director.

In 1962 after the CSO turned down his request to organize farmworkers, he resigned and returned to Delano. For the next three years, he crisscrossed the state, talking to farmworkers under the auspices of his new organization, the National Farmworkers Association. Many of them dismissed Chavez's ideas, saying that the growers were too powerful and that anyone caught talking about a union would immediately be fired. But drawing on his CSO experience, Chavez recruited workers by helping them with their legal, housing, and other problems.

A crucial turning point occurred in 1965. A small group of Filipino farmworkers, affiliated with the American Federation of Labor's struggling Agricultural Workers Organizing Committee, went on strike when the Delano grape growers cut pay rates during the harvest. Chavez persuaded his own union's members to support the strike. Soon the two groups merged into what became the United Farm Workers union.

The plight of America's migrant farmworkers had entered public consciousness right after Thanksgiving in 1960, when TV journalist Edward R. Murrow broadcast a documentary, *Harvest of Shame*, on CBS. For the next decade, Chavez used a two-pronged approach to build the UFW. Because food is perishable and needs to be harvested quickly, the union used strikes to disrupt the harvest and put pressure on the growers. But Chavez recognized that growers could rely on an almost limitless supply of migrant workers—including new arrivals from Mexico under the Bracero Program—who were recruited as strikebreakers. So the second strategy was to win the support of the general public, asking them to boycott grapes, wine, and lettuce until specific growers agreed to a contract.

Chavez called on allies in the labor movement, among religious congregations, and on college campuses to help with the national boycotts by picketing outside grocery stores and educating consumers. At its height, over 13 million Americans supported the grape boycott.

In the fields, on picket lines, and in meetings, UFW members faced violence from growers and their hired thugs. Another threat came from the Teamsters union, which had signed friendly "sweetheart" contracts with growers to represent the workers without the consent of the workers themselves—a maneuver that enriched Teamsters officials.

To keep their plight in the public eye and to raise the farmworkers' morale during these difficult times, Chavez used marches, civil disobedience, and prayer vigils to transform each strike into a protest movement. The grape strike became a cause célèbre among liberals and gained enormous media attention.

Chavez attracted a loyal cadre of organizers, lawyers, and others, who were paid less-than-poverty wages, as was Chavez and his top staffer, Dolores Huerta. Humble and self-effacing, Chavez became the UFW's public face and the country's most famous Mexican American. In 1969 *Time* magazine put him on its cover.

One of Chavez's key insights was that the union had to stake out the moral high ground—as the civil rights movement had done—in order to win public support. The backing of key clergy, including Catholic bishops and priests, was critical to its image. At one point, when a court prevented the union from picketing during a strike, the union held a religious vigil instead.

Maintaining a nonviolent approach was also central to winning public support. As local police and Teamster thugs resorted to physical violence against union members, some of them understandably wanted to strike back. Chavez was deeply influenced by Gandhian thought. When it appeared that union members might respond to violence with violence, Chavez sought to restore calm and discipline by engaging in hunger strikes, risking his health in the process. Chavez's fasts drew media attention that helped strengthen public sympathy for the workers' strike and for the boycott.

Chavez and the UFW also gained attention by attracting the support of high-profile politicians. The UFW's most important political ally was Senator Robert F. Kennedy of New York. In 1966 United Auto Workers president **Walter Reuther,** who had joined Chavez on picket lines and donated money to the UFW, asked Kennedy to visit Chavez. After meeting Chavez, observing the conditions in which farmworkers toiled, and recognizing the spirit of the organizing effort, Kennedy became a close ally of Chavez and the UFW. He arranged to hold a Senate hearing about farmworkers' conditions in Delano. When the local sheriff told Kennedy that his deputies arrested strikers who looked "ready to violate the law," Kennedy shot back, "May I suggest that during the luncheon, the sheriff and the district attorney read the Constitution of the United States?"

Kennedy made several other pilgrimages to visit Chavez—each time bolstering the union's image. The UFW repaid the favor. In 1968, when Kennedy announced he was running for president as an antiwar candidate against the incumbent, **Lyndon B. Johnson,** the union endorsed him, registered Mexican American voters, and helped secure a Kennedy victory in the California Democratic primary. UFW cofounder Dolores Huerta was at Kennedy's side when he was assassinated the night of his California victory.

Another key political ally was California's governor, Jerry Brown. As a young Catholic seminarian, Brown had supported the UFW boycott. Once in office, Brown engineered passage of the nation's first law giving farmworkers collective bargaining rights and protection from unfair labor practices. The California Agricultural Labor Relations Act (1975) led to a dramatic series of UFW election victories and contracts with growers.

By the late 1970s the UFW had close to 50,000 members (about one-quarter of the state's farmworkers) and contracts with most of the major table-grape and lettuce growers. Pay and working conditions had significantly improved. Growers were required to stop spraying the fields with toxic pesticides that endangered workers' and consumers' health. The Teamsters, under pressure from public opinion and other unions, withdrew from competing with the UFW. Migrant workers became eligible for medical insurance, employer-paid pensions, unemployment insurance, and other benefits. They had a grievance procedure to challenge employer abuses. Moreover, the threat of unionization led growers to improve agricultural wages for nonunion workers.

But within a few years the UFW had spiraled into chaos. This was partly due to the 1982 victory of a Republican governor who had close ties to growers and who failed to implement the new labor law. That failure made it harder for the UFW to win new elections and made it easier for growers to decertify the union. Equally important was Chavez's own weaknesses as a leader. He was not a good administrator, failed to delegate authority, and was suspicious of people who disagreed with him. Key staffers left. The union put fewer resources into organizing workers in the fields. Growers did not renew contracts. In the 1980s wages and conditions worsened. By the time of Chavez's death in 1993, membership in the UFW had declined to just a few thousand.

The UFW's legacy is not simply improved conditions for farmworkers. In the 1960s and 1970s, the UFW trained thousands of organizers and activists— boycott volunteers as well as paid staff. Many became key activists in the labor, immigrant rights, antiwar, consumer, and environmental movements. The UFW served as an incubator of movements, and activists on a wide variety of issues have embraced its strategies. In addition, Chavez inspired a nationwide upsurge of pride and political action by Latinos, most of whom were not farmworkers. For his efforts, Chavez received a posthumous Presidential Medal of Freedom. March 31, Cesar Chavez Day, is an official state holiday in California.

Michael Harrington
(1928–1989)

CREDIT: Courtesy of the Tamiment Library, New York University

FOR MOST of the 1950s, Michael Harrington barely made a living. He lived in voluntary poverty as a member of the Catholic Worker, sharing living space with homeless men and winos in the Bowery district, New York City's skid row, and wrote articles for tiny left-wing magazines. With his mentor **Dorothy Day** and others, he joined and sometimes helped organize protests against the Korean War and nuclear arms and for civil rights. Traveling by bus and thumb across the country, he spoke to small groups of students on college campuses as a representative of the Young People's Socialist League (YPSL). He spent many evenings at the White Horse Tavern in Greenwich Village, hanging out with poets, writers, bohemians, folksingers, and radicals. But by the early 1960s, Harrington was taking planes to Washington, DC, invited by President **Lyndon B. Johnson**'s top advisers to help develop a strategy to reduce poverty. He sat in on high-level meetings, drafted memos, and recommended policy ideas.

Harrington's journey from the White Horse to the White House started with the publication of his book *The Other America* in 1962. Although he was neither an economist nor a sociologist, the book gave him credibility as an expert on the most pressing economic and social issues of the day. One columnist called him "the man who discovered poverty," and the label stuck. The book became required reading for social scientists, elected officials and their staffs, college students, members of study groups sponsored by churches and synagogues, reporters and intellectuals, the new wave of community organizers, and the student activists who traveled to the South to join the civil rights crusade. Harrington was soon in great demand as a speaker on college campuses, at union halls, and before religious congregations. Reporters and television talk-show hosts wanted to interview him.

Throughout his life Harrington walked a political tightrope, both a reformer and a radical. He gave America a socialist conscience, and socialism an American accent.

The accent came from St. Louis, Missouri, where Harrington was raised in a middle-class Irish Catholic family. He attended Catholic schools, where he was popular and smart and where he edited the school paper and yearbook. He wanted to be a writer and a poet. At twenty-one, after fleeting experiences at Yale Law School and graduate school in English at the University of Chicago, he moved to New York in 1949, and soon joined the Catholic Worker.

After two years, Harrington decided that instead of ministering to the poor he wanted to work to abolish the system that produced so much misery. Harrington left Catholic Worker. Several Old Left socialists tutored him in Marxism and groomed him for a public role, recognizing that his midwestern boyish charm and his fiery speaking style made him a natural leader. But even in his twenties, Harrington rejected the tendency of his mentors to boil everything down to economics. He began writing for magazines like *Dissent, New Leader,* and *Commonweal* about war and politics but also about culture, movies, and novels. In the late 1950s and early 1960s, Harrington traveled to college campuses giving speeches about peace, civil rights, civil liberties, and other topics, meeting with small groups of activists, hoping to sign up recruits for YPSL. He discovered that there were a handful of radical students on many campuses, inspired by the civil rights movement, who were ready to confront America's political, economic, and moral problems but who were in need of guidance from older, experienced activists. Harrington, though only thirty-two years old in 1960, appointed himself to that job.

Few students joined YPSL, however. Many of the most talented student activists came together to form the Students for a Democratic Society (SDS). They admired Harrington, who was one of a handful of nonstudents invited to the SDS convention in Port Huron, Michigan, in 1962. Harrington could have had a big influence shaping the trajectory of the New Left. But he blew it by angrily attacking the first draft of SDS's manifesto, the Port Huron Statement, written primarily by **Tom Hayden,** a student leader at the University of Michigan. Harrington accused the manifesto of being inadequately critical of the Soviet Union and of American communism and too critical of the political complacency of labor unions. Even though Hayden and his coauthors revised the document to meet some of Harrington's concerns, Harrington's nasty assault and lack of respect created a deep rift between him and early SDSers. Eventually Harrington apologized and got back in the student radicals' good graces.

Harrington would have been content with being America's "oldest young socialist," as he often called himself, a somewhat marginal figure in American politics and culture. But after he had written a few articles about poverty for *Commentary* and other small magazines, an editor at Macmillan suggested that he expand his articles into a book. The book changed Harrington's life, and the country as well.

The Other America struck a nerve, in part because America was ready to hear its message. **John Kenneth Galbraith**'s best seller *The Affluent Society,* published in 1958, expressed concern that there were still Americans who were left out of the nation's prosperity. Edward R. Murrow's CBS television documentary *Harvest of*

Shame, broadcast in 1960, had drawn attention to the plight of migrant farm laborers. That year, when John F. Kennedy was campaigning for president, he was shocked at the suffering he saw in West Virginia, where the poor were mostly rural whites. JFK starting talking about the millions of Americans living in substandard housing and about the elderly living on inadequate incomes—statistics he probably got from Harrington's *Commentary* articles. After JFK took office, his economic adviser Walter Heller gave him a copy of Harrington's book, which came out in March 1962, or a lengthy review of the book published in the *New Yorker*.

The southern sit-ins, which began in February 1960, put a spotlight on the intertwined realities of racism and poverty. JFK was concerned that the exposure of widespread poverty and racism would embarrass the United States in the Cold War race with the Soviet Union for the hearts and minds of the world's people. Three days before he was assassinated, he told aides that he wanted to do something about poverty. On taking office, LBJ wanted to build on JFK's unfinished agenda. He told Heller that abolishing poverty was the kind of big, bold program he could get behind. He appointed Peace Corps director Sargent Shriver to head the new Office of Economic Opportunity. Shriver invited Harrington to join the program's planning committee.

It was not just good timing that made Harrington's book a hit with the public. His writing style—informal, accessible, morally outraged but not self-righteous—appealed to readers. *The Other America* challenged the conventional wisdom that the nation had become an overwhelmingly middle-class society as a result of postwar prosperity. He reported that almost one-third of all Americans lived "below those standards which we have been taught to regard as the decent minimums for food, housing, clothing and health."

Harrington did not rely primarily on statistics to make his argument. Instead, he told stories, humanizing the poor as real people trapped in difficult conditions not of their own making. He described people living in slum housing, people who got sick and lived with chronic pain because they could not afford to see a doctor, who did not have enough food for themselves or their children and lived with constant hunger.

"The fate of the poor," he concluded, "hangs upon the decision of the better-off. If this anger and shame are not forthcoming, someone can write a book about the other America a generation from now and it will be the same or worse." He added, "Until these facts shame us, until they stir us to action, the other America will continue to exist, a monstrous example of needless suffering in the most advanced society in the world."

Harrington was a committed socialist, but the word "socialism" did not appear in *The Other America.* He wanted the book to tug at people's consciences, to outrage them, and to push them to action. He wrote that poverty was caused and perpetuated by institutions and public policies, not by individuals' personal pathologies. But he did not argue that it was caused by capitalism or that the solution was socialism. The solution, he wrote, was full employment, more funding for housing and health care, and better schools and job training.

In February 1964 Harrington, his friend Paul Jacobs (a labor activist and writer), and US Labor Department official Daniel Patrick Moynihan (later a US senator from New York) wrote a background paper for Shriver's War on Poverty planning committee. The memo argued, "If there is any single dominant problem of poverty in the U.S., it is that of unemployment." The remedy, it said, was a massive public works initiative similar to the New Deal's Works Progress Administration (WPA) and Civilian Conservation Corps programs.

It was on this point that Harrington parted company from Johnson's aides. Jobs programs were expensive. The WPA had cost $5 billion in 1936. Johnson insisted that the "unconditional war on poverty" he had called for had to come in at under a billion dollars a year. The strategy was to help the poor improve themselves—a "hand up, not a handout," in Shriver's words. The War on Poverty legislation, passed in August 1964, included funds for preschool education, social services through community action agencies, and legal services, but no major jobs programs and no major direct cash grants to the poor.

Harrington complained to Shriver that America could not abolish poverty by spending "nickels and dimes." Shriver responded, "Oh really, Mr. Harrington. I don't know about you, but this is the first time I've spent a billion dollars."

The reality is that these policies (including Medicaid, subsidized housing, Head Start, legal services, and, later, food stamps), in combination with a strong economy, did significantly reduce poverty from the middle 1960s through the early 1970s. The biggest beneficiaries of LBJ's Great Society were the elderly, whose poverty rate declined significantly thanks to Medicare and cost-of-living increases for Social Security.

But Harrington was correct that the level of spending for antipoverty programs (less than 1 percent of the federal budget) was never sufficient to make a major dent in the problem. And as spending for the Vietnam War escalated, antipoverty programs suffered.

Harrington's stint as an adviser to the Johnson administration lasted about a month. But by then he had a platform as America's leading poverty expert. He mesmerized audiences, especially on college campuses, with his eloquent, funny, and morally uplifting lectures. He was also a talent scout, recruiting young activists and plugging them into different movement activities. When he talked about democratic socialism, he made it sound like common sense—rational, practical, and moral at the same time.

Harrington warned that campaigns for civil rights, union drives, and calls to withdraw US troops from Vietnam were not enough. They were necessary stepping-stones toward a better world, but they were not sufficient to end poverty, expand happiness, or stop imperialism. He told audiences, "You must recognize that the social vision to which you are committing yourself will never be fulfilled in your lifetime." In the meantime, though, socialists, radicals, progressives, and liberals had to fight today for what he called the "left wing of the possible."

What was possible depended on the specific political situation. When Democrats controlled the White House and Congress, "the possible" included raising the minimum wage above the poverty line, giving workers and their unions a voice on corporate boards, providing government-sponsored health insurance for every American, dramatically expanding public transportation, outlawing race and gender discrimination by employers, and increasing tax rates on the very rich. When Republicans controlled the levers of political power, it shrank to protecting existing liberal programs, exposing the GOP's ties to its corporate sponsors, and organizing to help elect progressive Democrats in the next political season.

Although he wrote eleven more books, *The Other America* was Harrington's calling card, and he used it to help build a "left wing of the possible" movement. Unlike **Eugene Debs** and **Norman Thomas**—his predecessors as the nation's leading socialists—Harrington never thought it was possible to create a radical third party that could succeed in electing candidates and gaining power. The task of socialists was to keep the flame of socialism alive while building coalitions among labor, civil rights, religious, and intellectual liberals and others to form a left flank within the Democratic Party. He worked closely with the leaders of the United Auto Workers, Service Employees International Union, and Machinists union. He wrote speeches for **Ted Kennedy** and **Martin Luther King Jr.** and drafted a Poor People's Manifesto for King in 1968.

In the aftermath of the 1960s and the decline of the antiwar movement, Harrington recruited students, professors, clergy, writers, and union activists to join the Democratic Socialist Organizing Committee, founded in 1973, and later Democratic Socialists of America (DSA), to make sure that the tradition of American socialism did not disappear. Although DSA never had more than 10,000 members, many of its members became key activists within unions, environmental groups, and other progressive organizations. During the last two decades of his life, Harrington was actively involved in the day-to-day activities of these organizations—a distraction from his writing and speaking, but a commitment he had made to himself years earlier. If he was to help keep socialism alive in the world's most capitalist country, he had to help maintain socialism's fragile infrastructure.

After Barack Obama was elected president in 2008, the word "socialism" made a curious comeback. Obama's opponents labeled anything Obama proposed, including his modest health-care-reform proposal, "socialism." Were Harrington still alive, he would have injected himself into the public debate, clarifying what socialism is and is not, and explaining that Obama was far from a socialist. Then he would urge liberals, progressives, and real socialists to push the Democrats to be bolder, to give Obama more room to maneuver, and to fight hard for the "left wing of the possible."

Rev. James Lawson
(1928–)

CREDIT: Courtesy of Vanderbilt University Special Collections and University Archives

ONE DAY in 1955 James Lawson was reading a newspaper in Nagpur, India, where he was serving a three-year stint as a Methodist missionary. When he saw photographs of masses of African Americans launching a bus boycott in Montgomery, Alabama, he began whooping, clapping, and dancing in joy. This shocked a colleague in the next hut, who only knew Lawson as a serious and cerebral man. But for Lawson, the photographs offered evidence that a nonviolent mass movement was taking hold back home, while he was in India to learn firsthand about Mohandas Gandhi's principles and tactics that had freed India from British colonialism. Moreover, the boycott movement was being led by a young Christian minister of about the same age as Lawson.

Pacifism had always been a defining feature of Lawson's life, thanks in large part to his mother. Lawson was born in Uniontown, Pennsylvania, and raised in Massillon, Ohio. His father came from Canada, to which his forebears, former slaves, had emigrated. His father was a strong-willed Methodist preacher, known for packing a pistol in his belt. He taught his son—the sixth of nine children— to fight for himself even if the odds were against him.

His mother, who had immigrated to the United States from Jamaica, saw strength in universal love. Once a little white boy much smaller than Lawson had called him a "nigger"; Lawson slapped the boy across the face. He proudly told his mother about the incident, but she admonished him, urging him always to be guided by love. The moment, he later reflected, was a "sanctification," an epiphany that there was a better way to be.

By the time he reached Baldwin-Wallace College, in Berea, Ohio, Lawson's ideas about nonviolence and political activism were rapidly coming together. He met **A. J. Muste** when the pacifist leader of the Fellowship of Reconciliation (FOR) spoke on campus, and he immediately joined FOR's local chapter.

In the spring of his senior year, Lawson received a draft notice. Although by then he had decided to pursue the ministry and could have received a deferment, he refused to request one. He thought it was unconscionable for the clergy to be deferred while others had to serve. He ended up in prison for thirteen months for refusing to fight in the Korean War.

After leaving prison, he was eager to return to his studies. He began working on his master's degree at Oberlin College. From there, he planned to go to Yale Divinity School, and then, he reasoned, he would be adequately prepared to go to the South and work for civil rights.

But in 1956, **Martin Luther King Jr.** came to Oberlin to speak, and the two men made an instant connection. King urged Lawson to abandon his plans and come immediately to the South, where events were moving more quickly than anyone had dared imagine.

In 1958 Muste appointed Lawson the FOR's southern field secretary, allowing him to move to Nashville, Tennessee, and to travel throughout the South conducting workshops in nonviolence for small groups of black teenagers, college students, and adults, many of them cosponsored with the Southern Christian Leadership Conference. King called Lawson "the greatest teacher of nonviolence in America."

In September 1959 Lawson began holding workshops in a church basement for students from Vanderbilt University and from four black colleges in Nashville—Fisk, American Baptist College, Meharry Medical College, and Tennessee Agricultural and Industrial State University. Drawing on both Christian and Gandhian principles, Lawson convinced students that they had the potential to overturn segregation through the righteousness of their ideas and the power of nonviolent protest. It had been five years since the US Supreme Court's ruling in *Brown v. Board of Education,* but not much had changed. Only a nonviolent movement, led by young people, Lawson said, would end segregation. It would require physical courage, unshakable conviction, and a willingness to forgive those who would beat them.

Lawson turned out to be a master strategist and careful planner. In his workshops, small groups of students, blacks and whites, engaged in role-playing exercises. Some played angry white racists pounding on protestors while calling them racist epithets. Lawson taught them to withstand the taunts, slurs, and blows of the segregationists and to protect themselves without retaliating. They began taking part in sit-ins at downtown businesses in 1959. Many of Lawson's protégés—including **John Lewis,** Diane Nash, Bernard Lafayette, James Bevel, and Marion Barry—became movement leaders.

In February 1960, inspired by the sit-ins in Greensboro, North Carolina, some 500 student volunteers crammed into Nashville's First Baptist Church, eager to join the crusade. The students wanted to stage a sit-in the next day, but Lawson was worried that without training in nonviolence, the action would be a disaster. He wanted first to raise bail money and to make sure the students understood how dangerous it was to take a stand. When he saw there was no turning back, he led a crash course in nonviolence that lasted well into the night.

The next morning, the 500 activists went en masse to Nashville's downtown stores, requesting to be served. They dressed impeccably and carried books to read. One group of students sat at a counter, were knocked down, beaten, and arrested. Then another group took their place, and the pattern was repeated. Some white thugs poured ketchup over the students and crushed lit cigarettes into their necks. As David Halberstam relates the incident in his book *The Children,* a white boy punched Rev. C. T. Vivian as the black minister knelt in prayer. One of the protesters, forgetting Lawson's teaching, raised his fists to retaliate. "Put your hands in your pockets!" Vivian commanded. The protester obeyed.

More than 150 students were arrested. In a lead editorial, the *Nashville Banner,* one of the city's two daily newspapers, quoted Lawson as urging students to "violate the law," which the paper called "the incitation to anarchy."

Outraged by the arrests and the brutal treatment of the student protestors, Nashville's African American community organized a boycott of downtown stores. Many whites also stayed away, some out of sympathy, others out of fear. Business leaders pressured the mayor and city council to resolve the controversy. In April, after the home of a prominent black lawyer was bombed, students led a march on city hall and confronted Nashville's mayor. To everyone's surprise, the mayor publicly acknowledged, in front of a large crowd of protesters and with the press looking on, that segregation was wrong. The next month, Nashville's lunch counters began to serve African Americans.

Ella Baker invited Lawson to deliver the keynote speech at the Student Nonviolent Coordinating Committee's founding meeting in April 1960. The sit-ins, Lawson told the assembled activists, represented a "judgment upon middle class conventional half-way efforts to deal with radical social evil."

At the same time he was leading the movement, Lawson pursued his master's degree in divinity at Vanderbilt University. He was one of only a handful of blacks at Vanderbilt, which had begun admitting black graduate students but not black undergraduates.

In the midst of the growing sit-ins, and under pressure from university board members, the dean of the Divinity School asked Lawson to withdraw. Lawson refused, and the board expelled him. But the university got more than it bargained for. Lawson's expulsion, reported on the front page of the *New York Times,* motivated ten Divinity School professors, including the dean, to resign in protest, forcing the school to eventually offer Lawson reinstatement. He opted instead to complete his degree at Boston University.

In 1961 Lawson and the Nashville students played a critical role in the Freedom Ride strategy. After the first wave of Freedom Riders were met with mob violence, including a bombing in Alabama, some activists thought the project should be halted. The Nashville students called Lawson, who endorsed the students' plan to send a new wave of Freedom Riders to Alabama to continue the campaign. Lawson told the students he would join them.

On Wednesday, May 24, the Nashville contingent—all "graduates" of Lawson's workshops—other activists, and about twelve reporters boarded the Trailways bus going from Montgomery, Alabama, to Jackson, Mississippi. Despite warnings of bomb threats along the way, the riders arrived safely in Jackson and, upon exiting the bus, filed into the "whites only" waiting room and were promptly arrested. The National Association for the Advancement of Colored People offered to pay their bail, but the riders refused the offer, preferring to remain in jail until their trial. On Friday Lawson and the other arrested riders appeared in court. The judge, an extreme segregationist, found all twenty-seven defendants guilty and sentenced each to a $200 fine and a sixty-day suspended sentence. He wanted them out of Mississippi and Mississippi out of the national media spotlight. But they refused to pay the fine and remained in jail, where some of them were beaten by the police. In the meantime, hundreds of other Freedom Riders had joined the crusade, making John F. Kennedy's administration increasingly concerned about the violent image of the United States being presented around the world.

On June 16 a delegation of Freedom Riders and their supporters, including Lawson, met with Attorney General Robert Kennedy at the Justice Department in Washington, DC. The delegation wanted Kennedy to intervene on behalf of the riders unfairly arrested in Mississippi. Kennedy wanted the activists to channel their energies into voter registration, promising to raise the money needed to make it feasible. Kennedy pressured the Federal Interstate Commerce Commission to issue new policies desegregating bus travel. The commission announced new rules in September 1961 whereby passengers would be permitted to sit wherever they pleased on interstate buses and trains, "white" and "colored" signs would come down in the terminals, separate drinking fountains, toilets, and waiting rooms would be consolidated, and lunch counters would be forced to serve people regardless of race.

In 1962 Lawson became pastor of Centenary Methodist Church in Memphis, where he continued his activism. In February 1968 he was asked to lead a strategy committee that was assisting black sanitation workers in Memphis, who toiled in dangerous conditions for pitiful wages and no benefits (see the profile of **Jerry Wurf**).

Union leader Jerry Wurf later said of that time, "What Lawson never understood was the degree to which he was hated in Memphis. They feared [him] for the most interesting of all reasons—he was a totally moral man, and totally moral men you can't manipulate and you can't buy and you can't hustle." Lawson persuaded King to come to Memphis to support the strikers and to generate national attention for the walkout. King's last speech was given at the Mason Temple, the day before he was murdered as he stood on the balcony of his room at the Lorraine Motel.

In 1974 Lawson left the South, accepting the position of pastor at the 2,700-member Holman Methodist Church in Los Angeles. There he became involved with the labor movement, the American Civil Liberties Union, and movements for reproductive choice and gay rights. He served as chairman of the Clergy and

Laity United for Economic Justice. He also served as national chair of the Fellowship of Reconciliation.

In 1989 he was one of thirty-six people arrested at the Federal Building in downtown Los Angeles while protesting US support for the government of El Salvador, which had committed massacres during the country's civil war. In 1997 he led a coalition of clergy in support of the city's proposed living-wage law and led protest rallies to push the Los Angeles City Council to approve an ordinance to raise wages for workers employed by private companies that got municipal subsidies and contracts. The next year, he marched onto the University of Southern California campus in support of unionized food service and facilities workers.

In 2000 Lawson was part of an interfaith delegation that traveled to Iraq to call for the end of sanctions, and following the September 11, 2001, attacks, he founded Interfaith Communities United for Justice and Peace, which brought together leaders of all the major faiths. In a November 2004 speech, he called on the world's religions to "stop blessing war and violence in all their various masks."

In 2003 Lawson joined with unions, immigrant rights groups, and civil rights activists to launch an Immigrant Workers Freedom Ride to mobilize public support to reform immigration laws in Congress and to challenge the widespread immigrant-bashing that occurred in the wake of the 9/11 bombings. The Los Angeles contingent's itinerary included several stops in southern cities, where they met with activists from the civil rights movement, including participants in the 1960s Freedom Rides, sharing stories of exploitation and struggle, prayers, and songs.

"No human being in the sight of God is illegal," Lawson explained at one of the rallies. "The fight for the civil rights of workers who come here from all over the world is the same as the Freedom Rides of 1961 and the continuing struggle for civil and human rights for all."

Noam Chomsky (1928–)

CREDIT: Associated Press/
Nader Daoud

IN SEPTEMBER 2006, while giving a speech at the United Nations, President
Hugo Chávez of Venezuela held up a copy of the Spanish edition of *Hegemony or
Survival: America's Quest for Global Dominance* by Noam Chomsky. Describing
it as an "excellent book to help us understand what has been happening in the
world throughout the 20th century," Chávez said, "I think that the first people
who should read this book are our brothers and sisters in the United States, because their threat is right in their own house." Chávez's endorsement stirred controversy and made headlines in the United States and throughout the world.
Chávez's comments dramatically boosted sales of the book, a stinging critique of
American foreign policy that had been published two years earlier. Within two
days it hit number 1 on Amazon's best-seller list.

In the mainstream media, Chávez—like Chomsky—has been vilified as an
anti-American left-winger. But to the many progressives who had been influenced
by Chomsky's writings, Chávez's remarks were hardly surprising. For four decades,
Chomsky, a professor at the Massachusetts Institute of Technology (MIT), had
been a persistent and influential critic of the political and economic establishment, particularly on issues of war and human rights. He first made his mark as a
brilliant linguist, but in the 1960s he became better known as one of the most
articulate opponents of the Vietnam War. Since then, he has written about genocide, terrorism, democracy, international affairs, nationalism, the media, propaganda, public opinion, militarism, and the history of the Cold War. Despite his
prolific pen, Chomsky's controversial views have been virtually ignored by the
mainstream media, which rarely review his books, publish his essays, or interview
him as an expert on foreign policy and human rights. Nevertheless, he has had a
major influence, in the United States and elsewhere, in shaping the progressive

analysis of American foreign policy. Chávez's tribute expanded Chomsky's visibility, leading many readers to discover his books for the first time, but it also heightened the debate over his views.

Chomsky was born in Philadelphia to Russian immigrant parents, who taught at the religious school of a synagogue. His father was also a highly respected expert on the Hebrew language. The Chomskys sent Noam, a brilliant and precocious student, to an experimental school inspired by the ideas of **John Dewey.** Young Noam would frequently visit his uncle, who was part of a circle of immigrant intellectuals and radicals in New York, including anarchists who published a Yiddish newspaper. At the University of Pennsylvania, Chomsky studied philosophy, logic, and languages. Already fluent in Hebrew, he was the only student at the university to study Arabic.

Somewhat bored with college, Chomsky considering moving to Palestine, where many idealistic radical young Jews were living on kibbutzim—collective farms—and hoping to built a secular socialist nation. But in 1947 Chomsky met Zellig Harris, a charismatic professor who founded the University of Pennsylvania's Linguistics Department (the first in the country). Harris reignited Chomsky's interest in academics. Chomsky wrote his honors thesis and his master's thesis on Hebrew linguistics, then completed his Ph.D. in linguistics at Harvard in 1955. MIT hired Chomsky that year, and he has taught there ever since. In the 1950s, Chomsky's theory of transformational grammar revolutionized the field of linguistics, philosophy, and cognitive psychology by challenging existing ideas about how humans learn and develop language skills.

As the Vietnam War escalated, Chomsky became involved in the antiwar movement. His 1967 essay "The Responsibility of Intellectuals," published in the *New York Review of Books,* challenged the complicity of academics, government bureaucrats, think-tank experts, and others in justifying America's right to dominate the world, and it established him as a leading critic of US foreign policy. The article was included in his book *American Power and the New Mandarins* (1969), a critique of US policy in Indochina that helped shift many Americans' thinking about the war.

Chomsky wrote numerous articles and other books documenting the American government's lies about the origins and execution of the war. He was in great demand as a speaker at rallies, forums, and debates. He had a significant influence on the antiwar movement's analysis of the war and of US foreign policy, but his dissenting views were rarely reported in the mainstream media. He was arrested on several occasions for engaging in antiwar protest and was included on President Richard Nixon's infamous "enemies list."

After the Vietnam War ended, Chomsky's books and articles focused on the roots of American foreign policy and the Cold War, US support for Third World dictatorships, and the role of the media in rationalizing American global domination and corporate priorities. In *Manufacturing Consent: The Political Economy of the Mass Media* (coauthored with Edward Herman in 1988) and *Necessary Illusions* (1989), Chomsky challenged the conventional view that the United States has a free press that acts as a watchdog on government. Instead, he viewed the media as more of a conveyor belt for government and corporate propaganda, which Americans do not recognize because they take it for granted.

Chomsky is generally less interested in the inner workings of the media than in the consequences of the media's domination by business and government elites. He has not closely examined *how* the media work on a day-to-day basis. This task has been take up by progressive watchdog groups such as Fairness and Accuracy in Reporting and Media Matters for America, whose thorough research routinely exposes the mainstream media's complicity with the powers-that-be. They have revealed, for example, the media's overreliance on establishment figures as guests on TV talk shows, or their bias toward conservative and centrist think tanks over liberal and progressive institutions as news sources. These watchdog groups use this research to embarrass and pressure editors and reporters to change how they report and frame the news.

Chomsky's view of American government makes little room for the battle of ideas or political agendas. Like **Ralph Nader,** Chomsky views both major political parties as captives of the larger system of business domination. He has little to say about the existence or potential of progressives within Congress or within government agencies. He sees them as exceptions to the rule who help maintain the chimera of real democracy. Chomsky has retained the anarchist instincts he imbibed as a teenager. He is suspicious of all governments. He views the workings of government—in democracies, military dictatorships, or Communist countries— as essentially the same. In Chomsky's worldview, politicians and government officials tend to horde and use power to expand their own influence, which leads them to be intolerant of dissent. Chomsky views the US government as a bulwark of global corporations. His writings recount America's military invasions and business control of Third World countries. American policymakers, he believes, generally follow the logic of imperialism—including a willingness to support dictators; to murder, annihilate, and control people in other countries; to use weapons of mass destruction; and to train and arm terrorists if doing so buttresses the empire.

In the 1970s and 1980s Chomsky was one of the few to speak out about the otherwise widely ignored genocide in East Timor, where Indonesian forces armed and supported by the United States were responsible for the deaths of more than 200,000 people. Chomsky's early Zionist sympathies were linked to support for decentralized cooperative farms (egalitarian kibbutzim) and the aspirations of Arabs. Since the 1960s, his consistent condemnation of US military and economic support for Israel has frequently ignited controversy.

Chomsky was pleased to see the Soviet Union crumble. But, he argued, the War on Terror offered the American military-industrial complex new enemies with which to justify its existence. In his book *9-11* (2002), Chomsky denounced the attack on the World Trade Center. At the same time, he traced the origins of the attack to the actions of the United States, which he labeled "a leading terrorist state." In *Failed States: The Abuse of Power and the Assault on Democracy* (2006), Chomsky argues that successive US governments, regardless of the party in power, have been involved in state terrorism.

Like **I. F. Stone** before him, Chomsky has a remarkable ability to dig out facts and examples, which he recites in his writings and speeches. In lectures, he is often able to disarm critics with his seemingly encyclopedic memory for details.

In "The Manufacture of Consent," written in 1984, Chomsky displays his ability to use a mundane everyday incident to challenge conventional wisdom. He wrote:

> During the Thanksgiving holiday a few weeks ago, I took a walk with some friends and family in a national park. We came across a gravestone, which had on it the following inscription: "Here lies an Indian woman, a Wampanoag, whose family and tribe gave of themselves and their land that this great nation might be born and grow." Of course, it is not quite accurate to say that the indigenous population gave of themselves and their land for that noble purpose. Rather, they were slaughtered, decimated, and dispersed in the course of one of the greatest exercises in genocide in human history, which we celebrate each October when we honor Columbus—a notable mass murderer himself—on Columbus Day. Hundreds of American citizens, well-meaning and decent people, troop by that gravestone regularly and read it, apparently without reaction; except, perhaps, a feeling of satisfaction that at last we are giving some due recognition to the sacrifices of the native peoples. They might react differently if they were to visit Auschwitz or Dachau and find a gravestone reading: "Here lies a woman, a Jew, whose family and people gave of themselves and their possessions that this great nation might grow and prosper."

Here Chomsky does not categorically identify who is responsible for the genocide of Native Americans, but it is not difficult to figure out who he is indicting: the original colonists, the land-grabbers, the federal government, the cowboys and military invaders, and the religious and secular thinkers whose writings portrayed Native Americans as subhumans or noble primitives, justifying their elimination or exploitation. At the same, he views almost the entire American public—"well-meaning and decent people"—as being so influenced by the American propaganda system that they are unable to see what Chomsky understands as the atrocity hidden by the gravestone's inscription.

Chomsky's loyal readers admire his prodigious research and his moral indignation in the cause of justice. But many progressives criticize Chomsky's analysis for providing little hope for change. Chomsky views "the state" as a system with its own logic. America is an empire, a war machine, a global police force. Its leaders, and much of its population, are blinded by ideology. He tends to view the US government, regardless of who is elected to office, as a force for evil.

Progressive movements succeed in part by taking advantage of disagreements and tensions within the elite. But in Chomsky's worldview, the "system" is a seamless web. Accordingly, there is little room for people—whether government officials, movements and their organizers, or liberal reporters—to make a difference. His supporters argue, however, that Chomsky's important role is to provide the ammunition so that others can organize movements to challenge the system.

CREDIT: Associated Press

Rev. Martin
Luther King Jr.
(1929–1968)

TODAY REV. Martin Luther King Jr. is viewed as something of a saint. His birthday is a national holiday, and his name adorns schools and street signs. In 1964, at age thirty-five, he was the youngest man to receive the Nobel Peace Prize. But in his day, in his own country, King was considered a dangerous troublemaker. He was harassed by the FBI and vilified in the media. In fact, King *was* radical, in terms of his critique of American society and his strategy for changing it. King helped change America's conscience, not only about civil rights, but also about economic justice, poverty, and peace, and in doing so he pushed the country toward more democracy and social justice.

King was born in Atlanta, Georgia, in 1929, the son of a prominent black minister. Despite growing up in a solidly middle-class family, King saw the widespread human suffering caused by the Depression, particularly in the black community. In 1950, while in graduate school, he wrote an essay describing the "anti-capitalistic feelings" he experienced as a result of seeing unemployed people standing in breadlines. During King's first year at Morehouse College, **A. Philip Randolph** spoke on campus. Randolph predicted that the near future would witness a global struggle that would end white supremacy and capitalism. He urged the students to link up with "the people in the shacks and the hovels," who, although "poor in property," were "rich in spirit."

After graduating from Morehouse in 1948, King studied theology at Crozer Theological Seminary in Pennsylvania (where he read both Mohandas Gandhi and Karl Marx), planning to follow in his father's footsteps and join the ministry. In 1955 he earned his doctorate from Boston University, where he studied the works of Reinhold Niebuhr, the influential liberal theologian. While in Boston, he told his girlfriend (and future wife), Coretta Scott, that "a society based on making all the money you can and ignoring people's needs is wrong."

When King moved to Montgomery, Alabama, to take his first pulpit at the Dexter Avenue Baptist Church, he was full of ideas but had no practical experience in politics or activism. But history sneaked up on him. On Thursday, December 1, 1955, Rosa Parks, a seamstress and veteran activist with the National

Association for the Advancement of Colored People (NAACP), decided to resist the city's segregation law by refusing to move to the back of the bus on her way home from work. She was arrested. Two other long-term activists—E. D. Nixon (leader of the NAACP and of the Brotherhood of Sleeping Car Porters) and Jo Ann Robinson (a professor at the all-black Alabama State College and a leader of Montgomery's Women's Political Council)—determined that Parks's arrest was a ripe opportunity for a one-day boycott of the much-despised segregated bus system. Nixon and Robinson asked black ministers to use their Sunday sermons to spread the word. Some refused, but many others, including King, agreed.

The boycott was very effective. Most black residents stayed off the buses. Within days, the boycott leaders formed a new group, the Montgomery Improvement Association (MIA). At Nixon's urging, they elected a reluctant King, only twenty-six years old, as president, in large part because he was new in town and not embroiled in the competition for congregants and visibility among black ministers. He was also well educated and already a brilliant orator, and thus would be a good public face for the protest movement. The ministers differed over whether to call off the boycott after one day but agreed to put the question up to a vote at a mass meeting.

That night, 7,000 blacks crowded into (and stood outside) the Holt Street Baptist Church. Inspired by King's words—"There comes a time when people get tired of being trampled over by the iron feet of oppression"—they voted unanimously to continue the boycott. It lasted for 381 days and resulted in the desegregation of the city's buses. During that time, King honed his leadership skills, aided by advice from two veteran pacifist organizers, **Bayard Rustin** and Rev. Glenn Smiley, who had been sent to Montgomery by the Fellowship of Reconciliation. During the boycott, King was arrested, his home was bombed, and he was subjected to personal abuse. But—with the assistance of the new medium of television—he emerged as a national figure.

In 1957 King launched the Southern Christian Leadership Conference (SCLC) to help spread the civil rights crusade to other cities. He helped lead local campaigns in different cities, including Selma, Alabama, and Birmingham, Alabama, where thousands marched to demand an end to segregation in defiance of court injunctions forbidding any protests. While participating in these protests, King also sought to keep the fractious civil rights movement together, despite the rivalries among the NAACP, the Urban League, the Student Nonviolent Coordinating Committee (SNCC), the Congress of Racial Equality (CORE), and SCLC. Between 1957 and 1968 King traveled over 6 million miles, spoke over 2,500 times, and was arrested at least twenty times, always preaching the gospel of nonviolence. King attended workshops at the Highlander Folk School in Tennessee, which connected him to a network of radicals, pacifists, and union activists from around the country whose ideas helped widen his political horizons.

King began his activism in Montgomery as a crusader against the nation's racial caste system, but the struggle for civil rights radicalized him into a fighter for broader economic and social justice. It is often forgotten that the famous 1963 protest rally at the Lincoln Memorial, where King delivered his "I Have a Dream" speech, was called the March on Washington for Jobs and Freedom. He was proud of the civil rights movement's success in winning the passage of the Civil Rights Act in 1964 and the Voting Rights Act the following year. But he realized that neither law did much to provide better jobs or housing for the masses of black poor in either the urban cities or the rural South. "What good is having the right to sit at a lunch counter," he asked, "if you can't afford to buy a hamburger?"

King had hoped that the bus boycott, sit-ins, and other forms of civil disobedience would stir white southern moderates, led by his fellow clergy, to see the immorality of segregation and racism. His "Letter from a Birmingham Jail," written in 1963, outlines King's strategy of using nonviolent civil disobedience to force a response from the southern white establishment and to generate sympathy and support among white liberals and moderates. "The purpose of our direct-action program is to create a situation so crisis-packed that it will inevitably open the door to negotiation," he wrote, and added, "We know through painful experience that freedom is never voluntarily given by the oppressor; it must be demanded by the oppressed."

King eventually realized that many poor and working-class whites had at least a psychological stake in perpetuating racism. He began to recognize that racial segregation was devised not only to oppress African Americans but also to keep working-class whites from challenging their own oppression by letting them feel superior to blacks. "The Southern aristocracy took the world and gave the poor white man Jim Crow," King said from the Capitol steps in Montgomery, following the 1965 march from Selma. "And when his wrinkled stomach cried out for the food that his empty pockets could not provide, he ate Jim Crow, a psychological bird that told him that no matter how bad off he was, at least he was a white man, better than a black man."

When King launched a civil rights campaign in Chicago in 1965, he was shocked by the hatred and violence expressed by working-class whites as he and his followers marched through the streets of segregated neighborhoods in Chicago and its suburbs. He saw that the problem in Chicago's ghetto was not legal segregation but "economic exploitation"—slum housing, overpriced food, and low-wage jobs—"because someone profits from its existence."

These experiences led King to develop a more radical outlook. King supported President **Lyndon B. Johnson**'s declaration of the War on Poverty in 1964, but, like the United Auto Workers' **Walter Reuther** and others, he thought it did not go nearly far enough. As early as October 1964, he called for a "gigantic Marshall Plan" for the poor—black and white. Two months later, accepting the Nobel Peace Prize in Oslo, he observed that the United States could learn much from Scandinavian "democratic socialism." He began talking openly about the need to confront "class issues," which he described as "the gulf between the haves and the have nots."

In 1966 King confided to his staff:

You can't talk about solving the economic problem of the Negro without talking about billions of dollars. You can't talk about ending the slums without first saying profit must be taken out of slums. You're really tampering and getting on dangerous ground because you are messing with folk then. You are messing with captains of industry. . . . Now this means that we are treading in difficult water, because it really means that we are saying that something is wrong . . . with capitalism. . . . There must be a better distribution of wealth and maybe America must move toward a democratic socialism.

Given this view, he was dismayed when **Malcolm X,** SNCC's Stokely Carmichael, and others began advocating "black power," which would alienate white allies and undermine a genuine interracial movement for economic justice.

King became increasingly committed to building bridges between the civil rights and labor movements. Invited to address the AFL-CIO's annual convention in 1961, King observed, "The labor movement did not diminish the strength of the nation but enlarged it. By raising the living standards of millions, labor miraculously created a market for industry and lifted the whole nation to undreamed of levels of production. Those who today attack labor forget these simple truths, but history remembers them." In a 1961 speech to the Negro American Labor Council, King said, "Call it democracy, or call it democratic socialism, but there must be a better distribution of wealth within this country for all God's children." Speaking to a meeting of Teamsters union shop stewards in 1967, King said, "Negroes are not the only poor in the nation. There are nearly twice as many white poor as Negro, and therefore the struggle against poverty is not involved solely with color or racial discrimination but with elementary economic justice."

King's growing critique of capitalism coincided with his views about American imperialism. By 1965 he had turned against the Vietnam War, viewing it as an economic as well as a moral tragedy. But he was initially reluctant to speak out against the war. He understood that his fragile working alliance with LBJ would be undone if he challenged the president's leadership on the war. Although some of his close advisers tried to discourage him, he nevertheless made the break in April 1967, in a bold and prophetic speech at the Riverside Church in New York City, entitled "Beyond Vietnam—A Time to Break Silence." King called America the "greatest purveyor of violence in the world today" and linked the struggle for social justice with the struggle against militarism. King argued that Vietnam was stealing precious resources from domestic programs and that the Vietnam War was "an enemy of the poor." In his last book, *Where Do We Go from Here: Chaos or Community?* (1967), King wrote, "The bombs in Vietnam explode at home; they destroy the hopes and possibilities for a decent America."

In early 1968 he told journalist David Halberstam, "For years I labored with the idea of reforming the existing institutions of society, a little change here, a little change there. Now I feel quite differently. I think you've got to have a re-construction of the entire society, a revolution of values."

King believed America needed a "radical redistribution of economic and polit-ical power." He kept trying to build a broad movement for economic justice that went beyond civil rights. In January 1968 he announced plans for a Poor People's Campaign, a series of protests to be led by an interracial coalition of poor people and their allies among the middle-class liberals, unions, religious organizations, and other progressive groups, to pressure the White House and Congress to ex-pand the War on Poverty. At King's request, socialist **Michael Harrington** drafted a Poor People's Manifesto that outlined the campaign's goals. In April King was in Memphis, Tennessee, to help lend support to striking African Amer-ican garbage workers and to gain recognition for their union. There he was assas-sinated at age thirty-nine on April 4, a few months before the first protest action of the Poor People's Campaign in Washington, DC.

Johnson utilized this national tragedy to urge Congress to quickly enact the Fair Housing Act, legislation to ban racial discrimination in housing that King had strongly supported for two years. He signed the bill a week after King's assassination.

The campaign for a federal holiday in King's honor began soon after his mur-der, but it did not come up for a vote in Congress until 1979, when it fell five votes short of the number needed for passage. In 1981, with the help of Stevie Wonder and other celebrities, 6 million signatures were collected for a petition to Congress on behalf of a King holiday. Legislation enacting the holiday was finally passed in 1983, fifteen years after King's death. But even then, ninety members of the House voted against it. Senator Jesse Helms, a North Carolina Republican, led an unsuccessful effort—supported by twenty-one other senators—to block its passage in the Senate. The holiday was first observed on January 20, 1986. In 1987 Arizona governor Evan Mecham rescinded Martin Luther King Day as his first act in office, setting off a national boycott of the state. Some states (including New Hampshire, which called it "Civil Rights Day" from 1991 to 1999) insisted on calling the holiday by other names. In 2000 South Carolina became the last state to make King Day a paid holiday for all state employees. Until then, em-ployees could choose between celebrating it or one of three Confederate-related holidays.

Allard Lowenstein
(1929–1980)

ON A warm October night in 1963, Allard Lowenstein was driving around Clarksdale, Mississippi, looking for a hotel with Steve Bingham and John Speh (two white Yale student volunteers) and **Bob Moses** (an African American organizer for the Student Nonviolent Coordinating Committee [SNCC]). They had been registering voters in the Mississippi Delta. As they headed toward the Alcazar Hotel, a black hotel, police arrested them on a bogus charge of loitering and violating the local curfew. They were taken to the county jail, where police taunted them about whether they would live to the next morning. "We were scared to death," Bingham recalled forty-eight years later. "We were worried that we were going to be 'disappeared.'"

The thirty-four-year-old Lowenstein, a graduate of Yale Law School, identified himself as an attorney and demanded that he be allowed to make a phone call, even though it was the middle of the night. Then he loudly placed a collect call to **Franklin D. Roosevelt**'s grandson Franklin D. Roosevelt III, a twenty-five-year-old Yale graduate. Lowenstein slowly spelled out the last name letter by letter. Roosevelt was barely awake, but Lowenstein pretended he was engaged in an intense conversation, saying, "No, don't call President Kennedy tonight, wait until tomorrow." Intimidated by the call, the police treated Lowenstein and the others with caution. The following morning, other civil rights workers bailed them out.

The incident revealed the traits that made Lowenstein one of the most effective civil rights and antiwar activists in the country. He was idealistic and courageous. He had an incredible network of contacts, whom he drew upon to support these causes. He also had the self-confidence—bordering on arrogance—of someone from a privileged background and with an elite education that allowed him to make the impossible seem possible.

Lowenstein was an inspirational and peripatetic political agitator, constantly on the move, embracing causes years before they generated broad support. His major contributions were raising awareness of apartheid in South Africa, mobilizing voter registration campaigns in Mississippi during the civil rights movement, and recruiting an antiwar Democrat to oppose President **Lyndon B. Johnson,** a move that forced LBJ to withdraw from his own reelection effort. Lowenstein's genius was in acting as an outsider and an insider at the same time, building bridges between protest politics and electoral politics, and linking the idealism of young radicals and the pragmatism of mainstream liberals. Lowenstein walked this difficult tightrope better than anyone.

Lowenstein's father Gabriel Lowenstein, a Jewish immigrant from Lithuania who admired **Eugene Debs** and **Norman Thomas,** gave up a professorship at Columbia Medical School to join his brothers in a lucrative New York City restaurant business. Allard lived in affluent comfort in suburban Harrison, New York, and went to the exclusive private Horace Mann School. The family business provided him with a regular income, so Lowenstein never had to worry about making a living, giving him the freedom to be a freelance organizer.

Lowenstein defied his father, who expected him to attend an Ivy League college, by attending the University of North Carolina, but he embraced his father's ideals by immediately jumping into student politics. When he arrived in North Carolina, he caused a stir by intentionally sitting in the black section of the bus from Durham to Chapel Hill. Frank Graham, the university's liberal president, took Lowenstein under his wing and encouraged him to shake things up. Within months of arriving on campus in 1945, Lowenstein was leading a group of students who challenged anti-Semitism and racism on campus and the domination of student government by fraternities. In the summer of 1947, after his junior year, Lowenstein attended a six-week Encampment for Citizenship in New York, sponsored by the Ethical Culture Society, which brought together a diverse group of college students from around the country, including a large number of blacks and Native Americans, to discuss human rights, the arms race, and social justice. The speakers included **Eleanor Roosevelt,** with whom Lowenstein would develop a close relationship.

In 1950 Lowenstein was elected president of the three-year-old National Student Association (NSA). He traveled to campuses, giving fiery speeches about racism, democracy, and idealism that inspired students to get involved in politics. Through NSA, Lowenstein met politicians, diplomats, activists, and student leaders who remained part of his web of influential contacts for the rest of his life. The small 1950s student movement laid the groundwork for the explosion of student activism in the 1960s.

Lowenstein began organizing against South African apartheid several decades before American campuses and liberal activists embraced the cause. He recruited two students from his NSA network and went on a covert fact-finding trip to South Africa to investigate racial oppression and social conditions. Hiding from police, they took clandestine photos, and after returning home, they issued a report for the United Nations, appeared on television and radio shows, and fed stories to major newspapers. A front-page *New York Times* story in April 1960 reported on documents Lowenstein had smuggled out of South Africa about a police massacre of antiapartheid protestors in Sharpeville. Two years later, Lowenstein revised the report into a critically acclaimed book, *Brutal Mandate*.

When he returned from Africa, Lowenstein spent a year teaching at Stanford, and then moved to North Carolina State. At both schools, he identified the idealistic students and urged them to get involved in campus politics. At North Carolina State, for example, he invited Angie Brooks, Liberia's UN ambassador, to speak on campus, and he arranged for an integrated group to meet Brooks for dinner at a segregated hotel, knowing that the hotel restaurant would refuse to serve her. Within days the incident had triggered what turned into weeks of protests (and consequent arrests) in downtown Raleigh, aimed at integrating local businesses and spearheaded by students from North Carolina State and Shaw University.

In July 1963 Lowenstein visited Mississippi to get a firsthand look at SNCC's voter registration efforts. The project was making little headway because of the brutal intimidation tactics used by local police, employers, and vigilantes. Lowenstein had thought about volunteering his services as a lawyer defending arrested civil rights activists, but he quickly realized that more dramatic action was needed. "We had to shake people on the outside out of thinking that Mississippi was just another state," Lowenstein said.

Lowenstein and Bob Moses came up with the idea of Freedom Vote, a plan to register black voters and hold mock elections for candidates running on an alternative party slate, holding the elections at churches, black schools, and clubs where they would not face harassment or arrest. Lowenstein raised the money for the project from his liberal friends in the North. He also recruited white college students to come to Mississippi and help with the voter campaign, a strategy that was guaranteed to draw media attention, northern white sympathy, money, and political support. Once America's "best and brightest" white students were risking their lives for their principles, he calculated, the major newspapers and newsmagazines would start paying attention. In three days more than 85,000 black Mississippians voted in the Freedom Vote elections, making a mockery of racist claims that blacks were politically apathetic.

The success of Freedom Vote led to a more ambitious project the next year— Freedom Summer—that brought over 1,000 college student volunteers to Mississippi. Lowenstein recruited students from Yale, Stanford, and other campuses. For many of the white student volunteers, working closely with African Americans in a tense and dangerous atmosphere, Freedom Summer was a life-changing experience. Many of them became prominent activists and organizers; a few, including future Congressman Barney Frank of Massachusetts, became elected officials. "I am prouder of being there than of anything else in my life," Frank said years later. Three of the volunteers—black Mississippian James Chaney and white radicals Andrew Goodman and Michael Schwerner—were murdered by segregationist vigilantes. That summer, hundreds of volunteers were arrested; sixty-seven churches, homes, and stores were bombed by racist thugs.

The summer campaign culminated in another mock election. Black voters elected an integrated slate, under the banner of the Mississippi Freedom Democratic Party (MFDP), which challenged the state's segregated delegation at the Democratic convention in Atlantic City, New Jersey, in August. President Johnson, fearful of alienating southern white voters, rejected the MFDP challenge but offered a compromise, offering them two seats in the state delegation. Led by **Fannie Lou Hamer** and Bob Moses, MFDPers rejected the compromise, which Lowenstein supported as a stepping-stone toward progress. Freedom Summer helped turn the nation's eyes on southern racism and repression of freedom fighters and helped guarantee passage of the Voting Rights Act.

Lowenstein's involvement in the antiwar movement, which began in 1965, was the climax of his activist career. In 1967 he helped draft **Martin Luther King Jr.**'s historic antiwar speech at New York's Riverside Church. Lowenstein admired antiwar activists who organized teach-ins and engaged in nonviolent civil disobedience, but he believed the best way to end the war was to elect antiwar candidates who would shut off the war's funding.

In 1968, as antiwar sentiment rose on campuses and voters became increasingly skeptical of US involvement in Vietnam, Lowenstein organized a Dump Johnson movement within the Democratic Party. He tried to talk Senator Robert Kennedy into challenging LBJ, but Kennedy refused. Lowenstein settled on Senator Eugene J. McCarthy of Minnesota and recruited an army of volunteers to work for McCarthy's New Hampshire Democratic primary campaign. They cut their hair, wore respectable clothes, and went "clean for Gene." McCarthy garnered 42 percent of the vote, exposing deep opposition to the sitting president. Four days later, Kennedy announced that he would run, also on an antiwar platform, and he soon outpaced McCarthy. Two weeks later, LBJ announced that he would not seek reelection. Had Kennedy not been assassinated in June, following his victory in the California primary, he would have won the Democratic Party nomination and would probably have defeated Republican Richard Nixon in the race for the White House. Instead, the Democrats nominated Vice President Hubert H. Humphrey, who lost his White House bid to Nixon.

Despite Nixon's victory, many antiwar candidates for Congress prevailed that fall, including Lowenstein, who won a congressional seat in a mostly Republican district on Long Island. Lowenstein's Dump Johnson movement had shown that antiwar candidates could win, and in 1970, 1972, and 1974 they won more and more congressional seats.

For Lowenstein, however, Congress proved to be a bad fit. His wife described him as providing "constituent services for the Western hemisphere," but he was not particularly interested in the day-to-day concerns of his Long Island district. Two years later he lost his reelection bid. He ran for Congress several other times, never successfully. His leadership of Americans for Democratic Action and his work as President Jimmy Carter's ambassador to the UN Human Rights

Commission kept him engaged, but they were not as satisfying as his civil rights and antiwar crusades. He might have eventually led another crusade, but his life was cut short in March 1980 when Dennis Sweeney, one of Lowenstein's former Stanford protégés who suffered from mental illness, showed up at his mentor's office in New York and shot and killed him. Lowenstein was fifty-one years old.

Harvey Milk (1930–1978)

Harvey Milk, left, with Mayor George Moscone in 1977.
CREDIT: Associated Press

SOON AFTER Harvey Milk was elected to the San Francisco Board of Supervisors in 1977—the first openly gay politician in a major public office—he sponsored two bills. The first outlawed discrimination based on sexual orientation. Milk was responding to his core constituency, San Francisco's gay community, which had endured years of bigotry from employers, landlords, and other institutions. The second bill dealt with an issue that, according to polls, voters considered the number one problem in the city: dog feces. Milk's ordinance, called the "pooper scooper" law, required dog owners to scoop up their pets' excrement. After it passed, Milk invited the press to a local park, where, with cameras rolling, he intentionally stepped in the smelly substance. The stunt attracted national media attention as well as extensive local press coverage, as Milk had anticipated. He later explained why he pulled off the photo op: "All over the country, they're reading about me, and the story doesn't center on me being gay. It's just about a gay person who is doing his job."

Milk was a flamboyant personality, but he was also a serious and brilliant politician. After his election, he was the most visible gay public figure in America. At a time when homophobia was still deeply entrenched in American culture, Milk encouraged gays and lesbians to come out of the closet. He received thousands of letters from gays around the country, thanking him for being a role model. "I thank God," wrote a sixty-eight-year-old lesbian, "I have lived long enough to see my kind emerge from the shadows and join the human race."

Milk knew that to win elections and pass legislation, he had to build bridges with other constituencies and with his straight colleagues on the Board of Supervisors. He cultivated support from tenants' groups, the elderly, small businesses, environmentalists, and labor unions.

Milk forged an unlikely alliance with the Teamsters union, which represented truck drivers. The Teamsters wanted to pressure beer distributors to sign a contract with the union to improve pay and working conditions for its members. They were particularly angry at Coors, which, of all the beer companies, was the most hostile toward unions. A Teamsters organizer approached Milk for help in reaching out to gay bars, a big portion of Coors's customer base. Within days, Milk had canvassed the gay bars in and around the heavily gay Castro District, encouraging them to stopping selling Coors beer. With help from Arab and Chinese grocers, the gay boycott of Coors was successful. Milk had earned a political ally among the Teamsters. At Milk's urging, the union also began to recruit more gay truck drivers.

A decade earlier, Milk had been a Wall Street analyst who had voted for conservative Republican presidential candidate Barry Goldwater in 1964. Milk's story—his personal transformation, his meteoric rise to political influence, and his tragic murder less than a year after taking office—reflects the merging of a man and a movement.

Milk grew up in a middle-class Jewish family on Long Island outside New York City. In high school he played football and developed a passion for opera. He graduated from college in 1951 with a degree in math. Although he knew he was homosexual while he was still a teenager, he kept it secret. A college friend recalled, "He was never thought of as a possible queer—that's what you called them then—he was a man's man." After college Milk joined the navy for four years, serving as a diving officer aboard a submarine rescue ship during the Korean War. He was discharged in 1955 with the rank of lieutenant, junior grade.

For the next fifteen years, Milk drifted, taking a series of jobs for which he had little enthusiasm. He taught high school, then worked as a statistician for an insurance company and as an analyst for a Wall Street brokerage firm. During that period he had a number of homosexual relationships.

One of Milk's long-term lovers was a successful director of countercultural 1960s Broadway plays, including *Jesus Christ Superstar* and *Hair*. He got Milk a job helping produce several plays, and Milk started hanging out with theater people and artists. He left Wall Street behind, let his hair grow long, traded his suits for jeans, and became part of the hippie subculture.

In 1972 Milk and his new partner, Scott Smith, joined the exodus of hippies and gays migrating to San Francisco. The city had long been a haven for nonconformists and bohemians. The 1950s beatnik scene, with its overlapping circles of radicals and folk music devotees, morphed into the hippie culture of the 1960s, centered in San Francisco's Haight-Ashbury neighborhood. After World War II, San Francisco had become a mecca for gay men. By the 1960s it had more gay people per capita than any other American city and a thriving gay scene of bars, businesses, and bathhouses. The Castro District became the city's gay ghetto, but the official culture still reflected mainstream antipathy toward gays. For example, landlords could legally evict tenants whom they discovered to be homosexual.

As their numbers grew, gays became a political force in the city. Two organizations—the Society for Individual Rights and the Daughters of Bilitis—began challenging the police department's arbitrary and sometimes brutal persecution of gay bars and entrapment of gays having sex in public parks. In 1971, 2,800 gay men were arrested for having sex in public restrooms and parks. That year, Richard Hongisto, a straight ex-cop who had fought the police department's bias against gays and minorities, ran successfully for county sheriff with the support of the gay community. Other liberal politicians began to court gay and lesbian support. Key gay leaders, including the publisher of the gay newspaper the *Advocate*, started the Alice B. Toklas Democratic Club in 1971 to mobilize gay voters.

Milk lived as an openly gay man, but he was not part of this early wave of gay activism. He and Smith had opened Castro Camera. The store's back room became a gathering place for Milk's widening circle of friends. He frequently complained about taxes on small businesses, underfunded schools (which he learned about when a teacher asked to borrow a projector because her school's equipment did not work), and ongoing discrimination against gays by employers, landlords, and cops. In 1973 Milk decided to run for supervisor. "I finally reached the point where I knew I had to become involved or shut up," he recalled.

Milk, who still looked like an aging hippie, ran a spirited but low-budget and chaotic campaign, drawing on patrons of gay bars angry about police harassment. His fiery speeches and flare attracted media attention, and he garnered 16,900 votes—winning the Castro District and other liberal neighborhoods, finishing tenth out of thirty-two candidates. It was not enough to win the citywide campaign, but it made Milk a visible presence.

Milk and other gay business owners founded the Castro Village Association, which chose Milk as its president. He also organized the Castro Street Fair to attract more customers to the area. By then, Milk had started referring to himself as the "mayor of Castro Street."

Milk ran a better campaign for supervisor in 1975. He cut his hair, wore suits, and stopped smoking marijuana (although he favored its legalization). His community organizing paid off. He had more money and more volunteers. Thanks to his work on the Coors boycott, he earned the support of key unions. This time he came in seventh, one spot away from winning a supervisor's seat.

Milk remained involved in grassroots gay activism, which was facing a backlash by the Religious Right across the country. The growing antigay climate had real consequences. Random attacks on gays in the Castro increased. Upset by the lack of police protection, groups of gays began patrolling the neighborhood themselves. On June 21, 1977, thugs attacked Robert Hillsborough, a gay man, yelling "Faggot!" while stabbing him fifteen times, killing him. A few weeks later, 250,000 people attended the Gay Freedom Day Parade, fueled by anger as well as by gay pride.

Milk's leadership in these mobilizations, plus his previous campaigns, gave him an advantage when he ran again for supervisor in 1977. Equally important, voters had just approved a city charter change to elect supervisors by geographic districts instead of citywide. The new District 5, centered in the Castro area, was Milk's home base. That November, Milk was finally elected to the Board of Supervisors, beating sixteen other candidates, half of them gay. This time he had an effective campaign manager, a large cadre of volunteers, and the endorsement of the *San Francisco Chronicle*.

Milk's victory made national news. He was not the first openly gay candidate to win public office. Voters in Massachusetts, Wisconsin, Minnesota, and Michigan had already elected gay and lesbian candidates. But Milk's victory, winning a powerful high-profile position in the nation's gay capital, made him an instant national figure. He compared himself to **Jackie Robinson,** the black baseball pioneer.

Milk became Mayor George Moscone's closest ally. They challenged the power of the big corporations and real estate developers that were gentrifying the city and changing its skyline. They supported rent control, unions, small businesses, neighborhood organizations, and a tax on suburban commuters. He made sure that he responded to constituency concerns, such as fixing potholes and installing stop signs at dangerous intersections.

Milk garnered headlines for sponsoring the antidiscrimination ordinance and the pooper scooper law. But much of Milk's eleven months in office—before he and Moscone were assassinated—was spent organizing opposition to a statewide referendum sponsored by State Senator John Briggs to ban gays from teaching in public schools. Milk went up and down California speaking out against the initiative. He debated Briggs on television. He crashed Briggs's events, generating media stories. When Briggs claimed that gay teachers abused their students, Milk countered with statistics documenting that most pedophiles were straight, not gay.

Opposition to the Briggs initiative mobilized gays and their liberal allies. They knocked on doors, wrote letters to the editor, and paid for TV and radio ads. More than a quarter of a million people attended that summer's Gay Freedom Day Parade in San Francisco. (Similar events in other cities attracted record numbers.) Milk rode in an open car and later gave an inspiring speech that, according to the *San Francisco Examiner*, "ignited the crowd." He said:

> On this anniversary of Stonewall, I ask my gay sisters and brothers to make the commitment to fight. For themselves, for their freedom, for their country. . . . We will not win our rights by staying quietly in our closets. . . . We are coming out to fight the lies, the myths, the distortions. We are coming out to tell the truths about gays! I'm tired of the silence. So I'm going to talk about it. And I want you to talk about it. . . . You must come out. . . . Come out to your parents, your relatives. . . . Come out to your friends.

On November 7, 1978, Briggs's initiative lost by more than a million votes, with 58 percent of voters—and 75 percent in San Francisco—opposing it. It was a stunning victory for the gay community, and Milk was its most visible leader.

Twenty days later, Milk and Moscone were dead. On November 27, former supervisor Dan White, carrying a gun, climbed into city hall through a basement window and shot both public officials. White had represented one of the city's more conservative neighborhoods and was the only supervisor to oppose Milk's antidiscrimination ordinance. Frustrated by his marginalization on the board, he abruptly resigned on November 10, only ten months after being sworn in. He quickly changed his mind and asked Moscone to reappoint him to his old position. Moscone refused to do so, in part because of Milk's lobbying against White.

White was charged with first-degree murder, making him eligible for the death penalty. A conviction seemed a slam dunk. But White's lawyer claimed that he was not responsible for his actions because of his mental state, which the lawyer termed "diminished capacity." On May 21, 1979, a jury acquitted White of the first-degree murder charge but found him guilty of voluntary manslaughter. He was sentenced to seven years in prison. The verdict triggered riots outside city hall as gays and their allies unleashed their fury.

Milk had anticipated his murder. Since his high-profile Assembly campaign, he had received many hate letters and death threats. He recorded his thoughts on tape, indicating who he wanted to succeed him if he were killed, saying, "If a bullet should enter my brain, let that bullet destroy every closet door." He added, "I would like to see every gay lawyer, every gay architect come out, stand up and let the world know. That would do more to end prejudice overnight than anybody could imagine. I urge them to do that, urge them to come out. Only that way will we start to achieve our rights."

The 2008 film *Milk,* which won Academy Awards for best actor (Sean Penn) and best original screenplay, triggered renewed and broad interest in Milk's life and legacy. In 2009 the California legislature established Milk's birthday, May 22, as Harvey Milk Day throughout the state. That year, too, President Barack Obama posthumously awarded Milk the Presidential Medal of Freedom for his contribution to the gay rights movement, stating, "He fought discrimination with visionary courage and conviction."

When Milk began his political career, the nation's laws and public attitudes still did not accept homosexuality as legitimate. His charisma and political savvy helped unleash the power of gay voters and advance the issue of gay rights, including the growing number of gay and lesbian elected officials and widening acceptance of same-sex marriage.

Ted Kennedy
(1932–2009)

EDWARD M. Kennedy, better known as "Ted" or "Teddy," made many rousing speeches, but his greatest was delivered after he had lost an election. In 1980, at the behest of liberals and unions, he tried to wrest the Democratic Party's presidential nomination from the incumbent Jimmy Carter, whose tepid support for national health insurance, labor law reform, and other issues disappointed the party's progressive wing. Kennedy's heart was not in it, he made a number of gaffes, and Carter won enough delegates to secure the nomination. Typically, candidates who lose their party nominations speak at the conventions and call for party unity behind the winner. That Kennedy did, but in his August 12, 1980, oration at Madison Square Garden he devoted only one sentence to endorsing Carter. For the rest of his half-hour speech, Kennedy made an impassioned case for progressive values and policies:

CREDIT: Associated Press/Toby Jorrin

> I am asking you to renew the commitment of the Democratic Party to economic justice.
>
> I am asking you to renew our commitment to a fair and lasting prosperity that can put America back to work. . . .
>
> Our cause has been, since the days of Thomas Jefferson, the cause of the common man and the common woman. Our commitment has been, since the days of Andrew Jackson, to all those he called "the humble members of society—the farmers, mechanics, and laborers." On this foundation we have defined our values, refined our policies, and refreshed our faith.

In this wide-ranging speech Kennedy affirmed the importance of full employment, women's rights, civil rights, and universal health care, the cause he had championed throughout his political career.

Kennedy ended the speech by declaring, "For me, a few hours ago, this campaign came to an end. For all those whose cares have been our concern, the work goes on, the cause endures, the hope still lives, and the dream shall never die."

The delegates leapt to their feet. Their ovation lasted more than a half hour.

Carter lost to Ronald Reagan that fall. Kennedy went on to become the longest-serving and most effective liberal senator in American history, serving for forty-seven years in the Senate, longer than all but two others—Strom Thurmond and Robert Byrd. During that period, Kennedy used his remarkable legislative skills to fight for the most vulnerable members of society. Whenever his Democratic colleagues began currying favor with big business and moving rightward on social policies, Kennedy worked to keep the progressive flame alive.

When he was growing up, and even into young adulthood, few expected Ted Kennedy to be a successful politician, much less the most accomplished politician in the Kennedy family. He was the ninth and youngest child of Rose Fitzgerald Kennedy and Joseph P. Kennedy. His autocratic father made millions in real estate, banking, and movies, on Wall Street, and in liquor during Prohibition. He served in **Franklin D. Roosevelt**'s administration as the first chairman of the Securities and Exchange Commission and then as ambassador to Britain, but he was never a New Deal liberal.

Ted Kennedy was overshadowed by his three older brothers and was often seen as a hand-me-down politician. His father expected the oldest son, Joseph P. Kennedy Jr., to run for Congress and even the White House someday, but Joseph Jr. was killed in World War II. Then John was elected to the US House of Representatives, then to the US Senate, and then, in 1960, to the presidency. Robert became JFK's attorney general and closest adviser.

Ted, who graduated from Harvard and then from the University of Virginia Law School, was never an outstanding student. He dutifully worked on JFK's campaigns. After JFK was elected president, Ted took a job as an assistant district attorney of Suffolk County, based in Boston.

In 1962, at age thirty, he ran for the Senate seat that John had once held. During one debate, his opponent, state Attorney General Edward J. McCormack Jr., ridiculed Kennedy, saying that the senatorial job "should be merited, not inherited" and that, given his qualifications, if Kennedy's name were "Edward Moore," his candidacy "would be a joke." Yet Kennedy beat McCormack in the Democratic primary and then bested George C. Lodge, the son of a former Republican senator, in the general election.

After the murder of John and Robert, Ted became the senior Kennedy politician and the head of the large Kennedy family. But his life zigzagged between numerous triumphs and tragedies, not only the deaths of his three older brothers but also the serious illnesses of two of his children and the deaths of three of his nephews. In 1964 he was almost killed in a plane crash, which left him with permanent back and neck problems. He also had to deal with an early reputation as a vacuous man of privilege and a playboy, most seriously in 1969 when, on vacation on Cape Cod, he drove his car off a narrow bridge and plunged into a tidal pool, which killed his passenger, a twenty-eight-year-old campaign worker, Mary Jo Kopechne. Kennedy survived the accident, but Kopechne's death, his failure to report the incident for almost nine hours, and his leaving the scene of an accident haunted him personally and politically for the rest of his life.

His triumphs, however, were numerous and made America a more humane and democratic society. He led the fight for the eighteen-year-old vote, the abolition of the draft, and campaign-finance reform. He supported the original Civil Rights Act of 1964, the Voting Rights Act of 1965 (sponsoring the amendment banning the poll tax), and the Fair Housing Act of 1968, and he was instrumental in legislation to strengthen them in subsequent years.

He played a key role in establishing the Occupational Safety and Health Administration. He pushed to expand school lunch programs, raise the minimum wage, and ensure that laid-off workers receive extended unemployment benefits while they search for new jobs. Despite being a religious Catholic, he embraced the cause of reproductive rights for women. Kennedy was one of the earliest supporters of gay rights. He championed AIDS research and treatment and guided the battle to enact the Americans with Disabilities Act of 1990. He sponsored legislation that increased funding for high school and college students and college graduates to participate in community service.

Some of Kennedy's most important legislative successes involved blocking efforts by Republicans to cut funding for social programs, restrict civil liberties, or approve the appointment of reactionary judges.

In 1981, when Ronald Reagan won the White House and the Republicans won a majority of Senate seats, Kennedy found himself in the minority for the first time. Over the years, he had established friendships with many GOP colleagues, with most of whom he had sharp ideological disagreements. But he was celebrated for being able to find enough common ground with some Republicans to support important legislation, even if it was watered down. In 1987 he led the opposition to Reagan's nomination of ultraconservative Robert Bork to the US Supreme Court. "In Robert Bork's America," Kennedy said, "there is no room at the inn for blacks and no place in the Constitution for women. And, in our America, there should be no seat on the Supreme Court for Robert Bork."

Conservatives poked fun at Kennedy for being the epitome of a "tax-and-spend" liberal. He never backed away from the label. He viewed himself not only as a legislator but also as part of a broader progressive movement. Kennedy met frequently with working families to hear their concerns, to relay their stories of both suffering and success, and to lend his support to their struggles. He was not only a regular and stirring speaker at labor union meetings but also a regular presence on picket lines and at rallies. In 2000, for example, he traveled to Los Angeles to march with striking janitors. The next year he showed up on the Harvard campus to support students protesting to pressure the university to pay janitors a living wage.

Kennedy's initial support for the Vietnam War shifted after he visited the country and as US involvement escalated. He called the war a "monstrous outrage" and began making antiwar speeches around the country, particularly opposing President Richard Nixon's "Vietnamization" policy as "war and more war." He led the congressional effort to impose economic sanctions on South Africa over apartheid. He worked for peace in Northern Ireland and successfully fought for a ban on arms sales to the dictatorship in Chile. In 2002 he voted against authorizing the war in Iraq, a move that he later called "the best vote I've made in my 44 years in the United States Senate." Although many Democrats worried about appearing unpatriotic, Kennedy opposed the impending invasion of Iraq, warning that it would "feed a rising tide of anti-Americanism overseas."

Kennedy called health care reform "the cause of my life." For years, while advocating a single-payer system of universal health care, he pushed for stepping-stone reforms to make health care more accessible. He began this long crusade in 1966, when he won a $51 million appropriation to create thirty community health centers to make it easier for poor Americans to get medical care. There are now thousands of such centers around the country. He helped establish the Women, Infants, and Children program, which helps low-income mothers have healthy, well-fed babies; the Consolidated Omnibus Budget Reconciliation Act, which permits workers temporarily to continue receiving health insurance between jobs; the Health Insurance Portability and Accountability Act, which limits the ability of insurance companies to cancel coverage; the Mental Health Systems Act, which allows the mentally ill to stay in their homes and communities instead of being institutionalized; the Children's Health Insurance Program, which provides health insurance for millions of poor and working-class children; and the Orphan Drug Act, which sponsors research into rare diseases.

In May 2008 he was found to be suffering from a brain tumor. Only weeks later, he left the hospital, against his doctors' orders, and secretly flew from Massachusetts to Washington, to vote for legislation to avert deep cuts to Medicare. When he arrived on the Senate floor, his colleagues gave him a standing ovation. According to a story in the *Washington Post*, "Several Republicans were so moved that they switched votes, assuring passage."

Kennedy was one of the first high-profile Democrats to endorse Barack Obama's presidential candidacy, calling for "a new generation of leadership." That support, in early 2008, was an important milestone in Obama's campaign.

It is one of the great tragedies of Kennedy's life, and of American social policy, that after Obama won the presidency, the senator became too ill to help shepherd a universal health care reform bill through Congress. He had geared up for the fight, hiring new staff, advising the new president, and writing articles to set the stage for what he hoped would be his ultimate achievement as a legislator. When he learned he had terminal cancer, he handed the reins to other senators, who were less skillful at legislative maneuvering. Shortly before he died, he wrote an article for *Newsweek,* proclaiming, "I am resolved to see to it this year that we create a system to ensure that someday, when there is a cure for the disease I now have, no American who needs it will be denied it."

Kennedy died before Congress passed the landmark health care reform law in March 2010. It was not the comprehensive bill he would have preferred, but it was the most important health care legislation in the nation's history, and it would not have happened without Kennedy's years of hard work.

Ralph Nader (1934–)

CREDIT: Associated Press

DURING THE 1970s, Ralph Nader was a household name, frequently interviewed and profiled in the media, regularly appearing in the Gallup Poll's annual list of most-admired men in America. Beginning in 1965 with his exposé of the auto industry, *Unsafe at Any Speed*, and for three decades after that, Nader inspired, educated, and mobilized millions of Americans to fight for a better environment, safer consumer products, safer workplaces, and a more accountable government. Americans viewed Nader as a selfless David fighting the greedy Goliath of corporate America.

Although sometimes seen as a Lone Ranger, Nader worked closely with the consumer, environmental, community organizing, and labor movements to push for progressive reforms. He built a huge network of nonprofit organizations designed to investigate and advocate for reform, training thousands of Americans to be more effective organizers, researchers, and public interest lobbyists. Many people who got their start with one of Nader's groups became influential activists, government officials, and journalists.

Thanks to Nader, our cars, airplanes, and workplaces are safer, our air and water is cleaner, and our food is healthier. We also have Nader to thank for seat belts and air bags. Over the years, millions of defective, unsafe cars have been recalled because of Nader's work.

Nader played a key role in campaigns for such important milestones as the Clean Air Act (1970), the Safe Drinking Water Act (1974), and the Superfund

Law (1980), which requires the cleanup of toxic-waste sites. He helped mobilize the public to get Congress to pass the Environmental Protection Act (1970), the Consumer Product Safety Act (1972), and the Occupational Safety and Health Act (1970) and to strengthen the Freedom of Information Act (1974). It is impossible to calculate the number of deaths and injuries prevented as a result of these landmark laws.

Nader was born in Winsted, Connecticut, to Lebanese restaurateur immigrants who instilled in him a strong belief in the importance of being an active citizen. He enjoyed reading copies of the *Congressional Record* (the speeches of members of Congress) that his high school principal gave him.

While studying at Princeton University, Nader tried but failed to stop the spraying of campus trees with the pesticide DDT, which he considered dangerous and harmful to the environment. (This was almost a decade before the publication of **Rachel Carson**'s *Silent Spring.*) He graduated magna cum laude from Princeton in 1955, majoring in government and economics. He attended Harvard Law School, where he was an editor of the *Harvard Law Review,* and upon graduation in 1958 he set up a small legal practice in Hartford, Connecticut.

While still at Harvard, Nader investigated automobile injury cases and came to believe that design flaws, rather than driver error, were responsible for most car accidents. He testified on the subject before state legislative committees and wrote articles for magazines, including a landmark 1963 article in *The Nation.* Nader's consequent book, *Unsafe at Any Speed: The Designed-In Dangers of the American Automobile* (1965) focused on the General Motors Corvair but indicted the whole auto industry for its indifference to safety. Nader testified before the Senate Government Operations Subcommittee's hearings on auto safety. He soon became a target of auto manufacturers, who were hit with lawsuits by victims of auto accidents.

In March 1966 General Motors president James Roche admitted, in response to charges by Nader, that his company—then the most powerful corporation in the world—had hired detectives to harass Nader and to investigate his private life in order to discredit his views on car safety. The controversy generated media attention, made Nader a public figure, and turned Nader's book into a best seller. This put the issue of auto safety on the public agenda, leading to the passage in 1966 of the National Traffic and Motor Vehicle Safety Act, one of the first auto safety laws.

Nader's effort to fund a network of nonprofit organizations dedicated to investigating corporate abuse got a big boost after he sued General Motors for $26 million for invasion of privacy and was awarded $425,000, which he used to hire a small army of young law students and college graduates, dubbed "Nader's Raiders."

During the late 1960s and 1970s, Nader's low-paid but dedicated researchers published a remarkable series of reports on irresponsible corporate practices and lax government regulation. Their early studies focused on mine safety, the dangers of oil and gas pipes, water pollution, nursing home fraud, pesticides in agriculture, and—like **Upton Sinclair**'s work several generations earlier—food safety. The resulting publicity led to the 1967 Wholesome Meat Act.

In 1968 Nader's task force of law students investigated the Federal Trade Commission (FTC), which had been created to protect consumers from shoddy products, fraudulent business practices, and deceptive advertising. They found that the agency was virtually held hostage by the industries it was supposed to monitor and regulate. The report triggered a congressional investigation and a major overhaul of the FTC.

In 1969 he founded the Center for the Study of Responsive Law, which examined incompetence and corruption at the Interstate Commerce Commission, the hazards of air pollution, and the Food and Drug Administration's lax oversight of the food industry. Nader recruited several hundred college students to profile every member of Congress and six key congressional committees. The resulting best-selling book, *Who Runs Congress?*, educated the public about Congress's inner workings. This project turned into Congress Watch, which for years advocated for sunshine laws that opened up congressional committees to public exposure and led to new rules that have weakened the power of entrenched committee chairpersons.

Nader has been a staunch critic of government subsidies for business, including the nuclear power industry, the aerospace industry, agribusiness, the synthetic fuel industry, and dozens of others. "Ours is a system of corporate socialism," Nader explained, "where companies capitalize their profits and socialize their losses. In effect, they tax you for their accidents, bungling, boondoggles and mismanagement, just like a government. We should be able to dis-elect them."

Time magazine called Nader the country's "toughest customer." The *New York Times* said, "What sets Nader apart is that he has moved beyond social criticism to effective political action." As Nader became increasingly well-known and his reform efforts more successful, business groups tried to tarnish his reputation, in part by challenging his findings (which they were rarely able to do successfully). Nader's own frugal lifestyle contributed to his image as a selfless and incorruptible crusader, a Pied Piper of citizen activism.

Nader's reports scrutinized the failures of federal agencies to protect consumers, workers and the environment, and they investigated the ties between big business and politicians. They named names, meticulously documented abuses, and proposed practical solutions. In the early 1970s Nader founded the Capitol Hill News Service, which pioneered investigative reporting about Congress. Nader's Freedom of Information Clearinghouse trained journalists in how to obtain government documents. In this way, Nader was following the tradition of such early muckrakers as **Lincoln Steffens** and Upton Sinclair and such postwar gadflies as **I. F. Stone.**

Nader did more than unmask specific scandals. His organizations became on-going watchdogs of big business and government, a role that the mainstream media, with greater resources, only occasionally played. He also started a network of campus-based organizations called public interest research groups (PIRGS) that have trained thousands of college students in the skills of citizen activism, published hundreds of reports, drawn attention to environmental and energy problems, and lobbied for hundreds of laws in state legislatures. Nader also led efforts to reform university governance, educational testing, legal services, and professional sports.

In 1980 Nader resigned as director of the consumer advocacy organization Public Citizen but continued his activism. Freed from the day-to-day oversight of his many nonprofit organizations, Nader took on wider issues of corporate power, including campaign finance, health insurance, trade, telecommunications, and banking. During the Reagan era and beyond, his challenges to big business became more radical as he indicted the whole corporate system rather than just specific industries. Increasingly, he attacked both major political parties as pawns of corporate America, dependent on contributions from big business and the very rich.

Had Nader retired in the early 1990s, his reputation and legacy as one of American history's most effective progressive leaders would have been secure. But he decided to run for president in 1996 and 2000 on the Green Party ticket and in 2004 as an independent.

Some Nader supporters encouraged him to run in the Democratic Party primaries, where he might have gotten considerable TV and radio airtime in the debates. They argued that although he would not have won the nomination, he could have helped strengthen the progressive wing within the party, as **Jesse Jackson** did in 1988 and 1992.

But because Nader saw both the Democratic and Republican Parties as essentially the same—as tools of corporate America—he chose to run as a third-party candidate. He claimed that his campaigns would help build a permanent progressive third party that could contest for power. But that influential third party never materialized, mostly because America's winner-take-all rules make it virtually impossible for third parties to gain traction, but also because Nader never devoted himself to the hard work of party building.

During his 2000 campaign, Nader argued that there was virtually no difference between Democratic candidate Al Gore and Republican candidate George W. Bush. He won nearly 3 million votes nationwide, close to 3 percent of the votes cast. After the scandalous miscounting of votes in Florida, Bush "officially" beat Gore by 537 votes (out of more than 5.8 million cast), making it the closest presidential election in the state's history. This gave Bush Florida's twenty-five Electoral College votes and, with the help of the US Supreme Court in *Bush v. Gore,* the presidency.

Nader won 97,488 votes in Florida. Polls showed that some of Nader's supporters would have stayed home if he had not been in the race, but most would have voted for Gore. A week before election day in November, when polls showed Gore and Bush neck and neck, many progressives urged Nader to encourage his supporters to vote for Gore in order to avoid a Bush victory. Many believe that had he done that, Gore would have beaten Bush.

Nader was unable to translate his reputation as an incorruptible reformer into support for his electoral campaigns, making him an increasingly marginalized figure in American politics.

Gloria Steinem (1934–)

CREDIT: Associated Press

GLORIA STEINEM became an active feminist in 1969, when the New York State legislature, considering a revision of its antiabortion law, convened a panel of "experts" that was made up of fourteen men and a nun. In protest, a feminist group called Redstockings held a counterhearing that was covered by Steinem, then a thirty-five-year-old journalist. She heard women talk openly about their experiences with abortions. One woman described the humiliation of being interrogated at a hospital by a committee of men, who asked her the details of how she got pregnant and then told her that they would give her an abortion only if she agreed to be sterilized.

"There was something about seeing women tell the truth about their lives in public, and seeing women take seriously something that only happens to women," Steinem recalled in an interview with *New York* magazine in April 1998. "In my experience, things were only taken seriously if they also happened to men. It made some sense of my own experience—I had had an abortion and had never told anyone. It was one of those moments when you ask, 'Why?'"

Since then, Steinem has been asking "Why?"—and encouraging others to do the same—about a wide range of issues, mostly dealing with women's roles in society, helping popularize feminist ideas as a writer and activist. Her frequent articles and appearances on TV and at rallies have made her feminism's most prominent public figure.

Steinem had a peripatetic childhood. Her father, Leo Steinem, an antiques dealer, spent winters selling his wares from a house trailer, usually with his wife,

Ruth, Gloria, and her older sister Suzanne. Gloria did not spend a full year in school until she was twelve. In the summers, her father ran a beach resort in Michigan. Her mother had gone to the University of Toledo and started a career as a journalist, but discrimination against women was so blatant (and so taken for granted) that she initially had to write her articles under a man's name. She eventually gave up her career and fell victim to depression.

After her parents divorced, Steinem, then eleven years old, became her mother's caretaker, cook, and housekeeper, and the family lived in difficult financial circumstances. In her teens, she worked as a salesgirl after school and on Saturdays, and also earned $10 a night dancing in local clubs. Suzanne persuaded their father to take care of their mother so that Gloria could move to Washington, DC, to live with her sister and finish high school.

Gloria's grandmother, Pauline Steinem, was a prominent women's rights activist, president of the Ohio Suffrage Association from 1908 to 1911, a leader of the National Woman Suffrage Association, and the first woman to be elected to the Toledo Board of Education. Pauline died when Gloria was five but left Gloria with vivid "sense memories" of her strength, courage, and intelligence.

At Smith College, Steinem majored in government, graduating magna cum laude. She was awarded a fellowship to study for two years in India, still in its first decade of independence from the British empire. Steinem moved to New York City in 1960 to pursue a career as a journalist. She worked for a new magazine of political satire, *Help!*, edited by Harvey Kurtzman, the creator of *MAD* magazine, and contributed short articles to women's magazines, such as *Glamour* and *Ladies' Home Journal.* After writing several pieces for *Esquire,* a men's magazine, without being credited, she finally published her first bylined article in 1962, about the then-new contraceptive pill. The article, published a year before **Betty Friedan**'s *The Feminine Mystique* appeared in bookstores, examined the fact that women often had to choose between a career and marriage. "The only trouble with sexually liberating women," Steinem ended the article, "is that there aren't enough sexually liberated men to go around."

Steinem made a big splash in 1963 with "I Was a Playboy Bunny," an article for *Show* magazine about working at a Playboy Club. The article exposed the decidedly unglamorous working conditions (including sexual harassment) faced by the club's waitresses—called "bunnies"—who were required to wear a corset, rabbit ears, cotton tails, and high heels.

Steinem made a living as a freelance writer—profiling celebrities and writing about popular culture for major publications—but she could not persuade editors to assign her serious political subjects. Eventually she began writing a column for *New York* magazine, which she helped launch in 1968. She wrote about Vietnamese leader Ho Chi Minh's years living in New York, Nelson Rockefeller's visit to Latin America on behalf of President Richard Nixon, wounded veterans returning from Vietnam, neighborhood battles over childcare centers, antiwar demonstrations, migrant workers, the New York City mayoral race, and the 1968 presidential campaign, among other subjects.

Two articles established her as a feminist spokesperson. The first was a 1969 article in *New York* magazine, "After Black Power, Women's Liberation," which profiled the burgeoning women's movement. The second was "What It Would Be Like if Women Win," a 1970 essay in *Time* magazine that predicted that feminism would liberate men as well as women. If women could have equal power, homosexuals had the right to marry, and women could refuse to have sex, men could no longer be "the only ones to support the family, get drafted, bear the strain of power and responsibility."

During her first several decades as a public figure, Steinem had to endure media stereotypes that called her the "pin-up girl of the intelligentsia" or a "willowy beauty, 34-24-34." And she also had to deal with some feminist leaders who resented her visibility in the media. But more than any other figure, she was the public face of modern feminism, a constant presence on college campuses, at union halls, in business meetings, at protests and rallies, on TV talk shows, and in media profiles. A kind of feminist diplomat, Steinem sought to build bridges between the radical or socialist and liberal wings of the women's movement. She was a bridge between the predominantly white feminist movement and African American feminists and, as a cofounder of the Coalition of Labor Union Women, among the women's movement, unions, and mainstream politicians. She explained feminism to the general public, including men, to change public opinion on such issues as job discrimination, sexual harassment, abortion, gender roles in marriage, and stereotypes about women in the media and religion.

Steinem consistently injected issues of race and class into the women's movement, pushing middle-class white feminists to recruit and embrace the concerns of working-class women and women of color. She never promoted the view that women are essentially different from men.

Feminism, she said in 1971, "is no simple reform. It really is a revolution. Sex and race because they are easy and visible differences have been the primary ways of organizing human beings into superior and inferior groups and into the cheap labor on which this system still depends. We are talking about a society in which there will be no roles other than those chosen or those earned. We are really talking about humanism."

Steinem often used outrageous ideas to shake up her readers and audiences. In 1971 she stunned parents and alums at the Smith College graduation by quoting her friend Flo Kennedy's observation that "there are only a few jobs that actually require a penis or vagina." She once told an audience of CEOs that a fair society would eliminate all inheritance. She has compared marriage to prostitution and said that unpaid housework "is the definition of women's work, which is shit work." In speeches, she frequently drew on the theme of her 1978 essay "If Men Could Menstruate."

Although Steinem wrote hundreds of articles and five books and gave thousands of speeches, her most significant accomplishments involve the creation of two institutions—*Ms.* magazine and the National Women's Political Caucus—that have become major influences in American culture and politics.

Ms. was the first modern feminist periodical with a national readership. Steinem served as editor from 1972 until 1987 and since then has served as a contributing editor. In its early years the magazine was considered so controversial that some conservative groups successfully sought to ban it from public libraries and some bookstores refused to carry it. Its very name was controversial, a new word invented by feminists to give women an option other than being identified by their status as married ("Mrs.") or unmarried ("Miss"). The word "Ms." raised awareness of how language reflected sexist thinking and stereotypes, leading to momentous changes in everyday speech.

From its earliest days *Ms.* challenged conventional wisdom in articles like "How to Write Your Marriage Contract," "Can Women Love Women?" "The Black Family and Feminism," "Welfare Is a Women's Issue," and "Down with Sexist Upbringing." In its first year, *Ms.* made history when it published the names of women, including **Billie Jean King,** who admitted to having had abortions before the US Supreme Court's *Roe v. Wade* decision, when it was still illegal in most of the country. Its 1976 cover story on battered women—which featured a photo of a woman with a bruised faced—was the first major exposé of the problem of domestic violence.

The magazine pioneered investigative stories about overseas sweatshops, sex trafficking, the wage gap, the glass ceiling, women's health (and the medical establishment's sexism), sexual harassment, and date rape. It explained and advocated for the Equal Rights Amendment, rated presidential candidates on women's issues, reported on feminist protests against pornography, exposed the influence of sexist advertising on women's self-images, and acknowledged race and class differences within the feminist movement.

Ms. injected these issues into the political debate at a time when they were considered too radical for the mainstream media to cover—or at least, to cover fairly.

In 1971 Steinem joined a bipartisan group of women—including **Bella Abzug,** Betty Friedan, former congresswoman Shirley Chisholm, and Dorothy Height (president of the National Council of Negro Women)—to launch the National Women's Political Caucus (NWPC). Unlike the National Organization for Women, which utilized diverse strategies, the NWPC's explicit goal was to increase women's participation in politics, particularly as elected officials, to make it easier to pass legislation to eliminate sex discrimination and bring about greater legal, economic, and social equality.

The NWPC has recruited women to run for office, sponsored nuts-and-bolts campaign training workshops for women candidates and campaign staffers, monitored the progress of women in public office and party positions, lobbied for rules guaranteeing women a greater voice in party activities, and endorsed female candidates. In 1985 feminists led by Ellen Malcolm, an heiress to the IBM fortune and a former NWPC press secretary, founded a parallel organization, called EMILY's List, to raise money for prochoice female Democratic candidates. In the 2009–2010 cycle, EMILY's List raised more than $38 million from over 900,000 members.

Both NWPC and EMILY's List, and the feminist movement in general, have contributed to a dramatic increase in the turnout of women voters and the number of women elected to office at every level of government.

Steinem's 1970 prediction—"if Women's Lib wins, perhaps we all do"—is not yet a reality. But a majority of Americans, men as well as women, and particularly those under forty, now take for granted the once-radical tenets of modern feminism.

Bill Moyers
(1934–)

BILL MOYERS and his colleague Marty Koughan were putting the finishing touches on a 1993 *Frontline* documentary investigating pesticides in food when a peculiar thing happened. As he related in his book *Moyers on America—A Journalist and His Times*: "The [chemical] industry somehow purloined a copy of our draft script and mounted a sophisticated and expensive campaign to discredit our broadcast before it aired. A *Washington Post* columnist took a dig at the broadcast on the morning of the day it aired—without even having seen it—and later confessed to me that the dirt had been supplied by a top lobbyist for the chemical industry." And in addition, the American Cancer Society distributed talking points to columnists and other opinion makers that were written by Porter Novelli, a public relations firm that also had several chemical companies as clients.

Later that year, the documentary, *In Our Children's Food*, won an Emmy for investigative journalism. But the experience was one more reminder to Moyers of the corrosive effect of corporate power on the common good.

Following in the footsteps of broadcaster Edward R. Murrow, Moyers used TV as a tool to expose political and corporate wrongdoing and to tell stories about ordinary people working together for justice. He introduced America to great thinkers, activists, and everyday heroes typically ignored by mainstream media. He produced dozens of hard-hitting investigative documentaries uncovering corporate abuse of workers and consumers, the corrupting influence of money in politics, the dangers of the Religious Right, conservatives' attacks on scientists over global warming, and many other topics.

Not content just to diagnose and document corporate and political malpractice, Moyers regularly took his cameras and microphones to cities and towns where unions, community organizations, environmental groups, tenants rights activists, and others were waging grassroots campaigns for change. Moyers gave them a voice. For example, on his April 30, 2010, show, he featured a segment on Iowa Citizens for Community Improvement, a grassroots community organizing group.

Moyers comes by his progressive class consciousness and moral outrage naturally. Neither of his parents went to high school. Dirt-poor, they worked as farmers until they could not make it anymore because of bad weather and the boll weevil.

When Bill was born, the family lived in southeast Oklahoma, where his father was making $2 a day working on highway construction. When he got a job driving a creamery truck, they moved to Marshall, Texas. In a 2008 show Moyers recalled,

> The Great Depression knocked him down and almost out, and he struggled on one pittance paying job after another, until finally, late in life, he had a crack at a union job. His last paycheck was the most he'd ever taken home in a week, $96 and change, and he was proud of it.
>
> I saw then how unions struggled to preserve the middle class, and can make the difference between earning a living wage and being part of the working poor.

Moyers and his older brother went to Sunday school at Central Baptist Church, where, as he recalls, "we didn't have baseball cards; we had Bible cards depicting scenes from the scriptures."

On his sixteenth birthday, Bill went to work for the local paper, the *Marshall News Messenger*. One of his first stories was the "Housewives' Rebellion," about a group of fifteen women who refused to pay Social Security taxes for their maids because they believed that the insurance program was unconstitutional. Their lawyer—former right-wing congressman Martin Dies Jr.—lost the case. Moyers was thrilled when the Associated Press picked up the story.

Only later did it dawn on him that that the newspaper never covered stories about Marshall's African Americans, who made up half the town's population. "For all practical purposes the staff of the paper pretended half of Marshall didn't exist," he wrote.

Moyers left Marshall in 1954 to attend North Texas State College (now University of North Texas). He spent a summer interning on then-senator **Lyndon B. Johnson**'s reelection campaign. Impressed with the young Moyers, LBJ suggested that he transfer to the University of Texas, Austin. There he majored in journalism and the liberal arts while working full-time as assistant news editor for KTBC-TV for $100 a week. Graduating in 1956, he studied theology at the University of Edinburgh in Scotland and at Southwestern Baptist Theological Seminary, where as the weekend pastor of two small rural churches he inflicted "amateurish wisdom on very patient and loving congregations of mostly farmers and their spouses," as he told NPR's Terry Gross in a 1996 interview. In 1959, he moved to Washington, DC, to work for Johnson. He helped run LBJ's 1960 vice presidential campaign as John F. Kennedy's running mate.

Moyers was a founding organizer of the Peace Corps in 1961 and was appointed its deputy director by President Kennedy. After Kennedy was assassinated, LBJ brought Moyers to the White House as his assistant for domestic policy with responsibility for shepherding the task forces that led to LBJ's Great Society program.

Moyers played a key role in helping LBJ pass the Civil Rights Act of 1964 and the Voting Rights Act of 1965. He was with LBJ when the president met with **Martin Luther King Jr.** at the White House and tried to convince the civil rights leader to call off further protests, arguing that they would harden white resistance and make it impossible for him to win over southern senators and representatives, with whom Johnson had often successfully negotiated as Senate majority leader. King disagreed, reminding LBJ of the history of murders, lynchings, and humiliation, insisting that the protests were necessary to draw attention to the need for civil rights legislation. As Moyer recalled: "LBJ listened, as intently as I ever saw him listen. He listened, and then he put his hand on Martin Luther King's shoulder, and said, in effect: 'OK. You go out there Dr. King and keep doing what you're doing, and make it possible for me to do the right thing.'"

By 1966 Moyers had reluctantly agreed to be the president's press secretary, but he found it increasingly difficult to defend LBJ's escalation of the war in Vietnam. "The things I really cared about—poverty, the Great Society, civil rights— were all being drained away by the war," he recalled. "The line that keeps running through my mind is the line I never spoke: 'I can't speak for a war that I believe is immoral.'"

Moyers resigned from the White House in 1967 and became the publisher of *Newsday,* a daily newspaper that primarily served New York's Long Island suburbs. "When I left the White House I had to learn that what matters in journalism is not how close you are to power, but how close you are to the truth," he said. With Moyers at the helm, *Newsday* expanded its news agenda, recruited a wide range of writers, and won many major journalism awards.

But Harry Guggenheim, *Newsday*'s conservative owner, disapproved of the paper's liberal innovations under Moyers, particularly what he called its "left-wing" coverage of the antiwar movement. In 1968 Guggenheim signed an editorial supporting Richard Nixon's presidential candidacy, while Moyers published his support of Hubert Humphrey.

Moyers resigned in 1970 and took a 13,000-mile bus trip around the country, armed with a notepad and tape recorder, interviewing people for his best-selling book *Listening to America: A Traveler Rediscovers His Country.* That year, he began his long relationship with public television, interrupted by a decade (1976–1986) at CBS News.

In order to maintain his journalistic independence, Moyers formed his own production company and raised all the funds for his many productions. At PBS, Moyers, a master of the long interview, had the freedom to craft his own programs, including *Now with Bill Moyers, Moyers on America,* and *Bill Moyers Journal.* He interviewed important thinkers and activists rarely seen on television, including community organizers like Ernesto Cortés, historians like **Howard Zinn,** scientists like René Dubos, philosophers like Joseph Campbell, and theologians like Karen Armstrong. He produced investigative documentaries on various topics, including the cost of the Iraq and Afghanistan wars on local communities, campaign finance, inadequate funding for public schools, the rise of the Religious Right, global warming, the dumping of hazardous waste, and, in *Trade Secrets,* the chemical industry's poisoning of American workers and communities. Moyers's 2007 documentary *Buying the War* reported how most of the press corps became complicit with the Bush administration's invasion of Iraq. "If the watchdog doesn't bark," Moyers said about the show, "how do you know there's a burglar in the basement? And the press is supposed to be a watchdog."

In a June 2008 show about America's "new Gilded Age," Moyers documented the fact that the nation's widening economic divide was making it harder and harder for working families to make ends meet. During the broadcast, Moyers said, "Can we put aside that old canard spouted by Wall Street apologists every time someone calls for greater equity between working people and the rich? Truth is, there's been a class war waged in America for thirty years now from the top down, and the rich have won."

The Nation called Moyers "the most radical presence on broadcast and cable television" but also pointed out that, to generate lively debate, he consistently invited conservative thinkers onto his show, including Richard Viguerie, Cal Thomas, and Ron Paul. Moyers often used his power as a broadcast journalist to uncover the unseemly entanglement of big business and politicians. "If a baseball player stepping up to home plate were to lean over and hand the umpire a wad of bills before the pitch, we would know what that was: a bribe. But when the tobacco industry stuffs $13 million in the pockets of the merry looters in Congress and gets protection in return, we call that a campaign contribution."

In a broadcast about the concentration of media ownership, he pointed to "the paradox of Rush Limbaugh, ensconced in a Palm Beach mansion massaging the resentments across the country of white-knuckled wage earners, who are barely making ends meet in no small part because of the corporate and ideological forces for whom Rush has been a hero."

Following a brief retirement, Moyers returned to weekly television with a new series, *Moyers & Company,* in 2012. Moyers has spent most of his broadcast career on public television, whose audience is considerably smaller than that of the major networks. But Moyers's influence—through his books, magazine articles, and speeches and because of the ripple effects of his calls for conscience—has been great nonetheless. He has received over thirty-five Emmy Awards and many other awards for his contributions to journalistic integrity and investigative reporting.

A gifted storyteller, Moyers's TV shows, speeches, and magazine articles have roared with a combination of outrage and decency, exposing abuse and celebrating the country's history of activism.

Bob Moses (1935–)

Moses, left, speaks to two men during a voter registration project in Greenwood, Mississippi, 1963.
CREDIT: Photo by Claude Sitton/New York Times Co./Getty Images
©2004 Getty Images

IN 1960 Bob Moses attended his first civil rights rally, in Newport News, Virginia. The fiery Rev. Wyatt Walker had just delivered a rousing speech extolling the virtues of **Martin Luther King Jr.** as the undisputed leader of the civil rights movement. Moses, then twenty-five, made his way to the front of the crowd. As Taylor Branch reports in *Parting the Waters,* Moses asked Walker, "Why do you keep saying one leader? Don't you think we need *a lot* of leaders?" Walker, somewhat mystified, ignored the earnest young man.

Within a year, Moses was working for the Student Nonviolent Coordinating Committee (SNCC) in Mississippi, devoting himself to bottom-up leadership, empowering ordinary people, challenging the top-down style practiced by King and others who emerged from the black church tradition. Moses saw himself as a catalyst, not a leader. Many students and Mississippi residents, inspired by Moses's example, joined SNCC's voter registration campaign.

Moses grew up in a Harlem housing project. His father, a post office worker, instilled in his son a belief in the basic dignity of "the common person." The gifted Moses passed a citywide examination to gain admission to Stuyvesant High School, a prestigious public school in Manhattan. In 1952 he earned a scholarship to Hamilton College in upstate New York, where he was one of three black students. There he was attracted to the writings of French philosopher Albert Camus, who stressed that individuals should refuse to be victims of circumstance and instead endeavor to act as agents of change. After his junior and senior years,

Moses worked at summer camps in Europe and Japan sponsored by the pacifist group American Friends Service Committee.

Moses went to Harvard for graduate school in philosophy. He earned his master's degree in 1957 but dropped out of the Ph.D. program after his mother died and his father suffered a nervous breakdown. He moved back to New York and found a job teaching math at the Horace Mann School, an elite private institution.

In 1959 he visited organizer **Bayard Rustin** in his New York office, hoping to find an outlet for his idealism. Rustin put Moses to work as a volunteer. While working with Rustin, Moses saw the newspaper stories about the student sit-ins in Greensboro, North Carolina, in February 1960. He was impressed by the defiant looks on the faces of the students, who appeared fearless and unflinching. "They were kids my age," he later said, "and I knew this had something to do with my own life."

Moses recalled that after participating in his first demonstration at Newport News, he had "a feeling of release" after a lifetime of accommodating himself to constant racial slights. "My whole reaction through life to such humiliation was to avoid it," Moses recalled, "keep it down, hold it in, play it cool."

Moses was keen to go to the South, so Rustin introduced him to **Ella Baker,** who was running the headquarters in Atlanta, Georgia, of the Southern Christian Leadership Conference (SCLC). In 1960 Moses moved to Atlanta, found a room at the YMCA, and reported to the SCLC office. Baker had allowed the SNCC volunteers to use the SCLC office, and Moses found the SNCC students more interesting than the SCLC ministers. Baker taught Moses about organizing, sharing her belief in the power of ordinary black people to change their lives if they could gain the self-confidence to do so.

Following the sit-ins, some SNCC leaders wanted to continue the direct action protest, including the Freedom Rides. But Baker and others believed that the next stage should be voter registration. To outsiders, this may have seemed a tamer approach, but in fact it was fraught with danger.

Mississippi's constitution included restrictions on voter registration, by measures such as literacy tests and poll taxes. The tests were administered by white voter registrars, who asked black would-be voters arbitrary and arcane questions, so that even well-educated blacks were typically refused registration on literacy grounds. Most blacks did not bother to try to register. In at least a dozen Mississippi counties, not a single black citizen was registered to vote.

If blacks, who represented a majority of adults in many Mississippi counties, had voted in large numbers, they would have controlled the schools, the police, the courts, and the other levers of government. Most whites would have done almost anything—inside and outside the law—to make sure that did not happen. Over the next four years, the quiet, philosophical Moses would be shot at, attacked, imprisoned, and beaten as he led the voter registration fight. His calm and courage inspired others to take a stand.

Moses used McComb, Mississippi, a town of 13,000 people near the Louisiana border, as his base, establishing an SNCC office in the black Masonic Hall. Word soon spread about SNCC's voter registration classes, and residents of nearby counties began asking for similar workshops.

On August 15, 1961, Moses accompanied three prospective voters to the Amite County Courthouse in Liberty, Mississippi, and stood by as they filled out forms. Driving back to McComb, he was arrested by police on a bogus charge. He was convicted, was given a ninety-day suspended sentence, and spent two days in jail. Moses's calls to the US Justice Department to protest this harassment went unanswered. On August 22, after bringing two other blacks to the Liberty courthouse, Moses was attacked with a knife handle by Billy Jack Caston, a cousin of the local sheriff, and was wounded badly enough to need nine stitches. Moses refused to back down and continued to the courthouse, covered in blood, where he was promptly arrested and jailed. Moses then did something almost unheard of: he pressed charges against Caston. But an all-white jury acquitted him.

Other SNCC staffers and volunteers faced similar violence in retaliation for their voter registration efforts. Local high school students responded by stepping up their resistance. After participating in SNCC's workshops on nonviolence, they began sitting in at the Woolworth's lunch counter, tried to register to vote, marched, and got arrested. In October, after the high school principal refused to readmit several students involved in the protest, more than 100 of them organized a prayer vigil in front of the city hall. As police began arresting the high-schoolers and as white thugs began attacking them, Moses and two other SNCC staffers, Bob Zellner and Charles McDew, tried to protect the students. Police arrested the three SNCC workers and sentenced them to four months in jail.

SNCC staff and volunteers found it increasingly difficult to persuade rural Mississippians to register to vote. Blacks in Mississippi knew that their homes could be burned and that they could be shot and killed by white segregationists while local law enforcement officials—some also belonging to the Ku Klux Klan or the White Citizens' Councils—sided with the vigilantes. Between 1961 and 1963, 70,000 Mississippi blacks tried to register. Only 4,700—5 percent of the state's voting-age blacks—succeeded. In December 1962 Moses told the Voter Education Project, "We are powerless to register people in significant numbers anywhere in the state."

John F. Kennedy's administration told SNCC that it liked its voter registration efforts, but when SNCC staffers called the US Justice Department appealing for protection or for prosecution of white vigilantes and local police, who assaulted and intimidated civil rights workers, it was to no avail. FBI agents in Mississippi looked the other way when local cops abused civil rights workers.

During the first half of 1963, it was clear that SNCC's voter registration campaign had stalled. In the fall of 1963 and again in the summer of 1964, SNCC expanded its paid staff and recruited white college students from prestigious universities to help register black voters. Their primary task was organizing the Mississippi Freedom Democratic Party (MFDP). In 1963 they held mock elections that gave blacks a chance to vote for an integrated slate of candidates.

The plan was significantly expanded the next summer. Whites retaliated with vicious violence. In June 1964 three SNCC volunteers were murdered in Neshoba County, Mississippi, just as hundreds of new recruits were being trained at a college in Ohio. On the last night of training, Moses spoke to the volunteers and urged anyone who might be uncertain to go home. Only a handful did. More than 1,000 Freedom Summer volunteers mobilized blacks to participate in "freedom schools" (where they discussed black history and current issues and learned about the Mississippi Constitution so they could pass the literacy test) and to vote in order to send an integrated delegation to the Democratic Party convention in Atlantic City, New Jersey. The murders and the presence of privileged white college students drew significant media attention to SNCC's efforts. But President **Lyndon B. Johnson,** worried about alienating southern whites in the November 1964 presidential election, refused to seat the MFDP delegates instead of the segregated delegation. Johnson offered the MFDP delegation only token seats in the delegation, which the MFDP rejected. (See the profile of **Fannie Lou Hamer.**)

At the end of 1964, Moses resigned from SNCC. He left Mississippi uncertain whether it, or the broader civil rights movement, had made much of a dent in the state's white political power structure.

It had. In 1965, the year Congress passed the Voting Rights Act, only 6.7 percent of Mississippi blacks were registered to vote. But four years later the number had jumped to 66.5 percent. The act, which outlawed literacy tests and other obstacles to voting, was an important tool for civil rights activists to challenge other barriers to black political participation, such as gerrymandering of city council, state legislature, and congressional districts in order to dilute black voting strength. By 2000, Mississippi had 897 black elected officials in local and state offices, plus Congress—the largest number of any state in the country.

In 1966 Moses moved to Canada to avoid the draft during the Vietnam War. In 1969 he moved to Tanzania, where he taught math. After President Jimmy Carter declared amnesty for draft resisters in 1976, Moses returned to the United States.

He picked up where he had left off at Harvard, completing his Ph.D. Then he joined his organizing work with his math expertise. When he discovered that his daughter's middle school in Cambridge, Massachusetts, did not offer algebra, he became a volunteer math teacher at her school and began to develop techniques for teaching the subject to low-income students.

In 1982 he was awarded a MacArthur Fellowship (the so-called Genius award), which he used to establish the Algebra Project. The project focuses on bringing high-quality public education to students who live in poor areas throughout the nation.

CREDIT: Associated Press/George Brich

Tom Hayden
(1939–)

INSPIRED BY Jack Kerouac's *On the Road*, Tom Hayden, the twenty-year-old editor of the *Michigan Daily* (the University of Michigan's student newspaper), took a cross-country hitchhiking trip during the summer of 1960.

During his trip, Hayden visited the San Francisco area, where he met activists who were organizing pickets in front of Woolworth's and Kresge five-and-dime stores to support the southern sit-ins. Some activists took Hayden to Delano, California, a rural agricultural area, where he encountered the near-slavery under which Mexican farmworkers toiled. He also interviewed Rev. **Martin Luther King Jr.,** who was walking a picket line outside the 1960 Democratic convention in Los Angeles to demand that the party endorse a strong civil rights platform.

"There I was," Hayden recalled years later, "with pencil in hand, trying to conduct an objective interview with Martin Luther King, whose whole implicit message was: 'Stop writing, start acting.' That was a compelling moment." King gently told Hayden, "Ultimately, you have to take a stand with your life." When Hayden returned to Ann Arbor that fall, he committed himself to the life of an activist.

No single figure embodies the spirit of that generation more than Tom Hayden. He played a part in almost every aspect of the decade's major battles for justice. He remained an activist during the 1970s, 1980s, and 1990s and into the 21st century, working to build a progressive movement based on values of social justice and grassroots democracy.

Named for St. Thomas Aquinas, Hayden went to Catholic schools in Royal Oak, Michigan, an all-white middle-class Detroit suburb. By the time he reached high school, Hayden was already an iconoclast. The editor of his school paper, Hayden was banned from attending his own graduation and kicked out of the National Honor Society for writing an incendiary editorial.

In the spring of 1960, thirty-two-year-old **Michael Harrington,** by then a veteran socialist activist, met Hayden in Ann Arbor at a student conference about civil rights. Harrington and Hayden had much in common—they were both midwestern middle-class Irish Catholics, with literary and journalistic bents—but Hayden resisted Harrington's efforts to recruit him to the Socialist Party's youth group, thinking that joining a group labeled "socialist" would immediately marginalize him, particularly at a time when the Red Scare was still a strong force in American politics. Hayden helped organize VOICE, a left-liberal campus political party that called for a greater "student voice in the decisions affecting our lives." Ann Arbor activists Al Haber and Bob Ross recruited Hayden to join Students for a Democratic Society (SDS), which began in 1960 as a vehicle to enlist white students on northern campuses to support the southern civil rights movement.

Along with the Student Nonviolent Coordinating Committee (SNCC), SDS became the decade's key catalyst for recruiting and radicalizing some of the baby-boom generation's most effective activists.

In late 1960 Hayden agreed to be SDS's first field secretary—or organizer. He worked on voter registration campaigns, joined protest marches in Mississippi, and participated in the Freedom Rides. In the South, he was inspired by the courage of SNCC volunteers (one of whom, Sandra Cason, he married), especially **Bob Moses.** He filed stories about these events for the *Michigan Daily*, *Progressive* magazine, and even *Mademoiselle.*

Hayden began writing the SDS manifesto—what would become the Port Huron Statement—while sitting in a jail in Albany, Georgia. (He had been arrested for trying to integrate the waiting room in the local train station.) His draft was circulated to SDS supporters around the country. A group of members convened at a union retreat center in Port Huron, Michigan, to debate the document and plot the organization's—and their generation's—future. The document reflected the early SDSers' hope for a new beginning in American political life, inspired by the nonviolent direct action of the southern civil rights movement and the growing protests against the nuclear arms race.

The Port Huron Statement begins: "We are people of this generation, bred in at least modest comfort, housed now in universities, looking uncomfortably to the world we inherit."

SDS believed that young people could play a role in changing America. It asserted a vision of society rooted in the concept of participatory democracy. Under Hayden's leadership, SDS played a significant part in four major issues:

- Lessening restrictions to free speech and political activism on college campuses
- Supporting the southern civil rights movement
- Mobilizing student opposition to the war in Vietnam
- Setting up community organizing projects to help mobilize the poor.

Hayden moved to New Jersey in 1964 to build the Newark Community Union. For over three years, Hayden and his colleagues knocked on doors in Newark's black ghetto, recruiting jobless and low-wage residents into the community group, which aimed to help them gain a voice over such problems as slum housing, police brutality, inadequate schools, and other issues. But progress was slow, and Hayden, like the poor residents trapped in Newark's ghetto, began to lose patience as corrupt local white politicians resisted change and as funding for **Lyndon B. Johnson**'s War on Poverty gave way to funding for the Vietnam War. In August 1967 Newark's ghetto exploded in riots, one of dozens of urban uprisings (including one in Detroit) during that "long hot summer." Hayden wrote a long analysis of the roots of the riot in his book *Rebellion in Newark*.

While living in Newark, Hayden devoted careful study to the history and culture of Vietnam and to US foreign policy in Southeast Asia. In 1965 he joined pacifist historian Staughton Lynd and Communist Party official Herbert Aptheker on a fact-finding trip to North Vietnam, a journey that violated US State Department rules and was attacked in the media. He and Lynd wrote a book, *The Other Side,* about their journey. In 1967 he returned to North Vietnam with other antiwar activists to investigate the human impact of US bombing. While they were there, the North Vietnamese government asked them to bring home several American prisoners of war. Because the United States did not recognize the Hanoi government, the Vietnamese wanted to release them to Americans involved in the peace movement. The release was viewed as both an act of humanitarianism and a propaganda gesture.

The optimism of the 1962 Port Huron Statement reflected the views of the early leaders of SDS, who were, like Hayden, born in the late 1930s and early 1940s. By the middle and late 1960s, many of these early SDSers, as well as many of the somewhat younger baby-boom generation of radicals, had lost faith in liberalism. The Kennedy administration's reluctance to reign in the vigilantes and law enforcement officials who perpetrated or condoned violence against civil rights activists, the conflict over seating the integrated Mississippi Freedom Democratic Party at the 1964 Democratic convention, the bloody escalation of the Vietnam War, America's opposition to anticolonial movements in the Third World, and the urban riots of the decade led some activists to embrace a strident attitude. They considered moderates and liberals as obstacles to progress, viewing them with almost the same disdain they held for segregationists, conservatives, and the military-industrial complex.

By 1967, America's growing military presence in Vietnam began to change public opinion and to increase opposition to the war. Many liberals and religious groups protested, but under LBJ the war and the death toll continued. To many frustrated and impatient antiwar activists, the United States felt like a war machine, not a democracy.

Hayden's antiwar activities embodied a distinctive combination of political pragmatism and moral outrage. He worked with SDS and other groups to organize protest rallies. He wrote for a variety of publications, attacking US policy and describing Vietnamese history and culture. In April 1968 he helped SDSers at Columbia University who occupied several buildings and shut down the university to protest both its no-longer-secret affiliation with research projects funded by the Defense Department and its plans to expand its campus into nearby Harlem.

By the late 1960s, many radicals had begun to view the war as an inevitable outcome of America's empire building, lust for profits, and racism toward the world's populations of color. Frustrated, some called for more-militant tactics, including burning draft cards (a federal crime). Hayden often shared this perspective, but he not only opposed violence and bombings, he also still had faith in the potential of electoral politics, particularly the promise of Robert Kennedy's 1968 antiwar and antipoverty campaign.

Kennedy's assassination that June was traumatic for the country and for Hayden. At Kennedy's funeral in St. Patrick's Cathedral in New York City, he cried over the tragic loss of the one politician who had the potential to unite the antiwar and antipoverty movements. That summer, Hayden joined other activists in planning protests at the Democratic convention, scheduled for late August in Chicago.

For eight days during the convention, protesters and the Chicago Police Department battled for control of the streets, while the Democrats nominated Vice President Hubert H. Humphrey as their standard-bearer. An official investigation would later describe the violence as "police riots." Despite this finding, the administration of newly elected Richard Nixon indicted Hayden and seven others for "conspiracy" to riot. The trial made headlines for months, as both sides used theatrics to turn the court proceedings into a political battleground. Hayden privately opposed some of the antics of his codefendants, particularly Jerry Rubin and Abbie Hoffman. Hayden nevertheless gained a reputation as a radical who condoned street violence. Hayden and five of the others were convicted in 1969 but were acquitted on appeal in 1973.

In the early 1970s Hayden began to rethink the antiwar movement's strategy. In 1972 he and other peace activists formed the Indochina Peace Campaign (IPC). They brought speakers, slide shows, and music to churches, campuses, and venues near military bases (to attract disillusioned soldiers) in order to educate the public about the war and to urge them to vote for antiwar candidates. During this period, Hayden met and married actress Jane Fonda, who had become a high-profile opponent of the war. IPC succeeded in pushing Congress to reduce war appropriations.

In 1971 Hayden moved to Santa Monica, California. He decided to challenge Senator John Tunney, a moderate Democrat who had supported the Vietnam War and who was running for reelection, in the 1976 Democratic primary. With Fonda's seed money, he knitted together a feisty statewide campaign, but he found himself attacked by some leftists for working within the system. The media also assailed Hayden for what they considered his radical views. Although no major daily newspaper endorsed him, Hayden shocked political pundits by garnering about 40 percent of the vote.

After the election, Hayden and others founded the Campaign for Economic Democracy (CED). In its decade-long existence, CED won local and statewide victories on rent control and solar energy, helped shut down a nuclear power plant through a referendum (the first successful antinuclear referendum), led a successful campaign to require labels on cancer-causing products, and won a statewide ballot campaign to triple tobacco taxes to fund public health and antitobacco initiatives. It also helped elect more than a dozen progressive candidates to office.

One of those candidates was Hayden, who was elected to the California State Assembly in 1982 and to the state Senate ten years later. Overall, he served eighteen years in the state legislature. The *Sacramento Bee* described Hayden as "the conscience of the Senate." While serving in the legislature, he worked closely with progressive groups to sponsor and enact legislation on a variety of environmental, educational, public safety, and human rights issues. Concerned about the upsurge of gang violence between African Americans and Latino immigrants in Los Angeles, he played a key role in negotiating a gang war truce and wrote a book about the experience, *Street Wars*, in 2005.

Ironically, the state legislature was Hayden's longest-lasting political home. Although he built a number of organizations over the years, none lasted long enough to sustain his career as an activist. Since leaving public office, he has earned his living by writing, speaking, organizing, and teaching. He has written eyewitness accounts of the global justice movements around the world, including moving firsthand accounts of the 1999 protests against the World Trade Organization (the "Battle in Seattle"). He played an important role in organizing opposition to the war in Iraq and penned a book on the subject, *Ending the War in Iraq.*

In 2008 Hayden helped launch Progressives for Obama, investing in the young Illinois senator some of the same hopes he had had for Robert Kennedy. After Barack Obama took office, Hayden supported his progressive initiatives but criticized what he considered the new president's weak policies to bolster the economy and his reluctance to quickly withdraw troops from Iraq and Afghanistan. Soon after the 2008 election, Hayden committed most of his energy to organizing opposition to the war in Afghanistan. Once again, Hayden understood the necessity of linking outsiders and insiders to bring about needed change. "No sooner had a social movement elected [Obama] than it was time for a new social movement to bring about a new New Deal," Hayden wrote. "Lest his domestic initiatives sink in the quagmires of Iraq, Afghanistan, and Pakistan, a new peace movement must rise as well."

John Lewis (1940–)

John Lewis, third from left, links hands with others during a march in protest of a scheduled speech by the pro-segregationist Alabama governor, George Wallace, Cambridge, Maryland, May 1964.
CREDIT: Photo by Francis Miller/Time & Life Pictures/ Getty Images © Time Life Pictures

ONLY A handful of the 250,000 people at the March on Washington in August 1963 knew anything about the drama taking place behind the Lincoln Memorial. Under **A. Philip Randolph**'s leadership, the march had brought together the major civil rights organizations. A representative of each group would address the huge crowd. **Bayard Rustin,** who was in charge of the event's logistics, required all speakers, even **Martin Luther King Jr.,** to hand in the texts of their speeches the night before. The speech submitted by the twenty-three-year-old chairman of the Student Nonviolent Coordinating Committee (SNCC), John Lewis, criticized President John F. Kennedy for moving too slowly on civil rights legislation. Rustin, Randolph, and others considered Lewis's text inflammatory, threatening the unity they had so carefully built for the event. It included these lines:

> The revolution is a serious one. Mr. Kennedy is trying to take the revolution out of the street and put in the courts. Listen, Mr. Kennedy. Listen, Mr. Congressman. Listen, fellow citizens. The black masses are on the march for jobs and freedom, and we must say to the politicians that there won't be a "cooling-off" period. We won't stop now. The time will come when we will not confine our marching to Washington. We will march through the South, through the Heart of Dixie, the way Sherman did. We shall pursue our own "scorched earth" policy and burn Jim Crow to the ground—nonviolently.

The evening before the march, Patrick O'Boyle—the archbishop of Washington, who was scheduled to give the rally's invocation—saw Lewis's speech. A staunch Kennedy supporter, he alerted the White House and told Rustin that he would pull out of the event if Lewis was allowed to give those remarks.

The next day, as the marchers assembled in front of the Lincoln Memorial, the controversy over Lewis's speech continued behind the stage. An intense argument, with raised voices and fingers shaking in each other's faces, broke out between Lewis and Roy Wilkins, the director of the National Association for the Advancement of Colored People. Rustin persuaded O'Boyle to start the program with his invocation while an ad hoc committee battled with Lewis over the language of his speech. Finally Randolph, the civil rights movement's beloved elder statesman, appealed to Lewis. "I've waited all my life for this opportunity," he said. "Please don't ruin it, John. We've come this far together. Let us stay together."

Lewis toned down the speech. His closing paragraphs no longer had the incendiary reference to William Tecumseh Sherman's march, but the address remained a powerful indictment of politicians' failure to deal boldly with discrimination. Lewis's skepticism toward the Kennedy administration was understandable. Lewis had risked his life as a Freedom Rider, but the White House had been reluctant to use federal troops to protect the protesters. Kennedy had referred to the SNCC activists as "sons of bitches" who "had an investment in violence." His brother, Attorney General Robert Kennedy, told a reporter that the violence surrounding the Freedom Rides provided "good propaganda for America's enemies."

Lewis was lucky to survive the Freedom Rides without permanent injury. Indeed, that Lewis was speaking at the March on Washington at all reflected a remarkable personal transformation and act of self-discipline. Born into a large family of sharecroppers in Alabama, Lewis was shy and suffered from a speech impediment. At fifteen he heard King's speeches and sermons on the family radio during the Montgomery, Alabama, bus boycott and decided to become a minister. He practiced preaching to chickens in his parents' barnyard and then preached at local Baptist churches.

At seventeen, after becoming the first member of his family to graduate from high school, he attended the American Baptist Theological Seminary in Nashville, Tennessee, which allowed students to work in lieu of tuition. He worked as a janitor and simultaneously attended the all-black Fisk University, graduating with degrees from both the seminary and the university.

Rev. Kelly Miller Smith, a local black minister and activist, introduced Lewis to **James Lawson,** a divinity student at nearby Vanderbilt University, who was conducting workshops on nonviolent social action through the Fellowship of Reconciliation. Lawson prepared his students intellectually, psychologically, and spiritually, assigning the works of Mohandas Gandhi, Henry David Thoreau, and theologian Reinhold Niebuhr. The students debated whether they could learn to forgive, even love, white segregationists who might beat them. They wondered if they had the self-discipline not to strike back, especially if they were called "nigger" or other epithets while being hit.

Lewis spent a weekend at a Highlander Folk School retreat, where he met **Myles Horton,** Septima Clark, and other activists who helped him visualize what could happen if thousands of poor working people—folks like Lewis's parents— were galvanized into direct action. "I left Highlander on fire," Lewis recalled. The fire got even hotter in the summer of 1959, when Lewis attended a workshop at Spelman College in Atlanta, Georgia, and heard veteran organizers Bayard Rustin, **Ella Baker,** Glenn Smiley, and Lawson discuss what it would take to dismantle Jim Crow.

When Lewis returned to college in the fall, the number of students attending Lawson's workshops had grown and included some white students from Vanderbilt. As Lewis wrote in his memoir, *Walking with the Wind,* "We were itching to get started." They planned to launch a full-scale nonviolent protest campaign targeting the major downtown department stores that refused to serve black people. But to their surprise, on February 1, 1960, four students from the Agricultural and Technical College in Greensboro, North Carolina, beat them to it, organizing a sit-in at the local Woolworth's. The news generated excitement on Nashville's campuses. Hundreds of students emulated their Greensboro counterparts and were threatened with arrest. Lewis wrote up a list of dos and don'ts to help out the students:

Do Not: Strike back nor curse if abused. Laugh out. Hold conversations with a floor walker. Leave your seat until your leader has given you permission to do so. Block entrances to stores outside nor the aisles inside.

Do: Show yourself friendly and courteous at all times. Sit straight: always face the counter. Report all serious incidents to your leader. Refer information seekers to your leader in a polite manner. Remember the teachings of Jesus Christ, Mahatma Gandhi and Martin Luther King.

Lewis was arrested at Woolworth's for the first of many times in his life. So too were hundreds of other protestors at other stores. Day after day, Lewis and the other students sat silently at lunch counters where they were harassed, spit upon, beaten, and finally arrested and held in jail, but the students insisted that they continue. The protests continued, with Lewis playing a key leadership role, and eventually Nashville's mayor and business leaders agreed to desegregate the downtown stores.

Lewis's physical and spiritual courage would be tested many times over the next few years. Each time, he revealed a remarkable, calm discipline, galvanizing others to follow his lead. The success of the sit-in movement led Lewis and his counterparts across the South to start SNCC in April 1960.

In May 1961, the twenty-one-year-old Lewis participated in Freedom Rides organized by the Congress of Racial Equality to protest the segregation of interstate bus travel and terminals. Lewis was on the first Freedom Ride, which left

Washington, DC, on March 4 destined for New Orleans, Louisiana. When they reached Rock Hill, South Carolina, and got off the bus, Lewis tried to enter a whites-only waiting room. Two white men attacked him, injuring his face and kicking him in the ribs.

Nevertheless, only two weeks later, Lewis was one of twenty-two Freedom Riders—eighteen blacks, four whites—on another Freedom Ride bus from Nashville to Montgomery, accompanied by a protective escort of state highway patrol cars. As they reached the Montgomery city limits, the state highway patrol cars turned away, but no Montgomery police appeared to replace them. When the bus arrived at the Greyhound terminal, several reporters approached Lewis to interview him. But they were quickly overwhelmed by a mob of angry whites carrying baseball bats, bricks, chains, wooden boards, tire irons, and pipes, screaming "git them niggers." As Lewis wrote in his memoir: "I felt a thud against my head. I could feel my knees collapse and then nothing. Everything turned white for an instant, then black. I was unconscious on that asphalt. I learned later that someone had swung a wooden Coca-Cola crate against my skull. There was a lot I didn't learn about until later."

When he regained consciousness, he was bleeding badly from the back of his head and his coat, shirt, and tie were covered with blood. Jim Zwerg, a white Freedom Rider, was in much worse shape. Lewis asked a police officer to help him get an ambulance, but the cop simply said, "He's free to go."

Two days later, the battered Lewis was back on another Freedom Ride bus, heading to Jackson, Mississippi, but this time with National Guard escorts. When they arrived at the terminal, a police officer pointed them toward the "colored" bathroom, but Lewis and the others headed toward the "white" men's room and were promptly arrested. Twenty-seven Freedom Riders were jailed. Lewis and others were later moved to the notorious Parchman Penitentiary state prison, which they had to endure for over three weeks.

Over the next few years, Lewis worked with SNCC to register voters, including in the Freedom Summer campaign in Mississippi. In 1965 he led 600 protesters on the first march from Selma, Alabama, to Montgomery. Police attacked the marchers, and Lewis was beaten so severely that his skull was fractured. Before he could be taken to the hospital, he appeared before the television cameras calling on President **Lyndon B. Johnson** to intervene in Alabama. The day, March 7, 1965, came to be known as "Bloody Sunday."

The Freedom Rides forced the federal government to implement laws and court rulings desegregating interstate travel. The voter registration drives, as well as public outrage against the violence directed at nonviolent protesters, helped secure passage of the Voting Rights Act.

The slow pace of change and the unrelenting attacks by southern whites led some SNCC activists to question the nonviolent and integrationist tenets preached by King, Lawson, Lewis, and others. Friction grew between various camps within

SNCC. Lewis lost his post as SNCC chair to the more militant Stokely Carmichael.

For the next seven years, Lewis directed the Voter Education Project (VEP), which registered and educated about 4 million black voters. President Jimmy Carter then appointed Lewis director of ACTION, the federal agency that oversaw domestic volunteer programs.

In 1981 Lewis was elected to the Atlanta City Council. Five years later, he was elected to Congress from an Atlanta district, and he has been reelected every two years since. After becoming an "insider," Lewis continued to advocate for progressive causes regarding poverty, civil rights, and foreign affairs. In 2009 he was one of several members of Congress arrested outside the embassy of Sudan, where they had gathered to draw attention to the genocide in Darfur. He was an early opponent of the US invasion of Iraq. In 2002 he sponsored the Peace Tax Fund bill, a conscientious objection to military taxation introduced yearly since 1972. In 2011 President Barack Obama awarded Lewis the Presidential Medal of Freedom.

In 1989 Lewis returned to Montgomery to help dedicate a civil rights memorial. An elderly white man came up to him and said, "I remember you from the Freedom Rides." Lewis took a moment to recall the man's face. Then he recognized Floyd Mann, who had been Alabama's safety commissioner. A committed segregationist, tough on law and order, Mann had been assured by Montgomery's police chief that no violence would occur. Seeing the white mob attack the Freedom Riders as they got off the bus, Mann realized he had been double-crossed. He charged into the bus station, fired his gun into the air and yelled, "There'll be no killing here today." A white attacker raised his bat for a final blow. Mann put his gun to the man's head. "One more swing," he said, "and you're dead." When they met again, Lewis whispered to Floyd Mann, "You saved my life." The two men hugged, and Lewis began to cry. As they parted, Mann said, "I'm right proud of your career."

Joan Baez
(1941–)

IN 1956, as a high school student, Joan Baez attended a conference on world issues sponsored by the Quakers. There she heard twenty-seven-year-old Rev. **Martin Luther King Jr.** speak about the Montgomery bus boycott and the strategy of nonviolence, a talk that brought tears to her eyes. The following year, Baez committed her first act of civil disobedience, refusing to leave her Palo Alto High School classroom during a mandatory air-raid drill.

It was the height of the Cold War. In affluent Palo Alto, students were expected to go home and hide in their cellars or in family air-raid shelters in the event of nuclear attack. The night before the drill, Baez checked her father's physics books. As she suspected, Soviet missiles would reach Palo Alto in less than half an hour, not giving students sufficient time to get home. At the start of the drill, Baez was in French class. As she recounted in her autobiography, *And a Voice to Sing With*, she told her teacher, "I'm not going," explaining that the drill was government propaganda. The next day the local newspaper ran a front-page story about her protest and quoted her as saying, "I don't see any sense in having an air raid drill. I don't think it's a method of defense. Our only defense is peace."

Since then, Baez, a celebrated folksinger, has been an activist for civil rights, human rights, environmental justice, peace, and nonviolence, participating in protest actions, raising money, speaking out, and using her musical fame to draw attention to these issues.

In 1962 she appeared on the cover of *Time* magazine, the folk music revival's first superstar. She has consistently helped the careers of others, including **Bob Dylan,** by introducing their songs and inviting them to tour with her.

Joan's parents were Quakers, and from an early age she displayed a strong social conscience. She inherited her father's dark complexion—he came to the United States from Mexico at a young age and became a physicist—and faced taunts and prejudice growing up. Blessed with a beautiful singing voice, she performed frequently for family and friends and at school events. When she was thirteen, her aunt took her to a **Pete Seeger** concert, and she was hooked. "It's like they gave me a vaccine, and it worked," she recalled in a *Rolling Stone* interview in 2009.

After her graduation in 1958, the Baez family moved to Boston, where her father had another faculty position. There she quickly became part of the Cambridge folk music scene, dropping out of Boston University after a few weeks.

Singer Bob Gibson introduced the eighteen-year-old Baez at the first Newport Folk Festival in 1959, where her haunting soprano voice, shy demeanor, and physical beauty mesmerized the crowd. This led to her first solo album, simply labeled *Joan Baez*, in the summer of 1960. It was followed by *Joan Baez, Volume 2*. Both were huge successes. These albums featured traditional ballads like "Silver Dagger" and "Barbara Allen," but her repertoire quickly expanded to include songs by **Woody Guthrie** and the Weavers, songs dealing with war and peace, civil rights, and spiritual redemption. Initially she mostly performed songs written by others, but she eventually started performing her own songs. She frequently recorded and performed songs in Spanish. She has had several popular hit singles, including her own "Diamonds and Rust," Phil Ochs's "There but for Fortune," and the Band's "The Night They Drove Old Dixie Down."

Although her commercial appeal has had its ups and downs through her more-than-fifty-year career, Baez has reliably been on the front lines of struggles for social justice, an unswerving advocate of nonviolence. In 1962, in the midst of escalating civil rights protests, she performed "We Shall Overcome" during a concert tour of colleges (including several black colleges) in the Deep South, insisting that blacks and whites be admitted to all her performances. In August 1963, at the March on Washington, she led the crowd of 250,000 in singing "We Shall Overcome." Baez joined King on his 1965 march from Selma to Montgomery, Alabama, singing for the marchers at the City of St. Jude (a Catholic school and hospital complex on the outskirts of Montgomery) as they camped the night before arriving in Montgomery. Baez became a regular ally of King's efforts. She later joined **Cesar Chavez** during his twenty-four-day fast to draw attention to the farmworkers' union struggle, and she participated in a Christmas vigil outside San Quentin State Prison, California, to oppose capital punishment.

In 1963 Baez was the first folksinger to refuse to appear on the television show *Hootenanny* to protest ABC's blacklisting of Pete Seeger, whom the network banned from the weekly broadcast. That year, with two gold albums already to her credit, she brought an unknown Bob Dylan to perform alongside her at the Newport Folk Festival (as Bob Gibson had done with her four years earlier).

In 1964, as the campus New Left was burgeoning, she sang at a Free Speech Movement rally in Sproul Plaza at the University of California, Berkeley. That year she also withheld 60 percent of her income tax to protest military spending. The next year she cofounded the Institute for the Study of Nonviolence near her home in Carmel Valley, California.

As the war in Vietnam escalated, Baez encouraged young men to resist the draft. In 1967 she was twice arrested for blocking military induction centers. "I went to jail for 11 days for disturbing the peace," she said. "I was trying to disturb the war." During Christmas of 1972, she joined a peace delegation traveling to North Vietnam, in part to deliver Christmas mail to American prisoners of war. While there, she was caught in the US military's bombing of Hanoi.

She helped start Amnesty International chapters in the West Coast's Bay Area in the early 1970s and has served on the human rights group's national board. During the 1980s she spoke out against South Africa's apartheid system and featured Peter Gabriel's song about antiapartheid activist Steven Biko at her concerts. In 1985 Baez opened the Live Aid concert in Philadelphia. In 1987 she traveled to Israel, the Gaza Strip, and the West Bank to sing peace songs with Jews and Arabs.

In 1993 she was invited by Refugees International to travel to Bosnia-Herzegovina to help draw attention to the suffering there. She was the first major artist to perform in Sarajevo after the outbreak of civil war in Yugoslavia. She has also lent her name to the gay and lesbian movement, performing at the National Gay and Lesbian Task Force's Fight the Right fund-raiser in San Francisco in 1995 and at other events.

In early 2003 Baez performed at two rallies of hundreds of thousands of people in San Francisco protesting the US invasion of Iraq. In 2005 she traveled to Crawford, Texas, to protest outside President George W. Bush's ranch with antiwar activist Cindy Sheehan, whose son had been killed in Iraq.

In 2008 she joined South African singer Johnny Clegg at a ninetieth birthday concert in London for Nelson Mandela. Although deeply involved in social causes, she avoided partisan politics until 2008, when she endorsed Barack Obama for the presidency. In 2010 she sang at a White House celebration of civil rights music, with President Obama in the audience.

Not surprisingly, her activism has triggered controversy and scorn. In the 1960s, cartoonist Al Capp parodied Baez as "Joanie Phoanie" in his *Li'l Abner* comic strip. In 2007 John Mellencamp invited Baez to perform with him at a concert for injured soldiers at Walter Reed Army Medical Center in Washington, DC, but the army barred her from the event.

Baez's personal life has been on full display throughout her career. In the early 1960s, she and Dylan had a two-year romance and were labeled the "queen" and "king" of folk music. In 1968 Baez married writer and antiwar activist David Harris. He spent the next twenty months in a federal prison in Texas for refusing induction into the military. They divorced in 1973. Her long career has ensured that Baez, like Pete Seeger, is now seen as the quintessential "protest singer." But she has always recognized that she is a part of an ongoing tradition of troubadours involved in movements for change. In an essay for Michael Collopy's *Architects of Peace,* a book on peace activists, Baez wrote, "Social change without music would be void of soul."

Bob Dylan
(1941–)

CREDIT: Associated Press/Ray Stubblebine

WHENEVER HOLLYWOOD movies, documentaries, or TV news programs try to evoke the spirit of the 1960s, they typically show clips of long-haired hippies dancing at a festival, marchers at an antiwar rally, or students sitting in at a lunch counter, with one of two songs by Bob Dylan—"Blowin' in the Wind" or "The Times They Are A-Changin'"—playing in the background. Journalists and historians often treat Dylan's songs as emblematic of the era and Dylan himself as the quintessential "protest" singer, an image frozen in time.

Dylan emerged as a public figure in 1961, playing in Greenwich Village coffeehouses after folk music revival was already under way. In less than three years, Dylan wrote about two dozen politically oriented songs whose creative lyrics and imagery reflected the changing mood of the postwar baby-boom generation and the urgency of the civil rights and antiwar movements.

At a time when the chill of McCarthyism was still in the air, Dylan showed that songs with leftist political messages could also be commercially successful. Unwittingly, he laid the groundwork for other folk musicians and performers of the era, some of whom were more committed to the two major movements that were challenging America's status quo, and helped them reach wider audiences. But in 1964 Dylan told friends and some reporters that he was no longer interested in politics. *Broadside* magazine asked folksinger Phil Ochs if he thought that Dylan would like to see his protest songs "buried." Ochs replied insightfully, "I don't think he can succeed in burying them. They're too good. And they're out of his hands."

He was born Robert Allen Zimmerman and raised in Hibbing, a mining town in northern Minnesota, in a middle-class Jewish family. As a teen he admired Elvis Presley, Johnnie Ray, Hank Williams, and Little Richard, and he taught himself guitar. In 1959 he attended the University of Minnesota but soon dropped out. He stayed in the Twin Cities to absorb its budding folk music and bohemian scene and began playing in local coffeehouses. A friend loaned Dylan his **Woody Guthrie** records and back copies of *Sing Out!* magazines that had the music and lyrics to lots of folk songs. He read Guthrie's autobiography, *Bound for Glory,* and learned to play many of Guthrie's songs.

By then Zimmerman had changed his name (apparently calling himself after Welsh poet Dylan Thomas) and had adopted some of Guthrie's persona. He mumbled when he talked and when he sang, spoke with a twang, wore work-men's clothes, including a corduroy cap, and took on what he believed to be Guthrie's mannerisms. At first Dylan seemed to identify more with Guthrie the loner and bohemian than with Guthrie the radical and activist.

Soon after the nineteen-year-old Dylan arrived in New York, he visited Guthrie, then suffering from Huntington's chorea, in his New Jersey hospital room. Dylan began weaving myths about his past, constantly reinventing himself, as he would continue to do throughout his life.

Greenwich Village was the epicenter of the folk music revival and of a growing political consciousness, and (along with San Francisco) it was the hub of the beat-nik and bohemian culture of jazz, poetry, and drugs. Dylan made the rounds of the folk clubs and made a big impression. His singing and guitar playing were awkward, but he had a little-boy charm and charisma that disarmed audiences. Dylan's initial repertoire consisted mostly of Guthrie songs, blues, and traditional songs.

Dylan got a huge break when music reporter Robert Shelton wrote a flattering review of his performance at Gerde's Folk City. In the *New York Times* on September 29, 1961, under the headline "Bob Dylan: A Distinctive Stylist," Shelton said that Dylan seemed like a "cross between a beatnik and a choir boy." The review put Dylan on the map and landed him a record contract, although his first album, *Bob Dylan,* had no songs that could be considered political, protest, or topical.

In July 1961 Dylan met and soon moved in with seventeen-year-old Suze Rotolo, the daughter of communists and a leftist herself. She introduced Dylan to the works of writers and poets (especially Bertolt Brecht and Arthur Rimbaud) that expanded his own horizons. She also raised his political awareness. She was working as a secretary at the Congress of Racial Equality's office and each night gave Dylan the latest scoop about the civil rights movement.

In January 1962 Dylan wrote his first protest song, "The Ballad of Emmett Till," about a fourteen-year-old African American who was beaten and shot to death in Mississippi in 1955 for whistling at a white woman. Within a year, he had written "Talkin' John Birch Society Blues" (poking fun at that right-wing organization), "I Will Not Go Down Under the Ground" (a critique of the Cold War hysteria that led Americans to build bomb shelters), "Oxford Town" (about the riots in Oxford, Mississippi, when James Meredith became the first black student admitted to the University of Mississippi), "Paths of Victory" (about the civil rights marches), and "A Hard Rain's A-Gonna Fall" (about the fear of nuclear war; he premiered the song at a Carnegie Hall concert a month before the Cuban missile crisis made that fear more tangible).

In April Dylan wrote what would become his most famous song, "Blowin' in the Wind." He took the tune from "No More Auction Block," an antislavery Negro spiritual. Unlike "Emmett Till," and "John Birch Society Blues," "Blowin' in the Wind" was not about a specific incident or public controversy. The lyrics reflected a mood of concern about the country's overall direction, including the beating of civil rights demonstrators and the escalating nuclear arms race.

By avoiding specifics, Dylan's three verses contain a universal quality that allowed listeners to read their own concerns into the lyrics. "How many times must the cannon balls fly before they're forever banned?" and "How many deaths will it take till he knows that too many people have died?" are clearly about war, but not any particular war. One could hear the words "How many years can some people exist before they're allowed to be free?" and relate it to the civil rights movement and the recent Freedom Rides. "How many times can a man turn his head pretending he just doesn't see?" could refer to the nation's unwillingness to face its own racism or other forms of ignorance. The song reflects a combination of alienation and outrage. Listeners have long debated what Dylan meant by "The answer is blowin' in the wind." Is the answer so obvious that it is right in front of us? Or is it elusive and beyond our reach? This ambiguity is one reason for the song's broad appeal.

Of "Blowin' in the Wind," Dylan said, "This here ain't a protest song or anything like that, 'cause I don't write protest songs." What Dylan said did not matter. The song caught the wind of protest in the country and took flight.

Dylan recorded "Blowin' in the Wind" on his second album, *The Freewheelin' Bob Dylan,* released in May 1963, but it was the version released a few weeks later by the trio Peter, Paul, and Mary that turned the song into a nationwide phenomenon. On July 13, 1963, it reached number 2 on the *Billboard* pop chart, with over a million copies sold. The song's popularity turned the twenty-two-year-old Dylan into a celebrity and confirmed his image as a protest singer who voiced the spirit of his generation. Dylan cemented that impression when, on July 5, he and **Pete Seeger** performed at a voter registration rally in Greenwood, Mississippi, sponsored by the Student Nonviolent Coordinating Committee. Dylan sang "Only a Pawn in Their Game," about the assassination, just the previous month, of Medgar Evers, a leader of the National Association for the Advancement of Colored People in Mississippi.

At the August 1963 March on Washington, Dylan sang several topical songs he had recently written, including "Only a Pawn in Their Game" and "When the Ship Comes In" (a song with biblical overtones about a coming apocalypse). A month or two after the march, Dylan penned "The Times They Are A-Changin'," which became his second-most-famous song, an angry anthem that challenged the political establishment on behalf of Dylan's generation. The finger-pointing song is addressed to "senators, congressmen" and "mothers and fathers," telling them that "there's a battle outside ragin'" and warning them, "don't criticize what you don't understand." The line "For the loser now will be later to win" sounds much like the biblical declaration that the meek shall inherit the earth, or it may mean that

America's black and poor people will win their struggle for justice. Like "Blowin' in the Wind," "The Times They Are A-Changin'" became an anthem, a warning, angry yet hopeful. It came to symbolize the generation gap, making Dylan a reluctant spokesman for the youth revolt.

Dylan's third album, called *The Times They Are A-Changin'*, recorded between August and October 1963, included the title song plus several other topical and protest songs, "With God on Our Side," "Ballad of Hollis Brown," "Only a Pawn in Their Game," "The Lonesome Death of Hattie Carroll," and "North Country Blues." The last song draws on Dylan's Minnesota upbringing and describes the suffering caused by the closing of the mines in the state's Iron Range, turning mining areas into jobless ghost towns—a theme that **Bruce Springsteen** would reprise years later. Remarkable, too, is the fact that Dylan tells the tale from the point of view of a woman.

Dylan was never comfortable being confined by the label "protest" singer. He disliked being a celebrity, having people ask him what his songs meant, and being viewed as a troubadour for an entire generation. "The stuff you're writing is bullshit, because politics is bullshit," Dylan told Phil Ochs, who continued to write and perform topical songs and identify with progressive protest movements. "You're wasting your time."

By his fourth album, the aptly titled *Another Side of Bob Dylan,* he had decided to look at "another side"—both inward for his inspiration and outward at other kinds of music. He began to explore more personal and abstract themes in his music and in his poetry. He also got more involved with drugs and alcohol. His songs began to focus on his love life, his alienation, and his growing sense of the absurd. In subsequent decades, with occasional exceptions, he abandoned acoustic music for rock and roll, country, blues, and gospel. His hit "Like a Rolling Stone" from the 1965 album *Highway 61 Revisited* revealed his talent as a rock musician.

Even after 1964, however, Dylan showed that he had not lost his touch for composing political songs. His absurdist 1965 song "Subterranean Homesick Blues" alludes to the violence inflicted on civil rights protesters by cops wielding fire hoses ("Better stay away from those / That carry around a fire hose") but also reflects his growing cynicism ("Don't follow leaders / Watch the parkin' meters"). The extremist wing of Students for a Democratic Society took its name— Weatherman—from another line in that song ("You don't need a weatherman to know which way the wind blows"). Other songs, such as "I Shall Be Released" (1967), the Guthrie-esque "I Pity the Poor Immigrant" (1968), "George Jackson" (1971), "Hurricane" (1975), "License to Kill" (1983), and "Clean Cut Kid" (1984), indicate that Dylan still had the capacity for political outrage.

On election night in 2008, Dylan was playing a concert at the University of Minnesota. As Barack Obama's victory was announced, Dylan said, "I was born in 1941. That was the year they bombed Pearl Harbor. I've been living in darkness ever since. It looks like things are going to change now." Then, deviating from his usual live encore of "Like a Rolling Stone," Dylan played "Blowin' in the Wind."

Dylan's off-and-on engagement with politics is intriguing. But his peace and justice songs have had a life of their own. "Blowin' in the Wind" and "The Times They Are A-Changin'," in particular, will forever be linked to the progressive movements of the 1960s and used to rally people to protest for a better world.

Barbara Ehrenreich
(1941–)

CREDIT: Sigrid Estrada

BARBARA EHRENREICH'S father had Alzheimer's disease, but his political memory remained sharp. During the mental assessment performed by a neurologist, he was asked the name of the president of the United States. As Ehrenreich wrote in her book *The Worst Years of Our Lives,* "His blue eyes would widen incredulously, surprised at the neurologist's ignorance, then he would snort in majestic indignation, 'Reagan, that dumb son of a bitch.'"

That same caustic irreverence marks Ehrenreich's many books of social commentary. A Ph.D. biologist, feminist, and socialist, Ehrenreich inherited her parents' working-class pride and suspicion of powerful elites. Since the 1980s, Ehrenreich has produced a stream of articles and books, including the best-selling *Nickel and Dimed: On (Not) Getting By in America* (2001) about the working poor. More than any other contemporary writer, she has balanced writing for progressive publications, such as *The Nation, The Progressive, Ms.,* and *Mother Jones,* and for mass-circulation mainstream publications, such as *Time, Atlantic Monthly, Harper's,* the *Guardian* in London, *Vogue, Esquire,* and the *New York Times.* Her wit, biting sarcasm, and underlying idealism make it easy for mainstream readers to accept, or at least take seriously, Ehrenreich's radical views on the economy, unions, women's rights, big business, and politics. Indeed, she makes radical ideas sound like common sense.

Ehrenreich was born in Butte, Montana, to a third-generation copper miner. Her mother, a homemaker, also came from a mining family. Both sides of her family were Scottish and Irish Americans, religious skeptics, and die-hard Democrats.

Ehrenreich's mother taught her children two primary lessons: never vote Republican and never cross a picket line. As an alternate delegate to the Democratic Party convention in 1964, her mother joined the protest by the Mississippi Freedom Democratic Party that tried to unseat that state's segregated delegation.

During Ehrenreich's childhood, her father pursued his education, graduated from college, became a corporate executive, and moved the family frequently for his work—from Montana to Pennsylvania, New York, Massachusetts, and finally California, to Los Angeles.

Ehrenreich graduated from Reed College in Oregon in 1963 with a major in physical chemistry. She earned a Ph.D. in cell biology from Rockefeller University in 1968. While in graduate school she married John Ehrenreich, and the couple had two children.

As she became immersed in the antiwar movement, the life of a scientist seemed less appealing than that of an activist. In 1969 she went to work for a small nonprofit organization, the Health Policy Advisory Center, which advocated for better health care for low-income people. She enjoyed writing investigative pieces for the organization's monthly newsletter. She helped write *The American Health Empire: Power, Profits, and Politics* (1971), an exposé in the tradition of muckrakers **Lincoln Steffens, Upton Sinclair,** and Ida Tarbell.

The birth of her first child in 1970 changed Ehrenreich's self-awareness. "The prenatal care I received at a hospital clinic," she recalled, "showed me that PhD's were not immune from the vilest forms of sexism." In the early 1970s, Ehrenreich's expertise in health care issues merged with her feminism. She became one of the founders of the women's health movement. She wrote many articles and several books, including *Complaints and Disorders: The Sexual Politics of Sickness* (1977) and *For Her Own Good: One Hundred Fifty Years of the Experts' Advice to Women* (1989), and helped popularize the idea that the health care system controls women's choices by mystifying the alleged expertise of (mostly male) physicians.

Ehrenreich has written eighteen books, many of them controversial, on topics ranging from women workers around the globe (*Global Woman: Nannies, Maids, and Sex Workers in the New Economy,* 2004) to men's lack of commitment (*The Hearts of Men: American Dreams and the Flight from Commitment,* 1987), the origins of war and humanity's attraction to violence (*Blood Rites: Origins and History of the Passions of War,* 1997), the human impulse for communal celebration (*Dancing in the Streets: A History of Collective Joy,* 2007) and, after getting breast cancer, a critique of the "think positive" movement in popular psychology, religion, and health (*Bright-Sided: How Positive Thinking Is Undermining America,* 2009).

In 1998 she began her most ambitious and best-known writing project, a book—*Nickel and Dimed: On (Not) Getting By in America*—on low-wage workers, based on her own experiences "passing" as one of them.

The working poor were not an alien species, as she noted in the book's introduction. Her sister had gone from one low-wage job to another—phone company representative, factory worker, receptionist—and Ehrenreich's ex-husband had been a $4.50 an hour warehouse worker before snagging an organizing job with the Teamsters union.

Ehrenreich set certain rules for herself: no relying on her education or writing skills to land a job, take the highest-paid job offered her, and find the cheapest accommodations she could. Her goal was not only to experience poverty but also to do the math: as a low-wage worker, could she actually make ends meet?

The project took her to Key West, Florida, where she waited tables; to Portland, Maine, where she toiled as a dietary aide in a nursing home and a maid for a cleaning service; and to Minneapolis, Minnesota, where she worked as a clerk for Walmart. She encountered a surprising reality. "You might think that unskilled jobs would be a snap for someone who holds a Ph.D. and whose normal line of work requires learning entirely new things every couple of weeks. Not so. The first thing I discovered is that no job, no matter how lowly, is truly 'unskilled.'"

She also earned about half a living wage, and she could not imagine supporting children or paying for medical expenses on the $7 an hour or so she earned. And, she added,

> what surprised and offended me most about the low-wage workplace was the extent to which one is required to surrender one's basic civil rights and self respect. I learned this at the very beginning of my stint as a waitress, when I was warned that my purse could be searched by management at any time. I wasn't carrying stolen salt shakers or anything else of a compromising nature, but still, there's something about the prospect of a purse search that makes a woman feel a few buttons short of fully dressed.

The book came out in 2001 and struck a nerve. Five years earlier President Bill Clinton and the Republican Congress had enacted so-called welfare reform, restricting family assistance for women and children and pushing many former welfare recipients into the labor market. After a few years, many economists and politicians celebrated the plan as a huge success, pointing to a dramatic decline in the relief rolls. But others noted that although the number of people on welfare had shrunk, welfare reform had not done much to reduce the poverty rate because so many of them ended up in dead-end low-wage jobs, usually without health insurance, leaving them worse off than before.

The book resonated with the nation's changing mood about inequality and poverty. Polls revealed that a vast majority of Americans wanted to raise the federal minimum wage. Local campaigns for living-wage laws and growing protests against Walmart (the nation's largest employer of low-wage workers) also reflected the changing tide of public opinion that *Nickel and Dimed* tapped and helped shape.

Nickel and Dimed sold more than 1.5 million copies. Many colleges assigned the book in classes. A small but vocal group raised objections. In July 2003, conservatives in North Carolina purchased a full-page ad in the *Raleigh News and Observer* complaining that students at the University of North Carolina were required to read "a classic Marxist rant" that "mounts an all-out assault on Christians, conservatives and capitalism." But other faculty, students, and politicians used the book to lobby for an increase in the minimum wage.

As late as 2010, *Nickel and Dimed* still made the American Library Association's annual list of the top-ten most frequently challenged books—books that some Americans sought to keep off library shelves and school reading lists.

In 2008 Ehrenreich published *This Land Is Their Land: Reports from a Divided Nation* about the widening gap between the nation's rich and everyone else. The following year, as the recession deepened, triggering an epidemic of layoffs and foreclosures, Ehrenreich wrote a series of four articles for the *New York Times*—"Is It Now a Crime to Be Poor?," "The Recession's Racial Divide," "Too Poor to Make the News," and "A Homespun Safety Net"—documenting and describing the plight of the poor, not only the downwardly mobile middle class but the people and families who had been poor before the downturn and for whom conditions had gotten even worse.

Like Jacob Riis, **Lewis Hine, Jane Addams, Florence Kelley, Carey McWilliams,** and **Michael Harrington** before her, Ehrenreich dares to remind the country about the reality of poverty in its midst.

In her books, columns, and speeches, she directs her audiences to grassroots community organizations, unions, and women's groups that are fighting for social justice. She has been arrested at a rally in support of Yale's blue-collar workers, joined picket lines with hotel workers and janitors, distributed leaflets for living-wage campaigns, and protested in favor of women's reproductive rights. On her Web site, Ehrenreich posts articles by activists describing their organizing campaigns. She has served as honorary cochair of the Democratic Socialists of America, the organization founded by Michael Harrington.

"If we are serious about collective survival in the face of our multiple crises, we have to build organizations, including explicitly socialist ones, that can mobilize this talent, develop leadership and advance local struggles," Ehrenreich wrote in *The Nation* in March 2009. "And we have to be serious, because the capitalist elites who have run things so far have forfeited all trust or even respect, and we—progressives of all stripes—are now the only grown-ups around."

Jesse Jackson (1941–)

ONE OF the most famous photographs of **Martin Luther King Jr.** shows him standing on the balcony at the Lorraine Motel in Memphis, Tennessee, with three of his top aides—Ralph Abernathy, Hosea Williams, and Jesse Jackson. The next night (April 4, 1968), on that same balcony, King was murdered. Jackson was one of several staffers with King at the hotel that fatal night.

Jackson had been drawn into King's inner circle at a young age. After King's death, some activists considered Jackson to be the slain leader's heir apparent, although others considered Jackson too young, inexperienced, and brash to assume King's mantle. By the 1970s, however, Jackson had become the nation's most visible civil rights leader. By the time he ran for president in 1984 and 1988, he had transcended the "civil rights" label to become the most visible progressive leader in the country, with a racially and economically diverse following that he called a "rainbow coalition."

Twenty years later, in 2008, another photo of Jackson symbolized the long journey that Jackson, and the nation, had taken. It was of Jackson standing in Chicago's Grant Park, holding a small American flag, with tears in his eyes, as he listened to Barack Obama speak to a huge crowd on the night he was elected president of the United States. The photo did not require a caption. Jackson had clearly paved the way for Obama's victory.

In the forty years that separated King's assassination and Obama's election, Jackson played a pivotal role in progressive politics, as a movement builder, a spokesperson, and a candidate for office.

Jackson was born in Greenville, North Carolina, in 1941 to high school student Helen Burns and Noah Robinson, a thirty-three-year-old married man who lived next door. When Jesse was a year old, his mother married Charles Henry Jackson, a post office worker. He adopted Jesse, who eventually changed his last name from Burns to Jackson.

Jackson attended Sterling High School, a segregated high school, where he was a good student and a football star. He graduated in 1959 and went to the University of Illinois on a football scholarship.

During the winter break of his freshman year, Jackson returned to Greenville and went to the city's segregated "colored" branch library to borrow books for a college assignment. The black library did not have the books he needed, but the librarian told Jackson that the all-white main library had them. She called her counterpart at the main library, who told her that the books would be there waiting for Jackson to pick up. He came in through the rear entrance and saw several police officers talking to the librarian. The librarian told Jackson that none of the books was available, and the police told him to leave the library.

Angry and humiliated, Jackson stared at the sign "Greenville Public Library" and cried. When he returned from Illinois the next summer, he and seven other students, under the tutelage of Rev. James Hall, an activist minister, staged a forty-minute sit-in at Greenville's downtown library. They were arrested, charged with disorderly conduct, and held for forty-five minutes in jail before Hall posted bail. The protest made the local television news that night.

Frustrated that he was not allowed to play quarterback at Illinois, he transferred to North Carolina Agricultural and Technical College in Greensboro, which gave him a chance to play the position. Although the campus was a hotbed of civil rights activism—its students had triggered the sit-in movement in February 1960—Jackson did not immediately join the movement, focusing on his demic and athletic endeavors. But leaders of the campus Congress of Racial Equality chapter recruited Jackson—who was student-body president and a football star—as they were planning to protest segregation in Greensboro's downtown businesses in the spring of 1963. As a gifted orator and charismatic figure, Jackson quickly became a leader of the demonstrations to integrate the theaters and cafeterias. For the second time in his life, Jackson was arrested, this time for "inciting to riot."

After completing a degree in sociology in 1964, Jackson attended the Chicago Theological Seminary. But Jackson's interest in activism won out over his formal studies. In March 1965 he traveled to Selma, Alabama, to participate in the civil rights marches. There he met King for the first time, and he was soon hired as an organizer for the Southern Christian Leadership Conference (SCLC).

After Jackson had helped organize the open housing marches in 1966 to challenge racial discrimination by landlords and real estate agents, King put him in charge of Chicago's Operation Breadbasket, an SCLC project to increase employment opportunities for blacks. Within a year, the project had obtained 2,200 jobs for African Americans in white-owned businesses.

By 1967 Jackson was Operation Breadbasket's national director. To secure agreements regarding fair employment practices, Jackson organized protests and boycotts of corporations that were heavily patronized by black consumers. To avoid bad publicity, some companies signed agreements to hire more African American employees and to do business with black-owned firms as suppliers. Conservative critics blasted such agreements as "shakedowns," but the civil rights movement had a long tradition of such boycotts, starting with the "Don't shop where you can't work" campaigns of the 1930s.

After King's death, SCLC leaders resented Jackson's visibility and ambition. Jackson, who was ordained as a minister in 1968, left SCLC in 1971 and founded Operation PUSH (People United to Serve Humanity) in Chicago. He would direct that organization until his 1984 run for the White House. It expanded Jackson's strategy of using the threat of boycotts to pressure companies to hire and promote black employees and to do business with black-owned firms. Operation PUSH signed agreements with many high-profile companies, including Coca-Cola, Anheuser-Busch, Southland Corporation, Heublein, Burger King, and Seven Up.

By the end of the 1970s Jackson had became a household name and was a major spokesperson for progressive views on a range of policy issues.

He condemned the Republican attacks on social spending and their support for increased military budgets. He also tied together the struggles for self-determination at home and around the world in a universal message of morality and self-respect.

As more blacks were elected to public office, white Americans got used to seeing blacks in powerful positions. A growing number of whites began to vote for black candidates. These trends and momentum made it possible for Jackson to consider running for president.

Jackson already had a track record of pushing the Democratic Party to be more inclusive. In 1972 he and Chicago alderman William Singer unseated Chicago mayor Richard Daley's Cook County delegate slate at the Democratic convention in Miami, Florida, replacing it with a more diverse group.

In 1983 Jackson gave a speech highlighting blacks' unrealized political influence, referring to the results of the 1980 election: "Reagan won Alabama by 17,500 votes, but there were 272,000 unregistered blacks. He won Arkansas by 5,000 votes, with 85,000 unregistered blacks. He won Kentucky by 17,800 votes, with 62,000 unregistered blacks. The numbers show that Reagan won through a perverse coalition of the rich and the registered. But this is a new day."

A growing segment of the Democratic Party's leaders were obsessed with winning back white middle-class suburban voters and attracting campaign contributions from business groups. Jackson wanted to stem the party's rightward shift and the growing influence of its "centrist" wing, embodied by the Democratic Leadership Council. His presidential runs in 1984 and 1988 achieved far more than many pundits had predicted. In 1984 he won over 3 million votes in Democratic primaries—nearly 20 percent of the total primary votes cast—finishing third (behind Walter Mondale and Gary Hart) in a field of eight candidates. He won about 80 percent of the black vote. He won several primaries in southern states with large black populations. The large black turnout for Jackson helped elect other Democrats to Congress, giving Jackson leverage as a party power broker.

By 1988 Jackson had become a crossover politician, appealing to black voters but also winning support from white voters, particularly white workers thrown out of their jobs by corporate mergers and outsourcing, and white farmers losing customers to food imports from abroad. He stressed the theme of economic opportunity for all Americans and the undue influence of big business.

In early 1988, two weeks after Chrysler announced it would be closing a large car assembly plant in Kenosha, Wisconsin, Jackson organized a rally outside the plant. He attacked Chrysler, saying, "We have to put the focus on Kenosha, Wisconsin, as the place, here and now, where we draw the line to end economic violence!" He compared the workers' fight to that of the civil rights movement. The United Auto Workers union local voted to endorse Jackson.

Jackson vigorously attacked American-based multinational companies that built plants in Asia, sending jobs overseas. He argued that the weakness of trade unions in Third World countries should be considered an unfair trade practice. "Let's stop mergin' corporations, purgin' workers," he told the Teamsters at their annual convention. "Let's shift, to reinvestment in America." As the *New York Times* reported in November 1987, "The overwhelmingly white audience roared its approval of Jesse Jackson, as most audiences he speaks to, black and white, generally do these days."

In 1988 Jackson won thirteen Democratic primaries and caucuses, doubled his total votes to 7 million, and garnered 29 percent of the total vote, finishing second to Massachusetts governor Michael Dukakis. He won the Michigan primary with 55 percent of the vote. Again, he won almost the entire black vote, but he also won 22 percent of the white vote in Connecticut and almost one out of four white votes in Wisconsin. Exit polls showed that more than half of Wisconsin's white voters had a favorable view of Jackson. Overall, he significantly increased his support among white voters. About 40 percent of the white voters who supported Jackson in 1988 had voted for Ronald Reagan four years earlier, indicating that his appeal was broadening beyond white liberals.

Jackson's campaign mobilized many activists around the country, which Jackson described as a "rainbow coalition" tying together diverse constituencies and causes. The campaign made Jackson an influential figure within the Democratic Party, but the campaign did not succeed in building a permanent progressive organization.

Jackson has remained a visible presence in American politics, speaking out on a wide range of issues. He has probably walked more picket lines and spoken at more labor rallies than any recent public figure. He traveled to Asia to investigate treatment of workers in the Japanese automobile industry and in apparel factories in Indonesia. He has played mediator in a whole host of hostage cases, most famously when he helped secure the release of hundreds of foreign nationals held in Kuwait by Saddam Hussein.

Jackson has been the recipient of numerous awards, including the Presidential Medal of Freedom, the nation's highest civilian honor. His son Jesse Jackson Jr. has served Chicago in Congress since 1995.

Muhammad Ali (1942–)

AT THE opening ceremonies of the 1996 Olympic Games in Atlanta, Georgia, Muhammad Ali suddenly appeared on a platform in the stadium. Janet Evans, a five-time Olympic medalist in swimming, passed the heavy Olympic torch to Ali. Shaking from Parkinson's disease and perhaps also from nervousness, he stood for a moment acknowledging the cheering crowd. Then he lit the cauldron that symbolized the official start of the Olympics. His role had not been announced in advance, so his appearance was a surprise to all but a handful of the spectators in the stadium and to the billions around the world watching on television. Already one of the most recognizable figures in the world, Ali had been selected to represent the United States, the host country.

This was a long way from the 1960s and 1970s, when, to many white Americans, Ali—the former Cassius Clay and one-time heavyweight champion of the world—was vilified as a menacing black man, a symbol of a "foreign" religion (Islam), and a fierce opponent of America's war in Vietnam who defied his government by refusing to be drafted, risking prison and the withdrawal of his boxing title.

Ali is regarded as one of the greatest boxers in history, even though his career was interrupted for more than three years. At his peak, powerful figures in government, media, and sports inflicted great hardship on the boxer-turned-activist for following his religious and political convictions. Eventually, Ali transcended his role as a sports figure to become a man acclaimed around the world as a person of conscience.

He was born Cassius Clay in Louisville, Kentucky, part of the Jim Crow South. His father was a house painter and his mother was a domestic worker.

When he was twelve, Clay's bike was stolen. He told a police officer, Joe Martin, that he wanted to beat up the thief. Martin, who also trained young boxers at a local gym, started working with Clay and quickly recognized his raw talent. Clay won the 1956 Golden Gloves Championship for light heavyweight novices and three years later won the Golden Gloves Tournament and the Amateur Athletic Union's light heavyweight national title. In 1960 the eighteen-year-old Clay won a spot on the US Olympic Boxing Team and returned from Rome a hero with the gold medal.

The next week, Clay went to a segregated Louisville restaurant with his medal swinging around his neck and was denied service. He threw the medal in the Ohio River.

He quickly turned professional and seemed unbeatable. He won his first nineteen bouts, most of them by knockouts. In 1964, in a match in which he was considered an underdog, he knocked out Sonny Liston to become the heavyweight champion of the world at age twenty-two.

Unlike most boxers, Clay was brash, articulate, and colorful outside the ring. He referred to himself as "The Greatest." He wrote poems predicting which round he would knock out his opponents. As a fighter, Ali was incredibly fast, powerful, and graceful. He told reporters he could "float like a butterfly, sting like a bee."

In his personal life, however, he was on a spiritual quest. In 1962 **Malcolm X** recruited him to the Nation of Islam, which was known to the public as the "black Muslims" and was almost universally condemned by the mainstream media, by white politicians, and by most civil rights leaders, who disagreed with the Nation of Islam's belief in black separatism. Clay waited until the day after he beat Liston in 1964 to announce that he had joined the Nation of Islam and that he had changed his name to Muhammad Ali.

At that point, the public turned against Ali. Most reporters initially refused to call him by his new name and attacked his association with Malcolm X. Even **Martin Luther King Jr.** told the press, "When Cassius Clay joined the Black Muslims, he became a champion of racial segregation and that is what we are fighting against." Many black Americans who disagreed with the Nation of Islam nevertheless admired Ali's defiance. In 1965, when some Student Nonviolent Coordinating Committee (SNCC) volunteers in Alabama launched an independent political party, the Lowdes County Freedom Organization, using the symbol of a black panther, the slogan on their bumper stickers and T-shirts came straight from Ali: "We Are the Greatest."

Ali's announcement jeopardized many commercial endorsement opportunities. The media pressed Ali to explain his convictions. "I'm the heavyweight champion," he said, "but right now there are some neighborhoods I can't move into."

Despite the controversy, he continued to dominate in the ring, besting all opponents who sought to topple him off his heavyweight throne.

Ali also found himself in another fight—a battle within the Nation of Islam between Malcolm X and Elijah Muhammad. When Muhammad suspended Malcolm X, Ali sided with Muhammad and broke off all relations with his mentor, with whom he had become close friends. When Malcolm X was assassinated in February 1965, Ali's public comments were chilling: "Malcolm X was my friend and he was the friend of everybody as long as he was a member of Islam. Now I don't want to talk about him."

Despite this break, Ali had absorbed Malcolm X's political views, which were more radical than those of the Nation of Islam. In 1966 Ali was drafted by the US Army. Had he agreed to join the military, he would not have had to fight in Vietnam but would instead have served as an entertainer for the troops. But Ali refused military service, asserting that his religious beliefs prohibited him from fighting in Vietnam. "I ain't got no quarrel with them Vietcong," Ali explained. Another Ali explanation—"No Vietcong ever called me nigger," which suggested that US involvement in Southeast Asia was a form of colonialism and racism—became one of the most famous one-line statements of the 20th century.

"When Ali refused to take that symbolic step forward everyone knew about it moments later," explained Julian Bond, a SNCC leader and later head of the National Association for the Advancement of Colored People (NAACP). "You could hear people talking about it on street corners. It was on everybody's lips. People who had never thought about the war—Black and white—began to think it through because of Ali."

The US government denied Ali's claim for conscientious objector status on the grounds that his objections were political, not religious. Ali reported to the induction center but refused to respond when his name was called. He was arrested and found guilty of refusing to be inducted into the military. He was sentenced to five years in prison, and his passport was revoked. He remained free pending many appeals. Even though he was not in prison, he was banned from boxing after its governing body stripped him of his boxing title and suspended his boxing license.

Ali was not permitted to box for over three years at the height of his athletic ability, from age twenty-five to twenty-eight. During those years he was a frequent speaker on college campuses, speaking out against the ongoing Vietnam War.

By 1970 public opinion about Vietnam, and about Ali, was changing, and the boxing establishment allowed Ali to fight again. Ali beat Oscar Bonavena at Madison Square Garden. But on March 8, 1971, also at Madison Square Garden, Ali failed in his attempt to regain the heavyweight title from the undefeated Joe Frazier.

Three months later, the US Supreme Court voted 8–0 to reverse his draft evasion conviction. But the Court could not give him back the three years and millions of dollars he lost during his boxing exile.

Ali kept fighting. Between 1971 and 1973, he beat Ken Norton, George Chuvalo, Floyd Patterson, and Frazier in a 1974 rematch. In October of that year the underdog Ali defeated the younger, hard-hitting champion George Foreman with an eighth-round knockout and reclaimed the heavyweight crown, in a fight in Zaire that the media called the "Rumble in the Jungle." The next year Ali defeated Frazier in the "Thrilla in Manila," one of the greatest battles in boxing history. In both Africa and the Philippines, Ali was greeted as a hero by people in the streets.

In February 1978 an overconfident Ali lost his championship belt to Leon Spinks, the 1976 Olympic champion. Friends urged Ali to retire, but he wanted to keep fighting. That September Ali defeated Spinks, becoming boxing's first three-time heavyweight champion. The next June he announced his retirement. He came out of retirement to fight again, revealing a dramatic decline in his skills. He retired for good in 1981 with an overall professional record of fifty-six wins and five losses.

By then, Ali was possibly the most recognized individual in the world, not only for his boxing achievements but also for his political views and courage. He left the Nation of Islam in 1975 (at the death of Elijah Muhammad), converting to Sunni Islam in 1982. He announced that he had Parkinson's disease in 1984.

Since his retirement, he has devoted much of his time to world travel and humanitarian work, such as his efforts with Amnesty International. In 1990 Ali traveled to Baghdad to negotiate for the release of US hostages held by Saddam Hussein. After ten days of negotiations, which included Ali's submitting to the indignity of a strip search prior to meeting with Saddam, he returned to the United States with the fifteen former captives.

In 1998 he was chosen to be a UN Messenger of Peace because of his work in developing countries. In 2005 he received the Presidential Medal of Freedom and in 2009 the President's Award from the NAACP for his public service efforts.

Political activism has never been widespread among athletes. Most dissident athletes have been African Americans. Ali was venturing into territory untried by any except **Jackie Robinson.** (Boxer Joe Louis quietly challenged racism in the military during World War II, but he never did so publicly.) The civil rights and antiwar movements, however, inspired some athletes to speak out. Bill Russell led his teammates on boycotts of segregated facilities while starring for the Boston Celtics. Olympic track medalists John Carlos and Tommie Smith created an international furor with their black power salute at the 1968 Olympics in Mexico City, which hurt their subsequent professional careers.

In 1969 All-Star St. Louis Cardinal outfielder Curt Flood refused to accept being traded to the Philadelphia Phillies. He objected to being treated like a piece of property and to the restriction placed on his freedom by the reserve clause, which allowed teams to trade players without their having any say in the matter. Flood, an African American, considered himself a "well-paid slave." With support from the players union, Flood sued Major League Baseball. In 1970 the US Supreme Court ruled against Flood, but five years later the reserve clause had been abolished and players became free agents, paid according to their abilities and their value to their teams.

Since the 1960s, a handful of athletes have challenged the political status quo. In the 1970s tennis great Arthur Ashe campaigned against apartheid well before the movement gained widespread support. In 1992 he was arrested outside the White House in a protest against American treatment of Haitian refugees. In the 1970s and 1980s tennis star **Billie Jean King,** followed by Martina Navratilova, spoke out for women's rights and gay and lesbian rights.

In 2003, just before the United States invaded Iraq, Dallas Mavericks guard Steve Nash wore a T-shirt during the National Basketball Association (NBA) All-Star weekend that said "No War. Shoot for Peace." Several other pro athletes—including NBA players Etan Thomas, Josh Howard, Adam Morrison, and Adonal Foyle, baseball's Carlos Delgado, and tennis star Martina Navratilova—raised their voices against the war in Iraq.

Billie Jean King (1943–)

Billie Jean King testifies before the US Senate in 1973 in support of the Women's Educational Equity Act.
CREDIT: Associated Press

ON SEPTEMBER 20, 1973, fifty-five-year-old Bobby Riggs, the 1939 Wimbledon champion and a top-ranked player through the late 1940s, played a match against twenty-nine-year old Billie Jean King, a star in the growing sport of women's tennis. The media dubbed the contest the "Battle of the Sexes." King was seen as playing for the honor of all women.

After months of advance hoopla, King entered the Houston Astrodome like Cleopatra, carried aloft in a chair held by four bare-chested musclemen dressed like ancient slaves. Riggs then entered in a rickshaw drawn by scantily clad women. Riggs gave King a giant lollypop; she handed Riggs a piglet, a symbol of male chauvinism. By the end of the day, King had defeated Riggs in three straight sets, 6–4, 6–3, 6–3.

The event became the most famous match in tennis history. Though clearly a publicity stunt, and a moneymaker for both athletes, it had enormous symbolic value, coming during the early years of the new women's movement. It was viewed by an estimated 50 million people around the world, and 30,000 attended at the Astrodome. King's solid victory significantly boosted the credibility of women's participation in major sports. Aided by Title IX, the federal antidiscrimination provision in the Education Amendments of 1972, and by the activism of King and other women athletes, the number of females involved in sports has grown steadily.

King is one of the greatest tennis players of all time, and her advocacy for women's sports in the 1960s and 1970s revolutionized school, amateur, and professional athletics. She helped make it acceptable for girls and women to be athletes. Later in her life, after she retired from competitive play, King also became an iconic figure in the lesbian and gay community. Like **Jackie Robinson,** she broke barriers in sports and then used her celebrity to break barriers in society. In 1975 *Seventeen* magazine polled its readers and found that King was the woman in the world they most admired.

Born in Long Beach, California, Billie Jean Moffitt's father was a fireman and her mother a homemaker. Her brother, Randy Moffitt, had a successful career in baseball as a major-league pitcher. Billie Jean was already an accomplished softball shortstop and enjoyed playing football when her parents decided that she should pursue a more "ladylike" sport. Her father suggested tennis. She picked up a racket at age twelve, played on public courts, and was soon identified as a tennis prodigy. Unlike today's promising young athletes, King did not have an elaborate network of coaches and clinics to nurture her talent. At fifteen, she made her debut at the US Championships. In 1961, at seventeen, she and Karen Hantze won the women's doubles championship at Wimbledon. In 1966 King won her first Wimbledon singles title and was ranked number 1.

King was ranked number 1 in the world five times between 1966 and 1972 and was ranked in the top ten for seventeen years, beginning in 1960. She won a record twenty Wimbledon titles, six of them in singles (1966, 1967, 1968, 1972, 1973, and 1975), won the US Open four times (1967, 1971, 1972, and 1974), and won the Australian Open in 1968. In 1972 she won Wimbledon, the French Open and the US Open. In total, she won 67 singles titles, 101 doubles titles, and 11 mixed doubles titles, amassing almost $2 million in prize money after turning professional in 1968 and before retiring in 1983.

In 1974 King was a founder of World Team Tennis and served as the player-coach of the Philadelphia Freedoms, becoming one of the first women to coach professional male athletes. She coached the US Olympic women's tennis team in 1996 and 2000.

In the late 1960s professional women's tennis was widely dismissed as a frilly sideshow. Male "amateur" tennis stars would get paid under the table, but women athletes were not taken as seriously. For winning her first two Wimbledons, she received nothing except the $14 daily allowance.

In 1970, when King and eight other female players defied the tennis establishment to form their own professional circuit, many experts doubted that they could attract big enough crowds to generate prize money. Women's tennis is now as popular as men's.

In addition to her dominance on the courts, King made significant contributions to women's sports and feminism in general. In 1972 she signed a controversial statement, published in *Ms.* magazine, that she had had an abortion, putting her on the front lines of the battle for reproductive rights. Also in 1972, she became the first woman to be named *Sports Illustrated*'s "Sportsperson of the Year."

King pushed for higher fees for women athletes, which led firms like Philip Morris and Virginia Slims to sponsor women's tournaments. When she won the US Open in 1972, she received $15,000 less than did the men's winner, Ilie Nastase. She threatened to boycott the 1973 US Open if it did not equalize prize money between women and men athletes. The tournament agreed to do so, setting a precedent.

In 1974 she was one of the founders and the first president of the Women's Tennis Association. That year, with support from **Gloria Steinem** and *Ms.,* King also founded *womenSports* magazine and the Women's Sports Foundation. With King's backing, the magazine and foundation became powerful voices for women in sports.

The foundation has helped women athletes obtain college scholarships, and it began its own grants programs to support summer camps and fund traveling and training scholarships for promising young female athletes. The foundation has played an important role in using Title IX to push for greater equality in athletic opportunities for men and women. Although women athletes still get fewer teams, fewer scholarships, and lower budgets than their male counterparts, since Title IX's passage, female athletic participation has increased by 904 percent at the high school level and by 456 percent at the college level.

This progress is the result of persistent pressure by advocates. The foundation has filed friend of the court briefs in support of women high school students seeking equity with male sports programs. In one case, resolved before reaching the courts, the foundation supported a teenage girl who wanted to try out for the men's high school baseball team instead of being restricted to softball. The foundation also advocates for greater sports participation by women of color and by those with disabilities.

By 1968 King realized she was attracted to women but could not bring herself to admit it to her husband or her parents. "The whole world was in tumult, and so was I," she said. "I was so ashamed."

"I couldn't get a closet deep enough. I've got a homophobic family, a tour that will die if I come out, the world is homophobic and, yeah, I was homophobic," King told a *Sunday Times of London* interviewer in December 2007.

In 1981 King was forced out of the closet by a former girlfriend who sued her, unsuccessfully, for palimony, while she was still married. She soon embraced her new role as the first openly lesbian major sports star. (She divorced her husband, Larry, in 1987.)

Elton John wrote "Philadelphia Freedom" to honor King and her World Team Tennis franchise. She serves on the Elton John AIDS Foundation and has received numerous honors for her work with the lesbian, gay, bisexual, and transgender (LGBT) community. King's foundation developed and promotes *It Takes a Team!,* an educational program to end homophobia in school sports.

Writing in *Sports Illustrated* in 1975, sports commentator Frank Deford observed, "[King] has prominently affected the way 50 percent of society thinks and feels about itself in the vast area of physical exercise. Moreover, like [what Arnold] Palmer [did for golf], she has made a whole sports boom because of the singular force of her presence."

Among her many honors, King was awarded the Presidential Medal of Freedom in 2009. The US Tennis Association has named its main facility in New York City the Billie Jean King National Tennis Center.

Paul Wellstone
(1944–2002)

CREDIT: Associated Press/Rodney White

SOON AFTER Paul Wellstone died while campaigning for a third term in the Senate, cars in Minnesota and elsewhere began sporting green bumper stickers that read, "W.W.W.D. What would Wellstone do?"

A college professor turned US senator from Minnesota, Wellstone's fiery speeches and dogged campaigning for progressive reform earned him the title "the conscience of the Senate." In 1991 he cast his first vote opposing US military action in the Persian Gulf; eleven years later, he cast his last vote against a resolution authorizing President George W. Bush to use force against Iraq.

Wellstone summed up his philosophy about why he was in the Senate by saying, "I don't represent the big oil companies, the big pharmaceuticals or the big insurance industry. They already have great representation in Washington. It's the rest of the people that need representation."

Born to Ukrainian Jewish immigrants, Wellstone grew up in Arlington, Virginia. His mother was a cafeteria worker and his father was a writer and federal employee. As a teenager, he was something of a juvenile delinquent, engaging in petty crime. He had difficulty in school because of what he later found out was a learning disability, and he did poorly on his College Board tests. As a senator he opposed educational measures that emphasized standardized test scores.

Wellstone's positive outlet was athletics. Only five foot five, he was a champion wrestler, undefeated in several high school seasons. At the University of North Carolina, he won the Atlantic Coast Conference championship in his 126-pound weight class.

Wellstone earned his undergraduate degree in 1965 and stayed at the University of North Carolina to earn a Ph.D. in political science in 1969. From 1969 to 1989 he taught political science at Carleton College in Minnesota, got involved in local organizing campaigns, and encouraged his students to do the same. While teaching at Carleton he was arrested twice—once at a Vietnam War protest at the federal building in Minneapolis and a second time at a local bank, where he was protesting farm foreclosures. He challenged the college's investments in companies doing business in South Africa, picketed with strikers at a meatpacking plant, and taught his classes off campus rather than cross a picket line during a strike by Carleton's custodians.

Wellstone's activism angered college administrators, who tried to fire him before he received tenure. Students waged an aggressive protest campaign to keep Wellstone. Eventually, political scientists from other schools were brought to campus to assess Wellstone's work, and they gave him a positive review. Ironically, instead of being dismissed, Wellstone was granted tenure a year early.

Wellstone became active with Minnesota's Democratic-Farmer-Labor Party, running unsuccessfully for state auditor in 1982. Wellstone cochaired **Jesse Jackson**'s 1988 presidential campaign in Minnesota and then worked for the Michael Dukakis campaign after Dukakis won the Democratic nomination.

In 1990 Wellstone ran against US Senator Rudy Boschwitz, a well-financed two-term Republican who outspent Wellstone nearly seven to one. Wellstone focused on grassroots campaigning. He made his lack of financing an issue by running a humorous low-budget television commercial in which he rapidly introduced himself to voters, saying he had to talk fast because he could not afford much airtime. The commercial became an immediate hit.

A fixture of Wellstone's campaign was a beat-up old school bus painted green and white with a speaker's platform rigged onto the rear exit. Despite some last-minute smears by his opponent attacking Wellstone's patriotism and religious integrity (supporters of the Jewish Boschwitz claimed that Wellstone was not a practicing Jew), Wellstone won 50.4 percent of the vote. He was the only challenger to defeat an incumbent senator that year.

When Wellstone met President George H. W. Bush at a White House reception for newly elected members of Congress, Wellstone, ignoring protocol, urged the president to spend more time on issues like education and cautioned him against invading Iraq. Irked by Wellstone's hubris, Bush asked an aide, "Who is this chickenshit?"

While serving in the Senate, Wellstone remained an organizer. In Washington, DC, and back in Minnesota, he was frequently seen on picket lines and at rallies sponsored by labor, community, environmental, and other progressive groups. His speeches, often appearing to be delivered completely off-the-cuff, would crescendo wildly into loud, short jeremiads expressing indignation at the wrongs the rally was addressing.

Wellstone spent the majority of his Senate career in the minority party. In his 2002 book *The Conscience of a Liberal,* he acknowledged that he spent nearly 85 percent of his time defending against Republican attacks on working families. When the Democrats were in the majority in 1993–1994, he pushed for a Canadian-style single-payer health care system, in contrast to President Bill Clinton's more modest reform proposal.

Wellstone opposed the North American Free Trade Agreement in 1993 and was an advocate of gun control laws and a proponent of abortion rights. He led legislative efforts to increase funding for vocational education, environmental protection, and teacher training. He fought for campaign finance and lobbying reforms. He criticized his fellow Democrat, President Clinton, for sending troops to Haiti without the consent of Congress. He was one of three senators to oppose the Bush administration's attempt to relaunch the Star Wars national missile defense program. He was the only Democrat to oppose his party's version of lowering the inheritance tax. He virtually single-handedly stalled proposed bankruptcy legislation that would have imposed onerous new burdens on the poor but would have benefited banks, credit card and car finance companies, and retailers.

In 1995 he and Senator Pete Domenici, a New Mexico Republican, cosponsored a successful bill to require insurance companies to treat mental health patients the same as those who suffer other illnesses. (Wellstone's older brother suffered from crippling depression.)

Even his senatorial colleagues who disagreed with Wellstone's views acknowledged his extraordinary human decency. He was one of the few senators who spent time with and remembered the names of the waiters, elevator operators, police officers, and other Capitol Hill workers.

In 1996 Wellstone was the only senator up for reelection to vote against an overhaul of the nation's welfare system, which Clinton signed that year. In a Senate speech, Wellstone predicted that low-income children would be hurt by the law. "They don't have the lobbyists, they don't have the PACs," Wellstone said at the time. As Wellstone predicted, his opponent—former senator Boschwitz, in a rematch—used that and other votes against him. Boschwitz's ads called Wellstone "Senator Welfare" and labeled him "embarrassing liberal and decades out of touch." Wellstone ran a feisty campaign, using clever TV ads and the green school bus again. But this time, running as an incumbent, he raised roughly $3 million more than Boschwitz and won a landslide victory.

In 1997 Wellstone visited Mississippi to begin a nationwide "poverty tour," similar to Robert F. Kennedy's visit to the rural South in the 1960s. He sought to remind his Senate colleagues, the press, and the public that poverty remained a serious problem in the United States, despite the economic boom and low unemployment of the period.

Wellstone consistently had the most progressive voting record of any senator, but on two occasions he angered his liberal supporters. After the 9/11 bombing of the World Trade Center, Wellstone failed to join Wisconsin senator Russ Feingold in voting against the USA Patriot Act. And in 1996 he voted for the Defense of Marriage Act, which allowed states to withhold legal recognition of same-sex unions from other states. He later questioned whether he had cast the right vote.

In 2002 Wellstone reneged on a promise to limit himself to two terms and ran for reelection. That year he also announced that he had multiple sclerosis, but he said it would not interfere with his campaign or Senate activities. He joked with journalists that it was fitting that he should be diagnosed with a "progressive" (that is, degenerative) illness.

The Republican Party and corporate lobby groups targeted Wellstone as the Senate's most vulnerable incumbent and raised a huge campaign war chest to help former St. Paul mayor Norm Coleman beat the progressive Democrat. President

George W. Bush visited Minnesota twice to campaign and raise money for Coleman, and Bush's father followed suit. Karl Rove, George W.'s key political adviser, oversaw the anti-Wellstone effort, steering money from the energy industry—upset by Wellstone's persistent opposition to oil drilling in the Arctic National Wildlife Refuge—to support Coleman's campaign. "There are people in the White House who wake up in the morning thinking about how they will defeat Paul Wellstone," a senior Republican aide confided at the time. "This one is political and personal for them."

Wellstone's first television ads criticized Bush's tax cuts for the wealthiest 1 percent of Americans. When Congress voted overwhelmingly to authorize military force against Iraq, Wellstone was the only senator facing a tough reelection challenge to vote no. On the Senate floor, he spoke out against Bush's "preemptive, go-it-alone strategy" and said it would undermine America's reputation around the world.

Polls showed that a few weeks before election day, Wellstone had pulled slightly ahead of Coleman. Then, on October 25, 2002, just eleven days before the election, on his way to a funeral and a campaign event in rural Minnesota, Wellstone's plane crashed near the Eveleth airport, killing the fifty-eight-year-old senator, his wife, Sheila, his daughter Marcia, three members of his staff, and two pilots. A memorial service for the Wellstones and other victims of the crash filled a 20,000 seat arena at the University of Minnesota. The Democrats picked former senator and vice president Walter Mondale to replace Wellstone in the campaign, but it was too late to wage an effective campaign. Minnesota voters elected Coleman.

Most obituaries described Wellstone as a quixotic radical, out of step with the times as a progressive in a conservative era. But Wellstone understood the importance of pushing the debate to the left while also fighting for concrete improvements in legislation. He was sometimes a lone dissenter, but at other times he used his position to rescue progressive amendments from oblivion. "He was always the last guy standing with the last amendment," Senator Byron L. Dorgan, a Democrat from North Dakota, told the *Los Angeles Times*. "It was always about children, or the poor." Wellstone liked to say that he represented the "Democratic wing of the Democratic Party."

Six years later, comedian Al Franken, a Minnesota native and one of Wellstone's closest friends, beat Coleman to take back the seat for the Democrats. The Wellstones' two surviving children, Mark and David, established Wellstone Action, a training center for progressive candidates and organizers, including college students.

Bruce Springsteen
(1949–)

IN A speech in Hammonton, New Jersey, in September 1984, during his reelection campaign, President Ronald Reagan invoked the name of the Garden State's favorite son: "America's future rests in a thousand dreams inside our hearts," the president said. "It rests in the message of hope in the songs of a man so many young Americans admire: New Jersey's own Bruce Springsteen."

At the time, Springsteen's song "Born in the U.S.A." was a huge hit, and Reagan's speechwriters obviously thought that the song, and its author, reflected the conservative patriotism of the voters the president was courting.

Reagan's speechwriters got the idea from a *Washington Post* column written two months earlier by George Will, the bow-tied conservative who had just seen Springsteen in concert. "I have not got a clue about Springsteen's politics, if any," Will wrote, "but flags get waved at his concerts while he sings songs about hard times. He is no whiner, and the recitation of closed factories and other problems always seems punctuated by a grand, cheerful affirmation: 'Born in the U.S.A.!'"

But even a casual listen to the song's first two verses would have provided a hint that the songwriter was angry about conditions in Reagan-land, which was then mired in deep recession:

> *Born down in a dead man's town.*
> *The first kick I took was when I hit the ground.*
> *You end up like a dog that's been beat too much.*
> *'Til you spend half your life just covering up.*

> *[Chorus] Born in the U.S.A.*
> *I was born in the U.S.A.*
> *[repeat]*

> *Got in a little hometown jam*
> *So they put a rifle in my hand*
> *Sent me off to a foreign land*
> *To go and kill the yellow man.*

The song tells a tragic story about a young man born into poverty in a dying city who is sent to Vietnam after a scrape with the law and returns to the United States embittered and disabled. It is inspired by the true story of Bobby Muller, a Vietnam vet who came home in a wheelchair and became an antiwar activist and advocate for veterans' rights. Three years earlier, Springsteen had headlined a benefit concert for Muller's group, Vietnam Veterans of America.

Shortly after Reagan's speech, Springsteen was performing in Pittsburgh, Pennsylvania. He mentioned Reagan during his introduction to the song "Johnny 99," about a man who goes on a crime spree after his factory closes and he can't find work. "The President mentioned my name the other day, and that got me wondering what his favorite album might be," Springsteen said wryly. "I don't think it's the *Nebraska* album. I don't think he's been listening to this one."

"Born in the U.S.A." is full of patriotism, but it is not the kind of xenophobic patriotism that Reagan had in mind. This was clear when Springsteen told *Rolling Stone* in December 1984, "You see in the Reagan election ads on TV, you know, 'It's morning in America.' Well, it's not morning in Pittsburgh," referring to one of the many industrial cities whose blue-collar families were struggling to survive in the wake of widespread factory shutdowns.

Springsteen's energetic stage performances and working-class songs—sometimes ebullient, sometimes mournful—have earned him an enormous following.

His songs look at the world from a working-class perspective, but his appeal ranges across the entire economic spectrum. Most of his songs tell stories of people paralyzed by heartbreak or calamity, some of their own making but more often due to economic and political forces beyond their control. But Springsteen does not succumb to the fatalism or cynicism that is pervasive among most pop culture stars and rock-and-rollers. Typically, though not always (as in "Glory Days"), he finds hope in personal redemption, political struggle, and community—people taking responsibility for and looking out for each other.

During his 1984–1985 Born in the U.S.A. tour, he introduced the song "My Hometown" with a speech about the poor, the homeless, and the working-class victims of America's economic hard times. He encouraged the audience to donate to or volunteer at a local homeless shelter, and he made sure that sign-up sheets were available after the show. Since then, Springsteen has donated a portion of the proceeds from every concert to a local food bank or homeless shelter.

In 1979 Springsteen and the E Street Band performed at a "No Nukes" anti–nuclear power concert at Madison Square Garden, along with Bonnie Raitt, Jackson Browne, James Taylor, and Crosby, Stills and Nash. In 1988 he was the headliner for an international concert tour raising funds for Amnesty International.

In 1994 he won an Oscar for the song "Streets of Philadelphia," a tender ballad composed for the movie *Philadelphia,* about a gay man dying of AIDS. His song "Dead Man Walking" for the film of the same name, about death penalty activist Sister Helen Prejean, was nominated for an Oscar. In 2004 Springsteen became directly involved in electoral politics for the first time when he openly backed Senator John Kerry's presidential race and played at large campaign rallies. Kerry's campaign used Springsteen's "No Surrender" as its theme song. On his 2007 antiwar album *Magic*, Springsteen sang "Last to Die," based on Kerry's statement when he returned from combat in Vietnam, "How do you ask a man to be the last man to die for a mistake?"

In 2008 Springsteen endorsed Barack Obama early in the election cycle and performed at campaign events. The following January, Springsteen joined **Pete Seeger** in singing "This Land Is Your Land" at Obama's preinaugural celebration concert in front of the Lincoln Memorial, with the new president and his wife sitting nearby on the stage.

Right-wing critics called Springsteen "unpatriotic" or "anti-American" for his critical comments about George W. Bush and the wars in Iraq and Afghanistan, particularly in his 2007 album *Magic*, which is filled with antiwar themes and critiques of the nation's violations of human rights. Springsteen explained in a February 2009 interview with CBS's *60 Minutes:* "Well, I think that we've seen things happen over the past six years that I don't think anybody ever thought they'd ever see in the United States." Springsteen added, "When people think of the American identity, they don't think of torture. They don't think of illegal wiretapping. They don't think of voter suppression. They don't think of no habeas corpus. No right to a lawyer . . . you know. Those are things that are anti-American."

"The American idea is a beautiful idea. It needs to be preserved, served, protected and sung out. Sung out on a nightly basis. That's what I'm going to try to do."

Growing up in a struggling blue-collar family in Freehold, New Jersey, which he described as a "redneck town," Springsteen performed in his first band in high school. Absorbed by his music, he was not politically active in the 1960s and 1970s. After dropping out of community college and failing his physical for the Vietnam draft, Springsteen began performing with rock bands in clubs on the East Coast in the late 1960s and playing acoustic folk songs in Greenwich Village coffeehouses to help pay the rent. He earned recognition for his songwriting and for his high-energy performances. He often has more words in a single song than many musicians have in an entire album.

Springsteen's first two albums, *Greetings from Asbury Park* (1973) and *The Wild, the Innocent, and the E-Street Shuffle* (1974), included elements that would be common throughout his career: portraits of working-class life and young adulthood in New Jersey and of the struggles of down-and-out men (and sometimes women) whose lives are pierced by glimmers of hope and redemption.

For instance "Lost in the Flood," from his first album, is a sparse song in three verses that tells the tale of a lonely "ragamuffin gunner" returning home from Vietnam. Themes from this early song—the brotherhood of underdogs who have been victimized by events beyond their control, the search for spiritual sanctuary (often with Catholic overtones), and references to the street life and culture of working-class Americans (including guns, cars, gangs, and drinking)—recur throughout Springsteen's work.

Born to Run (1975), his third and breakout album, made him an international star and put him on the cover of both *Time* and *Newsweek* the same week. The characters in his songs on *Born to Run* are often heroic, the music energetic. The title track paints portraits of young Americans born into bleak economic situations who want to fight the odds to win a better life: "We gotta get out while we're young, / 'Cause tramps like us, baby, we were born to run."

The acoustic album *Nebraska* (1982), which earned the Album of the Year award from *Rolling Stone,* further demonstrated his genius for addressing social issues with moving ballads about blue-collar figures caught in difficult points in their lives. Springsteen later explained that some of the album's themes were inspired by his reading of **Howard Zinn**'s *A People's History of the United States.*

Born in the USA (1984) was one of the best-selling albums of all time. Seven singles from the record made the Top Ten. Although the sound on *Born in the USA* is the most pop-oriented in Springsteen's work, the lyrics continue his themes from the past. The liveliness of the songs, and the repackaging of Springsteen himself as a heavily muscled rocker with an album cover featuring a giant US flag, may have overshadowed the album's radical politics. A few years later *Rolling Stone* magazine declared Springsteen the voice of the decade, largely for this album.

In 1995 Springsteen released *The Ghost of Tom Joad*, a (mainly) solo album that was partly inspired by John Steinbeck's *The Grapes of Wrath* about the plight of California's Depression-era migrant farmworkers. The album deals with politically explicit material in a manner that is more direct and persistent than in many of his previous songs. **Woody Guthrie,** one of Springsteen's musical heroes, also wrote a song about Tom Joad, the novel's protagonist. Springsteen's lyrics in the album's title song paraphrase the novel's famous passage where Joad explains the universality of his struggle:

> *Mom, wherever there's a cop beatin' a guy*
> *Wherever a hungry newborn baby cries*
> *Where there's a fight against the blood and hatred in the air*
> *Look for me Mom I'll be there*
> *Wherever there's somebody fightin' for a place to stand*
> *Or a decent job or a helpin' hand*
> *Wherever somebody's strugglin' to be free*
> *Look in their eyes Mom you'll see me."*

In 2002 Springsteen released *The Rising,* a studio recording with a full band, about the attack on the World Trade Center on September 11, 2001. During the tour, Springsteen criticized the Bush administration's violations of civil liberties. Asked about fans who do not want to mix their concert-going and politics, Springsteen replied, "I usually make that speech at the end of the show. I think after three hours of playing music, people can give me two minutes."

In 2006 he released *We Shall Overcome: The Seeger Sessions,* a tribute album of thirteen songs that Pete Seeger wrote or popularized, and Springsteen toured the world with a band he put together for the album. The following year he released the antiwar *Magic* album, which included "Long Walk Home," the story of a man who returns to his all-American small town but does not recognize it anymore.

"All you want is for your voice to be part of the record, at a particular time and place," Springsteen told *Rolling Stone* in February 2009. "You try to be on the right side of history. And maybe some other kid will hear that and go 'Oh, yeah, that sounds like the place I live.'"

Michael Moore
(1954–)

SOON AFTER the GOP won majorities in both houses of Congress in 1994, filmmaker Michael Moore flew down to Cobb County, Georgia, represented by House Speaker Newt Gingrich. In 1994, thanks in large part to Gingrich's influence, the prosperous county re-

CREDIT: Associated Press/Chris Pizzello

ceived $4.4 billion in federal funds, more than any other county in the country except Arlington County, Virginia (which houses the Pentagon) and Brevard County, Florida (home of Cape Canaveral). The federal funds amounted to about $10,000 per resident, almost twice as much as New York City received.

Moore slipped into the Cobb County Fourth of July parade with his film crew and wound up marching next to Gingrich. Later Moore interviewed him at a picnic. Moore listed the numerous projects in Gingrich's district that were funded by the federal government—a senior center, the public library, defense contracts for Lockheed Martin's aircraft factory (and a retraining program for laid-off Lockheed workers), research at Kennesaw State University (where Gingrich once taught history), a sewage treatment plan, railroad-crossing warning lights, school lunches, and the popular Allatoona Lake—and asked which should be eliminated or trimmed. Gingrich grew visibly more uncomfortable with each question and balked at identifying any item he thought should be cut.

Then Moore (filming this segment for his Fox network show, *TV Nation*) created a fictitious organization—the Cobb County Committee to Get Government Off Our Backs—and interviewed people who said they believed in cutting federal spending. He got into a boat in Allatoona Lake and used a bullhorn to warn the other boaters, "Leave this lake immediately. It is contaminated with federal dollars." None of the people riding motorboats, spending time at the senior center, or using the public library said they wanted to send the funds back to Washington. Students at Kennesaw State were not eager to give up their federally funded student grants. Moore drove past a street of large homes and called out, "Get rid of your federally funded mortgage insurance."

This nine-minute episode exemplifies Moore's approach to documentary filmmaking. Moore uses his humorous, hulking regular-guy persona (always complemented by his trademark baseball cap and jacket)—to feign sympathy for people of privilege and expose their hypocritical actions and rationalizations on camera. This method makes the targets of his outrage appear even more heartless and ridiculous.

Since making *Roger and Me*, his 1989 exposé on the fate of his hometown, Flint, Michigan, after General Motors (GM) closed its factories, Moore has produced a series of incendiary documentaries, abetted by frequent speeches, regular television interviews, and books (including *Downsize This!*, *Stupid White Men*, and *Dude, Where's My Country?*). He has revolutionized the industry by showing that political documentaries can not only win awards but also earn enormous profits. *Bowling for Columbine* won an Academy Award and was the highest-grossing documentary film in history. He followed that with *Fahrenheit 9/11*, which shattered the earnings record again. Like a modern-day **Upton Sinclair,** Moore has become our most important and controversial muckraking journalist, a fearless agitator who does not try to hide his progressive views behind a mask of objective journalism. His work is intended not only to entertain, educate, and stir outrage, but also to mobilize people to vote, join unions, and protest. Conservatives constantly demonize Moore as a misguided radical, but his regular presence on talk shows and other media outlets gives him a bigger platform than any other progressive public figure.

Michael Francis Moore was born and raised in Davison, a suburb of Flint, Michigan, the heart of the once-thriving US auto industry. Like most men in the area, his father worked for General Motors, in its AC Spark Plug division. His uncle was an early member of the United Auto Workers union and participated in the famous 1937 Flint sit-down strike.

At fourteen, Moore went to a youth seminary with the idea of becoming a Catholic priest. He admired Daniel and Philip Berrigan, radical priests who engaged in civil disobedience to protest the Vietnam War. Although he was a paper boy, an Eagle Scout, and a certified marksman through the National Rifle Association, his rebellious streak shone forth at a young age: he earned a merit badge by producing a slide show illustrating the poor environmental practices of local businesses. As a young teen, he wrote plays and an alternative newspaper, which were quashed by the nuns at his school.

He transferred to Davison High School, and in 1972, when eighteen-year-olds were granted the right to vote, he was elected to the Davison school board, making him one of the youngest elected officials in the nation. Supporting student rights and the teachers' union, he was a thorn in the side of his fellow board members. With the help of the local American Civil Liberties Union, Moore successfully fought to allow meetings to be tape-recorded and reported the board to the Michigan attorney general when it tried to meet without him. A referendum in 1974 to unseat Moore lost by more than 300 votes. "He asked questions nobody asked. He was willing to take the heat," recalled a high school teacher quoted in *USA Today* in June 2004, summarizing what would later become Moore's most important qualities as a filmmaker and writer.

After a year at the University of Michigan, Flint, Moore dropped out. In 1976 he organized a community hotline and crisis center and cofounded the *Flint Voice,* a successful alternative newspaper. With Moore as editor, the paper went statewide in 1983 and became the *Michigan Voice*. Based on the reputation of the *Michigan Voice*, Moore was appointed executive editor of *Mother Jones* magazine and moved to San Francisco in 1986. Five months later, he was fired for refusing to run an article critical of the Sandinista rebels in Nicaragua that he thought was inaccurate.

Moore sued, settling out of court for more than $50,000. With the settlement as seed money, and with money from the sale of his house, from two yard sales, and from contributions by his parents and others, he was able to finance *Roger and Me*, which wound up costing $250,000. The film juxtaposes shots of Moore interviewing Flint's unemployed workers with footage of happier times when the auto industry was the nation's biggest employer and a source of middle-class jobs. Moore's quarry is GM's chairman Roger Smith, whom he stalks throughout the film. His goal: to bring Smith to Flint to see the devastation GM's layoffs have wrought, even as the company made record profits.

Alternately laugh-out-loud funny and poignant, the film was a hit. After it was screened at the Telluride Film Festival, Moore sold it to Warner Brothers for $3 million and an unusual distribution agreement. The studio paid for housing for two years for families in the film who had been evicted from their homes, gave free tickets to people on unemployment, and paid $250,000 for Moore to take the film to depressed areas and show it for free in union halls and churches. *Roger and Me* was major critical success and one of the most financially successful documentary features ever made, earning $7 million.

The film launched Moore's career as a provocative, controversial, and funny filmmaker and author. In 1994 he tried his hand at television with *TV Nation*, a wacky look at current events along with comedy sketches and investigative pieces, such as the Gingrich segment. The show was canceled in 1995.

For his next film, *The Big One*, released in 1997, Moore pursued interviews with CEOs by showing up at their corporate headquarters and trying to argue his way past security guards and secretaries. He managed to interview Nike's CEO Phil Knight and confronted him about the morality of having all Nike sneakers manufactured outside the United States, particularly in Indonesian factories where workers, many of them children, earn just a few dollars a day and toil under terrible working conditions. Soon after the film's release, Nike—under pressure from campus antisweatshop activists and others, and embarrassed by Moore's exposé—changed its policies in Indonesian factories, requiring that employees be at least eighteen years old.

Moore's 2002 film *Bowling for Columbine*, which won the Oscar for best documentary, indicts America's obsession with guns and violence and attacks the National Rifle Association for its opposition to gun control. His Oscar-acceptance speech attacked President George W. Bush and the war in Iraq, generating controversy and publicity for the film.

Two years later, just in time for the 2004 presidential campaign, Moore released *Fahrenheit 9/11,* a scathing look at the Bush family's ties to the Saudi royal family and George W. Bush's motives for going to war in the Persian Gulf. When Michael Eisner, the CEO of the Walt Disney Company, refused to allow Miramax Films, which it owned, to distribute *Fahrenheit 9/11*, Bob and Harvey Weinstein, previously the owners of Miramax, personally bought the film back and distributed it on their own. It became largest grossing documentary in history, earning over $119 million at the box office.

When Moore announced that his next film, *Sicko,* would examine the American health care system, the country's major pharmaceutical lobby (Pharmaceutical Research and Manufacturers of America, or PhRMA) and health insurance lobby (America's Health Insurance Plans) created a phony front organization, Health Care America, to discredit Moore. Leading industry executives held top-secret meetings and amassed a huge war chest to destroy Moore's credibility. The business-sponsored hit job on Moore and *Sicko* was not exposed until July 2009, when Wendell Potter, a former public relations executive for the insurance giant Cigna, appeared on **Bill Moyer**'s PBS television program. Potter, who had become an industry critic, explained that the industry's public relations plan involved "an all-out effort" to "depict Moore as someone intent on destroying the free-market health care system and with it, the American way of life."

The industry recruited experts at conservative think tanks to attack Moore. The insurance and drug companies organized Moore-avoidance seminars for employees and ordered them to keep silent if Moore were to show up with a camera crew.

But Moore managed to find disgruntled former employees and victims of insurance industry abuses. He found both humor and outrage in the stories of America's health care victims. *Sicko* was a box office success and was nominated for an Academy Award. The film was released just before President Barack Obama announced his plans for a universal health plan, triggering a vigorous national debate, an expensive lobbying effort by the health care industry, and an energetic grassroots organizing campaign by unions, consumer groups, public health activists, and other progressives. Throughout 2009 and 2010, advocates on all sides constantly referred to *Sicko,* which had clearly influenced the national debate.

Moore's 2009 film *Capitalism: A Love Story* is an indictment of America's economic system. It ends with Moore wrapping the New York Stock Exchange building in yellow police-crime-scene tape. Although Moore supported Obama in the 2008 presidential race, the film criticizes both the Bush and Obama administrations for funneling hundreds of billions of tax dollars into bailouts of the same banks and corporations that caused the 2008 financial meltdown, the epidemic of foreclosures, and the resulting economic crisis. Moore contrasted the hedge-fund managers and CEOs who got bailouts and huge bonuses with working Americans who got layoffs and foreclosure notices. "We live in the richest country in the world," Moore says in the film. "We all deserve a decent job, health care, a good education, a home to call our own. It's a crime that we don't have it. And we never will as long as we have a system that enriches the few at the expense of the many. Capitalism is an evil and you cannot regulate evil. You have to eliminate it and replace it with something good for all people, and that something is called democracy."

In March 2011 Moore flew from New York to Madison, Wisconsin, to join government employees and their allies in fighting efforts by Scott Walker, Wisconsin's Republican governor, to repeal their collective bargaining rights, slash pension benefits, and cut public services. "The country is awash in wealth and cash. It's just not in your hands. It has been transferred, in the greatest heist in history, from the workers and consumers to the banks and the portfolios of the über-rich," he told the protesters. "You will live in the history books!" Moore shouted from the rotunda of the state capitol. "You have inspired so many people. You have inspired the whole country. I just had to come and thank you."

As Moore wrote on his blog: "The organizers told me this morning that my showing up got them more coverage yesterday than they would have had, 'a shot in the arm that we needed to keep momentum going.' Well, I'm glad I could help. But they need a lot more than just me—and they need you doing similar things in your own states and towns. How 'bout it? I know you know this: This is our moment. Let's seize it."

Tony Kushner (1956–)

CREDIT: Associated Press/Craig Lassig

IN THE 1990s, playwright Tony Kushner heard newspaper accounts of an oppressive fundamentalist regime that ruled a forgotten country in central Asia. He set his next play, *Homebody/Kabul,* in Afghanistan. The play mentions someone named Osama bin Laden, whom most Americans had never heard of. The play, which looked at the West's uneasy relationship with that troubled country, was in rehearsal in September 2001 when the World Trade Center was attacked. Americans would soon hear a great deal about the country, bin Laden, and the conditions Kushner was writing about.

Kushner's next play was a musical based on his experiences growing up in a Jewish family with an African American maid in Louisiana during the civil rights movement. *Caroline, or Change* opened in New York in November 2003. In the opening scene, Caroline sings,

> *Nothing ever happen underground in Louisiana*
> *'Cause they ain't no underground in Louisiana*
> *There is only underwater.*

Less than two years later, Hurricane Katrina burst the levees and New Orleans was flooded.

Kushner's plays focus on the oppression facing the poor, blacks, Jews, gays, and others. Kushner links his characters' fates to the conditions of the larger society and challenges his audience to consider the moral responsibilities of people in positions of power.

Kushner gained international acclaim as an unusually gifted, wide-ranging playwright with his *Angels in America,* which opened on Broadway in 1993. It earned Kushner a Pulitzer Prize and two Tony Awards. The two-part, seven-hour epic play is set during the beginning of the AIDS pandemic, when the disease was still called the "gay plague," there was no cure in sight, and most government officials refused to acknowledge its existence.

A sweeping denunciation of Reagan-era conservatism, *Angels* weaves together the stories of six characters, including a gay man who abandons his lover when the lover shows signs of AIDS; a married Republican Mormon lawyer who wrestles with his homosexuality; the real-life Roy Cohn, a ruthless right-wing attorney who worked for Senator Joe McCarthy during the Red Scare and who died of AIDS in 1986 without ever acknowledging his sexual identity; and Ethel Rosenberg, a rank-and-file Communist during the McCarthy era who was prosecuted by Cohn and then executed, along with her husband, Julius Rosenberg, for being a Soviet spy. In 2003 the play was made into an HBO television movie starring Meryl Streep, Al Pacino, and Emma Thompson. It won eleven Emmy Awards.

Angels in America—subtitled *A Gay Fantasia on National Themes*—is a moral report card on America in the Reagan era and beyond.

"What used to be called liberal is now called radical," Kushner said in 1995. "What used to be called radical is now called insane. What used to be called reactionary is now called moderate. And what used to be called insane is now called solid conservative thinking."

Kushner's political views have not changed dramatically over the years. His first play, *A Bright Room Called Day,* written in 1987, depicts the lives of young liberal and radical artists living in Berlin during the rise of Adolf Hitler. Kushner's left-wing politics have often stirred controversy. But during a career of challenging the status quo, Kushner is rarely doctrinaire. He celebrates the progress made by activists and the give-and-take of politics. "One of the painful rites of passage that everyone on the left goes through is to realize it's a lifelong struggle," Kushner once explained in a 1995 interview with *Mother Jones* magazine. But, he also noted, "I don't believe you would bother to write a play if you really had no hope."

Caroline, or Change, which looks at relationships between blacks and whites in Louisiana during the civil rights movement, "illustrates one of the ultimate cases in which American democracy achieved something great," Kushner told *Mother Jones* magazine in 2003. "I don't see how anyone can read that history and then turn their back on the system—how anyone can think it's not important who our justices are, who the president is, who's in Congress."

Having lived through the gay rights revolution, Kushner takes pride in the movement's accomplishments. "For gay people, the overturning of the sodomy laws is immensely significant. It's why I think politics is so extraordinary." Kushner, who married his partner in 2008, is a fervent advocate of marriage equality. Legalizing gay marriage, he told *Newsweek* in May 2009, would mean that gays were finally "complete citizens of this country."

The failure of liberals and progressives to rally behind the Broadway stagehands' 2007 strike inspired Kushner's play *The Intelligent Homosexual's Guide to Capitalism and Socialism with a Key to the Scriptures,* which opened in Minneapolis in 2009 and reached Broadway in 2011. "I thought all of us liberal-shmiberals would be out on the line with them," he explained to *New York* magazine in October 2010, but the creative class and the theater-going public turned their backs on Broadway's blue-collar workers. "It was stunning to me, because isn't the idea of labor unions that you get working-class people to live in nice houses and send their kids to college?"

The Intelligent Homosexual's Guide tells the story of Gus Marcantonio, a retired longshoreman, labor organizer, and Communist. In the summer of 2007, as the Wall Street meltdown is devastating the economy, he has lost political hope. He gathers his family around him to help him decide whether or not to commit suicide. (One of Gus's sons is named **Vito Marcantonio,** after the left-wing congressman from New York in the 1930s and 1940s.)

Like **Arthur Miller**'s works, Kushner's plays examine families who live in difficult times and have to make difficult choices. His own family background provides plenty of thorny dilemmas. Kushner was born in New York City to Jewish parents who were both professional classical musicians. His mother was one of the first women to have a major position—first bassoonist—in a major symphony orchestra. She had recorded with Igor Stravinsky and had played at the first Pablo Casals Festival. His father was a Julliard-trained clarinetist. When Tony was born, they were both playing for the New York City Opera.

Soon after Kushner was born in 1956, the family moved to Lake Charles, Louisiana, the small town where his father grew up. Kushner's father initially worked in his family's lumber business and conducted the local symphony. Kushner's mother had her own frustrations—a New Yorker living in a small southern town, her music career behind her, carrying the primary responsibility for raising the children, including their difficult-to-handle daughter, who was born with a severe hearing loss. Yet it was seeing his mother on stage in amateur productions that started Kushner's lifelong fascination with theater, especially when she transformed herself into the elderly Linda Loman in Miller's *Death of a Salesman*. "It was terrifying and wonderful. I don't think I ever saw her the same way again," Kushner told an interviewer for the *New Yorker* in January 2005.

Teased by other boys as a youngster, Kushner escaped into books. But he found his voice in high school, becoming a champion—and merciless—member of the debate team. He was also a rebel, refusing to stand for the Pledge of Allegiance, supporting feminism, even passing out leaflets for liberal George McGovern to Ku Klux Klan members. Tony had recognized since childhood that he was attracted to males—and that it was forbidden. In 1974 he headed back to New York to attend Columbia University, where he took a playwriting course and was a drama critic for the *Columbia Spectator*. He waited until he was twenty-five to tell his parents he was gay.

After Columbia, he earned a master's degree at New York University. A *New York Times* critic in May 2011 said Kushner is "perhaps the most intellectually far-reaching of all major mainstream American playwrights." All three major components of Kushner's identity—a Jew, a gay man, and a socialist—figure in his work. "It's much easier to talk about being gay than it is to talk about being a socialist," Kushner told *Mother Jones* in 1995.

Kushner's screenplay for Steven Spielberg's film *Munich* (for which he won an Oscar) triggered another controversy by questioning the morality of Israel's war on terrorism. The film first invites the audience to identify with the horror of the murder of eleven Israeli athletes by Arab terrorists during the 1972 Summer Olympics in Munich. Most writers would portray the Israeli government's attempt to avenge those murders—by hiring assassins to find and kill the terrorists—as a legitimate form of eye-for-an-eye justice. But Kushner questioned the extralegal tactics of the Mossad, Israel's intelligence agency, in hunting down and killing Arabs thought to be linked to the Munich massacre.

Kushner was criticized for condoning Arab terrorism. In response, Kushner explained to *Moment* magazine in 2007, "You can deplore someone's behavior without denying that the person is human and is motivated by recognizable and possibly even empathizable motives."

Kushner has been both a strong supporter of Israel's right to exist and a strong critic of its treatment of Palestinians. He has received many honors from Jewish organizations. But in May 2011 controversy erupted when the City University of New York's John Jay College of Criminal Justice rescinded its offer of an honorary degree after a prominent trustee, who had been appointed by former governor George E. Pataki, attacked Kushner for being anti-Israel. In a letter to the board, Kushner defended his views on Israel, accused his critics of slander, and demanded an apology. Several previous honorees, including writer **Barbara Ehrenreich,** said they would return their degrees if Kushner was denied his honor. The outcry on Kushner's behalf forced the university to backpedal and, within days, to reverse its decision.

In his remarks to the graduates upon receiving the degree, Kushner praised those who had organized on his behalf. "Behind [these efforts] there stands a shining community of people, of spirits of whom I'm proud to be able to call myself kindred," Kushner said, "who believe in the necessity of honest exchanges of ideas and opinions, who understand that life is a struggle to synthesize, to find a balance between responsibility and freedom, strategy and truth, survival and ethical humanity."

"There's injustice everywhere," he continued. "There's artificial scarcity everywhere. There's desperate human need, poverty and untreated illness and exploitation everywhere. Everywhere in the world is in need of repair, so fix it. Solve these things."

The 21st Century So Far

IN AUGUST 2010, the New York State Legislature passed and the governor signed a landmark Domestic Workers Bill of Rights. At least 200,000 domestic workers—nannies, housekeepers, and caregivers, almost all of them immigrants—were covered by the new law. Testifying before the legislature, some domestic workers described working twelve to fifteen hours per day and being paid only $135 per week. Under the new law, for the first time, domestic workers are entitled to a set workweek of forty hours, overtime pay, one day of rest per week or overtime pay if they work on their day of rest, and three days of paid time off after a year of employment. The law protects domestic workers, who are not covered by federal labor laws, against workplace sexual harassment and entitles them to temporary disability benefits and unemployment insurance.

The victory came after a five-year-long grassroots organizing campaign led by Domestic Workers United (DWU) and its thirty-seven-year-old founder and director, Ai-jen Poo. The daughter of immigrants, Poo frequently observes that domestic workers "do the work that makes all other work possible." At Columbia University, she had helped organize the student strike to push for an ethnic studies department. After working as a community organizer for several years, she started DWU in 2000, helping thousands of domestic workers to get back pay and challenge other abuses. In 2007 Poo founded the National Domestic Workers Alliance, which within a few years had grown into a national network of groups in seventeen cities and eleven states. Thanks to this organizing work, California and several other states are considering versions of the New York law.

One hundred years from now, anyone wanting to update this book to include the greatest Americans of the 21st century would have no shortage of candidates. The first eleven years of the century witnessed significant movements whose leaders, like Poo, are outstanding contenders for the Social Justice Hall of Fame. Fifty of these young activists, and a dozen successful campaigns, are identified below, but many more could be cited. They reflect another link in the chain of activists who have changed American history.

Signs of Progress

As the 21st century opened, many of the movements of the previous decades were bearing fruit. On a number of important fronts, the civil rights, feminist, gay liberation, and environmental and consumer movements had dramatically transformed and improved the country.

A decade into the new century, discrimination against African Americans remained a serious problem in employment, bank lending, and the criminal justice system. The poverty rate among African Americans is twice that among whites. The insidious police practice of racial profiling and the outrageous fact that more than 2 million Americans (disproportionately black and Hispanic men) are incarcerated reveals that the dream of racial equality remains unfulfilled.

Despite the persistence of racism, however, there is little dispute that America has made major strides in race relations since the modern civil rights movement began in the 1950s. A majority of black Americans have moved into the middle class. African Americans have broken barriers in every area of American society. They anchor the evening news, edit major newspapers, or serve in the cabinet, as college presidents, as chairman of the Joint Chiefs of Staff, or as CEOs of major corporations—achievements that many Americans considered unthinkable before the 1960s.

One of the civil rights movement's key victories, the 1965 Voting Rights Act, not only increased the number of black voters but also increased the number of black elected officials, many of whom had been active in the movement. In 1970 there were only 1,469 black elected officials in the entire country. By 2000, that number had reached 9,040. In the early 1960s, not a single major city had a black mayor. By 2000, many major cities, including many with relatively few African Americans, had elected black chief executives, including New York, Chicago, Los Angeles, Atlanta, Dallas, San Francisco, Denver, Seattle, and Philadelphia.

And in November 2008, Americans elected forty-eight-year-old Barack Obama—an African American, a former civil rights law professor, and a one-time community organizer—as their president, with 53 percent of the vote. The influence of Obama's organizing experience was evident throughout his presidential campaign. The campaign brought together first-time voters, young people, African Americans, Hispanics, and union members. In his speeches, Obama frequently used the United Farm Workers' slogan, "Yes, we can / Si se puede," and emphasized "hope" and "change." His stump speeches typically included references to America's organizing tradition. "Nothing in this country worthwhile has ever happened except when somebody somewhere was willing to hope," Obama said. "Change comes about," Obama said, by "imagining, and then fighting for, and then working for, what did not seem possible before." "Real change," he frequently noted, only comes about from the "bottom up."

Women battled and beat many barriers to economic, social, and political equality. The "second wave" women's movement, begun in the late 1960s, raised awareness among men as well as women about gender bias. Corporations, law firms, the media, advertising, the military, sports, and other core institutions could no longer exercise blatant discrimination without facing scrutiny and the risk of protest and lawsuits. Today most Americans believe that women should earn the same pay as men if they do the same job. Women are now running corporations, newspapers and TV stations, universities, and major labor unions. More men in couples share housework and child rearing than was the case two or three decades ago. Giving girls an equal opportunity to play competitive sports is now taken for granted. Employers now recognize the reality of sexual harassment, which did not even have a name until the 1970s. The right to have an abortion, legalized in the US Supreme Court's *Roe v. Wade* ruling in 1973, has come under attack but remains the law.

Since 1980, women's turnout at the polls has exceeded men's, according to the Center on American Women in Politics at Rutgers University. The number of women elected to office at every level of government has spiraled. In 1975, there were no women in the US Senate and only nineteen women in the House of Representatives. By 2011, seventeen women served in the Senate and seventy-two served in the House. Similar shifts have occurred at the local and state levels. Although a rise in women's turnout has spurred these gains, men are now more willing to vote for women candidates than ever before. By 1999, 91 percent of voters said they would vote for a woman running for president.

After the gay rights movement burgeoned in the 1970s, it took time for public opinion to shift. But as gay activism accelerated and as more people (including public figures) came out of the closet, attitudes changed. Public support grew for allowing openly gay and lesbian teachers to work in public schools, providing health benefits for gay partners, permitting gay couples to adopt children, ending antisodomy laws, outlawing job and housing discrimination against gays and lesbians, funding research to combat AIDS, and imposing penalties on people who commit hate crimes against gays and lesbians. The proportion of Americans who support allowing open gays and lesbians in the military increased from 44 percent in 1993 to 75 percent in 2010. In December 2010, President Obama signed a law repealing the military's "don't ask, don't tell" law, which went into effect the following September.

Support for same-sex marriage was not even an issue before the 21st century, but it made dramatic progress within a decade. In 2002, the *New York Times* began including gay and lesbian couples in its wedding announcements, and many other papers soon followed its lead. The proportion of Americans who told pollsters they endorsed giving gay and lesbian couples the legal rights of married couples in areas such as health insurance, inheritance, and pension coverage has increased from 40 percent in 2003 to 66 percent in 2010. Although only 30 percent of Americans over sixty-five believe gay marriages should be legal, 65 percent of those between eighteen and twenty-nine do, indicating that the tide of public opinion has dramatically turned. By 2011, Washington, DC, Connecticut, Iowa, Massachusetts, New Hampshire, Vermont, and New York issued marriage licenses to same-sex couples.

In 1991, 49 openly gay and lesbian Americans served in public office. In 2009, that number had increased to 445, according to the Gay and Lesbian Victory Fund. Gays and lesbians have been elected mayors of Houston, Providence, Chapel Hill, Cambridge, and Portland, Oregon. In 2010, John Pérez, an openly gay Latino labor activist from Los Angeles, was elected speaker of the California Assembly, the state's second-most-powerful official.

The environmental and consumer movements gained enormous momentum. Activists organized the first Earth Day in 1970. In response to President Nixon's plan to build 1,000 nuclear power plants by 2000, a new wave of activists began to engage in protest to thwart the expansion of the nuclear power industry and nuclear weapons. Large-scale anti–nuclear proliferation protests accelerated during the 1970s and 1980s. On June 12, 1982, a coalition of 130 organizations brought 1 million demonstrators to New York City's Central Park demanding a "freeze" of nuclear weapons and an end to the Cold War arms race. It was the biggest political demonstration in American history.

As a result of these efforts, many laws and activities that were once viewed as radical are now taken for granted. In response to grassroots pressure, Congress created the Consumer Product Safety Commission, the Occupational Health and Safety Administration, and the Environmental Protection Agency and passed the Clean Air Act. Led by Ralph Nader, the consumer protection movement pushed lawmakers to enact tough health and safety standards. New laws required corporations to give consumers more information about products and limited price-fixing and other monopolistic practices. Congress passed the Fair Packaging and Labeling Act in 1966 to ensure that labels carry such information as products' quantity and ingredients. The Wholesome Meat Act of 1967 required inspection of meat to ensure it meets federal standards. Congress passed laws requiring seat belts in cars, compelling factories to reduce pollution, and outlawing racial discrimination by banks in their mortgage lending, a practice called "redlining."

In 1976, Congress passed the Toxic Substances Control Act, which required manufacturers to test products for risk to human health or the environment before marketing them. Four years later it added the Superfund Law, which allocated federal funds to clean up abandoned hazardous-waste dumps and toxic spills and made dumpers and owners responsible for cleanup costs. That same year, the Alaska National Interest Lands Conservation Act preserved 104 million acres of wilderness in Alaska. In 1990, Congress strengthened the Clean Air Act and the regulation of air pollution by the Environmental Protection Agency. Starting in the 1980s, community, civil rights, and labor union organizations challenged the mainstream environmental groups to focus attention on the ways that pollution and other dangers disproportionately affect low-income areas and people of color. As a result, a new wave of "environmental justice" activism focused on issues such as the siting of toxic-waste facilities, public health, access to parks and open space, and land and water rights.

In 2000, 73 percent of Americans told pollsters that a candidate's support for environmental protection was "somewhat" or "very" important in determining their vote. At the start of the new century, 70 percent of Americans approved of international agreements in Kyoto, Japan, and Bonn, Germany, that would require countries to limit their emissions of carbon monoxide and other greenhouse gases. During the administration of George W. Bush, conservatives expanded their attacks on environmental science on behalf of business interests, particularly the oil industry. This propaganda campaign had an impact. The number of Americans who believed that the threat of global warming was a serious problem declined from 79 percent in 2006 to 63 percent four years later. Even so, a 2009 Gallup poll found that 80 percent of Americans wanted government to set higher fuel efficiency standards for automobiles and that 70 percent believed it should impose mandatory controls on carbon dioxide emissions by businesses. Two years later, a Gallup poll found that over 70 percent of Americans worried about pollution of air, rivers, lakes, reservoirs, and drinking water and about contamination of soil and water by toxic waste.

Government policies have made a big difference. America's air and water are now much cleaner than they were a generation ago. Americans now accept recycling as a standard everyday practice. They expect and want the government to require car manufacturers to build cars that are safe and energy efficient and that limit the emission of pollutants.

One of the most successful progressive movements of the past generation addressed the public health dangers of tobacco use. After starting slowly in the 1950s, by 1969 the antismoking movement had persuaded Congress to enact the Public Health Cigarette Smoking Act, which required cigarette companies to include the following warning on all packages: "The Surgeon General Has Determined That Cigarette Smoking Is Dangerous to Your Health." In 1970, Congress passed and President Nixon signed a measure banning cigarette advertising on radio and television. Public opinion shifted dramatically, especially after scientists documented that "secondhand smoke" posed a dangerous health risk to non-smokers. Cities, states, and the federal government adopted laws raising taxes on cigarettes and banning smoking in restaurants, schools, airplanes, and other public places. Between 1965 and 1990, adult smoking declined from 42 percent to 25 percent. By 2010, only 19 percent of American adults smoked cigarettes. The tobacco industry, once viewed as an invincible political force, had become an almost helpless giant, increasingly weakened by attacks from public health groups, politicians, and the general public.

A Turbulent Decade

The first decade of the 21st century was not simply a story of steady progress. It was full of turmoil, as conservative political forces and ideas competed with their progressive counterparts to shape American society. It began with the controversial

2000 presidential election in which the Supreme Court, not the voters, decided who would occupy the White House.

The Bush presidency was the culmination of several decades of successful political and ideological battle by business and conservative groups to reshape the public debate. In August 1971, Lewis Powell, a prominent attorney and member of the boards of eleven corporations (who later that year would be appointed to the Supreme Court by Richard Nixon), wrote an influential memo to the US Chamber of Commerce, "Attack on the American Free Enterprise System," calling on the business community to go on the attack against activists. He warned of a growing threat to the business establishment posed by consumer advocates, environmentalists, labor unions, and other voices and of the declining public support for business as reflected in opinion surveys. He particularly pointed to the growing liberalism on college campuses, in the media, and in the courts, which had become increasingly receptive to class-action lawsuits against big corporations. Powell argued that the American capitalist system was under attack. The changing mood, he warned, could ultimately threaten business's ability to operate freely and to generate adequate profits to survive. *Business Week* echoed this view in its October 12th, 1974, issue: "It will be a hard pill for many Americans to swallow—the idea of doing with less so that big business can have more. . . . Nothing that this nation, or any other nation, has done in modern economic history compares with the selling job that must be done to make people accept this reality."

The Chamber and business leaders took this advice to heart and began a "selling job" that changed American politics. They began funding a powerful network of organizations designed to shift public attitudes and beliefs over the course of years and decades. In 1972, the CEOs of General Electric and Alcoa founded the Business Roundtable, a lobby group made up of the heads of the nation's 200 largest corporations. Inspired by the Powell memo, Joseph Coors, the conservative head of the large brewery company, wrote a large check to establish a think tank called the Heritage Foundation to enlist academics and journalists to come up with conservative policy proposals. The memo inspired the creation of other conservative policy and lobby groups such as the American Enterprise Institute, the Manhattan Institute, the Cato Institute, Citizens for a Sound Economy, Accuracy in Academe, and other opinion-shaping institutions. The California Chamber of Commerce launched a conservative nonprofit law firm, the Pacific Legal Foundation, the first of about a dozen conservative litigation groups. In 1973, a conservative political operative, Paul Weyrich, started the American Legislative Exchange Council (ALEC) to provide a forum for state legislatures to share ideas for laws against abortion and in favor of school prayer. Within a few years, however, big corporations—including Coors, Amway, IBM, Ford, Philip Morris, Exxon, Texaco, and Shell Oil—began donating funds to ALEC, and the group shifted its focus toward promoting state legislation to limit government regulation of business. William Simon, former treasury secretary under Nixon, became head of the John M. Olin Foundation and began providing universities with donations to hire conservative faculty members and to fund conservative student organizations. Other corporate-funded foundations, such as the Scaife, Koch, Smith Richardson, and Bradley Foundations, soon followed Olin's example.

These long-term investments laid the groundwork for the election in 1980 of Ronald Reagan, who had a "hands-off business" philosophy. "Government is not a solution to our problem," Reagan said. "Government is the problem." Too many government regulations, too much taxation, and too many government employees stifled personal freedom and economic growth. The attack on "big government" and the notion of "getting the government off our backs," once viewed as extreme conservative ideas, moved from the margins to the mainstream.

During his first campaign for president in 1992, Arkansas governor Bill Clinton correctly observed that "the Reagan-Bush years have exalted private gain over public obligation, special interests over the common good, wealth and fame over work and family. The 1980s ushered in a Gilded Age of greed and selfishness, of irresponsibility and excess, and of neglect." Clinton initially had bold plans to expand the New Deal and Great Society legacies. These hopes were quickly dashed. Early in the Clinton administration, the Republicans (led by minority leader Senator Bob Dole) and the Democratic majority in Congress thwarted the president's efforts to enact a public investment plan to stimulate jobs, universal health insurance, and even a child-immunization program. After the November 1994 elections put a Republican majority in Congress, any significant progress on such matters was impossible. After a few years as president, Clinton proclaimed, echoing Reagan, that "the era of big government is over," which he carried out by slashing welfare benefits for poor children.

The business-sponsored attack on government reached a crescendo during the eight-year administration of George W. Bush, who took office in 2001. Bush will be remembered primarily for three things. First, during Bush's first year in office, terrorists attacked New York, Washington, DC, and rural Pennsylvania, the first foreign attack on US soil since Pearl Harbor in 1941. The attacks led to the US invasion of Iraq and Afghanistan (which lasted more than a decade) and the crackdown on civil liberties and immigrants as part of the "war on terrorism." Second, the Bush administration bungled the government's response to Hurricane Katrina, allowing the city and its people to suffer unprecedented displacement, economic hardship, and property destruction in the wake of the storm. Third, the Bush administration and bank regulators looked the other way while Wall Street banks triggered a meltdown of the nation's housing market and financial system, leading to a deep and prolonged recession that persisted after his successor took office in 2009.

During the Bush years, a combination of forces that had begun decades earlier triggered the worst economic crisis since the Great Depression. One force was the gluttony of merger mania and outrageous corporate compensation. Second was business's persistent assault on labor unions, which caused the weakening of this country's most effective bastion against economic inequality. Third was a dramatic cut in federal taxes for the wealthy and corporate America (resulting in the lowest tax burden on the rich in generations). Fourth was the political influence of big business, which persuaded Congress to weaken regulations designed to prevent banks from taking on too much risk or engaging in predatory practices. Finally, the conservative movement—led by corporate-backed think tanks, right-wing media like Fox News, the Republican Party, and the Tea Party—effectively led an all-out attack on government initiatives to address inequality and economic insecurity and to protect consumers, workers, and the environment from abusive businesses.

The Bush years saw dozens of corporate scandals that ripped off billions of dollars from the government, stockholders, and consumers. For example, top executives of Enron, a large energy corporation, hid billions of dollars of debt, the result of failed deals, from the company's shareholders. It also pressured its auditors, Arthur Andersen, to ignore these problems. As a result, shareholders lost more than $60 billion.

Bush rolled back regulations to limit greenhouse gas emissions, handed the pharmaceutical industry windfall profits by restricting Medicare's ability to negotiate for lower prices for medicine, and allowed the Food and Drug Administration to permit food companies to list health claims on labels before they had been scientifically proven. The Bush administration even used the war in Iraq as an opportunity for corporate profit making: it awarded defense contracts to Halliburton, a company once headed by Vice President Dick Cheney, and other politically connected firms, a practice that was soon labeled "crony capitalism."

No corporate sector acted as recklessly and irresponsibly as the financial industry. The newly deregulated banking sector had the freedom to charge usurious interest rates on mortgages and credit cards, to bundle and sell collateralized debt obligations and mortgage-backed securities, to take on astonishing amounts of toxic debt, and to make astounding profits while squeezing consumers. The majority of American families, suffering from decades of declining wages, had to borrow more and more money to pay for their mortgages, college tuition, and other basics. Banks invented new "loan products" with hidden costs and fees, low or no down payments, and low initial interest rates. They often rejected applications for conventional loans from families who had sufficient income and good credit, pushing them into taking out riskier loans. Black and Hispanic consumers were much more likely to be victims of such predatory practices than white consumers, including those with comparable incomes and credit worthiness. These risky "subprime" loans made up 8.6 percent of all mortgages in 2001 but had soared to 20.1 percent by 2006. After 2004, more than 90 percent of subprime mortgages came with adjustable rates that had initially low interest rates that exploded after several years. As these interest rates rose, the adjustable rate loans got more expensive and families could not make their mortgage payments. Soon, large financial institutions were holding portfolios of loans that were worthless.

Every part of the financial industry—mortgage companies like Countrywide Savings, commercial banks like Wells Fargo and Bank of America, Wall Street investment banks like Morgan Stanley and Goldman Sachs, and ratings agencies like Moody's and Standard & Poor's—played a part in this fiasco. Executives and officers of some of these companies cashed out before the market crashed, most notably Angelo Mozilo, the CEO of Countrywide Savings, the largest subprime lender. Mozilo made more than $270 million in profits selling stocks and options from 2004 to the beginning of 2007.

But borrowers were not so lucky. When the dust settled, millions of Americans were no longer able to make their monthly mortgage payments. Banks initiated a massive wave of foreclosures that touched low-income urban areas and middle-class suburban neighborhoods alike. According to the Center for Responsible Lending, from January 2007 through the end of 2009, banks completed 2.5 million foreclosures, most of them on owners who had taken out mortgages between 2005 and 2008. After the housing bubble burst, the wealth of American homeowners fell by some $9 trillion, or nearly 40 percent. Many families found themselves "under water," with mortgage balances that exceeded the values of their homes. The drop in housing values affected not only families facing foreclosure but also families in the surrounding community, because having a few foreclosed homes in a neighborhood brings down the value of other houses in the area. The neighborhood blight created by the housing crisis was much worse in African American and Hispanic areas. African Americans and Hispanics were almost twice as likely as whites to lose their homes to foreclosures.

The Widening Gulf

In July 2011, Michael Cembalest, the chief investment officer of J. P. Morgan Chase, issued a report to the giant banking firm's clients in which he observed that profit margins of the Standard & Poor's 500 companies were at their highest levels since the mid-1960s. How could that be, when the nation was mired in a deep recession and almost one in ten Americans were out of work? Cembalest's answer: "U.S. labor compensation is now at a 50-year low relative to both company sales and U.S. GDP [gross domestic product]." He explained that "reductions in wages and benefits explain the majority of the net improvement in margins."

We have seen this before. In 1928 the richest 1 percent of Americans received 23.9 percent of the nation's total income. When the gains of economic growth go to the very rich, the rest do not have enough purchasing power to buy goods and services. That is a recipe for economic disaster. The next year, Wall Street crashed, triggering the worst economic crisis in US history.

Thanks to the New Deal and then World War II, the United States climbed out of the Depression. Government spending—for highways, housing, schools, universities, and the military—catalyzed three decades of postwar prosperity. The growing influence of the labor movement assured that the prosperity would be widely shared, lifting a majority of Americans into the middle class. The incomes of the poor and the middle class grew faster than the incomes of the rich. Inequality declined. By the late 1970s, the top 1 percent had only 9 percent of the nation's total income.

After that, however, inequality grew. By 2008, the richest 1 percent of Americans—the 1.3 million families with incomes over $386,000—had a quarter of the nation's income and owned 40 percent of the nation's wealth. That widening economic divide has meant a declining standard of living and shrinking opportunities for most Americans, because the costs of basics, such as housing, health care, food, and college tuition, has increased much faster than wages. As a result, more Americans found themselves in debt. The median household income (in inflation-adjusted dollars) fell from $53,388 in 1999 to $49,777 ten years later. The number of Americans living in poverty grew from 31.5 million in 2000 to 46.1 million in 2010—from 11.3 percent to 15.1 percent of all Americans. During that period, the proportion of children under six living in poverty rose from 16.9 percent to 25.3 percent. Meanwhile, the number of Americans without health insurance increased from 36.5 million to 49.9 million—a jump from 13.1 percent to 16.3 percent of the population. According to the official statistics, 9 percent of Americans—14 million people—were unemployed in 2011. Nearly half had been jobless for more than six months—a record. If one adds workers who were so discouraged that they had given up looking for work and people who were underemployed (working part-time but wanting full-time jobs), the number of jobless Americans skyrocketed to more than 25 million.

Over the last quarter century, the super-rich gobbled up most of the economic gains. Between 1979 and 2007, the incomes of the richest 1 percent of American households grew by 224 percent. But the richest of the rich widened the gulf even more. The top 0.1 percent—one-tenth of 1 percent, or one out of a thousand Americans—saw their incomes grow by 390 percent.

It is hard to fathom the excessive wealth held by the handful of Americans in that stratosphere. Although sports and show business celebrities get the bulk of attention, most of the people in this category are top executives in the largest corporations. In 1979, the average compensation earned by the CEO of a major corporation was thirty-five times greater than that of the typical worker. By 2010, it was 325 times greater.

In 2010, the CEOs of the 500 largest corporations collected an average of $10.8 million in compensation. Even CEOs whose companies performed poorly, laid off workers, and saw declines in their stock prices received significant pay raises.

At the very top of the economic pyramid are the wealthiest 400 Americans, profiled each year by *Forbes* magazine. To make the list in 2010, an individual needed at least $1.1 billion in wealth. These 400 people have a total of $1.52 trillion in wealth. In a society of over 300 million people, these 400 people have more wealth than the bottom 150 million Americans.

Success Stories

On his weekly radio show on September 9, 2011, New York mayor Michael Bloomberg, one of America's richest people, warned that rising unemployment and poverty in the United States was a ticking time bomb that could explode in a wave of riots. "You have a lot of kids graduating college [who] can't find jobs," Bloomberg said. "That's what happened in Cairo. That's what happened in Madrid." He reminded listeners about the recent uprising that overthrew Egypt's president Hosni Mubarak and the protests against the Spanish government's austerity measures. "You don't want those kinds of riots here."

Eight days later, on September 17, a few hundred people gathered at Zuccotti Park near the city's financial district to protest corporate greed, income and wealth inequality, and the corrupting influence of major banks and global corporations on American politics. They did not riot. They engaged in peaceful, nonviolent protest. The organizers' initial idea was to camp out for weeks or months to emulate the large-scale demonstrations that had erupted earlier that year in Egypt, Spain, Israel, and elsewhere. The activists called their protest Occupy Wall Street and said they were speaking on behalf of the 99 percent of the population against the richest and most powerful 1 percent. Within a few weeks, similar demonstrations had spread to dozens of other cities across the country.

Riots are expressions of hot anger—outrage about social conditions—but they are not truly political protests. They do not have a clear objective, a policy agenda, or a strategy for bringing about change. They only bring more hardship. The Los Angeles riots in April 1992 left fifty-five people dead and caused more than $1 billion in property damage in inner-city neighborhoods. Almost twenty years later, many of the stores and other buildings in the riot-torn area had still not been rebuilt.

Social protest movements, in contrast, reflect cold anger. They are intentional, organized, and strategic. Activists carefully select the target to raise public awareness about an issue. A handful of people may engage in nonviolent civil disobedience, which could result in fines and jail time, but most participants find other ways to contribute to the cause. They attend rallies and marches, donate money, make phone calls and lick envelopes, distribute leaflets, write letters to newspapers, meet with and lobby elected officials, and encourage friends to vote.

Riots occur when people are hopeless. Protest takes place when people are hopeful—when people believe not only that things *should* be different but also that they *can* be different. The women's suffragists who chained themselves to the fence outside the White House in the early 1900s, the farmers who showed up at their neighbors' homes during the Depression and stopped banks from carrying out foreclosures, the auto workers who occupied the Flint, Michigan, GM plant in 1937 to protest wage cuts and layoffs, the college students who waged sit-ins at segregated lunch counters in the early 1960s, the antiwar activists who protested

the Vietnam War by disrupting military induction centers and defense contractors' offices, and the environmentalists who blocked the construction of nuclear
power plants in the 1970s helped bring about much-needed change.

The first decade of the 21st century witnessed similar movements for social
justice, important milestone victories, and momentum for future changes.

Florida, 2004

In Florida, where George W. Bush beat John Kerry by only 381,000 votes (winning 52 percent of the votes cast) in the presidential race, voters favored a ballot
measure raising the minimum wage to $6.15 an hour (a dollar over the federal
level) by 3.1 million votes (71.3 percent to 28.7 percent). A broad coalition of labor, religious, and community groups, initiated by ACORN, mounted the campaign, whereas major business groups—especially hotel, restaurant, and tourism
industry firms, including Disney World—sponsored expensive opposition efforts.
That same day in Nevada, Bush narrowly beat Kerry by 21,500 votes, but voters
backed a similar boost in the minimum wage by 293,328 votes (68.3 percent to
31.6 percent). The Nevada campaign was led by the state's labor movement. Obviously, many Floridians and Nevadans who voted for Bush also voted to raise the
minimum wage. Both states also saw a significant increase in turnout among low-
income and working-class voters, thanks to grassroots voter registration and get-
out-the-vote campaigns by coalitions of progressive groups.

Buoyed by these victories, ACORN and its union allies looked for other key
states where they could not only win ballot measures to hike the minimum wage
but also increase turnout among likely Democrats—a liberal counterpart to conservative efforts to put anti–gay marriage measures on the ballot. In 2006, voters
in Arizona, Colorado, Missouri, Montana, and Ohio approved measures to raise
state minimum wage levels by $1 to $1.70 an hour, joining Florida, Oregon,
Vermont, and Washington, which had not only increased their minimum wages
but also included annual cost-of-living adjustments.

These statewide campaigns were part of one of the most successful grassroots
crusades of the past several decades—the "living wage" movement. Baltimore
passed the first local law in 1994 following a campaign led by the American Federation of State, County, and Municipal Employees (AFSCME) and BUILD (a
federation of forty-six churches affiliated with the Industrial Areas Foundation
network of community groups). The law raised the base pay for workers employed by companies with city contracts to $6.10 an hour from $4.25, the federal
minimum at the time. The idea caught on. By 2007, 145 cities and counties—
including St. Louis, St. Paul, Minneapolis, Boston, Los Angeles, Oakland, Denver, Chicago, New Orleans, Detroit, Sacramento, and San Francisco—had passed
similar laws. In 2007, Maryland became the first state to pass a living-wage law.
As the new century opened, students at Harvard, the University of Miami, and

other colleges mounted successful campaigns to win living wages for campus employees.

The local grassroots campaigns helped inject the phrase "living wage" into the nation's vocabulary and consciousness. Barbara Ehrenreich's 2001 best-selling book, *Nickel and Dimed: On (Not) Getting By in America*, helped popularize the phrase "working poor." Community activists in Los Angeles, Chicago, and other cities waged campaigns to stop Walmart from opening new big-box stores, criticizing the company (the nation's largest employer) for paying employees poverty-level wages.

Polls consistently found that Americans believed that full-time workers should not have to live in poverty. By 2010, two-thirds of Americans (including a majority of Republicans) supported raising the minimum wage to at least $10 an hour at a time when the federal minimum wage was $7.25, which amounts to about $15,000 a year, far below the poverty threshold.

Los Angeles, 2006

More than 500,000 people marched in downtown Los Angeles to protest federal legislation that would build a 700-mile-long security fence on the US-Mexico border and penalize people who assist undocumented immigrants in obtaining food, housing, or medical services. Unions, religious organizations, and immigrant rights groups organized the rally and publicized it through Spanish-language radio shows and newspapers, which encouraged participants to bring American flags. The mobilization against the legislation was given a big boost when Cardinal Roger Mahony, leader of the Archdiocese of Los Angeles, announced that he would instruct his priests and parishioners to defy the legislation if it ever became law. The Los Angeles rally—orchestrated by labor leader Maria Elena Durazo and thirty-five-year-old Angelica Salas of the Coalition for Humane Immigrant Rights of Los Angeles—was part of an unprecedented nationwide effort to organize immigrants and their supporters.

In 2001, unions and immigrant rights groups, as well as the Mexican government, worked to persuade Congress and President Bush to grant legal status to many illegal immigrants. The September 11 attacks derailed the momentum for comprehensive immigration reform as the Bush administration shifted its focus to border security. Five years later, rallies in Los Angeles and other cities triggered a new phase in the immigrant rights movement. Much of its focus involved fighting a wave of anti-immigrant laws in cities and states, but the movement also pushed for laws to expand immigrants' rights. One of its signal victories was passage of the California Dream Act in 2011, allowing undocumented students who grew up in the United States to apply for and receive state-funded scholarships for college education. The activists viewed that success as a stepping-stone to winning a similar law at the federal level.

Houston, 2006

Even in antiunion Houston, the Service Employees International Union (SEIU) successfully organized 5,300 janitors, mostly immigrants, winning higher pay and better working conditions. Over several years, SEIU had built support among local religious leaders, elected officials, and community groups, who put pressure on the global investors who owned many of the city's largest office buildings. Unions also used the leverage of their pension funds, which were invested in the real estate companies that owned much of downtown Houston and that hired a handful of cleaning companies employing the majority of the city's janitors.

One year later, many of the janitors went on strike—which led to mass arrests—to win a decent contract. They won major raises as well as health insurance. Under the agreement, pay for janitors increased to $6.25 an hour, to $7.25 an hour a year later, and to $7.75 in 2009. Houston mayor Bill White disagreed with the union's militant tactics but still encouraged the cleaning companies to negotiate with the janitors. A year later, the union helped elect one of its own members to the Houston City Council. The Houston workers drew on lessons learned from SEIU's successful "Justice for Janitors" campaign, which began in the 1980s, spread to more than thirty cities, and combined worker mobilization and financial pressure on global office owners. More than 100,000 workers fought for and often won better wages, better conditions, and health insurance, often utilizing civil disobedience to gain public attention and sympathy. Led by SEIU organizer Stephen Lerner, the struggle was turned into a popular movie, *Bread and Roses*, directed by Ken Loach and released in 2000.

Los Angeles, 2008

An unlikely coalition of the Teamsters union, the Sierra Club, the National Resources Defense Council, and local public health and community groups waged an ambitious and successful effort to clean up the country's largest and filthiest port. More than 40 percent of the goods that come into the country use the adjacent ports of Los Angeles and Long Beach. The ships and trucks that carry the goods spew toxic pollutants that result in high rates of cancer and asthma (especially among children), particularly in the communities near the port. Every year 1,200 deaths in the Los Angeles area are caused by port-related pollution. As more than 10,000 trucks idle in long lines waiting to load goods from the ships, drivers inhale the pollution, leading to serious respiratory diseases. "After talking and meeting, we realized that issues affecting workers and communities are inextricably linked," explained Patricia Castellanos, the thirty-eight-year-old director of the Coalition for Clean and Safe Ports, which was formed in 2006 at the initiative of the Los Angeles Alliance for a New Economy.

Two years later, the mayor-appointed Harbor Commission, which oversees the Port of Los Angeles, passed the Clean Trucks Program. It required all pre-1994 trucks to be gone by the end of 2009, to be replaced by new clean trucks paid for largely by container fees. Three years after the program was implemented, diesel truck emissions had been reduced at the port by 80 percent. The coalition also sought to improve the living standards of the more than 15,000 port truck drivers, who were classified as independent contractors but who earned about $11 an hour, not enough to pay for gas and insurance, maintain their trucks, obtain health insurance, and pay themselves a living wage. The second part of the Clean Trucks Program required the Harbor Commission to set standards for trucking companies, who would employ the drivers and make them eligible, as employees, to unionize to improve their wages and benefits. The American Trucking Association sued to challenge the ban against independent trucking contractors, litigation that was still in the courts at the end of 2011. The Los Angeles effort sparked similar efforts by Teamsters, public health and environmental groups, and community organizations in other port cities around the country.

Chicago, 2008

For six days in early December 2008, 240 members of the United Electrical, Radio, and Machine Workers union illegally occupied their Chicago workplace after their employer, Republic Windows and Doors, abruptly told them that it was shutting down the factory and denying the workers severance pay or the vacation pay they had earned. Asked at a press conference about the workers' takeover in his hometown, Obama, still the president-elect, said, "When it comes to the situation here in Chicago with the workers who are asking for their benefits and payments they have earned, I think they are absolutely right. What's happening to them is reflective of what's happening across this economy."

By quickly endorsing the workers' protest, Obama showed the kind of bold leadership that progressives had been hoping for. His comment put pressure on the company's management and on Bank of America (its lender) to forge a solution. Following Obama's lead, local politicians sided with the workers. The Chicago police did not arrest the workers, despite their flagrant violation of the company's private property rights. The protest garnered national media attention, triggering donations and support from around the country. Emboldened by Obama's support, the workers—led by thirty-nine-year-old local union president Armando Robles and thirty-six-year-old organizer Leah Fried—pledged to keep their sit-down strike going. Eventually they reached a solution, the factory remained open, and the workers kept their jobs and their union contract.

Tar Heel, North Carolina, 2008

Also in December 2008, after a brutal fifteen-year organizing battle, workers at the world's largest hog-killing plant voted to unionize. The workers at the 5,000-employee Smithfield Packing slaughterhouse had rejected union membership in

1994 and 1997, after being subjected to the company's illegal harassment and intimidation, in a state known for its antiunion climate. The workers' vote to join the United Food and Commercial Workers (UFCW) was one of the largest private-sector union victories in many years and the biggest in UFCW's history. About 60 percent of the slaughterhouse's workers were African American. "It feels great," Wanda Blue, a hog cutter, told the *New York Times*. Blue, an African American, made $11.90 an hour after working at Smithfield for five years. "It's like how Obama felt when he won. We made history."

Nationwide, 2009

Following a year-long pressure campaign orchestrated by United Students Against Sweatshops (USAS), Russell Athletics, a clothing company, agreed to re-hire 1,200 workers in Honduras who lost their jobs when the company closed its factory soon after workers had unionized. Russell agreed to open a new plant in Honduras as a unionized factory and pledged not to fight efforts by workers to unionize at the company's seven other factories in the country.

After Russell had shut the factory the previous January, USAS mobilized student activists on about a hundred campuses—including Columbia University, the University of Michigan, Cornell, Boston College, the University of Miami, New York University, Stanford, and the University of North Carolina—who persuaded their universities to sever licensing agreements with Russell. The contracts had allowed the firm to put university logos on T-shirts, sweatshirts, and other articles of clothing and sell them in campus stores and elsewhere. USAS also picketed the National Basketball Association (NBA) finals in Orlando, Florida, and Los Angeles to protest the NBA's own licensing agreement with Russell. In addition, students distributed leaflets inside Sports Authority stores and sent Twitter messages to customers of the Dick's Sporting Goods chain, urging them to boycott Russell products. The group helped arrange a letter signed by sixty-five members of Congress, who voiced "grave concern about reports of severe violations" of workers' rights at Russell. The reports came from the Workers Rights Consortium (WRC), a nonprofit human rights group founded in 2000 to monitor conditions in clothing factories around the world.

"For us, it was very important to receive the support of the universities," Moises Alvarado, president of the union at the closed plant in Honduras, told the *New York Times*. "We are impressed by the social conscience of the students in the United States."

The student antisweatshop movement began in 1998, when Duke University students took over the university president's office. Within several years, about 200 colleges had adopted antisweatshop codes of conduct that required licensees to use factories that pay a living wage, follow adequate labor standards, and allow workers to form independent unions. Using those codes as leverage, students won some important victories, pressuring global apparel firms such as Nike to set limits on mandatory and unpaid overtime and to reduce sexual harassment of female employees (including requiring female workers to use birth control pills) in the factories making the company's clothes. USAS helped workers win recognition of their unions in some factories.

Implementing these standards proved difficult, however. College-bound goods, a $3 billion-a-year industry, are only a small fraction of the products made by the thousands of apparel factories around the world, and monitoring all those workplaces was an impossible task. In 2010, USAS embraced the Alta Gracia clothing brand. Alta Gracia clothing is produced in a unionized factory in the Dominican Republic. The brand was created with the help of WRC as a model to demonstrate that socially responsible clothing production was not only possible but also profitable. The factory opened in 2010, and its 120 workers earned three times the country's minimum wage, plus overtime pay. The Alta Gracia factory is cooler than other nearby workplaces, with good ventilation, plenty of windows, overhead lighting that helps workers avoid eye strain, and comfortable chairs to reduce workers' back pain. By the fall of 2011, several hundred colleges were carrying Alta Gracia's T-shirts and sweatshirts, which were sold at the same prices as clothing made by Nike, Russell, and other brands.

The student activists viewed their campaigns as part of the global fair-trade movement, mobilizing consumers to demand better treatment of the workers in Third World countries who produce food, clothing, and other products.

Washington, DC, 2010

On March 9, more than 5,000 protesters picketed outside the Ritz-Carlton Hotel, where America's Health Insurance Plans (AHIP), the powerful insurance industry trade association, was holding its annual lobbying conference. About fifty public figures—including writer Barbara Ehrenreich, AFL-CIO head Richard Trumka, the Center for Community Change's Deepak Bhargava, and former congressman Bob Edgar—participated in civil disobedience. The following day, twenty-four victims of insurance industry abuses—people who had lost family members, suffered because they were denied care, or gone bankrupt because of premium costs—confronted House Minority Whip Eric Cantor and other opponents of reform. Their question was simple: are politicians on the side of consumers or of the insurance industry?

The protest—led by Health Care for America Now (HCAN), a broad coalition of more than a thousand labor, consumer, civil rights, antipoverty, community, netroots (mobilizing via the Internet), and religious groups—was part of the endgame effort to salvage a victory from what appeared to be certain defeat. It represented an escalation in HCAN's efforts to spotlight the destructive role of the insurance industry.

In Obama's first year, an unholy alliance of the health care industry lobby groups (insurance, pharmaceutical, and hospital groups), the conservative media echo chamber (Fox News, the *Wall Street Journal*, Rush Limbaugh, and the right-wing blogosphere), extreme conservative forces within the Republican Party, and their allies among Tea Party ultraright groups threatened to stymie reform, in large part by influencing moderate Democrats either concerned about reelection or held hostage by campaign contributions from the medical industry. In the summer and fall, the Obama administration had lost momentum and wasted precious months as it encouraged Senator Max Baucus, a moderate Democrat from Montana and chair of the Senate Finance Committee, to pursue a futile bipartisan deal. From the beginning, Obama sent mixed signals on whether he truly supported a strong public option—a Medicare-like government insurance plan. In the meantime, the Tea Party movement seized the mantle of popular unrest, demonizing the administration's health care proposal. They stoked fear and confusion by warning that Obama's "socialized medicine" plan would create "death panels," subsidize health care for illegal immigrants, pay for abortions, and force people to drop their current insurance.

White House strategists, in regular contact with HCAN and other progressive groups, initially discouraged activists from mobilizing protests. In late August 2009, seeing defeat on the horizon, HCAN—whose largest members included SEIU, the American Federation of State, County, and Municipal Employees, ACORN, US Action, and MoveOn—regrouped. It mounted more than 200 increasingly feisty protest events in forty-six states, including demonstrations at insurance company offices and protests at the homes of the CEOs of the three largest health insurance corporations—CIGNA, United Health, and WellPoint. In some cities, protesters engaged in nonviolent civil disobedience and were arrested.

The large demonstration outside the AHIP conference was part of the activists' final push to rescue health care reform. The action coincided with Obama's cross-country speaking tour to energize voters to pressure members of Congress to vote for reform. "Let's seize reform. It's within our grasp," Obama implored his audience at Arcadia University outside Philadelphia. He denounced the insurance companies, which "continue to ration care on the basis of who's sick and who's healthy." Forgoing the bipartisan rhetoric that for months had frustrated activists, Obama taunted Republican critics who had stymied reform: "You had ten years. What happened? What were you doing?"

A few weeks later, Obama signed into law the Patient Protection and Affordable Care Act, extending health insurance to most Americans and ending the industry's policy of denying coverage to people with illnesses. Progressives were disappointed that it did not include a public option, but most agreed that, for all its shortcomings, it was one of the most important pieces of social legislation in the nation's history.

Immokalee, Florida, 2011

Following a decade-long battle, the Coalition of Immokalee Workers (CIW) signed an agreement with Florida tomato growers and several major fast-food chains to pay the farmworkers a penny more for every pound of fruit they harvest. Led by thirty-year-old Lucas Benitez, CIW scored its first major victory in 2005, when Taco Bell agreed to meet demands to improve wages and working conditions for the Florida tomato pickers in response to a national consumer boycott led by college students and religious groups. Students at twenty-one colleges persuaded their institutions to remove Taco Bell from their campuses, and students at more than 300 other colleges waged "Boot the Bell" campaigns. Taco Bell agreed to increase the amount it paid for Florida tomatoes by a penny per pound, with the increase to go directly to workers' wages.

It took more pressure to get McDonald's, Burger King, and other chains to reach a similar agreement, and several more years before the CIW pushed aside its biggest obstacle: the Florida Tomato Growers Exchange, a trade association that acts as a middleman; the association finally agreed to pass along the extra penny a pound to the workers. Florida growers produce $520 million worth of the nation's $1.3 billion annual tomato crop. "The impact of the penny per pound is a minimal addition to our purchase," an executive with Whole Foods told the *New York Times*, but it significantly improved living standards for farmworkers, who are not covered by federal minimum-wage laws. Under the agreement, Florida farmworkers' average earnings increased from $10,000 to $17,000 a year.

Albany, New York, 2011

In June, the New York State Senate approved a bill legalizing same-sex marriage by a 33–29 vote. Four members of the Republican majority joined all but one Democrat in supporting the measure. Gay rights activists, with the support of Governor Andrew Cuomo, mounted an intense, emotional, and effective campaign aimed at the handful of fence-sitting lawmakers. Having failed the previous year to win a legislative victory, the state's fragmented gay rights groups agreed to unite into a single coalition (New Yorkers United for Marriage) and adopt a common lobbying strategy.

Moments before the roll call, it was still unclear how some senators would vote. The tide appeared to turn when Senator Mark J. Grisanti, a Republican from Buffalo who had campaigned as an opponent of same-sex marriage, told his colleagues he now believed he had been wrong and would support the measure. "I apologize for those who feel offended," Grisanti said, adding, "I cannot deny a person, a human being, a taxpayer, a worker, the people of my district and across this state, the state of New York, and those people who make this the great state that it is the same rights that I have with my wife."

Twenty-nine states have enacted constitutional amendments blocking same-sex marriage. In eighteen of those states, the amendments also ban domestic partnerships or civil unions. New York became the sixth state (along with the District of Columbia) to legalize same-sex marriage. The victory in New York—which became the largest state where gay and lesbian couples can marry—gave the national gay rights movement a much-needed boost.

New York City, 2011

The Occupy Wall Street movement that began in New York soon spread to cities across the country, including Los Angeles, Chicago, Boston, Portland, Nashville, Atlanta, and San Francisco, as well as to many suburbs and small towns. Protesters created encampments in local parks, where dozens, hundreds, or thousands of people slept in tents at night and organized demonstrations and rallies during the day. Some protestors engaged in civil disobedience at bank offices and elsewhere, leading to arrests.

The protesters included veteran and first-time activists from a wide swath of social and economic backgrounds. The movement reflected Americans' pent-up frustrations and anger about big business's culpability for the nation's widening economic gap and declining standard of living. It also reflected the coming together of many separate movements and activists that had been fighting for social justice since the start of the 21st century—for workers' rights, financial reform, immigrant rights, women's equality, environmental justice, and other battles. It was fueled not only by the widening gap in wealth and income but also by outrage over the Bush administration's calamitous economic and military policies and by frustration over the inability of the Obama administration to make good on many of its promises to move America in a new direction.

The mainstream media initially ignored Occupy Wall Street. Then they ridiculed it, focusing on the spectacle of the protestors rather than on the issues. But after a few weeks, the media began taking the movement's concerns seriously. A growing number of stories, columns, and editorials addressed the problem of corporate influence and income inequality. The movement had obviously struck a nerve with the public. A *Time* magazine survey conducted a month after the establishment of the first encampment found that 54 percent of Americans had a favorable impression of the Occupy protests, whereas just 23 percent had a negative impression. By contrast, just 27 percent had favorable views of the Tea Party.

Many Americans who did not agree with the Occupiers' tactics or rhetoric nevertheless shared their indignation at the outrageous corporate profits and excessive executive compensation that were occurring side by side with an epidemic of layoffs and foreclosures. According to a Pew Research Center national survey released in mid-December, most Americans (77 percent)—including a majority (53 percent) of Republicans—agreed that "there is too much power in the hands of a few rich people and corporations." Pew also discovered that 61 percent of Americans—including 76 percent of Democrats, 61 percent of independents, and 39 percent of Republicans—believed that "the economic system in this country unfairly favors the wealthy." A significant majority (57 percent) of Americans—including 73 percent of Democrats, 57 percent of independents, and 38 percent of Republicans—thought that wealthy people do not pay their fair share of taxes.

The phrase "We are the 99 percent" became a much-repeated slogan. MoveOn, faith-based groups, and major labor unions embraced the Occupy movement. Around the country, union members joined Occupiers at rallies and protests. College students also joined in, organizing campus protests against sky-rocketing tuition costs. At Harvard, where students pitched tents on campus, the protests helped persuade the university to raise wages and benefits for the college custodians. At City University of New York, fifteen students protesting tuition hikes were arrested when they refused to leave a building where the university's trustees were meeting.

In Washington, DC, and in cities around the country, many Democratic politicians jumped on the bandwagon, voicing support for Occupy Wall Street's grievances, although Republicans were generally hostile. After being grilled during congressional hearings by Senator Bernie Sanders of Vermont, Federal Reserve chairman Ben Bernanke reluctantly expressed his agreement with the grievances of the Occupy Wall Street protest. In a speech in Kansas in December, Obama said that the nation's "gaping" economic inequality was "the defining issue of our time." He added, "This is a make or break moment for the middle class. At stake is whether this will be a country where working people can earn enough to raise a family, build a modest savings, own a home and secure their retirement." Obama criticized the "breathtaking greed" that has led to the widening income divide. "This isn't about class warfare," he said. "This is about the nation's welfare." Democrats in Congress invoked the "99 percent" to press for passage of Obama's jobs act, to raise taxes on the wealthy, to extend unemployment benefits, and to strengthen mine safety regulations. In contrast, Eric Cantor, the House majority leader, called the protesters "a growing mob," and GOP presidential candidate Newt Gingrich, former speaker of the House, described Occupy's protests as "un-American" and "class warfare."

Jackson, Mississippi, 2011

In November, Mississippi voters rejected Initiative 26, a "personhood" initiative that would have made the state the first to ban abortion by declaring that life begins at conception. The initiative, which proposed to give constitutional rights to a fertilized egg, would have banned emergency contraception, birth control pills, intrauterine devices (IUDs), and fertility treatments as well as all abortions, even in cases of rape or incest or to save the life of the woman or girl. For more than a year before the election, antiabortion activists had been pushing Congress to cut off funding to Planned Parenthood's family-planning clinics. By November 2011, every Republican candidate for president had endorsed the idea, as had many Republicans in Congress.

Reproductive rights supporters had defeated antichoice state ballot measures in South Dakota, Colorado, and California in 2006 and 2008 and in Colorado in 2010, but they were worried about the outcome in conservative Mississippi. Antiabortion crusaders expected Mississippi to be the first "personhood" victory. Two-thirds of Mississippians had identified themselves as "prolife" in a poll two years earlier. "If it can't pass here, it'd be hard to pass anywhere," said a University of Mississippi political science professor.

A month before election day, polls predicted the initiative would pass by 20 points, but a poll taken a few days before the election showed that the contest was a toss-up. The campaign against Initiative 26 was led by the American Civil Liberties Union and Planned Parenthood, which formed Mississippians for Healthy Families. Planned Parenthood members from across the country made phone calls to Mississippi voters, while local activists waged a campaign using television and radio ads, mailers, and door-to-door canvassing. The campaign was designed not only to make sure that prochoice voters went to the polls, but also to persuade many "prolife" Mississippians that Initiative 26 went too far. The Mississippi State Medical Association warned that doctors could be charged with murder or wrongful death for "employing techniques physicians have used for years." The strategy worked. According to Planned Parenthood, polls found that when voters were given information about the "personhood" amendment, support for it dropped significantly. "Concerns that the measure would empower the government to intrude in intimate medical decisions far afield from abortion— involving not just infertility, but also birth control, potentially deadly ectopic pregnancies and the treatment of pregnant women with cancer—were decisive in its defeat," the *New York Times* reported. Voters firmly rejected Initiative 26 by a 58 percent–42 percent margin.

Madison, Wisconsin, and Columbus, Ohio, 2011

In early February, Wisconsin's Republican governor Scott Walker unveiled proposals to scrap public employees' collective bargaining rights and slash funding for public education and services. Part of the GOP's ongoing war against unions, Walker's "budget repair" bill shifted pension and health insurance costs to state and local workers, even as he proposed cutting taxes for corporations and the rich by $200 million over two years. Walker also announced that he would refuse to bargain with the state's public employee unions.

Walker's actions triggered large-scale protests, including a rally with more than 150,000 protesters in March at the state capitol building, including thousands of high school students chanting "We support our teachers! We support public education!" The demonstrators then moved their protest from the streets to the ballot box, mounting recall efforts against Republican state senators. Pro-union Democrats picked up two state senate seats, but they fell one short of winning a majority in the Senate, which left the law still standing.

The events in Wisconsin rippled across the country, as public opinion polls showed growing support for public workers' right to join a union and to bargain collectively with employers by a nearly 2–1 margin. The Wisconsin uprising inspired similar demonstrations in Indiana, Maine, Michigan, Ohio, and other states with Republican governors who hoped to follow Walker's example.

On the same day in November that Mississippians stood up for women's rights, Ohio voters cast their votes for workers' rights. They overturned a controversial law that would have weakened public employee unions. Backed by newly elected Republican governor John Kasich and passed by the Republican-led legislature, the new law sharply curbed collective bargaining rights for 350,000 police officers, firefighters, teachers, snowplow drivers, and other government employees and increased public workers' share of health insurance payments. It also gutted unions' political clout by making it harder for them to collect dues and fund their political action committees.

We Are Ohio, a labor-funded coalition that led the repeal effort, collected nearly 1.3 million signatures during the summer to put the repeal of the law (SB 5) on the November ballot. (They only needed 230,000.) Large rallies and marches kept spirits high during the fall and winter months. More than 10,000 volunteers knocked on a million doors and made nearly a million phone calls. More than 2 million Ohioans came to the polls and voted by an overwhelming 61 percent–39 percent margin to repeal the antiunion law. A majority of voters in eighty-two of Ohio's eighty-eight counties supported repeal.

La Puente, California, 2011

Much to her own surprise, as the Occupy Wall Street movement gained momentum, Rose Gudiel became the public face of a growing protest movement to stop banks from foreclosing on families victimized by the economic crisis and abusive banking practices. Since the housing bubble burst in 2008, several million homeowners have lost their homes to foreclosure, many of them victims of banks' predatory and unscrupulous loans. When served with an eviction notice, homeowners routinely left quietly, embarrassed to have lost their homes after losing a job, getting their work hours cut, or having to pay for unforeseen medical emergencies.

In 2005, the twenty-nine-year-old Gudiel—a state employee—purchased a small one-story three-bedroom house in La Puente, a working-class suburb of Los Angeles, where she, her father (a warehouse worker), and one of her brothers cared for her disabled mother. They made steady mortgage payments until 2009, when the brother with whom she lived died unexpectedly and the family lost his income. The family was two weeks late on the next mortgage payment. When they sent in the payment, OneWest Bank would not accept it, telling Gudiel that she needed to apply for a loan modification instead. She spent over a year attempting unsuccessfully to get the bank to modify the loan—even though their income had long since recovered after another brother moved in with them. Eventually, Fannie Mae, the quasi-governmental housing finance agency, took over the OneWest mortgage and continued the foreclosure process. Fannie

Mae offered Gudiel $4,000 to give up her fight and leave voluntarily. She refused. Fannie Mae took her to court to evict her. Then the bank started foreclosure proceedings. "My parents instilled in me the idea that if you work hard and study you could live your American Dream," Gudiel told a local paper. "I was the first person in my family to graduate from college, and I worked hard so that I can own a home. And now these banks are taking my dream away."

Gudiel had never been politically involved before, but her experiences changed her views. She contacted the Alliance of Californians for Community Empowerment (ACCE), a community organizing group that had been helping homeowners deal with recalcitrant banks. With the guidance of Peter Kuhns, a thirty-five-year-old organizer for ACCE, Gudiel decided to join with others to resist eviction. Gudiel, her neighbors, coworkers, and supporters from the ACCE and her union (the Service Employees International Union) began a round-the-clock vigil at the house, pledging to link arms in front of the doorway to stop the sheriff from evicting the family, risking arrest. In early October, Gudiel joined members from ACCE and SEIU, as well as some Occupy Los Angeles activists, who protested at the $26 million Bel Air mansion of Steve Mnuchin, OneWest's CEO. The following day, Gudiel and other supporters occupied the Pasadena office of Fannie Mae, which had taken over the mortgage from OneWest. Gudiel and six others were arrested.

All this protest and media publicity put Los Angeles County sheriff Lee Baca in a bind. He obviously did not want to have to evict Gudiel and her family, including her disabled mother. The prospect of his deputies hauling off Gudiel's wheelchair-bound mother to jail did not sit well with the county's top law enforcer. So he stalled for time, contacted OneWest and Fannie Mae, hoping these giant institutions would do the right thing and modify Gudiel's mortgage so her family could stay in their home.

A week later, while leading several thousand Occupy Los Angeles protesters in a march in downtown Los Angeles, Gudiel received a message from Fannie Mae and OneWest Bank saying that the bank would modify the mortgage so the family could stay in its house. The protest and publicity had worked.

"I'm so happy and relieved, but this isn't over for the thousands of people out there on the brink of losing their homes," Gudiel told the media. "We were fighting against a big giant and people said we could not win this, but we proved them all wrong. What I've learned is that when you take a stand and fight against some of the richest and most powerful people in our country, you can win."

Gudiel's example—reported in the media and through union and community networks—inspired a growing number of homeowners facing wrongful evictions to take a bold stand. A coalition of religious groups, community organizations, and unions were mounting the Occupy Our Homes campaign, mobilizing homeowners who, when the banks or sheriffs came knocking on their doors, said, "We're not leaving." On one day in early December, homeowners in the Los Angeles, New York, Chicago, Philadelphia, Atlanta, San Francisco, Minneapolis, and Portland, Oregon, areas took similar actions. They hoped to catalyze a massive nation-wide campaign to resist foreclosures and block evictions; to create a mounting sense of crisis and urgency so that banks would change their routine practices and politicians would change government policy at the local, state, and federal levels; and to inject the foreclosure crisis—and Wall Street's culpability for the recession—into the 2012 presidential and congressional elections.

Activist Generations

Every generation of activists confronts new challenges and seeks to move the country in a new direction. But all social movements involve an overlap of generations. Older activists recruit and mentor the next generation. Younger activists learn from the successes and failures of their older counterparts. So, not surprisingly, many of the people included in the 20th century Social Justice Hall of Fame remained engaged in struggles for change in the new century. In addition, tens of thousands of baby boomers, born between 1946 and 1960, became politically active in the 20th century and continued their commitment to social justice into the 21st century.

But the future belongs to those born after 1960. *Ai-jen Poo*, the founder of the Domestic Workers United, is one of many people who have already made their mark. The fifty individuals listed here represent a new generation of activists, artists, thinkers, and politicians who have already become leaders of exciting movements for social justice. Many were involved in the 21st century movements described above. They offer hope that the 21st century will witness dramatic changes toward greater equality and democracy.

Key to any progressive resurgence is the growing wave of innovative community and union organizing. Among the most effective young organizers are *Cheri Andes* (Greater Boston Interfaith Organization), *Fred Azcarate* (AFL-CIO), *Aaron Bartley* (People United for Sustainable Housing in Buffalo), *Lucas Benitez* (Coalition of Immokalee Workers), *Deepak Bhargava* (Center for Community Change), *Jeremy Bird* (Wake-Up Wal-Mart and Organizing for America), *Joy Cushman* (New Organizing Institute), *Leah Fried* and *Armando Robles* (United Electrical Workers), *George Goehl* (National People's Action), *Simon Greer* (Jewish Funds for Justice), *Sarita Gupta* (Jobs with Justice), *Mary Beth Maxwell* (American Rights at Work), *Kirk Noden* (Mahoning Valley Organizing Collaborative), *Ethan Rome* (Health Care for America Now), *Amy Schur* (Alliance of Californians for Community Empowerment), *Liz Shuler* (AFL-CIO), and *Roxana Tynan* (Los Angeles Alliance for a New Economy). Since being chosen as its president in 2008, organizer *Ben Jealous* has helped reinvigorate the National Association for the Advancement of Colored People. *Teresa Cheng*, born in 1987, has helped lead several successful campaigns by United Students Against Sweatshops.

Young leaders of the burgeoning immigrant rights movement—including *Marissa Graciosa* (Fair Immigration Reform Movement), *Pramila Jayapal* (One

America), *Christine Neumann-Ortiz* (Voces de la Frontera), *Carlos Saavedra* (United We Dream), and *Angelica Salas* (Coalition for Humane Immigrant Rights of Los Angeles)—will continue to make waves as the century evolves, as will a new generation of environmental activists, such as *Phaedra Ellis-Lamkins* (Green for All), *Van Jones* (former Obama adviser and founder of Rebuild the Dream), *Erich Pica* (Friends of the Earth), and *Phil Radford* (Greenpeace).

Writers *Naomi Klein* (author of *No Logo* and *The Shock Doctrine*), *Ezra Klein* (*Washington Post* columnist), and *Tamara Draut* and *Heather McGhee* (both of the think tank Demos), television news analyst *Rachel Maddow* and *Daily Show* anchor *Jon Stewart*, media critic *David Brock* of Media Matters for America, Yale political scientist *Jacob Hacker* (coauthor of *Winner-Take-All Politics*, among many other books), New York University historian *Kim Phillips-Fein*, *Rinku Sen* (editor of *Colorlines*), sportswriter *Dave Zirin*, and singer and musician *Tom Morello* have been provocative interpreters and advocates for the progressive movement. *Robin Brand* (Gay and Lesbian Victory Fund) and *Jennifer Chrisler* (Family Equality Council) represent a young cohort of lesbian, gay, bisexual, and transgender leaders. *Eli Pariser* of MoveOn has been a pioneer in the fast-changing world of netroots activism.

Congresswomen *Tammy Baldwin* of Wisconsin, Tallahassee City Commission member *Andrew Gillum*, South Carolina state legislator *Anton Gunn*, New York City Council member and former community organizer *Brad Lander*, and activist *Darcy Burner* of Seattle are among the many young politicians who serve as the progressive movement's key allies inside the world of politics.

Many of these people are not well known to the general public, but each of them, as part of organizations and movements for change, has already shaped the contours of American society in the 21st century, and each is destined to keep reshaping it in the coming decades. Born in the 1960s, 1970s, and 1980s, they inherited an America that seems to be holding its breath, trying to decide what kind of country it wants to be.

Bibliography

I consulted hundreds of books and hundreds of articles in researching and writing the profiles of the 100 greatest Americans in this book. This bibliography includes books by and about these people. This list is provided as a starting point for readers who want to learn more about these fascinating individuals as well as the times in which they lived and the movements in which they participated. Some of them have not yet been the subject of a full-length biography or have not written an autobiography. In those cases, I have included books that offer some biographical information. I have also included biographical and documentary films about many of the individuals.

General References

Irving Bernstein. *The Lean Years: A History of the American Worker, 1920–1933*. Boston: Houghton Mifflin, 1972.

———. *Turbulent Years: A History of the American Worker, 1933–1941*. Boston: Houghton Mifflin, 1971.

Mari Jo Buhle. *Women and American Socialism, 1870–1920*. Urbana: University of Illinois Press, 1981.

Larry Ceplair and Steven Englund. *The Inquisition in Hollywood: Politics in the Film Community, 1930–1960*. Berkeley: University of California Press, 1983.

Dorothy Sue Cobble. *The Other Women's Movement: Workplace Justice and Social Rights in Modern America*. Princeton: Princeton University Press, 2004.

Ronald D. Cohen. *Rainbow Quest: The Folk Music Revival and American Society, 1940–1970*. Amherst: University of Massachusetts Press, 2002.

John D'Emilio. *Sexual Politics, Sexual Communities*. Chicago: University of Chicago Press, 1998.

Michael Denning. *The Cultural Front: The Laboring of American Culture in the Twentieth Century*. London: Verso, 1996.

Philip Dray. *There Is Power in a Union: The Epic Story of Labor in America*. New York: Doubleday, 2010.

Mary L. Dudziak. *Cold War Civil Rights: Race and the Image of American Democracy*. Princeton: Princeton University Press, 2002.

Sara Evans. *Personal Politics: The Roots of Women's Liberation in the Civil Rights Movement and the New Left*. New York: Vintage Books, 1980.

Eric Foner. *The Story of American Freedom*. New York: W. W. Norton, 1998.

Glenda Gilmore. *Defying Dixie: The Radical Roots of Civil Rights, 1919–1950*. New York: W. W. Norton, 2008.

Todd Gitlin. *The Sixties: Years of Hope, Days of Rage*. New York: Bantam Books, 1987.

Robert Gottlieb. *Forcing the Spring: The Transformation of the American Environmental Movement*, rev. ed. Washington, DC: Island Press, 2003.

Jonathan Hansen. *The Lost Promise of Patriotism: Debating American Identity, 1890–1920*. Chicago: University of Chicago Press, 2003.

Maurice Isserman and Michael Kazin. *America Divided: The Civil War of the 1960s*. New York: Oxford University Press, 2000.

Jonathan Katz. *Gay American History*, rev. ed. New York: Plume, 1992.

Michael Kazin. *American Dreamers: How the Left Changed a Nation*. New York: Alfred A. Knopf, 2011.

David M. Kennedy. *Freedom from Fear: The American People in Depression and War, 1929–1945*. New York: Oxford University Press, 1999.

Diana Klebanow and Franklin L. Jonas. *People's Lawyers: Crusaders for Justice in American History*. Armonk, NY: M. E. Sharpe, 2003.

Nick Kotz. *Judgment Days: Lyndon Baines Johnson, Martin Luther King Jr., and the Laws That Changed America*. New York: Houghton Mifflin, 2005.

Lawrence Lader. *Power on the Left: American Radical Movements Since 1949*. New York: W. W. Norton, 1980.

Nelson Lichtenstein. *The State of the Union: A Century of Labor in America*. Princeton: Princeton University Press, 2003.

Bradford Martin. *The Other Eighties: A Secret History of America in the Age of Reagan*. New York: Hill and Wang, 2011.

Michael McGerr. *A Fierce Discontent: The Rise and Fall of the Progressive Movement in America, 1870–1920*. New York: Oxford University Press, 2005.

Dan McKanan. *Prophetic Encounters: Religion and the American Radical Tradition*. Boston: Beacon Press, 2011.

Aldon Morris. *Origins of the Civil Rights Movement: Black Communities Organizing for Change*. New York: Free Press, 1984.

William O'Neill. *Everyone Was Brave: The Rise and Fall of Feminism in America*. New York: HarperCollins, 1969.

James Patterson. *Grand Expectations: The United States, 1945–1974*. New York: Oxford University Press, 1996.

William Preston Jr. *Aliens and Dissenters: Federal Suppression of Radicals, 1903–1933*. New York: Harper and Row, 1963.

Ruth Rosen. *The World Split Open: How the Modern Women's Movement Changed America*. New York: Viking, 2000.

Harvey Sitkoff. *A New Deal for Blacks*. New York: Oxford University Press, 1981.

Thomas Sugrue. *Sweet Land of Liberty: The Forgotten Struggle for Civil Rights in the North*. New York: Random House, 2008.

Cecilia Tichi. *Civic Passions: Seven Who Launched Progressive America*. Chapel Hill: University of North Carolina Press, 2009.

Zaragosa Vargas. *Labor Rights Are Civil Rights: Mexican American Workers in Twentieth-Century America*. Princeton: Princeton University Press, 2007.

James Weinstein. *The Decline of Socialism in America, 1912–1925*. New York: Vintage Books, 1967.

Lawrence Wittner. *Rebels Against War: The American Peace Movement, 1933–1983*, rev. ed. Philadelphia: Temple University Press, 1984.

Howard Zinn. *A People's History of the United States*. New York: Harper Perennial, 2005.

Tom Johnson (1854–1911)

Melvin G. Holli. *The American Mayor: The Best and the Worst Big-City Leaders*. University Park: Pennsylvania State University Press, 1999.

Tom L. Johnson. *My Story*. New York: B. W. Huebsch, 1911.

Robert M. La Follette Sr. (1855–1925)

David P. Thelen. *Robert M. La Follette and the Insurgent Spirit*. Boston: Little, Brown, 1976.

Eugene Debs (1855–1926)

Ray Ginger. *The Bending Cross: A Biography of Eugene Victor Debs*. New Brunswick, NJ: Rutgers University Press, 1949.

Nick Salvatore. *Eugene Debs: Citizen and Socialist*. Urbana: University of Illinois Press, 1982.

Louis Brandeis (1856–1941)

Louis Brandeis. *The Curse of Bigness*. New York: Viking Press, 1935.

———. *Other People's Money—And How the Bankers Use It*. New York: Frederick A. Stokes Company, 1914.

Philippa Strum. *Louis D. Brandeis: Justice for the People*. Cambridge, MA: Harvard University Press, 1984.

Melvin Urofsky. *Louis D. Brandeis: A Life*. New York: Pantheon Books, 2009.

Clarence Darrow (1857–1938)

Geoffrey Cowan. *The People v. Clarence Darrow: The Bribery Trial of America's Greatest Lawyer*. New York: Times Books, 1993.

Clarence Darrow. *Attorney for the Damned*. Edited by Arthur Weinberg. Chicago: University of Chicago Press, 1989. Originally published in 1957.

John A. Farrell. *Clarence Darrow: Attorney for the Damned*. New York: Doubleday, 2011.

Andrew Kersten. *Clarence Darrow: American Iconoclast*. New York: Hill and Wang, 2011.

Theodore Roosevelt (1858–1919)

H. W. Brands. *TR: The Last Romantic.* New York: Basic Books, 1998.

Douglas Brinkley. *The Wilderness Warrior: Theodore Roosevelt and the Crusade for America.* New York: HarperCollins, 2009.

James Chace. *1912: Wilson, Roosevelt, Taft and Debs—The Election That Changed the Country.* New York: Simon and Schuster, 2004.

Edmund Morris. *Theodore Rex.* New York: Modern Library, 2002.

Florence Kelley (1859–1932)

Dorothy Rose Blumberg. *Florence Kelley: The Making of a Social Pioneer.* New York: A. M. Kelley, 1966.

Josephine Goldmark. *Impatient Crusader: Florence Kelly's Life Story.* Urbana: University of Illinois Press, 1953.

Kathryn Kish Sklar. *Florence Kelley and the Nation's Work: The Rise of Women's Political Culture, 1830–1900.* New Haven and London: Yale University Press, 1995.

Kathryn Kish Sklar and Beverly Wilson Palmer, eds. *The Selected Letters of Florence Kelley, 1869–1931.* Urbana: University of Illinois Press, 2009.

John Dewey (1859–1952)

Jay Martin. *The Education of John Dewey: A Biography.* New York: Columbia University Press, 2002.

Alan Ryan. *John Dewey and the High Tide of American Liberalism.* New York: W. W. Norton, 1995.

Robert Westbrook. *John Dewey and American Democracy.* Ithaca, NY: Cornell University Press, 1991.

Victor Berger (1860–1929)

Sally Miller. *Victor Berger and the Promise of Constructive Socialism, 1910–1920.* Westport, CT: Greenwood Press, 1973.

David Shannon. *The Socialist Party of America: A History.* Chicago: Quadrangle Books, 1967.

James Weinstein. *The Decline of Socialism in America, 1912–1925.* New York: Monthly Review Press, 1967.

Charlotte Perkins Gilman (1860–1935)

Cynthia J. Davis. *Charlotte Perkins Gilman: A Biography.* Palo Alto: Stanford University Press, 2010.

Jane Addams (1860–1935)

Jane Addams. *Twenty Years at Hull-House.* New York: Macmillan, 1926.

Victoria Brown. *The Education of Jane Addams.* Philadelphia: University of Pennsylvania Press, 2004.

Jean Bethke Elshtain. *Jane Addams and the Dream of American Democracy: A Life.* New York: Basic Books, 2002.

Louise W. Knight. *Citizen: Jane Addams and the Struggle for Democracy.* Chicago: University of Chicago Press, 2005.

———. *Jane Addams: Spirit in Action.* New York: W. W. Norton, 2010.

Lincoln Steffens (1866–1936)

Peter Hartshorn. *I Have Seen the Future: A Life of Lincoln Steffens.* Berkeley, CA: Counterpoint, 2011.

Justin Kaplan. *Lincoln Steffens: A Biography.* New York: Simon and Schuster, 1974.

Lincoln Steffens. *The Autobiography of Lincoln Steffens.* New York: Harcourt, Brace, 1931.

Hiram Johnson (1866–1945)

William Deverell and Tom Sitton, eds. *California Progressivism Revisited.* Berkeley: University of California Press, 1994.

R. C. Lower. *A Bloc of One: The Political Career of Hiram Johnson.* Palo Alto: Stanford University Press, 1993.

George E. Mowry. *The California Progressives.* Berkeley: University of California Press, 1951.

Spencer C. Olin Jr. *California's Prodigal Sons: Hiram Johnson and the Progressives, 1911–1917.* Berkeley: University of California Press, 1968.

W. E. B. Du Bois (1868–1963)

David L. Lewis. *W. E. B. Du Bois: Biography of a Race, 1868–1919.* New York: H. Holt, 1994.

———. *W. E. B. Du Bois: The Fight for Equality and the American Century, 1919–1963.* New York: H. Holt, 2000.

William "Big Bill" Haywood (1869–1928)

Peter Carlson. *Roughneck: The Life and Times of Big Bill Haywood.* New York: W. W. Norton, 1984.

Melvyn Dubofsky. *"Big Bill" Haywood.* Manchester, UK: Manchester University Press, 1987.

William D. Haywood. *Bill Haywood's Book: The Autobiography of William D. Haywood.* New York: International Publishers, 1929.

J. Anthony Lukas. *Big Trouble: A Murder in a Small Western Town Sets Off a Struggle for the Soul of America.* New York: Simon and Schuster, 1997.

Alice Hamilton (1869–1970)

Alice Hamilton. *Exploring the Dangerous Trades: The Autobiography of Alice Hamilton, M.D.* Lebanon, NH: University Press of New England / Northeastern University Press, 1985. Originally published in 1943.

Barbara Sicherman. *Alice Hamilton: A Life in Letters.* Urbana: University of Illinois Press, 2003. Originally published in 1984.

Cecilia Tichi. *Civic Passions: Seven Who Launched Progressive America.* Chapel Hill: University of North Carolina Press, 2009.

Emma Goldman (1869–1940)

Richard Drinnon. *Rebel in Paradise: A Biography of Emma Goldman.* Chicago: University of Chicago Press, 1961.

Candace Falk. *Love, Anarchy, and Emma Goldman.* New Brunswick, NJ: Rutgers University Press, 1990.

Lewis Hine (1874–1940)

Kate Sampsell-Willman. *Lewis Hine as Social Critic.* Jackson: University Press of Mississippi, 2009.

Robert F. Wagner Sr. (1877–1953)

J. Joseph Huthmacher. *Senator Robert F. Wagner and the Rise of Urban Liberalism.* New York: Atheneum, 1968.

Upton Sinclair (1878–1968)

Anthony Arthur. *Radical Innocent: Upton Sinclair.* New York: Random House, 2006.

Kevin Mattson. *Upton Sinclair and the Other American Century.* Hoboken, NJ: John Wiley and Sons, 2006.

Greg Mitchell. *The Campaign of the Century: Upton Sinclair's Race for Governor of California and the Birth of Media Politics.* New York: Random House, 1993.

Film: "We Have a Plan." Season 1, episode 4 of *The Great Depression.* Documentary. Produced by Lyn Goldfarb. 1993.

Albert Einstein (1879–1955)

Albert Einstein. *Ideas and Opinions.* New York: Modern Library, 1994. Originally published in 1954.

———. *The World as I See It.* New York: Citadel Press, 1991. Originally published in 1935.

Jim Green. *Albert Einstein.* New York: Ocean Press, 2003.

Walter Isaacson. *Einstein: His Life and Universe.* New York: Simon and Schuster, 2007.

Fred Jerome. *The Einstein File: J. Edgar Hoover's Secret War Against the World's Most Famous Scientist.* New York: St. Martin's Press, 2002.

Fred Jerome and Rodger Taylor. *Einstein on Race and Racism.* New Brunswick, NJ: Rutgers University Press, 2006.

Margaret Sanger (1879–1966)

Ellen Chesler. *Woman of Valor: Margaret Sanger and the Birth Control Movement in America.* New York: Simon and Schuster, 1992.

Emily Taft Douglas. *Margaret Sanger: Pioneer of the Future.* New York: Holt, Rinehart and Winston, 1969.

Madeline Gray. *Margaret Sanger: A Biography of the Champion of Birth Control.* New York: R. Marek, 1979.

David M. Kennedy. *Birth Control in America: The Career of Margaret Sanger.* New Haven: Yale University Press, 1970.

Film: *Choices of the Heart: The Margaret Sanger Story.* Directed by Paul Shapiro. 1995.

Film: *Margaret Sanger: A Public Nuisance.* Documentary. Directed by Terese Svoboda and Steve Bull. 1992.

John L. Lewis (1880–1969)

Saul Alinsky. *John L. Lewis: An Unauthorized Biography*. New York: G. P. Putnam's Sons, 1949.

Melvyn Dubofsky and Warren Van Tine. *John L. Lewis: A Biography*. Urbana: University of Illinois Press, 1986.

Helen Keller (1880–1968)

John Davis. *Helen Keller*. New York: Ocean Press, 2003.

Dorothy Herrmann. *Helen Keller: A Life*. Chicago: University of Chicago Press, 1999.

Kim Nielsen. *Beyond the Miracle Worker: The Remarkable Life of Anne Sullivan Macy and Her Extraordinary Friendship with Helen Keller*. Boston: Beacon Press, 2009.

———. *The Radical Lives of Helen Keller*. New York: New York University Press, 2004.

Film: *Shining Soul: Helen Keller's Spiritual Life and Legacy*. Documentary. Directed by Penny Price. 2006.

Frances Perkins (1880–1965)

Adam Cohen. *Nothing to Fear: FDR's Inner Circle and the Hundred Days That Created Modern America*. New York: Penguin Press, 2009.

Kirstin Downey. *The Woman Behind the New Deal: Frances Perkins, FDR's Secretary of Labor and His Moral Conscience*. New York: Doubleday, 2009.

Richard Greenwald. *The Triangle Fire, the Protocols of Peace, and Industrial Democracy in Progressive Era New York*. Philadelphia: Temple University Press, 2005.

Frances Perkins. *The Roosevelt I Knew*. New York: Viking Press, 1946.

David Von Drehle. *Triangle: The Fire That Changed America*. New York: Grove Press, 2003.

Film: *Triangle: Remembering the Fire*. Documentary. Directed by Daphne Pinkerson. 2011.

Franklin D. Roosevelt (1882–1945)

H. W. Brands. *Traitor to His Class: The Privileged Life and Radical Presidency of Franklin Delano Roosevelt*. New York: Doubleday, 2009.

Adam Cohen. *Nothing to Fear: FDR's Inner Circle and the Hundred Days That Created Modern America*. New York: Penguin Press, 2009.

Frank Freidel. *Franklin D. Roosevelt: A Rendezvous with Destiny*. Boston: Back Bay Books, 1990.

Rose Schneiderman (1882–1972)

Gary Endelman. *Solidarity Forever: Rose Schneiderman and the Women's Trade Union League*. New York: Arno Press, 1982.

Annalise Orleck. *Common Sense and a Little Fire: Women and Working-Class Politics in the United States, 1900–1965*. Chapel Hill: University of North Carolina Press, 1995.

Rose Schneiderman. *All for One.* New York: P. S. Eriksson, 1967.

David Von Drehle. *Triangle: The Fire That Changed America.* New York: Grove Press, 2003.

Fiorello La Guardia (1882–1947)

Melvin G. Holli. *The American Mayor: The Best and the Worst Big-City Leaders.* University Park: Pennsylvania State University Press, 1999.

Thomas Kessner. *Fiorello H. La Guardia and the Making of Modern New York.* New York: Penguin Books, 1989.

Arthur Mann. *La Guardia: A Fighter Against His Times, 1882–1933.* New York: J. B. Lippincott, 1959.

Howard Zinn. *La Guardia in Congress.* Ithaca, NY: Cornell University Press, 1959.

Roger Baldwin (1884–1981)

Robert C. Cottrell. *Roger Nash Baldwin and the American Civil Liberties Union.* New York: Columbia University Press, 2000.

Samuel Walker. *In Defense of American Liberties: A History of the ACLU.* New York: Oxford University Press, 1990.

Eleanor Roosevelt (1884–1962)

Blanche Wiesen Cook. *Eleanor Roosevelt.* 2 vols. New York: Penguin, 1993, 2000.

Eleanor Roosevelt. *The Autobiography of Eleanor Roosevelt.* New York: Harper and Brothers, 1961.

Norman Thomas (1884–1968)

W. A. Swanberg. *Norman Thomas: The Last Idealist.* New York: Scribner, 1976.

Norman Thomas. *The Choice Before Us.* New York: Macmillan, 1934.

A. J. Muste (1885–1967)

Nat Hentoff. *Peace Agitator: The Story of A. J. Muste.* Indianapolis, IN: Bobbs-Merrill, 1967.

Maurice Isserman. *If I Had a Hammer: The Death of the Old Left and the Birth of the New Left.* New York: Basic Books, 1987.

Jo Ann Robinson. *Abraham Went Out: A Biography of A. J. Muste.* Philadelphia: Temple University Press, 1981.

Alice Stokes Paul (1885–1977)

Katherine Adams and Michael Keene. *Alice Paul and the American Suffrage Campaign.* Champaign: University of Illinois Press, 2007.

Amy E. Butler. *Two Paths to Equality: Alice Paul and Ethel M. Smith in the ERA Debate, 1921–1929.* Albany: State University of New York Press, 2002.

Linda Ford. *Iron-Jawed Angels: The Suffrage Militancy of the National Woman's Party 1912–1920.* New York: University Press of America, 1991.

Jo Freeman. *We Will Be Heard: Women's Struggles for Political Power in the United States.* Lanham, MD: Rowman and Littlefield, 2008.

Christine Lunardini. *From Equal Suffrage to Equal Rights: Alice Paul and the National Woman's Party, 1910–1928.* New York: New York University Press, 1986.

Mary Walton, *A Woman's Crusade: Alice Paul and the Battle for the Ballot,* New York: Palgrave Macmillan, 2010.

Sidney Hillman (1887–1946)

Steve Fraser. *Labor Will Rule: Sidney Hillman and the Rise of American Labor.* New York: Free Press, 1991.

Karen Pastorello. *A Power Among Them: Bessie Abramowitz Hillman and the Making of the Amalgamated Clothing Workers of America.* Urbana: University of Illinois Press, 2008.

Henry Wallace (1888–1965)

Adam Cohen. *Nothing to Fear: FDR's Inner Circle and the Hundred Days That Created Modern America.* New York: Penguin Press, 2009.

John C. Culver and John Hyde. *American Dreamer: A Life of Henry A. Wallace.* New York: W. W. Norton, 2000.

A. Philip Randolph (1889–1979)

Jervis Anderson. *A. Philip Randolph: A Biographical Portrait.* New York: Harcourt Brace Jovanovich, 1972.

Andrew E. Kersten. *A. Philip Randolph: A Life in the Vanguard.* Lanham, MD: Rowman and Littlefield, 2006.

Film: *A. Philip Randolph: For Jobs and Freedom.* Documentary. Directed by Dante James. 1996.

Film: *10,000 Black Men Named George.* Directed by Robert Townsend. 2002.

Earl Warren (1891–1974)

Ed Cray. *Chief Justice: A Biography of Earl Warren.* New York: Simon and Schuster, 1997.

Richard Kluger. *Simple Justice: The History of* Brown v. Board of Education *and Black America's Struggle for Equality.* New York: Vintage Books, 1977.

Jim Newton. *Justice for All: Earl Warren and the Nation He Made.* New York: Riverhead Books, 2006.

Edward White. *Earl Warren: A Public Life.* New York: Oxford University Press, 1982.

Floyd Olson (1891–1936)

George H. Mayer. *Political Career of Floyd B. Olson.* St. Paul: Minnesota Historical Society Press, 1987. Originally published in 1950.

Arthur M. Schlesinger. *The Politics of Upheaval, 1935–1936: The Age of Roosevelt.* New York: Houghton Mifflin, 2003. Originally published in 1960.

Richard Valelly. *Radicalism in the States: The Minnesota Farmer-Labor Party and the American Political Economy.* Chicago: University of Chicago Press, 1989.

Dorothy Day (1897–1980)

Robert Coles. *Dorothy Day: A Radical Devotion.* Reading, MA: Addison-Wesley, 1987.

Dorothy Day. *The Long Loneliness.* Chicago: Saint Thomas More Press, 1993.

Jim Forest. *Love Is the Measure: A Biography of Dorothy Day.* Maryknoll, NY: Orbis, 1994.

William Miller. *A Harsh and Dreadful Love—Dorothy Day and the Catholic Worker Movement.* New York: Liveright, 1973.

———. *Dorothy Day: A Biography.* San Francisco: Harper and Row, 1982.

Mel Piehl. *Breaking Bread: The Catholic Worker and the Origin of Catholic Radicalism in America.* Philadelphia: Temple University Press, 1982.

Film: *Dorothy Day: Don't Call Me a Saint.* Documentary. Directed by Claudia Larson. 2006.

Film: *Entertaining Angels: The Dorothy Day Story.* Directed by Michael Ray Rhodes. Paulist Pictures, 1996.

Paul Robeson (1898–1976)

Martin Duberman. *Paul Robeson.* New York: Alfred A. Knopf, 1988.

Philip Foner, ed. *Paul Robeson Speaks: Writings, Speeches, and Interviews: A Centennial Celebration.* New York: Citadel Press, 1982.

Paul Robeson. *Here I Stand.* Boston: Beacon Press, 1998.

Film: *Paul Robeson: Here I Stand.* Documentary. Directed by St. Claire Bourne. PBS, 1999.

William O. Douglas (1898–1980)

William O. Douglas. *The Court Years: 1939–1975.* New York: Random House, 1980.

Ann Gilliam. *Voices for the Earth.* New York: Random House, 1982.

Bruce Allen Murphy. *Wild Bill: The Legend and Life of William O. Douglas.* New York: Random House, 2003.

Lucas A. Powe Jr. *The Warren Court and American Politics.* Cambridge, MA: Belknap Press of Harvard University Press, 2000.

James Simon. *Independent Journey: The Life of William O. Douglas.* New York: Harper and Row, 1980.

Harry Bridges (1901–1990)

Stanley Kutler. *The American Inquisition: Justice and Injustice in the Cold War.* New York: Hill and Wang, 1982.

Charles Larrowe. *Harry Bridges: The Rise and Fall of Radical Labor in the United States.* New York: Lawrence Hill, 1972.

Frances Perkins. *The Roosevelt I Knew.* New York: Viking, 1946.

Film: *Harry Bridges: A Man and His Union.* Documentary. Directed by Berry Minott. 1992.

Langston Hughes (1902–1967)

Langston Hughes. *The Big Sea: Autobiography.* New York: Alfred A. Knopf, 1940.

―――. *I Wonder as I Wander: An Autobiographical Journey.* New York: Hill and Wang, 1964.

Arnold Rampersad. *The Life of Langston Hughes.* New York: Oxford University Press, 1986.

Vito Marcantonio (1902–1954)

Gerald Meyer. *Vito Marcantonio: Radical Politician, 1902–1954.* Albany: State University of New York Press, 1989.

Annette T. Rubinstein, ed. *I Vote My Conscience: Debates, Speeches, and Writings of Vito Marcantonio, 1935–1950.* New York: Marcantonio Memorial Fund, 1956.

Alan L. Shaffer. *Vito Marcantonio, Radical in Congress.* Syracuse, NY: Syracuse University Press, 1966.

Virginia F. Durr (1903–1999)

Anne Colby and William Damon. *Some Do Care: Contemporary Lives of Moral Commitment.* New York: Free Press, 1992.

Virginia Durr. *Outside the Magic Circle: The Autobiography of Virginia Foster Durr.* Tuscaloosa: University of Alabama Press, 1985.

Joan Marie Johnson. *Southern Women at the Seven Sister Colleges.* Athens: University of Georgia Press, 2008.

Patricia Sullivan, ed. *Freedom Writer: Virginia Foster Durr. Letters from the Civil Rights Years.* New York: Routledge, 2003.

Donnie Williams. *The Thunder of Angels: The Montgomery Bus Boycott and the People Who Broke the Back of Jim Crow.* With Wayne Greenhaw. Chicago: Lawrence Hill Books, 2005.

Ella Baker (1903–1986)

Clayborne Carson. *In Struggle: SNCC and the Black Awakening of the 1960s.* Cambridge, MA: Harvard University Press, 1981.

Joanne Grant. *Ella Baker: Freedom Bound.* New York: John Wiley and Sons, 1998.

Barbara Ransby. *Ella Baker and the Black Freedom Movement.* Chapel Hill: University of North Carolina Press, 2003.

Film: *Fundi: The Story of Ella Baker.* Documentary. Directed by Joanne Grant. 1981.

Theodor Geisel (Dr. Seuss) (1904–1991)

Jonathan Cott. *Pipers at the Gates of Dawn: The Wisdom of Children's Literature.* New York: Random House, 1981.

Henry Jenkins, Tara McPherson, and Jane Shattuc. *Hop on Pop: The Politics and Pleasures of Popular Culture.* Durham, NC: Duke University Press, 2002.

Julia Mickenberg and Philip Nel, eds. *Tales for Little Rebels: A Collection of Radical Children's Literature*. New York: New York University Press, 2008.

Richard H. Minear. *Dr. Seuss Goes to War: The World War II Editorial Cartoons of Theodor Seuss Geisel*. New York: New Press, 1999.

Judith and Neil Morgan. *Dr. Seuss and Mr. Geisel: A Biography*. New York: Da Capo Press, 1996.

Philip Nel. *Dr. Seuss: American Icon*. New York: Continuum, 2004.

Myles Horton (1905–1990)

Frank Adams. *Unearthing Seeds of Fire: The Idea of Highlander*. With Myles Horton. Winston-Salem, NC: J. F. Blair, 1975.

John Glen. *Highlander: No Ordinary School*. Knoxville: University of Tennessee Press, 1996.

Myles Horton. *The Long Haul: Autobiography of Myles Horton*. With Herbert and Judith Kohl. New York: Doubleday, 1991.

———. *The Myles Horton Reader: Education for Social Change*. Edited by Dale Jacobs. Knoxville: University of Tennessee Press, 2003.

Myles Horton and Paulo Freire. *We Make the Road by Walking: Conversations on Education and Social Change by Paulo Freire and Myles Horton*. Edited by Brenda Bell, John Gaventa, and John Peters. Philadelphia: Temple University Press, 1990.

Howell Raines. *My Soul Is Rested: Movement Days in the Deep South Remembered*. New York: G. P. Putnam's Sons, 1977.

Eliot Wigginton, ed. *Refuse to Stand Silently By: An Oral History of Grassroots Social Activism in America, 1921–1964*. New York: Doubleday, 1992.

Carey McWilliams (1905–1980)

Carey McWilliams. *The Education of Carey McWilliams*. New York: Simon and Schuster, 1979.

———. *North from Mexico: The Spanish-Speaking People of the United States*. Philadelphia: J. B. Lippincott, 1949.

Peter Richardson. *American Prophet: The Life and Work of Carey McWilliams*. Ann Arbor: University of Michigan Press, 2005.

William J. Brennan Jr. (1906–1997)

E. Joshua Rosenkranz and Bernard Schwartz, eds. *Reason and Passion: Justice Brennan's Enduring Influence*. New York: W. W. Norton, 1997.

Seth Stern and Stephen Wermiel. *Justice Brennan: Liberal Champion*. New York: Houghton Mifflin Harcourt, 2010.

Rabbi Abraham Joshua Heschel (1907–1972)

Abraham Joshua Heschel. *Moral Grandeur and Spiritual Audacity*. Edited by Susannah Heschel. New York: Noonday Press, 1996.

Edward K. Kaplan. *Spiritual Radical: Abraham Joshua Heschel in America, 1940–1972*. New Haven: Yale University Press, 2007.

Rachel Carson (1907–1964)

Martha Freeman, ed. *Always, Rachel: The Letters of Rachel Carson and Dorothy Freeman, 1952–1964*. Boston: Beacon Press, 1995.

Linda J. Lear, ed. *Lost Woods: The Discovered Writing of Rachel Carson*. Boston: Beacon Press, 1999.

———. *Rachel Carson: Witness for Nature*. New York: Henry Holt, 1997.

Mark Hamilton Lytle. *The Gentle Subversive: Rachel Carson, "Silent Spring," and the Rise of the Environmental Movement*. New York: Oxford University Press, 2007.

Peter Matthiessen, ed. *Courage for the Earth: Writers, Scientists, and Activists Celebrate the Life and Writing of Rachel Carson*. New York: Houghton Mifflin, 2007.

Film: *A Sense of Wonder*. Documentary. Produced by Kaiulani Lee. Sense of Wonder Productions, 2010.

Walter Reuther (1907–1970)

Kevin Boyle. *Organized Labor and American Politics, 1894–1994: The Labor-Liberal Alliance*. Albany: State University of New York Press, 1998.

Nelson Lichtenstein. *The Most Dangerous Man in Detroit: Walter Reuther and the Fate of American Labor*. New York: Basic Books, 1995.

Film: *Sit Down and Fight: Walter Reuther and the Rise of the Auto Workers Union*. Documentary. Directed by Charlotte Zwerin. 1993.

Film: *With Babies and Banners: Story of the Women's Emergency Brigade*. Documentary. Directed by Lorraine W. Gray and Lyn Goldfarb. 1978.

I. F. Stone (1907–1989)

D. D. Guttenplan. *American Radical: The Life and Times of I. F. Stone*. New York: Farrar, Straus and Giroux, 2009.

Myra MacPherson. *All Governments Lie! The Life and Times of Rebel Journalist I. F. Stone*. New York: Scribner, 2006.

I. F. Stone. *The Best of I. F. Stone*. Edited by Karl Weber. New York: Public Affairs, 2006.

———. *In Time of Torment, 1961–1967*. Boston: Little, Brown, 1989.

———. *Polemics and Prophecies, 1967–1970*. New York: Vintage Books, 1972.

Film: *I. F. Stone's Weekly*. Documentary. Directed by Jerry Bruck Jr. 1973.

Thurgood Marshall (1908–1993)

Rawn James Jr. *Root and Branch: Charles Hamilton Houston, Thurgood Marshall, and the Struggle to End Segregation*. New York: Bloomsbury Press, 2010.

Richard Kluger. *Simple Justice: The History of* Brown v. Board of Education *and Black America's Struggle for Equality*. New York: Alfred A. Knopf, 1975.

Thurgood Marshall. *Thurgood Marshall: His Speeches, Writings, Arguments, Opinions, and Reminiscences*. Edited by Mark V. Tushnet. Chicago: Lawrence Hill Books, 2001.

Mark Tushnet. *Making Constitutional Law: Thurgood Marshall and the Supreme Court, 1961–1991.* New York: Oxford University Press, 1997.

Juan Williams. *Thurgood Marshall: American Revolutionary.* New York: Times Books, 1998.

Film: *Thurgood.* Directed by Michael Stevens. HBO. 2011.

Lyndon B. Johnson (1908–1973)

Robert Caro. *Master of the Senate: The Years of Lyndon Johnson.* New York: Alfred A. Knopf, 2002.

———. *The Years of Lyndon Johnson: Means of Ascent.* New York: Alfred A. Knopf, 1990.

———. *The Years of Lyndon Johnson: The Path to Power.* New York: Alfred A. Knopf, 1982.

Robert Dallek. *Flawed Giant: Lyndon Johnson and His Times, 1961–1973.* New York: Oxford University Press, 1998.

———. *Lone Star Rising: Lyndon Johnson and His Times, 1908–1960.* New York: Oxford University Press, 1991.

Doris Kearns Goodwin. *Lyndon Johnson and the American Dream.* New York: Harper and Row, 1976.

John Kenneth Galbraith (1908–2006)

John Kenneth Galbraith. *The Affluent Society.* Boston: Houghton Mifflin, 1958.

———. *Money: Whence It Came, Where It Went.* Boston: Houghton Mifflin, 1975.

Richard Parker. *John Kenneth Galbraith: His Life, His Politics, His Economics.* Chicago: University of Chicago Press, 2005.

Saul Alinsky (1909–1972)

Saul Alinsky. *Reveille for Radicals.* New York: Vintage Books, 1946.

———. *Rules for Radicals.* New York: Vintage Books, 1971.

Sanford D. Horwitt. *Let Them Call Me Rebel: Saul Alinsky. His Life and Legacy.* New York: Alfred A. Knopf, 1989.

Nicholas Von Hoffman. *Radical: A Portrait of Saul Alinsky.* New York: Nation Books, 2010.

Film: *The Democratic Promise: Saul Alinsky and His Legacy.* Documentary. Directed by Bob Hercules and Bruce Orenstein. PBS. 1999.

Film: *Encounter with Saul Alinsky: Parts I and II.* Documentary. Directed by Peter Pearson. National Film Board of Canada. 1967.

Bayard Rustin (1912–1987)

Jervis Anderson. *Bayard Rustin: Trouble I've Seen.* Berkeley: University of California Press, 1998.

Raymond Arsenault. *Freedom Riders: 1961 and the Struggle for Racial Justice.* New York: Oxford University Press, 2006.

John D'Emilio. *Lost Prophet: The Life and Times of Bayard Rustin.* Chicago: University of Chicago Press, 2003.

Film: *Brother Outsider: The Life of Bayard Rustin*. Documentary. Directed by Nancy D. Kates and Bennett Singer. 2003.

Harry Hay (1912–2002)

Harry Hay. *Radically Gay: Gay Liberation in the Words of Its Founder*. Edited by Will Roscoe. Boston: Beacon Press, 1996.

Stuart Timmons. *The Trouble with Harry Hay: Founder of the Modern Gay Movement*. Boston: Alyson Publications, 1990.

Film: *Hope Along the Wind*. Documentary. Directed by Eric Slade. 2002.

Studs Terkel (1912–2008)

Studs Terkel. *P.S.: Further Thoughts from a Lifetime of Listening*. New York: New Press, 2008.

———. *Talking to Myself: A Memoir of My Times*. New York: Pantheon Books, 1977.

———. *Touch and Go: A Memoir*. New York: New Press, 2008.

David Brower (1912–2000)

David Brower. *Let the Mountains Talk, Let the Rivers Run*. New York: HarperCollins, 1995.

———. *Work in Progress*. Layton, UT: Gibbs Smith, 1991.

John McPhee. *Encounters with the Archdruid*. New York: Farrar, Straus and Giroux, 1971.

Film: *For Earth's Sake: The Life and Times of David Brower*. Documentary. Directed by John de Graaf. Bullfrog Films. 1989.

Woody Guthrie (1912–1967)

Ronald D. Cohen. *Woody Guthrie: Writing America's Songs*. New York: Routledge, 2012.

Ed Cray. *Ramblin' Man: The Life and Times of Woody Guthrie*. New York: W. W. Norton, 2004.

Will Kaufman. *Woody Guthrie: American Radical*. Urbana: University of Illinois Press, 2011.

Joe Klein. *Woody Guthrie: A Life*. New York: Alfred A. Knopf, 1980.

Robert Santelli and Emily Davidson, eds. *Hard Travelin': The Life and Legacy of Woody Guthrie*. Hanover, NH: University Press of New England, 1999.

Arthur Miller (1915–2005)

Susan C. W. Abbotson. *Critical Companion to Arthur Miller*. New York: Facts on File, 2007.

Christopher Bigsby, ed. *The Cambridge Companion to Arthur Miller*. 2nd ed. Cambridge: Cambridge University Press, 2010.

Enoch Brater, ed. *Arthur Miller's America: Theater and Culture in a Time of Change*. Ann Arbor: University of Michigan Press, 2005.

Martin Gottfried. *Arthur Miller: His Life and Work*. Cambridge, MA: Da Capo Press, 2003.

Arthur Miller. *Timebends: A Life*. New York: Penguin, 1995.

Jane Jacobs (1916–2006)

Anthony Flint. *Wrestling with Moses: How Jane Jacobs Took on New York's Master Builder and Transformed the American City.* New York: Random House, 2009.

Roberta Brandes Gratz. *The Battle for Gotham: New York in the Shadow of Robert Moses and Jane Jacobs.* New York: Nation Books, 2010.

C. Wright Mills (1916–1962)

G. William Domhoff. *Who Rules America? Challenges to Corporate and Class Dominance.* 6th ed. New York: McGraw-Hill, 2010.

Daniel Geary. *Radical Ambition: C. Wright Mills, the Left, and American Social Thought.* Berkeley: University of California Press, 2009.

Tom Hayden. *Radical Nomad: C. Wright Mills and His Times.* Boulder, CO: Paradigm Publishers, 2006.

C. Wright Mills. *C. Wright Mills: Letters and Autobiographical Writings.* Edited by Kathryn Mills with Patricia Mills. Berkeley: University of California Press, 2000.

John H. Summers, ed. *The Politics of Truth: Selected Writings of C. Wright Mills.* New York: Oxford University Press, 2008.

Barry Commoner (1917–)

Barry Commoner. *The Closing Circle: Nature, Man, and Technology.* New York: Alfred A. Knopf, 1971.

Michael Egan. *Barry Commoner and the Science of Survival: The Remaking of American Environmentalism.* Cambridge: MIT Press, 2007.

Robert Gottlieb. *Forcing the Spring: The Transformation of the American Environmental Movement,* rev. ed. Washington, DC: Island Press, 2003.

Fannie Lou Hamer (1917–1977)

Chris Myers Asch. *The Senator and the Sharecropper—The Freedom Struggles of James O. Eastland and Fannie Lou Hamer.* New York: New Press, 2008.

Kay Mills. *This Little Light of Mine: Fannie Lou Hamer.* New York: Penguin Books, 1993.

Film: *Standing on My Sisters' Shoulders.* Documentary. Directed by Laura Lipson. 2002.

Jackie Robinson (1919–1972)

Arnold Rampersad. *Jackie Robinson: A Biography.* New York: Ballantine Books, 1998.

Jackie Robinson. *I Never Had It Made: The Autobiography of Jackie Robinson.* New York: Putnam, 1972.

Jules Tygiel. *Baseball's Great Experiment: Jackie Robinson and His Legacy.* New York: Oxford University Press, 1983.

Pete Seeger (1919–)

David King Dunaway. *How Can I Keep from Singing? The Ballad of Pete Seeger,* rev. ed. New York: Villard Books, 2008.

Pete Seeger, Bob Reiser, Guy Carawan, and Candie Carawan. *Everybody Says Freedom: A History of the Civil Rights Movement in Songs and Pictures.* New York: W. W. Norton, 1989.

Alec Wilkinson. *The Protest Singer: An Intimate Portrait of Pete Seeger.* New York: Alfred A. Knopf, 2009.

Alan Winkler. *To Everything There Is a Season: Pete Seeger and the Power of Song.* New York: Oxford University Press, 2009.

Film: *Pete Seeger: The Power of Song.* Documentary. Directed by Jim Brown. 2007.

Jerry Wurf (1919–1981)

Joseph C. Goulden. *Jerry Wurf: Labor's Last Angry Man.* New York: Atheneum, 1982.

Michael Honey. *Going Down Jericho Road: The Memphis Strike, Martin Luther King's Last Campaign.* New York: W. W. Norton, 2008.

Bella Abzug (1920–1998)

Bella Abzug. *Bella! Ms. Abzug Goes to Washington.* Edited by Mel Ziegler. New York: Saturday Review Press, 1972.

————. *Gender Gap: Bella Abzug's Guide to Political Power for American Women.* With Mim Kelber. New York: Houghton Mifflin, 1984.

Suzanne Braun Levine and Mary Thom. *Bella Abzug: How One Tough Broad from the Bronx Fought Jim Crow and Joe McCarthy, Pissed Off Jimmy Carter, Battled for the Rights of Women and Workers, Rallied Against War and for the Planet, and Shook Up Politics Along the Way.* New York: Farrar, Straus and Giroux, 2007.

Betty Friedan (1921–2006)

Stephanie Coontz. *A Strange Stirring: The Feminine Mystique and American Women at the Dawn of the 1960s.* New York: Basic Books, 2011.

Betty Friedan. *The Feminine Mystique.* New York: W. W. Norton, 1963.

————. *It Changed My Life: Writings on the Women's Movement.* New York: Random House, 1976.

————. *Life So Far: A Memoir.* New York: Simon and Schuster, 2000.

Daniel Horowitz. *Betty Friedan and the Making of the Feminine Mystique.* Amherst: University of Massachusetts Press, 1998.

Kate Weigand. *Red Feminism: American Communism and the Making of Women's Liberation.* Baltimore: Johns Hopkins University Press, 2000.

Howard Zinn (1922–2010)

Howard Zinn. *You Can't Be Neutral on a Moving Train: A Personal History of Our Times.* Boston: Beacon Press, 1994.

————. *The Zinn Reader: Writings on Disobedience and Democracy.* New York: Seven Stories Press, 1997.

Film: *You Can't Be Neutral on a Moving Train.* Directed by Deb Ellis and Denis Mueller. First Run Features. 2004.

Rev. William Sloane Coffin (1924–2006)

Taylor Branch. *Parting the Waters: America in the King Years, 1954–63*. New York: Simon and Schuster, 1988.

Warren Goldstein. *William Sloane Coffin, Jr.: A Holy Impatience*. New Haven: Yale University Press, 2004.

Film: *William Sloane Coffin: An American Prophet*. Documentary. Directed by John Ankele and Anne Macksoud. 2004.

Malcolm X (1925–1965)

David Gallen. *Malcolm as They Knew Him*. New York: Ballantine Books, 1995.

Malcolm X. *The Autobiography of Malcolm X*. With Alex Haley. New York: Grove Press, 1965.

Manning Marable. *Malcolm X: A Life of Reinvention*. New York: Viking, 2011.

Film: *Malcolm X*. Directed by Spike Lee. 1992.

Cesar Chavez (1927–1993)

Marshall Ganz. *Why David Sometimes Wins: Leadership, Organization, and Strategy in the California Farm Worker Movement*. New York: Oxford University Press, 2009.

Jacques E. Levy and Cesar Chavez. *Cesar Chavez: Autobiography of La Causa*. New York: W. W. Norton, 1975.

Miriam Pawel. *The Union of Their Dreams: Power, Hope, and Struggle in Cesar Chavez's Farm Workers Movement*. New York: Bloomsbury Press, 2009.

Randy Shaw. *Beyond the Fields: Cesar Chavez, the UFW, and the Struggle for Justice in the 21st Century*. Berkeley: University of California Press, 2008.

Film: *The Fight in the Fields: Cesar Chavez and the Farmworkers Movement*. Documentary. Directed by Rick Tejada-Flores and Ray Telles. Paradigm Productions. 1997.

Michael Harrington (1928–1989)

Gary Dorrien. *Economy, Difference, Empire: Social Ethics for Social Justice*. New York: Columbia University Press, 2010.

Michael Harrington. *Fragments of a Century: A Social Autobiography*. New York: Saturday Review Press, 1973.

———. *The Long Distance Runner: An Autobiography*. New York: Henry Holt, 1988.

Maurice Isserman. *If I Had a Hammer: The Death of the Old Left and the Birth of the New Left*. New York: Basic Books, 1987.

———. *The Other American: The Life of Michael Harrington*. New York: PublicAffairs, 2000.

Frank Stricker. *Why America Lost the War on Poverty–And How to Win It*. Chapel Hill: University of North Carolina Press, 2007.

Rev. James Lawson (1928–)

Raymond Arsenault. *Freedom Riders: 1961 and the Struggle for Racial Justice*. New York: Oxford University Press, 2006.

David Halberstam. *The Children.* New York: Fawcett Books, 1999.

Michael Honey. *Going Down Jericho Road: The Memphis Strike, Martin Luther King's Last Campaign.* New York: W. W. Norton, 2008.

Film: *At the River I Stand.* Documentary. Directed by David Appleby, Allison Graham, and Steven John Ross. 1993.

Noam Chomsky (1928–)

Robert Barsky. *The Chomsky Effect: A Radical Works Beyond the Ivory Tower.* Cambridge: MIT Press, 2007.

———. *Noam Chomsky: A Life of Dissent.* Cambridge: MIT Press, 1997.

Noam Chomsky. *The Chomsky Reader.* New York: Pantheon Books, 1987.

Film: *Manufacturing Consent: Noam Chomsky and the Media.* Documentary. Directed by Mark Achbar and Peter Wintonick. Humanist Broadcasting Foundation. 1993.

Rev. Martin Luther King Jr. (1929–1968)

Taylor Branch. *Parting the Waters: America in the King Years, 1954–63.* New York: Simon and Schuster, 1988.

Michael Eric Dyson. *I May Not Get There With You: The True Martin Luther King, Jr.* New York: Free Press, 2001.

David J. Garrow. *Bearing the Cross: Martin Luther King, Jr., and the Southern Christian Leadership Conference.* New York: W. Morrow, 1986.

Thomas F. Jackson. *From Civil Rights to Human Rights: Martin Luther King Jr., and the Struggle for Economic Justice.* Philadelphia: University of Pennsylvania Press, 2007.

Film: *King: A Filmed Record. Montgomery to Memphis.* Documentary. Directed by Sidney Lumet. 1970.

Allard Lowenstein (1929–1980)

Alan Brinkley. *Liberalism and Its Discontents.* Cambridge, MA: Harvard University Press, 2000.

William Chafe. *Never Stop Running: Allard Lowenstein and the Struggle to Save American Liberalism.* New York: Basic Books, 1993.

David Harris. *Dreams Die Hard: Three Men's Journey Through the Sixties.* San Francisco: Mercury House, 1993.

Gregory Stone and Douglas Lowenstein, eds. *Lowenstein: Acts of Courage and Belief.* New York: Harcourt Brace Jovanovich, 1983.

Bruce Watson. *Freedom Summer.* New York: Viking Penguin, 2010.

Film: *Citizen: The Political Life of Allard K. Lowenstein.* Documentary. Directed by Julie M. Thompson. 1983.

Harvey Milk (1930–1978)

Randy Shilts. *The Mayor of Castro Street: The Life and Times of Harvey Milk.* New York: St. Martin's Press, 1982.

Film: *Milk.* Directed by Gus Van Sant. 2008.

Film: *The Times of Harvey Milk.* Directed by Rob Epstein. Black Sand Productions. 1984.

Ted Kennedy (1932–2009)

Peter Canellos. *The Last Lion: The Fall and Rise of Ted Kennedy.* New York: Simon and Schuster, 2009.

Adam Clymer. *Edward M. Kennedy: A Biography.* New York: Harper, 2009.

Edward M. Kennedy. *True Compass: A Memoir.* New York: Twelve, 2009.

Ralph Nader (1934–)

Nancy Bowen. *Ralph Nader: Man with a Mission.* Brookfield, CT: Twenty-First Century Books, 2002.

Kevin Graham. *Ralph Nader: Battling for Democracy.* Denver, CO: Windom, 2000.

Patricia Cronin Marcello. *Ralph Nader: A Biography.* Westport, CT: Greenwood Press, 2004.

Film: *An Unreasonable Man.* Directed by Henriette Mantel and Steve Skrovan. 2007.

Gloria Steinem (1934–)

Carolyn Heilbrun. *The Education of a Woman: The Life of Gloria Steinem.* New York: Dial, 1995.

Sydney Ladensohn Stern. *Gloria Steinem: Her Passions, Politics, and Mystique.* Secaucus, NJ: Carol, 1997.

Film: *Gloria: In Her Own Words.* Directed by Peter Kunhardt. HBO. 2011.

Bill Moyers (1934–)

Bill Moyers. *Bill Moyers Journal: The Conversation Continues.* New York: New Press, 2011.

———. *Moyers on Democracy.* New York: Doubleday, 2008.

Bill Moyers and Julie L. Pycior. *Moyers on America: A Journalist and His Times.* New York: New Press, 2004.

Bob Moses (1935–)

Taylor Branch. *Parting the Waters: America in the King Years, 1954–63.* New York: Simon and Schuster, 1988.

Eric Burner. *And Gently He Shall Lead Them: Robert Parris Moses and Civil Rights in Mississippi.* New York: New York University Press, 1995.

Clayborne Carson. *In Struggle: SNCC and the Black Awakening of the 1960s.* Cambridge, MA: Harvard University Press, 1981.

Nicolaus Mills. *Like a Holy Crusade: Mississippi 1964—The Turning of the Civil Rights Movement in America.* New York: Ivan Dee, 1993.

Robert Moses and Charles Cobb. *Radical Equations: Civil Rights from Mississippi to the Algebra Project.* Boston: Beacon Press, 2002.

Charles Payne. *I've Got the Light of Freedom: The Organizing Tradition and the Mississippi Freedom Struggle.* Berkeley: University of California Press, 1995.

Barbara Ransby. *Ella Baker and the Black Freedom Movement.* Chapel Hill: University of North Carolina Press, 2003.

Bruce Watson. *Freedom Summer.* New York: Viking, 2010.

Film: *Freedom on My Mind*. Directed by Connie Field and Marilyn Mulford. California Newsreel. 1994.

Tom Hayden (1939–)

Tom Hayden. *The Long Sixties: From 1960 to Barack Obama*. Boulder, CO: Paradigm Publishers, 2009.

———. *Reunion: A Memoir*. New York: Random House, 1988.

———. *Writings for a Democratic Society: The Tom Hayden Reader*. San Francisco: City Lights Books, 2008.

James Miller. *Democracy Is in the Streets: From Port Huron to the Siege of Chicago*. New York: Simon and Schuster, 1987.

Kirkpatrick Sale. *SDS*. New York: Random House, 1973.

John Lewis (1940–)

Raymond Arsenault. *Freedom Riders: 1961 and the Struggle for Racial Justice*. New York: Oxford University Press, 2006.

David Halberstam. *The Children*. New York: Fawcett Books, 1999.

John Lewis. *Walking with the Wind: A Memoir of the Movement*. New York: Harcourt, Brace, 1998.

Film: *Freedom Riders*. Directed by Stanley Nelson. PBS. 2011.

Joan Baez (1941–)

Joan Baez. *And a Voice to Sing With*. New York: Summit Books, 1987.

David Hajdu. *Positively Fourth Street: The Lives and Times of Joan Baez, Bob Dylan, Mimi Baez Farina and Richard Farina*. New York: Farrar, Straus and Giroux, 2001.

Bob Dylan (1941–)

Guy and Candie Carawan. *Sing for Freedom: The Story of the Civil Rights Movement Through Its Songs*. Montgomery, AL: New South Books, 2007.

David Hajdu. *Positively Fourth Street: The Lives and Times of Joan Baez, Bob Dylan, Mimi Baez Farina and Richard Farina*. New York: Farrar, Straus and Giroux, 2001.

Dorian Lynskey. *33 Revolutions per Minute: A History of Protest Songs, from Billie Holiday to Green Day*. New York: HarperCollins, 2011.

Anthony Scaduto. *Dylan: An Intimate Biography*. New York: Grosset and Dunlap, 1971.

Michael Schumaker. *There but for Fortune: The Life of Phil Ochs*. New York: Hyperion, 1996.

Robert Shelton. *No Direction Home: The Life and Music of Bob Dylan*. New York: William Morrow, 1986.

Sean Wilentz. *Dylan in America*. New York: Doubleday, 2010.

Film: *No Direction Home: Bob Dylan*. Documentary. Directed by Martin Scorcese. PBS. 2005.

Barbara Ehrenreich (1941–)

Barbara Ehrenreich. *Nickel and Dimed: On (Not) Getting By in America*. New York: Metropolitan Books, 2001.

———. *The Worst Years of Our Lives.* New York: Pantheon Books, 1990.

Jesse Jackson (1941–)

Frank Clemente. *Keep Hope Alive: Jesse Jackson's 1988 Presidential Campaign.* Boston: South End Press, 1999.

Marshall Frady. *Jesse: The Life and Pilgrimage of Jesse Jackson.* New York: Random House, 1996.

Muhammad Ali (1942–)

Muhammad Ali. *The Greatest: My Own Story.* With Richard Durham. New York: Random House, 1975.

Thomas Hauser. *Muhammad Ali: His Life and Times.* New York: Simon and Schuster, 1992.

Mike Marqusee. *Redemption Song: Muhammad Ali and the Spirit of the Sixties.* New York: Verso, 1999.

David Remnick. *King of the World: Muhammad Ali and the Rise of an American Hero.* New York: Random House, 1998.

William C. Rhoden. *Forty Million Dollar Slaves: The Rise, Fall, and Redemption of the Black Athlete.* New York: Crown Publisher, 2006.

David Zirin. *Muhammad Ali Handbook.* Chicago: Haymarket Books, 2007.

———. *People's History of Sports in the United States: 250 Years of Politics, Protest, People, and Play.* New York: New Press, 2009.

Billie Jean King (1943–)

Billie Jean King. *Autobiography of Billie Jean.* With Frank Deford. New York: HarperCollins, 1982.

———. *Pressure Is a Privilege: Lessons I've Learned from Life and the Battle of the Sexes.* With Christine Brennan. New York: LifeTime Media, 2008.

Selena Roberts. *A Necessary Spectacle: Billie Jean King, Bobby Riggs, and the Tennis Match That Leveled the Game.* New York: Crown Publishers, 2005.

Susan Ware. *Game, Set, Match: Billie Jean King and the Revolution in Women's Sports.* Chapel Hill: University of North Carolina Press, 2011.

Film: *Billie Jean King: Portrait of a Pioneer.* Documentary. Produced by Margaret Grossi. HBO. 2006.

Paul Wellstone (1944–2002)

Bill Lofy. *Paul Wellstone: The Life of a Passionate Progressive.* Ann Arbor: University of Michigan Press, 2005.

Dennis J. McGrath and Dane Smith. *Professor Wellstone Goes to Washington: The Inside Story of a Grassroots U.S. Senate Campaign.* Minneapolis: University of Minnesota Press, 1995.

Paul Wellstone. *The Conscience of a Liberal: Reclaiming the Compassionate Agenda.* Minneapolis: University of Minnesota Press, 2002.

Film: *Wellstone.* Documentary. Directed by Pam Colby. 2004.

Bruce Springsteen (1949–)

Eric Alterman. *It Ain't No Sin to Be Glad You're Alive: The Promise of Bruce Springsteen.* New York: Little, Brown, 1999.

Dave Marsh. *Bruce Springsteen: Two Hearts.* New York: Routledge, 2004.

David Masciotra. *Working on a Dream: The Progressive Political Vision of Bruce Springsteen.* New York: Continuum, 2010.

Michael Moore (1954–)

Matthew Bernstein, ed. *Michael Moore: Filmmaker, Newsmaker, Cultural Icon.* Ann Arbor: University of Michigan Press, 2010.

Michael Moore. *Here Comes Trouble: Stories from My Life.* New York: Grand Central Publishing, 2011.

Michael Moore and Kathleen Glynn. *Adventures in a TV Nation.* New York: Random House, 1997.

Roger Rapoport. *Citizen Moore: The Life and Times of an American Iconoclast.* Muskegon, MI: RDR Books, 2006.

Emily Shultz. *Michael Moore: A Biography.* Toronto, Canada: ECW Press, 2005.

Tony Kushner (1956–)

James Fisher. *Understanding Tony Kushner.* Columbia: University of South Carolina Press, 2008.

Robert Vorlicky, ed. *Tony Kushner in Conversation.* Ann Arbor: University of Michigan Press, 1998.

Permissions

About the Author

PETER DREIER is the Dr. E. P. Clapp Distinguished Professor of Politics and chair of the Urban and Environmental Policy Department at Occidental College in Los Angeles. He teaches courses on urban politics and policy, community organizing, movements for social justice, and work and labor. In addition to being a scholar and teacher, he has been a journalist, community organizer, and government official. He earned his Ph.D. from the University of Chicago and his B.A. from Syracuse University.

At Occidental he created and coordinates Campaign Semester, a program that since 2008 has provided students with a full semester credit to work full-time on election campaigns around the country.

He is coauthor of three other books—*The Next Los Angeles: The Struggle for a Livable City*, with Regina Freer, Bob Gottlieb, and Mark Vallianatos (University of California Press, 2006); *Regions That Work: How Cities and Suburbs Can Grow Together*, with Manuel Pastor, Eugene Grigsby, and Marta Lopez-Garza (University of Minnesota Press, 2000); and *Place Matters: Metropolitics for the 21st Century*, with John Mollenkopf and Todd Swanstrom (University Press of Kansas, 2nd ed., 2005). *Place Matters* won the Michael Harrington Book Award, given by the American Political Science Association for the "outstanding book that demonstrates how scholarship can be used in the struggle for a better world." Dreier also coedited, with Jennifer Wolch and Manuel Pastor, *Up Against the Sprawl: Public Policy and the Making of Southern California* (University of Minnesota Press, 2004).

Dreier writes frequently for the *Los Angeles Times*, the *Nation*, *American Prospect*, and the *Huffington Post*. His articles have also been published in the *New York Times, Washington Post, Boston Globe, Newsday, Chicago Tribune, Philadelphia Inquirer, New Republic, Dissent, Washington Monthly, Progressive, Forward, Commonweal, Chronicle of Higher Education*, and elsewhere.

His scholarly articles have appeared in many edited books as well as in such journals as the *Harvard Business Review, Urban Affairs Review, Social Policy, Journal of the American Planning Association, North Carolina Law Review, Perspectives on Politics, Columbia Journalism Review, Housing Policy Debate, National Civic Review, Planning, International Journal of Urban and Regional Research, Journal of Urban Affairs, Cityscape, Social Problems, Housing Studies, Humanity and Society, New Labor Forum,* and other professional journals.

Dreier is chair of Cry Wolf Project, a nonprofit think tank that examines the accuracy of statements by business groups, politicians, and the media that have predicted economic disaster if health, safety, and environmental protections became law. Dreier is also on the boards of the Los Angeles Alliance for a New Economy, the National Housing Institute, Invest in Kids, and the Pasadena Educational Foundation. He served on the executive committee of Housing LA, a broad coalition of labor, community, and faith-based groups, and on the board of the Southern California Association for Non-Profit Housing. Over the years he has worked closely with many unions, community groups, public interest organizations, and others on campaigns for social justice. He has been a member of Los Angeles City Council task forces on economic development and on affordable housing, a member of the Bring LA Home blue-ribbon task force on homelessness, and a member of the Community Reinvestment Task Force of United Way of Los Angeles.

Dreier is married to Terry Meng, a nurse practitioner, and lives in Pasadena. They have twin daughters, Amelia Marsh Dreier and Sarah Michaela Dreier.